**Sefton Libraries Bookface**  **@seftonLibraries**  **Sefton Libraries**

# Your library Sefton

## Please return this item by the due date:

24. 10. 17

06. 11. 17

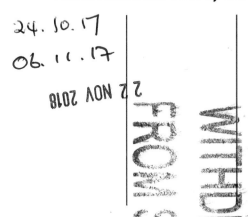

2 2 NOV 2018

Please return this item by the due date
or renew at **www.sefton.gov.uk/libraries**
or by telephone at **any** Sefton library:

Bootle Library **0151 934 5781**
Crosby Library **0151 257 6400**
Formby Library **01704 874 177**
Meadows Library **0151 288 6727**
Netherton Library **0151 525 0607**
Southport Library **0151 934 2118**

**your Library** Sefton

Sefton Council

# PASSCHENDAELE

www.**penguin**.co.uk

# PAUL HAM
# PASSCHENDAELE
## REQUIEM FOR DOOMED YOUTH

Doubleday

LONDON · TORONTO · SYDNEY · AUCKLAND · JOHANNESBURG

TRANSWORLD PUBLISHERS
61–63 Uxbridge Road, London W5 5SA
www.penguin.co.uk

Transworld is part of the Penguin Random House group of companies
whose addresses can be found at global.penguinrandomhouse.com

First published in Australia in 2016 by William Heinemann
an imprint of Penguin Random House Australia

First published in Great Britain in 2017 by Doubleday
an imprint of Transworld Publishers

Maps by Alicia Freile, Tango Media Pty Ltd

Internal design by Xou Creative

The subtitle of *Passchendaele: Requiem for Doomed Youth* was
inspired by Wilfred Owen's poem, 'Anthem for Doomed Youth'.

A CIP catalogue record for this book
is available from the British Library.

ISBN 9780857525291

Typeset in 11.5/14.5pt Adobe Garamond Pro
Printed and bound by Clays Ltd, Bungay, Suffolk

Penguin Random House is committed to a sustainable
future for our business, our readers and our planet. This book
is made from Forest Stewardship Council® certified paper.

MIX
Paper from
responsible sources
FSC® C018179

9 10 8 6 4 2

To Dad, Ollie and Ian

# CONTENTS

# LIST OF MAPS

# Western Front — Third Ypres

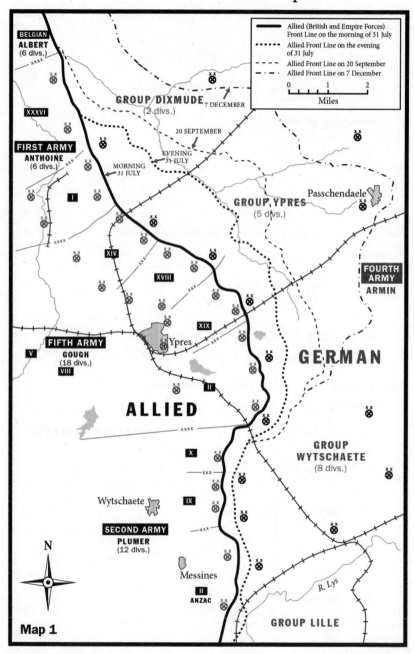

**Legend:**
- ——— Allied (British and Empire Forces) Front Line on the morning of 31 July
- ••••••• Allied Front Line on the evening of 31 July
- – – – Allied Front Line on 20 September
- –·–·– Allied Front Line on 7 December

0   1   2
Miles

BELGIAN
**ALBERT**
(6 divs.)

GROUP DIXMUDE 7 DECEMBER
(2 divs.)

20 SEPTEMBER

XXXVI

EVENING
31 JULY

**FIRST ARMY**
ANTHOINE
(6 divs.)

MORNING
31 JULY

I

Passchendaele

GROUP YPRES
(5 divs.)

XIV

XVIII

FOURTH
ARMY
ARMIN

XIX

**FIFTH ARMY**
GOUGH
(18 divs.)

V

VIII

Ypres

**GERMAN**

II

**ALLIED**

X

GROUP
WYTSCHAETE
(8 divs.)

Wytschaete

IX

**SECOND ARMY**
PLUMER
(12 divs.)

N

Messines

II
ANZAC

R. Lys

GROUP LILLE

**Map 1**

# The Flanders Campaign — Final Sketch Plan

*Handed by Field Marshal Sir Douglas Haig to General Philippe Pétain on 18 May 1917*

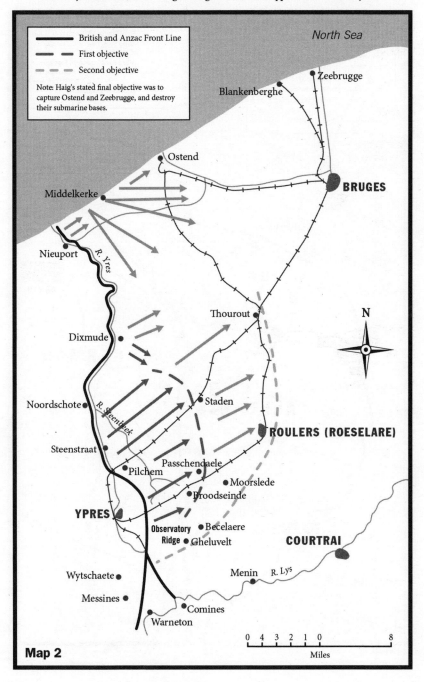

British and Anzac Front Line
First objective
Second objective

Note: Haig's stated final objective was to capture Ostend and Zeebrugge, and destroy their submarine bases.

North Sea

Zeebrugge
Blankenberghe
Ostend
BRUGES
Middelkerke
Nieuport
R. Yres
Thourout
Dixmude
N
Noordschote
R. Steenbeek
Staden
ROULERS (ROESELARE)
Steenstraat
Passchendaele
Pilchem
Moorslede
Broodseinde
YPRES
Observatory Ridge
Becelaere
Gheluvelt
COURTRAI
Wytschaete
Messines
Menin
R. Lys
Comines
Warneton

0  4  3  2  1  0        8
Miles

**Map 2**

# Messines: The End of the Battle, 14 June 1917

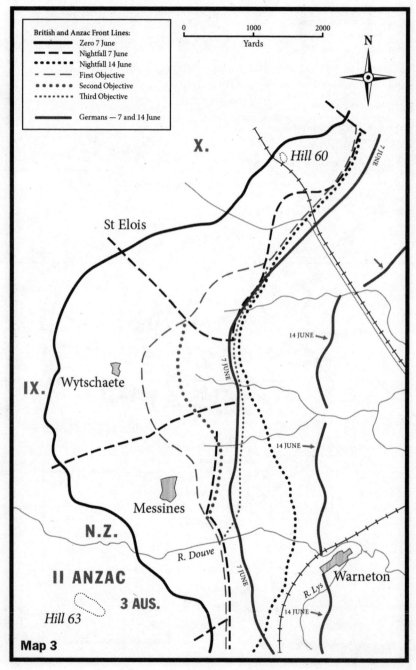

British and Anzac Front Lines:

- Zero 7 June
- Nightfall 7 June
- Nightfall 14 June
- First Objective
- Second Objective
- Third Objective

Germans — 7 and 14 June

0     1000     2000
Yards

N

X.

Hill 60

St Elois

IX.    Wytschaete

14 JUNE →

7 JUNE

14 JUNE →

Messines

N.Z.

R. Douve

7 JUNE

II ANZAC

3 AUS.

Hill 63

Warneton

R. Lys

14 JUNE →

Map 3

# The Fifth Army Offensive, 31 July 1917

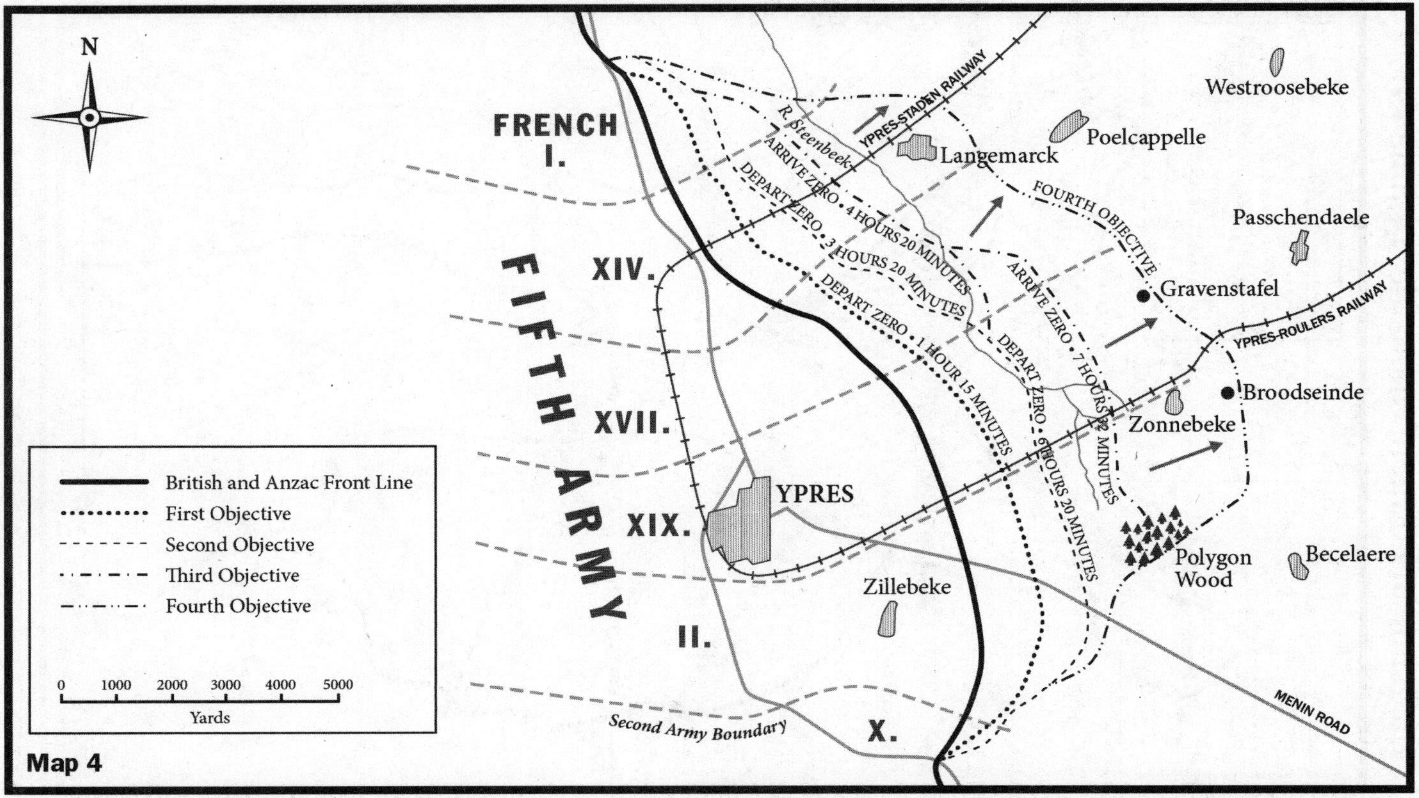

Westroosebeke

Passchendaele

Becelaere

Poelcappelle

Gravenstafel

Broodseinde

Zonnebeke

Polygon Wood

YPRES-ROULERS RAILWAY

MENIN ROAD

FOURTH OBJECTIVE

Langemarck

ARRIVE ZERO · 7 HOURS 22 MINUTES

DEPART ZERO · 6 HOURS 20 MINUTES

DEPART ZERO · 1 HOUR 15 MINUTES

R. Steenbeek

ARRIVE ZERO · 4 HOURS 20 MINUTES

DEPART ZERO · 3 HOURS 20 MINUTES

YPRES-STADEN RAILWAY

Zillebeke

YPRES

X.

FRENCH
I.

XIV.

XVII.

XIX.

II.

FIFTH ARMY

Second Army Boundary

N

| | British and Anzac Front Line |
| | First Objective |
| | Second Objective |
| | Third Objective |
| | Fourth Objective |

0 1000 2000 3000 4000 5000

Yards

Map 4

# The Battle of Polygon Wood, 26 September 1917

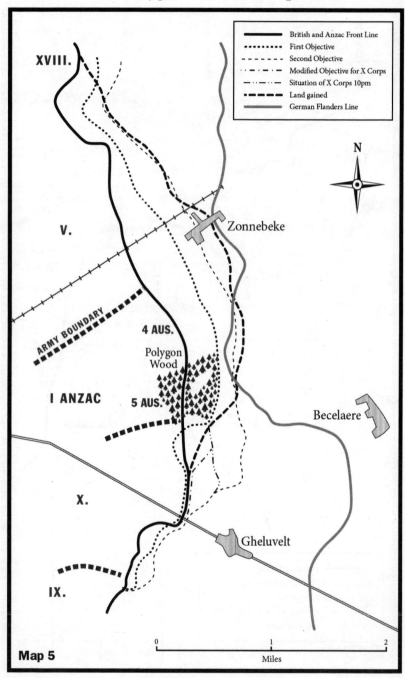

**Legend:**
- British and Anzac Front Line
- First Objective
- Second Objective
- Modified Objective for X Corps
- Situation of X Corps 10pm
- Land gained
- German Flanders Line

N

XVIII.

V.

Zonnebeke

ARMY BOUNDARY

4 AUS.

Polygon Wood

I ANZAC

5 AUS.

Becelaere

X.

Gheluvelt

IX.

0    1    2
Miles

**Map 5**

# The Battle of Broodseinde, 4 October 1917

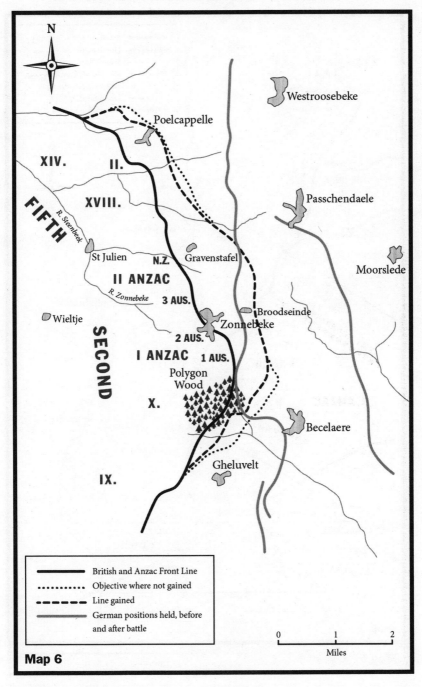

N

Westroosebeke

Poelcappelle

XIV.

II.

XVIII.

Passchendaele

R. Steenbeek

St Julien

N.Z.

Gravenstafel

Moorslede

II ANZAC

R. Zonnebeke

3 AUS.

FIFTH

Broodseinde

Wieltje

Zonnebeke

2 AUS.

SECOND

I ANZAC

1 AUS.

Polygon
Wood

X.

Becelaere

IX.

Gheluvelt

British and Anzac Front Line
Objective where not gained
Line gained
German positions held, before
and after battle

Map 6

0          1          2

Miles

# The First Battle of Passchendaele, 12 October 1917

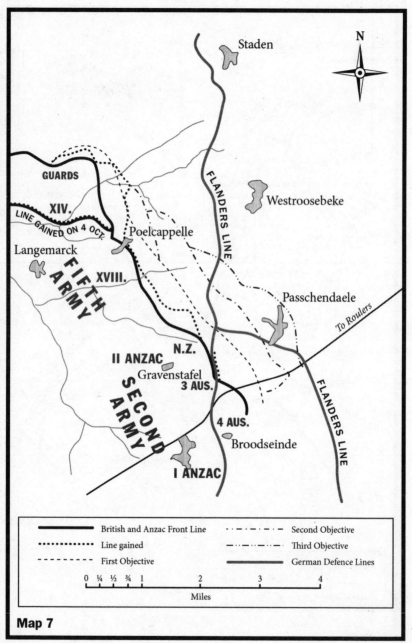

Staden

N

FLANDERS LINE

Westroosebeke

GUARDS

XIV.

LINE GAINED ON 4 OCT.

Poelcappelle

Langemarck

FIFTH ARMY

XVIII.

Passchendaele

To Roulers

N.Z.

II ANZAC

Gravenstafel

3 AUS.

SECOND ARMY

FLANDERS LINE

4 AUS.

Broodseinde

I ANZAC

| | |
|---|---|
| —— British and Anzac Front Line | ·—·—·— Second Objective |
| ·········· Line gained | —··—··— Third Objective |
| - - - - - First Objective | ▬▬▬ German Defence Lines |

0  ¼  ½  ¾  1          2          3          4

Miles

**Map 7**

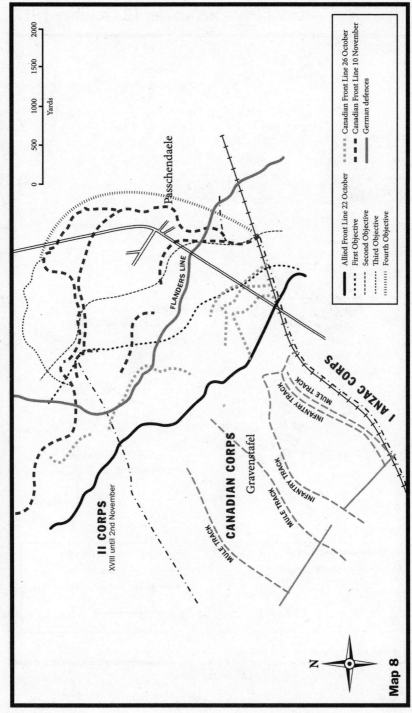

The Second Battle of Passchendaele, 26 October — 10 November 1917

Passchendaele

FLANDERS LINE

II CORPS
XVIII until 2nd November

CANADIAN CORPS
Gravenstafel

I ANZAC CORPS

INFANTRY TRACK

MULE TRACK

INFANTRY TRACK

MULE TRACK

MULE TRACK

Yards

0   500   1000   1500   2000

Allied Front Line 22 October
First Objective
Second Objective
Third Objective
Fourth Objective

Canadian Front Line 26 October
Canadian Front Line 10 November
German defences

N

Map 8

# INTRODUCTION

—

THEY CLAIM A SMALL PLACE in our minds, a century on, in memorial services and on poppy days. 'We are the dead,' they announce in the poem 'In Flanders Fields', like regiments of ghosts whose spirit won't rest.[1] More than half a million of them lay dead, wounded or missing on those fields in 1917, mostly British, Australian, Canadian, Irish, New Zealanders and their German counterparts, a few of whose voices survive in letters and diaries. They tell of one of the bloodiest battles of the Great War – indeed, of any war – with fear and love, humour and pathos, and sometimes with a kind of urgency, as if conscious that theirs would be the only eyewitness accounts of 'Passchendaele'.

The Flemish town that bears this name seems unable, or unwilling, to carry the burden of what happened here. The local spirit is more inclined to look forward than back: there is no general monument here. The historical and emotional freight is probably too heavy for one small community, let alone a city or country. (The larger, neighbouring town of Zonnebeke hosts the new Passchendaele Museum.)

Officially they called it the Third Battle of Ypres, or 'Third Ypres'. In fact, it was a series of immense clashes on the plains to the east of

1

the mediaeval city of Ypres, between 31 July and 11 November 1917. The people and the press fastened instead on the village at the heart of these events, five miles north-east of Ypres: 'Passchendaele', a word evoking Easter and the Passion of Christ (from the Latin verb *pati*, to suffer). Here, the word suggests, lies more than a little Flemish community; here lies a dale of martyrdom, a soldiers' Calvary, a land of tortured souls.

This is what 'Passchendaele' has come to mean in the civilian mind: an epic of pointless butchery that, even by the standards of the Great War, entered the realm of the infernal and monumentally futile. Soldiers, animals, artillery and pouring rain were thrown together in a maelstrom of steel and flesh in the name of a strategy that anticipated hundreds of thousands of casualties – and all for nothing.

Some military specialists disagree with this 'popular' view of Third Ypres, arguing that most of its battles were necessary, achieved some of their goals and were worth the cost. For these self-described 'revisionists', Passchendaele was part of a just and inevitable war against tyranny, and not another massacre in an avoidable tragedy that destroyed the best part of a generation (we shall address this endless controversy in Chapter 17).

We may be sure of one thing: the huge casualties were not some epic blunder; they were expected, they were *planned for*. To understand why is to understand the meaning of a total war of attrition. That effort may be more than the twenty-first-century mind can bear, living as we do in the super-sentimental West, where a body bag is treated as a political opportunity. Many of us approach the Great War not through primary historical records but through the lens of literature, films, photographs or the entertainments of *Blackadder* and *Oh! What a Lovely War*, cultural phenomena that soften, ridicule or set at one remove the truth. That is not to demean these interpretations. It is to say that the finest war literature, some of the funniest satire, and the work of cultural historians such as Paul Fussell, Jay Winter and Modris Eksteins, have transformed the perception of this tragedy into a kind of elevated cultural experience. It is almost as if art has become our reality of the Great War, and the Great War a reflection of art.[2] To borrow the famous Platonic metaphor, that is to look at the War as a shadow thrown against the wall of a cave, the shadow of its true Form.

To open our minds to this tragedy, to understand *what happened* in Flanders in 1917, is to turn our eyes from the shadow and gaze at the Form. It means journeying into a different world, a kind of hell, no doubt, but also a realm in which people lived at extremes, captive to the emotions of hope, love, terror and hubris. The journey is hard and horrifying, and yet also profoundly moving. The following symphony of witnesses, gathered into a narrative, will tell us something of the truth of Passchendaele, and something of the political imperative that drove humanity to that terrible place. Stay the distance and we shall meet on the other side, with a deeper understanding of what human beings are capable of doing to their fellow creatures, and why. For only by reasoning why can we hope for a wiser, perhaps kinder, future. My conclusions, some of them novel, appear in Chapter 17; for now, we shall confine ourselves to the narrative.

# 1

# SERVANTS OF ATTRITION

*You are the War generation. You were born to fight this War,
and it's got to be won . . . So far as you are concerned as
individuals it doesn't matter a tinker's damn whether you are
killed or not. Most probably you will be killed, most of you.*
A British staff officer to a meeting of subalterns, quoted in
Richard Aldington's autobiographical novel, *Death of a Hero*

---

A VISITOR TO PASSCHENDAELE today would struggle to imagine this small Flemish town as the object of a field marshal's obsession and the pivot of the great Flanders Offensive of 1917. In the centre, a few clothes shops and a couple of cafes give onto a desolate square. By the kerb, curiously isolated, stands a bronze relief of the stages of the battle, sculpted by Dr Ross Bastiaan. Opposite stands the church, rebuilt since the war in red, yellow and white stones. British and German artillery destroyed the previous one, along with its cemetery, churning up the remains of the pre-war dead with the casualties of battle. The elaborate graves crowding the grounds post-date the armistice, on 11 November 1918, when the local people returned to reclaim the scab of bones and rubble that had been their home.

A closer look helps us to understand the town's military relevance: Passchendaele sits on the highest (only about 200 feet above sea level) of a series of concentric ridges, arcs of slightly elevated ground that radiate east of Ypres like the terraces of an enormous, shallow stadium. The Passchendaele-Staden section of the ridge offered a good view and 'jumping off' point into German-held territory to the north-east: i.e. the village of Roulers (Roeselare), which served as a vital German supply base, and the plains of Flanders peeling away to the Belgian coast.

Passchendaele village had no strategic importance in its own right; the ridge was merely the first stage of a vast offensive that aimed to liberate Belgium, realising Britain's original case for entering the war. The Flanders Offensive would be a distinctly Commonwealth campaign. In 1917, the exhausted and mutinous French Army were reduced to playing a defensive role on the Western Front; the Russians were in the throes of revolution; and the Americans had not yet arrived. So the British Army and their Australian, Canadian and New Zealand allies (with small French, South African and Belgian units in support) would confront the most powerful concentration of German troops on the Western Front, who were then being reinforced with fresh troops from the east. On British orders, they were to capture Passchendaele Ridge within weeks (see Map 1), seize Roulers and swing north to the Belgian coast, to fulfil one of the chief aims of the offensive: to destroy the German submarine bases at the ports of Ostend, Zeebrugge and others, whose U-boats were waging unlimited war on Allied shipping.

This would be the prelude to the total rout of the German forces in Belgium, a war-winning scenario dependent on a run of incredible victories, daunting in their ambition even with the help of brilliant command, fine weather and a lot of luck (none of which was forthcoming or guaranteed). The great French marshal Ferdinand Foch was not the only commander who had little faith in what he called a 'duck's march' through the Flanders mud. As we shall see, there were other reasons why, between August and November 1917, the British and Dominion commanders drove their men beyond the edge of the humanly possible to capture the village of Passchendaele, and why the Germans were similarly driven to defend it.

The lessons of the immediate past might have counselled against the offensive. This would be *Third* Ypres. The First was a defensive battle fought in October and November 1914, in which the Franco-British forces just held the city, though at a huge cost in blood. The Second, from 22 April to 25 May 1915, ended in a stalemate, with Allied casualties of 87,000 against German casualties of 35,000. By the war's end, there would be *five* battles of Ypres. With the exception of a single day in 1914, the British and their allies would never yield the once-beautiful mediaeval town of Ypres itself to the Germans. And not until October 1918, at the Fifth Battle of Ypres, would they remove the German forces from the edges of the city's eastern hinterland, the 'immortal salient' – a blister of Allied-controlled territory that swelled up and subsided, but never burst, during four years of war. Hundreds of thousands would be killed or wounded defending or attacking the Ypres Salient; many more would live to remember marching past Ypres' shell-cratered streets, past the ruins of the thirteenth-century Cloth Hall and cathedral, to the front. In time, defending 'Wipers', as the Tommies rejoiced in mispronouncing it, became a rite of passage more terrible than the Somme. The Germans, too, would remember this place with special loathing.

—

Prior to Third Ypres, at the start of 1917, Europe was exhausted, brutalised, locked in a conflict that had consumed the lives of millions. A young man might be forgiven for refusing to enlist in a war that had already killed two million out of nearly seven million total casualties on the Western Front, the rest wounded, missing or taken prisoner.[1] The casualty lists at the end of 1916, after the Somme and Verdun, had shocked and then benumbed the British, French and German people. In many homes, the mounting losses, intractable trench lines and ghastliness of the wounds had engendered a kind of dazed acceptance of war as an unstoppable force beyond the human agency to control.

'You knew the horrors of war,' recalled Norman Collins, a young subaltern on his way to Flanders in 1917. 'We knew that 60,000 men had become casualties on July 1st [1916]. We went not thinking we'd come out of it, we didn't think we'd live.'[2]

The mood of foreboding that marked 1917 was a far cry from the exuberance at the outbreak, in August 1914, when the British Expeditionary Force (BEF), a band of 150,000 professionals whom the Kaiser had scorned as a 'contemptible little army' (hence their nickname, the 'Old Contemptibles'), sailed for France. At the time, they were the best-trained soldiers and finest marksmen in the world. By 1917, with the exception of a few diehards, they were dead, wounded, exhausted or retired. They had not gone easily: in August 1914, this force held the line at Mons until forced to join the great French retreat towards Paris. In September that year, they had plugged a critical gap in the French lines at the Marne and helped, in an important symbolic way, to drive the Germans back to the Aisne and confound the Prussian Schlieffen Plan to conquer France within six weeks. In October 1914, vastly outnumbered, the Old Contemptibles held Ypres against waves of young German recruits, sustaining 58,000 casualties. And from 25 September to 13 October 1915, they marched to their doom at Loos, in one of the worst defeats in British military history.

The unspeakable scenes at Loos might have shelved forever the idea that huge frontal attacks could break the German lines. What happened at Loos revealed a breed of man, the British Tommy, whose courage, unquestioning sense of duty and fear of failure persuaded him to march head-on into enemy machine guns. A German witness, the historian of the 26th Infantry Regiment, famously described the result:

Never had the machine guns had such straightforward work to do . . . with barrels burning hot and swimming in oil, they traversed to and fro along the [British] ranks unceasingly; one machine gun alone fired 12,500 rounds that afternoon. The effect was devastating. The enemy could be seen literally falling in hundreds, but they continued their march in good order and without interruption. The extended lines of men began to get confused by this terrific punishment, but they went doggedly on, some even reaching the wire entanglement in front of the reserve line . . . Confronted by this impenetrable obstacle, the survivors turned and began to retire.[3]

Field Marshal Sir John French, the BEF's serially inept commander, and the then lieutenant general Sir Douglas Haig were jointly responsible for this debacle.[4] Sir John bore the brunt of the blame, for failing to send up reserves in time to hold the British gains, exposing his forward troops to devastating German counter-attacks. The toll was 59,247 British soldiers killed, wounded or missing, including three major generals and the only son of the poet Rudyard Kipling, whose death would inspire the poem 'My Boy Jack' ('"Have you news of my boy Jack?" / *Not this tide.* / "When d'you think that he'll come back?" / *Not with this wind blowing, and this tide.*'). Many soldiers inhaled British poison gas, blown back onto their trenches when the wind changed, killing or incapacitating them. Sir John was sacked, and he returned to Britain to command the Home Forces, a bitter and resentful man. Haig replaced him.

News from the wider war offered little respite in that dismal year. In the Dardanelles Campaign (April 1915–January 1916), the Allies hoped to carve a third front against the Germans, from the south. To do so, they would conquer the Turks and combine with the Russians from the east and the French from the west to crush Germany and Austria-Hungary in a three-way vice. Winston Churchill's brainchild was a disaster: nearly half a million British, French, Turkish and Commonwealth soldiers were killed or wounded over six months of futile carnage. The Australians and New Zealanders would henceforth romanticise Gallipoli as a 'nation-forming' sacrifice. Their decent intent is understandable, but their annual commemorations amount to a rite of denial of what Gallipoli actually meant: the useless occupation of a few Turkish beaches that achieved nothing other than a flourish of pointless heroics and the dispatch of grief into hundreds of thousands of homes. The Allies spent the rest of 1915 nursing their wounded, regrouping, launching sporadic trench raids and training the vast intake of new recruits.

—

When 1916 began, the war was still young, the adventure real, and everyone wanted to be in it. The middle classes of all the respective nations were loudly receptive to the idea that they were fighting for the motherland, for King, Kaiser, Emperor or Tsar. Every side had God on their side. This would be the 'decisive' year, declared the Triple Entente (France, Russia, Britain and their colonial allies), a refrain they would repeat at the start of every year. The coming battles would be unlike anything the world had seen, fought at Verdun, on the Meuse, on the Somme, in Italy and on the Eastern Front, where Russia's Brusilov Offensive prepared to unleash the most lethal military operation to that point in history.

Britain, France, Russia and Germany had cranked up the war effort to a level of intensity unimaginable twelve months earlier. Factories chugged away night and day to deliver the instruments of death. Millions of rounds of heavy explosive, hundreds of thousands of rifles, machine guns, uniforms, gas shells, gas masks, grenades, trenching tools, and all kinds of newfangled equipment poured off the assembly lines. Governments and military commanders adopted new ways of managing their huge new armies: the British forces were being reorganised, under the deep reforms of Viscount Haldane and Haig. The appeal from Lord Kitchener – field marshal and secretary of state for war – to fill his 'New Armies' had raised the largest volunteer force in the world. Almost 2.5 million British men voluntarily enlisted between August 1914 and December 1915. The promise of a square meal and the King's shilling, more than god or country, persuaded the unemployed and malnourished to enlist. They made up the majority. Even this immense force was not enough, and from 2 March 1916 the British Government began conscripting single men for frontline duty, under the first Military Service Act; on 25 May, another Act extended conscription to married men.[5]

Germany was similarly moving to a total war footing. On 31 August 1916, General Field Marshal Paul von Hindenburg instructed the War Ministry to ratchet up production to unprecedented levels. 'Men – as well as horses – must be replaced more and more by machines,' he wrote. Women, the wounded, prisoners, social misfits and minors would be compelled to work in war industries. The war effort was a 'screw without end', Hindenburg said: victory would go to the power that turned the screw tightest at the right moment.[6] Henceforth, he called for the monthly output of gunpowder to double, to 12,000 tons, and of machine guns to triple, to 7000 pieces. Those rates of production were scheduled to remain in force until at least May–June 1917, when, a German colonel confidently declared, 'the war would have ended'.[7]

By 1916, Europe had turned into a vast armed camp. Great armies, millions strong, gazed across no-man's-land, bristling for action. No, it would not be over by Christmas, not this year or the next. The trenches were no longer the shallow, hastily dug scrapes of 1914. Solid wooden A-frames and duckboards, deep tunnels, reinforced dugouts and cement bunkers locked down the front lines, behind which a labyrinth of support and communication trenches, like subterranean cities, wound back to the railheads, encampments and training grounds in the tented rear areas, brimful of fresh troops and shipments of weapons and supplies. Food, ammunition and medical provisions were produced, packaged and delivered by millions of civilians, mostly women, working day and night in darkened factories on the home front. These oceans of toiling humanity lapped either side of that great fissure of black earth running from the Belgian coast to the Swiss Alps, where, on this 'Western Front', the contest of the world would be decided.

—

Verdun almost broke the spirit of the belligerents. The memory of that ghastly confrontation, fought over ten months (21 February–18 December 1916), disabused thousands of troops of their faith in the war and indelibly scarred the historical soul of France and Germany. 'Like Auschwitz . . . Verdun came to symbolise a breach of the limits of the human condition,' wrote the French historian Antoine Prost.[8] The 299-day bloodbath transformed the meaning of war. The 'noble sacrifice', the 'fight for freedom and country', had become a program of indifferent extermination. Verdun killed or wounded between 600,000 and 900,000 men (depending on the source), 315,000–542,000 French and 281,000–434,000 German. At the end of it, 160,000 French and 143,000 German soldiers lay dead.[9] Neither side 'won': the German strategy amounted to a series of limited attacks on French border forts aimed at drawing the blue-uniformed *poilu* into a narrow killing zone and then pulverising them with artillery of such intensity that 'not even a mouse could live'. Those were the words of the chief of the German general staff, General Erich von Falkenhayn, for whom it was immaterial whether the Germans actually took Verdun. The main objective of the battle, as he assured the Kaiser, was to 'bleed France white' (*Blutabzapfung*).[10] Not for nothing was Falkenhayn known as the 'Blood-Miller of Verdun', and the Great War's first exponent of a strategy of pure attrition.

To relieve the French at Verdun, and divert the German forces, the British and Dominion armies launched the Somme Offensive (1 July–18 November 1916). The Somme was a *diversion*. Haig had preferred to fight in Flanders, but he bowed to the political imperative of aiding Britain's chief European ally. We need not dwell on this catastrophic struggle, which has produced more literature than any other Anglo-Saxon battle. As we know, or should know, the holocaust killed or wounded more than 1.3 million men, in one of the bloodiest confrontations in history. The Somme claimed 57,470

British casualties on the first day (of whom more than 19,000 were killed); the Germans lost 40,000 over the first ten days. The ensuing battles, of Albert, Fromelles, Delville Wood, Pozières, Thiepval Ridge, Ancre and many more, surged and flowed over the plains of Picardy, killing or wounding the Allies at the rate of almost 3000 men per day.[11]

Haig later described the Somme as the start of 'the wearing-down war', or the war of attrition, a term that broadly meant slowly grinding down the enemy's strength and resources, until it became possible to break through to open ground and destroy their residual strength. Attrition, reckons a US military writer, Dr J. Boone Bartholomees, 'strategically favors the attacker since he can regulate his own pain; he can select when, where, and how hard he attacks and thus control to at least some extent his losses'.[12] That may be true, yet the 'body count' in an attritional war almost always favours the defenders, as the great Prussian strategist Carl von Clausewitz (1780–1831) explained in his book *On War* (a lesson taught to generations of Sandhurst men): i.e. men defensively employed in well-entrenched positions had an inherent advantage over their attackers.[13] In 1916 and 1917, the Germans acted on this: they chose not to initiate any major offensives, instead defending their gains of 1914 and 1915. And so, entrenched in their fortified redoubts, their dugouts and concrete pillboxes, the German infantry prepared to exploit their Clausewitzian advantage: they simply sat and waited for the enemy to charge, aiming to bleed the attackers to death.

Britain, France and their allies more than obliged, hurling wave after wave of recruits at the German lines. The Somme killed or wounded many more British, French and Dominion troops than German troops, in line with von Clausewitz's grim equation: 794,000 versus 540,000 (according to a consensus of scholars).[14] Again, no side 'won' this series of gruesome encounters: the Germans withdrew and were reinforced; the British consolidated their modest gains.

Certain military experts now calmly remind us of the chief

'benefit' of the Somme: it taught Allied commanders useful tactical lessons, chiefly the correct application of the creeping barrage, without which they could not have won the war. The Great War would be a steep and bloody learning curve. Of course, Germany could cite the same lessons: the learning curve proceeded at a similar pace for both sides, ceding no ultimate advantage. In any case, the Allied armies did not fight the Somme purely to learn 'lessons' and educate the commanders. The more intelligent and innovative generals (Britain's Herbert Plumer, Australia's John Monash and Canada's Arthur Currie) did not need the Somme to teach them the point of the creeping barrage, or evidence of its failure in the mass graves of the Anglo-Saxon and Celtic dead. In this light, one can't help wondering how families who'd lost their sons on the Somme would have reacted to this *ex post facto* justification for the battle: 'Oh, we had to fight the Somme to teach the generals how to fire the heavy guns. Sorry about your boy.'

The third year of the Great War ended in stalemate after the bloodiest contests in history. Censorship could not shield the public from the casualty lists, which crowded the newspaper columns and reduced whole communities to despair. Some towns, such as Accrington, in East Lancashire, were rumoured to have lost nearly all their young men. The Somme had annihilated many 'pals battalions' – i.e. drawn from the same communities or industries – nourishing an impression that an entire generation was being systematically wiped out.

British High Command defended their actions on the grounds that the Germans must never be allowed to rest; the offensive spirit must be kept high; the German Army must be worn down. At the end of this 'wearing-down war', whenever it finally came, the victor would be the last man standing. That prospect did not unduly trouble the Allied generals. In 1917, the British commanders knew they were losing men at a faster rate than Germany, but they also knew they would soon draw on a far deeper pool of manpower, once France had recovered and the Americans had arrived. Yes, they would probably lose more men in absolute terms, but Germany and Austria-Hungary would exhaust their reserves more quickly. By that brutal logic, the Entente would win the war.

—

On the trains and ships bound for France they came, the usual bois-terous, overconfident young men, keening for battle and 'killing the Boche' (or 'Tommies', on the German side). Many found refuge in jokes; others were thoughtful, ruminant, or immersed in their books. Many were quietly terrified. If most had shared Norman Collins's feelings in 1914 – 'I felt I had to defend our country'[15] – and the writer A. P. Herbert's sense that he'd been 'calmly persuaded' to go to war 'for a just cause',[16] fewer felt that way in 1917. The thrill of the declaration of war had dissipated, and the patriotic affection of ear-lier years had cooled into something harder, more ruthless, or, at any rate, less self-deceiving. The men who had trained the new recruits had served on the Western Front and seen the carnage, after all.

By 1917, their illusion of invincibility had waned. The romance of war, the boyish hero-worship, the glory of the charge, their faith in the cause had come unstuck. The soldiers had heard all about the Somme and Verdun. They'd seen the wounded in the streets – the lucky ones – or heard about the rest: shellfire could disembowel, decapitate and castrate you. If your friend beside you took a direct hit, you'd be covered in his blood and entrails. Artillery would tear apart 'the pleasant fringes of war . . . and drinking in strange towns' with the indiscriminate power of an epidemic.[17] Chlorine and phos-gene gases would kill you slowly, in great agony (mustard gas would not be used until July 1917).

To say you'd enlisted for god, king or country invited ridicule from hardened veterans. The soldiers were no longer 'duped by the War talk', wrote Richard Aldington, an officer in the Royal Sussex Regiment in 1917, in his autobiographical novel of the war: 'They laughed at the newspapers. Any new-comer who tried to be a bit high falutin was at once snubbed with, "Fer Christ's sake don't talk patriotic!" They went on with a sort of stubborn despair . . .'[18]

Others shared Private Neville Hind's hardened sense of duty: 'from the first day I put on Khaki, I accepted the moral responsibility for killing Germans, just as the Conscientious Objector refuses from the outset'.[19] There was little glory in it; it was a job. Hind's low-key departure, like most, was bereft of the euphoria of earlier years: a small crowd saw his regiment off. Some troops sang and shouted from the carriages, 'though others were silent'[20] – such as the Cardiff City ex-professional footballer and the Northumberland miner, 'very kind, generous and soft-hearted; getting on for 40, leaving home, maybe for the first time, and feeling it very acutely, leaving a wife and family'.[21] 'Old' soldiers just back from the front had told the men what to expect. Hind's 25-year-old platoon sergeant, puffing away on a Woodbine at the station, cried 'like a child at the brutality of men' as his unit departed. Hind's regimental chaplain, who had also 'been out', stood on the platform looking 'grave, yet in a sense cheery'.[22]

They travelled all night to Folkestone and boarded a packed troop ship escorted by a destroyer: the submarine threat was at its height in 1917. During the crossing to France, they passed a hospital ship, a reminder of what 'all knew, tho' none said, that there were some of us would never return'.[23] The songs had changed. Few sang the rousing tunes that piped them into battle in 1914 and 1915: 'Take Me Back to Dear Old Blighty' had replaced 'It's a Long Way to Tipperary'.[24] But their sense of humour, 'the great safety-valve of a soldier', never deserted them.[25] On New Year's Eve of 1916–17, to the tune of 'Auld Lang Syne', they sang:

> We're here because we're here,
> Because we're here, because we're here,
> We're here because we're here,
> Because we're here, because we're here.[26]

—

The Seabrook brothers, George, 25, Theo, 24, and Keith, 20, sailed from Sydney aboard the troop ship *Ascanius* on 25 October 1916 and landed at Devonport, Plymouth, on 28 December. The eldest of eight children, the brothers formed the core of a close-knit, if peripatetic family. George was an apprentice painter, Theo a fireman, and Keith a telephone operator. Pre-war photos show their father, William, padded up and playing cricket with his sons, like any other Australian dad, in the backyard of their inner-city cottage.

Their mother Fanny (née Isabel Ross) came from a prosperous family of staunch Methodists, proprietors of the general store in Grafton, a town in northern New South Wales. This determined young woman became the rock on which her growing brood relied. 'I've never heard anyone in the family say a harsh word about her,' recalls one relative. 'She held the family together.'[27] Her elfin face and small frame belied a strong-willed woman of stoic calm, in marked distinction to the erratic, vulnerable disposition of her husband, William.

In 1916, the Seabrooks settled in Petersham, a working-class suburb of Sydney, where William resumed his trade as a railway carpenter, offering Fanny a welcome respite from his exhausting delusions. William had hitherto persuaded himself, Micawber-like, that his fortune lay around the next bend, in pursuit of which he'd dragged the family across the country on various doomed excursions – to Fremantle, in Western Australia, to invest in a dolomite mine; back to New South Wales, to the town of Armidale, to open a bookshop; and elsewhere, with new ideas and get-rich-quick schemes, none of which amounted to much.

George and Theo enlisted for service abroad in the Australian Army in August 1916; their younger brother Keith, aged nineteen, required his parents' 'full permission to enlist for active service abroad', which he received the same month. Despite his youth, Keith had had experience as a junior officer in the militia, and would receive an acting sergeant's and later a lieutenant's rank. They signed the oath that bound the Dominions to defend the British realm:

> I [name] swear that I will well and truly serve our Sovereign
> Lord the King in the Australian Imperial Force . . . and
> that I will resist His Majesty's enemies and cause His
> Majesty's peace to be kept and maintained . . .[28]

They then passed their medical examinations – free of scrofula, phthisis, syphilis, impaired constitution, defective intelligence, defects of vision, voice or hearing, haemorrhoids, severe varicose veins, marked varicocele with unusually pendant testicle, inveterate cutaneous disease, chronic ulcers, traces of corporal punishment or evidence of having been marked with the letters D. [Deserter] or B.C. [Bad Character], contracted or deformed chest, and abnormal curvature of the spine – and were pronounced 'fit for active service'.[29]

The voyage to England took them via Colombo, South Africa and Dakar. The day after their arrival, they marched into a training camp at Rollestone, near Salisbury. On leave, they visited London. Their postcards offer a glimpse of their characters: George had recovered from the death of his wife, in January 1916, and he wrote home with great enthusiasm. Theo lacked his brothers' self-confidence yet 'loved to poke fun' at them all.[30] Keith was the more responsible, and wrote of his brothers' health and plans.

They were all having a 'glorious time' in London. 'This place is very cold, we had a good fall of snow yesterday,' Keith told his grandmother.[31] They had 'had a great time riding on the buses, no doubt you would too,' they told their little sister Jean.[32] 'My word,' they wrote to their youngest brother, Clarrie, 'you would jump with glee if you where [*sic*] in London . . .'[33]

—

At about this time, a young Englishman with a markedly different background to the Seabrooks was serving as a junior officer in the King's Royal Rifle Corps. Like so many former public school boys, the Old Etonian Desmond Allhusen had enlisted as soon as he left school, in August 1914. At news of the declaration of war, Allhusen and his friends rejoiced. 'There were scenes of wild enthusiasm,' Desmond noted in his diary. 'A form of parting much used among the cadet school-leavers was "Good-bye. See you again in Hell".'[34] Later that evening, Desmond found his brother Rupert in his room, 'sharpening his sword'.

On 15 August 1914, Allhusen was gazetted as a second lieutenant. He attended the Royal Military College, Sandhurst the following year. 'I can't recollect having learnt anything there,' he wrote, 'but the time passed very pleasantly . . . The Old Etonian coterie was exempt from most of the orders . . . and we amused ourselves without much interference.'[35]

He left Sandhurst shortly before his nineteenth birthday and sailed for France on the night of 5 October 1915, in charge of a platoon of working men several years older. At Le Havre, he discovered that he'd already drunk most of the brandy that he'd brought for the battlefield. His regiment camped on a hill above Honfleur, the scene of Henry V's 'once more into the breach' scene, he remarked.[36]

Allhusen suffered from recurring jaundice, yet he repeatedly persuaded medical boards to pass him fit. 'This was not very difficult,' he wrote in 1916, after a three-month convalescence, 'as at this time Boards took the view that if anybody said he was fit he was certain to be.' Another man, he noticed, passed fit and 'could hardly walk'.[37]

Allhusen spent the first half of 1917 either in hospital or on sick leave. His frequent Channel crossings showed how total war had transformed the voyage. In 1915, he'd been 'shown to my cabin by a steward, asking unnecessary questions about breakfast next morning. I had slept between sheets and had, in general, travelled to the war like a gentleman.' In 1917:

I was bundled onto a small, smelly, overcrowded boat, hermetically sealed to stop the slightest glimmer of light showing. It was just a question of getting as many human beings on board as the ship would carry. There was barely standing room for everybody, and no question of lying down.

After hours at sea, 'the atmosphere was indescribable'.[38]

———

Nineteen-year-old Corporal John Ronald Skirth, of Eastbourne, had had a protected, Christian upbringing. He excelled at maths and enjoyed reading the Romantic poets. A few weeks before he left for France, in March 1917, he realised that he'd 'fallen in love' with Ella, a fifteen-year-old schoolgirl. The couple promised to devote their lives to each other when he came home – a common enough dream. He sailed on the *Mona's Queen*, an antiquated old bucket of a paddle steamer from the Isle of Man, which would be sunk by a German submarine on her return trip.[39]

Skirth arrived at Le Havre at dawn on 1 April and spent the first two nights under canvas bell tents in pouring rain. In his wallet, he carried a photo of Ella, 'wearing the spotted white dress she wore the day I fell in love with her'.[40] According to his identity disc, Skirth was officially '120331 Corporal Skirth, J.R., B.C.A., C. of E., 239 Siege Battery, Royal Garrison Artillery'. B.C.A. stood for 'battery commander's assistant', whose job was to gather the information on weather, wind, distance, topography and other variables necessary to calculate the target range for the guns. His battery operated the 'heavies' – heavy guns that fired 6- or 9.2-inch-calibre shells – as well as four howitzers, 'stubby fat-looking monsters', weighing two tons each, which had to be towed to the front behind tractors.

Skirth's naivety made him an easy target for his friends, the 'Tyneside Twins' Geordie and Bill, who mocked him for his two stripes, 'posh' accent and 'because I was barmy enough to read poetry'.[41] They quickly fastened onto Skirth's sexual inexperience (he was a virgin): '[T]hey were a decade ahead of me in . . . their familiarity with every detail of the female anatomy.' Skirth's other 'best friend' was a red-haired, six-foot amateur Scottish boxing champion from Glasgow, called Jock Shiels. In a few months, Jock would drag Skirth out of a gas-filled shell hole, 'in which, but for him I would have died a painful death'.[42]

Skirth grew to hate his commanding officer 'more than any of my country's enemies', a man who 'in every way possible sought to humiliate me'.[43] This officer, a public school and Camberley Staff College-educated '100% professional' and recipient of the Distinguished Service Order (DSO), wore a neat, steel-grey moustache on a face 'desiccated into parchment' by the suns of India and Aden. Clearly, he had little time for men like Skirth, whom he regarded as delicate examples of the 'New Army'; yet he valued Skirth's maths brain, which served as the battery's 'calculating machine'.[44]

In turn, the commanding officer was apparently unpopular throughout the ranks. 'Everyone,' Skirth recalls, 'from senior officers down to the humblest ranked gunner feared [him]. I never saw him smile. I never heard him utter one word of praise to anyone. I never saw him perform one act of kindness. In addition I never saw his face register emotion of any kind – until one terrible day at Passchendaele.'[45]

—

Fathers faced a tough choice: should they avoid the risk of denying their children a father's love and care? Or should they offer their country their able bodies in its time of need? In 1914, the 34-year-old E. C. Allfree was 'just a peaceful solicitor' living in Broadstairs, east Kent, 'with a wife and three children to keep'. When Britain declared war, he was sitting in the Country Inn near Canterbury 'watching the cricket during the Canterbury Cricket Week'. He had had no military training, never fired a rifle and didn't know how to ride. What good would I be as a soldier, he wondered. How could I leave my wife and family? Who would support them? What would happen to my business?[46]

Posters and the press warned him that Britain needed every fit man, and he hurt his wife's feelings when he said, 'This is the first time I have ever wished I was not married.'[47] He was not being unkind: 'I meant that if one was single, one would be relieved of that horrible indecision as to what one's duty was.' As a married man, he enlisted in the Derby Scheme's reserves, composed of those willing to go but not yet needed. He served as a 'special constable', drilled and practised shooting, guarded the local waterworks in case enemy aliens poisoned the water and wandered around at night 'looking for spies and landing parties and finding none . . .'[48]

The demands on manpower soon came knocking. On 10 June 1916, his group were ordered to present themselves at Canterbury Barracks. By then, Allfree's wife, Dolly, had given birth to a fourth child, now six months old. Allfree moved the family from Broadstairs – then vulnerable to German air raids – to a cottage in Herne Bay and drew up his will.

Noting Allfree's above-average intelligence, the army awarded him a commission, and he joined the Royal Garrison Artillery. On 27 April 1917, the new Lieutenant Allfree sailed from Southampton aboard the SS *King Edward*, which was 'absolutely packed . . . soldiers everywhere as tight as sardines'. They crossed the Channel in darkness, escorted on either side by 'torpedo boats' to protect them from enemy submarines. Men slept in their lifebelts, in the gangways and on the decks, 'everywhere and on everything'. Allfree did not sleep: 'there seemed no spot that invited sleep. I leant over the side of the ship and drank in the weirdness of it all.'[49] All through the night, the only sounds were the chunck, chunck, chunck of the engines and the swish of the black water along the ship's sides.

—

At first sight, Lieutenant Patrick Campbell, nineteen, seemed another sensitive middle-class young man prone to fall prey to his imagination and crack up. Like many junior officers, Campbell was barely a man: his voice had not yet fully broken, he lacked self-confidence and his platoon's carnal sense of humour shocked him.

In April 1917, he was saying goodbye to his parents on the platform at Oxford Station. It was 'very disagreeable', he recalls.[50] They had already lost one son and their eldest was stationed in Mesopotamia. The previous night, his father had read to him from St John's Gospel, 'Let not your Heart be Troubled, neither let it be Afraid,' and advised him that he could do 'what any Tom, Dick or Harry' had done. His mother offered more practical advice: 'You have to go, I know you wouldn't be happy if all the others went and you were left behind.'[51]

From the ship's deck, Campbell looked down on the near-deserted wharves: 'Nobody . . . was interested, no-one was seeing us off, there would be no waving from the shore.'[52] The thought that he would not make a good officer tormented him. He felt afraid, not of death, but of fear itself. Touching in its pathos is his youthful idea that a prefect's beating or a game of football would prepare him for artillery fire: 'I had been able to bear these things as well as anyone else, I should be able to bear shellfire. But a slight doubt remained, I could not entirely banish the feeling of unease.'[53] Campbell gazed at the stars and looked forward to 'my first view of a foreign country' and the beginning of 'a Great Adventure'.[54]

Over many of these men, observed Richard Aldington, 'hung a sense of doom', which a British staff officer 'admirably if somewhat ruthlessly expressed' to a meeting of subalterns. 'You are the War generation,' he said. 'You were born to fight this War, and it's got to be won . . . So far as you are concerned as individuals it doesn't matter a tinker's damn whether you are killed or not. Most probably you will be killed, most of you.'[55]

# 2

# THE HUMAN FACTOR

*I am 'meant to win' by some Superior Power.*
Field Marshal Sir Douglas Haig, in a letter to wife, 27 December 1915

---

*I am not prepared to accept the position of a*
*butcher's boy driving cattle to the slaughter.*
Prime Minister David Lloyd George, 9 February 1917

---

At what cost was the war worth winning? Would the great struggle extirpate the European powers, their empires and Western civilisation itself? For what were they fighting: king and country, freedom, the privileges of the ruling class, the war profiteers? If they were winning, why did they have so little to eat? At the start of 1917, people of all political persuasions and social backgrounds, from Liverpool factory workers to liberal intellectuals, German housewives to Russian Bolsheviks, were asking such questions. The huge losses on the Somme, at Verdun and in the eastern theatre had traumatised European society, and rumblings of dissent were growing: workers were refusing to work in war industries; civilians were turning against the war; even rogue conservatives were rethinking whether the huge cost was worth it. The Australian people upset Britain (and infuriated the Labor prime minister, Billy Hughes, who lost his seat as a result) by narrowly rejecting conscription in a national referendum on 28 October 1916, sending a clear message that the little dominion would not jump to fulfil British demands for more men.

And men were precisely what the British war effort needed. 'The overwhelming preponderance in man power,' David Lloyd George later wrote, 'which had given the Allies such a false sense of security and lured them in 1915 and 1916 into enterprises where human life was thrown lavishly and recklessly into the conflagration to feed the flames as if there was an endless store of available men in reserve, had now practically disappeared.' Militarily, the Central Powers looked 'stronger and more unbreakable than they had ever been'.[1]

By 1917, the belligerents' 'war aims' had fundamentally shifted. The Entente Powers (Britain, France and Russia) continued to insist on their 1914 goals – that they were at war to punish German aggression and liberate Europe from tyranny. Germany and her allies continued to insist that they were fighting a defensive war, a 'preventive strike', to secure the Reich and their empires against the three-way vice of the Triple Entente. By now, however, the world had changed, and the powers adjusted their policies and propaganda accordingly. Tsarist Russia teetered on the brink of collapse, and France and Britain were gravely weakened: the Triple Entente looked like crumbling, and deep pessimism infected the three governments. Britain and France used state propaganda and an acquiescent press to reassure their people that they were engaged in a sacred struggle to avenge the immense sacrifices of 1916. Germany had come through 1916 in a stronger state, and the Prussian High Command believed they could win the war and implement the fantastic program for European conquest that they'd unveiled in September 1914, to which the German government had not committed.

In fact, the European powers were in a state of crystallising panic. They had *everything* to lose if they lost – their empires, markets and financial power. A new enemy, the 'enemy within', was threatening to overthrow the very systems of government that had prevailed for centuries, founded on the divine right of kings, imperial rule (and partial democracy), and the concentration of capital in the hands of a small elite. The new socialist and liberal parties were determined to overturn the political order that had tolerated systemic inequity and social exclusion. Extremists in Russia and Germany went further: they aimed to dismember the ruling classes and reorder society along communist lines. A spectre was indeed haunting Europe, as Karl Marx had warned: workers were organising and unions railing against their employers. The shortage of food and huge casualties were political gifts to opposition parties such as Germany's Social Democratic Party (SPD) and the British Labour Party. On the extreme fringes, the Bolsheviks, Anarchists and other militant movements welcomed the prospect of their nations' military collapse as the handmaiden of revolution and the decapitation of the bourgeoisie. Lenin, the Bolsheviks' self-exiled leader, longed for his country's defeat as an opportunity to seize power and destroy Tsarism forever. The authoritarians in power in Russia, Germany and Austria-Hungary played into their hands by refusing even moderate social reform.

Even that relatively docile political species, the British worker, had begun to place class loyalty ahead of loyalty to country. Socialist leaders exploited the widespread feeling that the English aristocracy who had taken Britain to war in 1914 had more in common with their German and Russian counterparts than with the ordinary people of their country. The perception exacerbated extreme social tension. Relatively liberal Britain, driven by rising political stars David Lloyd George and Winston Churchill, had made concessions to social reform: the introduction, for example, of a collective labour law (*Trade Disputes Act 1906*), a nod at security for the elderly (*Old Age Pensions Act 1908*) and provision of assistance to the unemployed (*National Insurance Act 1911*). The irony of the state caring for the old and unemployed while killing off the young was not lost on many soldiers.

If Britain was a beacon of social progress in the leaden,

authoritarian facade of Europe, her government postponed deeper reforms: to extend votes to women, improve public healthcare and alleviate extreme poverty. Mothers had no say in the choice of government that would force her sons to fight and die, if necessary. Many workers were outraged at the profiteering of war-related businesses at a time of extreme food shortages: a record number of strikes would animate 1917. All of this alarmed the richest echelons and capital-owning classes. A glance at the graphs in Thomas Piketty's *Capital in the Twenty-First Century* shows just what was at stake for Europe's upper orders: in 1914, total net private wealth in Europe was worth about 600–700 per cent of national income.[2] The elites had everything to lose if they lost the war.

Governments were thus acutely aware that they were fighting two wars: against the enemy without, who wanted to carve up their empires and extract a big war dividend; and against the enemy within, who wanted social reform, votes and higher wages (or the 'redistribution of capital'). The year of 1917 would see the most acute expression of this inner-outer tension, especially in Russia. Only total victory would give the German, Russian and Austro-Hungarian regimes the authority they needed to defeat their internal enemies and preserve their empires. Having refused to liberalise their otiose systems, they had little choice other than to fight to the bitter end, for their ancient privileges and financial power, the preservation of which they continued to sell to their people as a noble sacrifice for god, the Fatherland and the incumbent crowned head.

In sum, the Great Powers' war aims now boiled down to 'victory at all costs', as the German historian Holger Herwig concludes:

> the more the war cost in blood and treasure and the longer
> it went on, the greater the clamour for post-war gains. The
> conservative regimes of the Central Powers feared that
> failure to bring home vast indemnities and annexations
> would endanger their near-exclusive rights to rule.[3]

The crowning irony is that the imperial dynasties of Russia, Germany, Austria-Hungary and the Ottomans were *genuinely* at risk just as their people were losing interest in defending them.

—

While most governments and their press pulpits continued to bellow for war, a rising number of moderate, middle-class people were beginning to disagree with them, on moral and religious grounds. Shocked by the huge losses on the Western Front, many British, French and German people no longer believed the costs justified the aims of the war, whatever they happened to be. The Catholic Church had made its opposition to the war very clear, and would make several doomed appeals for a peaceful settlement. Indeed, one of the church's most outspoken anti-war voices was Daniel Mannix, the Irish-born Catholic archbishop of Australia, who provoked uproar in 1917 by damning the global conflict as 'just an ordinary trade war'.[4] In Germany, middle-class women who couldn't feed their children were taking to the streets in violent protests, stealing and attacking shops. For them, a looted ham meant far more than news of the fall of Bucharest.[5]

Powerful government officials felt moved to find a peaceful solution. An eminent British example was the former Conservative foreign secretary and statesman Lord Lansdowne (Henry Petty-Fitzmaurice, 5th Marquess of Lansdowne), who, in November 1916, privately circulated a letter in the Cabinet urging the government to seek a negotiated peace with Germany. No war aims could be advanced after the Somme, Lansdowne argued, that would recompense Britain for the cost of victory in the blood of the nation's youth.[6] The British Government were aghast that so prominent a Conservative should put forward a 'defeatist' position. It was considered exceedingly bad form, notwithstanding the fact that several powerful figures, including Herbert Asquith, the embattled Liberal prime minister who had recently lost his son on the Somme, were 'in complete concurrence' with Lansdowne.[7]

Lansdowne's plea fell on barren ground. A strong majority in Cabinet supported the war, and would accept nothing less than Germany's unconditional surrender. A peace deal that failed to secure this, they declared, for which so many had paid the supreme sacrifice, was not worth the paper it was printed on. The huge casualty lists reproached both sides of the argument: those who would politicise the soldiers' sacrifice to justify further slaughter in the guise of vengeance; and those who would undermine the sacrifice by negotiating an 'unworthy' peace.

Lansdowne looked forlorn when, on 12 December 1916, the Allies received Berlin's notorious 'Peace Note', signed by Chancellor Theobald von Bethmann-Hollweg. From a position of 'indestructible strength', having won 'considerable successes', it declared, Germany, Austria-Hungary and Turkey would 'not seek to crush or annihilate' their adversaries. On the contrary, 'conscious of their military and economic power' and their readiness 'to carry on to the end, if they must, the struggle that is forced upon them', they proposed 'to enter even now into peace negotiations'.[8]

The tone of haughty triumphalism struck entirely the wrong note: the German Peace Note was risible, London, Saint Petersburg and Paris swiftly decided. It made no concessions, failed to mention the restoration of Belgian and Serbian sovereignty, and amounted to a display of Teutonic chest thumping. Russia rejected the Note on 15 December, followed by France and Britain two weeks later. It coincided with the appointment of a new British Liberal prime minister who would attempt to rejuvenate the nation and transform the mood of despair into a new faith in victory.

—

A formidable political leader with the hide of a rhino and the personal drive to bind the Liberal–Conservative coalition in an all-out effort to defeat Germany: that was how David Lloyd George sold himself as the fittest man to rule Britain at war – and, by extension, the Dominion armies. We haven't the space to navigate the full circumference of this colossus of British politics. (I recommend biographies by Roy Hattersley, John Grigg and Peter Rowland.)[9] We aim chiefly to distil the personal attributes of this immensely gifted, exceptionally self-confident and deeply duplicitous character that helped or hindered his leadership in the darkest year of the war, after which the memory of Passchendaele would weigh on his conscience for the rest of his life.

David Lloyd George was a genuine radical of British politics. The English instinctively distrusted this Welsh firebrand. And yet, to call him 'the Great Outsider' is half-accurate: his huge ambition, forceful personality, soaring oratory and divisive political style compelled others to conform to him, rather than he to them. Iconoclastic, contemptuous of (English) tradition, Lloyd George used his points of difference to bend the establishment to his will and recreate the political order in his image. By 1917, 'the Great Insider' more accurately described his central place in British power, dominating the four-man War Cabinet that he appointed to run the war: the great outsider would soon turn the inside out.

Lloyd George's ability to slash away at impediments to action and bully his opponents into submission won the grudging support of his harshest critics and most avowed enemies. These were the personal attributes with which, as minister of Munitions (a department he created), he had broken the shell famine, launched the tank-building program and reorganised procurement; as chancellor, introduced old-age pensions and laid the foundations of the modern welfare state; and as prime minister, transformed the Cabinet and the nation into a war-winning political machine. That is the familiar, outward character of Lloyd George. To cut a keener profile of his leadership during Third Ypres requires a sharper scalpel.

Born in Manchester and raised in a Welsh village, David George lost his father as a boy and grew up under the powerful influence of his uncle, Richard Lloyd, who was determined to ensure that his gifted nephew received a solid religious education. We need not dwell on the small Baptist sect in which the Georges worshipped, except to say that the Children of God, or the 'Campbellites', as they were known, gave the boy his first taste of English 'oppression'. Young David found it intolerable that the Welsh nonconformist faith should be subject to the laws and traditions of the Church of England and would later deploy his sense of outrage at this 'injustice' as a political weapon.

As he rose in the world, by stages a journalist, lawyer and politician, Lloyd George honed his talent for speech-making into a crushing ad hominem style. His political oratory sizzled with personal rancour, burning off much of the substance that lay within it. His speeches advanced like an artillery barrage and were 'almost entirely destructive', observed Hattersley: 'Demolition of his opponents' arguments was rarely followed by the construction of something to put in their place. There was never a suggestion of an underlying ideology or philosophical principle – both of which were alien to his nature.'[10] As Lloyd George himself observed, he was never quite sure what he really stood for. In spirit a pacifist – he had opposed the Boer War – he abandoned any outward show of pacifism during the Great War. He entertained no ideology or set of guiding principles. 'I know I have the religious temperament,' he wrote as a young man, 'but if an angel from Heaven came to demand it, I could not write down what my convictions are.'[11] He cleaved to his own gut feel and ideas rather than to those of any political party or creed.

As a mature politician, Lloyd George relished the role of fixer and arch manipulator, for whom everything was in flux and nothing beyond his will to amend or reverse. Under Lloyd George, 'Was it rule by a dictator or a democrat?' wondered the Welsh historian Kenneth O. Morgan. 'Did any consistent principle animate the "man in the saddle", or was it all opportunism gone berserk?'[12] Even Lloyd George's closest associates were unable to answer with certainty. John Maynard Keynes later alleged that the values of Wales's 'Great Commoner' were 'rooted in nothing'.[13] The prime minister's friendships were as fragile as his sense of loyalty, a virtue he used sparingly. Nowhere would he find a natural 'fit' in the partisan swim of politics; rather, he sought to enmesh the fish that surrounded him in his school of thought. One idea that possessed him was the iniquity of unearned income (rentiers, inheritors, investors, and so on), and he waged a lifelong campaign against inherited wealth of the kind that had enriched his future commander-in-chief, Douglas Haig.

—

On 10 April 1908, Prime Minister Asquith formally offered Lloyd George the job of chancellor of the exchequer. Despite Lloyd George's many enemies, who accused him of leaking the news to the press in order to pre-empt a royal veto (King Edward VII disapproved of his philandering), his success as president of the Board of Trade couldn't be overlooked. Lloyd George's letter of acceptance revealed the man in full: 'Men whose promotion is not sustained by birth or other favouring conditions are always liable to be assailed with suspicions of this sort.'[14]

Germany's invasion of Belgium in August 1914 won Lloyd George over to the hawks, whose war he'd hitherto opposed. Some construed his conversion as brazen self-interest masquerading as principle; yet who in politics has not mixed principle with self-interest? His decision to back the war combined his abhorrence of military aggression, his support for Britain's treaty obligations to Belgium, and his political ambitions. Suddenly, the war was very popular, and so was Lloyd George.

Once he'd declared his hand, he threw all his verbal and political powers at rallying the people to the war effort. 'It will be a terrible war,' he boomed, in his great speech at Queen's Hall, London, on 19 September 1914. 'But in the end we will march through terror to triumph.' Invoking his homeland in the famous metaphor 'I know a valley in North Wales between the mountains and the sea . . . a beautiful valley, snug, comfortable, sheltered',[15] he warned the British people that they had been living in a valley like it for too long and had turned selfish and indulgent. The war would shake them to their senses.

Lloyd George took a close interest in military strategy – close enough (he felt) to pass judgement on the authority of Field Marshal Horatio Herbert Kitchener. The hero of the Battle of Omdurman (1898), commander-in-chief of India, and now war secretary knew a thing or two about drill. By contrast, Lloyd George had spent a testing week or so in the militia. That did nothing to dissuade the latter from pressing Kitchener to open a third front outside France, an idea Winston Churchill embraced. Intensely irritated, Kitchener knocked the idea down. (Churchill would soon bring it disastrously back to life, in the Dardanelles.)

Kitchener's aristocratic hauteur did little to inhibit the Baptist upstart from the Welsh hills, who would later describe the war secretary as 'a good poster but a bad general',[16] and uncharitably dismiss him, after his death in 1916, as 'a driving force' with 'no mental powers'.[17] Lloyd George's scornful assessment of the then highest ranking British soldier was a mere shadow of his bruising relationship with the soft-spoken, straightforward Scot soon to become commander-in-chief of the British forces on the Western Front, Field Marshal Sir Douglas Haig.

Lloyd George quickly came to be seen as the war leader in waiting: who else had the energy and mental toughness to lead Britain to victory? Who else could win over the people? The glaring answer took shape in his mind, until 'winning the war became . . . an aspect of his destiny which had to be fulfilled'.[18] Even his Tory enemies accepted his accession as inevitable. The former Conservative prime minister Lord Balfour disagreed with his policies yet came to see Lloyd George as the saviour of the nation: '[T]he only man who can, at this moment, break down the barriers of red tape and see that the brains of the country are made use of'.[19] Indeed, if he believed in anything, Lloyd George believed in action, in getting things done. At 7.30 pm on 7 December 1916, Lloyd George 'accepted' the prime ministership from the incumbent, Herbert Asquith, as head of a precarious Liberal–Conservative coalition.

The war, not Lloyd George, had destroyed Asquith. The death of his son Raymond, an officer in the Grenadier Guards, on the Somme in September 1916 had reduced the Liberal prime minister to a ghostly presence in Westminster. Unbearable grief rendered him unfit to govern the nation at war, as he later admitted. 'Whatever pride I had in the past,' he wrote of his son's death, 'and whatever hope I had in the future, by much the largest part was invested in him. Now all that has gone.'[20]

Lloyd George had secured the leadership of the Conservative-dominated coalition government, in cahoots with several powerful Conservatives and two press barons.[21] A condition for the Tories' support carried a heavy hostage to fortune: they would not abide the sacking of Douglas Haig, the commander-in-chief of the British and Dominion forces in France. That condition grated, for Lloyd George had repeatedly made public his abhorrence of Haig's methods. There would be no more Sommes, he had warned, in November 1916. Glaring at the journalist Charles à Court Repington, the new prime minister repeated the message on 9 February 1917: 'I am not prepared to accept the position of a butcher's boy driving cattle to the slaughter.' Repington dismissed this as sentimentality.[22]

Lloyd George's revulsion at the losses on the Somme was sincere, and he would spend the rest of the war championing a third front, in an effort to minimise British casualties. The prime minister failed or refused to accept his commanders' conviction that the war must be fought and won on the Western Front, at Germany's strongest point, and that the only way was to continue battering away at the enemy's trench lines with vast armies, machine guns and heavy artillery. The seeds of a disastrous relationship were sown.

—

The new prime minister took charge of a nation reeling from her recent 'victories'. A pall of grief hung over thousands of British and Dominion homes. The very real fear of defeat animated the highest officers in the realm: German and Austro-Hungarian forces had stalled Russia's advance, held the Italians, and overrun Romania; German U-boats were sinking a rising toll of British shipping; the French were mutinous and exhausted; and the Americans would not arrive in strength until mid-1918. Lloyd George would have none of this defeatism. His greatest political asset was his war-winning confidence and calm in the face of destruction. He flourished in adversity. There would be 'no compromise, no deals done, no talk of peace' under a Lloyd George government. 'How shall we win' was the only counsel the War Cabinet listened to.[23]

In his first weeks in power, the prime minister moved to put the nation on a total war footing. The primacy of supply was second nature to the man who had created the Ministry of Munitions. In this spirit, he cut the size of the War Cabinet, to make it more responsive, and able to make fast decisions. Almost immediately, he created a string of new ministries to address the emergency: Shipping, Labour, Food and Pensions – and, later, National Service and Reconstruction – all of them radiating outwards from the 'supreme arbiter', the prime minister.[24] With admirable pragmatism, he struck up an effective partnership with the Conservative leader and chancellor, Andrew Bonar Law, who would remain quietly loyal to his ideological opponent even as Lloyd George bypassed him and assumed increasingly dictatorial powers.

The War Cabinet met every day or so, to confront the myriad challenges of the war effort. Their immediate concerns were pooling manpower, fixing the prices of the 1917 harvest and putting down strikes. The most exigent was the soaring cost of the war: Britain would have to borrow US$1.5 billion from America (an enormous sum at the time, equivalent to US$30.5 billion in today's money) to finance the war up to March 1917, the War Cabinet learned on 9 December 1916. 'We must strain every nerve to obtain the money,' advised Morgan, Grenfell & Co., the government's agents in New York, whose agents confessed that they were 'staggered' by the amount.[25]

Lloyd George's gravest political concern was manpower. The

shortage of fighting men threatened to derail the great offensives planned for the summer of 1917. In late 1916, Haig had requested 500,000 more, infuriating Lloyd George. In the prime minister's eyes, Haig had already wasted hundreds of thousands of lives, for meagre results; he should not be allowed to do so again. The prime minister's preferred strategy was to use non-British troops on his proposed third front; to join France's defensive war; or to inflict a knockout blow that would end the war soon. Of one thing he was clear: Haig's war of attrition was politically unacceptable, and somehow must be stopped or changed.

In Haig's eyes, Lloyd George misunderstood the nature of the war and the sacrifices necessary to win it. Indeed, a contradiction lay at the heart of the prime minister's war: he would never reconcile this determination to win it with his condemnation of the way his commanders were fighting it. Not until many years after the armistice would he put these feelings on public display (see Chapter 17).

—

Intensifying the British manpower crisis was the German decision on 5 December 1916 to conscript all males aged between seventeen and sixty, with the exception of those employed in vital war-related industries. The forcible recruitment of able-bodied German men – passed by 235 votes to fourteen in the Reichstag – deeply disturbed the British War Cabinet. Earlier in 1916, Downing Street had relaxed constraints on employees in war industries, in order to 'comb' the nation for new recruits. Now Britain would match Germany and conscript them: on 12 December 1916, the War Cabinet approved the adoption of compulsory national service for all men between the ages of eighteen and sixty. It came into force on 2 March 1917. Thus far, the Military Service Act had prevented, as far as possible, the dispatch of anyone under nineteen to the front line. Henceforth, grandfathers, school-leavers and those with physical defects (poor eyesight, flat feet, etc.) were deemed eligible for overseas service. If an eighteen-year-old wanted to serve at the front, he should be sent, the

War Office advised the government on 9 January 1917.[26] At a stroke, school-age boys could be dispatched to the Western Front.

On 18 December, the government went further, withdrawing war service badges and certificates that had exempted men with jobs in war industries. Now they, too, were eligible for combat duty, and punished with up to six months' hard labour and a fine of £100 if they refused.[27] Nor was the 'dad's army' of half a million men deemed necessary to defend the home front: two divisions of these, too, were released for active service.[28]

These measures would never deliver Haig's 500,000. At any rate, Lloyd George refused to send so many British troops. He fastened instead on Britain's overseas allies as the next best source of manpower: the Dominions of Australia, Canada, New Zealand and South Africa, and the colonies of India and parts of Africa. On 23 January, the War Cabinet approved the recommendations of the Army Council to shake down the 'Available Resources of Man-Power, both White and Coloured, in the Overseas Dominions and Dependencies of the Empire'. The Australian Government should 'be urged to take steps at once for the formation of a sixth Australian Division'; New Zealand encouraged 'at once' to form a second New Zealand Division; and the Canadian Government persuaded to dispatch as soon as practicable a fifth division to France and 'to examine the possibility of raising a sixth'.[29]

Australia disobliged the Mother Country. In vain, Britain pressed the government of Billy Hughes to deliver up the 'large reserve' of Australian manpower, but a slim majority of people voted against conscription at a referendum on 28 October 1916 (and again in December 1917), removing any hope of the country of 4.75 million sending a further division and even putting at risk the maintenance of the existing five then serving in France. The New Zealanders were less reluctant. Here, the British Government had identified a further 30,000 men 'for disposal', enough to form a division with five months' reserves. The New Zealand people were 'extremely alive' to the importance of a bigger contribution, reported

*The Dominion* newspaper. That, noted the British Army Council contentedly, 'could hardly fail to stimulate similar efforts from other Dominions'. Canada, Newfoundland, India and South Africa also sent troops, to the extent that they were able, though the Canadian Corps would not exceed four divisions. In the event, Britain would shoulder the burden of the Anglo-Saxon war effort, enlisting 16.08 per cent of its male population of 22,485,501; compared with about ten to twelve per cent in Australia, Canada and New Zealand (see Appendix 2).[30] By these measures, Haig would get most of the men he needed for his huge 1917 offensive.

—

Field Marshal Sir Douglas Haig comes down to us as one of those wintry British commanders who placed duty, victory and loyalty to the king above all else, no matter the cost in lives and human misery. Like a surgeon in the days before anaesthetics, Haig at war was 'entirely removed . . . from the agony of the patient', Churchill would write.[31] Haig's methods have since provoked the wrath of regiments of critics, some of whom tend to portray the British field marshal as a rogue butcher, over whom the War Cabinet had no control. That impression, whose chief architect was Lloyd George, is false. Like Turner's sea monster, monstrous truths lurk beneath the surface of the water, all-seeing if barely seen. As we shall see, one man alone cannot have borne the weight of responsibility for 1917; rather it was the dysfunctional relationship between Haig and Lloyd George that kindled and fomented the tragedy of Passchendaele.

Current impressions of Haig conjure two extremes: the bungling, blimpish cavalryman, indifferent to the soldiers' suffering, who sent wave after wave of young men to certain death; and the hard-working 'educated soldier', the professional commander, who did his best in dreadful circumstances and felt genuine concern for the men under his command. The second image is the more accurate.

And there is a third, lesser known, dimension to Haig. The field marshal's implacable calm – his only sign of anxiety in the worst of the fighting was a tendency to stroke his moustache, remarked one general[32] – belied an intensity of feeling of which few people out-side his family and staff were aware. This 'inner Haig' was a man of deep emotion and acute religious feeling. On the eve of an offen-sive, he would pray quietly to his Presbyterian god and confide in his favourite chaplain. His religious belief was a source of deep con-solation, as was his family. At the height of his personal crisis on the Western Front, he would turn for emotional solace to his beloved wife, Doris, to whom he confided in a series of letters; to his loyal sister, Henrietta, who helped his career and to whom he was devoted; and to the spirit of his late mother, Rachel, who died when he was eighteen, the memory of whom he would revere to the end of his days. In a sense, Haig was a 'woman's man', more at ease with female love than with the knockabout company of men.

Douglas Haig was born on 19 June 1861, the eleventh son of John and Rachel Haig (née Veitch), in a large town house on Charlotte Square, in Edinburgh. He was a direct descendant of the Norman knight Pierre de la Hague, who had settled in the Scottish lowlands near Bemersyde in the twelfth century. By the early nine-teenth century, the family's aristocratic pedigree had deteriorated to the merchant class, reflected in the rough brogue and manners of Douglas's alcoholic father, a wealthy whisky distiller. Such defects were no block to social advancement in Victorian Britain so long as you were rich, and the Haigs were very rich.

Like many families of the lowland Scottish elite, the Haigs felt at least as 'British' as they were 'Scottish', and were among the stoutest defenders of the Empire. Privately educated, young Douglas wore the trappings of his class a bit too seriously, like a man trying to adapt to an ill-fitting garment. He lacked the ease with which the aristocratic young men of his acquaintance deigned to move in any social milieu, and perhaps this explained his need to distinguish himself, to get on, to succeed. He was suspicious of outsiders (be they Catholics, French or 'foreigners') and disdainful of uppity new men like Lloyd George, whom he tended to dismiss as ill-bred opportunists. He felt a genuine affection for the 'real' men under his command, such as the ordinary British and colonial troops – he especially admired the Anzacs – although this often went unreciprocated.

Early on, Haig proved himself an exemplary soldier with outstanding promise: in December 1884, he passed out first of 129 Gentleman Cadets at Sandhurst and received the Anson Sword of Honour. He enjoyed hunting and excelled at polo and horsemanship – a career in the cavalry beckoned. In one marked respect, Haig differed from his fellow graduates: he was a deeply serious young man who considered soldiering a career, not an enjoyable pastime or a sort of 'blood sport'. He had little of the irreverence of his fellow junior officers. For one thing, he was certainly 'educated' in a way most of them were not. His regimental nickname, 'Doctor', referred to his unusual attendance at Oxford and the impression he gave as a 'thinking soldier'.[33]

Haig certainly thought a lot, and rose through the ranks with a mixture of will, ability and powerful friends. This cannot be dismissed as crude 'nepotism': Haig's friends were smart enough to discern and reward genuine ability. G. F. R. Henderson, a professor of military history at Camberley Staff College at the time of Haig's attendance (1896–97), rated him as the 'coming man in the army' and 'a future commander in chief'.[34] In 1896, Haig co-wrote the 'Cavalry Drill Manual' with John French, 'the tactical bible for cavalry operations'.[35] He received a commission with the illustrious 7th Queen's Own Hussars and served with distinction as the regimental adjutant in India.

His determination to excel as a professional soldier distinguished him from the British military tradition of 'gentleman amateurs', who tended to regard too much 'success' as a bad thing. Not if you were Douglas Haig. He was an innovative and adaptable commander who would embrace the use of new technology (e.g. the tank, the machine gun, the artillery barrage, aircraft and poison gas) no matter how controversial, belying the popular impression of a buffoonish cavalryman. He studied and learned from history, approving of Napoleon's 'wearing down' war as the prelude to the decisive, pitched battle. He preferred the German Army's command system of delegating responsibility to junior officers over the British 'top-down' approach.[36] In recognition of his precocious ability, Lord Kitchener made him inspector general of cavalry in 1903, conferring the rank of general on Haig at the age of 42.

To top off this accomplished résumé, Haig was physically brave, a quality conspicuous by its absence from Lloyd George. During Haig's first taste of combat at the Battle of Atbara in Egypt in 1898, he galloped onto the field to rescue a wounded Egyptian soldier – a Victoria Cross–winning feat had the Egyptian been British, according to one biographer.[37]

In 1906, he was recalled to England to serve as Lord Haldane's right-hand man in reforming the British Army. Between them, they created the BEF, of one cavalry and six infantry divisions, conceived to serve anywhere in the Empire, supported by a home reserve, the Territorial Force (later the Territorial Army). It was the most radical reform of the British Army since the age of Wellington. Knighted for this work, Haig returned to India in 1909 to serve as chief of staff of the Indian Army with the rank of lieutenant general.

As an army commander, in October 1914, Haig co-led the defence of Ypres from repeated German attacks. At Second Ypres, in April 1915, the hideous effects of chlorine gas – then first used in combat, by the Germans – persuaded him of its utility as an offensive weapon, not for its destructive power (gas caused relatively few casualties) but for the sheer panic it spread among the ranks. He felt similarly about 'liquid fire', primitive flame-throwers, then also in use for the first time. Haig was nothing if not a great learner, and ruthlessly pragmatic. His determination to win the war silenced any qualms of conscience he might have felt over the use of gas, then banned under the Hague Conventions of 1899 and 1907, which explicitly forbade the use of 'poison or poisoned weapons'. He ordered up great quantities of the stuff for use at Loos and the Somme, insisting that gas factories work '*night* and day' (his emphasis) to deliver the necessary supplies.[38] He studied the evolution of gas technology and was an early adopter of gas shells, in 1916, a great improvement on the wind in sending lethal clouds into enemy trenches.

Haig's moral outlook was inherently Victorian, circumscribed by his social class and his belief in the superiority of the British race. Honour, chivalry and respect were, for him, the highest personal virtues, sharpened by privilege and a sense of *noblesse oblige* to the lower orders. This outlook was not suited to a world war, whose polyglot racial and class mix tended to level social distinctions. The ordinary soldiers respected him; they did not love him. The ranks called him 'Duggy', with little enthusiasm, one wrote: 'He was too remote – but that was not his fault. The show was too big.'[39] The soldiers denied him the affection they felt for more 'human' commanders such as Plumer, Birdwood, Byng, Monash and Currie, whom they saw a lot more of. Yet, if Haig lacked the 'common touch', he took a genuine interest in the men and their families, and the dead and wounded deeply aggrieved him. He regularly visited the field hospitals.[40]

As befitted this career soldier, Haig always dedicated himself to the *task* at hand, because the completion of every task advanced the fulfilment of his *orders*.[41] That is what made this commander tick. He tended to place efficiency (and personal ambition) ahead of loyalty. He would thus abandon his friends, the chief of the Imperial General Staff, 'Wully' Robertson, and Lord Derby, the secretary of state for war, when they were no longer useful or hindered his work; he sacked many subordinates, not all of them inept. He justified his pivotal role in the downfall of Sir John French on the grounds that Sir John was wholly responsible for the botched offensive at Loos. In his diary, Haig blamed Sir John's 'unreasoning brain' and 'ignorance of the nature of the fighting' for the disaster.[42] Yet Haig shared responsibility for Loos and many other costly errors, as Dr John Paul Harris reveals in his masterful study of Haig's war.[43]

Haig succeeded French as commander-in-chief of the BEF on 10 December 1915. In accepting the command of the British and Dominion forces on the Western Front, on 28 December 1915, Haig relished his 'special task' set by Lord Kitchener: to drive the German armies out of France and Belgium (see full text, Appendix 3).[44]

—

Field Marshal Haig now had the power to run the war as he saw fit. His large, liquid eyes and solid frame, his quick step and handsome, reliable face, brought renewed confidence to the British and Dominion armies in France. Moderate in his habits, calm and inscrutable, he 'tended to speak only when he had something important to say', observed one biographer. 'He would not have been the life and soul of a cocktail party, but . . . one does not have to be a jolly good chap to win wars.'[45] He measured every action, however harsh, against his determination to forge an army with the resolution to win. On Wednesday 3 March 1915, for example, 'I recommended that 3 men of the Loyal North Lancs who had deserted deliberately (one found in Paris) . . . should be shot. The state of discipline in this battalion is not very satisfactory . . .' In the event, the accused were spared.[46]

In January 1917, Haig, now 55 and recently promoted to field marshal (having served as a corps commander for the past two years), was about to embark on the greatest test of his career. He commanded, for better or worse, the lives of more than a million men. He believed in his bones in the offensive war, of never letting the enemy rest. His bold plans, important meetings and impressive moustache suggested he exerted great control over the war; less often examined is the extent to which the war exerted control over him. And one thing is important to understanding him, in light of what follows: he would always act in accordance with the instructions of his government. Only in this context can we understand the reasoning of a commander who would be held personally responsible for the death or wounding of the best part of a generation.

Haig's gravest weaknesses, as seen at the Somme, were his failure to intervene to prevent needless slaughter and his inclination to overestimate the physical endurance of his men. He tended to believe in what he wanted to believe (he unquestioningly accepted, for example, his intelligence chief John Charteris's exaggerated reports of the enemy's weakness), and he seemed unable to communicate clear, direct orders (a striking exception being his 'backs to the wall' order of April 1918) or terminate or amend bad ones. His notorious inarticulacy provoked cruel jokes and anecdotes (that he was at least as fluent in French as in English said little for his French, ran one). Countering these flaws were his ready willingness to learn and adapt to the exigencies of war, and to listen to the advice of others. He delegated to a fault, sometimes failing to rein in errant generals or ideas. A defining trait of his command was his apparent optimism, a 'mask of command' that rode out news that might have unhorsed a more self-reflective man.

Whence arose Haig's iron imperturbability, his reassuring sanguinity? The field marshal's Christian faith and doting wife had much to do with it: on finding General Gough 'downhearted' at Loos, for example, Haig reminded Gough that trust in God alone would deliver victory.[47] In this spirit, he urged his chaplains to preach the cause of the war to the men, that 'we . . . are fighting for the good of humanity'.[48] Unlike the impersonal, pragmatic Anglicans on his staff, Haig drew on a deep well of personal feeling that placed God and his Presbyterian faith at the heart of his decision-making. In his lonely position, carrying an immense burden, Haig understandably sought the consolations of a spiritual authority. He usually read a chapter of the Bible before going to bed and confided weekly in his favourite chaplain, the erudite Reverend George Duncan, in whom he placed a near mystical trust. For a hard-headed commander, Haig could be curiously superstitious: when Duncan considered leaving his service, Haig persuaded him to stay, comparing the chaplain to Aaron who held Moses' hands aloft to ensure the Israelites were victorious in battle.[49]

At times, Haig suggested that God had selected him to lead the Allies to victory. 'All . . . somehow give me the idea that they think I am "meant to win" by some Superior Power,' the field marshal confided in a letter to his wife, soon after his promotion.[50] At the time, this was not outlandish or bizarre: powerful, proud men of the day often supposed themselves to be the instruments of the Divine. The trouble with this way of thinking was that the thinker could validate any outcome, no matter how disastrous, as the mysterious workings of the Lord. On the eve of the first day of the Somme, 30 June 1916, for example, Haig told Doris that 'whether or not we are successful lies in the Power above. But *I do feel* that in my plans I have been helped by a Power that is not my own.'[51] Such power deserted the British the next day, at the end of which almost 60,000 men lay dead, wounded or missing. 'A day of downs and ups!' was how Haig responded, conceding that 'the news about 8 am was not altogether good'.[52] When he was informed of the casualties of the Somme, he wrote that they 'cannot be considered severe in view of the numbers engaged, and the length of front attacked'.[53]

If Haig was 'not a religious fanatic', as the Reverend Duncan assures us,[54] his faith in Calvinistic predestination seems to have been a dangerous psychological disposition in a man at the head of an army: what scale of sacrifice was necessary to win the war and realise the will of the Lord? How many casualties would justify the ways of God to men? A singular goal animated everything he did and said: the defeat of Germany. In this, he shared something with David Lloyd George: both men were driven by an insatiable desire to win, and to be seen to have won.

That is all they shared. In truth, it is hard to imagine two more different men in command of the British war on the Western Front: Haig, the privately educated Oxford and Sandhurst man, a friend of the King's, married to Queen Alexandra's maid of honour, and closely connected with the Conservatives in Cabinet; and Lloyd George, the cottage-bred Welsh lawyer turned Liberal prime minister, with a reputation as a philanderer and no respect for English traditions.

Their relations began to slide in September 1916, when Haig learned to his fury that Lloyd George, then secretary of state for war, had gone behind his back and asked Ferdinand Foch, the French commander-in-chief, for his opinion of British generals and why – if the British had gained no more ground than the French forces – they had suffered such heavy casualties. 'I would not have believed that a British Minister could have been so ungentlemanly as to go to a foreigner and put such questions . . .'[55] Later that year, their dislike intensified over the cost of the Somme. 'I have no great opinion of L. G. as a man or a leader,' Haig wrote to his wife in September 1916.[56] In 1917, their relationship would reach new depths of mutual loathing, poisoning a vital liaison at the heart of power and endangering soldiers' lives.

# 3

# DEATH BY WATER

*Potential famine is the most powerful weapon*
*in the army of the belligerents.*
Prime Minister David Lloyd George

---

*We need the most energetic, ruthless methods which*
*can be adopted. For this reason, we need the . . .*
*U-boat war to start from February 1, 1917.*
Field Marshal Paul von Hindenburg

---

By January 1917, the face of European power had changed utterly. Lloyd George had replaced Asquith as British prime minister. A new French Government under Prime Minister Aristide Briand moved at once to replace Marshal Joseph Joffre, commander-in-chief of the French forces: the legend of the Marne had no lives left after Verdun. His successor, General Robert Nivelle, appointed on 12 December 1916, brought forward plans for another huge French offensive.

In Germany, von Falkenhayn's Verdun 'strategy' had lost all credibility – even the muddle-headed Kaiser ceased to believe in it – and in August 1916 the legendary Generalfeldmarschall Paul

Hindenburg, hero of Tannenberg, replaced him as chief of the general staff. The ageing Hindenburg was a figurehead; real command continued to be exercised through Erich Ludendorff, general of the infantry. Along with Haig's December promotion to field marshal, the European powers entered the new year in the hands of hugely ambitious men who would accept nothing less than total victory and the unconditional surrender of their enemies.

The winter of 1916–17 was the coldest in memory. The troops, ice-caked and sick, were being rotated along the line; the guns were quiet for the winter months. Warmer weather, everyone knew, heralded the resumption of battle and the roar of the howitzers, severing any vestigial association of spring with joy. At home, the exuberance of earlier years was flagging. New Year's Eve parties were frowned upon. High society tangoed and frolicked behind closed doors. The gossip columns were muted. The university halls were near deserted, and traditional male enclaves – clubs, sports events, pubs and non-war factories – bereft of younger men. Those not working in vital war industries were being trained, or were serving in France or Belgium. The rest were dead or wounded. London, Paris, Berlin and Moscow were cities of the elderly, women and children – and the walking wounded, whose nervous disorders and hideous injuries alerted the home fires to an unprecedented phenomenon: the effects of heavy artillery on the mind and body. Insensate politicians and pub warriors continued ranting about the nobility of war and reciting the old lie, how sweet and right it was to die, etc. In this war, for a rising number, the holocaust of 1916 had crushed those illusions.

—

In Britain, the war still held most people in its trance, abetted by political propaganda and a grossly irresponsible press. If a form of collective amnesia obscured the original case for going to war, there could be no doubt now about the reasons for staying in it, according to the new pitch: the Great War had become an epic struggle of vengeance. The Germans must pay for what they have done to our boys, fulminated members of parliament and soapbox orators. The militarists in the Reichstag railed in a similar vein: the perfidious English must be vanquished. The lives of so many young men have not been lost in vain, the rival governments declared; the supreme sacrifice must be avenged. This was thought to be politically popular: the families of the fallen should settle for nothing less than all-out war, the governments implied, and so should the people. Nobody asked when or whether the quality of forgiveness had deserted the British and German people. This popular appeal, carefully synchronised between politicians and journalists, amounted to a call for more violence to avenge past violence, implying a never-ending spiral of bloodshed.

The German bombing of London and other cities, first with zeppelins and then, in 1917, with Gotha bombers, ratcheted up the war of revenge. In June, a Gotha raid struck a school in Poplar, East London, killing eighteen children and maiming thirty. The air raids would continue until May 1918, killing nearly a thousand Londoners and wounding three times as many. All this militated against any talk of mediation or a negotiated surrender. Terms such as 'peaceful settlement' and 'understanding' had no traction.

Hate-filled lies spilled off the German and British presses. None could match the British newspapers for sheer inventiveness, and their squalid line in Hun-bashing enraged the public against the enemy. Everyone heard the stories of the abominable Germans who had crucified Canadians with bayonets and boiled down the bodies of the dead for use as pig-feed, fertiliser and soap. This nonsense, peddled in Lord Northcliffe's *Times* and *Daily Mail*, horrified the public and poured oil on the furnace of vengeance.[1] The 'public interest' had rarely been so gravely abused.

At the subtler end of the spectrum of indoctrination, the British War Propaganda Bureau, incorporated into the Department of Information in February 1917 under the direction of John Buchan, with the secret assistance of some of Britain's most famous writers, was determined to preserve the public mind from softening. It published more than a thousand pamphlets enunciating the case for war, the horror of German aggression, the honour of the British Empire and the freedom of the nation.[2]

Appeals to civic duty, to lend all hands, entrenched the idea of war as a normative, daily struggle that must be fought to the bitter end. Everyone must do his or her bit: knitting socks and mittens; sending blankets and letters to the men at the front; collecting scrap for recycling; naming new babies after French and Flemish towns; volunteering in every way possible. British middle-class women had joined the workforce for the first time, as nurses, ambulance drivers and non-combat soldiers: the Voluntary Aid Detachment (VAD), the First Aid Nursing Yeomanry, and the formation in early 1917 of the Women's Auxiliary Army Corps and the Women's Royal Naval Service. The people were enmeshed in the conflict at every level. The war was no longer viewed as a passing tempest; it had become a way of life. In 1917, that way of life would get a lot tougher, especially for the German people, for whom the 'war of hunger' was about to enter its most extreme phase.

——

The presence of German submarine bases on the Belgian coast exerted a powerful hold on the minds of the British Government, the military command and the people. Enemy U-boats threatened the free passage of ships in the English Channel, which was crucial in supplying provisions to Haig's armies in France and food to the British Isles. 'There is no measure to which the War Cabinet attaches greater importance than the expulsion of the enemy from the Belgian Coast,' noted a Cabinet Minute on 26 October 1916.[3]

As early as January 1916, Haig had begun planning an offensive in Flanders to achieve that goal. He conceived of a war-winning blow that would not only destroy the U-boat bases on the coast but also crush the German Army in Belgium. It would involve six stages and seven corps (350,000-400,000 men). Passchendaele Ridge would be taken within the first week or so. The fall of Roulers would follow,

freeing Haig's armies to march on the Belgian coast, where, with the
help of an amphibious land invasion, they would destroy the submarine bases at Ostend and Zeebrugge. The battle for Belgium would
end, fittingly enough, with the return of mobile warfare and a cavalry charge over the remnants of the enemy.[4] It would all be over by
Christmas – a familiar refrain.

Verdun postponed Haig's Belgian plan, and the Somme intervened. The Flanders Offensive resurfaced at the end of 1916, in
commanders' discussions of the war plans for 1917. All agreed that
a knockout blow should be inflicted on Germany. The decisive struggle would unfold on the Western Front, where a massive French-led
Spring Offensive on the Aisne would culminate in Haig's *coup de
grâce* in Flanders. The British and French commanders persuaded
themselves that the resumption of the 'wearing down' war would
kill, wound or exhaust so many German troops that victory would
be theirs before the year was out.

In other words, nothing had happened in 1916 to dent the generals' enthusiasm for further massed frontal attacks. The commanders looked back on the Somme and Verdun not as disastrous warnings but as tactical lessons in new methods of waging attritional
war. With the resumption of offensive action, they planned to apply
those lessons, with modifications, chiefly in the use of the creeping
barrage.

—

The peculiar misery of the German people impinged ever more
acutely on the war, driving the German regime to revive a 'strategy' that would have fatal consequences. Berlin's decision to resume
unlimited submarine warfare cannot be seen as an isolated atroc-
ity. It was a direct response to the British naval blockade, which was
slowly starving the German nation. The Royal Navy had slashed the
country's food supply. Most available food went to Germany's armed
forces. The elderly, women and children were severely malnourished.

The British blockade was ruthless but necessary, claimed Lloyd

George (and a string of post-war apologists). 'Potential famine is the most powerful weapon in the army of the belligerents,' he later wrote. 'War is organised cruelty . . . savagery is of its essence.'[5] According to this argument, anything went in total war. Lloyd George was parroting the usual justification for barbarity, so long as it was 'our' barbarity, the cruelty of the righteous.

He lacked the honesty to confront the truth: the British blockade was illegal according to any fair interpretation of international law. Within a fortnight of declaring war, the British Government had reneged on two international agreements, the first to the letter, the second in spirit. The Treaty of Paris (1856) stipulated that sea blockades were permissible only if they visibly ringed a port or harbour; blockades from a 'distance', in open waters – such as the Royal Navy's of Germany – were illegal. The Declaration of the London Naval Conference of 1909 – which Britain had not signed but was expected to honour (it had been a British idea) – distinguished between shipping used for military purposes (arms and military equipment, or 'absolute contraband') and solely for civilian purposes (food, clothing, etc.). The British redefined all food bound for Germany as 'absolute contraband' and seized it.

The effects of the blockade were immediate and devastating: by the end of 1914, the Allies had impounded more than 60 per cent of German merchant shipping, leading to a grave shortage of green vegetables that winter. In January 1915, the Bundesrat (the Upper House) urged every German community of 5000 people or more to store canned meat, unleashing the Great Hog Murder (*Schweinemord*). In March 1915, Britain banned neutral vessels from calling at German ports, abolished any distinction between contraband and non-contraband, and insisted on the right to board all neutral vessels. 'Guilty until proven innocent' became the British law of the sea.[6]

The 'turnip winter' of 1916–17 was the harshest in German memory. The early frost and heavy rains halved the potato harvest. Ordinary German people ate swede turnips, the loathed 'Prussian pineapple', a coarse root crop hitherto used for animal fodder. The author Ernst Glaeser witnessed children stealing each other's rations and heard women in food queues talking 'more about their children's hunger than the death of their husbands'.[7] Mobile field kitchens, or 'goulash guns', rushed to feed the hungriest but did little to assuage the fury of German mothers, who formed a 'new front' against the authorities: in 1916, women committed 1224 acts of violence against the German police.[8]

By 1917, malnutrition and related diseases – dysentery, scurvy and tuberculosis – ravaged the cities. Hunger oedema, characterised by gross swelling of the limbs, proliferated among the poor. Long lines of starving women and children were a daily occurrence at soup kitchens. Food prices soared on the black market. Riots and wholesale theft overrode German loyalty to the war effort, in what Berlin described as the British 'hunger blockade'.

'Once I set out for the purpose of finding in these food-lines a face that did not show the ravages of hunger,' reported an American correspondent in Berlin near the end of 1916. 'Four long lines were inspected with the closest scrutiny. But among the 300 applicants for food there was not one who had had enough to eat for weeks. In the case of the youngest women and children the skin was drawn hard to the bones and bloodless. Eyes had fallen deeper into the sockets. From the lips all color was gone, and the tufts of hair which fell over the parchmented faces seemed dull and famished – a sign that the nervous vigor of the body was departing with the physical strength.'[9]

—

German rage brooded on a response that would immeasurably worsen their plight. In the summer of 1916, the German admiralty, desperate to prove their usefulness and break the British blockade, advocated a return to unlimited submarine warfare, to 'drive all neutral shipping from British shores' and starve the British Isles into submission.[10] In other words, a German war crime would match a

British war crime, and so the 'war of starvation' would dramatically escalate.[11] The Berlin regime defended the U-boat war on neutral shipping as an act of national survival – even if it risked bouncing America into the war.

That was a risk worth taking, concluded Admiral Reinhard Scheer, the German fleet commander.[12] An unlimited U-boat war, he believed, would crush the British economy and reduce the English to the wretchedness to which the Royal Navy had reduced the German and Austro-Hungarian people. Admiral Henning von Holtzendorff, chief of the admiralty staff of the German Navy, shared this sentiment. 'The blockade of Germany is becoming more and more oppressive,' he told the U-boat conference at Pless Castle on 31 August 1916, attended by Bethmann-Hollweg, Hindenburg, Ludendorff, senior admirals and the ministers of the Interior and Foreign Office.[13]

The admirals were solidly in favour of the new U-boat offensive, conceding nonetheless that submarines were unlikely to be able to break the British blockade or impose one on Britain. 'U-boats can undertake nothing in the night time,' warned Chancellor Theobald von Bethmann-Hollweg, who had curiously metamorphosed into a submarine expert.[14] Even so, the admirals believed an unlimited underwater offensive offered a golden opportunity to force Britain to surrender before America entered the war.

The ineffectual Bethmann-Hollweg and his soon-to-be-retired foreign minister, Gottlieb von Jagow, were initially unpersuaded. Attacks on neutral shipping would merely provoke neutral nations to declare war on Germany, Jagow warned: 'Germany will . . . be looked upon as a mad dog against whom the hand of every man will be raised for the purpose of finally bringing about peace . . .'[15] Bethmann-Hollweg worried about alienating Germany's allies, and advised postponing a decision. He dreaded another international backlash.

In December 1916, Holtzendorff again pressed the case for a resumption of unlimited submarine war. Only if 'we can break

England's backbone' – i.e. her shipping power and unchallenged naval supremacy – could Germany win the war. The point that Britain would lose the war if she lost the Channel was high in the minds of the Prussian admirals, who had far bigger ambitions for the submarine offensive: they saw it as the first strike in Germany's long-held plan to supplant Britain as the world's leading naval power.

In a strategic paper submitted to the chancellor and general staff on 22 December, Holtzendorff calculated that if, from 1 February 1917, German submarines sunk 600,000 tons of enemy shipping per month (deterring a further 1.2–3 million tons from sailing, he esti- mated), Britain would be forced to surrender within six months and Germany would win the war on 1 August, the start of the 1917 har- vest. Had he announced the very hour of the armistice, the assem- bled top brass, accustomed as they were to Prussian military preci- sion, would probably have nodded in concurrence.

The all-powerful German Army commanders applauded the idea. If it worked, it would avoid another Somme, thought Ludendorff. One grim fact animated Germany's actions on the Western Front in the opening phases of 1917: Britain and France possessed far more men, heavy guns, machine guns and other equip- ment than Germany did. Against Germany's 154 divisions, the Allies had 190 – 'an exceedingly unfavourable balance of forces', Ludendorff later wrote.[16] That meant Germany had little choice other than to fight a defensive war on the Western Front, undermining the argument that if Britain hadn't attacked in Flanders the Germans would have crushed the French. If Ludendorff's men could hold on for six months, while German submarines sank British ships, denied Haig his supply line across the Channel and starved the British people, Berlin had a good chance of winning the war before America arrived.

'It has to be,' Field Marshal Paul von Hindenburg told the meet- ing, silencing dissent. 'We expect war with America and have made all preparations for it. Things cannot get any worse.'[17] He added, 'We need the most energetic, ruthless methods which can be adopted.

For this reason, we need the . . . U-boat war to start from February 1, 1917.'[18] The jar-headed Ludendorff, the supposed brains behind Hindenburg's brawn, echoed these sentiments with his own note of defiance. 'I don't give a damn about America,' Ludendorff said; for him, the starving of England was all that mattered as it would spare the German Army another Somme.[19]

Already, the German commanders had begun shifting reinforcements to Flanders to defend the submarine bases at Ostend and Zeebrugge. As early as 30 December 1916, 'definite information' reached the War Cabinet that a German division (of about 14,000 men), 'fresh from training' with 'a specific purpose', had relieved an exhausted one stationed at the Ypres Salient. The item was first on the agenda at the meeting the prime minister chaired that morning.[20] In early 1917, British military intelligence reported a further German troop build-up in Flanders. Between 1 January and 8 March, six fresh German divisions – about 85,000 men – were sent to reinforce the Western Front (including Flanders), with evidence of 'large numbers' of enemy troops moving to eastern Belgium.[21]

The German civilian leaders succumbed to the military imperative. Fearful that the U-boat offensive would bring America into the war, Bethmann-Hollweg now resigned himself to the inevitable, in a statement of lethal stupidity and rank cowardice: he would strive to keep America out of the war while supporting the decision to resume the unlimited submarine offensive. The chancellor failed or refused to see that the pursuit of the latter ensured the failure of the former. Just as he had blinded himself to the truth about British 'neutrality' during the crisis of July 1914, so now he blinded himself to the absurdity of his policy towards America. America would assuredly be in the war the moment the first German torpedo struck the belly of a neutral vessel. Bethmann-Hollweg even deluded himself into believing that the Entente's rejection of his worthless 'Peace Note' could be used to justify the submarine war and appease Washington.

Ultimately, it mattered little what Bethmann-Hollweg did or

said, because he had limited if any power left. Like the Kaiser, he functioned in name alone, a plaything of the militarists after years of dysfunctional civilian leadership: 'Step by step, the generals roped off the Chancellor's freedom of manoeuvre and worked to nail him to their standard.'[22] He now yielded completely to their will, abrogating any shred of responsibility for the country in its encroaching catastrophe. The U-boat war was Germany's 'last card' and 'a very serious decision', Bethmann told the meeting, echoing the Kaiser's view that the offensive was a strictly military decision. His next sentence epitomised the helplessness of this political marionette: 'But if the military authorities consider the U-boat war essential, I am not in a position to contradict them.'[23] The ceding of civilian authority to the Prussian military was complete, and Bethmann-Hollweg and Germany entered their 'darkest hour': 'the literal capitulation of political authority before the military in the most decisive question of the entire World War', noted the historian Gerhard Ritter, one of the chancellor's strongest apologists.[24]

A few months later, in April 1917, Bethmann would justify the U-boat war on the grounds that 'England not only did not give up her illegal and indefensible policy of blockade, but uninterruptedly intensified it'.[25] That at least made an arguable ethical point.

The decision went out that night, 9 January; the Kaiser and chancellor celebrated with champagne. German submarines would fire their first torpedoes into neutral shipping on 1 February. On that day, just 23 of the German Navy's 105 operational U-boats embarked from bases on the Flanders coast. Ostend and Zeebrugge were never as critical to the submarine war as the Allies supposed.

—

Hope for peace lay with one great power: America, still neutral at the end of 1916. Inconveniently for the Entente, on 20 December President Woodrow Wilson made a genuine peace proposal, albeit modified from an earlier, more robust version. The president's letter was not an open call to end hostilities; it merely appealed to the belligerents to sit down and 'compare views' so that 'soundings may be taken' as to what 'ultimate arrangements' must precede the 'peace of the world'.[26]

London and Paris paused to consider their reply on account of the proposal's powerful provenance; the Entente could not ignore the White House. The president's naive hopes for a negotiated peace were misguided, of course, and would have to be shot down. Yet deflecting Wilson had to be handled with the utmost diplomatic care, as they desperately needed America in the war. Somehow, the Americans must be made to see that they misunderstood the war and required an education, Lord Robert Cecil, the undersecretary of state for Foreign Affairs, advised the War Cabinet on 23 December. Both sides were 'not fighting for the same objects', as Wilson had claimed.[27] Germany was the aggressor; Germany had breached Belgium's neutrality and invaded France. It was for Germany to make sincere proposals of peace, not the Allies.

Cecil urged the government to engage the president with a vigorous explanation of the origins and goals of the war. Above all, Britain must be seen to be the reasonable party. 'Englishmen do not mind doing violent things,' Cecil wrote, 'but they like to persuade themselves that they are all the while models of moderation.'[28]

On 10 January 1917, the British rejected the president's peace gambit with a litany of examples of German perfidy, such as the earlier waging of unlimited submarine war, the execution of the British nurse Edith Cavell, accused of being a spy, and the 'enslavement' of the Belgian workforce. If Wilson failed to see that those crimes necessitated the continuation of the war, he certainly grasped the logic of attrition, fearing that 'million after million of human lives' would be offered up if the war continued, until one side or the other 'had no more to offer'.[29]

One issue, however, would persuade Washington to join the war: the resumption of unlimited submarine warfare. Berlin had abandoned this tactic in 1916 after international condemnation of the sinking of the *Lusitania*, a passenger ship, by a German U-boat on

7 May 1915, killing 1198 passengers and crew. To resume the submarine offensive would not only be barbarous, Wilson later said, but also foolish. On 1 February 1917, Berlin's leaders offered ample evidence that they were both.

—

In the opening months of 1917, many British people feared that German U-boats would win the war. The British Admiralty seemed helpless to protect the country from hundreds of underwater predators: German submarines had sunk 632,000 tons of British (i.e. non-neutral) shipping in the last four months of 1916, easily outpacing the shipbuilding rate of 52,000 tons a month. Britain 'could not carry on much longer' and 'a complete breakdown in shipping would come before June 1917', Walter Runciman, president of the Board of Trade, warned the Cabinet on 9 November 1916. He later revised this deadline, fearing that the collapse of the nation must come sooner.[30] Admiral of the Fleet Lord 'Jacky' Fisher of Kilverstone even warned of a U-boat invasion of Britain, the danger of which bubbled up in his letter to the prime minister on 15 March 1917: 'in view of the development by the enemy of submarines of great size and power . . . the Germans were likely to undertake an invasion of this country'.[31] Few ministers took the threat of invasion seriously, yet they pandered to Fisher's eminence by asking him to flesh out his warning.

From Germany's viewpoint, the success of the U-boat war would rely on the accuracy of its own navy's estimates of the British shipping schedule. The admirals had complete faith in their arithmetic, the fruit of months of analysis of the shipping news. The statistics and timetables failed, however, to account for the frustrating tendency of the real world to change, to adapt to expectations, rather than stay conveniently inert in deference to what Germany planned to do. The German admirals tended to ignore or play down factors that hobbled their pristine plan, such as British retaliation or food stockpiling. Their blindness reprised the army's slavish obedience to the Schlieffen Plan of 1914, investing their blueprint with the quality of a self-fulfilling prophecy. But a 'prophecy' is only as accurate as the information being fed into it.

In this case, the U-boat planners lacked a correct inventory of British food supplies and failed to account for the determination of David Lloyd George to outwit and stall the underwater war. Nor had the German Navy considered the extent to which they would imperil their own army by exposing it to the full onslaught of General Haig's Flanders Offensive, the case for which, at least in part, was the destruction of the submarine bases in Belgium.

—

The British Admiralty monitored the ensuing disaster with a statistician's fetish for numbers. Lord Jellicoe, the first sea lord, presented a daily tally of shipping losses to the War Cabinet, which revealed that Germany had been sinking neutral vessels well before 1 February 1917: of 304,000 tons of shipping sunk in November 1916, 93,000 tons had sailed under a neutral flag.[32] On 19 January, Britain established a 'restricted area' covering most of the North Sea, 'which will be dangerous to all shipping and should be avoided'.[33]

In February 1917, as feared, German U-boats sent thousands of tons of British and neutral ships to the ocean floor. The new campaign was immediately successful, alarming the War Cabinet. In the week ending 25 February 1917, German submarines sank 34 neutral and Allied vessels, a total of 65,677 tons. Merchant vessels were encouraged to arm themselves: 1681 were armed by 11 February, up from 1194 two months earlier.[34] Many ships refused to venture out of port, fulfilling Germany's secondary goal of deterring them. Still, the losses rose: in the first two weeks of March, 192,863 tons (109 British and neutral ships) were sent to the seabed, compared with 204,860 tons (116 ships) in the same period in February.[35] U-boats destroyed 499,430 tons of shipping in February and 548,817 in March, rapidly approaching the threshold for an August victory.[36]

The campaign unleashed terror on the ships at sea: a torpedo ripped open its hull with a terrific submarine explosion; the men scrambled for life rafts as the ship filled with water and began to list; the seamen caught below deck drowned; and thousands of tons of food and supplies were lost. On the German side, the submariners, in their hot, cramped metal tubes, endured mind-shattering conditions. '[S]ubmarine men,' said one German account, 'were likely to break down with nerve strain of some kind or other and were constantly being sent away to recuperate . . . Some went mad.'[37]

April's record losses drained the faces of the War Cabinet: a staggering 841,118 tons of shipping were sunk that month, 169 British and 204 other nations' ships, the worst month of the U-boat campaign.[38] The stunned Jellicoe announced that, in the first nine days, 192,000 tons were lost, almost double that of the corresponding period in March.[39] The exchange ratio was one U-boat to 53 merchant ships in February, one to 74 in March and one to 167 in April. That loss rate easily exceeded Britain's capacity to fix damaged ships, build new ones or find extra tonnage elsewhere.

The U-boats were also finding their ultimate target: the British civilian. By mid-April, Britain had nine weeks' supply of wheat and flour stocks (compared with fourteen weeks' the previous December).[40] Total British imports of food, drink and raw materials had fallen to 2,503,000 tons in March 1917, compared with 3,567,000 tons in the same month in 1916.[41] By May, the net annual rate of depletion of British shipping had reached 25 per cent, which, if continued, would have seriously threatened British survival. Haig's armies relied on the lifeline across the English Channel. 'Britain would lose the war, if it lost the Channel,' writes the British naval expert Geoffrey Till. For Jellicoe, the rising losses pointed to the 'absolute necessity of turning the Germans out of northern Belgium at the earliest possible moment. It must be done during the present summer.'[42]

Spurred by this success, Berlin decided to devote its entire shipbuilding resources to building submarines, according to a captured

U-boat captain (whose statements were presented to the War Cabinet in May). Output would soon reach twenty submarines per month; already 300 submarines were in use, he claimed (not all were operational). By then, a special U-boat training school was turning out crews within three months.[43]

All this added huge impetus to the case for Haig's Flanders Offensive, with three caveats. First, the submarine bases in Flanders played a relatively minor role in the U-boat war, because Germany had more important bases in the Baltic. Second, shipping losses would never reach their April peak thanks to the effectiveness of a new convoy system championed by Lloyd George (see below). The losses fell to 590,729 tons (287 ships) in May 1917, 669,218 tons in June (290 ships), and 534,799 tons in July (227 ships) – a total of 3.7 million tons of world shipping since 1 February.[44] Third, the British people were better off than Jellicoe feared and these figures suggested. The government had acted quickly to raise domestic food production, stockpile food and relieve the nation's dependence on imports. The food controller pressed the public to curb waste and 'extravagant consumption',[45] and urged every eating-place to observe one 'meatless day' per week and bakers to use only 'straight-run flour'. Posters exhorted the public to 'Eat Less Bread', 'Save the Wheat, Help the Fleet' and 'Save Two Slices every day and Defeat the U-Boat'.[46] The Germans had failed to factor into their calculations the huge grain reserves on hand in Australia, Canada and the Americas, which was more than enough to feed the nation. The British people would never experience the severe malnourishment and, in some regions, starvation of their counterparts in Germany. The wealthy could afford to ignore these restraints, and many continued gorging themselves as if it were peacetime. Nor would British racehorses receive less corn and oats, so plentiful were the grain supplies.

—

As anticipated, the U-boat offensive accelerated America's entry into the war. On 31 January 1917, Ambassador Count Johann von Bernstorff, with all the bumbling menace that passed for German diplomacy, told Robert Lansing, US secretary of state, that German submarines would stop all sea traffic 'with every available weapon and without further notice in the . . . blockade zones around Great Britain, France, Italy and in the Eastern Mediterranean'.[47] US ships, he warned, should henceforth display prominent markings to ensure their safe passage. Most would distrust that warning and confine themselves to port: German submarines sank two ships bearing US flags that month, bringing back memories of the *Lusitania* and hardening American opinion against Germany. The president promptly condemned the U-boat war as illegal and indefensible, and froze all diplomatic contact with Germany.

The moment that confirmed US entry was the interception by British intelligence of the 'Zimmermann Note', a cypher telegram sent on 11 January 1917 by Arthur Zimmermann, German foreign secretary, to Heinrich von Eckardt, the German ambassador in Mexico. It proposed a military alliance between Germany and Mexico should America enter the war, and that Mexico, in return, would share in the spoils of victory, including the disputed border states. When Edward Bell, secretary of the US Embassy in Britain, first saw the note on 19 February, he thought it a fake. His incredulity turned to rage when Zimmermann himself confirmed the telegram's authenticity.

'We intend to begin on the 1st of February unrestricted submarine warfare,' the Note told the Mexicans. 'We shall endeavor in spite of this to keep the United States of America neutral. In the event of this not succeeding, we make Mexico a proposal of alliance on the following basis: make war together, make peace together . . . an understanding on our part that Mexico is to reconquer the lost territory in Texas, New Mexico and Arizona . . . [T]he ruthless employment of our submarines now offers the prospect of compelling England in a few months to make peace. Signed, Zimmermann.'[48] Within two months, America was at war with Germany.

—

While German and British commanders respectively defended the submarine war and naval blockade as legitimate weapons, powerful civilians were not persuaded. The 'immorality' of the two offensives drew the concern of the Vatican. In a message to the British Government on 28 February, Pope Benedict XV urged Britain and Germany to cease waging 'warfare by means of starvation', and offered to mediate to reach an agreement.[49]

Downing Street dismissed the Vatican's intervention. 'The Pope's proposal was not one that could be accepted,' reasoned the War Cabinet on 2 March. 'It was doubtful whether . . . Germany could be trusted to adhere to any such arrangement. The danger would be that, after accumulating a certain stock of food, Germany would find some pretext for throwing the arrangement over and reverting to unrestricted submarine warfare.'[50]

The Vatican failed to see that the blockade lay at the heart of British military strategy, as the War Cabinet noted in its response:

> [T]o accept the [Vatican's] proposal would be to
> abandon the whole of our military policy, of which the
> blockade formed an essential part, and even to consider
> it would be an admission on our part of the success of
> the submarine campaign and of our own weakness.[51]

Germany dismissed the Pope's intervention on similar lines: national survival was at stake. Both responses revealed the callousness of governments unwilling even to consider mediation and determined to use any weapon, regardless of whether it broke international laws or slaughtered civilians.

—

Compounding the threat of submarines in early 1917 was the alarming prospect of Russia abandoning Britain and her allies. Russia's domestic turmoil was steadily undermining the Allied war effort. The revolution of March 1917 forced the Tsar to abdicate, installing a provisional, 'democratic' government, first under Prince Georgy Lvov and then under Alexander Kerensky. The next month, the new regime moved to reassure the Entente governments of Russia's commitment to the war, promising to continue the struggle against Germany. Huge Bolshevik-inspired protests against the war, by Russian workers and soldiers, countermanded any such promise; in May and July, the soldiers would 'vote with their feet' and desert en masse.[52]

There was a 'deplorable lack of discipline' in the Russian Army, the British consul in Odessa cabled the War Cabinet on 11 May, 'and very poor prospects of any offensive on the part of the Russian forces'.[53] Deserters had exceeded two million before the March Revolution, and doubled after it, Major General Alfred Knox, the British military attaché (and spy) in Russia, reported at the end of May. A mere 100,000 had returned to the colours.[54]

In response, the French and British Governments wrote off hopes of their eastern ally contributing anything further to the war effort. Britain's High Command 'quite plainly believed that nothing could be expected of Russia in the future'.[55] (The wounded Russian bear would keep grumbling until September, when the Germans put it out of its misery for good, at the Battle of Riga.) Lord Robert Cecil (whose avowed pacifism had not dissuaded him from serving as minister of blockade), failed to see how Britain and France could win the war alone. Several top officials dwelled once more, in the privacy of their clubs and offices, on finding a peaceful settlement with Germany.

Yet France, too, had become an unreliable ally, for reasons peculiar to the experiences and culture of the French Army. Many of France's finest regiments had expired in the fires of Verdun, and the country needed time to recoup her huge losses. That much was clear at the start of 1917. Less clear was how the brooding beast of French morale would hold up to another huge offensive, planned on the Aisne. Already, there were dark mutterings in the French ranks about the terrible food and short leave, among other complaints. Yet nobody in French High Command – certainly not its new commander, General Robert Nivelle – anticipated the speed and thoroughness with which the genie of mutiny would spread through the *poilu.*

—

Meanwhile, Lloyd George had devoted much of his time to finding a way of neutralising the German submarine offensive. This cohered with the idea of himself as an amateur expert in strategic matters who could countermand his admirals and generals through sheer genius and force of will. In this case, the prime minister would be proved perfectly correct. He championed a system of 'scientifically organized convoys', first proposed by the Cabinet secretary, Maurice Hankey, in a memo in February 1917, on the recommendation of Admiral Reginald Henderson, a quiet renegade in the upper ranks of the navy. Simply put, the system worked in the same way as a herd of wildebeest: the herd presented a moving, collective target to the lion, and the biggest protected the weakest. In the same way, merchant ships would sail in convoy formation, protected by destroyers, denying the U-boats a lone target. If the submarines attacked the convoy, they risked immediate exposure and destruction. It was a fairly obvious solution, which Lloyd George came to cherish as his pet project.

Yet the prime minister's enthusiasm for convoys had not counted on the intransigence of the admiralty, whose grandees frowned on the notion of a British destroyer *escorting* a fishing trawler. Had the Royal Navy, monarch of the oceans, ruler of the waves, been reduced to this? Jellicoe and other top sailors agreed over breakfast with Lloyd George on 13 February to 'conduct experiments' in convoys, but argued that merchant captains lacked the discipline to keep their stations.[56]

On 8 March, having completed his 'experiment', Jellicoe moved to torpedo the idea. The captains of ten 'tramp steamers', he grandly informed the War Cabinet, had said they were 'strongly against convoy' and 'would very much prefer to sail alone'.[57] The 'survey' failed to persuade Lloyd George. The prime minister, to his credit, was determined to force the idea on the admiralty, even if that meant removing Jellicoe.

—

On 2 April 1917, President Woodrow Wilson delivered a War Message to Congress. 'The present German submarine warfare against commerce is a warfare against mankind,' he declared. 'It is a war against all nations. American ships have been sunk, American lives taken . . . There has been no discrimination. The challenge is to all mankind. Each nation must decide for itself how it will meet it . . .'[58] Four days later, the United States declared war on Germany.

Immediately, Britain sent Lord Balfour with an urgent shopping list for troops, guns, medical supplies, wheat and steel.[59] With America in the war, the British were no longer reliant on the long and dangerous delivery of Australian wheat: US battleships would join the convoys in helping to combat the submarine threat.[60]

Meanwhile, Lloyd George was close to proving the admiralty dead wrong over the submarine menace. His first 'experiment' in convoy protection tore up the admiralty's case that escorts wouldn't work. On 10 May, several British destroyers escorted seventeen merchant ships out of Gibraltar; twelve days later, all reached British ports safely, with their cargo intact. It was a shining moment for the British war effort amid all the gloom.

By mid-1917, most merchant ships were sailing in protected convoys across the Atlantic. Germany would never again repeat the record strike rate of April, the only month in which her submarines sank more than 600,000 tons of British shipping – the threshold on which Berlin's 1 August victory deadline relied. From July 1917 onwards, the U-boat campaign would fall well short of Germany's war-winning tally.

That posed the question: why launch a huge land offensive

against German U-boat bases on the Belgian coast when the convoy system showed every sign of defeating the enemy's submarines? Third Ypres was scheduled to begin in July 1917. Yet as early as May, the U-boats were being deterred and the convoys protected. Why go ahead with Third Ypres at all if the submarines could be defeated at sea, as seemed likely? Haig and his generals had their reasons, as we shall see. The War Cabinet was silent on the issue. It was never pursued.

# 4

# KNIGHTS AND PAWNS

*And so we went to bed, thoroughly disgusted with*
*our Government and the Politicians.*
Field Marshal Sir Douglas Haig, 26 February 1917, at the Calais conference

---

At first, their relationship seemed workable. Haig spoke well of the prime minister, as a man he thought he could work with. Neither knew that their feelings would soon degenerate into a state of mutual contempt that would fester for the rest of their lives. This was not a passing power struggle between a political leader and his commander; this was viscerally personal, as one story reveals. After Haig gave an ill-advised interview to French journalists that came across as vainglorious in *The Times*'s English translation, infuriating Lloyd George, the prime minister tried to persuade Lord Northcliffe to turn his arsenal of ink on the popular commander. '[Lloyd George] made the proposition,' the press baron recounted, 'that I should attack [Haig] in my group of newspapers and so render him unpopular enough to be dealt with. "You kill him and I will bury him." Those were his very words.'[1] (At the time, Lloyd George was the more likely target of Northcliffe's press.)

At the heart of the dispute lay the question of how best to win the war: Lloyd George and Haig had very different ideas. The prime minister had no faith in Haig's strategy of attrition, which he saw as pointless butchery. Lloyd George preferred to use the British Army in defence and on a third front in Italy, to limit losses. He later professed that he and the War Cabinet were not told of Haig's Flanders Plan until June 1917, a month before the ground offensive began, implying that, had he known, he could have stopped it, and that he, at least, was not responsible. (This whitewash is one of several barefaced lies in Lloyd George's otherwise riveting memoir.)

For one thing, Lloyd George had known of the Flanders Plan as early as 21 November 1916, when the War Committee fastened on 'the very great desirability . . . of military action designed either to occupy Ostend or Zeebrugge, or at least render those ports useless as bases for destroyers and submarines,' according to Asquith's account. 'There was no difference of opinion . . . that the submarine constitutes by far the most dangerous menace to the Allies at the present . . .'[2] On the 23rd, the Committee reinforced the point: the 'expulsion of the enemy from the Belgian coast' was of the highest importance.[3] Lloyd George was not then prime minister, but it is inconceivable that a politician with his ego and hankering to be at the centre of events was unaware of the planning of the most important Allied offensive of 1917.

In January, General Sir William 'Wully' Robertson, the hotheaded, popular chief of the imperial general staff (CIGS), apprised Haig of the *government's support* for an offensive in Flanders, and the 'great importance' it attached 'to the capture of Ostend and Zeebrugge before next winter'. In whose name was he acting if not in the name of the government of the new prime minister?

Robertson's letter, dated 1 January 1917, raised the question of whether General Nivelle's plan for a new offensive in Champagne would prevent Haig 'from undertaking the operations which you contemplate in Belgium'.[4] The issue was extremely sensitive, because Haig's hopes of attacking in Flanders hinged upon the support of his prime minister, which was never a given. Soon it would become clear that Lloyd George saw in Nivelle's reckless plan for a lightning breakthrough a far more appealing alternative to Haig's gradual attritional war.

—

On 5–7 January 1917, Lloyd George attended the Rome conference of Allied leaders and their military advisers to discuss the year's war plans. True to his flamboyant form, the prime minister stole the show with an idea that tore up everything his advisers thought they had privately agreed before the meeting. Lloyd George had, in fact, been studying an alternative to Haig's wearing-down war, which he had not discussed with anyone. Even members of his own Cabinet were in the dark, showing just how much the prime minister ran the war as he pleased.

Why not hurl the brunt of the Allied attack at Germany's weakest point, on the Italian front, along the Isonzo River, Lloyd George asked the conference. 'Would it not be possible,' he said, 'to make a great and sudden stroke against the enemy on the Isonzo front . . . to inflict a decisive defeat on him, and to press forward to Trieste and get astride the Istrian Peninsula?'[5]

'No', the delegates variously said or thought, 'it would not'. The idea defied all conventional military sense. The British military advisers, led by Robertson, were 'completely taken aback at finding their own Prime Minister putting forward a plan they had never heard of'.[6] Robertson bit hard on his humiliation and calmly opposed the idea.

The French officials firmly rejected it. The British leader's Italian 'strategy' was wrong-headed on several grounds, the commanders pointed out, not least because 130 of Germany's 200 divisions, including the enemy's best units, were then stationed along the Western Front – and any weakening of Allied pressure risked provoking an enemy offensive. The war would be won or lost in France and Belgium, the French and British delegations argued. To shift guns and men to Italy would denude the French and Belgian lines of defence and encourage the Germans to attack.

Even the callous and incompetent General Luigi Cadorna, the Italian commander-in-chief, who would fight a string of failed offensives on the Isonzo, was reluctant to agree to the reinforcement of the Italian front, despite his own government's delight at the prospect.

Lloyd George refused to release his Italian bone: 20,000 railway wagons, he said, could safely transport the Anglo-French forces to Italy without fear of submarine attack, and Britain could spare much of its heavy artillery for a third front in Italy. Had the man lost his senses? Was Lloyd George seriously suggesting that they dismantle their vital defensive positions on the Western Front? And pack off the heavy guns in France and Flanders, then holding back the German steamroller, to Italy?

The delegates consigned the idea to a respectful oblivion, at least for now: the three governments' military advisers agreed to examine the proposal and respond in good time.[7] If they hoped the idea would sit and gather dust, they underestimated the British leader. He would never abandon his cherished Italian offensive (not even to appease Lord Northcliffe, who, on 2 January, had threatened to bring down the government if Lloyd George dared to move two divisions from the western theatre). It was a measure of Lloyd George's extraordinary self-confidence – a union of wilful ignorance and sincere determination to spare Britain another Somme – that he reckoned he could turn the great ship of war to Italy.

—

For now, at least, the prime minister was obliged to stick with the Western Front, where his gaze settled on a fresh plan that owed nothing to Haig and promised fewer casualties: the lightning offensive envisaged by the dashing new French commander, General Robert Nivelle, the hero of Verdun. The Nivelle Offensive, when he heard of it, was music to Lloyd George's ears. It aimed to break the German line on the Aisne River in a matter of days, heave the enemy out of France and end Haig's war of attrition.

Robert Nivelle, 61, was a supremely self-confident artilleryman who had convinced himself, if not his fellow generals, that the artillery barrages with which he'd won the last battles of Verdun would work in the wider, better-defended theatre of the Aisne valley. Saturation shelling on an unprecedented scale followed by a concentrated, creeping barrage in advance of waves of shock troops would rupture the German lines and win the war. Best of all, in the politicians' eyes, the Nivelle Offensive would be a short sharp blow with comparatively few casualties. All Nivelle needed was 48 hours, the Frenchman promised, and if the breakthrough took longer he promised he'd call the whole thing off.

Nivelle laid his plan before Haig on 20 December 1916. It aimed, Nivelle wrote, 'to destroy the main body of the enemy's armies on the Western Front'. The French forces, with British help, would 'pin down as large a portion as possible of the hostile forces' in the Somme and Arras–Bapaume sectors, while an *attaque brusquée* would 'break the enemy's front in such a manner that the rupture can be immediately exploited'.[8] If it failed, 'it will still be possible', Nivelle reassured Haig, 'to carry out in fine weather (*á la belle saison*) the operations projected in Flanders'.[9]

At first, Haig gave his French counterpart the benefit of the doubt (he would later change his mind). The British commander agreed that 'a decisive blow' should be 'struck by surprise' now that 'the Enemy's morale is weakened'.[10] Brigadier General John Charteris, Haig's unreliable intelligence officer, spoke in awe of Nivelle's self-confidence and how the Frenchman 'sees big'.[11]

Nivelle was strong on grand statements but short on detail. Who would lead the Anglo-French forces? Would there be a unity of command? At what point would the British and Dominion troops be released from the French offensive and entrained to Flanders? The transfer would involve a gigantic logistical operation, moving hundreds of thousands of men and huge amounts of ammunition and supplies. How would this be achieved?

With these questions high in mind, Haig told the French general (on 6 January 1917) that he would support the attack on the Aisne on the condition that it had a strict time limit: the decisive attack, Haig reminded Nivelle, would be of short duration (up to fourteen days in the opening bombardment phase, and 24–48 hours in the second phase). If Nivelle failed to get results in this time frame, Haig reserved the freedom to break off the offensive and move his troops to Flanders. '[T]he clearance of the Belgian coast,' he wrote, 'is of such importance to the British Government that it must be fully provided for before I can finally agree to your proposals.'[12] Haig henceforth planned two offensives in 1917: on the Vimy, Arras and Ancre sectors in France, in support of Nivelle's left flank, scheduled for April; and in Flanders, on the Ypres Salient, scheduled to start in late July.

Haig proceeded on the assumption that his prime minister, whatever their personal differences, retained faith in his operational ability. For a commander of such experience, Haig could appear strangely guileless. He saw himself as a man of his word, an upholder of the Victorian values of honour and self-respect. He disdained the strange, slithering beast of the politician. Haig despised the political type, their venality, their molten nature, the ease with which they poured themselves into a new vessel and threw out the old. If you had told Haig then that Lloyd George was about to cast aside the strategic priority of the Belgian coast, he would have disbelieved you. If you had told Haig then that his prime minister was secretly working with the French to subordinate him to Nivelle, he would have thought you mad.

—

Lloyd George's infatuation with Nivelle reached a high point on 15–16 January, when the Frenchman arrived at a conference in London to present his plan for victory. Nivelle was a great success. His dash and pluck charmed the ladies and enthralled the men. A smallish man, with a well-pruned moustache and an excellent command of English (the gift of his English mother), Nivelle deeply impressed Lloyd George, who, playing the amateur phrenologist, remarked that he liked the Frenchmen's head. 'He often judged men in this way,' observed Brigadier General Edward Spears, the Anglo-French liaison officer. '[H]e either liked the shape of a man's head or he did not'.[13] Lloyd George also liked the way Nivelle spoke, and he quickly persuaded himself that the Frenchman's plan was the right one.

In Nivelle, the prime minister espied a fellow man who got things done. Nivelle's all-or-nothing gamble on the Aisne spoke to Lloyd George's penchant for decisive, fleet-footed action over Haig's long 'bleeding' war. What's more, Nivelle was easier to comprehend, Lloyd George cruelly joked, than his famously inarticulate commander-in-chief. The Nivelle Offensive appealed to him for another reason: ever mindful of the rising body count, Lloyd George assumed that French troops would bear the brunt of the fighting – and the casualties.

Not everyone shared the prime minister's faith in Nivelle. The Frenchman's victory-clenching battle plan failed to persuade the experts in the War Office, who refused to believe that saturation bombing, however concentrated, could destroy nine to twelve lines of trenches set in a defensive system five to twelve miles deep. Nor were they convinced that the French guns could be moved up in time to support the advancing infantry, who, without artillery cover, would be cut to pieces. Yet the Nivelle Plan hinged on a breakthrough within 48 hours, a feat that neither side had accomplished in two years. The boffins in the War Office were ignored: Nivelle so impressed the British Cabinet that Lloyd George dismissed the criticisms as signs of weakness. He even ordered Robertson to send a special instruction to Haig to back Nivelle's proposal 'in the letter and in the spirit' and on no account to keep the Frenchman waiting.

—

The Nivelle Plan gathered the support of powerful civilians. Soon, in

Lloyd George's mind, it had eclipsed the Flanders Plan. The U-boat menace on the Belgian coast, once thought so dangerous, receded as a priority. Nivelle himself dismissed the attack on the submarine bases as 'an *idée fixe*': a British obsession that would merely push the submarines eastward. The real war was in north-eastern France, he insisted. Only after the defeat of Germany on French soil, he granted, would the lesser glory of clearing Belgium fall to the British.

As the terrible day approached, Nivelle made ever more strident claims for his plan, propelled by the unwavering support of Colonel d'Alenson, his *chef de cabinet*, 'a Napoleon without genius' who was dying of phthisis and who burned for victory over Germany before he expired.[14] Yet Nivelle's nerves began to tell: he had never commanded an army on this scale; he received slender political support, in the form of Prime Minister Aristide Briand, himself in a fragile political state; and he enjoyed none of the affection the French people had bestowed on Joffre and Foch.

Nivelle overcompensated for his anxiety with a puffed up sense of his own importance, displaying a dangerous tendency to treat Haig as a subordinate (as field marshal, Haig easily outranked the French general). On 25 January, Nivelle wrote to his British counterpart in dictatorial tones, heavy with the presumption that the British and Dominion armies were a part of the French Army. This deeply rankled at Haig's headquarters, where the issue of command had not yet been resolved.

As yet unknown to Haig, these were the opening salvoes of a 'wearing-down war' against the British commander, conducted behind the scenes by Lloyd George in concert with the French Government. The prime minister had privately decided to place Haig and his forces at the beck and call of Nivelle. If Lloyd George could not sack his commander-in-chief, under his pledge to the Conservatives, he could so humiliate him that Haig's pride would do the rest and he would resign.

On the face of it, a more despicable act of sabotage of a commander-in-chief by his prime minister is difficult to imagine. For his part, Lloyd George had persuaded himself that his intentions justified this act of gross disloyalty: he wanted No More Sommes. That meant taking the reins of the British Army out of Haig's blood-soaked hands and putting them in the Frenchman's.

—

The prime minister delivered the body blow at the Calais conference on 26–27 February 1917, innocuously convened to resolve an Anglo-French dispute over railway lines in the British zone of operations. Well in advance, Lloyd George had made the true agenda of the meeting clear to the French Government but not to his own commanders: that was, to hand over command of the British forces in France to the French.

An unappealing feature of Lloyd George's character was the puerile way in which he relished the coming destruction of his rivals, real or imagined. Buoyed by the blow he was about to inflict, he laughed and joked on the journey across the Channel. Yet the shooting down of Haig had an ingredient of calculated malice extreme even by Lloyd George's methods.[15]

Haig and Robertson travelled to Calais suspecting nothing. Unusually, Robertson had not been invited to attend the War Cabinet two days earlier, because he would have opposed the scheme to dethrone Haig and blown the plot. Lloyd George merely suggested to the four-man meeting that agreements reached in London about the command structure would be formalised in Calais. Maurice Hankey, the formidable secretary of the War Cabinet, mildly minuted this as an endeavour to adopt 'such measures as might appear best calculated . . . to ensure unity of command'.[16] The Calais meeting would complete Haig's deception in the most destructive way.[17]

The conference began at 3.30 pm in the Hotel of the Gare Maritime, a harbour-side haunt of illicit lovers, recently seasick passengers and anxious immigrants, flung up in the path of a restless, moaning wind. Lloyd George and Hankey represented the British Government; Prime Minister Aristide Briand and Minister for

War General Hubert Lyautey, the French. Between them sat Haig and Nivelle, and fellow generals and staff members. The minds of the French and British commanders moved in different orbits. Haig and Robertson arrived expecting a robust discussion about logistics and railway timetables, involving Auckland Geddes, the director of recruiting at the War Office – though the presence of such powerful personages must have alerted them to the likelihood of a far more important agenda. Nivelle arrived expecting to hear the confirmation of his appointment as supreme commander of the French and British forces, which he presumed a fait accompli. (Nivelle would soon tearfully claim that he knew nothing of the plot to unseat Haig, and that it shocked him to find that he'd been used as the unwitting instrument of a politician's dirty work. In fact, Nivelle had known the French were plotting to seize command of the British Army in late December 1916, though in fairness he may not have known the extent of Haig's ignorance.)[18]

The mood rapidly deteriorated when the meeting reconvened at 5.30 pm, and Lloyd George raised the question of unity of command. 'The enemy has but one army,' he said. 'The Entente Powers should secure for themselves the same advantage, especially in battle. If we do not do this we cannot hope for success.'[19] He asked for complete frankness, and invited Nivelle to present his plan and to raise any differences of opinion he had with 'Marshal Haig'. The prime minister urged Nivelle 'to keep nothing back'.[20]

After a little prefatory padding on the strengths of his relationship with Haig, the Frenchman rather hesitantly advanced the idea that unity of command was indispensable. Goaded by Lloyd George to force the point, Nivelle bluntly declared that France should have full command of the British forces.

Haig's camp met this with astonished silence. Haig then opened his mouth, firmly declaring that *he* would decide '*where* and *how* I would dispose of my troops . . .'[21] To relieve the tension, Nivelle was asked to put his terms in writing. The meeting adjourned.

The slow humiliation of Field Marshal Haig and his commanders resumed at 8 pm that night, when General Nivelle handed his written terms to Lloyd George, in the prime minister's rooms. Haig and Robertson were not then present. These terms stated that the French commander-in-chief 'will, as from March 1st, have command over the British forces operating on [the Western Front], in all matters affecting the conduct of operations'.[22] The extraordinary document sought to give the French commander absolute power over planning, operations, munitions and supplies of the British Army, leaving Haig in command of discipline and arranging reinforcements – the powers, in effect, of little more than a provost marshal. A British 'Quarter Master General' would be installed at the French headquarters in Beauvais, through whom Haig would have to communicate to reach London.

Under this 'unity of command', the British Army, along with its Australian, New Zealand, Canadian and South African components, would henceforth cease to exist as a distinct entity and would become a mere appendage of the French, rather like the colonial forces of Morocco or Algeria. Lloyd George professed himself satisfied with the document, apparently unaware of the extent to which he would be handing over the camel of the British forces to France and leaving Haig barely holding its tail. The Dominions had had little say in the transaction that would bargain away the control of their soldiers. (Australia's prime minister Billy Hughes had been unable to attend the Imperial War Cabinet meetings in early 1917, leaving him in a state of 'complete ignorance' of negotiations that would have a direct bearing on Australia's army.)[23]

Digesting the translation of Nivelle's statement over dinner that night, Robertson turned a deep shade of red and showed 'every sign of having a fit'.[24] 'Get 'Aig!' he yelled. On reading it, Haig was speechless with rage at the connivance of his prime minister with the French in his effective removal from command of the British Army. Spears would later compare this 'monstrous farce' to a Borgia family dinner at which the guests were pronounced poisoned upon the arrival of dessert.[25] 'Seldom in history,' his florid account continued, 'can Englishmen have been asked to subscribe to such abject conditions. It seemed incredible that the greatest army we had ever sent abroad, now at the height of its power and absolutely confident of its superiority over the enemy, should be confronted with terms such as might be imposed on a vassal state.'[26]

The execrable terms would be rejected, of course. The two commanders carried their rage – Haig's silent and wounded, Robertson's sulphuric – to the prime minister's rooms at 10 pm that night. A violent row ensued. '[I]t would be madness to place the British under the French,' Haig told the prime minister, adding that he 'did not believe our troops would fight under French leadership'.[27] Lloyd George hit back with the insulting insinuation, 'I know the British soldier very well. He speaks more freely to me and there are people he criticises a good deal more strongly than General Nivelle.'[28] Lloyd George concluded by shouting that Nivelle would command the British forces, and he showed his top soldiers the door.

They retreated to Robertson's rooms for a post-mortem, joined by Lieutenant General Launcelot Kiggell, chief of the general staff of the British Armies in France. Aghast at their treatment, but braced by Hankey's revelation that Lloyd George had not received 'full authority' to act from the War Cabinet, Robertson proposed the mass resignation of the top brass. He quickly thought the better of it. He was needed now, as never before, to defend the British Army. Instead, the commanders decided to disobey the plan, even though that meant disobeying their own government. They would 'rather be tried by Court Martial than betray the Army' by placing it under the French. 'And so we went to bed,' Haig brooded in his diary, 'thoroughly disgusted with our Government and the Politicians.'[29]

That night, Hankey prevailed upon Lloyd George to soften the arrangement, to preserve a semblance of cooperation. The prime minister reluctantly agreed, and Hankey and Major General Frederick Maurice found themselves deputed to stay up all night and hammer out a solution.

The next morning, in a meeting with Robertson (which Haig

refused to attend), Lloyd George tabled a modified proposal: Nivelle would command the British Army only for the planning and duration of his offensive, after which Haig's powers would be reinstated. Robertson rejected this, and fought tooth and nail for the army's independence. Haig fired off a memo, warning that the proposal to subordinate the British forces to the French 'must involve the disappearance of the British commander-in-chief and GHQ': 'So drastic a change in our system seems to me to be fraught with the gravest danger.'[30]

Lloyd George thrashed about in a rage, and refused to compromise. After much coming and going between hotel rooms, a deal was reached: Nivelle would command the French and British forces on the Western Front for the duration of the offensive; Haig would have the right to challenge French orders if he believed they 'would compromise the safety of his army' and be free to choose the means of deploying his troops in the 'zone of operations [the French] allotted him'.[31] It was the best the British commanders could hope for, and they signed. From that moment, until the end of Nivelle's campaign, the British Army would be a unit of the French.

Haig left Calais bridling with unconcealed disgust at the proceedings. He lunched at Boulogne, where he overheard a remark by General Joseph Micheler, commander of the French reserves, who happened to be sharing his doubts about the Nivelle Offensive: 'it does not matter what the politicians decide', Haig later quoted Micheler as saying, 'the French soldier is not going to fight after the autumn!'[32]

—

Haig and Robertson would never forgive Lloyd George for what they saw as an act of gross disloyalty. They were soldiers, above all; their loyalty to the army was indivisible. And so, on their return to London, Robertson at once informed the Army Council of what had happened, turning the 'icy douche' of responsibility on the government.[33] Ministers, he stressed, would now be held accountable for the safety of the troops and the consequences of a decision taken without his or Haig's agreement. He made violently clear that his signature on the paper did not indicate concurrence.[34] His anger festering, Robertson later wrote to Haig, 'I cannot believe that a man such as he can remain for long head of any Government. Surely some honesty and truth are required.'[35]

Haig offered his resignation to the King, who rejected it. The old friends agreed that it was 'a calamity for the country to have such a man at the head of affairs in this time of great crisis'.[36] Haig's diary summed up the weight on his mind: 'All would be so easy if I only had to deal with the Germans.'[37] 'LG,' he told his wife, is 'looking about to find something else to increase his reputation as the "man of the hour" and the saviour of England. However I am doing my best and have a clear conscience. If they have someone else who can command this great Army better than I am doing, I shall be glad to hand over to him, and will be *happy* to come back to my darling wife and play golf and bring up the children.'[38]

The War Cabinet regrouped on 28 February, and the prime minister made a half-hearted effort to patch things up. The Calais agreement, he back-pedalled, 'merely' sought to secure a 'clearly defined unity of control', and in no sense cast aspersions on Haig's ability and qualifications, 'in whom the War Cabinet continued to entertain full confidence'.[39] One can almost hear Wully Robertson's heart thumping with Scottish rage at this twisted representation.

Unity of command should have devolved upon an overarching commander to whom Haig and Nivelle were equally answerable, under an Anglo-French war committee. Instead, the British commanders now faced the complete immersion of their beloved army into the French one. What neither man fully realised was that the subordination of Haig was the first blow in Lloyd George's personal campaign against his 'unsackable' commander-in-chief. On either side, feelings were incandescent.

—

The war that had seemed like 'noises off' in this tawdry drama of power and control was allowed to resume. On 8 March, Haig was told that he 'enjoyed the full confidence of the War Cabinet'; a week later, fresh words were inserted into the agreement, according to which 'the British Army and the Commander-in-Chief will be regarded by General Nivelle as Allies and not subordinates, except during the particular operations . . . explained at the Calais Conference'.[40] Haig set aside his personal misgivings and resolved to enact the agreement to the letter.

Nivelle, however, nonplussed at not getting full control over the British, now revealed himself as the kind of man who sought power for its own sake. He continued to dispatch orders to Haig's head-quarters, eliciting the latter's contempt for this 'junior *foreign* commander', a remark that did Haig no favours.[41] The French general added to Haig's woes by requesting that General Sir Henry Wilson, the bellicose Francophile schemer whom Haig deeply distrusted, be made head of the British Mission at Beauvais, through whom Haig would have to liaise.

Haig shot off a letter steaming with indignation at Nivelle's 'dictatorial language' and bid to 'grasp more power over our Armies' than was agreed at Calais. He demanded that the British Government inform the French that their commanders had no authority to issue orders to British units other than through himself; and that Nivelle had no right to inspect British or Dominion units, 'visit them' or remove their troops from the line without his consent. He was even reduced to asking the Cabinet to dispatch an 'expression of confidence in myself' to the French authorities, painfully revealing just how little confidence Haig felt his government had in him.[42]

Clearly, it was an unworkable arrangement, and the friction escalated. A 'dangerous divergence of views' now arose between Haig and Nivelle, the War Cabinet heard on 8 March. Haig had refused to cooperate, the French Government complained. Haig found it galling to be at the beck and call of a French officer of lower rank, in whose plans he had little faith; and with every slight, every humiliation, Haig's contempt for Lloyd George deepened.

The next day, the British Government meekly complained to the French that Nivelle's office had treated Haig as a subordinate (no surprise, surely, as that was exactly what the prime minister had reduced him to) and not an equal temporarily under Nivelle's orders, itself a meaningless notion.[43] The fallout could imperil the Allied cause if the dysfunctional arrangement continued, so Lloyd George proposed another meeting to resolve the crisis.[44] This came to nothing; the French Government declined to attend.

On 14 March, the War Cabinet struck a conciliatory note. Haig (in one of his rare appearances) was asked whether he felt he had the 'personal freedom of action' necessary to deal with a surprise attack by the enemy on the Flanders front. He replied through gritted teeth that his freedom to act in Flanders would be assured so long as Nivelle didn't take his troops 'out of my hands at the critical moment'.[45]

A few days later, Jellicoe, the first sea lord, posed a similar question: were British ground troops prepared for a possible enemy attack by sea, to the rear of Haig's forces, at Nieuport? Jellicoe calculated that the Germans could land 20,000–30,000 troops using tugs and lighters assembled in the canals of Zeebrugge and Ostend.[46] A man less self-disciplined than Haig might have barked back that a disloyal prime minister had removed his power to act. Again, Haig kept his composure. No, he had not detected signs of enemy preparations for a seaborne invasion, he replied, warning however that 'our coastal defences were not designed to deal with anything more than small raids'.[47]

—

A month before the French offensive, Nivelle's brittle confidence took a battering. In March, Briand lost power to his declared enemy Paul Painlevé, who became minister for war. A socialist intellectual, Painlevé thoroughly disliked Nivelle and thought his battle plan a recipe for 'mass manslaughter'.[48] He threw his support behind Nivelle's rival, General Philippe Pétain, the 'Lion of Verdun' and a national hero, who had consistently argued that the French infantry should dig in and wait until the Americans arrived. When Painlevé took office, on 19 March, however, Nivelle's plans were too far advanced to halt. The new minister yielded to the momentum and hoped for the best.

Nivelle's great moment approached. Heavy rains postponed zero hour well into April. The French train system groaned under the vast logistical exercise, and the target itself – the German forces stationed along the Aisne – seemed to be thinning out. The weary French Army began moving up, and the British diversionary battles, at Vimy Ridge and Arras, were set in motion.

Neither Nivelle nor Lloyd George, in their enthusiasm for the two-day miracle, had paused to consider the state of the French soldiers who were supposed to achieve it. Lloyd George's readiness to accept huge French (and Italian) casualties ahead of British ones underscored the political over the humanitarian motive that prevailed. Yet any commander, or politician, with an ounce of compassion should have been able to see that the French troops were not up to the job. After their staggering losses at Verdun, these men were being ordered, again, to charge into the furnace.

That scarcely troubled Nivelle, who assumed the poilu would never tire of throwing his blue-uniformed body at German guns. Exhausted, badly fed and utterly demoralised, many had not had leave in months. Most had lost friends, brothers and sons at Verdun. Since 1914, between 2,560,000 and 3,285,000 French soldiers (depending on the source) had been killed or wounded, compared with 1,120,204 British and Dominion troops. The French people were numb with grief and the French Army close to collapse.[49]

—

Meanwhile, on the other side of no-man's-land, the Germans were fully aware of what the French were about to attempt. Nivelle had unwisely circulated his plan to the lower ranks. On 3 March, the Germans captured a French sergeant who happened to possess 'a memorandum . . . of extraordinary value', noted Crown Prince Rupprecht, commander of Army Group Rupprecht, 'as to the particular nature of the surprise which the attacker has in view'.[50] On 6 April, a German raid captured the order of attack of France's Fifth Army, laying out the Nivelle Plan in detail. The Germans immediately deployed 30 fresh divisions (about 400,000 men) to reinforce the vulnerable sector, and extended and fortified the wire and trench lines.

At this point, the Germans were able to draw on hundreds of thousands of fresh troops, thanks to mass conscription and the imminent arrival of reinforcements from the Eastern Front. The March Revolution had heralded the end of Russia's participation in the war, and the redeployment west had begun. By April 1917, 151 German divisions (almost two million men) were entrenched on the Western Front, compared with 119 at the start of the Somme. The number of German rifles 'opposing us' was 100,000 greater than the total on the first day of the Somme, Robertson warned the War Cabinet on 10 April 1917.[51] That said, the combined French and British forces exceeded four million, and they had many more guns than the Germans.

Bedevilling Nivelle's hopes were reports of the curious *absence* of the German front line. The enemy seemed to be deserting his posts. The Australian forces first noticed it: a strange silence issuing from various points along the front. Patrols were sent to investigate, and, sure enough, the enemy were abandoning their posts. Word arrived of agricultural work ceasing, and plant and equipment being destroyed. The reports gradually formed a pattern, and the pattern conformed to an order. They had detected the early signs of a massive defensive withdrawal.

All along the entire front, the German forces were pulling back, under Operation Alberich, ordered by Ludendorff on 4 February. Between 9 February and 19 March, the German Army steadily withdrew to the heavily fortified 'Siegfried Line' (the Allies would soon call it the Hindenburg Line), a ribbon of steel that German engineers had been constructing for months. It comprised a system of wire, trenches and concrete pillboxes twenty to thirty miles deep and in places extending as far back as fifty miles. The withdrawal, timed to coincide with the resumption of the submarine war, was a shrewd defensive move designed to narrow the German front and ease the pressure on the army.

The scorched earth policy that preceded it brought the opprobrium of the world down on Berlin's head. The French and British forces witnessed the wretched result, as they moved onto formerly German-occupied territory to get close enough to attack: terrified French villagers disgorged from the rubble of their homes. For two years, these French border towns had hosted the German forces; now the residents had become refugees in their own country. Many women bore the evidence of occupation, in the fair-haired babies of German fathers. 'Can you love me still, who have loved you always?' some would appeal to their French husbands on being reunited. 'No physical suffering I saw or heard of during the war,' wrote Spears, 'equalled or even approached that raw agony.'[52]

The British journalist Philip Gibbs witnessed the gutting of 'the cottages of the peasants, and all their farms and all their orchards' across the Somme valley. At Réthonvillers, one village of many, he saw 'how each house was marked with a white cross before it was gutted with fire. The Cross of Christ was used to mark the work of the Devil.' Witnessing the women and children in the streets, and staring at him out of windows, 'I was stuck with a chill of horror. The women's faces were dead faces, sallow and mask-like, and branded with the memory of great agonies. The children were white and thin – so thin that their cheekbones protruded. Hunger and fear had been with them too long.'[53]

The Germans left nothing edible or useable: the fields were devastated; livestock slaughtered; villages and towns depopulated and burned; the wells polluted. 'Nearly every tree in the Aisne

Department has been felled,' reported one observer.[54] Booby traps primed to explode were attached to shovels, doors and displaced duckboards. Delayed-action bombs destroyed buildings, such as the town hall in Bapaume after the British occupied it. A recent environmental study of warfare described the German withdrawal as the 'cold-blooded and systematic devastation of the countryside'.[55]

Ludendorff would justify it as a painful strategic necessity – 'we had no choice' – admitting that it implied 'a confession of weakness bound to raise the morale of the enemy'. He claimed his forces had not poisoned the wells, and had salvaged any valuable works of art.[56] His objectives were to narrow the front and 'avoid battle', salvage German guns and equipment, and destroy 'highroads, villages, towns and wells' to prevent the enemy 'establishing himself in force . . . in front of our position'.[57] In pure strategic terms, the German pullback was a stroke of brilliance: the soldiers' entrenchment along a slimmer, better-fortified front plugged the gaps in their line and transformed them into a far more dangerous defensive force.

—

Even as the German Army dematerialised, Nivelle insisted that his plan would triumph. He would outflank the Germans, if necessary, from the other side of the Hindenburg Line: 'In this respect the German retirement may be entirely to our advantage.'[58] Nivelle reckoned on advancing twenty miles in three days. None of his senior commanders, not Pétain or Micheler or the howitzer-shaped General Franchet d'Espèrey, had any confidence in its success: the Nivelle Plan was unravelling before their eyes. On 6 April, beset by doubts, Nivelle presented French president Raymond Poincaré with an ultimatum: approve my plan or accept my resignation. Poincaré gave Nivelle the nod, and the French commander repaired at once to his new headquarters in a chateau near Chantilly, a former residence of Marie Antoinette, trailed by his wine cellar and chefs.

The British 'diversion' at Arras followed a week-long artillery barrage. At first light on 9 April, British and Dominion forces surged over the top, in a series of attacks aimed at diverting German reserves from the much bigger action soon to erupt in Champagne. It started well. The Canadian Corps stormed Vimy Ridge and captured it, at the cost of 10,500 casualties, in perhaps the greatest set-piece battle of the war. Further south, General Edmund Allenby's Third Army advanced three-and-a-half miles in a day, the 'greatest distance accomplished at a bound since the onset of trench warfare',[59] and pierced the Hindenburg Line in several places. By 11 April, the British, Canadians and Anzacs had taken 11,000 prisoners – a record in so short a time. The War Cabinet were delighted; Haig should receive a telegram of congratulations, they decided.[60]

Bad news soon arrived, and with it despair. In a pattern that would soon scar battle after battle, German counter-offensives reclaimed much of the lost ground, and dogged trench warfare resumed. While the Canadians held Vimy, the British were forced back and lost most of their gains at Arras. The casualties between 9 April and 16 May were 159,000, a daily average of 4076 killed, wounded and missing, which would prove to be the worst daily casualty rate of any major battle of the First World War.[61] If Arras wore down the Germans, taught the British lessons on the 'tactical learning curve'[62] and amounted to 'a victory of sorts',[63] as some claim, it is hard to imagine what a real setback would look like.

At the same time came news of the Anzac disasters at Bullecourt. The unpopular British general Hubert Gough, who led the attacks, cursed his soldiers' chances from the start. Exhausted after their long march to the front, the Australians and New Zealanders were sent straight into battle across open ground without artillery cover. To maximise the element of surprise, Gough ordered them to advance behind a dozen tanks, despite the fact they had no experience in tank tactics. The Anzac commander, Lieutenant General William Birdwood, expressed his gravest reservations; Gough overruled him. When only four tanks arrived in time, the attack was postponed and the forward troops streamed back from the jumping-off points, 'disappointed, exasperated . . . like a crowd returning from a football match'.[64]

Bullecourt resumed the next day: Gough made no allowance for the complete loss of surprise. At 3 am on 11 April, the Anzacs again moved into position behind the tanks, over a field drenched in German gas. The tanks advanced slowly, like lumbering tortoises, easy targets for shellfire and armour-piercing bullets. All were out of action by 7 am, and half the crews dead or wounded. Unprotected by tanks or guns, the Anzacs continued advancing. They were mown down. Those who reached the German lines, in scenes reminiscent of Loos, died on the wire. Some briefly penetrated the Hindenburg Line before the Württembergers, fighting 'like demons', reclaimed the lost ground.

Thus ended the First Battle of Bullecourt, another heroic failure: the Australian 4th Division lost 3000 officers and men. The Anzacs would never forgive Gough, whose 'almost boyish eagerness to deliver a death blow', wrote Charles Bean, 'broke at every stage rules . . . recognised even by platoon commanders'.[65] Second Bullecourt would further poison relations between the Anzacs and their British commander (though, in fairness, the Anzac generals made their own errors in the second battle). The memory of the Somme and Bullecourt made up the minds of the Australians, New Zealanders and Canadians: they would never serve under Gough again, if they could help it.

—

Meanwhile, a tragedy of epic proportions was unfolding in Champagne. Here, the world was about to witness the spectacular folly of a man whose mind had lost touch with reality and whose obsession with his war-winning plan appeared to intensify with every premonition of its failure. A commander absorbed in his plans must at times take the enemy into consideration, Churchill had icily observed. Schlieffen, Joffre and Holtzendorff had been deaf to this advice. Now Nivelle would join their ranks – on a similarly devastating scale. Every word of dissent, Nivelle had rejected; every plea to reconsider – from Pétain, Painlevé and his own generals – he flung to the wind, wildly confident of his belief in Germany's imminent defeat. 'No consideration should intervene of a nature to weaken the élan of the attack,' Nivelle told Micheler on 1 April. By then, Nivelle was beyond recall to a saner world.

His forces were immense. Nivelle drew on almost a million Frenchmen in the Aisne River valley, supported by 4800 guns and an estimated 1000 aircraft. The Germans on the opposing heights fielded 480,000 men, 2431 German guns and 640 German aircraft. At dawn on 16 April, the first waves of French troops advanced under sheets of sleet into a stretch of the most difficult terrain on the Western Front – steep gorges, swampy river valleys and sandy rock faces. Enemy machine guns commanded every ridge and spur. German intelligence had been precise: the French attacked exactly where and when expected. They were cut to pieces. The Senegalese colonials fled the field. Nivelle's men gained 600 yards on the first day; he'd promised six miles.[66]

As the news came in, Nivelle tried to soften expectations. His first reports were models of military obfuscation. Gradually the whole ghastly enterprise revealed itself to the French and British Governments: the much-touted breakthrough, the darling of Lloyd George, had failed according to all its benchmarks. During the first four days, almost 30,000 French troops had been killed, 100,000 wounded and 4000 captured, more than ten times Nivelle's original casualty estimate for the first day.[67]

The walking wounded fell back through a great pall of smoke and thunder, their faces disfigured with despair. 'It's all over,' some variously told Spears. 'We can't do it. We shall never do it. *C'est impossible.*' That day, Spears witnessed something he thought he'd never see in the French lines: 'These men were broken in spirit as well as body.'[68] Nivelle had foolishly promised a breakthrough within 48 hours. His pride would not accept defeat, and he flogged the offensive for three more weeks, exterminating some of the finest units in the French republic. He called it off on 9 May, an absolute slaughter: 187,000 French men killed, wounded and missing, against 163,000

German losses. It was France's worst casualty rate since November 1914, for a few miles of useless ground.[69]

—

Nivelle was sacked and dispatched to North Africa. On 15 May, Marshal Philippe Pétain took command of the French forces, an army on its knees. Pétain moved quickly to salvage what was left of their self-esteem. He spoke personally to the men, anxious to rebuild some of their famous *esprit de corps*. Yet the French Army were finished as a fighting force, at least for the rest of the year. On 19 May, Pétain decided to postpone future offensives and rest his men in defensive positions until more tanks and the Americans arrived.[70]

The French Army, Pétain realised, had further to fall. For almost three years, France had been devouring the best of her young men. She had thus far suffered the greatest loss of life in any battle in military history. Verdun had been monstrous, but Nivelle's fiasco proved the last straw. The soldiers felt ill-used, hungry and furious at their conditions: French soldiers were paid a fraction of the daily rate of factory workers. From 3 May, the growl of mutiny spread through the ranks. Two regiments of a colonial division deserted, brandishing placards in their barracks: 'Down with the War! Death to those who are Responsible!'[71]

The mutiny spread like a bushfire. Nivelle's most damaged divisions led the insurrection. Soldiers singing 'The Internationale' threw down their weapons and ransacked their commanders' headquarters. 'Sympathy strikes' erupted among workers in Paris, Soissons and Chalon. In time, 115 regiments from 45 divisions mutinied.[72] A record 27,000 French soldiers would desert in 1917. By an astonishing piece of luck, or rare German incompetence, Berlin never discovered the extent of the mutiny, missing a perfect opportunity to attack Paris when just two reliable regiments were guarding the city's gates.

—

At the time of Nivelle's Waterloo, in London, the first sea lord held a finger to the wind. On 23 April, at the height of the U-boat war, Jellicoe presented a paper, 'The Submarine Menace and the Food Supply', to the War Cabinet. It warned of an extremely dire situation. An immediate investigation began into food stocks, likely future losses and minimum imports required to sustain the armed forces and the country.[73] The government, unaware that April would be the worst month for shipping losses, drew the worst conclusions. Haig's Flanders Offensive refocused their minds, and a tic of humiliation alighted on Lloyd George's brow.

Cometh the hour . . . Haig emerged from the smoke and failure of Champagne like a condemned man who had been granted a reprieve. His powers were now thoroughly restored. 'Sir Douglas Haig has come out on top in this fight between the two Chiefs,' noted Lloyd George's private secretary, in her diary on 12 May. She feared that her boss would 'have to be very careful in future as to his backings of the French against the English'.[74]

A rare spectacle then ensued, of Lloyd George feeling obliged to appear humble, even contrite. Insofar as the prime minister was capable of humility, he conveyed less the fawning attentiveness of Uriah Heep than the importunate countenance of a Cheshire Cat. At the Inter-Allied Conference in Paris, 3–5 May, he presented himself as an innocent civilian ignorant of military matters, with 'no pretensions to being a strategist', despite his recent barnstorming interventions in strategy. He expressed his complete confidence in his military chiefs, and fully authorised Haig to attack when and where he thought best.

Back in command, Haig seized the reins of the Flanders Offensive with fresh gusto. On 7 May, he presented a new plan for Third Ypres at the army commanders' conference at Doullens, north of Amiens. It divided the offensive into two stages. First, in early June 1917, he would attack Messines Ridge, the critical high ground to the south of Ypres that the Germans had more or less possessed since 1914. Next, at the end of July – a gap of seven weeks – he would launch the main offensive against the ridges radiating north and east of Ypres: Pilckem, Gheluvelt, Broodseinde and Passchendaele. Two simultaneous operations would assist the march on the coast: General Rawlinson's forces at Nieuport would attack the Germans at Middelkerke, while an amphibious landing would strike behind the German lines, blocking their retreat. The combined British and Dominion forces would then destroy the U-boat bases at Ostend and Zeebrugge and drive the enemy out of Belgium.

Previously, these two stages – Messines and Passchendaele – had been part of a unified plan. Their separation in time would have immense repercussions, not least because the gap handed the enemy almost two months to prepare their defences for the Passchendaele onslaught.

Haig's ideas met a mute, sullen response. Robertson thought them over-ambitious; Henry Wilson disapproved of anything Haig did or said. Only the Royal Navy welcomed the infantry's help in defeating the U-boats. Yet nobody raised a hand against it – certainly not the contrite Lloyd George, who privately detested it and later claimed not to have head of it until June. He did ask the South African General Jan Smuts to review the plan, hoping for an answer that countermanded Haig. Instead, Smuts gave the 'wrong' answer: a defensive campaign would be disastrous. Smuts saw 'more advantage in an offensive intended to recover the Belgian coast and deprive the enemy of their advanced submarine base'.[75]

In the end, Haig's was the only plan on the table. The British and Dominion commanders, facing Germany alone on the Western Front, believed they had no choice other than to attack and keep on attacking. As Lloyd George had told his French allies in Paris on 4 May, 'We must go on hitting and hitting with all our strength until the Germans ended . . . by cracking.'[1] (With Nivelle's failure, however, the prime minister now quietly revived his plan to 'hit' them in Italy.)

And so, in May–June 1917, as the mutinous French Army rested, the British and Dominion powers turned their eyes once more to the windswept plains of the Ypres Salient. Though Flanders had been a 'dormant' sector for the past two years, the Germans were well aware of Britain's strategic interest in the Belgian coast, and were reinforcing their positions. On the Allied side, as we've seen, Haig had demanded half a million more men.

Hundreds of thousands of soldiers now began to pour into this little patchwork of Flemish farmers' fields, an area far smaller than the Somme and a fraction of the size of the great battlefields on the Russian front. That meant an unusual density of firepower, implying an exceedingly high force to space ratio – i.e. the number of shells fired per square yard – which, every commander knew, would churn up the battlefield and concentrate the casualties.

# 5

# THE BLOODY SALIENT

*Of this man little was heard, possibly because he had a habit of
going into places a thousand strong and coming out a remnant of a
hundred and fifty or so. Dead men tell no tales of their own glory.*
Sergeant Charles Arnold, on the British Tommy

---

*You people stop . . . I can't take anymore.*
The voice of 'Death', on the cover of the German
magazine *Simplicissimus*, 19 June 1917

---

On the map, the Salient resembled a half-oval of British-held territory that bulged into the German lines east of Ypres. In the minds
of the men, it was the 'bloody Salient', a land of screaming shells and
hissing gas, waterlogged trenches and scuttling rats. By 1917, it had
earned its reputation as the most loathsome place on the Western
Front.

The Salient swelled and shrivelled with the ebb and flow of battle,
like a bladder under pressure from either side. The Allies had held it,
in a bigger or smaller form, since the First Battle of Ypres, in October
1914, when the British and French pushed its eastern extremity as

far as the plain beneath Passchendaele Ridge. By January 1917, the German forces had reclaimed the bladder to within a mile or two of Ypres, and clung to the horseshoe of 'high' ground that surrounded it on three sides, from Langemarck and Saint Julien north-east of the city, along the ridges of Pilckem and Gheluvelt (Geluveld) Plateau due east, to Messines Ridge and a string of hills to the south (see Map 1). Beyond this front line, the Germans occupied successive ridges fanning out from the city of Ypres, the most prominent of which were Broodseinde, Poelcappelle and Passchendaele.

In 1917, this land was unrecognisable from what it had been before the war, a region of gently rising pastures and farmlands interrupted by villages and forests. '[Y]ou could not see half a mile for woods,' recalled Lieutenant Guy Chapman. When Ferdinand Foch arrived in Ypres in 1914, he looked out from the tower of the Cloth Hall over a sprinkling of white hamlets set in fields of tobacco and beetroot, interspersed with hedgerows and barns and heaps of manure, 'a sea of green, with little white islands marking the location of the rich villages with their fine churches and graceful steeples'.[2] It was a land of monotonous rains and misty dawns, an atmosphere of 'melancholic sadness melting almost imperceptibly into the grey waters of the North Sea'.[3] The gently rising plains were broken here and there by small woods of ash, chestnut and oak, and by rows of poplars, set in heavy, blue Ypres clay. The terrain was criss-crossed by a network of little canals and creeks that drained the fields. Multitudes of poppy seeds would germinate during the ploughing season, dabbing the dark brown soil in little splashes of red paint. Shellfire had the same effect, bringing to the soldiers' minds an image of the blood of the dead and wounded streaming up from the earth below.

By 1917, the scene was 'as bare as a man's hand', Chapman recalled. 'Were these puke acres ever growing fields of clover, beet or cabbage? Did a clear stream ever run through this squalmy glen?' A 'magnate's estate' of lawns and ornamental fountains was now 'a quag of islands and stagnant pools over which foul gases hang'.[4] A network of trench lines extended east and west of the front lines, interspersed with wire, human and horse remains, wreckage and shell craters. Two years of sporadic shellfire had reduced most of the chateaux, hunting lodges, stately homes, villages and churches to rubble. The stamp of hundreds of thousands of boots and the advance and withdrawal of heavy machinery, gun carriages, horse-drawn carts and truckloads of supplies had turned the land into a fortified labyrinth reaching back to the supply depots of Poperinghe (spelled Poperinge today) on the British side and Roulers on the German (see Map 1).

A few reminders of peace were still visible in mid-1917: ragged copses and hedgerows, a few broken farmhouses, remnants of villages and isolated clumps of forest whose names – Sanctuary Wood, Polygon Wood, Nonne Bosschen, Crest Farm – would soon lose their obscurity forever. The fragile drainage system still partly functioned; the little canals and ditches that had drawn off the surface water for centuries and rendered this former swamp cultivable were not yet completely destroyed.

Nowhere on the Western Front was trench life as miserable as here. Trench foot and other diseases were endemic, and rats were plentiful, bloated on the flesh of corpses. Winters were bone-rattlingly cold, usually around freezing and as low as −15C; summers were hot and wet and fly-blown. Water threatened both armies' trench systems, from above and below. Rain fell with seasonal certainty here, in great, depressing sheets, drenching the trenches and dugouts. The shallow water table seeped through the soil and over the duckboards, limiting the trenches' depth. The infantry had faced the same difficulties every year in Flanders. This year, however, would be far worse, the result of unprecedented shellfire and unusually heavy rain.

In such conditions, the construction of deep trenches had proved extremely difficult. In the wettest areas, the parapets were heightened with sandbags, to protect the soldiers' heads. The Germans had been quick to realise the value of an above-ground defensive system, in the form of rows of concrete pillboxes. Throughout 1916 and early 1917, supplied by an old cement factory at Roulers, they had built up a defensive network of squat cement bunkers that housed shock troops – trained to inflict sudden, lightning attacks – and heavy machine guns. The pillboxes were carefully sited along the ridges, with interlocking fields of fire. Only a direct hit by the heaviest shell would seriously damage these squat excrescences of ferro-concrete. Advancing platoons would have to destroy most of them.

—

For centuries, the beautiful city of Ypres had been the urban heart of Flanders, the Flemish province in western Belgium. The city once rivalled Paris in wealth, as the home of Europe's textile trade, and as a progressive religious centre. Cornelius Jansen, founder of Jansenism – scourge of the French Jesuits – was made Bishop of Ypres in 1636. It was no stranger to conquest, drawing a succession of marauding armies throughout its boisterous history, for religious, economic and strategic reasons. The Romans had attacked and occupied the ancient settlement. There followed the English, French, Spanish, Dutch and English again, in the march of power through time. The city provided troops for the uprising against the French occupying forces at the Battle of the Golden Spurs in 1302. In 1383, Henry le Despenser, the Bishop of Norwich, led an English army to occupy Ypres, as part of the 'Norwich Crusades'. He remarked upon 'a nice old town, with narrow, cobble-stoned streets and some fine buildings' and then besieged it for four months until French relief arrived.[5] During the seventeenth and eighteenth centuries, Ypres fell under the sway of advancing and retreating armies: in 1678, the French Army conquered the city and the engineer Vauban installed a series of ramparts to deter further invaders (the very ramparts that protected the British dugouts and to this day buttress the edge of the moat). They didn't stop the Spanish, who occupied Ypres in 1679. The Austrian Netherlands then wrested control from the Spanish in 1713, and held it until the Napoleonic Wars rid the low countries of the Habsburgs. The Belgian revolt against the Netherlands in 1830 bestowed freedom on the city as part of an independent Belgium.

In the early twentieth century, Ypres had the misfortune of finding itself of strategic value to the British/French and German armies. In 1914, it stood in the path of the Schlieffen Plan, the great wheeling offensive devised by Count Alfred von Schlieffen, according to which the German Army would conquer France in six weeks. In putting this improbable gamble into effect in August 1914, and despite pounding scores of Belgian towns to rubble, the Germans failed to capture the city during First Ypres in October of that year.

The British forced them back, in one of the most heroic actions of the war, and got as far as attempting an attack on Passchendaele Ridge, on 21 October. 'Fighting was hard and came to bayonet work,' Haig recorded in his diary.[6] But Sir John French had overextended his forces. The German counter-attack drove the Allies back to the Ypres line, where British, French and Belgian forces held the city – respectively sustaining 85,000, 58,000 and 21,500 casualties. The Germans, too, suffered tens of thousands of losses at the hands of Britain's Old Contemptibles, notably at the battle of Langemarck, in which Lance Corporal Adolf Hitler participated. (He would return as Führer to lay wreaths on the mass graves of the German dead, whose sacrifice had become known in Germany as the 'Massacre of the Innocents', a reference to the high proportion of young men, just out of school, who died there.)

The Germans tried and failed to take the city at Second Ypres, in April 1915. This time, a resolute defence, led by Canadian and French forces, prevailed against waves of German shock troops and the first use of poison gas. The Canadian 3rd Brigade and the French Algerian 45th Colonial Division were the first to feel the agonising effects of chlorine gas, dispersed from canisters and carried on the wind. 'The French troops,' wrote Arthur Conan Doyle, then a 55-year-old infantryman, 'staring over the top of the parapet at this curious screen which ensured them a temporary relief from fire, were observed to suddenly throw up their hands, to clutch at their throats and to fall to the ground in agonies of asphyxiation. Many lay where they had fallen, while their comrades, absolutely helpless against this diabolical agency, rushed madly out of the mephitic mist and made for the rear . . .'[7] The masked German infantry burst out of the cloud and forced the Allies to withdraw to a new defensive line. By 1 May 1915, the Salient had collapsed to just two-and-a-half miles at its widest point, within easy enemy artillery range. The battles of Second Ypres cost the Allies a further 58,000 and the Germans 38,000, dead and wounded.

Thereafter, the British held the city, under the command of General Herbert Plumer. Two years later, the enemy were still hunkered down on the ridgelines and surrounding hills, in their newly constructed concrete pillboxes and elaborate trench systems, with a commanding view of the city and the Salient.

By 1917, the city was a smouldering ruin, the most bombed target on the Western Front. The spire of the cathedral and the tower of the Cloth Hall poked out of piles of slate and smashed brick, the detritus of two years of war. All seemed dead on the surface, yet underneath a hive of military activity buzzed. German shellfire had failed to dislodge the British dugouts, merely bouncing the rubble on the city's ramparts, beneath which hundreds of soldiers maintained supplies and transmitted orders to the forward units.

The traffic of men and matériel continued to pour through the rubble of the market place, defying the shellfire, 'streams of men, vehicles, motor lorries, horses, mules, and motors of every description, moving ponderously forward, at a snail's pace, in either direction, hour after hour, all day and all night . . . a reek of petrol and smoke everywhere'.[8] The witness was General John Monash, commander of the 3rd Australian Division, who saw a body of fighting troops pass, 'tin-hatted and fully equipped, marching in file into the battle area', followed by 'perhaps a hundred motor lorries, all fully loaded with supplies; a limousine motor-car with some division staff officer . . .', horse and mule-drawn vehicles, ambulance wagons, 'a great 12-inch howitzer, dragged by two steam traction engines', thousands more infantry, more trucks and machines, then 'a long stream of Chinese coolies', dispatch riders on motorbikes, horse-drawn artillery 'clattering and jingling', an anti-aircraft gun ('Archie'), and a Royal Flying Corps truck carrying parts of aeroplanes to forward hangars . . . all this through the wreckage of a city under periodic shellfire.[9]

—

Why hold this 'bump' in the line, whose three sides made the defence of Ypres such a hellish trial? Why risk so many lives for a city of rubble and a stretch of apparently useless terrain? General Horace Smith-Dorrien was not the only commander to have suggested the Allies surrender the Salient and withdraw to a more defensible position, possibly behind the Ypres Canal, which ran north–south through the city (he was relieved of his command for his temerity). On the face of it, the Salient did not seem worth the candle. It demoralised both sides. 'I always had a horror of the name . . . Flanders,' wrote a German soldier after the 1914–15 battles. Most shared his feelings in 1917, prefiguring the Wehrmacht's hatred of the Russian front in the Second World War. 'Death' appeared on the cover of the German magazine *Simplicissimus* on 19 June of that year, personified by a skeleton in a great coat sitting on a pile of corpses amid a field of bodies. Death has laid down his scythe and is holding his skull in his hands: 'You people stop,' the grim reaper weeps, 'I can't take anymore.'[10] The 'Bloody Salient' inspired a similar revulsion in the British. The soldiers' spirits lifted when they heard they were leaving this place; even the open valley of the Somme seemed preferable, to both privates and generals.

There were good reasons to hold the city and blister of terrain to the east. Ypres had stirring symbolic value as the last Belgian city before the Channel, a powerful reminder of the *raison d'être* for Britain's entry into the war, as the liberator of Belgium. The press played up its importance. Stories of its heroic defence went down well back in Britain. Ypres also offered protection and underground supply caches unavailable elsewhere so far forward: its ancient ramparts proved surprisingly resilient to modern artillery, and thousands of British soldiers owed their lives to the sturdy construction of the casements beneath them.

Most importantly, there were sound strategic reasons for holding Ypres. Commanders on both sides saw the city as a useful jump-off point, from which the British could launch attacks on the vital German positions in Flanders, the supply route into France; and from which the Germans could try to break the British supply line on the French coast. Ypres was a mere 30 miles from the Channel port of Dunkirk, and 55 miles from Calais, between two and four times the range of the German heavy guns – almost thirteen miles, at their outer limit.[11]

And possession of the city was a great morale booster. Its loss would have been a monumental psychological blow to the British, who had held it for so long. It was in Ypres, under the city's ramparts, that the famous trench newspaper *The Wipers Times* was published. A fine example of British stoicism under fire, the newspaper offered an entertaining mix of satire, poetry, spoof columns and advertisements. Hence an ad for the Tunnel & Dug-Out Vacuum Cleaning Company: 'Why Suffer from Trench Feet? . . . We guarantee a well-drained aired and Tunnel or Dug-Out . . .'[12] And the column 'A Few More Military Terms Defined': 'DUDS: There are two kinds. A shell on impact failing to explode [and] the other kind, which often draws a big salary and explodes for no reason. These are plentiful away from the fighting area.'[13]

—

The trench lines had been transformed since 1914. On the British side, the desultory shell scrapes of the start of the war – the work of an army that believed it would be leaving by Christmas – were now solid A-framed trenches topped with sandbags and held together with revetments of woven wattle. The trenches ran in a zigzagged pattern to limit an enemy occupant's field of fire into the zig (or zag).

They were six feet deep and three and a half feet wide at the top, but their dimensions varied. Drainage sumps were dug under the duckboards on the trench floors, but these failed to prevent the constant seepage and would prove useless in heavy rain.

The trenches had special functions. Fire trenches, the frontline fighting trenches, were fitted with firing slits in the parapet, periscopes every few yards and 'fire steps', platforms from which to aim and fire. The soldiers slept in 'funkholes' dug into the trenches' sides. In the coming battles, the advancing British would have to 'reverse' German fire trenches moments after occupying them, to defend themselves from terrific counter-attacks.

Behind the fire trenches were the supervision and support trenches, fitted with larger bays for supplies. Behind these were rows and rows of reserve trench lines connected to the front, every hundred yards or so, by perpendicular communication trenches. The whole arrangement formed a single defensive network that extended several miles to the rear.

If he gazed through a periscope, or dared to look over the top, the British soldier saw features on the map that earlier units had 'colonised' with homely names – e.g. Glencorse Wood, Inverness Copse, Black Watch Corner, Tower Hamlets, Clapham Junction, Surbiton Villas, Maple Lodge or Leinster Farm – all of which were now in German hands. None of these were recognisable as topographical features, as the artillery officer Huntly Gordon recalled; they were just, 'lines and lines of sandbags alternating with hedges of rusty barbed wire, brown earth and grey splintered tree trunks'.[14]

Such were the German front lines of what would soon become the most formidable defensive system on the Western Front, developed according to the new doctrine of 'elastic defence' or 'defence in depth'. This was the brainchild of Major Max Bauer and Captain Hermann Geyer, authors of 'Conduct of the Defensive Battle', one of the most influential manuals on infantry defence.

Elastic defence worked like this: a small number of troops occupied the front lines, with orders to fall back under British artillery attack, drawing the enemy into their territory, whereupon well-trained reserves in the rear would counter-attack, swiftly falling on the exposed enemy and reclaiming the lost ground. The Germans made an improvised attempt at elastic defence at Arras, which succeeded, winning over the sceptical General Fritz von Lossberg, who would soon became its most powerful champion. 'The fireman of the Western Front' (as von Lossberg was known, thanks to his penchant for dealing with crises) arrived in Flanders in April 1917 with orders to build up an impenetrable defensive barrier in this critical theatre.

—

Throughout 1917, boatloads of British and Dominion troops arrived at the French ports, and their German counterparts at railheads in the western theatre, where the dreaded spectre of another Flanders 'stunt' rose in every soldier's mind. On arrival in France, the British and Dominion soldiers found themselves in the 'bullring', one of the vast training camps that stretched from Le Havre to Étaples ('Eat Apples', as the Tommies called it), and from Calais to Boulogne: hectares of canvas tents and Nissen huts, officers' messes, canteens, hospitals, lecture theatres and training areas. They stood in lines of thousands, waiting to be counted off into battalions and marched off to their regimental base (see Appendix 4 for the structure of the British and Dominion Armies in 1917).

Each battalion comprised four companies each of about 200 men; each company comprised four platoons each of about 50 men, the basic fighting unit.[15] In 1917, as part of far-reaching reforms, each platoon would contain four sections, dedicated to specialist roles: one comprised riflemen (including sniper and forward scout); a second bombers, or grenade-throwers; a third 'rifle-grenades'; and a fourth Lewis light machine gunners. These four highly agile infantry 'teams' formed a platoon 'capable of waging its own little battle in miniature, using a variety of modern weapons'.[16] The reforms would make a critical difference in the coming battles.

The British Army's culture had changed dramatically too since the start of the war. By 1917, the rich identities of the old British regiments had lost their definition under a perpetual round of reinforcements who were, for the most part, conscripted men with little feeling for the grand traditions of the units to which they'd been posted. A Tommy might wind up as a Lancashire Fusilier, a Northampton, a Manchester, in the Duke of Wellingtons, or in any one of dozens of other ancient British regiments. While one can safely say the members of the famous Guards Division, the Royal Scots (the 1st of Foot) and the Queen's Royal Surrey Regiment retained their historical identities, most of the rest were diffuse and blurred. New recruits found themselves with a body of strangers, marching, training and fighting. They formed close relationships with men in their sections and platoons, and gave little thought to anyone else – least of all higher command, who were so remote as to be invisible. They lived on laughter, mateship, Woodbines, bully beef, tea and jam. Their chief daily concerns were their comrades-in-arms and whether they'd live another day.

Since 1915, nearly a million officers and men had passed through the tented colonies that stretched along the sand dunes of the French coast. British and Empire soldiers retained distinct memories of those training days, the last before battle. They spent weeks learning how to throw Mills bombs, use a bayonet, survive gas, fire Lewis guns and rifle-grenades, and defeat the enemy in hand-to-hand combat.

The point of bayonet drill was chiefly psychological, to produce a 'lust for blood' – according to the Officers' Training Manual – and engender the killer instinct (the weapon would have limited use in battle).[17] The bayonet's chief proponent was the Gordon Highlander Lieutenant Colonel Ronald Campbell, whose lecture 'The Spirit of the Bayonet' his students would never forget. This ferocious sermon did the rounds of the bullring and thereafter appeared in much war literature, expressing Campbell's obsession with the weapon and its correct use.[18] There would be no mercy, he explained: 'When a German holds up his hands and says: "Kamarad – I have a wife and seven children," what do you do? Why, you stick him in the gut and tell him he won't have any more!'[19]

The men received Campbell's lessons with a mixture of revulsion, mirth and excitement. 'We rushed, with raucous yells, and stabbed straw-stuffed bodies,' Private Bernard Livermore recalled.[20] Robert Graves had vivid memories:

> [T]he men had to make horrible grimaces and utter blood-curdling yells as they charged. The instructors' faces were set in a permanent ghastly grin. 'Hurt him, now!' 'In the belly! Tear his guts out!' they would scream, as the men charged the dummies. 'Now that upper swing at his privates with the butt. Ruin his chances for life! No more little Fritzes!' . . .[21]

Norman Collins was told to stick his bayonet into a skull, one or two of which were 'lying about', in order to experience how hard it is to remove a bayonet stuck into bone: only by planting your foot on the skull and pulling.[22] Notwithstanding Campbell's enthusiasm for the evisceration and castration of surrendering Germans, he made a persuasive point. 'Get the bayonet into the hands of despondent troops,' he later said, 'and you can make them tigers within hours. I found nothing better to introduce recruits to the terrible conditions which awaited the poor devils up the line.'[23] On the other hand, as the officer and later historian Basil Liddell Hart witnessed, troops who took Campbell at his word and put on their 'killing face' to charge the enemy were often shot before they got close enough.[24] Officers were inured to these methods; their own training manual instructed them to foster a bloodthirsty spirit in their men, to encourage them to be 'forever thinking of how to kill the enemy'.[25]

Gas drill involved sitting in a gas chamber 'filled with various kinds of poison gas' with your box respirator on, recalled Lieutenant Allfree. The gas clouds were denser and more lethal in the chamber than on the battlefield. An instructor always sat with the men, Allfree recalled, because some were apt, on account of 'a sense of 'suffocation' caused by 'nervousness' or 'a sort of hysteria', to want to 'pull their masks off'.[26] They'd all heard stories of the horror of gas, of phosgene and chlorine. One type, known to doctors as diphenyl-chloroarsine, was the only weapon used in the war in which 'pain *per se* was the sole effective agent'.[27] Inhalation, even in a concentration of one part in 200 million of air, produced such agony as 'to wholly disable' the victim.[28] Since it could penetrate gas masks, the soldier in his confusion would tear off his mask, only to suffer a greater dose (the Germans nicknamed the gas the 'maskbreaker'; both sides used it). Perhaps the cruellest stroke was that it did not kill you.

Injuries during training were frequent, and accidents often deadly. Graves recalled a sergeant of the Royal Irish Rifles advising a platoon on the use of the grenade: 'He picked up a No. 1 percussive grenade and said: "Now lads, you've got to be careful here! Remember that if you touch anything while you're swinging this chap, it'll go off." To illustrate the point, he rapped the grenade against the table edge. It killed him and the man next to him and wounded several others more or less severely.'[29]

The officers' insistence on petty discipline struck many soldiers, especially the better-educated conscripts, as self-serving or a waste of time. Allfree, for example, found himself 'in a large dining hut with an elderly, white-haired Major . . . He gave us a sort of lecture – the gist of which . . . was the extreme importance of saluting senior officers. Some one had failed to salute him on passing by.'[30] The bull-ring inspired terror in sensitive men. Fearful, homesick or under-confident boys latched on to their officers or stronger men. 'A quaint youth' called 'Soddy' who shared Allfree's tent 'attached himself to me in a most friendly way, much as a lost dog might'.[31]

Private Neville Hind would never forget the load the men bore in full marching order, summoning a portrait reminiscent of Baldrick, the overburdened, mud-caked Tommy in the Blackadder series:

Army boots, socks, trousers, tunic, puttees, cap, pants, cardigan
(if not in pack), shirt, belt, braces, pouches with ammunition,

sandbags, rifle, bayonet in scabbard, entrenching tool and handle, water bottle, haversack, iron rations, day's ration, valise (containing overcoat, change of under-clothing, extra socks, shaving tackle . . .), oil sheet, steel helmet, two gas helmets.

At the front, the soldier would abandon a lot of this, and take on 'a good deal more' in ammunition, Mills bombs, a club, wirecutters and perhaps an entrenching tool or spade.[32] The officers carried a cane, a revolver and a few grenades.

These few weeks' training ended with the 'final assault course' in full equipment, 'a series of rushes from trench to trench', observed Private Joseph Maclean, 'the intervening space being strewn with barbed wire, high wire, shell holes etc, and they have fellows throwing huge fire cones at you all the time to represent bombs'.[33]

Meanwhile, the gunners tested and ranged their guns. In Flanders, the devout Corporal Skirth was in the process of losing a stripe. He'd been told to range his guns on a distant target; the French maps had infuriated a visiting staff officer, who was unable to do the necessary calculations. Skirth easily converted the metric measurements and plotted the range of a target he thought a farm at first, but then realised it was a church.

'Sir,' Skirth addressed the staff officer, 'I think there has been a mistake. The target you have ringed is a church.'

'What the hell has that got to do with it?' the staff officer retorted.

'It's the tower of a church. There must be a mistake . . . Only the Germans destroy churches.'

'Are you a bloody conchie [conscientious objector]?' said the officer.

'I don't know,' Skirth mumbled. 'Perhaps I am. I don't think –'

'Listen Corporal,' the officer interrupted, 'what you think has nothing to do with it. I shall report your insolence to your Commanding Officer . . . Hand me those figures.'

Later, Skirth was able to confirm that no shell had landed within

250 yards of the church: 'My calculations must have been very inaccurate.'[34]

—

The archetypal British soldier, 'Private Tommy Atkins', was the 'British working man in uniform'.[35] He tended to do as he was told, without complaint. Like all soldiers, he grumbled and joked his way through the war. Tommy was the 'clodhopper from Suffolk, or Devon, or Durham – the man who obeyed orders and stuck it out . . .'[36] He volunteered in huge numbers and went to war with a doggedness of spirit that astonished his officers, some of whom unkindly (and wrongly, as we shall see) attributed the British soldiers' resilience to the triumph of ignorance over reality, the failure to imagine the consequences of his actions.

There he stands, in photos, smiling through the gaps in his yellow teeth, sitting in a trench or on a truck. Tommy Atkins probably sports a moustache, as decreed by the King's Regulations: 'The chin and the lip will be shaved, but not the upper lip. Whiskers, if worn, will be of moderate length.'[37] He wears a 1902 Pattern Service Dress of khaki tunic and trousers, with puttees (Urdu for 'bandages') wound from the ankle to the calf, which prevent him from snagging his trousers on wire but can induce frostbite if they freeze. On his head, during combat, is his Mk I 'battle bowler', the broad-rimmed steel helmet, covered in stretched hessian. A first-aid kit, or shell dressing, is sewn inside his tunic, containing bandages, iodine and safety pins. From his webbing and waist belt hang a water bottle, entrenching tool, bayonet, ammunition pouches, and grenades; in his haversack, he probably keeps the 'unexpired' portion of the day's ration, his gas cape, and a spare pair of socks.[38] On his feet are a pair of 'B5' ammunition boots, in strong, rough leather with metal-studded soles. A greatcoat or sleeveless goatskin jerkin protects him from the cold, and a rubberised gas cape from gas and rain. At the sound of the 'gas gong', he'll sling on a small box respirator, connected by a tube to a full-face waterproof gas mask.

The Empire troops are similarly equipped and attired, with a few national exceptions, such as the Australians' kangaroo-hide webbing and slouch hats. The Scots go into battle in kilts camouflaged with khaki skirts, which were essential for clans of bright tartan such as the distinctive red of the Cameron Highlanders and the Royal Stewart.

Theories abound to explain the British soldier's unerring sense of duty. 'To the war writers and their middle class readers,' observed Corelli Barnett, the English historian, 'it was this squalor of trench life that constituted not the least . . . unpleasant aspect of the Great War. Yet nearly a *third* of the British nation lived their entire lives in the slums, contemporary descriptions of which remarkably echo those of the living conditions of the trenches . . . Many of the rank-and-file were in fact better off in the trenches than at home.'[39] Barnett suggests the pleasure Tommy Atkins derived from the relative comfort of a water-filled shell hole over a Tyneside slum explained his cheerful stoicism. This reeks of the sort of middle-class condescension Barnett otherwise scorns; it also ignores the breakdown in morale across all units, regardless of class, in the closing months of 1917. They were all men, made of flesh and blood, in the end.

While the small Anzac and Canadian units gained a reputation for inordinate courage in a series of set-piece battles, the Tommies' performance appeared less consistent, chiefly because there were so many of them: they were everywhere and did everything, and their units varied in quality. They *were* the war in Flanders, in the sense that they far outnumbered the Dominion forces, and their casualties were greater (see Appendix 2). At his best, Tommy Atkins was capable of astonishing courage and endurance, as he showed at Loos and First Ypres. The English foot soldier and his Scottish, Welsh and Irish versions stayed the distance where the Russian, French, Austrian and ultimately the German armies would give up. His morale never broke – though it would come very close at Passchendaele.

'Of this man little was heard,' writes Sergeant Charles Arnold (himself a quintessential Tommy), 'possibly because he had a habit of going into places a thousand strong and coming out a remnant of a hundred and fifty or so. Dead men tell no tales of their own glory.'[40] The Tommies essentially won the war, reckons Arnold, with some justification: 'He won it by sheer dogged pluck.'

—

A reputation for invincibility grew up around the Dominion forces, much of it deserved. The Canadian Corps drew on a string of unbroken victories, at Vimy, Arleux, Fresnoy, Avion and Hill 70, and a series of brutal facts: they had withstood the first use of gas in war, in 1915; fought (with a regiment from Newfoundland, then not part of Canada) alongside the British and Anzacs on the Somme in 1916, with 24,700 losses;[41] and driven the Germans off Vimy Ridge in April 1917, sealing their renown as the first army to crack the German lines on the Western Front. In 1918, they would cap these triumphs with a brazen stand at Amiens, without which the tide of war might not have turned so soon against Ludendorff's Spring Offensive.

A similar legend sprang up around the Anzacs, the insubordinate diggers who had boldly gone wherever their British commanders had ordered them: Gallipoli, the Somme and now Flanders. There were tangible reasons for the extraordinary offensive spirit of the Dominion armies: they were very well led, in the main, under the exceptional British generals Plumer, Birdwood and Byng and the far-sighted 'colonial' commanders, Monash and Currie; they swiftly embraced new tactics, technology and weapons; their officers planned every battle down to the smallest detail; and they trained damn hard. The better units in the British Army shared all these attributes, of course, and excelled in similar circumstances.

Something more, however, lay behind the Dominions' irrepressible, near-reckless aggression, their willingness to slog it out beyond the limits of what their commanders thought possible. One explanation is that the officers and men in the Dominion armies enjoyed a far better relationship than their British counterparts. The Anzacs and Canucks were comparatively free of the burden of 'class' that cascaded down the British ranks and landed with a crushing thud on the head of the ordinary Tommy, who rarely spoke his mind to his superiors. The Australian, New Zealand, Canadian and South African forces were a rough-hewn lot among whom the officers and men tended to speak with the same thick accents and think within similar frames of reference. They understood each other's worlds. Friendships between officers and men were more 'equal' in the Dominion than in the British ranks, creating a special kind of loyalty. Irreverent and unruly the colonial armies may have been – Richard Aldington was amazed to find that the Canadians 'never salute' – but their performance on the battlefield gave the lie to the idea that soldiers would only fight under a punitive regime ruled by the fear of one's superiors or the threat of execution for cowardice.

Psychologically, the Dominions drew strength from the fact that they were small foreign armies, rugged outsiders sent to assist the Mother Country in her hour of need. They were determined to prove themselves in the eyes of the world. The Canadian Corps, uniquely among the Dominions, was a national formation (the Australians would not be organised into a national corps until 1 November 1917), and this imbued the men with a powerful sense of patriotic unity, acutely aware that they were carrying the honour of Canada in their kitbags. By any measure, they had lived up to that expectation. 'With such men,' a captured German battalion commander told his interrogator, he would 'go anywhere and do anything'.[42] It was of a piece with the respect that the Germans paid all the Dominion armies, whom they tended to regard as their most lethal and resilient foes.

While under the ultimate control of the British command structure, the Dominion armies had their own regimental headquarters and a very different culture. The commanders of the Australian, New Zealand and Canadian forces had begun the war as amateurs, and were promoted for their exceptional gifts and personalities – and willingness to learn. As Haig observed after inspecting the Anzacs in 1916, 'They are undoubtedly a fine body of men, but their officers and leaders as a whole have a good deal to learn . . .'[43]

On 14 May 1917, three of those men, George, Theo and Keith Seabrook, left England for France. 'Well me Nipper,' they wrote to their little brother, 'In a very short time we all will be in the Fray smacking the Germans right & left.'[44] At Étaples, the three brothers were posted to the same company in a battalion that had lost 340 men, a third of its strength, during the battle of Bullecourt. Like hundreds of thousands of reinforcements, the Seabrooks filled dead men's shoes. They stayed for a month at a village near Arras, where they trained and relaxed, playing soccer, cricket and boxing.[45] Word passed around that 'this type of training was intended as preparation for operations . . . north-east of Ypres'.[46] Soon enough, after a final rehearsal for a large-scale attack on German trenches, they were ordered to travel to the front in Flanders. In high spirits, the battalion 'marched away from Clairmarais Forest and its beautiful surroundings' and, 'with the band playing the rousing quick-step El Abanico', the Seabrooks headed for the Ypres Salient.[47]

—

The German soldier on the Western Front, whom the Allies generally referred to as Fritz, Boche or the Hun, was either a young recruit of seventeen to twenty years; a veteran of the Eastern Front, deployed west as Russia teetered; or one of the dwindling number of hardened Prussian professionals. Fritz was certainly a 'valued commodity', given the shortage of manpower in the Reich.[48]

He wore a field-grey tunic of thick wool, trousers of coarse grey cloth, a traditional waterproof satchel and, for shock troops, an assault pack, carrying essential gear. His cloth-covered 'Stalhelm', the new chromium-nickel helmet, offered all-round protection of the head, and was a great improvement on the leather, spiked Pickelhaube, which officers still wore behind the lines. His calf-length greatcoat was probably the warmest of the war. Sentries, 'static infantry' and some machine gunners wore steel-plated body armour over their chest and abdomen.[49] From the German soldier's waist belt and webbing hung his bayonet, water bottle, mess tin, breadbag and ammunition pouches. From his neck dangled a gas mask made of sheepskin, to preserve the Reich's rubber resources.[50]

The new German recruit was poorly trained at this stage of the war; typically he received one to three months in German bases and two weeks in Flanders before being rushed into battle. His rifle skills were no match for the British and Anzacs. Yet he had machine guns in abundance, lines of pillboxes, and perhaps the best engineering, medical and logistical support in the field. He sorely lacked enough artillery and shells, but he had been ordered to defend, not to attack, so the shortage was less important. He was likely of Württemberg or Bavarian origin, as most of those forming the three armies of the Kronprinz Rupprecht (Crown Prince Rupert) von Bayern Army Group on the Flanders front were. The start of the influx of battle-hardened veterans from the Russian front raised his spirits and forged a do-or-die mentality that persisted well into 1918. In short, Fritz was far from 'worn down', no matter how often Haig and Charteris insisted that the Somme and the Aisne had exhausted him.

———

A few basic comforts lay between an army in high spirits and one in the doldrums. The lack of food, warm clothes and cigarettes struck down morale more forcefully than fear or exhaustion. The British and Dominion troops lived off the same dreary rations of bully beef (from *boeuf bouilli*, on which Napoleon's armies marched), biscuits, bread, jam and tea, the staple of the British Army for more than 50 years. In the trenches, the men typically ate canned, cold rations, and perhaps a dixie of hot food brought up from horse-drawn cookers in the rear. They also carried 'iron rations' in their rucksacks – to be eaten in emergencies – consisting of tins of bully beef and biscuits. The Germans survived largely on sausage, sauerkraut and black or rye bread.

British dieticians set 4193 calories a day as ample for frontline troops; their German equivalents received just 4083 (well short of the best fed army in Europe, Americans, who would receive 4714).[51] Soldiers' families supplemented this meagre diet with dispatches of fruitcake, tinned fish and meat, cheeses, biscuits, chocolates, sausage and, of course, the ubiquitous cigarettes. Most men on the Western Front spent their waking hours longing for a smoke: the cheap Woodbine for the Tommies and Players and Goldflake for the officers.

'The brightest moment' of the British soldier's day was his tot of rum at dawn, without which his 'resistance weakened'.[52] The double rum ration in his coffee before he went into battle was thought to help forge a fighting spirit. Rum 'saved thousands of lives', claimed Colonel Walter Nicholson. 'It is an urgent devil to the Highlander . . . a solace to the East Anglian countryman before the fight.'[53]

—

The British infantryman carried a .303 short-magazine Lee Enfield rifle (SMLE), which proved more accurate over long ranges than the German 7.92-millimetre Mauser Gewehr, and had a ten-round magazine against the German five-round. Both were effective sniper's rifles at ranges of 1000 yards. Bayonets were standard, but rarely used in combat, inflicting only 0.32 per cent of combat wounds (see above).[54]

The attacking infantrymen carried an array of clubs, knives, knuckledusters and even sharpened spades for use in hand-to-hand fighting. The most effective weapon for 'clearing' trenches or pill-boxes was the hand grenade, of which a huge range were developed, including the first firebomb, known as P-bombs or phosphorus bombs, and the British Mills bomb, the most reliable, first used in the British Armies in 1917. Only the officers were issued with revolvers: the heavy-recoil British Webley or the reliable German Luger.

Machine guns were the most lethal firearms, capable of scything through waves of advancing troops and dropping lines of horses. Light machine guns such as the Lewis gun (strictly speaking, a large automatic rifle) were standard in every British platoon in 1917, and fired off a 47-round drum magazine. The Lewis's mobility and power made it the ideal weapon for attacking pillboxes. Heavy belt-fed machine guns could fire up to 600 rounds per minute: three men operating a British Vickers or German MG08 machine gun could inflict as many casualties as a platoon of riflemen.[55] 'Serried ranks of infantry could be chopped down in a single traverse,' writes the historian Chris McNab, 'and an infantry squad bunched together could be dispatched in seconds.'[56] In action, the Vickers 'felt like a living animal' in the hands of the operator, 'as the blowback of gas from the previous round discharging drew in the next'.[57]

The big guns were the war-winning weapons. Artillery had thus far caused 70 per cent of casualties on the Western Front, and would inflict a higher percentage in Flanders. Never had so much steel fallen on human flesh. Heavy explosive shells tore bodies in half and decapitated men who a moment ago had been chatting or filling a pipe. A soldier who took a direct hit was blown to pieces, showering his comrades with his blood and entrails. Shrapnel shells, bursting overhead, scattered tiny balls, like shot, that cut down advancing platoons. Those whose bodies survived a bombardment often lost their self-control, reduced to 'nervous cases', though surprisingly few fled or went mad – such was the pressure not to break.

There were dozens of kinds of cannon, ranging from small trench mortars to heavy guns. The Stokes mortar, developed by Wilfred Stokes, could send 25 bombs per minute in a high, near-vertical arc into the enemy trenches; a quick adjustment in the angle extended the range up to 800 yards. The Germans had earlier developed the hated '*minenwerfers*' ('minnies', the Tommies called them), whose fat, sluggish rounds could smash open trenches.

The medium field artillery covered a great assortment of guns of various power and sizes. Two prolific models were the Royal

Field Artillery's Ordnance QF (Quick Firing) 18-pounder, and the German 7.7-centimetre *Feldkanone*. Both had a range of about 9000–10,000 yards, and their ubiquity meant they dominated the battlefield. Throughout 1917, on the Western Front, the British QF shot 38 million shells out of an available 42 million manufactured.[58]

The heaviest guns and howitzers pumped shell after shell onto the enemy lines in an unbearable, deafening continuum. These monsters were capable of cracking open pillboxes and 'delivering localized earthquakes' at ranges of up to 15,000 yards.[59] One of the most powerful British heavy guns was the Ordnance BL 60-pounder, capable of firing two 60-pound shells (5 inches in diameter) per minute. Larger, road- or rail-mounted howitzers could fire 9.2-inch or even 12-inch shells, destroying especially stubborn targets such as bunkers, buildings or fortifications. Germany's Krupp guns – notably 'Big Bertha', in 1914 the largest cannon ever fired – had smashed open Belgium's forts and alerted everyone to the fact that heavy artillery would decide who won the war.

The scale of this onslaught beggars the imagination. By April 1917, the Royal Artillery fielded about 2300 heavy guns on the Western Front, firing about five million rounds in the second quarter of the year (compared with 706,222 in the same period in 1916).[60] Between July and November 1917, the Royal Artillery would expend two to three million shells *per week*, a total of about 33 million during Third Ypres, two-thirds of which were fired into the Salient.

The Germans were outnumbered in artillery by three to one, and in shells by six to one.[61] Being on the defensive, however, they could afford to sit and wait, and pack their firepower into devastating counter-battery attacks, which, if well timed and aimed, could cut down the enemy as they left their trenches (as happened to many British troops on the first day of the Somme). The Germans also happened to have a threefold advantage in gas shells with which to terrorise attacking troops. No army had yet faced the impact of such concentrated shellfire in so small an area, and the density of the barrages is what would make the coming battle a uniquely terrifying experience.

—

The British invested great hopes of cracking open the enemy lines in two new weapons, whose destructive potential would not be realised until the Second World War: tanks and aircraft. Primitive tanks had been available since the Somme, and were now hailed as a war-winning weapon. Yet the soft Flanders soil, soon to turn to liquid mud, would quickly end their effective use in 1917, with the exception of a few dry weeks.

Aircraft flew incessantly overhead, on thousands of sorties, mostly combat and photoreconnaissance missions. They would play a critical role in Third Ypres. This was the era of the Royal Flying Corps' Sopwith Camel, the famous biplane that would shoot down 1294 enemy aircraft – more than any other Allied fighter – and whose crews used to joke that sorties offered them a choice between a wooden cross, a Red Cross and a Victoria Cross;[62] and the Fokker Eindecker, the best known German aircraft, whose dominance would end in 1917, as well as the Albatros series, famously flown by Manfred von Richthofen, the 'Red Baron' and 'ace of aces', credited with shooting down 80 enemy planes.

Pilots tended to come from the privileged classes, young men who saw themselves as part of a rare elite, superior to the troglodyte world in the trenches below. The Germans were initially the better pilots: 70 of their aircraft shot down 300 British planes in 'Bloody April' 1917, killing or wounding 200 men. The balance would be levelled during Third Ypres, largely due to the reckless courage of pilots such as Old Etonian Lieutenant Arthur Rhys Davids DSO, MC (with bar), who seemed to think the whole thing a daring game. Rhys Davids, who had loathed his brief stint in the army – 'My darling Ma,' he wrote home, 'everyone is so common and so sordid' – could not contain his delight on being selected by the 56th Squadron, Royal Flying Corps: 'Gee! ain't I bucked? Just think Mums: I shall be with my friends Muspratt and Potts; we have for flight commanders two of the best fighting pilots in the RFC . . .'[63]

Flying aces like Rhys Davids and von Richthofen tended to speak of 'bagging' an enemy plane and racking up 'kills'. The pilots' chief weapon was the cockpit-mounted machine gun, with which they engaged each other in spectacular duels in the sky. British aircraft were also used to identify their troops' locations during battle, relying on klaxon horns or white flares to mark the soldiers' forwardmost lines, and were critical as artillery spotters, guiding the guns to their targets from the air.

Communication between headquarters and the front lines was otherwise limited to telephone lines – whose wires were always being cut – runners, carrier pigeons and even semaphore flags, a relic of the nineteenth century. The bulky, primitive wirelesses were of little use on the battlefield; no radios or helicopters were yet available, of course. 'The era of the First World War stands as the only period in history in which high commanders were mute,' concludes one historian.[64] Junior officers, leading their men into the attack, revolvers at the ready, were responsible for relaying orders and making decisions under fire; many were killed or wounded before they could do so. The average life expectancy of a lieutenant on the Western Front, hitherto no more than a few months, would soon be measured in weeks.

—

The great challenge facing the generals was how best to deploy such destructive firepower. Being almost always on the attack in 1916 and 1917, the Allies were preoccupied with trying to find a way of using their superior firepower to break the German lines. Deep trenches, dugouts and bunkers protected the enemy from the biggest projectiles. Only the infantry could destroy the enemy in detail, yet how could they advance across exposed terrain? The Somme and other battles had taught the generals that only a barrage of great density and destructive power could shield the infantry as they advanced, break up the enemy wire, and keep the German counter-attack divisions at bay.

The artillery barrage had come a long way since 1914. Back then, the static barrage hammered away at a single target, such as a trench line or pillbox. The more advanced 'box' barrage bracketed a position on several sides, with the aim of protecting the British infantry in the boxed-off area from counter-attacks. Yet these barrages failed to achieve their aims, as shockingly demonstrated at the Somme.

The new concept of the 'creeping barrage' aimed to shield the advancing infantry behind a slow-moving wall of exploding shells. It was used to stunning success at Vimy Ridge, in April. To produce a moving barrage, the medium and heavy gunners fired together in carefully controlled belts, which moved forward in precisely timed increments or 'lifts'. This diabolical configuration would advance like a slow-moving wall of steel, chopping up everything in its path, throwing up geysers of soil, pocking the field in craters. No soldier would ever forget the sound of its approach, in which the mass of exploding shells merged into a constant din dubbed 'drumfire'.

To succeed, the creeping barrage required exact calculation, taking in the density of fire, rate of extension of fire, and positions of friendly infantry and enemy. The gunners would launch as many as eight successive belts of shell, carefully timed to lift in increments of perhaps 50 yards a minute. The infantry would advance behind this protective curtain to the edge of the enemy trenches, charge out of its smoky embrace and kill or capture the stunned survivors, most of whom would be stupefied with shock.

If the barrage advanced too quickly, or lacked the density to destroy entrenched enemy positions, the defending Germans would be able to recover and shoot down the attacking troops stranded in the open – as happened to the British Army on the Somme. Or, the barrage might prove too dense and slow, churning up the battlefield and rendering it impassable to troops, horses and gun carriages, especially if accompanied by torrential rain.

No battle had been fought in such conditions, or with such firepower, forcing many hard questions on the British and Anzac commanders: how would they bring up the artillery fast enough to resume the barrage once the infantry had captured their objectives? How would they aim and fire guns in muddy, unstable soil? How would the vital sound-rangers (who used pairs of microphones to pick up and fix on targets) and topographers (who carried their maps and tripods up to the front) operate in such conditions? And how would that new species of soldier, apparently impervious to fear, the forward observation officer, perform in a treeless wasteland? What if it rained and bogged down the advance? Preoccupying the German soldier were questions of how long he could withstand successive waves of shellfire followed by waves of infantry. All these questions, and many others, had no easy answers: both sides were learning how to fight the war as they went.

—

And both sides were now on the march, or travelling in lorries or light rail, moving through northern France towards Flanders. Great lines of men coursed through the French and Belgian countrysides. Throughout the night, in the distance, the forward soldiers heard the distant crump of the guns and saw flares burst and illuminate the sky, sweeping to earth in red, green and white sparks. The pipers were playing at the head of the Scottish regiments, as the men sang and waved their hats for photojournalists.

Here came Lieutenant Patrick Campbell, the anxious young officer who itched to prove himself in action, but for whom the low boom of guns sounded 'terrifying . . . more sinister than anything I had ever imagined': 'If there had been someone with me that I loved I could have endured it. But there was no one . . . to endure fear and loneliness together was more than I could bear . . . what hope for me was there when I was up in the middle of it? And what would happen to me if I failed?'[65]

Campbell reached Flanders in June, on a clear summer's night. All the countryside was lit up in silver starbursts:

I saw the flat plain, the low willows bordering the dykes, the

taller poplars . . . then the beautiful light went out, and it was
so dark for a moment that I could not see the ears of the horse
I was riding. I made friends with the stars overheard, I had no
other friends. They encouraged me, they seemed to talk to me.[66]

A few nights later, his platoon tried and failed to take ten wagon-
loads of stones, for road-building, up to the front; shellfire forced
them back, among the sound of larks and scenes of Flemish farmers:

That was the strange thing about the war in Flanders, so
short a distance separated peace from war. You could go
up from the world of ordinary men and women, cattle
and green fields, up into the very mouth of destruction,
and back again to the same clean sights and smells and
quiet noises, all in the space of a short summer night.[67]

In their headquarters, the commanders fixed their minds on their
maps. Contours marked the high ground at Messines Ridge, barely
150 feet above sea level, which the Germans had held since 1915: this
they must capture first.

# 6

# THE MINES OF MESSINES

*It is said that the detonation of the gigantic mines*
*could be heard in London. . . . All around Messines the*
*ground was said to have been covered by the bodies of*
*Bavarian soldiers (our poor, brave 3rd Division!).*
Crown Prince Rupprecht, commander of the Bavarian Army

---

A slight ridgeline wrinkled with hills, of which the highest is a mere 60 metres above sea level, runs through the villages of Messines and Wytschaete (which the British dubbed 'White Sheet' and the Germans called 'Wijtschate') on the southern limit of the Salient. Sleepy little market towns before the war, in 1917 they were mostly rubble. The British forces were entrenched on the western side of the ridge, with their base at Ploegsteert ('Plugstreet') Wood. They had held this position more or less since 1915; from January to May 1916, Winston Churchill had served here, as commanding officer of a battalion of Royal Scots Fusiliers. The plain rising gradually to the ridge was now a mass of trench lines and shell holes.

The Germans were dug in on top of the ridge and down the eastern slopes, where the plain runs gently into the Lys valley, interrupted by hedgerows and woods, green and undisturbed. They had held this nine-mile curve of high ground, from Saint Yves to Mount Sorrel, since 1915 (see Map 3). It had obvious military value: from here, looking north, the Germans enjoyed a perfect vantage point over Ypres and the Salient, with a bird's-eye view of the Gheluvelt Plateau to the east of the city, where the German commanders had correctly concluded that Haig would launch the main Flanders Offensive. From Messines, 'the Germans could watch every detail of any preparations the British make for an offensive eastwards between Ypres and the Belgian Coast'.[1] And all of it was within German artillery range.

In short, the British and Empire forces had to capture Messines Ridge, to 'straighten' this S-bend in the Salient before they could open the battle for Flanders proper.[2] It posed a formidable obstacle: British forces had tried and failed to capture Messines Ridge several times since 1914, chiefly around the bloody sentinel of Hill 60, where the soil was heavy with Allied and German dead. In 1917, von Lossberg's flexible defensive system presented a more difficult barrier: the German trench lines radiated back from the high ground in great depth, interspersed with wire and peppered with concrete pillboxes.

Haig had no choice: the ridge had to be taken if his main offensive was to have a chance of success. The man he selected for the job was General Herbert Plumer, commander of the Second Army, who had been commanding the Allied defence of Ypres for almost two years. Haig regarded Plumer as too cautious; he preferred more aggressive generals like Gough and Rawlings. At Messines, however, Plumer was seen as the best choice because he knew the area so well. Determined to reward Haig's faith in him, in June 1917 Plumer threw himself at the task with every sinew in his ageing body.

Plumer was among Haig's more astute and capable generals; he was certainly no donkey. Despite his unpromising appearance – his white walrus moustache, pink face and pot belly – Plumer was a superb planner who left nothing to chance. A master of trench warfare, his watchwords were 'Trust, Training and Thoroughness'. A careful and compassionate man, he tried to find ways of minimising

Allied casualties while maximising the enemy's.

He elicited the admiration of those who worked with him, not least the Australian commander General John Monash, who shared Plumer's fastidious attention to detail. The two men met no less than eight times in the weeks before Messines, poring over the plan. Plumer owed much of his success to a close meeting of minds with his intelligence officer, Major General Sir Charles 'Tim' Harington. The two men worked so well together, 'it was impossible to see where one ended and the other began'.[3] Their relationship went back to the start of the war and would have a great impact on the outcome of Messines: as early as 1915, for example, Plumer and Harington had had the foresight to authorise the start of deep tunnelling under the German positions on Messines Ridge with a view to blowing them up.

—

Plumer started planning the attack on Messines in January 1917, five months before it was scheduled to begin. Using a huge scale model of the terrain – 'the size of two croquet lawns'[4] – at Scherpenberg, he ran through every possible scenario and ensured every man knew his specific job. He presented his plan to Haig in April: the offensive would start with a preliminary bombardment over four days (later extended to almost two weeks); then, at 'zero' hour, a series of huge mines would blow up under the German positions; the creeping barrage would burst forth; the infantry would attack and seize – 'bite and hold' – Messines Ridge. On the second day, they would capture the village of Wytschaete, dig in and defend their gains from German counter-attacks. The whole operation would advance the Allied line no further than 1500 yards.

Haig was unimpressed; he wanted more emphasis on 'bite' and less on 'hold'. He insisted that Plumer capture Wytschaete and Messines villages on the first day, and then advance as far as the Courtrai–Roulers line, beyond Passchendaele, a distance of between 20 and 30 miles, surely an impossible task.[5] At this stage, Haig envisaged the Messines and Passchendaele operations as a continuous offensive. That was plainly unworkable, Plumer felt, and he made his views clear. In early May, Haig revised his plan: Messines would now be confined to a single battle, the first in a two-stage attack, Haig told a conference of army commanders on 7 May. The great Flanders Offensive, proper, would begin several weeks later, with the capture of Gheluvelt Plateau and Passchendaele before the clearing of the Belgian coast. There would be no more talk of Plumer's men reaching Roulers within a few days; instead, they would take Messines and Wytschaete, advance down the German side of the slope and secure the whole Messines position – within the first day.

To execute the plan, Plumer issued a list of demands. He would need another hundred medium cannon, bringing the total to 1510 field and 756 heavy guns, and 142,000 tons of ammunition to ensure they produced the densest possible barrage. Against this immense arsenal, the Germans were thought to possess just 344 field and 404 medium and heavy guns, giving the Allies a five to one advantage in field guns and two to one in heavy guns.[6] A critical task for the artillery, Haig said, was to obliterate the rolls of wire in front of the German lines, the existence of which had obstructed the infantry at Loos and the Somme.

—

That month, Crown Prince Rupprecht's Bavarian Army Group were ordered to move to Messines to relieve the exhausted units stationed there, mostly Saxons and Württembergers, who had occupied the ridge for several months. Since January, Rupprecht and his staff had assumed that Flanders (Flandernschlacht) would be the scene of Haig's next great offensive, and correctly judged that the opening blow would land here, at Messines, on what German topographers called Wijtschatebogen (the Wijtschate Salient). At least two British prisoners 'had spoken with certainty of it'.[7] One, captured on 29 May, told the Germans that the attack on Messines 'would take place on 7th June after eight days' bombardment'.[8]

The Germans had also correctly divined that the Messines Offensive would probably start with some sort of mine explosion. They had had hard experience of the British penchant for tunnelling at various points beneath the Messines ridgeline. In previous years, mine blasts had preceded British assaults on the hills in the area, chiefly at Hill 60 in 1914 and at Saint Eloi on 27 March 1916, when six huge mines killed 300 Germans and blasted a hole in the front line.[9] On the Somme, too, a series of massive mine explosions warned the Germans of the coming attack. 'From this time [late 1916] onwards,' noted a German history of Flanders, 'the Germans knew what they were in for at the Wijtschate Range. They had observed the activities of the English mine layers . . .'[10] But the Germans would have no idea of the extent of Allied tunnelling under Messines, which surpassed anything yet attempted in the underground war.

Alert to the mine risk, in April 1917 Rupprecht considered abandoning Messines altogether and withdrawing to a safer line, 'in order to avoid heavy losses' from 'a large-scale enemy attack' on the ridge, which was 'exceedingly endangered due to its protruding front alignment and [British] mining preparations', states the German history.[11] He chose not to; the high positions along the ridge were too valuable. The German commanders 'believed that it was not permissible to give up the important hillside lines of Wijtschate and Mesen [Messines] without a fight, and decided to retain the current front'. In so doing, the Germans 'severely underestimated' the 'English mining preparations' at Messines. The German history adds, with melancholy hindsight, 'By early June, it was too late to take any such measures, and things took their fateful course.'[12]

——

On 21 May 1917, the British heavy gunners opened up on the German lines. The 'softening up' involved all 2266 guns, including 1158 18-pounders and 352 4.5-inch howitzers. During the next fortnight, the British guns fired about 3.5 million shells onto German lines around the Salient, concentrating heavily on the Messines area. At the same time, some 300 Allied aircraft, about double the German number, flew low over the enemy, photographed their artillery positions, strafed the high points and attacked German observation balloons.[13] On the ground, 72 Mark IV tanks rumbled forward to prepare for their first action: to help the infantry capture the ridge, which they were expected to accomplish a few hours after 'zero', just before dawn on 7 June (in the event, the tanks would prove of little value at Messines).

One British artillery officer about to head to Messines was Lieutenant Allfree, the solicitor and father of four, whom we last saw at Étaples. He was presently 'loafing about' with his fellow officers in the Counter-Battery Room at VIII Corps Heavy Artillery headquarters, in a chateau in northern France, enjoying a whisky and soda.[14] Here, he could overhear the anguished telephone calls of battery officers in the field, who were then coming under German fire and were seeking advice. The HQ commander, a Colonel Walters, replied with the size and direction of retaliatory fire; e.g., as he told one gunner, 'Ring up Colonel J. and tell him to put 30 rounds from a 6 inch into X3, and we'll see if it has any effect.' Or he would order planes to 'shoot 300 rounds' on an enemy gunner's position.[15] The coordination of artillery and aircraft had made great advances since the days of the Somme.

The next day, Allfree travelled to his battery position, through a desolation of craters, British guns and enemy shells, 'bursting to my left and now somewhat behind me'. At last, at Soyer Farm, just west of Ploegsteert ('Plug Street'), he encountered a smallish officer with a fair moustache and glasses, standing in a sunken road. 'Is this 111th Siege Battery?' he asked him.

'Yes, are you Allfree? We have been expecting you. My name is Marshall. Come and see Cripps – he is in the Mess.'[16]

Within a week, Allfree and his men were blasting away at Messines Ridge, shelling the wire in front of the German lines. The rounds were fitted with the new 106 fuses, which exploded more reliably on impact – essential to the destruction of barbed wire. They were a great improvement on the unreliable fuses used at the Somme, with which a third of some calibre rounds failed to explode and 'an alarming number' detonated prematurely.[17]

———

Possessing fewer guns, the German batteries responded by trying to pick off each British battery one by one, the results of which Allfree had just heard on the telephone. The German counter-bombardment succeeded in destroying or damaging several gun placements and igniting ammunition dumps, which went up in great blazes, but it fell well short of inflicting serious damage.[18] So the German gunners resorted to gas, blanketing the plain beneath them in clouds of phosgene and chloropicrin. This had more serious consequences.

Allfree's battery was caught in the thick of the gas attack. '[T]he place reeked,' he recalled. 'It would have been fatal to have removed one's gas mask. . . . We longed for a breeze to spring up to blow the foul stuff away, but it remained dead calm.' He and two comrades spent the night on higher ground to escape the huge gas cloud, which was heavier than air. At one point, they briefly removed their gas masks and lay down in a meadow. One officer thrust his head into a patch of grass, which seemed gas-free, and he even got some sleep. 'We went and looked at him from time to time,' Allfree recalled, 'to see that he was still alive.'[19] Finally, 'day broke, the sun came out, the shelling ceased and the gas gradually dispersed, till at last we could take off those beastly gas masks. What a relief it was to . . . light a cigarette!'[20]

———

At around this time, twenty-year-old Captain Harry Yoxall arrived at his divisional HQ in the Messines area, determined as ever to take the fight to the Boche. '[D]aily the bombardments are becoming heavier,' he wrote to his mother on 1 June, 'and nightly the raids more frequent. We're hitting the Boche with both hands now and I must say that on the whole he takes it like a little gentleman.'[21] As a staff officer, Yoxall worked well back from the front line. Here, he observed how quickly nature reasserted itself outside the battle zone:

> There are not many flowers in this part of the world but
> there is plenty of blossom, lilac . . . hawthorn, cherry
> & pear. The birds too are going it good . . . and seem
> to have been very prolific this year. In one tree alone in
> the garden of Divisional Hqs there are 18 nests.[22]

On 3 June, he climbed a hill and witnessed 'one of our stunts',[23] a dress rehearsal of the creeping barrage. At 3 pm, the 18-pounders fired three belts of shellfire, 700 yards deep, on the German trench lines.[24] The barrage advanced slowly across the field like a dust storm. 'It was a wonderful sight,' Yoxall wrote in his diary. '[T]he broad barren patch of the [German] trench lines [were] transformed into an inferno of twisting shells, so that the view became obliterated with the smoke and dust & the sky grew heavy overhead on that bright day of early June. . . . It was difficult to realize that there were human beings in the midst of that tornado of steel & explosive. Still, they were Germans: they asked for this, and now they've got it.'[25] He described the same sight, less aggressively, in a letter to his mother: 'I do not think that there has ever been so great a weight of metal thrown about . . . certainly the gunfire on both sides is heavier than it ever was while I was down on the Somme . . .'[26]

The next day, Yoxall turned 21 and reflected gratefully:

> Life has been kind to me: personally I can have very
> little to complain of, save in the way of so many good
> friends gone. . . . If death should come to me I hope
> I may meet it as well as they: & why should I fear to
> follow where so many better men have gone.[27]

War had sharpened his feelings for his family into something tangible, expressible:

Dear people, I thank you: now that the little quarrels and jealousies of childhood are past, I love you all with a very great love: & esteem it a great privilege that by being out here to fight for you I can in some measure repay the great debt I owe you.[28]

Meanwhile, 'the day approaches', he wrote: 'Daily and nightly the bombardments become more severe.'[29]

———

In the early hours of 7 June, the first waves of 80,000 British and Dominion troops – of Plumer's Second Army – moved into position along the taped 'jump off' point. For many, the journey had been traumatising. The eight attack battalions of Monash's 3rd Australian Division, who had left their billets at 11 pm the previous night, were passing through Ploegsteert Wood when high explosive, incendiary and gas fell amid them, killing or wounding many and disorientating the column. Gas shell landed with a seemingly harmless 'plop', followed by the hissing sound of the chlorine or phosgene escaping into the atmosphere – in this case, beneath a forest canopy. The unfortunates who failed to get their masks on in time fell retching to the ground. Horses and mules 'were passed on the road gasping piteously in the poisonous air'.[30] The gas killed or disabled an estimated 500–1000 Australians, about ten per cent of their force, before they reached the front.[31] Most reached the jump-off point within 40 minutes of zero hour. Some late arrivals headed straight over the top and into battle. Several gassed soldiers even joined the fight until their poisoned lungs disabled them.[32]

At 2.10 am on 7 June, British aircraft flew low overhead to drown the sound of the advancing tanks. A 3.05 am, a faint glimmer of dawn shone on the eastern horizon. The sun would not challenge the moon, just past full, for at least an hour. So far, the Germans had failed to detect the huge forces gathering in the dimness on the plain beneath them. At one point, a few New Zealanders who'd crept into no-man's-land drew a burst of machine-gun and rifle fire. Then all turned quiet again, and the soldiers awaited the signal, to be preceded by the detonation of a string of huge mines buried deep under the German positions on Messines Ridge.

—

The Allied impetus for this astonishing military feat arose from the dogged persistence of one of those talented mavericks the British always seem to find in a crisis: in this case, Major John Norton Griffiths. At the outbreak of war, Griffiths was 43, a Boer War veteran and a Conservative member of parliament. He had spent many years working in remote African and American mines as a mining engineer and was now operating a successful structural engineering firm that specialised in big projects such as drainage systems and underground rail networks. He had a tunnel vision, literally.

At the time, his men were participating in the construction of the Manchester sewer system and the London Underground, where they had developed a technique called 'clay-kicking'. While lying on their backs in tunnels too small to swing a pick, they'd deliver a sharp kick to a specially designed spade, which dislodged the clay. In December 1914, Griffiths offered a few 'clay-kickers', or 'moles', to the War Office for frontline work. The then commander-in-chief, Field Marshal Sir John French, ignored the offer, shutting the door on the lessons of centuries of military tunnelling, which had repeatedly demonstrated its efficacy against fortified positions. No doubt, the explosive shell had made tunnelling under besieged castles superfluous. Now, however, destroying rows of trench lines containing tens of thousands of troops required a revival of the tunnel, Griffiths believed, and he pressed his atavistic vision on the British Army.

The failure of conventional mining methods spurred him to take firmer action. In December 1914, the Allies had tried, and failed, to detonate 45 pounds of gun cotton in a 20-yard trench a few yards from the German lines. The Germans responded by igniting ten charges along the front near the village of Le Plantin, killing an estimated 3000 Indian soldiers. Many suffocated in their trenches, and morale collapsed among the survivors, so much so that elements of the Indian Corps refused to stay in the line. 'The fear of being swallowed suddenly by a massive explosion beneath their feet' sapped morale among troops already enduring the frightful conditions of the winter trenches.[33] Few had any confidence in the early British tunnellers, who failed to grasp the rudiments of tunnel drainage and construction. The Germans, however, seemed well advanced. On 3 February 1915, German tunnellers again succeeded in detonating mines under Allied positions, this time at Saint Eloi, on Messines Ridge, of all places, with heavy casualties.

Griffiths was apoplectic, 'like a maniac', his wife recalled, 'frantic for action' to get his moles to France.[34] This time, the War Office responded to his entreaties. In mid-February, Griffiths received a telegram from his old friend, Lord Kitchener, then war secretary, to come in for a chat. Griffiths got straight to the point, demonstrating how clay-kicking would greatly speed up the tunnellers' progress, enabling the construction of deeper and longer tunnels. In one of the most extraordinary scenes of the war, the heavily built engineer grabbed a coal shovel from his Lordship's fireplace, prostrated himself on the sumptuous carpet and kicked away at the air with all his might.

It worked. 'Get me ten thousand of these men,' Kitchener said. 'Immediately.'[35]

Within the month, the War Office had approved the formation of the first tunnelling unit, as part of the Royal Engineers, and by mid-1915 230,000 British miners, a quarter of the total, would volunteer.[36] A delighted Griffiths left for the front at once, with eighteen volunteers.

On 23 February, Griffiths' men, who 'had been safely digging sewers beneath Manchester' five days earlier, found themselves tunnelling towards the German lines near Givenchy.[37] Within weeks, eight mining companies, each comprising six officers and 227 men, had materialised, thanks largely to Griffiths' frantic recruitment drive.

They had their first success in April 1915, at Hill 60, one of several man-made hills flung up during the construction of the Belgian railway. Hill 60, an important tactical high point, had changed hands several times during the war. The clay-kickers dug about three to four yards a day (double the previous British average of two yards), outpacing the Germans and enabling them to place explosives under the enemy positions sooner. The charges blew on 17 April. The infantry rushed in and took Hill 60 from the stupefied survivors. Within weeks, however, the Germans retaliated. They smothered the area in chlorine gas, killing 90 British troops and leaving hundreds more incapacitated. Then they reclaimed the mound.

—

In September 1915, the then British engineer-in-chief, Brigadier General G. H. Fowke, recommended the adoption of Griffiths' ideas at Messines, but with an inspired innovation: the tunnellers, he suggested, should drive deep galleries 60–90 feet beneath the German trench lines. Not until Haig became commander-in-chief at the end of the year would official approval of the idea be forthcoming. By then, Griffiths' confidence had bloomed and tunnels were back in favour as a battle-winning tactic.

In early January 1916, Griffiths told a meeting of astonished British generals that his tunnellers would create an 'earthquake' under Messines that would blow up the ridge and swallow the enemy.[38] The tunnellers had, in fact, been working on the deep tunnels for six months. Since August, General Plumer had authorised them to dig 'wells', half a dozen deep shafts. The successful blast at Saint Eloi in March 1916 had accelerated their work, not least because it converted Haig to the underground war.

Haig threw his support behind a tunnelling project of staggering scale: to bury at least twenty huge mines deep under critical sections of Messines Ridge. That would require a much bigger tunnelling effort, and in 1916 Australian and Canadian specialist tunnelling companies brought new resources and fresh talent to the job.

Many were miners, used to the extreme conditions of working deep underground.

Thereafter, the underground war in Flanders escalated into a terrifying back-and-forth struggle in the darkness, as Will Davies and Ian Passingham show in their accounts of the Australian and British operations at Messines. Moles on either side descended with torches and revolvers into this subterranean battle zone, planting explosives and risking the collapse of tunnels and shocking collisions with the enemy that often ended in frantic hand-to-hand combat. New listening technology enabled Allied and German tunnellers to hear each other digging several metres apart, whereupon they'd often try to blow each other up. Few combat jobs were as nerve-wracking; few men could bear repeated descents. (Their story has inspired recent novels and films, for example Sebastian Faulks' *Birdsong*, the TV series *Peaky Blinders* and the biopic *Beneath Hill 60*, based on Davies' biography of Oliver Woodward, the commander of the Australian tunnelling company that blew up Hill 60 in 1917.)

The German tunnellers were at a disadvantage because, holding the high ground, they were forced to dig deeper to reach the stable blue clay. This 'Ypres' clay was firmer than the sandy layers of topsoil, enabling Allied tunnellers to dig horizontal galleries 80–120 feet beneath the German trenches, from shafts starting 300–400 yards behind the British front line.[39] No German tunnel had reached that depth; nor would the Germans on the ridge suspect the existence of the blue clay galleries, because they ran beneath a series of 'decoy' tunnels the British had dug in the shallower soil. To keep the secret, the tunnellers hid the excavated blue soil in woods or 'under sandbag parapets', out of sight of German aircraft and lookout balloons.[40] In April, a German raiding party retrieved a sample of blue clay and suspected the existence of a deeper tunnel, but it dismissed the find as an isolated instance.

In the months before the battle, then, a little underground city was taking shape, of vertical shafts, horizontal galleries, connecting tunnels and crowded dugouts, bristling with human moles, digging, listening, scraping and fighting. The tunnellers' extraordinary progress in the year before Messines not only involved the excavation of 5000 yards of subway, six foot by three foot, but also the digging of underground accommodation, in which 6000 men could sleep and 10,000 shelter; as well as 24 deep dugouts for brigade HQ and 28 for battalion HQs, averaging 700 square feet each.[41] Some 200 Australians under Woodward's command had taken nine weeks to dig the largest dugouts, nicknamed 'The Catacombs', beneath Hill 63, which could accommodate 1200 men.

All along the front lines, the tunnels were the scenes of fierce underground clashes. Nowhere was the tunnelling war as ferocious as under Hill 60, a slag-heap excavated from the Ypres–Comines railway cutting that had special importance as an observation point. Here, the underground battle was 'of a severity unsurpassed of its kind on the British front throughout the war'.[42] The Royal Engineers' 175th Tunnelling Company dropped the first deep blue clay shafts here on 22 August 1915; the 3rd Canadian Tunnelling Company took over the work in April 1916. Their objectives were to excavate large cavities deep beneath Hill 60 and a nearby mound nicknamed the Caterpillar (due to its shape), and pack them with explosives. In July 1916, the Canadians, fighting off repeated German tunnelling attacks, succeeded in ramming 53,500 pounds of high explosive into Hill 60's deep gallery; three months later, they filled the Caterpillar gallery with 70,000 pounds (the Caterpillar crater, one of the biggest, is well preserved today).[43]

On 9 November, the Canadian tunnellers officially handed over responsibility for maintaining Hill 60 to the 1st Australian Tunnelling Company, whose jobs were to maintain and defend the huge mines until their detonation. They needed to protect the deep galleries in which the charges lay from damp, corrosion and marauding German tunnelling parties. Of immediate concern, just before Messines, were signs that the enemy was starting to dig a deeper gallery, 'which ultimately would have cut into the gallery leading to the Hill 60 mines', Haig reported later that year. 'By careful listening it was judged that, if our offensive took place on the date arranged, the enemy's gallery would just fail to reach us. So he was allowed to proceed.'[44] By early 1917, writes Will Davies, 'a necklace of enormous mines was being created along nine kilometres of German frontline'.[45]

—

Unaware of what lay beneath them, the defending Germans weathered the opening bombardment in a state of frozen apprehension. Their forward zone consisted of two trench lines running just in front of or on the ridge, and rows of pillboxes manned with machine guns. Thinly spread, these frontline Germans anticipated a terrific onslaught. Their main forces were positioned on the eastern slope of the ridge, and included two reserve Eingreif (counter-attack) divisions, poised to maul the advancing troops and drive them back.

At that moment, a Württemberg and three Saxon divisions of Group Wijtschate, under the command of General der Kavallerie Maximilian von Laffert, awaited the arrival of the Bavarian divisions assigned to relieve them. The Saxons and Württembergers had borne the job of defending Messines for several weeks and were exhausted. Now, however, the British bombardment had delayed the Bavarians. So von Laffert's men had little choice other than to stick it out in their trenches and pillboxes, or in the rubble of Messines village, the monastery and Saint Nicholas church (in the crypt of which the wounded Lance Corporal Adolf Hitler had been treated in November 1914).

For days, the bombardment continued. Sitting around a table inside their pillbox, Reserve Oberleutnant Scheele and his men were 'almost blinded by debris, dust and flying earth', he recalled. 'None of us believed any longer that we should escape this witch's cauldron in one piece . . . Our situation was desperate but it did draw us together.'[46] Scheele and his comrades passed the time by re-reading their letters from home and sharing photos of their families while speculating 'when we should be hit'.[47]

And then suddenly, in the early hours of 7 June, the British guns ceased. An unusual silence followed. Every German soldier tensed in anticipation of the infantry assault which had to come at any moment.

At 1 am, Reserve Leutnant Wendler, lying awake in his dugout, felt a strange stillness. At 2.45 am, he went up to the observation post (OP), from which he had a complete view of the front. The bombardment had paused. He expected to see thousands of British soldiers scrambling over the distant plain, coming towards him. But tonight, everything was deathly quiet. The German sentries were being rotated, as usual, and officers were moving up and down the lines, checking their defences and encouraging the men. In his pill-box, Scheele and his friends ate a little tinned meat, as the ration parties could only get cold food through. They lay down to get some sleep.

—

At 3.10 am on 7 June, the first mine exploded, seven seconds early. Eighteen followed (two failed to detonate) in close succession, at Hill 60, Saint Eloi, Hollandscheshuur, Petit Bois, Maedelstede Farm, Peckham, Spanbroekmolen, Kruisstraat, Ontario Farm and Trenches 122 and 127 (see Map 3). Residents of London and parts of England claimed to have heard them. In Lille, fifteen miles away, 'terrified Germans rushed panic-stricken about the streets'.[48] Great mounds of earth rose out of the ground 'like colossal mushrooms', wrote a German witness.[49] The ridge blew apart in nineteen places, flinging thousands of German soldiers and huge chunks of earth into the sky. Caverns opened up under the enemy trench lines, turning them into instant mass graves.

Nineteen seconds passed between the first and the last explosion, an unintended delay that had a crushing impact on German morale. Feeling and hearing the huge blasts on either side of him, the German soldier realised, horror-struck, that his position would be next. Many scattered like 'a herd of wild animals', recalled Reserve

Leutnant Freiherr Kress von Kressenstein. One man, 'his left arm left dangling', was 'racing around the cratered area like a lunatic'.[50] 'The local German garrison, already overstrained by the week's bombardment, was entirely unstrung,' wrote Charles Bean, Australia's official historian.[51]

As the dust fell, the creeping barrage began: three belts of bursting shell, a wall of shrapnel, fire and smoke 700 yards deep, moved towards the devastated German positions. Visibility fell to 50 yards, as the barrage blocked out the light of the moon. In despair, the Germans fired green and white flares into the night sky in the hope of drawing down their own artillery. Little was forthcoming: an earlier, well-aimed British bombardment of gas and heavy explosives had disabled most of the German guns.

In their pillbox, Scheele and his men 'looked in horror at one another, believing initially that there had been an earthquake'. Through the loopholes, Scheele witnessed the approach of the barrage, 'a massive cloud of dust . . . rolling towards us . . . lit up by a great display of light signals'. The battlefield 'was eerily empty apart from dead horses, dead men and wrecked wagons . . .'[52]

—

Then came the infantry. The whistles blew and the first waves, more than a hundred battalions, rose out of their trenches and charged across the plain behind the barrage, which was moving at the rate of 100-yard lifts every two minutes.[53] The enemy wire lay in fragments as they approached and overwhelmed the German lines: 'the leading assault groups rushed or outflanked the many strongpoints and machine gun nests'.[54] The attackers found 'a sprinkling of the enemy cowering there, mostly in the numerous rectangular concrete shelters. . . . Many others had fled, a litter of accoutrements, rifles, ammunition, cigars, and scraps of food in the shell-holes showing where their line had been.'[55] They killed or captured the survivors, many of whom pleaded for mercy, inert with shock.

Near the top of the ridge, the British and Anzacs came upon the aftermath of the detonations: burning debris strewn with thousands of corpses, many of them mutilated beyond recognition. Huge craters between 220 and 440 feet in diameter and 20 to 30 feet deep gaped between mounds of earth, 'like ant-heaps and saucers'.[56]

Through their loopholes, Scheele and his men glimpsed the lines of steel hats coming at them from beyond the barrage: 'Whenever there was a brief gap in the endless clouds of dust and smoke, we could make out massive numbers of attackers, followed by dismounted cavalry leading their horses.' Scheele's men tried to form a rough defensive line, 'determined to sell our lives dearly'. He waved his pistol and even took 'the odd pot shot' at aircraft flying 'ten to 20 metres' overhead. The situation was hopeless. As the barrage swept over them, they raced to the rear, 'through the showers of earth and shell splinters from shell hole to shell hole'. Rounds with delayed-action fuses hurled up great geysers of earth.

Though the mine blasts did not reach the Germans garrisoned to the east of the ridge, 'the moral shock was naturally terrific'.[57] Sparks of German resistance rallied and died. Major Hans Ritter von Kohlmüller refused to yield. A stern, respected officer, recipient of the Knight's Cross at Loos, von Kohlmüller was determined to fight to the last man. His wish was soon granted: he led his little band of survivors – five wounded officers, two machine guns and a few men – in hand-to-hand combat, beating back several British attacks until, at 7.30 am, a direct hit from a heavy shell blew him up; his men surrendered or were shot.

Few Germans followed his suicidal example: most of the front lines surrendered. Some emerged from their pillboxes 'cringing like beaten animals'. A few made 'fruitless attempts to embrace us', reported Lieutenant William Garrard, of a Tasmanian battalion. 'I have never seen men so demoralised.'[58]

—

Further back, in Messines village, the Germans put up a stiffer fight. The New Zealand Division enveloped and overran this fortified husk, crushing the diehard German stand with 'acts of great gallantry' that involved rushing enemy machine guns. They smoked the occupants out of the village cellars. The New Zealanders captured 50 Germans and eight machine guns at a desolate point on the map, fittingly called Hell Farm, 700 yards north-west of Messines.[59] British forces mopped up pockets of German survivors in fierce skirmishes in the surrounding farms and woods, now desolate and skeletal, bereft of the ancient oak and larch trees that once stood there.

Meanwhile, two Irish brigades – one Protestant, one Catholic, fighting side by side – overran the heavily fortified Wytschaete village with the help of howitzers, gas and a tank. Fierce opponents over Home Rule, the men of the 16th Irish and 36th Ulster divisions had set aside their grievances here, tending to each other's wounded and praising each other's courage (a stone 'Peace Tower' at Messines today commemorates this unique collaboration). And while the Ulstermen protested that they 'couldn't possibly agree with his religious opinions', they felt nothing but the greatest admiration for Father Willie Doyle of the 8/Royal Dublin Fusiliers, who was killed after Messines. 'He didn't know the meaning of fear and didn't know what bigotry was,' wrote one. 'He was as ready to risk his life to take a drop of water to a wounded Ulsterman as to assist men of his own faith and regiment.'[60]

—

The sun shone red through a veil of smoke on the morning's carnage. All over the field, German survivors, broken in body and spirit, were picking their way back to the rear lines. A father met his blood-smeared son, wandering along with a shrapnel wound to the head, begging to be taken to hospital: 'Father . . . I can't stand this pain anymore.' The boy soon died of his wounds.[61] Most were utterly demoralised. Some sat down and prayed. Some suffered complete nervous breakdown, reduced to incoherent muttering, rocking back and forth and clutching their heads.

Reports of the slaughter filtered back to the German command posts. At around 7.30 am, a runner reached the headquarters of a Bavarian Infantry Regiment to inform the adjutant, Oberleutnant Eugen Reitinger, that his entire battalion had just been 'blown sky high', with total casualties of 1185 officers and men and three horses.[62]

The Second and Third Bavarian Infantry Divisions were the worst hit, with the latter losing 3600 men and 98 officers instantly, according to one estimate.[63] Several battalions of the 3rd Bavarian Division were completely wiped out. The next day, Scheele found that he was one of only two officers left standing in his battalion. Many had expired of shock, or suffocation, as the blasts sucked the oxygen out of the surrounding atmosphere.

'It suddenly dawned on everyone that the British . . . had blown up the entire front,' recalled Leutnant Dickes, of another Bavarian regiment.[64] Within 30 minutes, his regiment's forward battalion had ceased to exist: the mines and artillery barrage had killed 29 officers and more than 1000 men. The survivors evacuated. To have stayed any longer would have been suicidal.

Reserve Leutnant Hermann Kohl, the battalion's liaison officer, went forward to see for himself:

> Everywhere I bumped into stragglers from the division,
> leaderless and wandering like lost sheep. Totally apathetic
> they lay in shellholes or by the side of the road . . . I came
> across a Saxon leutnant, who had obviously suffered a
> nervous breakdown. He kept bawling at me that I ought
> to be in the front line and taking part in an attack. He
> spoke incoherently and in a pitifully agitated fashion.
> I was just waiting for him to draw his pistol . . .[65]

—

By mid-morning on 7 June, the ridge and the villages of Messines and Wytschaete were in Allied hands, as were 7000 German prisoners. For the first time since 1914, the Allies could move unhindered on the western slope.[66] Thus far, Plumer had met Haig's demands. The next day, Yoxall excitedly told his mother:

> we have straightened out the Salient . . . that terrible
> charnel house of British life, is no more. Our success was
> so easy that we are wondering why we did not attempt
> something more ambitious. . . . The mine explosions
> seem to have stunned the German infantry.[67]

One of the craters, he wrote, 'is about three times as big as our two gardens'.[68]

Plumer decided not to advance down the eastern slope at this point. He chose instead to utilise the five-hour pause that his plan allowed to consolidate his gains and bring forward the artillery. Several heavy guns and 40 field guns were dragged up, each with 300 rounds. The gun carriages were hitched to horses, the mules loaded with ammunition. In addition, 146 machine guns were placed along the ridge. Men with huge 'Yukon packs' (Canadian packs that distributed the load using a strap across the forehead, enabling a man to carry up to 65 pounds), carried the belts of machine-gun ammunition.

The offensive would resume at 3.10 pm that day, led by the 4th Australian Division. In the meantime, the British and Dominion forces crowded cheerfully along the ridgeline, reversed the German trenches, and dug themselves in, in readiness for the coming counter-attack. Behind them, a mangle of wire, equipment and corpses lay in and around the gigantic craters and piles of earth; ahead, to the east, the wonder of grassland, hedgerows and woods with leaf-bearing trees, and, further, the villages and meadows of the green valley of the Lys.

No Germans were to be seen – yet. Most of their remaining guns were hidden, in the forest at the base of the slope, and the Eingreif had not yet appeared. Every man lay waiting, thinking: when will the Huns return? When will the counter-blow come?

—

It struck with unexpected ferocity. Every Allied soldier had anticipated savage reprisals, but they had not yet confronted the enemy's new elastic defensive system – under which thousands of shock troops, held back in reserve, were to be sent pouring into battle to regain lost ground.

By mid-morning, the Allies saw them coming, lines of German troops closing on Messines from the east and north. At 11 am, a long file of enemy was seen coming up the road from Wervik about two-and-a-half miles away. New Zealand forward posts saw ten lines of Germans 'approaching them across the open fields, giving excellent targets to their machine guns'.[69] At 1.45 pm, waves of German infantry had assembled along the Oosttaverne Line, a 1000-yard front across the valley. Since 9.55 am, British artillery had been pounding this front; now it intensified its fire. Soon, thousands of German reinforcements were seen in the distance, and the dreadful spectre of another Arras arose in Allied heads.

The British guns began pounding away at the advancing hordes, easily identifiable from the newly claimed high ground. Wave after wave of German attacks failed to surmount the slopes to the east, thanks also to the rows of machine guns that blazed down on the enemy. By 2.30 pm, the counter-offensive was 'completely spent', wrote Bean.[70] The German infantry melted back to the Oosttaverne Line, and beyond.

The German batteries whose medium guns sat hidden in woods in the valley floor now came alive, shelling the Messines ridgeline and inflicting thousands of casualties on the Allied forces crammed into that small space. At the same time, a German plane penetrated the 23 British aircraft keeping guard over the ridge like a swarm of wasps, and reported the troop locations on the southern part of the ridge. Alerted, the German artillery adjusted their range and pounded this area, causing further heavy casualties.

Plumer's plan had anticipated the counter-attacks. At 3.10 pm, as planned, the barrage resumed, creeping down the eastern slope at 100 yards every three minutes. The Australian infantry rose again, this time behind tanks. It would be close-quarter fighting, and the men were ordered to 'fix bayonets'. The sight was too much for the Germans: having beheld tanks and Anzac infantry through the gaps of a fresh barrage, 'many lay on the ground crying for mercy or embracing the knees of the Australians', according to the British official history.[71] Those who fled were cut down by the barrage. Many stayed in their pillboxes, and machine-gunned the approaching waves in last desperate stands.

Two Queensland battalions advancing behind three tanks – and often, to the dismay of the tank crews, in front of them[72] – overran an outlying German trench and took 120 prisoners. Inspired, the Anzac platoons began attacking the pillboxes, one by one. In this, their first taste of blockhouse fighting, the Australians would quietly surround the targeted pillboxes and hurl Mills bombs in the back doors or fire through the loopholes. In many cases, shellfire had smashed open the bunkers' concrete roofs like eggshells, into which they tossed grenades.

Captain Robert Grieve led by example. Creeping up alone on a bunker at 'Hun House' that had pinned down his company, he single-handedly attacked and silenced two machine-gun crews inside (for which action he was awarded the Victoria Cross).[73] These individual attacks on pillboxes became the stuff of legend; so would the discoveries inside them: cigars, whisky, sausages were all part of the spoils. A story, widely believed, did the rounds of a beautiful woman with blonde hair found dead in one bunker.

The advancing Anzacs gave no quarter in these frenzied assaults. Hand-to-hand combat raged around the pillboxes. German machine gunners spilled out of the rear doors with their hands raised, pleading 'Mercy!', 'Kamerad!' They were often dispatched in a hail of bullets: few prisoners were taken. A moment ago, these men had been slaughtering the Australians' friends, so tensions were exceptionally high. The diary of Private Gallwey, whose battalion had suffered miserably at Bullecourt, reflected the incendiary mood. Finding a group of wounded Germans lying in a pillbox, his platoon fired point blank into the huddle: 'There was a noise as though pigs were being killed. They squealed and made guttural noises . . . after which all was silent.' The five bodies were then hauled out and dumped in a pile to confirm they were dead. 'It was a good thing this hornets [*sic*] nest had been cleaned out so easily,' Gallwey wrote. 'Nearly all were young men. It is an impossibility to leave wounded germans [*sic*] behind us because they are so treacherous. They all have to be killed.'[74]

If true, this case of Australians slaughtering wounded men constituted a war crime; it was also an 'inevitable' consequence of war, as Bean later explained:

> The tension accompanying the struggles around these
> blockhouses, the murderous fire from a sheltered position
> followed by the sudden giving in of the surrounded garrison,
> caused this year's fighting in Flanders to be marked by
> a ferocity that renders the reading of any true narrative
> peculiarly unpleasant. When such tensions exist in battle
> the rules of 'civilized' war are powerless. Most men are
> temporarily half mad, their pulses pounding at their ears,
> their mouths dry . . . With death singing about their ears
> they will kill until they grow tired of killing . . . It is idle
> for the reader to cry shame upon such incidents, unless
> he cries shame upon the whole system of war, for this
> frenzy is an inevitable condition in desperate fighting.[75]

The Australians moved on, and captured the Oosttaverne Line and dozens of pillboxes, aided by 24 tanks, sixteen of which crossed the line. For II Anzac Corps, these days of 'consolidation' were far deadlier than the attack on Messines Ridge itself.

—

At a conference of the German High Command on 9 June, Crown Prince Rupprecht, commanding the Bavarians, and General Sixt von Armin, commanding the Fourth Army, decided to abandon any hope of recovering Messines. Between 10 and 14 June, the Germans withdrew.

For the rest of the month, the British and Anzac forces fortified the captured ground, shelled the withdrawing Germans and completed the occupation of one of the most important positions in the Salient. Telephone wires were laid, connecting the new front line with rear command.

One telephone party included Ronald Skirth, the gunner, and his two friends, Geordie and Bill, none of whom was a telephonist. Their mission bewildered them. They headed east across no-man's-land on 8 June through the aftermath of battle. Skirth held a basket containing a carrier pigeon, the purpose of which eluded him. He presumed he was meant to send the bird back with the message that the telephone worked, but surely that was the point of the telephone, he questioned. He carried on:

> [W]e reached the site of the enemy's old trenches . . . It was a ghastly sight which met our eyes. I cannot attempt to describe what shapes and colours, things which once were human bodies and parts of human bodies assume after they have been blown sky high. Some looked like bluish-green replicas of the Michelin Tyre-men in the old advertisements – only inflated to twice life-size. Others were . . . incomplete . . .[76]

In shock, the party stumbled on: 'I had the utmost difficulty in forcing myself forward . . . I turned my head to see where my two pals were. One was being violently sick . . . we were the only living creatures in that nightmarish landscape.' Skirth saw something a few yards from the track that compelled him to take a closer look. What it was, he could not bring himself to write down: 'I was about to faint. I crouched and pulled my head low between my knees.'

Soon the German bombs began falling near the party: 'A dozen times we had to flatten ourselves or jump instantly into a shell-hole.' Bill and Geordie were both killed while trying to fix the phone line; the fourth member of the party was already dead. On finding their broken bodies, Skirth 'burst into uncontrollable tears. I remember crying out, "Oh God! Why couldn't you have let them die less horribly?"'

He lay in a shell hole alone with the carrier pigeon, wondering whether to continue towards the British trenches or go back. He decided to attach a message to the pigeon – 'Report three of our party killed . . .' – but lacked paper and pencil. He opened the lid of the basket: 'There wasn't any pen, pencil or paper. Only a dead pigeon.'[77]

—

The Battle of Messines Ridge was a complete Allied victory. In terms of vital territory gained, it was the most decisive of the war thus far. Vimy Ridge alone bore comparison.[78] For once, the euphoria in the press seemed justified: 'Great victory at Messines! Read all about it! Great victory at Messines!' shouted the newsboys at Piccadilly, as theatregoers spilled onto the streets that night.

The victory opened up a great expanse of German territory to Allied eyes for the first time in two and a half years, chiefly the Gheluvelt Plateau, due east of Ypres, the destruction of which would be vital to the success of the Flanders Offensive. That success relied, however, on the ruthless exploitation of the victory: the enemy should be given no breathing space. Instead, as we shall see, the British commanders dithered and delayed, giving the Germans ample time to erect the most formidable defensive shield in the western theatre.

For now, Haig could be forgiven for dwelling on the victory. He proudly reported to the War Cabinet, 'over one million pounds of explosives were used . . . The simultaneous discharge of such an enormous aggregate of explosive is without parallel in land mining, and no actual experience existed of the effects which would be produced.'[79] The impact on German morale had been 'tremendous', the War Cabinet heard on 11 June.[80] King George V sent his congratulations to Haig and Plumer.

Victory came at a high cost, in men and morale. The British and Empire body count, at 24,562 killed or wounded (of whom the Anzacs incurred more than half),[81] was higher than the German count of about 22,900 (including 7200 prisoners). And German artillery had knocked Allied morale: the rate of shell shock rose rapidly after Messines, from 50 cases admitted to hospital on 7 June to about 1800 cases by the end of the month[82] – a grim warning to High Command, who continued to ignore or downplay the 'nervous cases'.

If fewer enemy guns could do this to the British and Australians, the effect on the German soldier's nervous system of a creeping barrage was devastating: the blow to German morale at Messines was 'simply staggering', Ludendorff later acknowledged.[83] Rupprecht wrote dejectedly in his diary on 9 June, 'It is said that the detonation of the gigantic mines could be heard in London . . . All around Messines the ground was said to have been covered by the bodies of Bavarian soldiers (our poor, brave 3rd Division!).'[84]

# 7

# A FATAL DELAY

*Never has an army been in a better position*
*before a defensive battle.*
General Fritz von Lossberg, German defence expert known as 'the
fireman of the Western Front', before the start of Third Ypres

---

*You are out here for one purpose and one purpose*
*only – to kill Boches. From what I have seen every*
*man here today is good for two or three Boches.*
Major General Sir Geoffrey Percy Thynne Feilding

---

Haig's buoyant mood at this time led him to make decisions that misread the reality around him. Prone to recurring visions of Germany's collapse, he laboured under the delusion that the enemy's forces were *completely* demoralised. Their finest divisions were decimated, he believed – even as evidence to the contrary emerged, of a revivified and lethal foe.

This had obvious consequences for the men on the ground. Haig's strategy of wearing down the enemy made a huge call on manpower, as we've seen. It was not for him to answer the awkward political question of *how* the nation would tolerate 'normal wastage' of 35,000 casualties a month. That was a question for the politicians. The War Cabinet dared not publicly say what they all knew: that Allied casualties had exceeded Germany's at every major battle thus far – Second Ypres, Loos, the Somme, Verdun, Arras, the Aisne – chiefly because forces attacking fortified positions sustained higher losses than those defending them. This brutal arithmetic boiled down to the fact that the British and Dominion troops were being killed or wounded at a faster rate than Germany's.

In purely strategic terms, the casualty rate did not overly concern Haig because the British were able to draw on a much deeper pool of manpower than the Germans. By that calculus, Germany's defeat was simply a matter of time – and body count. Even with the Russians a virtual spent force, and France in the doldrums, Britain could rely on her doughty Dominion partners – who had proven so solid in battle – and the arrival of America's vast reserve of recruits, half a million men strong. In short, Haig could afford to 'waste' more lives than the enemy.

All this alarmed Lloyd George. The prime minister would never accept the logic of Haig's war. Preserving British lives had led Lloyd George to support the Nivelle Offensive and promote his Italian adventure. The former had failed; the latter was mothballed. That left the prime minister with no other choice than to bend an ear to the victor of Messines, a man he had damned as monstrously profligate with soldiers' lives, and whom he had tried to subordinate to the French to avoid the political fallout of another Somme.

This was the psychological backdrop to Haig's appearance, on 19 June, at the first meeting of the prime minister's Committee on War Policy, set up to concentrate power over the direction of the war in the prime minister's hands. It contained a further four men: Andrew Bonar Law (the Conservative leader), Alfred Milner (the 1st Viscount Milner, statesman and a former South African high commissioner), George Curzon (1st Marquess Curzon of Kedleston, leader of the House of Lords and a former Viceroy of India) and Jan

Smuts (temporary lieutenant general in the South African Army, a founding spirit of Apartheid and the smartest man in the room). Robertson would dismiss Milner as a 'tired and dyspeptic old man' and Curzon as a 'gas bag', adding in a letter to Haig dated 9 August that Smuts 'has good instinct but lacks knowledge'.[1]

The Committee's military experience amounted to the prime minister's week in the militia and Smuts's hit-and-run raids in the Boer War and questionable command of the South African forces against the Germans in Africa. Into their inexperienced hands passed the responsibility for the entire British war effort, on land, sea and air. For Lloyd George, it was a political ploy: he meant to use this nimble-footed committee as a means of bending the leadership of the war to his will. His four colleagues were not chosen for their readiness to defy him: Smuts proved to be the only member willing, on occasions, to challenge the prime minister, but all would duly fall into line under Lloyd George's dominance.

And so, about six weeks before the Flanders Offensive was due to start, Haig and Robertson were summoned to appear before the War Policy Committee in Lord Curzon's Privy Council Office at 10 Downing Street. Haig arrived in a confident mood, with all the runes in his favour: he had won Messines and Lloyd George had lost Nivelle. At first, the prime minister put on a good show of contrition: he possessed in abundance the politician's reptilian ability to adapt to changing scenery. He began the meeting by saying that he recognised the 'very powerful statement' Haig had made in favour of the Flanders Offensive, in recent days.[2] The trouble was, he disagreed with them . . .

—

Let's briefly review those statements. Just after Messines, on 12 June, Haig had sent Robertson an outline of his thinking on the coming Flanders campaign. Scornful of Lloyd George's Italian strategy, Haig pressed the case for fighting the war primarily on the Western Front: 'to fail in concentrating our resources in the

Western theatre, or to divert them from it, would be most dangerous. It might lead to the collapse of France. It would certainly encourage Germany.'[3] Most military minds agreed with him. Haig's unfailing optimism then led him to cast several hostages to fortune. He reckoned that he could clear the Belgian coast 'this summer', and that victory in Belgium 'might possibly lead to [Germany's] collapse'.[4]

Two conditions attached to that achievement: sufficient forces and speed of action, he told Robertson. At that moment, Haig reckoned his forces were adequate, numbering 42 divisions, but he would soon need many more men. And they 'must act promptly' to attack before Germany could transfer its eastern divisions to the western theatre. The Germans were demoralised, he claimed, with scant evidence. They would be unable to shift more than twenty divisions from east to west (two a week), he wrote. Forty per cent of their infantry – 105 German divisions – had been wiped out in recent battles, he claimed. All things considered, Haig argued that Germany would 'be forced to conclude peace on our terms before the end of the year'.[5]

Haig's wishful thinking was divorced from the facts, Robertson concluded. The CIGS 'could not possibly agree' with Haig's views on German morale, he wrote in a cable the next day: the Germans had, after all, won all their battles, with the exceptions of Vimy and Messines, in the sense that they had successfully defended their lines. Robertson added:

> What I do wish to press upon you is this:- Don't argue that
> you can finish the war this year, or that the German is already
> beaten. Argue that your plan is the best plan – as it is – that
> no other would be safe, let alone decisive, and then leave them
> to reject your advice and mine. They dare not do that . . .'[6]

Robertson warned Haig not to circulate his views before the big meeting with Lloyd George's committee. For now, Haig took that advice: instead of winning the war that year (as he told an army commanders' conference on 14 June), the Allies would continue to 'wear down and exhaust the enemy', while capturing Passchendaele Ridge and securing the Belgian coast.[7] At the very least, he would seize Passchendaele, after which, if circumstances ran afoul, 'it may be necessary to call a halt [to the offensive]'.[8] Haig thus covered himself in the event of failure. That seemed unlikely, he believed, after the great example of Messines. Success, he said, would depend on speed and secrecy, and a series of diversionary attacks. '[T]he best plan,' Haig reminded himself in his diary, 'seems to be to prepare simultaneously several points of attack: thus the situation becomes similar to the case of the pea under one of three thimbles.'[9]

———

Haig submitted his written case for the Flanders Offensive to the government two days before the 19 June meeting (see Appendix 6 for the full text). In defiance of Robertson's advice, he claimed that a 'limited advance' would protect Dunkirk from long-range hostile gunfire, bring the Roulers railway station within range of British artillery, and render Ostend useless to the German Navy. A 'short further advance' would place Bruges within range of his heavy guns and 'most probably induce the evacuation of Zeebrugge and the whole coastline'.[10] Germany would then have to choose between accepting defeat, undertaking a disastrous retreat, or violating Dutch territory. The Flanders Offensive, in sum, opened up 'sufficient prospects of success this year',[11] so long as the bulk of Allied forces were concentrated on the Western Front, he stressed, in a broadside at Lloyd George's Italian distraction. 'Amid the uncertainties of war one thing is certain,' he concluded, 'viz, that it is only by whole-hearted concentration at the right time and place that victory ever has been and ever will be won.'[12] That time would be 31 July, less than six weeks away; that place, the plain rising gently towards Passchendaele, north-east of Ypres.

In buoyant spirits, the field marshal set off for London on Sunday

17 June to sell his plan to the War Policy Committee. He enjoyed a fillip at Calais, over lunch with Admiral Sir Reginald Bacon, commander of the Dover Patrol, who was 'wholeheartedly with us', Haig wrote. Bacon had written to the Admiralty of 'the absolute necessity for clearing the Belgian coast before winter'.[13] Haig left by destroyer for Dover and reached Charing Cross by special train at 5.20 pm.

—

Haig, Robertson, the four members of the War Policy Committee and Bonar Law met at 10.45 am on 19 June around a plush wooden table in Curzon's rooms. The prime minister struck a courteous, slightly deferential note, in recognition of the ascendancy of his commander and softened by thoughts of his daughter's wedding, which was to take place later that day.[14]

Haig got off to a bad start, mumbling about a successful Russia offensive that would hearten the Russian people. Lloyd George dismissed this as incorrect: Russia was on the brink of abandoning the war altogether. Haig ploughed on: the Germans were demoralised, the German submarine offensive failing. If so, wondered Lloyd George, what was the case for launching the Flanders Offensive? Haig seemed to want to have it both ways: if the U-boats were failing, we should strike while the enemy is vulnerable; if the U-boats were succeeding, then we should strike to destroy their submarine bases. 'Since Haig scored a point either way,' the historian Leon Wolff observed, 'something must be wrong with his premise.'[15] Up to a point: Wolff overlooks the fact that the whole purpose of the battle, in Haig's mind, involved much more than destroying U-boat bases.

Unruffled, Haig laid out a map to explain the offensive, stage by stage. Years later, Lloyd George would famously lampoon his commander's presentational style:

[Sir Douglas] spread on a table or desk a large map and made a dramatic use of both his hands to demonstrate how he proposed to sweep up the enemy – first the right hand brushing along the surface irresistibly, and then came the left, his outer finger ultimately touching the German frontier with the nail across.[16]

No doubt, the prime minister's lurid imagination embellished this scene, to enliven his memoirs years later; on the other hand, Haig had a way of coming alive over his colourful maps.

Haig deflected a barrage of questions with his sunny optimism: yes, the French would participate in the offensive, despite their demoralised condition; yes, German morale had collapsed (Haig cited the blow at Messines and an American committee's report, claiming the Germans 'realize they are beaten'); no, the Germans did not enjoy artillery superiority and, in any case, their guns were inaccurate. At which Robertson harrumphed to life and argued on Haig's side that German artillery supremacy was 'a myth': the Germans were not even able to supply enough ammunition.[17]

The meeting turned to the likely casualties, a subject over which the prime minister glowered with proprietorial menace. Deeply concerned about the nation's ability to replace the dead and wounded, Lloyd George asked Haig for an estimate of the losses (dead, wounded, missing and captured), reminding him 'that on the Somme our losses had amounted to an average of 100,000 a month'.[18]

To this, Haig unwisely replied that he had anticipated a loss of 100,000 men a month on the Somme. The idea that such losses were somehow planned deeply rankled Lloyd George. Haig reassured him that there were no grounds to fear such casualties in the Passchendaele offensive, citing the 'small rate of loss' at Messines. To which Lloyd George sharply reminded him that since 7 April – a period encompassing the battles of Arras, Bullecourt and Messines – total British losses were 'not much less than 200,000 [182,000, to be more precise], which was not very far short of 100,000 a month'.[19] In reply, Haig calmly reminded the prime minister that the heavy casualties at Arras followed the decision at Calais to compel the British Army to support the Nivelle Offensive (and everyone in the room knew who had been the most vocal backer of Nivelle).

Slightly taken aback by Haig's quiet confidence, the War Committee continued probing manpower needs, German strength, and other matters. At the same time, Lloyd George hankered to press on the meeting the case for shifting guns and men to the Italian front. Anticipating this, Haig and Robertson rammed home the importance of striking now, in Flanders, on the Western Front, with everything they had. Only then, Haig claimed, could he capture the Belgian coast and liberate Belgium.

To most of those in the room, Haig's ambition for the Flanders Offensive seemed fantastic, and it elicited silence. Robertson ruminated that Haig had gone out on the limb he had warned him not to. The room fidgeted and shuffled their papers, heavy with the realisation that their commander was deadly serious. Years later, Lloyd George would recall the moment in his memoir, in prose dripping with incredulous sarcasm: 'If this attack were . . . successful, that would enable us to reach a portion of Passchendaele Ridge . . . in the course of a single day without any serious casualties.'[20] In fairness to Haig, Lloyd George then had the benefit of knowing the outcome.

Bonar Law wondered whether the price justified the cost in likely casualties, to which Lord Milner offered the depressing calculation that ridding the Belgian coast of the Germans 'was worth half a million men'.[21] Milner did not explain how he reached this astronomic number. 'Curious indeed,' Lloyd George later observed, 'must be the military conscience which could justify an attack under such conditions.'[22] No Australian, Canadian or New Zealand politician or military chief was present to influence their forces' involvement in the coming attack; Australia's then representatives in Britain had 'no authority to contribute to [Cabinet] decisions'.[23] The sacrifice of young men from the Dominions was simply assumed and factored into 'normal wastage'.

Misinformation, exaggeration and wilful ignorance rattled the room like a squadron of disruptive poltergeists. A lot of what Haig told the Committee was sheer wishful thinking and plain wrong.

Not that he dissembled or lied; he simply chose to believe in the best possible outcome. Haig's plan, for example, had *not* persuaded the French commanders Marshals Philippe Pétain and Ferdinand Foch, who had forcefully criticised it; German morale had *not* collapsed; and enemy reinforcements were starting to pour into Flanders from the east. And yet, Haig insisted that his offensive must go ahead, or the Germans would attack and 'we should then probably lose the same number of men and guns without any advantage'. That denied the fact that the defenders of attrition almost always suffered fewer casualties, as the German experience had shown. Lloyd George echoed this, suggesting 'we could hold the enemy even if he did attack' – his preferred course of action on the Western Front being Pétain's defensive strategy: dig in and wait until the Americans arrived.[24]

For his part, Lloyd George was just as fast and loose with the truth. He would later claim, falsely, that this was the first time the government had heard of or studied the Flanders Offensive. A variation of the plan had been in the works since January 1916, and had been tabled in November that year.

They reached a stalemate. Lloyd George, Bonar Law and Milner emerged from the meeting strongly opposed to Third Ypres, with Curzon undecided and Smuts warmly in favour. The prime minister wanted the offensive postponed until 1918, when France had recovered and the Americans had put boots on the ground. (Washington had recently informed the British Government that the United States hoped to have 120,000–150,000 men in France by January 1918 and 500,000 by the end of that year.)[25]

The meeting would resume the next day. As he prepared to leave for his daughter's wedding, the prime minister pitched a few verbal grenades into the room: manpower wasn't a limitless resource, he warned; the government had been 'scraping up men' from war factories, farms and lists of medical rejects; the people were resentful and turning against the war. 'Every time we scraped any in there was trouble in the House of Commons or a strike,' he added. Britain and the Dominions were bearing 'the whole burden of the War', and the government 'had to consider whether it would not be better to hold our hand until the French Army had been resuscitated by the intervention of America'.[26]

Later that day, Lloyd George continued drilling the point. The government could not gamble with so many lives, he wrote to Haig and Robertson, 'merely because those who are directing the War can think of nothing better to do with the men under their command'. In saying so, the prime minister seemed to have forgotten who was ultimately holding the reins: he was, and he had the power to overrule his commanders.

Would the Flanders Offensive bring anything better than Messines or Vimy Ridge, he wondered, whose 'brilliant preliminary successes [were] followed by weeks of desperate and sanguinary struggles, leading to nothing except perhaps the driving of the enemy back a few barren miles – beyond that nothing to show except a ghastly casualty list'.[27] The Flanders Plan would not, he concluded: it had little to commend it, would be very costly and therefore ought to be discouraged. 'I earnestly entreat our military advisers as well as the Cabinet to think again before they finally commit the British Army to an attack . . .'[28]

—

The meeting reconvened on the morning of 20 June (and would meet several times in the next few weeks to discuss every aspect of the campaign – no offensive was more thoroughly analysed, at political and military levels; no battle more anticipated and feared). The prime minister now presented his formal alternative to Third Ypres, worked up the night before. It was a variation on his Italian plan, with the aim of knocking Austria out of the war.[29] His case boiled down to this: why pitch our strongest against their strongest and our weakest against their weakest? We should strike the Central Powers at their feeblest point, on the Italian front, using Italian reserves and 75 batteries of British heavy artillery. Trieste would swiftly fall, followed by the collapse of Austria, which would be compelled to sign a separate peace, and then Bulgaria and Turkey, leaving Germany naked to the storm.

A single sentence betrayed the prime minister's strategic incoherence: 'What does it matter whether we fight Germans in the north of France or in Italy?' It mattered because fighting the enemy in Italy would have severely weakened the British forces where the Germans were strongest, with the very liberty of France at stake. In any case, the prime minister's reply to his own rhetorical question gave away his chief motive. Attacking on the Italian front, he said, will mean 'we can use the enormous reserves of the Italians'.[30]

Haig and Robertson had a well-prepared response.[31] The chief of staff argued that Austria would not sign a separate peace without Germany. In any case, Robertson icily explained, defeating Austria would be extremely unlikely: the Germans had five railway lines into Italy; the Allies had two. Thus Germany would easily win the race to reinforce the Italian front, as it would take French trains six weeks to move 75 batteries to Italy: 'The enemy can therefore always hope to beat us if he wishes to, in concentrating superior forces on the Italian front.'[32]

Moreover, Robertson argued, to denude the Western Front of so many guns would force the British forces to adopt a defensive strategy (which, ironically, was exactly what Lloyd George wanted). A 'sinister sentence' then struck the prime minister's ears. 'We should follow the principle of the gambler who has the heaviest purse,' Robertson said, 'and force our adversary's hand and make him go on spending until he is a pauper.'[33]

Robertson concluded:

> our chances of obtaining good results are certainly no
> greater in Italy than they are in the North [i.e. Flanders],
> while the risks involved are much greater in the former
> . . . [W]e must continue to be aggressive somewhere on
> our front, and we ought of course to do this in the most

promising direction [i.e. towards the Belgian coast] . . .[34]

Britain's top soldiers then made a concession: they would undertake to halt the Flanders Offensive should progress falter or should they fail to achieve their goals. Lloyd George's ever-active mind latched on to this proposal, as Haig took the baton from Robertson. Haig similarly dismissed the Italian adventure, as likely to lead to disastrous reversals in the west. He then went on the attack. He would defeat the Germans in Flanders because he possessed twice their troop numbers, he claimed. Not even Robertson, aware of German reinforcements arriving from the east, believed this. Haig then dazzled his listeners further, by suggesting that maximum pressure on the Western Front might well win the war by the end of the year. He reprised his claim that the Germans were exhausted, and that defeating the enemy in Belgium in 1917 ran a 'reasonable chance of success'. What had seemed fanciful yesterday was starting to sound like an arguable, if not realisable, goal.

The seven men sat and pondered: should they fight in Flanders, as Haig insisted; or Italy, the prime minister's choice? Or should they sit still, using the defensive tactics of Pétain, of 'a punch here and a punch there'[35] – while 'pulling faces at the Boches', as Sir Henry Wilson had unhelpfully suggested – until the French recovered and the Americans arrived?[36] The meeting reached another stalemate. Neither side was willing to back down. Lloyd George, Bonar Law and Milner remained resolutely opposed to Third Ypres; the two most senior soldiers were just as strongly opposed to the Italian option. Was a compromise possible? Upon their decision lay the hopes and lives of millions.

—

Into this frigid moment sailed Admiral Sir John Jellicoe, summoned the next day to offer an opinion. Premonitions of defeat beleaguered the First Sea Lord: the Ancient Mariner of Jutland had come to reprise the threat of the German U-boats, the horror of which seemed to rise in his mind as it receded in everyone else's. He spoke with great urgency of 'the grave need' to destroy the German submarine bases in Belgium before the winter, or 'we could not go on with the War next year through lack of shipping'. The war would be lost unless Zeebrugge were taken, Jellicoe insisted. 'There is no good discussing plans for next Spring – We cannot go on.'[37]

Nobody agreed with Jellicoe. Lloyd George 'indignantly challenged' this 'startling and reckless declaration'.[38] The prime minister, who had virtually taken control of the Admiralty,[39] placed great confidence in the convoy system's defeat of Germany's underwater war: the first experimental convoys had survived, and 300 submarine-chasing destroyers were soon to enter service. British food stocks were, in any case, healthy: 'we could continue the war until the harvest of 1918', Lloyd George would soon say in a speech in Scotland.[40] The First Sea Lord's claim was 'wholly fallacious', Churchill later argued: a dozen small U-boats were 'not a worthy objective for a grand land offensive'.[41] Haig himself privately rubbished Jellicoe's 'bombshell', as he called it in his diary on 20 June: 'No one present shared Jellicoe's view, and all seemed satisfied that the food reserves in Great Britain are adequate.'[42]

Again, this raised the questions that nobody explored: if the German U-boats no longer posed a serious threat to Britain's survival, what was the case for launching an immense ground offensive to destroy the submarine bases? Hadn't capturing the ports of Ostend and Zeebrugge hitherto been a vital aim of the offensive? No longer, it seemed: the government showed little interest in the ostensible purpose of the Flanders Offensive. Two long Cabinet debates about the submarine threat, on 13 and 20 July, did not even mention the great battle due to start at the end of that month, with the stated goal of destroying the U-boat bases.[43] In any case, Haig had far bigger ambitions than a few submarine pens: the defeat of the Germans in Belgium, no less, the culmination of his 'wearing down' war. For this reason, Haig did not openly challenge Jellicoe (confining his doubts to his diary). However little Haig credited the First

Sea Lord's fears of Britain's death by submarines, it certainly buttressed his case for Third Ypres.

On 21 June, at the 10th meeting of the War Policy Committee, Lloyd George made his final case against the Flanders Offensive – and for an attack on Austria through Italy. It was a bravura performance, powerfully delivered:

> I made a final effort to persuade Haig and Robertson to
> abandon this foolhardy enterprise. I felt they were plunging
> into a perilous hazard when the conditions demanded unusual
> circumspection and preparation . . . I then turned to an
> examination of the prospects of success. I pointed out that
> failure would be very serious business. All the world would
> recognise, if Sir Douglas Haig only succeeded in reaching his
> first objective [Passchendaele Ridge], that our operations had
> failed to realise their full scope . . . What reason, I asked, was
> there to believe that we could first drive the enemy back fifteen
> miles and then capture a place ten miles away? For a success
> on this scale one of the following conditions was essential:
>   1. An overwhelming force of men and guns;
>   2. That the enemy should be attacked so strongly
> elsewhere that his reserves would be drawn off;
>   3. That the enemy's morale should be so broken
> that he could no longer put up a fight.
>   None of the above conditions obtained at that time.[44]

Lloyd George's analysis was correct. Haig did not possess, and never would, the overwhelming superiority in guns and men necessary to heave the Germans out of Belgium; nor was German morale close to collapse. Yet, having laid down a forceful argument against the offensive, the prime minister did nothing further to oppose it. Instead, he proposed a compromise, which reprised Haig's earlier offer to end the campaign if it failed to meet his goals. The decision of whether to proceed with Third Ypres, Lloyd George said, should

fall on Haig and Robertson, 'on the understanding that if the progress they made with the operation did not realise the expectations
they had formed, it should be called off'.[45] Cabinet ministers, he later
wrote, 'attached great weight to the undertaking given them by both
Sir William Robertson and Sir Douglas Haig that the attack would
be abandoned as soon as it became evident that it was not likely to
succeed . . .'[46]

This brazen shifting of responsibility conveniently belayed Lloyd
George from a bad fall if the offensive failed. Well might he later
use his professed ignorance of military matters as an excuse not to
intervene; but that had not stopped him meddling in strategy when
it suited him. As the supreme elected authority, the prime minister
had the power to decide if and when an offensive should proceed or
end. He protested that the Conservative forces opposing him, in the
parliament and press, prohibited him from making such a stand,
and he would later hold Haig solely responsible for the carnage of
Passchendaele.

—

Obstacles of a strategic and tactical nature already beset the offensive: two prerequisites for its success were speed and surprise, as Haig
had stressed. Neither was forthcoming after Messines. Haig broke
his own conditions by acceding to the demands for more time, from
the general he appointed to command the offensive, Hubert Gough.
It was Gough who, after Messines, had persuaded Haig that he
needed at least six to seven weeks to redeploy and prepare his forces.
This long delay was now in progress, giving the Germans more
than enough time to prepare for the coming onslaught. The tragedy
of Passchendaele may be sourced, in large part, to this fateful gap
between the end of Messines and the start of Third Ypres.

A youthful commander, aged just 47, General Hubert de la Poer
Gough had a polarising, aggressive style of leadership that failed
to engender loyalty in his junior officers yet made him a favourite
of Haig's. Of Protestant Irish extraction – he would proudly call

himself 'Irish by blood and upbringing' – Gough had a pedigree English army officer's background: public school (Eton) and Royal Military College, Sandhurst. The Boer War interrupted his training at the Staff College, Camberley, and in South Africa he served as an intelligence officer and commanded a regiment of mounted infantry, whom he led on a reckless offensive against the Boers in September 1901 that resulted in his capture (along with most of his regiment), and his later escape, from a Boer prison.

On his return to Britain, he shot up the ranks, reaching lieutenant colonel by 1902, at the age of 32. Rapid promotion brought out his personal shortcomings. Gough had a 'tedious habit of questioning regulations' and an inability 'to control his temper', his then superior officer, Brigadier General Scobell, complained.[47] These were understandable traits in so young and promising a commander. To his credit, Gough was painfully aware of his shortcomings, which he attributed to his impulsiveness and aggression: 'All his life he regretted that he was prone to wound or wrong others when angry.'[48] These characteristics were on unseemly display during the Curragh Incident, when Gough and 57 officers, fierce opponents of Irish independence, threatened to resign their commissions at Curragh rather than obey orders to coerce Protestant Ulster into accepting Home Rule.

His steely, unsympathetic eyes and haughty disdain for those he considered his inferiors sharpened his reputation as a bullying, 'top-down' commander with little feeling for the ordinary soldier. By 1917, a deep well of unpopularity had formed around Gough's name, synonymous with 'heavy losses and complete failure' and with terrorising his subordinates to the extent that they were 'afraid to express their opinions for fear of being [sacked]'.[49] His thriving reputation for launching precipitate offensives with callous disregard for casualties persuaded the Anzac and Canadian commanders who had served under him at the Somme and Bullecourt never to do so again. He was a frequent sacker, and undermined, bypassed or removed commanders 'whom he did not wholly trust'. His style was spit and polish, the kind of commander who would tour the trenches looking for dirty rifles.[50] Gough, wrote Brigadier General Hodgkins in his diary on 14 March, 'does not care a button about the lives of his men'.[51]

It was a heavy charge, and could easily have been applied to other generals, of course, but Gough's unfortunate character drew a disproportionate share of junior officers' scorn. On the credit side, he could be charming among his friends and those in whom he placed confidence. He performed well at First Ypres and arguably received an unfair spray of the blame for disasters that often originated in higher places or were driven by political motives.

Yet, he seemed to learn little, slowly, of the nature of this ever-changing war, contends Simon Robbins: Gough 'does not seem to have learned' anything from his experiences in 1915 and 1916.[52] Where generals Plumer, Allenby, Currie and Monash scaled the learning curve and adapted to the fast-changing circumstances of the war, Gough seemed stuck in the mind of Loos and the Somme. In July 1917, he was eager to launch another spectacular frontal assault, of Nivellean dimensions. In this light, Ian Beckett's seems a fair assessment of the man charged with the command of the opening battles of Third Ypres:

> Ironically, [the] independent traits that Gough abhorred in
> his subordinates he embodied in practice. His inability to
> take direction, and his wholehearted and often unjustified
> confidence in his own planning, led him to overestimate his
> army's abilities and contributed to his disastrous operations . . .[53]

In the months before Third Ypres, Gough's methods impressed the one man who might have restrained him: Haig. Haig admired Gough's uncompromising spirit; it was the right stuff to achieve the breakthrough that Haig had so long sought. Like Haig, Gough was a 'cavalry man', and cavalrymen were less inclined to tolerate the 'wearing down' war of the trenches (Haig's Olympian patience being the exception): the cavalry spirit yearned to gallop across distant plains in the direction of a drawn sword.

Gough's Fifth Army Headquarters was an unlovely square block north of Poperinghe, called Lovie Chateau. His chief of staff was a 'harsh and unsympathetic individual' called Neill Malcolm, who would soon poison relations between Gough and his corps commanders, and contribute to the atmosphere of terror that reigned over the Fifth Army during the campaign.[54]

—

And so, an aggressive and unpopular cavalryman took charge of planning the first battle. And yet, instead of pouncing on the chance Messines presented, Gough curiously prevaricated. At an army commanders' conference at Lilliers on 14 June, he effectively tore up the original Flanders Plan and insisted on six weeks to prepare, to which Haig acquiesced. At first glance, this defied common sense and military reason. General Rawlinson had told Haig in January that no more than 48–72 hours should divide Messines from the main attack.[55] The Allies should exploit the enemy's confusion to the maximum, Rawlinson had said. Plumer, too, advised Haig to seize on Messines' success at once. He would need three days, he said, to get his guns into position to make a limited attack on Gheluvelt. In the minds of Plumer and Rawlinson, mounting a swift attack after Messines, even a limited one, was not a logistical 'impossibility'. The cavalrymen, however, were thinking on a different scale . . .

Why Haig failed to expedite the offensive has excited much speculation. The fairest answer is that Haig needed additional time to prepare for the more ambitious campaign that he and Gough envisaged. In Gough's mind, the battle plan was clear: after an artillery pounding of unprecedented force, his Fifth Army would smash open the German lines east of Ypres and break out into the wide, green plains beyond Passchendaele; the ridge would be his within a week or so. The consequences of so swift an advance, of placing his men beyond the protective range of their artillery, were not examined.

Victory at Messines emboldened Haig to adopt Gough's more aggressive tactics. By acceding to the revised plan, Haig counter-manded his own advice (Haig tended to advise rather than order his generals, delegating tactical authority to the commander in the field) that he had offered at the Doullens meeting on 3–4 May: first, attack the high ground on the Gheluvelt Plateau, and then progress by stages – 'bite and hold' – a kilometre or two, dig in, and defend your gains while your artillery moves up to cover the next bite. By mid-June, his thoughts chimed with Gough's rather than those of the more experienced Plumer: the Germans were on the brink of col-lapse, and a final, almighty blow would finish them off. In this light, the bite and hold tactics that had proved so effective at Messines were to be relegated: the situation demanded a decisive thrust. And temperamentally, 'Goughie' was a 'thruster', not a biter.[56] His break-through would demand many more guns and men, and they would take time to put in place. And so, the tactical urgency of delivering an immediate, if limited, strike against the Germans was lost, and the Messines advantage squandered. In lunging for the highest fruit, Haig left the rest to rot, and risked gaining none.

—

Haig tended to fashion his orders, or advice, according to his com-manders' temperaments, sometimes blurring the ultimate purpose of the battle.[57] Clearly, he wanted to cover himself against all outcomes. He told Gough on 30 June, 'the object of the Fifth Army offensive is to wear down the enemy, but, at the same time, to have an objective: I have given two: the Passchendaele-Staden ridge and the coast.' The steady-handed Plumer, who would support Gough, should 'be ready to act offensively on the right, north of the Lys'.[58] Gough lacked the subtlety of mind to see that if one objective failed, the other should be pursued. He interpreted this as a green light to make up his mind as he went.

Of all the myriad considerations on Gough's desk, from the length of the bombardment to the composition of forces, the most critical was: to what depth should he advance, and how should his men hold the ground captured? On the first day, Gough intended to capture 3000–3500 yards of German-held ground in three stages, followed by further 'jumps' of up to 2000 yards if the situation permitted. The British troops were to seize the territory bracketed inside three lines on his maps (see Map 4): blue (1000 yards), black (2000 yards) and green (3500 yards). The blue line ran just beyond the front line, and embraced Pilckem Ridge, part of the Frezenburg Ridge and Westhoek. The black line ran before Saint Julien and Langemarck in the north, and Polygon Wood and Tower Hamlets in the south. The green line enclosed the entire Wilhelm Stellung (the Germans' 'Wilhelm Position'), at which point the officer in charge would have to decide whether to press on to the red line, 1500 yards further on, past Broodseinde and Gravenstafel to the threshold of Passchendaele Ridge.

Capturing all this in a single day, and Passchendaele within a week, was a heavy demand. And it raised the question of whether Gough's artillery could advance at the same pace as the men. The barrage was vital in shielding the men as they charged and destroying the German wire on the way. Ominously, Gough's pre-battle planning failed to answer it.

And there was the thorny issue of Gheluvelt Plateau. Everything relied on seizing the high ground at Gheluvelt, as Haig had stressed. Gheluvelt stood at the midriff of the Salient's eastward bulge. Here, the German gunners enjoyed an unrestricted view over the plains before Ypres. Driving them back in a broad line would force the bulge further east, lengthening the sides and thrusting the advancing troops deeper into the German noose. Ideally, then, Gough should first concentrate on the Germans on Gheluvelt, to remove their flanking fire. The heavy German artillery at Gheluvelt imperilled this plan: indeed, Gough had received fairly solid aerial intelligence telling him where to expect most of the enemy. The German presence on the plateau was a direct obstacle to the success of the offensive. In the end, Gough decided to attack along a single, wide line, to attempt to destroy everything in his path, 'straighten' the Salient and ultimately break through to open country.

At the same time, Haig had reverted to favouring the more cautious, step-by-step approach. He failed to communicate this to Gough, who proceeded in the belief that a swift breakthrough remained the chief aim of the offensive – and even revised upwards his expectations, hoping for a gain of 6000 yards on the first day.

If Gough was 'not subtle enough to understand the dual nature of the offensive', as Andrew Wiest concludes[59] – i.e. the capture of the Belgian coast in tandem with the wearing down of the enemy – then so too were most others involved in the plan, notably the prime minister. The problem lay in Haig's failure to clarify his orders and insist they be obeyed, a failure the historian Gary Sheffield has called 'a dreadful abdication of command responsibility'.[60] And so the Flanders campaign continued towards its terrible denouement, and those who had the power to stop it, or influence the outcome, still misunderstood, or disagreed on, why it should proceed and what it should achieve.

In early July, King George V visited Flanders to congratulate the men on the victory at Messines. For his Majesty's entertainment, several battalions mocked up a re-enactment of the battle: a drum roll took the place of the guns and mine blasts, and lines of flag-bearing men on horseback enacted the creeping barrage. The advancing British swept all before them, and hundreds of 'Germans' surrendered, emerging from their 'trenches' with their hands in the air. The show delighted the King's party so much the men gave a second performance.

—

In the German camp, Rupprecht and Ludendorff had been aware of Haig's plan as early as May, a month *before* the British Government claimed it knew (that is, if we believe Lloyd George's story that Cabinet had been ignorant of the Flanders Offensive until 19 June). The German press had been fully informed: *Frankfurter Zeitung* reported on 1 July, 'the renewal of an ambitious land operation [in Flanders] with far-reaching strategic aims is doubtless to be expected. . . . [F]or a long time . . . we have contemplated these things in a state of preparation'.[61] Local Flemish farmers also got wind of the coming attack before Lloyd George, simply by noticing the huge build-up of men and matériel. When one farmer asked the Germans for permission to move his livestock, the po-faced military police snapped, 'What? An impending offensive? How do you know that? How dare you give away military preparations!'[62]

The Crown Prince knew the attack was coming, but was greatly relieved by the delay. His greatest fear – that the Allies would launch a series of sudden attacks in the Salient within days of Messines – had not materialised. On 12 June, six weeks before it struck, he described the British Flanders Offensive as 'certain', precisely forecasting its object, the Belgian coast.[63]

Every day of British inaction handed the Germans a great opportunity.[64] The day Messines ended, Ludendorff acted at once to fortify the German defences in Flanders. On 14 June, he dispatched General von Lossberg, his man for all crises, to German headquarters at Courtrai. Promoted to chief of the general staff of the Fourth Army, von Lossberg set about transforming Germany's lines into the strongest defensive system on the Western Front (a task he'd already been hard at). The curious absence of British action after Messines gave him all the extra time he needed.

Von Lossberg developed a series of trench systems within a defensive zone six to seven miles deep, interspersed with rolls of wire, snipers' nests and concrete bunkers that formed a near-impenetrable barrier. British troops entering this labyrinth would first encounter 'great wedge-shaped masses of rusty metal', the belts of wire, 30 yards deep.[65] Anyone caught in the wire would be machine-gunned.

Those who penetrated beyond the wire would reach the German frontline trenches, the thinly manned sections of the Albrecht Stellung. Beyond these, they would encounter fresh trench lines interspersed with concrete pillboxes containing machine guns and knots of shock troops. All of this would have to be destroyed before the Allies reached the battle zone proper, the Wilhelm Stellung and the Flandern Stellungen I, II and III (Flanders Positions 1, 2 and 3), each of which consisted of trench systems hundreds of yards deep, set about 2000 yards apart, under the protective gaze of more rows of concrete bunkers positioned with interlocking fields of fire. Unlike the elastic defence at Arras, where the forward troops fell back, all these forward forces were ordered to 'fight it out in situ, and to break up the enemy attack . . . until help arrived'. They were to remain in place 'however severe the attack',[66] under orders that effectively condemned tens of thousands of German men to a uniquely horrible death.

The German defensive bands ran broadly parallel, but the first two crossed each other at Glencorse Wood, on Gheluvelt Plateau, perhaps the most heavily fortified position on the German front. The final trench systems straddled either side of Passchendaele Ridge. Carefully positioned to the rear of each stage, and on the eastern side of Passchendaele, unseen by Allied eyes, were further regiments of Eingreif reserves. The whole defensive system was about five miles deep, from the thinly defended front lines at the foremost lip of Gheluvelt Plateau to the thickets of the German forces proper, heavily concentrated near and beyond Passchendaele.

And the Germans had greatly increased their troop numbers in the time Haig had allowed them: 65.5 divisions now fought under Rupprecht's Heeresgruppe, of which General Sixt von Armin's Fourth Army counted for sixteen divisions (frontline and reserve), up from twelve in early June. Supporting them were scores of new machine-gun nests, and batteries of artillery, carefully hidden behind the ridges with a clear view of the Salient. Their guns had trebled in number, from 389 to 1162.[67]

Most of these reinforcements had arrived between mid-June and the end of July 1917, just before the start of Third Ypres. No doubt, the Allies retained their supremacy in manpower (1.5 men to one) and artillery (three guns to one), yet these were not enough to defeat a heavily entrenched enemy.[68] Von Lossberg's improvements threatened a bloody and infuriating stand, aided by a new form of gas, an invisible, highly toxic vapour that eluded detection and, though usually not fatal, was 'extremely painful'.[69] The vapour emanated from an oily fluid that settled in the trench floors and in the creases of clothing, burning through uniforms and blistering the skin. The worst cases suffered temporary blindness and sloughing of the scrotum. The fluid's strange, mustard-like smell soon gave the gas its name.

In sum, the German commanders could not have hoped for a more helpful interlude between the thunder of Messines and the start of the British offensive in Flanders. Rupprecht was optimistic: 'I am awaiting the attack with great calmness, since on an attacked front we never have been provided with reserves so strong and well trained.'[70] And von Lossberg was supremely confident. Surveying his newly fortified lines, the fireman of the Western Front echoed the Crown Prince: 'never has an army been in a better position before a defensive battle'.[71]

And never was an army better primed for an offensive battle. In the British camp, in late April, the elite Brigade of Guards (a divisional unit comprising eight battalions of Coldstream, Grenadier, Scots, Irish and Welsh guards) were enjoying a sports day, and rejoiced in the news that they were heading for Ypres 'very soon'. At the day's end, their commanding officer, Major General Sir Geoffrey Percy Thynne Feilding, addressed them:

> I want to say how pleased I have been with your bayonet
> fighting today. . . . You are out here for one purpose and one
> purpose only – to kill Boches. From what I have seen every
> man here today is good for two or three Boches. That's what
> I want. You all of you put any amount of viciousness and beef
> into your work today, with no fancy work. That's what I want
> . . . Also that you may have an opportunity of showing very
> soon what you can do against the real thing in the open!

To which hundreds of his men cried, 'That's what we want!' And the general roared with laughter.[72]

# 8

# AUGUST 1917

*The entire earth of Flanders rocked and seemed to be on fire. This was not just drumfire; it was as though Hell itself had slipped its bonds. What were the terrors of Verdun and the Somme compared to this grotesquely huge outpouring of raw power?*
General Hermann von Kuhl, recalling 31 July 1917

---

*British prisoners are saying – and this has never been heard before – that they wished that they had shot their own officers who were leading them into the slaughterhouse. They have had enough of this butchery!*
Crown Prince Rupprecht, 16 August 1917

---

And now Gough's infantry were moving into position. Throughout June and July, a quarter of a million men of the Fifth Army approached the central section of the 15-mile front, which ran from Diksmuide in the north to Westhoek and Hooge in the south. Thousands came marching through northern France, en route to Belgium. 'A lovely moon was shining,' recalled the medical officer Captain Harold Dearden, of the Grenadier Guards, 'and the battalion looked like a great dusky caterpillar along the white road, the stretch-ers carried by the company stretcher bearers giving an added affect of horns along the creature's back.'[1]

Tens of thousands came up by light railway, open trolleys packed with men, waving their tin hats for the cameras and singing. A favourite was 'Good Old Whiskey': 'Here's to good old whiskey, mop it down / Here's to good old whiskey, mop it down / Here's to good old whiskey / It makes you feel so friskey [*sic*] . . .' etc.[2] Others came by lorry, travelling by night with the headlights off, jolting through the flash of shells and the starburst of Very flares, towards the Ypres front. 'It was just fumes and dust and smells all the time,' recalled Driver L. G. Burton, 'and sometimes there was gas too, sometimes incendiary shells. You could see them glowing red among the brick ends.'[3]

The march had moments of strange, earthly beauty, dashed by the sudden intrusion of war, noticed Captain Dearden. 'The trench,' he wrote in his diary near Elverdinghe, on 21 July, 'was passing under some beautiful willows . . . and the sides of it were all spar-kling in dewy grasses and flowers, while the duckboards stood out under your feet almost as if phosphorescent. I thought how lovely to smell the dampness of the grasses and put my hand to the elbow in them – they smelt of sulphur and gas only!'[4]

Gough's Fifth Army comprised four corps; a corps contained three infantry divisions, each of 20,000 men, nearly twice as large as a German division. Flanking them were six divisions of the First French Army, to the north, and several divisions of Plumer's Second Army to the south, incorporating the Anzacs. Lines of bell tents accommodated them in the forward areas, from where they would soon advance up the communication trenches to the fire trenches and jumping-off points at the front line. Behind the infantry, two cavalry divisions assembled – at Dickebusch, south-west of Ypres, and Elverdinghe, north-west of Ypres – ready to charge to the Passchendaele-Staden ridge once the infantry had broken through.

'[N]o one has any idea when, if ever, we are going to pop

the parapet,' wrote the Australian colonel Alex Wilkinson to his younger sister, Sidney ('Sid') on 8 June. 'If we do I shall be a certain starter . . . I should hate to be left behind. Nowadays we wear exactly the same clothes as the men when we attack. I don't like the idea much but we have no choice. I far prefer to be dressed as a gentleman!'[5]

German artillery tried to spread panic in the British ranks throughout July, firing thousands of gas rounds. Gas gongs rang out somewhere in the British lines almost every night. The men slept with their masks always by their sides; the officers in their dugouts behind heavy gas curtains. On 12 July, the Germans used mustard gas for the first time. It incapacitated about 1200 troops that day, and many more later.[6] Post-mortems of the lethal cases revealed severe internal ulceration of the throat and abdomen; the health of those who survived was often permanently impaired.[7]

Nobody saw the mustard gas coming, wrote Private Neville Hind:

> [T]he poor fellows who were in the first attack . . . got
> excited, rushed about, snatched up their rifles – and each
> time they touched anything, were badly burned and blistered
> . . . The gas thereupon attacked eyes, nose, mouth, and
> throat. They breathed it, with disastrous internal results
> . . . I am not exaggerating when I say that . . . a great many
> battalions were left with only a remnant of their men.[8]

The effects of the new weapon shocked the field hospitals. 'They cannot be bandaged or touched,' said a British nurse working with mustard gas cases. 'We cover them with a tent of propped-up sheets. Gas burns must be agonizing because usually the other cases do not complain, even with the worst wounds, but gas cases are invariably beyond endurance and they cannot help crying out.'[9]

—

Among those pouring into the British lines was nineteen-year-old Lieutenant Desmond Allhusen, the Old Etonian whom we last saw at Messines. Allhusen now commanded an 'unlucky platoon for officers', as his sergeant cheerfully informed him: his predecessor had gone mad. His regiment's role in the coming offensive was to launch diversionary attacks, to make the enemy think the offensive was starting here, north of Messines. They served as lures, sitting ducks for enemy guns: '[E]very day we were treated to at least one barrage'.[10]

Allhusen led a working party up to the front line:

> an endless toiling in the dark . . . always losing the man in front,
> or being lost by the man behind; everybody hurrying, trying
> to pass some special danger point before the inevitable shell
> came; then, the agonizing suspense when a flare went up and
> everybody stood motionless, cursing everybody else for moving,
> a long line of giant-like figures standing in absurd attitudes,
> the centre of a landscape as light as day; then, as the light died
> down, a sigh of relief and a hurrying forward again, men now
> cursing each other in whispers for making too much noise;
> worst of all perhaps the handing over of stores at some Company
> Headquarters, probably a well-known shell trap, sorting and
> counting things in the dark, signing receipts and hanging
> about . . . with the somewhat chilling knowledge that Germans
> were watching and listening somewhere in the darkness.[11]

On the night of Saturday 16 June, Allhusen and his men reached the frontline trenches. The Germans were 300 yards away, across a turnip field overgrown with coarse grass. He shared a hole cut in the trench wall that he compared with 'the once popular torture of putting people in a cage too small either to sit up or lie down in'. By night, the trenches came alive with patrolling, digging, setting wire, receiving deliveries, dispatching runners, preparing for the coming attack. By day, the men rested and did comparatively little. Both sides tended to greet the dawn with a 'light' bombardment of gas and heavy explosives, during which Allhusen and his platoon 'sat in our gas masks watching our breakfast getting cold'.[12]

Three days later, he noticed 'certain sinister preparations': sappers had begun installing a long line of 'dummy men', realistic models of soldiers made of wood and canvas, which they laid face down, ready to be pulled up by a rear cord. The next day, these armies of manikins were sent into battle: they 'rose' and 'advanced' through smoke flares, drawing German retaliatory fire. Within minutes, just one dummy was left standing. While the ruse distracted the Germans, a brigade of real British riflemen attacked the enemy lines, 'killed a lot of Germans' and captured many prisoners.[13]

In July, Allhusen's men were relieved – 'food, drink and water to wash in, and beds were all waiting for us' – pending their next rotation to the front. Within a few weeks, they would hear a lot about 'Menin Road', a name that sent 'a nightmare throughout the whole army'. Soldiers returning from it 'shivered when the Menin Road was mentioned', Allhusen wrote, 'and talked of it with a horror that I could not understand. I wondered vaguely what it was like.'[14]

—

For weeks, the batteries had been hauling up the guns, fixing the gun platforms into the spongy soil, firing off ranging rounds, and unloading thousands of cases of ammunition. There were 3000 guns, of all sizes – howitzers, 18-pounders and auxiliary weapons – the heaviest borne by truck or horse-drawn carriages. 'Massed artillery was drawn together the like of which the history of warfare had never seen before,' records a German historian. 'Enormous piles of munitions were stacked up everywhere . . . The whole might of the British Empire was mustered in methodical preparation to enter into a battle the duration, extent and means of which followed new principles hitherto unheard-of.'[15]

One battery commander then approaching the front was Lieutenant Allfree, the country solicitor and father of four, who arrived at corps headquarters in Poperinghe, three miles west of Ypres, on 24 June with his twenty-man advance party. One Colonel Budgeon showed him his designated battery position, in woods just short of Woesten. The colonel insisted that the guns be half-buried in pits to conceal them, rather than set on platforms.[16] Major Bell, Allfree's commanding officer, objected that the guns would sink if it rained. Budgeon wouldn't budge: the guns must be placed in pits.[17]

On 13 July, Allfree and his battery got their Movement Order, and were trucked to their billets in the village of Reninghelst, south of Poperinghe. Told to move his guns into position that night, he set off in a jeep, towing his gun carriage behind it, up the road out of Poperinghe. His lorries had already departed. Diverted by shellfire to Elverdinghe, he soon caught up with his trucks, which had stopped by the side of the road. The drivers were reluctant to continue: shelling up ahead had knocked out several vehicles and horse-drawn wagons. Allfree could hear the rounds exploding, but 'I had to go on. So I spoke to each of the lorry drivers, and told them what they had to face . . .' He ordered them 'to get on with all speed, and not to stop for anybody or anything'.[18] It was crucial to get the guns and supplies forward by daybreak, before the lorries became visible targets.

His driver proceeded carefully; the spokes on the wheel of the gun they towed had 'jarred loose'. Already, they had been forced to leave another gun behind due to a mechanical fault. They soon reached the scene of the shelling ahead – 'disembowelled horses and smashed up wagons and lorries and the smell of blood and high explosive'.[19] There was so much traffic the German guns couldn't miss striking a lorry if they got the range of the road right. Allfree drove around the mess. Two shells burst just behind and ahead of his vehicle. Then the gun carriage's axle came loose on the pot-holed road, and he abandoned it. He arrived without any of his guns, which were brought up the next day. Such was the exhausting journey to his position of just one British artilleryman.

Allfree's men set up the battery on the dead flat, soggy ground north of Ypres, near the ruins of the village of Boesinghe. Beside them, to the north, were the light-blue-uniformed French gunners, veterans of Verdun, with whom he and his men shared rations. Due east was the Steenbeek Canal, running north to south, the wettest section of the front, and beyond it 'Bocheland'.[20] The battery hid their guns in a small copse behind a clearing that contained the officers' mess, cookhouse, office and phone exchange. The officers slept in two huts erected under trees to the rear; the men tried to sleep in shallow dugouts near the battery, but nightly shelling forced them to move. Exhausted from lack of sleep, they were given the basement in the ruins of a nearby house.[21]

On 14 July, Allfree prepared for action. 'The feature of this offensive we are about to engage in,' he wrote in his diary, 'is to be a most intense artillery bombardment of the Enemy's trenches, wire and strong points for about a fortnight before the infantry attack.'[22] The next day, he visited his forward OP in a bombed house in Boesinghe, a few hundred yards from the German front lines, 'crouching and hurrying past the open gaps'.[23] Inside the ruin, he climbed a heap of bricks to the OP, a chamber of iron girders and concrete on the upper level, from where he raised a periscope covered in a sandbag slowly over the concrete wall: 'Through the eyepiece . . . I now saw for the first time the face of the ridge on the other side of the canal . . . and systems of Boche trenches.'[24] He began to check off the features of the landscape against those on his map: the edge of a wood, a crossroads, the ruins of a farmhouse – yes, they were all there.

His telephonist, sitting below, received a call from the battery commander, who wanted to know if he could 'range the battery on trench junction at [he read off the coordinates] . . . will you let him know if you can see it all right, Sir.' Allfree found the reference and, using his protractor, measured off the degrees between it and the nearest features, the crossroads and the corner of the wood.

Five minutes later, they fired the first round on the target. It exploded slightly short and to the left. '45 minutes to the right and plus,' Allfree instructed the telephonist, who relayed the message.

The battery fired another round: '1 degree right and minus.' After six to ten rounds, the guns were ranged accurately.[25]

—

In the German camp, the Fourth Army in Flanders had swollen to 65.5 divisions by mid-July, 43.5 of which had arrived since Messines, supported by 600 aircraft and 1162 guns (550 heavies).[26] Commanded by General Friedrich Sixt von Armin it deployed four combat groups strung out between the North Sea and the River Lys: a Marine Corps, defending the line from the coast to Schorbakke; the Diksmuide Group, holding the line to the Staden-Ypres railway; the Ypres Group, with its right flank near Pilckem and left flank two miles due east of Ypres, embracing the villages of Langemarck, Poelcappelle, Zonnebeke and Passchendaele; and the Wijtschate group, with its left flank near the ruins of the Hooge Chateau, defending the line across the Menin Road passing Zillebeke to the east up to the canal bend near Hollebeke.

On the ground, tens of thousands of German soldiers lined the ridges of the Salient. Every day, they fired mustard gas and explosive rounds onto the British and Dominion positions on the 'stage' below, where the first waves lay in wait for the order to attack.

By now, Haig had lost any shred of surprise. In mid-June, 'there was complete clarity on the German side that a major British offensive in Flanders was to be expected', General Hermann von Kuhl, Rupprecht's chief of staff, wrote. 'What was completely uncertain, however, was when the offensive was due to begin.' Clearly it was going to be something very big. For von Kuhl, it was obvious the British had imposed an operational pause in order to complete their preparations: 'The signs that intensive and long lasting battles were ahead were clearly visible. The main effort would be in the Flanders [sic].'[27]

The Germans waited and wondered when the blow would fall. Late July seemed likely: German patrols had reported the steady British build-up during the month – the arrival of tanks, guns and men, the construction of a new light railway – all pointing to an imminent attack. Ludendorff responded by authorising further reinforcements: eastern veterans and swiftly trained recruits were flung into the Albrecht Stellung, the front line of the German trench systems, or into the Eingreif divisions, held back in reserve ('Eingreif' literally meant an *automatic* application of extreme force – *Gegenstoss* – against any breach in the line, rather like plugging holes in a dyke.)[28]

July drew on. The long anticipation sapped morale. By midmonth, both sides were impatient for battle, to end the deleterious play of the imagination on the spirit. Unleashed by inaction, the mind revelled in phantoms, summoning hideous visions of dying alone in a shell hole, toppling forward into mud. Action would expunge them.

—

The opening bombardment fell on the German lines in the early hours of 15 July – a week *before* Haig would receive Cabinet approval to proceed with Third Ypres. Britain's massed artillery now revealed its terrific power: 752 heavy cannons, 324 4.5-inch howitzers and 1098 18-pounders unleashed the most powerful bombardment hitherto known to the history of war. For the next two weeks, they would fire 4.5 million projectiles onto the German trenches on the plains beneath Passchendaele Ridge, more than twice the number of rounds that had preceded the Somme.

In Allied eyes, the sight was one of preternatural beauty. '[T]he sky was heavy with black and very low lying clouds,' Captain Harold Dearden wrote in his diary on the night of 19 July. 'There was no moon, and every gun flash was thrown onto the clouds like a limelight in a theatre, the whole vault of the sky being ablaze with transient waves of fire – orange, red, yellow and violet . . . All along the front Verey [*sic*] lights danced, too, some white, some red, some blue, while from time to time a "golden rain" would bathe the whole area near it in a perfectly beautiful rose pink colour. The trees stood out jet black against the flaming sky, and the whole scene was one of simply appalling beauty.'[29]

A hail of shellfire, 'far worse than anything we had experienced on the Somme' fell on the German lines, recalled Vizefeldwebel Wellhausen. 'Shells, shrapnel balls and their pots rained down around our heads.'[30] The 'softening up' ranged across the German positions, shattering, cutting down, fragmenting every obstacle, every village, house, tree, human, animal caught within 2000–3000 yards of the British front. Blankets of British gas interspersed the hail of explosives, smothering the German soldiers' movements and stifling the delivery of relief, rations and ammunition.

The air war roared to life during gaps in the shell storm. Dozens of low-flying British aircraft 'circled our positions', recalled Fusilier Guard Häbel:

> Wherever an individual was seen, British airmen were on hand to direct the fire of their guns onto him. A sentry stood stock still, hidden by a groundsheet so that he could not be seen from the air in front of each dugout. Every few moments someone called to him to see if he was still alive ... The British were trying to extinguish all signs of life.[31]

German reserve battalions staggered up in gas masks. Like the Australians at Messines, several were annihilated before they reached the front. On their arrival, they found only utter desolation: no wire, no machine guns, no grenades, and no signs of proper trenches. The sparsely defended line had virtually ceased to exist. The surviving platoons and sections were cut off. Many had abandoned their mashed trenches and lay in shell craters. One company (of 88 men) were ordered to defend a 300-yard section of trench. At such low density, that was impossible. These men were not expected to live. Their role was to confuse and hinder the attacking British infantry; the real battle would occur further back.

Desperate survivors sent up red and green flares, the signal for immediate protective fire. The Germans had too few guns to sustain an effective counter-bombardment. Instead, they directed harassing fire at British troop concentrations: bridges, supply sections, railway lines, billets and munitions depots. They fired 533,000 rounds during the week starting 13 July, and 870,000 the following week. British firepower was about four times that.[32] The German gunners depended heavily on mustard gas, which brought them some 'relief': between 12 and 27 July, the British lost 13,284 dead, wounded and missing to enemy gas, artillery and aircraft attack.[33]

Many survivors of the bombardment, on both sides, suffered shell shock and 'windiness' (sheer terror). 'I have never seen anyone so hopelessly terrified,' Dearden observed of one lad, just out from England, who sat in his trench 'deathly pale', sweating and breathing hard, while 'his legs literally knocked together every time a shell came'. Dearden tried to reassure the youth, but resigned himself to the fact that 'he'll never do anything. He's just the type to desert . . .' Indeed, the company sergeant major expected it at any time, amusing himself by asking the lad whether he would prefer 'to be shot by the Boche or be shot by the English'. This line of questioning had not, Dearden noticed, 'steadied him any!'[34]

———

On 25 July, Haig received a cable from Robertson on behalf of the War Cabinet, authorising the commander-in-chief to proceed with the offensive he had already started. 'War Cabinet authorizes me to inform you,' Robertson stated, 'that having approved your plans . . . you may depend on their whole-hearted support; and that if and when they decide to reconsider the situation they will obtain your views before arriving at a decision as to cessation of operations.'[35] Haig replied that 'even if my attacks do not gain ground . . . we ought still to persevere in attacking the Germans in France. Only by this means can we win.'[36] That would be his guiding principle for the rest of the campaign: keep attacking.

On the cusp of battle, the relationship between Haig and Lloyd

George reached a new low – at the very moment when its healthy functioning was most needed. In a letter to Lord Derby, Haig drew a dark comparison between the government's lacklustre, mean-spirited support offered him and the 'whole-hearted, almost unthinking support given by our government to [Nivelle]'.[37]

Haig's bitterness was understandable, but his psychological disposition regrettable. His motives for action were turning dangerously personal. A garrulous political monkey sat in judgement on his shoulder, watching, waiting for him to fail. Haig would win this offensive and silence Lloyd George. How many young lives must be ruined or lost as a result of hasty decisions perverted into action by the smouldering hatred between two proud and wounded men?

———

In the days before the infantry charged, the guns fired virtually without pause. On 28 July, nineteen trainloads of rounds were unleashed on the German trenches and pillboxes. Dozens of British aircraft swooped on them. Soldiers lying in their trenches witnessed dogfights in the sky: bright red German aircraft came sweeping down to attack the British hornets that were strafing their positions. Notwithstanding a valiant effort from the Ypres Group's fighters, who managed to shoot down twelve British planes that day, it was all in vain: British superiority in guns, rounds and aircraft soon forced the Germans to abandon a strip of territory a mile wide and half a mile deep, the token front line. 'The first gap had been opened up,' noted the German history.[38]

In late July, British night patrols mounted a series of daring raids on the German lines, to gather some last intelligence on enemy positions. In one raid, 200 Highland Light Infantrymen captured 80 German prisoners and much information for very few losses (one killed, three missing and seventeen lightly wounded).[39]

On the 29th, two days before zero, British gunners ratcheted up the torment to a level beyond words. Many German soldiers broke or deserted. The rate of self-inflicted wounds rose. Despite all this, the bulk of the German Army stayed in their places, in the path, they all knew, of their destruction.

Mighty interests deigned to smile on this hellish place, to thank the men on the eve of battle. That day, the Kaiser sent his commanders a telegram (forwarded via Hindenburg):

> From the battlefields of Galicia . . . my thoughts turn, with a grateful heart, to the unforgettable deeds of the armies of the west; which, through their sacrificially tough endurance, are holding back the enemy . . . I am thinking especially of the courageous troops in Flanders, who have already been under artillery fire for weeks, unflinchingly awaiting the coming storm. You have my complete trust, together with that of the entire Fatherland, whose borders you are defending against enemies from all over the world. *Gott mit uns!*

On the eve of zero hour, the bombardment rose to a shrieking, crashing, whizzing pitch. Incendiary grenades, gas, smoke projectiles, heavy mortars, heavy explosives and shrapnel were flung at the German lines in what survivors would recall as 'a hurricane from hell'.[40] It was 'beyond anyone's experience', witnessed General von Kuhl:

> The entire earth of Flanders rocked and seemed to be on fire. This was not just drumfire; it was as though Hell itself had slipped its bonds. What were the terrors of Verdun and the Somme compared to this grotesquely huge outpouring of raw power? The violent thunder of battle could be heard in the furthest corner of Belgium. It was as though the enemy was announcing to the world: Here we come and we are going to prevail! [41]

Oberstleutnant Freiher von Forstner's cement pillbox rocked like a boat at sea. For the regimental commander, 30 July was the worst night he had experienced, when the shelling rose to an intensity that was incomprehensible, unbearable.

Flying shrapnel chopped into anyone who dared venture outside. A medical officer issued opium to calm nerves. At one point, a dense cloud of gas enveloped the bunker, sending long fingers of vapour into the vault-like rooms. Lacking enough gas masks to go around, the men in the outer shelters collapsed and died. Well before the British infantry attacked, artillery and gas had already inflicted more than 30,000 German casualties.[42]

The stunned survivors hoped and prayed for the enemy to advance; anything but this. The Eingreif counter-strike divisions were 'drawn up to the front in the highest readiness for action'.[43] Many ardently wished for battle, to escape 'the terrible effects of the barrage fire'.[44]

—

Haig's bombardment had wiped out the thinly defended German front but failed to destroy crucial points in von Lossberg's defensive shield. Most of the German pillboxes (and their machine guns), as well as the artillery at Gheluvelt and the heavy guns beyond Passchendaele Ridge, remained intact: 'in the crucial area of the Gheluvelt Plateau,' conclude Prior and Wilson, 'the preliminary bombardment failed comprehensively.'[45]

Haig knew this. Between 19 and 30 July, Fifth Army intelligence reports repeatedly warned of 'heavy fire' issuing from enemy batteries along the Gheluvelt higher ground, where the German guns were protected and hidden.[46] Instead of heeding his field commanders' accounts, Haig chose to believe the optimistic counsel of Lieutenant General Sir Noel Birch, artillery adviser at GHQ. British gunners had gained 'the upper hand over the German artillery', Birch claimed on 28 July, a point Haig underlined in his diary.[47] Plainly, they had not.

Past midnight, in the early hours of 31 July, the 3000 British guns fired as one, turning the whole front line between Boesinghe and the Lys into a 'blazing and shrapnel-belching strip slowly being wrapped in artificial mist'.[48] At 3.50 am, their roar drowned the commander's whistle. 'It sounded like all the guns in the world,' wrote Lieutenant Campbell, 'as though the sky was falling . . . as though the world itself was breaking into pieces.' Exploding British shells flashed across the eastern sky; in reply, helpless enemy SOS flares in red, green and yellow lit up the brawling world and showered earthward in 'a beautiful golden rain'.[49]

At that moment, in the German rear area, two leutnants, Höllwig and Boldt, were out riding. Boldt raised his hand and pointed to the western horizon, which seemed on fire. They heard a low rumble, like thunder. Boldt turned and said, 'That is the start of the battle of Flanders, Höllwig.'[50] Moments later, the first British infantrymen stormed over the parapets. From the shaking lips of German runners and down the few connected telephone lines came the code word, *Scharnhorst*. The ground battle had begun.

—

In the British camp, Gough's first wave of about 100,000 men slung on their equipment, tossed back their tot of rum, dragged on a Woodbine and urinated. Each man wore full battle dress, with bayonets fixed, and carried a sandbag of Mills bombs around his neck. Every second man had a spade or trenching tool 'shoved down his back'. Every third man carried a pair of wirecutters. Their regiments hailed from the English shires, the Midlands and the North, the Scottish Highlands and the Welsh hills. They included Guardsmen, Regulars, Territorials and New Army men, with French, Australian and New Zealand troops in support. (See Order of Battle, Appendix 5.)

At 3.50 am, the creeping barrage began. A six-minute storm of steel – millions of shrapnel balls – burst over the German lines. It paused. The whistles blew. The leading infantrymen scrambled up the fire steps and poured across no-man's-land, heading for the German lines, 300 yards away.

The barrage moved ahead of the men, at the pace of 100 yards every four minutes. None had experienced drumfire of this density. It stunned the attackers as much as the defenders, as Private W. Lockey of The Sherwood Foresters recalled: 'It was an inferno. Just a solid line of fire and sparks and rockets lighting up the sky.'[51] Within moments, one German commander witnessed the destruction or scattering of his entire company.

Heavy, low clouds obscured the seam of sunlight on the eastern horizon, and removed the hope of air support. For now, the attacking army navigated by compass. Ahead of them, a haunting, unnatural glow fell over the field. Red and green flares, the smoke of the barrage and the distant flash of guns lent a wonderland sensation to the scene: this was surreal, the stuff of dreams, not a battlefield. Long shadows loomed and coloured lights flickered through the curtain of fire, revealing the shapes of stumps, ridges and ruins. The British pressed on, a swarm of little khaki creatures, miniaturised among the craters over which they scrambled, up and down, in a frantic effort to keep pace with the inside arc of bursting bombs.

—

At first, the Allies advanced with minimal trouble: in the north, the six French divisions made great progress, moving quickly against light resistance. Little had been expected of these veterans of Nivelle's disaster, on Gough's far northern flank. They redeemed themselves, destroying most of the enemy's concrete bunkers and advancing further than their allocated 2500 yards.

The Fifth Army encountered scant resistance – at first. Most of the frontline Germans who were not dead or wounded simply surrendered. By 4.40 am, Gough's men had reached their first goals, advancing 800 yards 'across shell-hole pitted Pilckem ridge'.[52] They encountered a dazed and confused enemy. '[W]hat had once been the German front line . . . didn't exist,' W. Lockey recalled. 'There was not a bit of wire, hardly a trench left, that hadn't been blown to smithereens by our barrage.'[53]

Well-trained platoons silenced the concrete bunkers with grenades, trench mortars and Lewis guns, concentrating fire through the loopholes or rear doors. They seized Hollebeke village and Pilckem Ridge, and reached their designated lines. In the south, the Anzacs captured German outposts west of the Lys and at La Basse-Ville. 'Moppers up' cleared the enemy trenches and pillboxes, and fresh troops came up to relieve the first wave. Their task: to carry the offensive baton to the next line, some 1000 yards ahead.

Seizing on gains at Pilckem Ridge, the Guards managed to lay rough bridges of wire matting over the Steenbeek, a marshy creek beyond the village. By 5.20 am, the Coldstream and Grenadier Guards had forded it behind a barrage of smoke canisters. Later, British forces made steady advances along a 3000-yard front, crossing the Steenbeek, and by 8 am had reached their designated coloured line and captured the village of Saint Julien. By 9.30 am, the Coldstream Guards had established outposts on the eastern bank of the creek, but the heavy German presence along the road to Langemarck dissuaded them from pressing on.

———

That sketch of the opening attack passes over the appalling scenes on the ground. The famous Highlander Division, the 51st, for example, were in the van of the attack. Crossing the Yser Canal, with the Gordons out in front and the Royal Scots close behind, they suffered few casualties until they reached 'Minty's Farm', as Lieutenant J. Annan recounted:

> [T]he shells started falling all around. We got a slashing there all
> right. As we were struggling up to it one of the boys got hit with
> a huge shell fragment. It sliced him right in two. He dropped
> his rifle and bayonet and threw his arms in the air, and the
> top part of his torso fell back to the ground. The unbelievable
> thing was that the legs and the kilt went on running, just
> like a chicken with its head chopped off! One of my boys – I

think it was his special pal – went rushing after him.[54]

Past Minty's Farm, Annan saw, for the first time, a man going berserk:

> He came running back towards us like a spectre waving its
> arms, and shouting and yelling, 'Mother! Mother! Mother!'
> . . . [I] got hold of him and said, 'Come on. Come on over
> here, till we see to you.' But he was like a mad thing. He
> just shook me off and ran on yelling, 'Mother! Mother!'
> completely off his head. That was the last we saw of him.[55]

The Northamptonshire Regiment entered the tortuous terrain around the Bellewaerde Lake, which split them in two: '[T]he entire area was also covered in exploded trees, which were perfect hiding places for machine gun nests.'[56] They captured the frontline trenches, where the severely demoralised enemy surrendered, but heavy German counter-attacks held them off the 'blue line', with heavy losses. They eventually prevailed, thanks to several acts of astonishing courage, notably that of Thomas Riversdale Colyer-Fergusson, a 21-year-old captain who led ten men in storming a trench, captured an entire company of German soldiers, and went on to seize two machine guns, killing 35 Germans with one of the guns. A little later, a sniper shot him. For 'an amazing record of dash, gallantry and skill for which no reward can be too great having regard to the importance of the position won', Colyer-Fergusson was awarded a posthumous Victoria Cross.[57]

The Notts & Derbyshire Regiment (The Sherwood Foresters) were to take the village of Westhoek, past the Bellewaerde Lake. 'We weren't so much running forward,' said Lockey, 'as scrambling on over fallen trees and shell-holes . . . the German field artillery was firing back, so there were shells exploding all around. The chap on my right had his head blown off, as neat as if it had been done with a chopper . . . My pal, Tom Altham, went down too, badly wounded, and Sergeant-Major Dunn got a shell to himself.'[58]

In German eyes, the 'dark figures' of the Tommies came at them in ceaseless waves, survivors recalled. When a man fell dead or wounded, another instantly filled the gap in the line.

Faced with annihilation by the oncoming infantry, many German soldiers tried to break *back* through the creeping barrage, and reform in the rear. In one such action, Fusilier Guard Musolf shouldered his wounded officer and carried him safely through the British artillery shield, earning an Iron Cross First Class for bravery.

Leutnant Wiemes and his men were not so lucky, finding them-selves surrounded by a pack of 'drunk British soldiers' (for which there is no evidence) who 'came at us with fixed bayonets'. Only the intervention of a British corporal who 'leapt between us and his men' ensured that 'we were not cut down'.[59] It seems they had witnessed the results of Campbell's bayonet lessons rather than the effects of too much rum.

A Bavarian battalion was left stranded as battle swirled around them, with no means of communicating: they had no flares or sig-nals; the runners couldn't get through; the messenger dogs were dead or wounded; the telephone lines destroyed; and two of their four car-rier pigeons incapacitated. In desperation, the commander laid out panels for aircraft to read: 'There is a battalion command post here . . . Support is needed.'

—

The seizure of Pilckem Ridge denied the Germans an observation point over Ypres, in that section of the front – ominously, Gheluvelt retained that advantage. Yet Gough failed to consolidate his new possessions, to allow time for the guns to catch up with the men. Third Ypres was supposed to open with a series of incremental attacks, Haig had belatedly advised, 'limited to the range of the mass of supporting artillery',[60] not a frantic rush beyond the limit of the guns into enemy-infested country. Instead, Gough wanted to accel-erate, to take more territory. He ordered his armies to push on. This defied the wisdom of his own intelligence, who warned that the enemy's 'defence in depth' would immeasurably stiffen the deeper the British advanced. It was a great, gaping trap.

Nor had the British penetrated the higher ground at Gheluvelt Plateau. Here, the Germans held on, and were yet to reveal their hidden strength, held well back on the plateau. Gough had decided not to concentrate his attack here, against Haig's advice. His men were about to face the consequences. Gough well knew the enemy's strength at Gheluvelt (Fifth Army intelligence had been thorough): three defensive lines, each 1500 yards deep, bristling with German troops, heavily supported by Eingreif in the rear, and all obscured behind the remains of three blasted forests on the western edge of the ridge, dubbed Shrewsbury Forest, Sanctuary Wood and Chateau Wood, 'a wilderness of fallen tree trunks, shell holes and debris', impassable to tanks.[61] Well-hidden pillboxes clustered at vital points, such as the Lower Star Post and Clapham Junction, with clear views across the attacking terrain.

Haig and Gough could not know the extent to which the German forces on Gheluvelt had survived the two-week bombardment. British artillery had failed to destroy the massed ranks of guns and men that lurked on the plains beyond the broken tree lines. This failure would have dire consequences. At first, however, the results seemed promising – too promising. In places, the Germans were luring the British towards the narrow defiles between the woods; elsewhere, they put up ferocious resistance, funnelling them into the gaps. The Worcestershire Regiment, for example, moved relatively easily, reached the blue line, captured or shot the few Germans they found in the trenches, and continued to the black line, eliminating en route a pillbox on the Menin Road. Far tougher resistance met the unfortunate 21st Brigade, whose troops won the ruins and ridge of Stirling Castle after a bloody ordeal up the slopes beneath well-placed machine-gun nests.

Could tanks break the Germans at Gheluvelt? They gave it a go, with devastating results. The huge, lugubrious machines rumbled down the Menin Road, in an attempt to destroy the giant pillbox at Clapham Junction. Their great tracked bodies made slow progress and were easy targets for German armour-piercing rounds. Of 48 tanks involved in this action, nineteen reached the front lines, and 'all but one became casualties'.[62] The rest were abandoned or hit by shells or anti-tank guns. A 'tank graveyard' of burned-out steel hulks lay strewn along the road for the duration of the war.

—

God and Nature intervened: God, in the form of a papal plea to halt the hostilities. The British victory the Lord had ordained had not persuaded the Catholic Church. On 1 August, Pope Benedict XV put forward a peace proposal.

'To the Heads of the Belligerent Peoples', he declared:

> ... Whoever has followed Our work during the three unhappy years which have just elapsed, has been able to recognize ... Our resolution of absolute impartiality ... We have never ceased to urge the belligerent peoples and Governments to become brothers once more ... Shall, then, the civilized world be naught but a field of death? And shall Europe, so glorious and flourishing, rush, as though driven by universal madness, towards the abyss, and lend her hand to her own suicide?'[63]

Futile in bending the minds of the belligerent governments, who ignored it, the Vatican irritated Britain by singling out the naval blockade as an obstacle to peace; and angered Germany by offering them no spoils.

The London *Times* thundered that the Pope's appeal was 'pro-German', 'anti-Ally' and 'permeated with German ideas'.[64] Ludendorff described the Pope's actions as having 'an evil influence on the conduct of the war'.[65]

Nature intervened, in the form of torrential rain. The rain had started spitting down at dawn, soon after the whistles blew. Other than a brief spell of sun at around 10 am, it rained for the rest of the day. The rain fell in heavy, sidelong sheets upon a field churned and cratered over two weeks of bombardment. The shelling had destroyed the fragile drainage system of creeks and canals that emptied the former marshes between Ypres and Passchendaele. The commanders on the spot saw at once that the undrained ground west of Passchendaele Ridge would soon turn into a brown soup, a man-made swamp. A human tragedy of staggering proportions was about to unfold in Flanders fields.

The little 'beeks' or streams that traversed the line of attack overflowed their banks. The putrid liquid merged with the rainwater that filled the shell holes, until the natural and man-made boundaries between earth and water ceased to exist, and the drains and conduits sat gathering water without beginning, direction or end. The Salient was slowly turning into a mud pan, pocked with thousands of shell craters of unknown depth that oozed brown slime. The attack began to seize up on this man-made bog. Soldiers scrambling over water-logged craters couldn't keep pace with the barrage, which started to thin out for lack of guns – leaving the men naked to German retaliation.

At 7 am Campbell's gun battery arrived at the stream near Bellewaerde in pouring rain. They stopped, unable to advance further. His commanding officer joked whether headquarters 'had got any boats. We could take the guns up by boats if they still want us to advance.' He could 'hardly wait' for *The Times*, he added, to read about another great victory.[66]

Nor had the British gunners any clear idea where the furthermost men were, because most of the British telephone lines were cut, and the runners couldn't get back in time. At Sanctuary Wood, an entire British division fell outside the barrage's protective cover, leaving them severely disorientated and exposed to terrific fire. A whole brigade got lost, and entered Chateau Wood instead of Glencorse Wood, sustaining huge casualties.

—

The rain benefited the Germans on the less wet, higher ground, at the very moment when von Lossberg's counter-strike forces were moving up. A British forward observer spotted the first of them, at 11.30 am: 'a vast amount of German infantry going along the Passchendaele Ridge'.[67]

They attacked soon after 2 pm. Thousands rushed forward to reoccupy trenches and pillboxes they had earlier lost. In a series of humiliating setbacks, the Eingreif bundled back whence they came some of Britain's most famous regiments. Even the Guards that had forded the Steenbeek were forced to retire, blaming their failure on the weakness on their flanks.

Low-flying German aircraft relayed the new British positions to enemy batteries at Gheluvelt, who replied with a storm of well-aimed rounds. By late afternoon, the British forces astride the Saint Julien–Poelcappelle road, including the Black Watch and Hertfordshire Regiments, had been forced back to their second starting line. Saint Julien was lost (though regained two days later).[68] The Hertfordshires were wiped out. One of their quartermasters, sent to deliver 600 rations to the regiment, found only the brigadier in a captured German pillbox that was 'rocking like a boat in a rough sea'. 'He just stood and looked at me,' said the quartermaster. 'After a while he said, "I'm sorry, Quarters, I'm afraid there isn't *any* Hertfordshire Regiment."'[69]

Chaos ensued. Nobody in the rear knew what was happening at the front, or where the front was. The rain steadily worsened. The telephones failed. German and British guns bombed their own sides. More Eingreif divisions appeared out of nowhere. British platoons scattered. The Germans were up to their knees in water, trying to retake the Steenbeek.

All down the front, the British were being forced back. The Lincolnshires and Irish Rifles lost the ground they'd gained that morning, and recaptured it by 5 pm. The Cameron Highlanders, short of ammunition, alone at the green line and facing a torrential counter-attack, had no choice other than to abandon the ground they'd won at such cost in the morning. By late afternoon, the British forces held a tenuous grip on a jagged new line, vulnerable to enemy artillery as long as Gheluvelt remained in German hands. Stragglers and the shell-shocked were found wandering the field, lost, demented, laughing or crying, and easy prey to the provost marshals who scoured the lines for deserters.

—

The afternoon rain turned into a torrential downpour, a prelude to the heaviest August precipitation in Flanders in decades.[70] It rained almost an inch that day, more than had fallen in the previous 30. Darkness fell. It rained all night. The battle resumed the next morning in a downpour. The rains fell all day for the next four days. With nowhere to drain, the water overran the shell holes and formed putrid little lakes that obscured the corpses of men and horses. Duckboards were laid between shell holes, forcing the men to advance in single files.

Moving up the guns and supplies in these conditions challenged the toughest constitutions. It had to be done: if the artillery could not maintain contact with the advancing infantry, all was lost. Teams of horses were unable to haul the guns over mud. Limbers proved useless. A tug of war with the mud ensued, as artillerymen heaved their guns yard by yard. The hardy mule, a gas mask looped over its head, carried up rations and ammunition.

'Liquid mud' filled the craters, Yoxall wrote to his mother on 2 August. Four men had drowned, he had heard: '[T]hey must have been stuck in the mud, become exhausted, and fallen face forward.'[71] That day, the *Daily Mail* reported scenes of men scarcely able to walk in full equipment, 'much less dig'. 'Every man was soaked through and was standing or sleeping in a marsh.'[72]

The heavy guns sank, as Lieutenant Allfree had feared, 'very deep in the mud, and caused a great deal of trouble'.[73] His men rammed bundles of faggots and brushwood behind the trails. The battery moved forward to the village of Boesinghe that night. Leading the advance party, Allfree came upon a horse harnessed to a French wagon 'with its hind legs so deeply sunk in the mud, that it could not move'.[74] The horse's stomach was level with the ground, and the animal had to be dug out.

Allfree found the ruined village in 'a ghastly state! . . . Everything was wet, dirty and miserable.' After two days of fighting, 'the Hun . . . had been pushed back to beyond the ridge on the other side of the canal', and now Red Cross men, wagons, ambulances and guardsmen thronged the cleared street. 'Stretcher parties were bearing in wounded from the shelled, desolate mud swamps,' he recalled. Many 'had been lying out there since yesterday in the rain and half-buried in mud'. A stretcher party usually took six hours to bring in a single wounded man, he calculated, and then went straight back out 'to recover another poor fellow'.[75]

On 6 August, Allfree went out with a fellow officer and five telephonists to fix the broken telephone line between the battery and the new OP:

> It was the first time I had been across the Canal into that
> desolate, muddy, shell-strafed area . . . It would have been
> impossible to find one square yard without a shell hole . . . How
> on Earth [*sic*] the Infantry had advanced over such country
> is beyond my comprehension. But they had done so . . .[76]

Shellfire had cut the wire in five places. They joined up each break and bound it with insulation tape.

The dreadful state of the terrain alarmed the Tank Corps, whose machines had not experienced such conditions. A tank intelligence officer, Major Fuller, drew up maps showing the flooded areas, in blue, deemed impassable to tanks. He had it sent to Haig's office. Charteris intercepted and returned the map with a curt note containing the now infamous phrase: 'Send us no more of these ridiculous maps.'[77] Haig's intelligence chief was said to have remarked to an aide, 'I'm certainly not going to show *this* to the commander-in-chief. It would only depress him.'[78]

Haig had dreaded the weather turning against him, but he had not anticipated an inch and a half in the first four days (and five inches for the month, almost double the average).[79] Yet his marked facility for finding a dram of good news in a barrel-load of bad kept his spirits up: to advance 'a bit', even in this deluge, he wrote, 'was all to the good'.[80] 'A bit', as it proved, was all they could manage. On 4 August, Haig called off the attack; it would resume on the 10th, after the fields had a chance to dry.

———

In the lull, Haig received a gloomy cable from Robertson, reporting on the Anglo-French-Italian conference that had taken place in London on 7–8 August. Lloyd George and the Italian Government were 'anxious to get heavy artillery out of us, and even divisions', Robertson wrote, in time for a fresh offensive on the Isonzo, scheduled for 15 September. To his chagrin, the British Government 'showed that they attached no importance to the great and serious operations now taking place on the West [*sic*] Front . . .' He summed up the meeting as 'the usual waste of time'.[81]

In fact, Lloyd George had said much worse, according to a letter to Haig from Robertson's deputy. The prime minister had told the entire conference that he had 'no confidence' in the British general staff or their plans, and that 'he had known all along that this latest offensive [in Flanders] was doomed to failure'. The prime minister added that 'he'd backed the wrong horse. We ought instead to have reinforced the Italians.'[82] For now, Robertson persuaded the War Cabinet to adhere to Haig's Flanders Offensive, a gesture of loyalty that Haig would fail to repay.

———

The 10th was another miserably wet day. Two British divisions (the 18th and 25th) dragged themselves forward beneath a down-pour that drenched what little had dried. Great pools of stinking mud greeted them. In a triumph of will, the 25th Division captured Westhoek village, the only success of the day; the 18th stormed Glencorse Wood and struggled in vain to clear Inverness Copse. The attack stalled, after German guns and Eingreif units had inflicted 2200 British casualties. General Sir Ivor Maxse's 18th Division were 'bundled back' to the starting line, 'a rare defeat for the justly renowned division which . . . had been unbeatable on the Somme'.[83] Haig misinterpreted the result as 'most satisfactory': 'our guns killed vast numbers of the enemy when forming up for counter-attacks. Six of these were attempted but all failed.'[84]

The 10th was a shocking day for Lieutenant Patrick Campbell. Taking his turn as forward observation officer, he reached his des-tination, Bank Farm, a captured pillbox just across the Steenbeek, where the setting sun shone through Ypres 'in the saucer below us', like the ruins of an ancient city.[85]

A line of shell-shocked men came down the slope towards him: 'They didn't seem to be walking properly, they looked as though they were walking in their sleep.' A colonel addressed them, but they filed past without saluting or noticing him.[86]

To escape German shelling, Campbell sat with his men in a trench lined with a concrete wall. The wounded kept coming in, but there was no room for all of them. The hopeless cases were left out-side: 'They were a long time dying . . . Their crying rose to a scream as they heard the sound of [a round] coming, then fell away to a moan after the shell had burst.'[87]

Stuck in a trench beside the dead and dying, under incessant bombardment, Campbell's nerves almost broke. He would never forget his 'paralysing fear'. He closed his eyes: 'I was conscious only of my own misery. I lost . . . all count of time. There was no past to remember or future to think about. Only the present. The present agony of waiting, waiting for the shell that was coming to destroy us, waiting to die . . .' He could not move: 'I had lost all power over my limbs . . . fear of that sort was horrible, debasing, abject.'[88]

The only man he told of this experience at the time was a soldier called Vernon, for whom he 'felt an extraordinary affection': 'I wanted to have him always by my side. Together we had been down into the valley of the shadow, together we had climbed a little way out of it, a little way out of the pit. But we had nothing else to say to each other. We parted on the road, in the place where we had met, just eighteen hours earlier.'[89]

Campbell survived this debilitating fear, the cumulative effect of a sequence of horrifying events: the hundreds of dead faces in the shell holes; the shell-shocked 'puppets of men' who shuffled down the hill; and the incessant German bombardment. Millions of troops had or would share his experience, of the demoralising effect of concentrated shellfire, the fear of which he rationalised in later days as 'another pain' he had to endure but would never conquer.[90]

—

Haig's bludgeoning was scheduled to resume on the 14th, but a heavy thunderstorm delayed it for two days, giving the commander-in-chief a chance to reply to Robertson. Haig's letter, on 13 August, expressed with unusual clarity his belief, at that point, in how the war should be fought (the emphases are his): '[T]he only *sound* policy is for the government to support me whole-heartedly, and concentrate all possible resources here. And do it *now*, while there is time, instead of continuing to discuss other enterprises.' If he received the men and matériel needed to keep his units up to strength, 'we are convinced we can beat the enemy'. He based his confidence in victory on three '*facts*': 'the poor state of the German troops, high standard of efficiency of our own men, [and] power of artillery to dominate enemy's guns . . .'[91]

The fresh attack (the Battle of Langemarck) began at 4.45 am on the 16th, across the whole front, in a virtual rerun of the plan of 31 July. The morning was mysteriously bright and sunny. And then, later that day, as if on cue, the skies opened. Had the very guns punctured the heavens, the troops joked? In the north, the British did well, advancing beyond Langemarck and claiming the village. The French divisions also captured their objectives – 1.2 miles of mud – thanks to weak German defences in their sector to the north of the Salient.

On the crucial Gheluvelt Plateau, however, the Germans still held firm. The British guns had not dominated here; nor were the Germans demoralised. Well-trained British troops, veterans of the Somme and Messines, bashed away at the ridgeline for twelve hours, gaining little ground. One brigade attacked with inadequate artillery protection and was virtually wiped out. Even before one division went over the top, it had suffered 2000 casualties to enemy shells and gas; it attacked anyway, with 330 instead of the normal 750 men per battalion.[92]

—

A tragedy befell the two Irish divisions – the 36th (Ulster), formerly the Ulster Volunteer Force, and the 16th (Irish), formerly John Redmond's 'Irish Brigade' – in the attack on Zonnebeke Ridge. It was the second time the 'Protestant' and 'Catholic' divisions went into battle side by side, after their triumph at Messines. They attacked again with the same great camaraderie, but after a few hours both had virtually 'ceased to exist as fighting formations'.[93] A chaplain, the Jesuit Father William Doyle, spent all day on 16 August in no-man's-land administering last rites, to soldiers of both faiths. He found one young soldier 'lying on his back, his hands and face a mass of blue phosphorus flame smoking horribly in the darkness'.[94] Doyle had earned the Military Cross at the Somme, and 'many of the men believed him to be immortal'.[95] He died a few days later, struck by a shell while comforting the wounded; three officers recommended him for a Victoria Cross but he received nothing: 'the disqualification of being an Irishman, a Catholic and a Jesuit, proved insuperable,' according to one witness.[96]

The heavy Irish losses marked a cruel end to one of the bravest commitments on the Western Front. Since entering the line, the

Irish division had lost 7800 men, almost half their number; both divisions had suffered terribly on the Somme. Their latest sacrifice earned them little more than Gough's scorn and an entry in Haig's diary: 'Gough was not pleased with the action of the Irish divisions,' Haig wrote. 'They seem to have gone forward but failed to keep what they had won . . . The men are Irish and apparently did not like the enemy's shelling, so Gough said.'[97]

Gough, an avowed loyalist, deeply distrusted the Catholic division. A corps commander had told him (he later claimed) that the Catholics under his command were 'no longer politically reliable'.[98] Neither man produced any evidence. In truth, both Catholic and Protestant Irishmen were physically exhausted, their ranks heavily depleted: 200 Ulstermen had fallen dead or wounded in the first half-minute of the offensive, according to the historian Cyril Falls.[99] The survivors of both units were soon relieved.

Unsure of the state of the terrain at this time, and thus the consequences of his orders, Haig continued to press Gough to send more demoralised men into battle: the 53rd Brigade of the 8th Division, for example, whose commander, General Higginson, had vigorously protested four times that his men were 'not fresh enough to carry out an attack' ('not fresh' being a euphemism for utterly spent). Pitched against well-intact German positions, his men soon found themselves being bombed by both German and British artillery. The attack failed.

The London Territorials elected to charge through to their final objectives rather than hold their positions until relief arrived. Their aggressive spirit pleased Gough, until he saw the result: an entire battalion vanished in a blaze of German guns. Most of the Royal Fusiliers and London Rifle Brigade 'pressed boldly through Glencorse Wood and on into Polygon Wood and were, quite simply, never seen again'. A company of the 8th Middlesex similarly 'just disappeared' into the maw of the Eingreif.[100] The rest were thrust back to the start line, with the enemy in hot pursuit. So serious and chaotic was the situation, writes McNab, that British shells were brought down just in front of the original start line, to hold off the Germans, even though many

British troops were still forward.[101] Such were the results of attacking without artillery protection – a lesson learned at the Somme, Loos and other battles, and forgotten or ignored here.

The Battle of Langemarck ended in a bloody fiasco. Gough's army had gained 1500 yards of swamp in the north, fragments of bog in the centre and nothing at Gheluvelt in the south, for the cost, thus far, of 15,000 dead, wounded and missing. Haig cast this debacle as 'most successful' in the north and centre, while conceding 'only moderate' gains on the right flank at Gheluvelt. Nonetheless, 'many Germans had been killed'.[102]

That afternoon, before the extent of the failure had been revealed, Robertson's staff car swept into Haig's headquarters at Chateau de Beaurepaire in Montreuil, bearing unusually upbeat news: the prime minister had relayed a friendly message of confidence in his commander. Haig brushed this off with a curt thank you and told Robertson to relay to Lloyd George the army's core demands: 'what I want is tangible support. *Men, guns, aeroplanes.* It is ridiculous to talk about supporting me "wholeheartedly" when men, guns, rails, etc. are going in quantities to Egypt for the Palestine expedition; [and] guns to the Italians . . .'[103]

—

The disaster at Gheluvelt soon reached GHQ. Haig blamed the failure on sheer haste, 'due to commanders being in too great a hurry!!!' Three more days of bombardment would have destroyed the enemy's guns and concrete defences, he claimed.[104] He had argued for haste prior to the attack, however, making the complaint self-incriminating. As Prior and Wilson assert, Haig had failed 'to act on his insight and assert his authority'.[105]

A truthful picture seemed unable to penetrate the thickets of manipulated intelligence (Charteris's dubious dispatches), scapegoating (Gough's 'Irish card') and self-deceit (Lieutenant-General Claud Jacob's mistaken assertion that II Corps had captured important ground at Gheluvelt). On four occasions, Charteris visited the front, and noted the dreadful conditions; but he consistently underrated the German defences.

Gough continued bizarrely to blame his men (not only the Irish ones), and even suggested that officers and non-commissioned officers (NCOs) who had failed to hold their captured ground be court-martialled for dereliction of duty. Frontline soldiers were being relieved too soon, he added, a practice that must stop to avoid a troop shortage. He did not clarify when the men should be relieved.

At this point, common sense (if not ordinary compassion) might have intruded and suggested the blindingly obvious: that thousands of soldiers' lives were being wasted; that the methods were not working; and that it was time to adopt different tactics or call off a battle that had literally bogged down. In a moment of clarity, Gough saw this: 'tactical success was not possible' in such conditions, he told Haig on 16 August, and he urged his commander to abandon the attack.[106] Haig decided to press on.

—

A rare tank breakthrough on the 20th along the St Julien–Poelcappelle road, which was firm enough to bear their weight, encouraged Haig to resume the battle two days later. One last push, he reckoned, should do the trick. The tanks destroyed a few pockets of German resistance, clearing the area for the British infantry. The machines were unserviceable elsewhere, sinking whenever they left the few tracts of solid ground. And relief was at hand, in the form of the inexperienced 61st Division, who came up to fill the gap left by the broken Ulstermen. They joined a series of smaller, no less lethal, attacks on the 22nd, which persisted throughout the day, with heavy casualties for the capture of Inverness Copse.

With dreary inevitably, the rain pelted down on 23 August, and it wouldn't let up for another four days. The relieving soldiers had to advance in single file along the duckboards laid between the craters. Anyone who slipped into a shell hole risked drowning, borne down by the total weight of his pack and battle dress (60–70 pounds). An unknown number, probably several thousand, perished this way, because it was extremely difficult to drag a heavily burdened soldier out of the sucking slime. Among them was Lieutenant Colonel Edgar Mobbs DSO, 35, of Northampton, whose battalion called themselves Mobbs Own, such was the immense popularity of this former English rugby international. As he lay sinking in a shell hole with a wound to the neck, Mobbs managed to send a runner back with details of his position. The runner never reached his destination, and Mobbs's body was never recovered.[107]

The long files of men were easy targets. Many were shot off the duckboards and bled to death as they drowned. Would-be rescuers could find no traction, or trees from which to attach ropes, to drag them out. None would forget the sound of a man drowning slowly in mud, 'a terrible kind of gurgling noise [of] . . . the wounded, lying there sinking, and this liquid mud burying them alive, running over their faces and into their mouth and nose'.[108]

Scenes of drowning horses were similarly horrifying. Unaware of what was happening to them, the poor creatures bucked and jerked about in the grip of the mud. Most were shot before they drowned – a mercy not extended to drowning men.

The German horses, foaming with fear at the approach of the barrage, reared up and often slipped and fell into shell holes. One officer, unable to shoot his beloved horse, saw 'a spray of mud' where the poor animal 'was still fighting and losing the battle against suffocation'.[109] In time, the rigid corpses of men and horses protruded from the swamps, and 'inside them, oblivious to the din of battle, the rats were at their disgusting work'.[110]

A pathetic symbol of the effects of the weather was a carrier pigeon, with an important message attached to its leg, so wet and caked in mud 'it just flapped into the air and then came straight down again', as noted by a member of the Yorkshire company to whom the pigeon belonged. To the soldiers' horror, the bird then started 'walking towards the German line', 100 yards away, bearing its secret message. So they shot it.[111]

—

Haig had been alert to the possibility of a wet month, but he could not have expected the wettest August in Flanders in 75 years. Five times as much rain fell that month as in the same period in 1915 and 1916.[112] Not since Marlborough's 1707 Flanders campaign against the French had soldiers fought in such conditions near Ypres in August. Marlborough had himself written, 200 years before, that he 'could scarcely stir out of his quarters, the dirt being up to the horses' bellies, which is very extraordinary this month'; and when he was able to advance, many of his soldiers perished in the sloughs along the roadsides.[113]

Haig's own report echoed Marlborough's experience:

The low-lying, clayey soil, torn by shells and sodden
with rain, turned to a succession of vast muddy pools.
The valleys of the choked and overflowing streams were
speedily transformed into long stretches of bog, impassable
except by a few well-defined tracks, which became
marks for the enemy's artillery. To leave these tracks
was to risk death by drowning . . . In these conditions
operations of any magnitude became impossible . . .[114]

Haig's post-war critics claim that he should have expected and prepared for this. Their case hinges on Charteris's gross exaggeration in his memoir that the clouds in Flanders opened in August 'with the regularity of the Indian monsoon'. (Charteris then contradicted this, claiming that 1917 was the wettest August in Flanders in 30 years.)[115] Haig haters would insist, years later, that the British commander had 'made a reckless gamble . . . on the chance of a rainless autumn' (Lloyd George); that he was well aware of the likelihood of a deluge (Liddell Hart and Leon Wolff); or that his offensive 'relied on a drought of Ethiopian proportions to ensure success' (Gerard de Groot).[116] None of these criticisms was fair.

The man whose job it really was to predict the weather also mis-judged it. Haig's weatherman, Lieutenant Colonel Ernest Gold, a fellow of Trinity College, Cambridge, and an outstanding meteor-ologist, had reckoned on 'bright [i.e. clear] weather' for early August. He recanted as the clouds drew in, but gave Haig no cause to expect a biblical deluge. In fact, August was usually the drier summer month, and October the wettest of the year, according to the evidence of 30 prior summers.[117] Gold's forecasts for September and October were less inaccurate, encouraging Haig to hope that he 'had no reason to anticipate an abnormally wet October'.[118] What all these arguments miss, however, is the effect of even normal rainfall on a battlefield covered in shell holes that lacked a working drainage system.

—

More attacks went forward on 24 August, under more rain. This time, the infantry would have no effective barrage because the artil-lerymen could not get their guns up in time. In scenes reminiscent of the Somme, Gough pressed ahead, as ordered, though he knew it was 'impossible' for his men to advance.[119] He hoped sheer num-bers might defeat the Germans but he underestimated the resil-ience of von Lossberg's defensive shield. The attack degenerated into another slog through mud: thousands were left flailing about, shot up, bombed, dismembered and slaughtered beneath the command-ing heights of an unreachable foe. Inverness Copse was lost, and Haig lost confidence in Gough. If this was the point at which Haig gave up on the Fifth Army, it was also the point at which many Fifth Army officers gave up on Haig.

By the end of August, the British and Dominion forces had lost 70,000 men (3424 officers and 64,586 other ranks),[120] of whom 31,850 had been killed, wounded or lost in the first three days, accord-ing to Edmonds' figures (officially, at the Battle of Pilckem Ridge, 31 July–2 August). Of the 22 divisions involved, fourteen were with-drawn, deemed unfit to continue.[121] Some units got the brunt of it, such as the Irish and Hertfordshires. The 8th Division suffered 3160 officers and men killed, wounded or missing during their failure to capture the high ground around the ruins of Stirling Castle.[122]

Thirteen Victoria Crosses were awarded during the month's fighting: three went to the 51st (Highland) Division of Seaforths, Argyll & Sutherlands, Gordons and the Black Watch; two to the Guards; and two to Welsh regiments.[123]

Haig and Gough satisfied themselves that the casualties fell well within their expected range. The opening days had been 'highly satisfactory', Haig wrote to the War Cabinet on 4 August, 'and the losses slight for so great a battle'.[124] Previous offensives had set the norm for what constituted 'slight'. By this macabre calculus, the 31,850 casualties of the first three days were 'moderate', notes the official historian (conceding, nonetheless, that they were 'in themselves severe').[125] Edmonds' litmus test for 'moderate', however, was the first day of the Somme, when Haig lost 57,000 men for a gain of 3.5 square miles.

Haig wrongly believed that the Germans had lost as many men, if not more. The battle had 'pinned down' 37 German divisions, he claimed, exhausting many of them, and it had concentrated 70 per cent of German artillery fire that might have been spent on the Russians or French. By that measure, some historians have judged the first month of Third Ypres a success.[126] In territorial terms, the Allies had gained eighteen square miles and the high ground at Pilckem Ridge.

The Germans saw the battle very differently. They claimed a series of great victories. At the end of the first day, Rupprecht praised his men for thwarting the British attack. He took particular comfort from the fact that his commanders had scarcely drawn on the battle reserves of Group Wijtschate. His infantry held on for the rest of the month, thanks to their astonishing defensive system and the weather. 'Yesterday's attacks,' Rupprecht wrote on 28 August, 'were utterly defeated.'[127]

German losses that August were about 50,000 (20,000 fewer than the Allies), and seventeen of thirty divisions were withdrawn, exhausted.[128] That is not to suggest the Germans were deluded into scenting victory: 30,000 men had been killed or wounded in the artillery barrage, as Rupprecht warned the Kaiser. Their counter-attack reserves were depleted; their reserves thinning out; and adequate rations had failed to arrive.

—

Morale reached a new low, in both armies, at the end of August. The opening battles of Flanders had surpassed 'the Hell of Verdun', wrote von Kuhl, and signalled 'the greatest martyrdom of the World War'. The German defenders had cowered for weeks in 'water-filled craters . . . without shelter from weather, hungry and cold, abandoned without pause to overwhelming artillery fire'.[129]

Their appalling losses alarmed even Ludendorff, no stranger to battles of annihilation. 'The fighting on the western front,' he would write, 'became more severe and costly than any the German Army had yet experienced. From July 31 till well into September was a period of tremendous anxiety [and] caused us very considerable losses in prisoners and stores and a heavy expenditure of reserves . . . In spite of all the concrete protection they seemed more or less powerless under the enormous weight of the enemy's artillery. At some points they no longer displayed that firmness which I, in common with the local commanders, had hoped for. I myself was being put to a terrible strain. The state of affairs in the West appeared to prevent the execution of our plans elsewhere. Our wastage had been so high as to cause grave misgivings and exceeded all expectation.'[130]

Yet despite their commanders' alarm, and Haig's convictions to the contrary, the German soldiers were not close to breaking, reckoned Colonel Macleod, a Fifth Army officer, in mid-August. Indeed, the German 'frontline hogs' were proving astonishingly resilient. One Eingreif company commander said at this time:

If I live to be one hundred, the memories of the days [in

Flanders] will never be extinguished. Here the true greatness
of the defensive battle revealed itself in full. It requires
enormous reserves of morale and courage to hold out in
muddy shell holes for seven long days on end despite bad
weather and ceaseless concentrated artillery fire. What
each man in his lonely shell hole achieved deserves to be
set down in letters of gold in the history of this war.[131]

If German morale held, British spirits appeared to be slipping. Many
soldiers fathomed their darkest place thus far in the war. Many lost
faith in the offensive. British captives were starting to express disillusionment. 'British prisoners,' Rupprecht wrote on 16 August, 'are
saying – and this has never been heard before – that they wished
that they had shot their own officers who were leading them into
the slaughterhouse. They have had enough of this butchery!' A week
later, fresh captives told their German interrogators how little faith
they had in their officers; and captured officers blamed the failure on
their commanders. None thought 'there is any chance of defeating
Germany without American assistance'.[132]

The wanton losses, the rain and mud, had dragged proud British
units to their knees. 'How could all these dashed hopes fail to dis-
hearten us?' wrote an officer of the London Rifle Brigade. 'After
seeing the pitiful remains of the battalion . . . something like disgust
with the British tactics made itself felt.'[133] Captain Yoxall was not the
only officer to report 'several cases of attempted desertion and some
self-inflicted wounds'.[134]

A bitter joke began to circulate. Who, the Tommies wondered,
would take rations up to the last man? A morbid fatalism took
hold of some. It was no longer a case of 'When I go on leave' but
rather 'If I get out of this'. The Dominions, too, were underwater.
The morale of the Australian 4th Division was at 'its lowest ebb'[135]
even before Third Ypres, after their brutal encounters at Bullecourt
and Messines. Many Anzacs were unable to withstand shellfire
any longer, 'due to the long and continuous strain they had been

under'.[136] If this was how they felt before August, one can only imagine their state of mind at the end of it.

Even Britain's sanguine official historian was moved to write:

> [T]he strain of fighting with indifferent success had
> overwrought and discouraged all ranks more than any
> other operation fought by British troops in the War
> . . . The memory of this August fighting, with its heavy
> showers, rain-filled craters and slippery mud, was so
> deeply impressed on the combatants . . . that it has
> remained the image and symbol of the whole battle.[137]

The possibility that conditions might get worse was simply inconceivable. Distressed the men surely were, but they had not yet reached the lower circles of Passchendaele. Through his reddening rage, Lloyd George saw only further, futile carnage.

# 9

# THOSE WHO WALKED
# BESIDE YOU

*My own darling Mother,*
    *Death is no horror to me . . . I look forward to it though*
*one would not be human if one did not shrink from the*
*actual ordeal. Even the Master shrank for a moment in*
*Gethsemane but he won the day . . . So farewell dear old*
*Mum and AU REVOIR for if you get this letter I shall have*
*passed into that other and more glorious sphere . . .*
Reverend E. Victor Tanner, in a letter to be sent home in the event of
his death

---

Who accompanied the soldier, in body or spirit, on his journey
into this hell? Certainly not the generals or the politicians, many
of whom were largely ignorant of the actual conditions at the front
(Winston Churchill, who had commanded a battalion in Flanders in
1916, was an exception). Post-war generations have seized on images
of blimpish generals luxuriating in chateaux ten to twenty miles
behind the front, quaffing French red and sucking on cigars, while
the men slogged away in the mud. The commanders never visited the

trenches, it is claimed, and relied on battle reports and eyewitness accounts, many of which they dismissed as inaccurate or too alarming for circulation – for example, Charteris's dismissal of the Tank Corps report.

In fairness, Haig and his staff familiarised themselves with the terrain, and moved GHQ to the forward areas before battle.[1] Haig himself complained as early as November 1914 of the French generals' refusal to 'go forward to visit their troops . . . They rely too much on telegrams and written reports on regiments.'[2] Plumer, Birdwood and Gough were well aware of the general conditions, as were the divisional commanders. Most officers, from brigadier down to second lieutenant, had seen or fought in the Salient. And Charteris, Haig's intelligence chief, visited the front several times in 1917 and was well aware of the conditions. On 4 August, for example, he described the battlefield as 'a sea of mud churned up by shell-fire'.[3] With what degree of urgency he transmitted this to Haig is less clear.

The senior commanders could hardly be expected, in a total war, to lead from the front. Their responsibilities far exceeded those of today's commanders. They measured their power in vast armies and weapons systems spread over hundreds of square miles, demanding a multitude of visits, dispatches and telephone calls per day. They beheld a battleground conforming to broad contours on huge coloured maps. They could not possibly have commanded all this by candlelight in a frontline dugout. Their gaze traversed horizons, far beyond the trench lines. Modern communications, chiefly the telephone, had transformed the role of commander into a kind of conductor (as Monash saw himself), who stood back to survey the big picture.

Nor were the generals always safe; their lives were more at risk during the First than in the Second World War. Prized sniper targets, many of them were easily identifiable by their red tabs, paunches and white moustaches. Of 1252 British generals in World War One, 78 were killed in action or died of wounds, and 146 were wounded or taken prisoner, according to a recent BBC report.[4] They included General Tom Bridges, who would lose a leg at Passchendaele. The last thing on their minds was the thought that they would be condemned or satirised a century on for failing to rub their noses deep enough in the mud of Ypres.

The direction of the war, for better or worse, depended on keeping them alive. Haig's headquarters was sensibly situated at Montreuil-sur-Mer, on the river Canche, near Étaples, a castle embedded in a hillside within a two-hour drive of Ypres and easy access to the Channel. He resided three miles south-west, in the Chateau de Beaurepaire, modest by French standards, and far less opulent than the Chateau de Querrieu, General Rawlinson's sprawling billet on the Somme.

On the other hand, the defenders of High Command seem to have let the pendulum swing to the other extreme, almost as if the older men in the rear could not be expected to feel sympathy or concern for the men at the front. Part of the trouble was the generals' experiential ignorance of the combat conditions. Modern battle was unrecognisable from the days of their youth. None had fought in a gas mask or inhaled poison gas; none had seen a heavily burdened soldier drown in a shell hole; none had attacked behind, or sat in the path of, a creeping barrage; none had thrown a modern grenade in anger or ridden a tank into battle. They were too old and too highly ranked to participate in combat. That hardly exonerated their failure to fully comprehend the reality of what they were asking their men to do. This chasm between the commanders' and the soldiers' battle experience began to sow resentment, especially between young officers who had lost most of their platoons or companies, and the generals who had ordered them to attempt a plainly impossible task.

There is a well-told story of General Launcelot Kiggell, who visited the front after the awful month of August. As his chauffeur pulled up on the threshold of the battlefield, Kiggell gasped through tear-filled eyes. 'Good God,' he is reported to have said, 'did we really send men to fight in that?'[5] Haig's haters have used the story to prove how out of touch the generals were; Haig's defenders have discredited it. There is no record of Kiggell making the remark. That does not mean he did not say it (not everything a commander said was taken down or minuted, of course). The larger point, however, is that regardless of *whether* the conditions shocked Kiggell, they certainly *should have* bothered him – the implication being, if Haig and his corps commanders had been similarly aware of the extremity of the conditions, they might have paused to think harder about whether to persist.

A more credible high-level discussion about the state of the terrain proceeded between Colonel C. D. Baker-Carr and a group of British generals. Baker-Carr was trying to impress upon them an understanding of the front, of which he had had close experience. Afterward, Brigadier John Davidson drew Baker-Carr aside and reprimanded him for his effrontery.

Baker-Carr: You asked me how things really were and I told you frankly.

Davidson: But what you say is impossible.

Baker-Carr: It isn't. Nobody has any idea of the conditions up there.

Davidson: But they can't be as bad as you make out.

Baker-Carr: Have you been there yourself?

Davidson: No.

Baker-Carr: Has anyone at O.A. been there?

Davidson: No.

Baker-Carr: Well then, if you don't believe me, it would be as well to send someone up to find out.[6]

Later, Baker-Carr would write, with disgust:

I am absolutely convinced that the department responsible
for the staging of the Ypres offensive had not the remotest
conception of the state of affairs . . . To anyone familiar with
the terrain in Flanders it was almost inconceivable that this
part of the line should have been selected. If a careful search
had been made from the English Channel to Switzerland,
no more unsuitable spot could have been discovered.[7]

—

The politicians were ignorant of the conditions in this battle of mud, to which they had sent so many thousands of young men. The matter was barely discussed. In the privacy of the War Cabinet, one might have expected to hear a full and frank debate about the terrible proceedings in Flanders. Instead, Third Ypres merited little comment at the top table. Conspicuous by its absence from the minutes between August and the end of the year was any serious discussion of the terrain, casualties and tactics over which the prime minister would later express so much vitriol, guilt and regret; and no examination of whether the offensive should be terminated, as the Cabinet had promised to do if it hit a snag. The War Policy Committee did not even meet that month, and would not reconvene until 24 September. Un-minuted, off-the-record discussions were held in committee rooms and corridors, and over telephones. But at the highest level of government, a curious silence reigned over Third Ypres, interrupted now and then by passing remarks on Haig's latest lunge.

Certainly, the ministers were exceedingly busy. A queue of demands preyed on their time: the collapse of Russia, the oil supplies, manpower, the U-boat war. On the other hand, they often found themselves steeped in arcane debates that seemed, at best, a misplaced sense of their priorities and, at worst, a case of thoughtless indifference to the suffering of the troops. On 2 August, for example, the morning after the disastrous first day of Third Ypres, the Cabinet raised, as the first subject for discussion, whether to grant the King's commission to Indian soldiers, hitherto denied an officer's rank 'owing to the unwillingness of the War Office to concede the principle of giving Indians command over Europeans'.[8]

The packed Cabinet heard every angle of this essentially racist policy. Conceding that thousands of Indian soldiers had given their lives for the Empire, the Cabinet nonetheless felt that no British, Anzac or Canadian soldier would serve under a 'coloured' officer. There would be 'trouble'. An agenda item that should have been swiftly decided in the Indians' favour, granting them the same rank as Anglo-Saxons, absorbed several hours and reached the wrong conclusion. The Flanders Offensive, the greatest land battle since the Somme, merited a single paragraph of comment that day, containing the line, 'The British casualties up to noon yesterday were 25,000.'[9] No sign there of Lloyd George steaming up about the methods of attrition he later claimed he had so vehemently opposed.

As August dragged on, the Cabinet had many other things on their minds. On 11 August, they devoted hours to the wording of a personal letter against Labour leader Arthur Henderson, who had had the temerity to propose an international conference on settling the war. Ministers were determined to find ways of keeping Britain in the fight, yet they barely discussed the fighting. The Cabinet briefly reviewed operations and debated alternative strategies, but the progress of the campaign, by which Lloyd George later claimed to have been so horrified, was rarely examined. On 17 August, at the peak of the nightmare in Flanders that month, a single paragraph in the minutes concluded, 'The weather on the Western Front was bad.'[10]

Yet by any measure – body count, failure to advance, German resistance – the first month of Third Ypres had been an unmitigated disaster and warranted serious Cabinet attention. The Battle of Pilckem Ridge formed a template for the whole month, as Prior and Wilson attest: 'The most that could follow from what had been achieved was a succession of similar operations, carried out spasmodically as guns could be brought forward.'[11] The guns could not be brought forward through mud in pouring rain; troops who outpaced (or fell behind) the creeping barrage were slaughtered. Haig would soon act on his disappointment, and replace Gough's wasteful methods with Plumer's 'bite and hold' tactics. That lesson, however, had involved a month of avoidable carnage.

August's failures acquire a Nivellean dimension when stacked against the grandeur of Haig's ambitions, because whatever advantage a few ridges in a drenched corner of Flanders yielded, it fell well short of the master plan he had so confidently presented to the War Cabinet. In that scenario, Passchendaele was supposed to have been in his hands by now.

Lloyd George had given an undertaking to halt the offensive if it failed to progress. Instead, he sat on his hands and watched. Often, he failed to attend Cabinet meetings, preferring to stay at the estates of powerful friends. He tuned in when the Italian alternative captivated him. On 27 August, for example, he telegraphed the Cabinet, urging the immediate transfer of guns to Italy. Robertson struck this down as disastrous for morale and an admission of defeat on the Western Front.[12]

—

The press, as so often in wartime, underplayed or misreported the truth. But censorship could not incubate the British, Dominion and German people for long. Rumours of dozy generals sending thousands to needless deaths, of men wading into battle through fields of mud, of men sitting in shell holes waiting to die, filtered home. The slaughter met with incomprehension and anger, fuelled by the anti-war left, the fledgling British Labour and German Social Democratic parties.

Senior politicians were losing faith in the war, as news of Third Ypres reached home. Some came around to Lord Lansdowne's view that the case for continuing was not worth the sacrifice. Even the Conservative leader Andrew Bonar Law succumbed to a bout of defeatism, confiding in the prime minister that he felt the great Flanders Offensive doomed. '[I]n speaking to Robertson yesterday,' he wrote on 18 September, 'I said to him that I had absolutely lost all hope of anything coming of Haig's offensive and though he did not say so in so many words, I understand that he took the same view . . . It is evident, therefore, that the time must soon come when we will have to decide whether or not this offensive is to be allowed to go on . . .'[13]

Yet the war would go on. Parliament and the press would not tolerate a negotiated or, as the War Cabinet saw it, a 'dishonoura-ble' peace. The German regime was of the same mind. Nothing less than unconditional surrender would satisfy the belligerents, imply-ing the reduction of Europe's greatest civilisations to insensate husks. Until that was achieved, it was treasonable or socialist to question the point of the war.

When Lloyd George snapped, in an impromptu speech, 'we shall just win', a radical journal had the gall to reply, 'Win What?'[14] Nobody had a clear answer, because the war aims had shifted beyond those invoked when the Entente Powers declared war: to punish German aggression, liberate Belgium, reclaim Alsace-Lorraine, avenge an archduke's murder. Now, they were fighting for vague or open-ended goals, of a very different magnitude: pure vengeance, and to defend their regimes, empires and economic systems – within which less than one per cent of the people controlled or owned the capital of Europe[15] – from both the enemy without and the enemy within.

A subversive spirit was sweeping Europe, summoning the force of an insurrection in Russia and Germany: the huge waste and appar-ent pointlessness of the war had sown disillusionment and cynicism. Five and a half million days were lost to strikes in Britain in 1917, 1.5 million in May alone, emboldening the King to tour the country to engender loyalty among the working men, in which he secured the 'royalist' affections of hard-bitten unionists. This, accompanied by pay rises, tax breaks and rationing, gave an impression of unity and went some way towards healing a nation on the brink of social fragmentation.

These great arguments scarcely impinged on the minds of the British soldiers and their colonial counterparts. The revolutionary fer-vour and demoralisation that had led millions of Russian troops to desert; the outrage at their treatment that drove the French Army to mutiny: neither would distract the British and colonial soldier from his duty, even though they were ignorant of the evolving reasons why they had to keep fighting. Fear and survival were now their chief concerns.

—

Writing letters home eased the men's fears and calmed their minds. Writing home let them put their experience into a friendly, familiar context, as if to normalise it. The euphoria of being involved in tremendous events animated their early letters; later correspondence tended to acquire a darker tone, and a pointed optimism – 'Don't worry about me!', 'I'll be all right!', 'It's just a scratch!' Others wrote of the sheer exhilaration of war, of the 'tremendous fun' of battle.

Most soldiers sent postcards or brief letters: Dear Mum . . . My Own Darling Wife . . . Dear Old Girl . . . Auntie May, Nellie, Ada, Gwen . . . Thank you for the parcel . . . Don't get in a state when you see I'm in hospital . . . Thanks for the smokes, cake, pork pie, parcel from Fortnum's . . .[16]

Duty officers read unsealed correspondence, and blacked out or destroyed any letters that gave away military locations, unit names, deployments, or the general mood and morale. Pre-scripted field postcards were distributed on which the soldier simply struck out the sentences that were incorrect. For example:

> I am quite well.
> I am coming home on leave.
> I received your letter.
> I have been wounded.

And the home front responded, as best they could, but not always to the soldiers' liking. 'Dear John' letters informing a soldier that his wife or fiancée had found someone else left many men feeling recklessly suicidal. Some threw themselves at the enemy, falling on the mercy of a bullet to escape the pain of rejection. Or the war broke the woman's faith. A friend of Neville Hind's received a letter from a 'heart-broken wife' to which he angrily replied that 'if she couldn't f_____ well write a better f_____ letter than that, she'd better not write at all'.[17] Of course, it was hardly her fault that the war had left her desolated.

The letters that survive tend to convey the experiences of the better-educated middle classes, chiefly officers. The Australian-born Colonel Alex Wilkinson, son of a British doctor, went to Eton and University College Oxford, and served as a reserve officer with the Coldstream Guards for the duration of Third Ypres. His letters home, to his sister and father, offer a rare glimpse of the world through the eyes of a young Guards officer.

Wilkinson spared his parents none of the danger. On the night of 28 June, when the Germans started shelling his position while he was writing to his father, he had to take 'a short interlude', he wrote, 'as the Hun dropped [a bomb] about 50 yards away. While I write another has followed, but fortunately a dud. And another! I sincerely hope he won't put 50 yards more onto his fuse.'[18] A few weeks later, he tried to reassure his father on the eve of battle: 'if you have not received a wire [informing him of Wilkinson's death or wounding] by the time you get this, all will be well . . . You can be absolutely certain that I am all right.' He added that he was 'really looking forward' to the battle: 'I think it will be a walk over.'[19]

For Wilkinson, as for many men, the Great War was the defining experience of his life. The opening battle of Third Ypres was 'splendid fun', he wrote, talking it up to ease his father's concerns: 'we all enjoyed it immensely'. The 'weather side' of it was something else: 'I never thought that the human frame could endure such hardship.' In places, the water was up to his knees, 'yet there we stayed for another 48 hours!' Eventually they were relieved: 'Yet never for a moment did the men lose heart. . . . The only thing they wanted was a chance to kill more Huns . . .'[20]

Afterwards, he looked forward to another 'show': 'They were the greatest three days I have lived and had it only kept fine we could have gone much further . . .'[21] In late August, Wilkinson received the Military Cross, of which he wrote to his family, 'It seems strange that a decoration should be awarded to one who merely showed a marked ability in dodging missiles.'[22]

Captain Harry Yoxall similarly wrote of his pleasure in the war, to reassure his beloved mother. He described German shellfire as 'beastly' and addressed his mother as 'dear little mummy'.[23] He read *Tatler* magazine in the trenches. Battle was 'good fun', he told her: 'for sheer excitement there's nothing to top a trip into no-man's land'.[24] Or he was dead bored: 'I was rather bored', 'bored stiff', 'fed up', 'how bored I am', etc.[25]

Like many officers, Yoxall tended to portray himself as careless of danger, though the grittier entries in his diary tell a truer tale. A bleak note occasionally intrudes: 'I think if you did ruminate much on the real meaning of the things you do and the things that are done to you, your nerves would crack in no time.'[26]

He entered 1917 with high hopes of action: 'War is a very thrilling game if only something happens.'[27] It soon did: in February, he witnessed a shell explode on a group of men, and had to postpone his leave. 'It is not to be,' he told his mother. 'This is sad, but we must keep smiling. Somehow when you have seen a shell fall into the midst of five men and packed three of them away in a sandbag little things like leave don't seem to matter. In fact, one wonders whether anything matters – but that way madness lies. One must at least believe that we are fighting for something or the whole ghoulish business becomes so preposterously criminal that one couldn't carry on . . .'[28]

He carried on: 'Things are never so black that one cannot hope.' Like many officers, he found solace in literature, quoting Arthur Hugh Clough's 'Say Not the Struggle Naught Availeth' to his mother:

And not by eastern windows only,
When daylight comes, comes in the light;
In front the sun climbs slow, how slowly!
But westward, look, the land is bright!

Of which he concluded, 'it is not always from the direct source that the things which are more excellent are brought to us . . . it is a long and wearying business. – I grow very wise, in my old age . . .'

In time, he grew harder, and spared his mother little. 'The kindest thing you can do to a German,' he told her on 5 April 1917, 'is to kill him, to save him from himself.'[29]

———

In his solitude, brooding on his private fears on the eve of battle, many soldiers turned to God. God will always be by your side, the Before Action services promised him. They were held in the field, and in the rear areas. The Anglicans formed the largest congregations in the British ranks, followed by the Catholics, whose padres heard the troops' confessions before battle. The Germans attended Lutheran or Catholic services. Rabbis served the comparatively few Jewish soldiers. The prayers of Hindus and Muslims, recruited from the British and French colonies, were similarly hopeful of divine intervention.

Services were scripted to inspire an offensive spirit and blunt the fear of death. The Anglican service typically began with lines from Psalm 27: 'Though an host of men were laid against me, yet shall not my heart be afraid: though thee rose up war against me, yet will I put my trust in Him.' Or 'The Lord is my light, and my salvation; whom then shall I fear?'[30]

They read the General Confession: 'So let us ask His forgiveness for . . . any malice of ill-feeling that we have entertained towards others . . .'[31] And they sang from their Field Service Hymn Book, hymns such as 'Onward Christian Soldiers', 'Fight the Good Fight' and 'Jerusalem'.

'I certainly did not admire their choice of hymns,' Lieutenant Allfree recalled. 'The unfortunate Tommy was always expected to sing hymns about soldiers and fighting . . . you could not get away from it. I suppose he was not given credit . . . for being capable of any other sentiment. Having been fighting all the week, he must sing about it on Sunday.'[32]

The services ended with a prayer that aligned the soldiers' sacrifice with Christ's:

Holy Jesus, Thou pattern of true manhood, grant to
us Thy sons that we may throughout this time of trial
keep Thy great example before us, and, in a spirit of self-
sacrifice, give ourselves to the service of our King and
Country, with a devotion such as inspired Thee to lay
down Thy Life for the eternal welfare of the world . . .[33]

In Neville Hind's observation, 'sinners' were more receptive to the
padres' prayers: 'those who had lived the most immoral lives are
those who are most terror-stricken in the face of sudden death. The
first to throw themselves on the Mercy of God.'[34]

Reverend E. Victor Tanner was one of the more dedicated army
chaplains. He never seemed to have doubted God's will, not in the
worst of Third Ypres. Ordained in 1909, Tanner was chaplain to
Weymouth College, Dorset, when the war broke out. In January
1915, he delivered a sermon to the boys that left none in any doubt
that he should enlist as soon as he was old enough. 'War would be
the test of your character,' Tanner told the boys, and Christ 'the
Captain of your soul'.[35]

In Flanders, Tanner frequently put his own body on the line,
and keenly volunteered for frontline service: 'I want to be where the
lads are and to share their experiences – and their dangers.'[36] Posted
to the Worcestershire Regiment of the 33rd Division, he felt privileged to be among the men, 'at this, their time of deepest need'. His
message to the troops was that Christ had given each of His flock
a divinely appointed twelve hours in which to perform His sacred
duty. Until that duty was done, 'nothing untoward can happen
to him'.[37] On the Somme, Tanner witnessed the results, in a daily
round of burials of men who had gone forth to perform their sacred
duty, and died well short of their allotted twelve hours. Now, he prepared to face the same ordeal at Passchendaele.

The day of his departure, Tanner wrote but did not send two letters, to his mother and sister. He marked the envelopes, 'To be delivered only in the event of my death':

My own darling Mother,
Time is short as we are going into the line this afternoon and
into action tomorrow morning . . . I am going up into the fight
voluntarily & of my own free will, firstly because I feel that
my presence may be a help to these brave Worcester lads and
secondly because the honour of Christ's Church is entrusted to
us Chaplains and we must be worthy of so great a privilege.
       Death is no horror to me . . . I look forward to it
though one would not be human if one did not shrink
from the actual ordeal. Even the Master shrank for
a moment in Gethsemane but he won the day.
       This thought however gives me as much
confidence as anything – that I have dedicated
myself to the Master's work & that nothing can
happen to me unless my earthly task is done . . .
       So farewell dear old Mum and AU REVOIR
for if you get this letter I shall have passed into
that other and more glorious sphere . . .
       Be very brave, Mother darling
Your devoted
Sonnie[38]

The Worcesters moved up to the Ypres Salient in mid-September 1917. They would soon play a central role in the battle for Passchendaele Ridge.

—

Not all the chaplains displayed Tanner's mettle. Some refused to venture beyond the transport lines; a few bolted, disillusioning the men. While Lieutenant Allhusen's unit waited for a train to take them beyond Ypres,

we discovered that the Padre had deserted. He was a Roman
Catholic, and a wretched creature, reliably reported to

wash in bed. Most Roman Catholic Padres were better
men than the Church of England ones, but this one was
well down to the average. The Colonel promised to do his
best to get him shot, but I am afraid without success.[39]

The beliefs of the devout young Anglican Ronald Skirth soon col-
lided with what he saw as the godlessness of the war. Skirth had
refused to aim his guns on a church. He invoked God as his witness
in disobeying the order, but the army disagreed and demoted him.

His faith in institutional religion began to fray, and tore apart
one morning as he queued to take Holy Communion 'al fresco' in a
field service. Three clergymen had set up a gilded crucifix, a chalice
and containers of consecrated bread and wine. The danger of enemy
artillery had reduced the group of waiting communicants to a dozen
or so. Soon enough, an enemy Fokker appeared in the distance and
fired on a British blimp.

As Skirth approached the altar, he noticed the queue had dwindled to one – 'me'. A series of German shells flew harmlessly overhead and 'crumped' in the distance. At this point, the chaplains:

> whipped their ecclesiastical gear off the table, threw that onto
> a lorry . . . and had the site cleared in 30 seconds flat. The two
> padres scrambled onto the tailboard . . . and the lorry made
> the quickest standing start I've ever remembered seeing.

The young Skirth felt 'morally shattered': the churchmen who had
'given us their blessing when we went off to war, told us patriotism
was noble', had 'scuttled away like rabbits' at the first approach of
danger. He shouted after them, 'Bloody Hypocrites!'[40]

After this episode, Skirth rejected all invocations to God to justify the war: 'At nineteen I found my standards of conduct obsolete,
my ideals shattered. I had lost all faith in institutional religion.'[41]
Henceforth, he prayed daily that God would 'stop the war going
on, and end the misery it caused'. When the Almighty failed to

intervene, Skirth blamed the 'wickedness' of the war on mankind, 'not the indifference of God'.[42]

He drew solace from the memory of his girlfriend, Ella, and wrote to her daily: 'All I wished to see in her schoolgirl handwriting was "I still love you".'[43] He loved her 'more than ever', even if she was 'the idealised girl of my hopes and dreams'.[44] She sent him cakes and a hand-knitted scarf, as he prepared to join the Autumn battles.

—

In the end, many men found a repository of hope and comfort in the animals who accompanied them to the front. The armies relied on horses and mules to haul the cannons forward and carry up rations and ammunition. Gas-masked mules ran the gauntlet of shellfire to deliver rounds and food across terrain impassable to lorry or cart. The vital carrier pigeons were also a source of deep affection.

The animals were literally the soldiers' lifesavers. They were all in this nightmare together, like Noah's Ark in a maelstrom.

The horses in particular became the soldiers' dearest companions. Their warm hides and swishing tails, their blameless, frightened eyes, endeared them to the soldiers in a way their fellow human beings could not.

In 1917, there were nearly a million horses in the British and Dominion armies, with more than 440,000 of them on the Western Front, of which just 27,000 served as cavalry mounts (giving the lie to the claim that the generals expected to fight a cavalry war). They died in huge numbers. Of some 1.4 million horses Germany sent to the war, 400,000 would be killed by fire and 500,000 expire of illnesses relating to malnutrition, a sixty-five per cent casualty rate. European farms were denuded of horses and mules rather like the universities and factories were bereft of men.[45]

The affection these magnificent animals inspired was extraordinary. 'The killing and wounding of horses is one of the most detestable phases of the war,' wrote the Australian Private Edward Lynch, 'and one we'll never get hardened to, tough though we are.'[46]

When hostile aircraft killed 'Billy', the pet stallion of a British heavy battery, on 5 July 1917, an anonymous poet wrote:

> He was only a bloomin' heavy,
> Only a battery horse
> But if there's a heaven for horses
> Billy will not be lost . . .[47]

Perhaps the most astonishing case of a soldier's devotion to his horse was that of a young Canadian who, despite losing his nose, one eye, an entire cheek and upper jaw, stayed by his horse, itself wounded in the same attack: 'His fore leg was smashed, so I could not leave him,' the soldier told the Reverend Charles Doudney at a base hospital. 'Had him all the time since we left Canada.' Not until the horse was shot did this young man deliver his message (demanding more ammunition) and seek medical aid for himself.[48]

# 10

# SEPTEMBER 1917

*Our troops are elated and confident; those on the enemy's
side cannot but be depressed and we have good evidence of it.
In the circumstances it is beyond question that our offensive
must be pursued as long as possible . . . the enemy's man
power will be running out next May or June at the latest.*
Haig to Lloyd George, 26 September 1917

---

In the lull, fear preyed on the soldiers' minds and fired their imagina-
tions. The best advice was to try not to think about tomorrow, what
might happen. 'Look here, lad,' an old soldier advised the Australian
Edward Lynch. 'You give up thinking too much or this war will get
you down. It will beat you. I've been in it since Gallipoli and I know.
The man who thinks is done . . . Don't look too deep and above all
don't think too deeply. Try to see the funny side of everything . . .
Take my tip . . . and although I can't say you'll live longer you'll certainly live happier.'[1]

Lynch tried to apply this advice, to limit 'the self-torture of a too
lively and vivid imagination': 'If we could only be inoculated against
thinking, how much more bearable this war would be.'[2]

An overactive imagination often instilled 'dugout disease', a crippling state of inertia, as Australian Lieutenant H. R. Williams recalled:

> Put men out into holes in the ground where they could see the shells bursting around them and could hear plainly the rattle of machine guns, inure them to exposure of weather and battle, and they would fight whenever occasion arose. Take those same men and put them in a dugout . . . and let them stew in their fears for several days and they would soon get windy . . . In the midst of danger and death the man who will force himself to look the unpleasantness straight in the face will retain his courage, but he who tries to cover up his eyes will probably become a gibbering coward. Nothing in war is so cruel, so terrible, so ghastly, as shattered nerves working on the imagination.[3]

His superior officers tended to think 'Tommy Atkins' could not imagine his situation, and his ignorance explained his astonishing durability. '[M]ost of them are not cursed with an imagination, and so don't worry about what's coming,' one officer remarks in *The Secret Battle*.[4] Such observations, common enough, said more about the ignorance of the upper echelons of Britain's army than the average British soldier's mental powers. The Tommy was no automaton: his sense of humour pricked the most pompous drivel, his subversive spirit rumbled in the wings of his orders. If he rarely challenged his superiors, or openly 'reasoned why', that was not through lack of imagination.

—

As the men waited for fresh orders, their daily discomforts persisted: the shrieking shells, the hideous scenes, the soft 'give' of rotting flesh underfoot, the cold, wet trenches and long, hot days. And when the guns were quiet and darkness fell, the smells remained, the 'penetrating and filthy stench', recalled Frank Hawkings, 'which assailed our noses and filled the atmosphere, a combination of mildew, rotting vegetation and the stink which rises from the decomposing corpses of men and animals. This smell seems to be a permanent fixture in the firing line and there is no mistaking it.'[5]

Rats fat with the flesh of horses and the unburied dead scuttled along the little 'dykes' that separated the shell holes. At night, they loitered among the men, nibbling at their hair and feet. One captain awoke to find a fully grown rat 'swinging from his nose', with its teeth sunk in the cartilage.[6] Shooting and bayoneting the vermin never seemed to deter them. They penetrated the deepest dugouts and even swam across the shell holes: 'at night one could see the snouts of rats as they pushed their way across', Stuart Dolden recalled. 'We were filled with an instinctive hatred of them, because however one tried to put the thought out of one's mind, one could not help feeling that they fed on the dead. We waged ceaseless war on them . . . they were easy prey because owing to their nauseating plumpness they were slow of foot.'[7]

The rats and lice, the disgusting condition of the trenches, the long hours of intimacy with death, wore down morale and induced a stupefied, eye-hanging exhaustion from which the adrenalin of battle offered a welcome respite: anything was better than shivering in a waterlogged hole.

But no hardship could dislodge the soldier's craving for sleep. Lieutenant Carlos Paton ('C. P.') Blacker of the 2/Coldstream Guards (and future eugenicist), described the sensation:

> If you leaned against the side of the trench for more than
> a short moment, your consciousness would insidiously and
> insensibly dissolve. Your brain seemed to melt and you
> slid down into the region of unstable mists. When you felt
> yourself in danger of slithering into this state, you welcomed
> a noise of war – a shell or a rifle bullet which roused you.[8]

—

Haig remained optimistic, and reconciled to the casualties of August. '[I]f we can keep up our effort, final victory may be won in December,' he wrote on the 19th[9] – suggesting, as one critical history observes, that he 'was quite unaware of what had been occurring'.[10] If his optimism seemed faintly macabre, even bizarre, in the circumstances, it was all of a piece with Haig's iron refusal to let bad news corrode his will to win.

The popular portrayal of the commander-in-chief as callous and out of touch – impassively stroking his moustache, opining on the weather and confiding in his chaplain while the civilised world tore itself apart – overlooks the enigmatic, many-faceted nature of Haig. He was a dedicated soldier who worked ceaselessly in search of a path to victory, a task that eluded every other commander on the Western Front. None had yet found a way to make a decisive breach in the German lines. Messines and Vimy were cracks. What distinguished Haig from the rest, rightly or wrongly, was his determination to act: actions were what counted for him, so long as they were offensive actions, the incessant battering of the enemy's lines.

In his report to Cabinet on 21 August, he pronounced himself 'well satisfied' with the latest operations, 'although the gain of ground would certainly have been more considerable but for the adverse weather conditions'. The Germans were being worn down, he insisted, and had suffered 'heavy wastage' (many years later, he would have the satisfaction of reading Ludendorff's remarks that bore at least some of this out). Yet Haig's optimism ran well ahead of events. He utterly misread the strength of the Russian Army, which most commanders had given up on. Indeed, 'the great mass of Russian soldiers did not want to fight,' Major General Sir Alfred Knox, the British military attaché in Russia, informed the War Cabinet on 7 September.[11] Haig continued to express the hope that 'very considerable results' would soon accrue that would 'greatly facilitate the clearing of the coast'.[12]

Alas, on 24 August, Haig received news of the failure of the third attempt to capture Gheluvelt Plateau. Even he could not wring something positive from the disaster, and resolved to inject fresh thinking and verve into his generalship. Gough's reluctance to continue the offensive eased Haig's task of relieving him. According to a story sourced to the telephonist at Fifth Army Headquarters, when Gough received the sealed envelope containing his fresh orders to attack, he scrawled 'IMPOSSIBLE' over the first page, 'BLOODY IMPOSSIBLE' on the second, and 'BULLSHIT' over the timetable, in thick blue pencil, and sent the pages straight back to Haig.[13] Gough was sacked the next day.

On 25 August, Haig transferred the field command to Lieutenant General Plumer, handing responsibility for taking Gheluvelt and Passchendaele to the Second Army, incorporating the Anzacs. It was a blow for Gough, who kept slogging away into early September, with forlorn small-scale missions that achieved nothing, until Haig intervened. Complete control of the offensive now fell to his older, slower, fellow commander.

—

Even the harshest critics of British High Command concede that Plumer was not a donkey, a butcher or a bungler. Liddell Hart went so far as to call Plumer the closest thing to military genius in a war 'singularly devoid' of that quality.[14] The red-faced little general with the drooping white moustache took centre stage at a time of serious disenchantment. He was the right man at the wrong time; the tragedy is that Haig failed to choose him first. Even Gough later claimed that Plumer should have commanded Third Ypres from the start, given the latter's intimate knowledge of the terrain. That oversight may well have been Haig's biggest mistake of the war, some claim, even though some of Plumer's offensives would prove costlier than Gough's.

Belatedly, then, Haig now turned to the champion of Messines. At the commanders' conference on 25 August, Haig asked Plumer to prepare at once for a new attack, along a frontage of 6800 yards, between the Ypres–Comines Canal and the Ypres–Roulers Railway.

Haig insisted that Plumer do what he had advised Gough to do: concentrate every effort on throwing the Germans off the high ground of Gheluvelt between Zonnebeke and Zandvoorde. This area included the most stubborn 'Boche' strongholds on the plateau: Inverness Copse (said to have changed hands nineteen times in August), Glencorse Wood, Nonne Bosschen and, beyond them, a patch of blasted stumps that aspired to the name of Polygon Wood. Plumer's Second Army would spearhead this renewed onslaught over the same ground on which Gough had fought in August; the latter's Fifth Army would play a supportive role on the northern (left) flank. The first phase of this onslaught would be remembered as the Battle of the Menin Road.

Plumer wisely aimed for modest results, and said so, making his achievements look greater than they actually were (Nivelle's and Gough's error was to promise much more than they delivered). He led by example, and inspired great loyalty in his staff officers. He and his chief-of-staff, Major General Tim Harington, worked like the cogs of a well-made timepiece, an indispensable element in the Second Army's success. An emotional, affectionate man, Plumer felt an affinity with the soldier's lot and intense loyalty to his staff. He would fall into 'tearful incoherence' when farewelling them (before he left for Italy, later that year). He enjoyed a fatherly place in the hearts of the men, who nicknamed him 'Daddy' and 'Old Plum'.[15]

Plumer requested three weeks to prepare; he applied the same meticulous planning as for Messines. He introduced 'an intensive system of training such as we had never known', remarked Anthony Eden, the future prime minister, then a young adjutant.[16] Plumer insisted on applying the gradual tactics he had advanced from the start: a succession of sharp blows with clearly defined goals, in jumps of no more than 1500 yards a day, focusing all his forces on the Gheluvelt Plateau. They would advance in four stages, or 'bites', with a six-day pause ('hold') between each.

First advanced by General Rawlinson, and applied successfully at Vimy Ridge and Messines, the concept of 'bite and hold' would now take central importance and undergo detailed modifications. In its basic form, as Rawlinson had explained, the attacking troops seized a piece of the enemy's front, held it against counter-attacks while the guns were brought forward. They would then bite off another chunk of terrain, hold on, wait for the guns, and so on – until they broke through. In this way, the infantry would always stay inside the protective barrage, sealing them off from German counter-attacks. Plumer transformed this rough concept of bite and hold into a meticulously configured plan, mathematically tuned to ensure the precise synchronisation of men and guns. For him, it was the only way to defeat von Lossberg's system of flexible defence.

Here is how the advanced form of bite and hold worked from the German perspective, as described by the German official history of Flanders:

> Take a section of the enemy front twenty kilometres wide and three kilometres deep, batter it for fourteen days with a few thousand guns of all calibres, cover it in a few hundred thousands of gas shells, turn everything completely upside down, until nothing could possibly be still moving as far as is humanly possible – then occupy it by way of ten waves [of infantry] supported by machine guns, tanks and planes proceeding in sequence one after the other and protected by a fiery dome. Then advance the artillery through the shell hole area and prevent the enemy from taking any effective counter-action by continuous barrage fire and unceasing individual attacks. After ten days, you take another section twenty kilometres wide and some kilometres deep and repeat the same calculation. And repeat it until you have reached your goal.[17]

Indeed, Plumer's war would be slow and exhausting, across extremely difficult, cratered terrain. And God help them if it rained – a scenario every British and Dominion commander dreaded and every German welcomed. Plumer, a devout Christian, prayed for fine weather in the weeks before the attack. Whatever the outcome, there would be no more talk of reaching Roulers or the Belgian coast before the end of the year. Even the capture of Passchendaele Ridge would involve weeks if not months of bitter fighting, Haig knew. His best hope was to take the village before winter, and hold it until the fighting resumed in the spring of 1918. To that task he now set his mind.

—

World events were closing in on Flanders, denying Haig any hope of support from Russia and offering little from France. Russia's armies were 'fast disintegrating': July's Kerensky Offensive had failed, and the spirit of revolution proliferated in the Russian ranks. Thousands were deserting. Lenin's calls for insurrection were curdling into reality, easing pressure on the German units along the Eastern Front, many of whom were now packing up and heading west. In France, Pétain's armies were not expected to resume full strength until early 1918, even though six divisions were already serving in Flanders and many more were recovering. The Americans were delayed, and not due to arrive until mid-1918.

The British and the Dominions thus remained the only forces capable of offensive action. This might have counselled restraint, even a defensive war. Instead, Haig felt the imperative to attack, and attack again, even though the original goal, the Belgian coast, could not be reached. Few supported him, or pressed him to persist. The French generals, notably Foch, were against the Flanders Offensive; or, like Pétain, they went along with it because it bought more time for their forces to recover. Haig's own commanders, notably Gough, had advised against continuing in the conditions. And the prime minister and War Policy Committee were, of course, consistently opposed (even if they failed to act). According to the latest statement to this effect, issued on 20 July, 'on no account' should Flanders degenerate into 'protracted, costly and indecisive operations' like the Somme.[18] Results should be frequently reviewed and the offensive terminated if the casualties were too high or unjustifiable. But nobody in government had closely reviewed the results, and, in a manifest failure of political leadership, the Cabinet did nothing. Government inertia, rather than any overt support, gave Haig and Robertson the nod to keep bashing away.

Then, on 4 September, the thorn in Haig's side made its presence felt: Lloyd George summoned his commander-in-chief to a meeting of the War Cabinet in London. The prime minister was deeply disturbed. A military strategist he may not have been, but Lloyd George could read a map. August, he noticed, had produced little or no gains for a great many dead and wounded, amid rumours of unspeakable conditions that had shocked the home front.

To his alarm, Haig found himself being assailed by the ghost of an old idea he had thought long dead: moving the attack to the Italian front and fighting a defensive, 'waiting' war in the west. Lloyd George disinterred the plan with a fresh proposal: that Haig transfer 100 heavy guns to the Italian front, to assist General Cadorna's attack on the Austrians.[19] The guns were desperately needed, the prime minister said, to reinforce Italian gains made at the *eleventh battle* of the Isonzo, on the 17th. In the meantime, Haig's armies should fight a defensive war alongside the French: 'husband resources during the remainder of 1917' and 'embark only on minor operations' until the French Army recovered and the Americans arrived.[20]

Haig was contemptuous of the plan: to withdraw a single man or gun from Flanders – or the Western Front at large – would be most unsound policy.[21] If the Germans knew the Allies were going to sit and wait, he reasoned, the enemy would attack in great strength – a course that might prove 'disastrous'. A mere six German divisions had defeated the Kerensky Offensive back in July, he argued (and within a few weeks they would break the Russian lines at Riga).

Nor were the French forces ready for offensive action, he claimed: enervated, gloomy and despondent, the French Army, according to Pétain, fielded not a man on whom he could rely between Switzerland and the British flank. Prone to exaggeration, Pétain (*'trop negatif, trop timide,'* Joffre called him) could be expected cynically to buy time for France at the cost of British lives. Haig took Pétain's diagnosis on face value in his case against his prime minister. 'From September on, Haig used the argument of French weakness up to the hilt,' argues the historian Leon Wolff.[22]

Haig prevailed, and a majority of the Cabinet cautiously approved the continuation of the Flanders Offensive. The prime minister retained the option of shutting it down should it fail to 'progress' to the government's satisfaction. Haig's only concession was that he would talk to Pétain about the transfer of guns to Italy. The Cabinet asked him to consider sending 50 medium-calibre guns; in the event, he sent a single heavy.

Meanwhile, to Haig's alarm, the flow of recruits was drying up. Volunteers had disappeared and just 8000 British men had been drafted to arrive in France through September, according to Robertson's dispatch to GHQ on 17 August. Those numbers would barely replace normal wastage, at present casualty rates. At the commanders' conference on the 21st, Haig warned that, by the end of October, the British Army would be 100,000 below 'establishment', i.e. the prescribed level of men per unit (then 52 divisions of twelve battalions each, or 605,280 men).[23] Somehow, more men had to be found.

—

On 29 August, Plumer submitted his plan for the capture of Gheluvelt Plateau. It would involve four steps, with a break of six days between each to allow time to bring up the guns and supplies. The Australians and New Zealanders would spearhead the offensive. The I Anzac Corps and Second Army's X Corps would lead, with II Anzac Corps in reserve. At the heart of these vast formations, the restructured 40-man platoon would fulfil the pivotal combat role. As at Messines, every man was trained in a specific job (rifleman, grenade thrower, Lewis gunner, etc.) and integrated into the whole. And if the front line buckled under the blows of the Eingreif, the reserve Anzacs would be ready to counter-attack the counter-attackers.

Leading the Anzacs was a British general of formidable character. At 52, General William Riddell Birdwood – 'Birdy' – was the youngest of the field commanders. Privately educated, a Sandhurst man, the son of a colonial administrator in India, Birdwood seemed anything but the right man to lead a bunch of unruly colonials. But he was held in surprising affection among the Australians and New Zealanders, and Charles Bean described him as 'one of the greatest leaders of men possessed by the British army during the war'.

Bean explains this 'fit' with his usual acuity, boiling it down to a single, winning formula: Birdy saw the man, not the manner. He looked beyond accent, dress, rank, name, title, quality of boots, hair style – outward shows by which an English officer might instantly assess an English soldier – to the character of the man himself. He chatted with and moved among the Aussies and New Zealanders under his command. He had a rich sense of humour, goading them to write to their wives and sweethearts – 'because if you don't they will write to me'.[24] He wore a big slouch hat, and loved to swim off Anzac Cove at Gallipoli, often within range of Turkish fire. Perhaps his most appealing features, in the eyes of the Australians, were his extreme, even foolhardy bravery – 'only once was he known to "duck"' – and his willingness to get out in the field.[25] Birdwood cleaved to notions of honour, self-respect, loyalty and fairness, and vigorously opposed any action that degraded those ideals. This appealed straight to the Anzac heart at Gallipoli, where he commanded the Australian and New Zealand Army Corps, and bravely led their evacuation of the beaches, ironically the greatest success of that doomed venture, from which the Anzacs emerged with honour intact.

If Birdwood was later criticised for not protesting enough against orders to enact the impossible, his men would never scorn to serve under him as they had Gough, whom they now accused of using them as 'storm troops'.[26] (With tearful eyes, Birdwood later explained to an Australian brigade how he had tried to dissuade Gough from the disastrous attack at Bullecourt.) Other generals deserved similar recognition – notably, at divisional level, the Australian Sir John Monash and the Canadian Sir Arthur Currie. Yet Plumer and Birdwood would play the critical role in the coming September offensives, and the way in which they inspired their men helped deliver a series of stunning victories.

—

Plumer decided, at first, to concentrate the main thrust along a 4000-yard front, handing 2800 yards to Gough's men on the left flank to the north. The battle's spearhead would emerge from a triangle whose axes, like a pair of open scissors, began at Ypres and diverged at Hellfire Corner, a fittingly named, perennially bombed point a mile east of the city. The northern blade ran along the Ypres–Roulers railway to touch the Gheluvelt Plateau at Broodseinde, and the southern blade ran along the Menin Road, to touch the plateau at Clapham Junction (see Map 5).[27]

On the ground, the grassy ramparts and dirty moat of Ypres' eastern edge gave onto abandoned fields, covered in thickening clusters of craters and the occasional ruin. Further east, the names on the maps bore little relation to the scene on the ground: a few leafless, broken trunks remained of the forest that had surrounded Bellewaerde Chateau, itself a ruin, and the nearby lake 'resembled some foul pool left in a hollow of an upheaved ocean bed'.[28] Beyond, the terrain and its few identifiers had surrendered so completely to the machinery of war that the word 'stream' or 'beek' meant a stinking swamp of detritus and decomposition; a 'village', a graze of bricks and tiles flung amid unburied corpses (Hooge, for example, had been 'completely erased', the site marked by a cluster of mine craters and the original road untraceable);[29] and a 'wood' or 'copse', snatches of beheaded saplings hanging like mutilated scarecrows over the dead countryside. Such was the state of Polygon Wood, a vital point on the Plateau and the ultimate goal of the offensive. Packed inside this Gheluvelt triangle were the usual German strongholds, the ubiquitous pillboxes lining the distant spurs, amid lines and lines of trenches rolling back to Passchendaele Ridge and beyond. All of it was 'exceptionally important' to the Germans, as Ludendorff later wrote, for observation and cover.[30]

Upon this blameless scrape of earth, Plumer now meant to visit a torrent of fire on a scale mankind had never inflicted on his fellow man, at the end of which all German soldiers caught inside the triangle should be dead, mutilated or incoherent. To this end, he ordered up an unprecedented number of heavy and medium guns. His astonishing demands were largely met, thanks to the efforts of the new minister of munitions, the precociously talented Winston Churchill, rehabilitated to the Cabinet after taking the fall for Gallipoli.

Under Churchill's dispensation, Plumer would receive a further 1295 guns (575 medium and heavy, and 720 field guns and howitzers)[31] – 350 fewer than he ordered but more than double the number allocated to Gough to attack the same stretch of front on 31 July. This time, the British guns would fire 1.65 million of three million available rounds into a smaller area, over just seven days, amounting to a shell density of about three to four times the density of 31 July, and almost double the concentration (a ratio of one gun to every 11.8 yards of front, against the previous one to eighteen yards).[32]

The heaviest (9.2-inch, 12-inch and 15-inch howitzers) would target the blockhouses. They began firing at the end of August, and built to a crescendo over the following three weeks. An improved fuse system ensured that each shell burst the moment the nose hit the ground, minimising the 'cratering' effect and maximising the destruction.[33] If that were not enough, Plumer planned to blanket the enemy batteries in gas, and intersperse the barrage with machine-gun fire (I Anzac, for example, would deploy eleven machine-gun companies, equipped with 174 guns). The ultimate aim of this conflagration was the destruction or disabling of every soldier, pillbox, machine-gun position, wire belt, OP and telephone exchange in the path of the attack.

In short, the Allies were about to witness, and the Germans to feel, the most concentrated bombardment ever wrought in warfare, a veritable wall of flame and steel hurled at the strongest point of the enemy lines on the Western Front. And while it prescribed hell on earth for Crown Prince Rupprecht's men lining the Gheluvelt Plateau, it aimed to preserve British and Anzac lives.

—

The three-week delay deceived the Germans into thinking Third Ypres was over. 'The Flanders fight seems actually to have ended,' Rupprecht wrote in his diary on 12 September. 'We can consider pulling out several divisions.' His chief of staff, General von Kuhl, agreed, though he found it hard to believe the 'stubborn English' had given up.[34] British prisoners attested to the 'fact', however, claiming that an offensive further south was planned. The sporadic sound of the heavy guns had not, yet, portended anything unusual – bombardments were common – and the strange lull bred dreams of an armistice.

The rain stopped. The sunlight and the drying ground, the return of familiar sounds – birdsong, the neigh of horses, or just the novelty of calm – dared many soldiers to hope for a reprieve.

The Germans were deceiving themselves. Plumer packed every ounce of energy and action into those few weeks. Within the next seventeen days, 156 trainloads carrying 54,572 tons of matériel arrived at the railheads, all of which had to be trucked, entrained, dragged or carried on mule-back to the front.[35] Light tramways were hastily reconstructed and roads rebuilt out of wooden planks. Shell holes were filled in and stamped down; gun emplacements firmly laid; telephone lines unrolled and buried; rations and medical supplies prepared and brought forward – all of which proceeded within range of German shellfire. Miles of duckboards were laid, latticing the drying plain, connecting little islands and ridges of high ground in the hardening mud. The men trained all day, rehearsing new platoon tactics, pillbox flanking manoeuvres and how to coordinate their advance with the creeping barrage, worked out to mathematical certainty.

Overhead, 26 squadrons of the Royal Flying Corps buzzed about the skies, mostly on reconnaissance missions to locate and photograph German targets, or on strafing raids of the enemy's reserve lines and railheads. The mosquito-like whine of the British planes was easily distinguishable from the phut-putting beat of the twin-engine German aircraft. Daily, they engaged in great aerial duels, the 'flying circuses' of the sky that produced the 'aces' of legend. Among the British: Rhys Davids, James McCudden, Mick Mannock and Billy Bishop. And the Germans: Werner Voss, Hermann Goering and, the greatest of them all, the 'Red Baron', Captain Manfred von Richthofen. Rhys Davids achieved the most lethal – and reckless – reputation of the British, notching up more than twenty 'kills', including the shooting down of Voss.[36] Daily the infantry, lying back in their trenches, witnessed the aerial theatrics of these agile little aircraft, spinning, diving and chasing each other, the loser hurtling to earth in flames and exploding in a pall of smoke.[37]

The weather answered Plumer's prayers and shone on his deliberations, teasing him with hopes of a dry month. His commanders were similarly buoyant. Two weeks before 'zero' – dawn, on 20 September – the 'softening up' intensified, and soon reached a level of unparalleled destructive power.

—

The first waves moved up on the nights of 18 and 19 September: 65,000 men of eighteen assault brigades, armed to the teeth, advanced quietly along a four-mile line of trenches and shell holes.

Zero was fixed for 5.40 am. A light drizzle turned to rain around 11 pm, and Gough advised Plumer to delay the offensive. Plumer consulted 'Meteor', Ernest Gold, for the weather report: fair in the immediate future, and the ground 'go-able', he said. The rain ceased after midnight. The stars were visible. The attack would proceed.

In the pre-dawn hours, the troops moved up to the jumping-off tapes – in some places, a mere 150 yards from the enemy OPs.

By 4.30 am, most units were in place: thousands of men grounded in trenches and shell holes, ready to rise at the sound of the whistle. Some spilled into no-man's-land, so congested were the lines. German guns were busy firing throughout this advance, killing or wounding at least half the officers of one Australian battalion before they reached the front.

The German ranks heard rumours of an imminent attack, and nervously fired bright-coloured flares into the night to try to locate the enemy spreading out on the plain below them. The capture that morning of an Australian officer in possession of the battle plan confirmed their fears, and a blast of German 'annihilation fire' tore into the British front at 5.36 am, four minutes before zero. It caused confusion and light casualties. At any rate, the German wireless warnings were too late: Plumer's creeping artillery barrage had begun.

The barrage was like a mechanical hurricane, of a density 'beyond all precedent', flailing the earth and air with heavy explosive, smoke and shrapnel in a 1000-yard band divided into five belts, each 200 yards wide, lifting in 100-yard increments every four minutes (later slowing to 100 yards every six minutes). Behind this protective curtain, tens of thousands of troops, relieved to be in action at last, a cigarette on the lips of every man,[38] rose 'like spectres out of the mist' and made for the German front.[39] The conditions were very different from those Gough's men had encountered a month ago: the barrage was far denser; the limit of the advance half as far; and the battlefield dry and hardened by the September sun.

—

September started badly in the German lines. An epidemic of gastro-intestinal illnesses had depleted the reserves: 'The cause,' noted a report on their fighting ability, had been 'wet conditions in the craters and dugouts and the stink of rotting corpses which is poisoning the air. Despite clearance of the area many corpses must be concealed in the mud and water-filled craters.'[40] Virtually every man in one regiment suffered from illness.

Fresh Bavarian units began arriving on 10 September to relieve the exhausted Württembergers in the frontline shell holes, who dissolved into the night, happy to be released at last. And now, as the British bombardment increased the Bavarians climbed into the craters. They got no sleep. Their immediate job was to link the craters with 'crawl trenches'. They started digging, swapping their guns for their trenching tools. They had no barbed wire to their front, the troops noticed, with mounting despair. They felt as though they had been abandoned. And, in a sense, they were right.

In the hours before dawn on the 20th, the British guns crashed down on the German lines with 'ludicrous violence'. The survivors were numb with shock: 'utter chaos' . . . 'dead and wounded lay everywhere' . . . a 'hell of steel splinters', as a few survivors later recalled. Some went raving mad, reported one eyewitness. When a direct hit killed fourteen of his comrades, all of whom died instantly, 'with hardly a murmur', a signalman standing nearby 'went off his head': 'We had to restrain him, binding him tightly, because he had been rushing around, lashing out and foaming at the mouth.'[41]

As the sun rose, members of a German machine-gun company then coming up the line passed through the ruins of Zonnebeke. They witnessed 'nothing but death': 'Rotting, stinking horses were sprawled all over the roads and wagons simply drove over them.' They arrived at the 'Red House', a ruin in a massive crater field not far from the front, and 'sat in silence', wondering when they would receive a direct hit. '[M]y men stared glassily into the middle distance, their cigarettes smouldering,' wrote Reserve Leutnant Kotthoff. 'We were surrounded by crashes, explosions and an unbelievable racket as though we were in the midst of Hell.'[42]

The German forward command posts telephoned for flares, to help guide in their own artillery. But the shelling had mutilated the phone lines. Instead, runners raced to and fro with orders, and message dogs and pigeons were dispatched. Few lived to deliver their messages. The men huddled like animals, locked together in terror in their craters. 'Normal command' ceased to exist. The barrage levelled all rank. In Passchendaele village, a soldier witnessed heavy rounds exploding around a large crucifix – 'Christ covered in filth' – exposed through the gaping roof of the church.[43]

—

At last, the Germans saw in the distance the approach of waves of Anzac and British troops, their hunched forms visible through the gaps in the smoke-shell and the dawn mist. Two Anzac divisions formed the arrowhead, and their *esprit de corps* was at its height. The rest of the infantry came forward fast on their heels, to escape the German shells, which fell harmlessly behind them. The fact that German gunners were still in operation was an astonishing testament to their resilience.

The Anzac arrowhead advanced in thousands of little groups of seven to eight men known as 'worm columns', filing along the duckboards, scrambling in and out of the craters, creeping beneath the ridgelines.[44] Each man carried a waterproof sheet, 220 extra rounds, two rifle-grenades, four empty sandbags, an extra ration, an iron ration and two full water bottles, as well as his usual kit.[45]

They emerged from the smoke with bayonets fixed and hand grenades raised. The first Germans they encountered were broken. 'For us it was all over,' recalled Unteroffizier Ludwig Schmidt. 'It was a matter of hands up, drop equipment and throw away ammunition.' Schmidt claimed that some British (or Anzacs) had been 'drunk'; he was struck in the groin with a rifle butt for keeping bullets in his pockets. A comrade was shot in the back while making his way to the rear.

When they saw the outline of a pillbox through the smoke, every Anzac in the vicinity concentrated on it, flanking and disabling it with Lewis guns or grenades. As the pillboxes burned, great palls of black smoke rose over the battlefield.

At the Albrecht lines, the attacking troops found Germans sitting, dazed and demoralised beside their unfired machine guns, surrounded by the dead and dying. Many were eager to surrender, and greeted the arrival of the Anzacs and Tommies with a flutter of white handkerchiefs and streaming bandages.

A string of German bunkers fell to Plumer's men: the British 23rd Division captured the infuriatingly resistant Inverness Copse, overcoming fierce pockets of German resistance. The 1st Australian Division walked into Glencorse Wood virtually unopposed. The enemy amounted to a knot of machine guns, which were swiftly silenced.

By 7.45 am, two hours after zero, the Anzac and British forces had captured Nonne Bosschen (Nun's Wood), a wasteland of mud-filled craters, and the western fringe of Polygon Wood. Shocked German garrisons spilled out of their concrete shelters, with their hands raised: 'at least nine machine guns were captured unfired, together with the crews, listless alongside them'.[46] The 2nd Australian Division had equal success in the Hanebeek swamp, where the Germans gave up after perfunctory resistance. Several drowning men had to be dragged out of the mud. The Australians gained the far slope, the Anzac House spur, and captured the huge pillbox, a vital observation point. The surviving Germans ran away.

—

The Seabrook brothers were there. They entrained for Flanders in September, and reached Dikkebus, south-west of Ypres, on the 13th. All three were in the same unit: the 17th Battalion of the 5th Brigade, 2nd Australian Division. On the morning of the 20th, the battalion faced an extremely difficult task: to pierce the Wilhelm Stellung between Westhoek and Garter Point, just north of Polygon Wood, and capture the green line. Every man wore a piece of green cloth on the back of his helmet to designate his goal. The huge, well-defended pillbox 'Anzac' lay in their path.[47]

'Troops left at midnight for the firing line,' Tom Bowman, a friend of Keith Seabrook's, wrote in his diary that morning. 'Keith very pale and anxious . . . final handshake very spontaneous and affectionate.'[48] They moved up in drizzle, 'in single file along the slippery duck-board tracks laid over the uptorn country-side, towards the Menin Road'.[49]

Bowman never saw Keith alive again. A few days later, he heard that en route to the front, a mile beyond Hellfire Corner, fragments of a phosphorus shell had seriously wounded the young lieutenant and killed or wounded eight of his men.[50] '[W]e were in single file walking along the duckboard,' said a witness. '[Keith] was marching first of the platoon.'[51] Corporal James Abbey later told the Red Cross that he had personally dressed Keith's wounds, 'but they were of such a nature that I do not think it advisable to let his people know what they were'.[52] Stretcher-bearers bore the wounded man to a dressing station, and thence to a casualty clearing station near Poperinghe. His skull had been fractured in several places. It was Keith's first day in the line.

Brothers George and Theo marched on with the battalion, passing through Glencorse Wood. At 3.30 am, they made their last preparations for the attack. Whether they had seen their younger brother's body is unknown, but 'surely they must have heard that Keith was seriously wounded and was being transported to a dressing station'.[53]

The two brothers were among the second wave of attacks. Theo and George moved forward. At around 9 am, they closed on Polygon Wood under heavy German shellfire. Theo took a direct hit, which wounded him in the head, stomach and legs; he died moments later. '[Theo] Seabrook was killed by the same shell that wounded me, in fact I fell across him when I was hit,' Private E. Cooper later told the Red Cross.[54]

George, standing nearby, saw his brother's lifeless body but had to keep moving, to survive German shellfire. A moment later, he too lay dead, most likely from a direct hit. The next day, their younger brother Keith succumbed to his wounds. Within a day, the three brothers were dead; their fellow soldiers later described them as popular and 'good sorts'. Sets of brothers were commonly killed, but rarely all at once, in the same action.

—

By about 9.45 am, the first day's goals were almost in Anzac and British hands. They dug in to defend the new front line, reversing the captured German trenches and occupying the pillboxes, where they happily lit up German cigars. None yet thought of victory: every man knew that the real front line lay ahead, in the ruins of Zonnebeke and the plains beyond, where Eingreif formations bristled for action in the intensifying light.

This time, however, the German counter-strike units had to contend with something they had not expected. The creeping barrage kept coming at them, advancing 2000 yards deeper than anticipated, well into their rear positions. They had no answer to this. Their earlier successes had depended on a near-lightning response. Yet the density and depth of the drumfire killed their hopes of a swift counter-blow. The Allies had bought valuable time to fortify their new lines and bring forward the supplies and guns so crucial for the next bite.

The barrage resumed at 9.53 am. Machine guns were brought up to support the last 400 yards, the limit of the day's attack. The Anzac divisions reached their final goals within half an hour, completing the capture of the Anzac House spur, and digging in. Only the rows of German gunners at Tower Hamlets, atop the spur beyond Bassevillebeek, had withstood the barrage, and continued to pour fire down onto the British attackers.

The northern and southern flanks told their own stories, too numerous to recount. In sum, all along the line the Allies made decisive gains; the German presence on the vital plateau crumbled away. In one amazing example, a company of the King's Own Scottish Borderers managed to bypass the German garrison huddled in Hanebeek Wood, turn and storm the pillboxes and trenches from the enemy side.[55]

By noon, English, Scottish, Anzac and South African brigades had taken their allotted objectives, gained 1500–2000 yards and captured more than 3000 German prisoners. In British and Dominion hands now were: Hanebeek, Berry Farm, Potsdam House (whose surviving pillboxes put up furious resistance), key positions in the Zonnebeke valley, and footholds on the Gravenstafel and Poelcappelle spurs. And throughout it all, the heavy guns kept firing away.

—

Every man, from Plumer down to the youngest private, prepared for the German counter-attack. The forward troops strengthened their lines using enemy wire and laid new telephone lines. In the meantime, runners, flags, messenger dogs and carrier pigeons conveyed their positions back to the rear command centres, so the guns could reorder the targets (the pigeons had proved so effective that sixteen were allocated to each infantry brigade and twelve to the forward observers).[56]

By 1 pm, the dreaded Eingreif still had not appeared. The British guns kept firing. Many gunners had been laying down constant fire for eight hours, and would continue into the night. At around 2 pm, the barrage paused, the clouds cleared and British aircraft reported thousands of enemy reinforcements moving along the Flandern III line between Menin and Westroosebeke.

By the time they reached the front, the afternoon sun was shining in their eyes, low over Ypres, silhouetting the British positions and casting long shadows up the Salient. The early evening light made any movement on the plain easily detectable to the artillery observers, who relayed the enemy's position to the guns. The result fell on the German positions with terrible accuracy.

One group of Australians 'sat down and laughed' at the effects of their artillery on the counter-attack, an officer recalled. As the Eingreif's ranks disappeared in distant puffs of smoke, the Australians even felt disappointed: they were looking forward to the battle. Some were reported to have been praying for the Germans to get through. None would. Between noon and 7 pm, the Germans launched eleven counter-attacks, of which ten failed completely and only one managed to make a dent in the Allied lines.[57]

'The day drew to a close,' remembered a German reserve leutnant called Zimmer. 'As the sun sank . . . it created a scene of weird beauty and the entire horizon appeared to glow. To our front a wrecked concrete bunker blazed as the flares that had been stored inside shot into the air in a series of red and green streaks.'[58]

Night fell. The Eingreif withdrew, with heavy casualties. The quiet seemed surreal after hours of deafening noise. Over the next five days, the British and Dominion troops rooted themselves on the Gheluvelt Plateau, for so long a source of despair, now an exhilarating possession.

———

Haig was delighted. His generals were euphoric. For once, the German counter-attack had failed. His forces had taken a bite out of the toughest section of the German front, and held it. All along the line, they had broken von Lossberg's system. The barrage had won the day. 'Excellent – the best ever put up,' said an Australian officer later.[59] The density of the explosive curtain was the main cause of defeat, Prince Rupprecht himself acknowledged, because it wiped out the German communication lines and created havoc. Bean concluded: 'the advancing barrage won the ground; the infantry merely occupied it . . .'[60]

Bean's 'merely' seems unfair given the infantry's huge sacrifice: total British and Dominion casualties that day were about 21,000 – for the capture of 5.5 square miles, or 3800 casualties per square mile, according to Prior and Wilson's calculations. In fact, Plumer had lost more men per square yard gained than the much-maligned Gough, whose forces had suffered 27,000 losses for the capture of eighteen square miles, or 1500 men per square mile.[61] Some units were decimated. The South African brigade had lost almost half its strength: 1255 of its 2576 men were killed, wounded or missing. Their sacrifice nonetheless achieved a 'brilliant advance', wrote Jan

Smuts.[62] The survivors were relieved from combat duties.

Success led to hubris. They had gained one and a half miles, the first of Plumer's terrible steps towards Passchendaele. Bean rapturously concluded that the Allies were now using their supremacy in men and weapons 'in a way which, granted fine weather, made success certain'.[63]

Spirits rose everywhere except at home, where the Cabinet and the public could not imagine the cost in blood and bombs needed to capture a small slice of front. The politicians fastened on the casualty lists and failed to appreciate this milestone in the coordination of infantry and artillery. 'We have done a good offensive, which is much appreciated,' Lord Bertie, the British ambassador in Paris, wrote in his diary. 'But will it lead to anything really important.'[64] In London, Robertson reported Haig's 'excellent progress' to an underwhelmed War Cabinet: 'We had succeeded in gaining a ridge which included Inverness Copse, a point of great importance,' for which the casualties were 'about 5,000'.[65]

—

The men rested and smoked, and prepared for the next bite. Rations, supplies and small-arms ammunition arrived on mule-back. The heavy guns were hauled up over the steaming earth. Stretcher parties under Red Cross insignias fanned out across the brown land. 'Suddenly I saw flags,' recalled Kotthoff, 'Red Cross flags! Slowly they came, stretcher after stretcher . . . What an amazing, overwhelming sight!'[66]

The Germans also regrouped in new positions, and dug in. Their headquarters conducted a post-mortem, and reached the wrong conclusion. 'All that was left to the enemy,' according to an Order of the Day at Group Ypres headquarters on 23 September, 'were small territorial gains in the form of a shell-shattered crater field. His intention of breaking through our line has failed utterly with heavy casualties.'[67]

Plumer, of course, had not intended to break through; only

to bite off a valuable chunk. The next bite would start on 26 September, precisely in line with his schedule. It planned to capture all of Polygon Wood. A victory here would haul the British front to within striking distance of Broodseinde and Gravenstafel, just shy of Passchendaele Ridge. Only two to two-and-a-half miles of gently rising plain separates Polygon Wood and Passchendaele, a pleasant few minutes' bicycle ride in peacetime. Over this little slice of territory, the world's mightiest armies now prepared to unleash all their available firepower.

Polygon Wood had once been a densely forested area; it was now a scrawny, unnatural landscape of gnarled stumps and 'thin stubble of sapling stalks barely breast high',[68] pocked with muddy ditches and corners of damp, mouldering vegetation in which German machine guns and pillboxes lay wedged and refused to yield.

The task of taking it fell to I Anzac, many of whom relished the chance. Others were less pleased to serve once more as Haig's battering ram. Some jeered at the news; the officers of one battalion resigned en masse when their commander called the men 'dopey', forcing an apology, according to the account by the Australian Captain Albert Jacka VC MC (with bar).[69] The whole front was just 8500 yards wide (compared with 14,500 yards in the first stage); the offensive was entering a bottleneck. The Australians would be spread across 2100 yards at the start, broadening to 2750 yards at the objective – the line between Zonnebeke and Gheluvelt village. They were to advance just 1200 yards, because enough guns could not be brought forward in time to support a deeper attack. 'So in a continuing display of sanity,' write Prior and Wilson, 'the infantry plan was reduced to what could be supported by the artillery.'[70] Gough's battered Fifth Army would capture the ruins of Zonnebeke, to the north. If the Tommies seemed less enthusiastic about this than their Antipodean comrades, they drew on deeper, bitter experience of the enemy's shock troops, the full ferocity of which the Anzacs were yet to experience.

To bring the guns up, the engineers laid new plank roads, a

light railway, mule-tracks and even a short, experimental length of monorail[71] – all in a week. Daily, 240 tons of elm and beech plank were sent to Australian engineers, to build roads over what had been 'Menin Road' and other barely discernible tracks between Hooge and Birr Cross Roads.[72] Eighty lorries and 120 horse-drawn wagons, moving through the nights, transported the planks from the railhead at Ouderdom to the working parties. Long mule trains carried the ammunition and rations. Enemy artillery targeted these files of mules: a direct hit forced the drivers and animals to linger in the open while stretcher parties cleared the casualties, and the able-bodied fixed the track.

A shock came early on the 25th: German troops launched a powerful counter-attack, with artillery and mustard gas, serious enough to disrupt the engineers' work and breach the line on the Menin Road. It struck at the worst possible time: just when fresh British troops were relieving an exhausted division. The Highland Light Infantry were sent forward to crush the breach, with dreadful results. 'Many of the platoons . . . disappeared forever,' a witness wrote.[73] The German offensive was repelled, at heavy cost, mauling several Allied battalions. The losses brought total British casualties between 20 and 25 September to 20,255, of which Plumer's Second Army accounted for 11,460 (of whom 1774 were killed) and Gough's Fifth Army 7923 (1317 killed).[74]

Mustard oil lingered in the craters and pools, blistering the engineers' skin as they resumed their work. Notwithstanding these awful conditions, the engineers laid the planks, and enough guns were brought forward in time. Throughout the night of 25–26 September, the troops silently waited in the trenches and shell holes for dawn to arrive and the second bite to begin.

Meanwhile, at Montreuil-sur-Mer, Haig and his staff were fastening on the bigger picture should the Germans crumble and withdraw from Flanders. Every Allied unit in France and Belgium was poised to exploit this 'turning point', thought to be imminent after recent successes. Rawlinson's Fourth Army would attack across the

Yser, near the Belgian coast. Reinforcements were preparing to land, if possible, at Ostend and Middelkerke. And Haig's five beloved cavalry divisions were marshalling in the rear, champing to charge and complete the enemy's destruction on the plains rolling away from Passchendaele.

—

At 5.50 am on the 26th, the first waves of Australians rose behind a renewed barrage – five belts of heavy explosive, 1000 yards deep – and poured over the top. '[T]housands of shells screamed through the air and burst in a long straight line of flame and destruction about 200 yards ahead of the waiting infantry', said one witness. 'Released simultaneously from the bonds that had held them silent and motionless, the 4000 men of the six attacking battalions dashed forward at a run.'[75]

The sun had dried the field, and the drumfire slammed into crumbling mud, raising 'a dense wall of dust and smoke' that headed for the German lines 'like a Gippsland bushfire'.[76] Geysers of dry, dusty soil spouted in fountains where the shells burst. Little balls of shrapnel tore about the air like neutrons in search of a home. Behind this monstrous creation, the men raced forward in broad waves, a few tanks blasted into view over the ridges, cannons thundered and recoiled, and biplanes buzzed among the flares and smoke, vying for control of the sky.

Hugging the barrage, the Australians reached the first stage with little resistance. '[S]o closely did the Australians follow the dust cloud,' wrote the official British historian, 'that most of the German machine gun detachments were rushed or outflanked before they could fire a shot'.[77] 'The barrage,' wrote Bean, 'was the most perfect that ever protected Australian troops.'[78]

They paused in the captured holes, strewn with enemy corpses, and waited a few minutes for the barrage to lift. Some men kept running, straight into the inside edge of the exploding shield, to their deaths. Their officers, it seemed, had not properly synchronised their watches with the timing of the lift. Albert Jacka and others tried to steady the men, most of whom 'restrained themselves'. They paused and lit up: 'Hundreds of matches flickered feebly along the line in the misty grey dawn, and keen eyes watched the barrage as second after second of its three minute wait ticked away.'[79]

The attack resumed, and victory was swift. The Anzacs quickly outflanked and emptied the pillboxes. Most of the little garrisons surrendered. Lines of ashen-faced German men in field-grey uniforms came blinking into captivity with their hands up, mumbling '*Kamerad, Kamerad*'. 'From some came whimpering boys, holding out hands full of souvenirs.'[80]

By 9.45 am, all of Polygon Wood was in Anzac hands, largely due to the driving attacks of Pompey Elliott's 15th Brigade, who overturned a near-desperate situation at Hooge and drove the enemy off. By 11 am, they had dug into excellent positions overlooking the Polygonebeek valley. The captured German observation bunker (now the site of the Polygon Wood memorial obelisk) offered a crowning view of the surrounding area. Another line on the map had been bitten off and held. The British units on the flanks had also reached their goals. 'The men were full of confidence' and even started lighting fires to boil pots of tea.[81]

———

The Eingreif appeared on the plains beneath Passchendaele at about 4 pm, spotted by British aircraft. These were not the usual fleet-footed shock troops; they edged forward, dazed, and in disarray, through a storm of artillery. Their officers led them stumbling westward through the fiery wall of the barrage, searching for weak points, skirting wired-off swamps and hedgerows, testing the streams for crossing points and picking their way towards the front.

They made a few perfunctory lunges before Allied shellfire broke them up: 'the counter attack . . . did not materialize'.[82] Many were seen running back to their starting lines, shocked by the wall of bombs, gas and machine-gun fire. The Anzacs amused themselves again, by taking pot shots at low-flying German aircraft, and even brought down a plane, which crashed near their trenches.

Leutnant Heider tried to rally his men. In despair, he appealed to God: 'The hour has come when I have to trust each and everyone of you . . . I shall go first and you must follow me . . . We shall meet up again in the front line. Go forward with God!' A young runner took him at his word, sped off shouting 'Praised Be the Lord Jesus Christ', and collapsed, mortally wounded.[83]

German grenadiers who attempted to retake Polygon Wood were so badly shot up they lost all sense of orientation, falling into trenches and wandering off in confusion. Two officers were killed and twelve wounded, with severe casualties among the rest. The commander of another Eingreif unit reached the front by moonlight, only to find:

> an officer with some tens of men looking up at me with blank,
> white faces from the shell hole where they were huddled. The
> company commander, utterly exhausted and apathetic, talked
> in a confused manner about defensive fire and men being buried
> alive; responding to my questions concerning how? and why?
> with ironic, stupid giggles. The poor wretch was at the end of
> his tether. He could give no information about his position,
> the situation to his left or right, or concerning the enemy.[84]

There were frequent reports of extraordinary German courage, of gunners who had chained themselves to their guns, of infantry dragging the wounded to aid posts under fire, of stretcher-bearers racing onto the battlefield to disinter soldiers who'd been buried alive, and officers quietly trying to reassure men on the brink of insanity. An *obergefreiter* (lance corporal) called Kolmich tried to raise morale by playing his harmonica as the shells fell around his men.

Another German counter-attack had failed, and a rattled Ludendorff phoned von Kuhl and von Lossberg at German headquarters: how would they respond to the new British tactics?[85]

Ludendorff was already in a dreadful state after the loss of his eldest stepson, a pilot, shot down over the Channel. He had also suffered a railway accident in which his carriage overturned. Now this: the German Army was being forced to fight the war on Allied terms. Their failure that day would forever trouble Ludendorff, who was still brooding years later: '[T]he enemy managed to adapt himself to our method of employing counter-attack divisions.'[86] 'The Eingreif divisions,' concluded a German history, '. . . in the face of the British barrages, took 1½ to two hours to advance one kilometre, their formations broken and their attack-power lamed.'[87]

—

The fighting ceased at 8.15 pm. A silent night ensued. The men rose from their holes like ghosts. The capture of Polygon Wood was the most complete Allied victory after Messines. Again, it came at a huge cost: 15,375 men killed, wounded and missing, for the capture of 3.5 square miles; in other words, 4400 casualties per square mile, far worse than Menin Road.[88]

Among the dead was Lieutenant Colonel Oswald Croshaw, a British officer serving with the Australians, whose chaplain called him 'the bravest soldier, the most God-fearing christian, and the most perfect gentleman I have ever known'. 'Gentlemen, your men before yourselves,' Croshaw had told his officers before the attack. 'God bless you lads, till we meet again.' Unusually, he led from the front, until a German shell struck and killed him.[89]

The number of Germans killed, wounded and missing that day is unclear, though likely to be fewer than the Allies'. A German history calculates total German losses between 11 and 30 September at 38,500, and the British/Anzac at 36,000.[90] Allied losses were in fact higher. Yet, in the last days of September, German casualties had been so severe that fresh formations were rushed to Flanders to relieve the exhausted troops: such was the importance the German commanders placed on Passchendaele Ridge.

—

Nine Victoria Crosses were earned that day, most of them posthumous. Among them was the Australian Private Patrick Bugden, 22, who led a small party to capture a machine gun and pillbox that were delaying the advance. He took several prisoners, and rescued five wounded men, under fire, dragging them to safety. Two days later, a sniper shot him. 'He kept fighting until he was killed,' notes the Australian War Memorial.[91] Sergeant William Burman went forward alone, killed a German gunner and carried the gun to his objective, where he 'used it with great effect'. Later, he outflanked enemy troops who were enfilading his battalion, killed six and captured two officers and 29 other ranks.[92] Corporal Ernest Albert Egerton raced through heavy mist to silence a German dugout, killing three enemy troops, after which 29 surrendered, 'relieving in less than 30 seconds an extremely difficult situation'. Second Lieutenant Hugh Colvin single-handedly entered and cleared several dugouts that were blocking his battalion's advance, taking about 50 prisoners – an act that largely ensured the 'complete success' of the attack.[93]

There were crimes of vengeance, as in all wars. When a burst of gunfire from a surrendered German pillbox wounded Captain F. L. Moore, a much-loved officer, his men surrounded the prisoners and would have exterminated the lot had Australian officers not intervened. In this murderous moment, uninvolved German soldiers were bayoneted. One Victorian grimly fixed his bayonet while his tearful prisoner sat pleading for mercy. 'The Germans in this case,' writes Bean, 'were entirely innocent, but such incidents are inevitable in the heat of battle, and any blame for them lies with those who make wars, not with those who fight them.'[94] Moore later died of his wounds.

On 28 September, Robertson informed the War Cabinet of the string of victories. All the German counter-attacks had been repulsed and 'our troops retained all the ground that they had captured'. He chose not to reveal that the September battles had gained 2750 yards at a cost of more than 36,000 casualties. Nor did he comment on the fact that the Belgian coast could not be won that year. Haig had known this since 23 September, when he cancelled the amphibious attack on the coast, a centrepiece of the plan to destroy the U-boat bases. From that point on, unknown to the soldiers, the Allies were fighting not to seize geographic objectives but to 'attrit' – to kill or wound as many of the enemy as possible.

—

Lloyd George visited Haig's headquarters in Montreuil-sur-Mer on the 26th, and dined with the field marshal. Haig took pains to show the prime minister his recent victories on a map. He was determined to buttress the case for continuing the offensive, even though both men knew the original goal of the Belgian coast had been abandoned.

'The enemy is undoubtedly considerably shaken,' Haig told the prime minister. 'Our troops are elated and confident; those on the enemy's side cannot but be depressed and we have good evidence of it. In the circumstances it is beyond question that our offensive must be pursued as long as possible . . .' The enemy had suffered 'considerable wastage' and would most likely commence the new year with '500,000 to 600,000 reserves at his disposal', of low fighting value. At the present rate of attrition, Haig delighted in informing the prime minister, 'the enemy's man power will be running out next May or June at the latest'.[95]

Lloyd George was unconvinced. 'I found there an atmosphere of unmistakable exaltation,' he later wrote. 'It was not put on. Haig was not an actor. He was radiant. He was quiet, there was no swagger . . .' He added, with characteristic disdain:

It naturally pleased Haig to have carefully chosen and nicely cooked little titbits of 'intelligence' about broken German divisions, heavy German casualties, and diminishing German morale served up to him every day and all day. He beamed satisfaction and confidence. His great plan was prospering. The whole atmosphere of this secluded little community reeked of that sycophantic optimism which is the curse of autocratic power in every form.[96]

Lloyd George penned these venomous vignettes many years later. At the time, he listened and looked impressed, but his mind was far from Flanders. Haig's plans ceased to engage his active interest, at a critical moment in the September battles, when a tactical victory looked feasible. The prime minister's thoughts orbited Italy, and had done for weeks, spurred on by General Cadorna's success on the Italian front on 26 August.

During his visit, Lloyd George asked to see the German prisoners, of whom he'd heard poor reports. He was shown over a suitably bedraggled mob, corralled in cages. He thought them a 'weedy lot . . . deplorably inferior to the manly samples I had seen in earlier stages of the War', and noted the 'good spirit' of 'our own army'.[97]

# 11

# ODYSSEY OF THE WOUNDED

*[P]erhaps the most terrible thing of all was the laughter
and tears of the shell-shocked cases. I found that hard
to stand. Every effort to quiet them failed.*
Reverend Julian Bickersteth

---

*The poor gassed beggars kept grabbing at things and I saw one man
grab at his own hand and smash his fingers out of joint. One man tore
his mouth nearly back to his ear trying to pull the gas out of his throat.*
Private Edward Lynch

---

The battles of August and September posed an unprecedented challenge to the stretcher parties: the sheer concentration of casualties, scattered across a moonscape of mud. Never before had the bearers encountered so many wounded inside a few square miles. There was about one stretcher case to every three walking-wounded; and for every man killed, three or four were wounded.[1] Eight thousand more stretchers were sent for, and thousands had to be replenished when they broke up, were blown apart or lost. Relay teams were organised to carry men over terrain that was impossible for mule or cart.

The wounded soldier's journey home often began in a shallow shell crater in no-man's-land, into which he had crawled or been blown. His first thoughts were 'to save himself, if possible, from further harm', wrote one medical officer. 'If he is able, he will walk, crawl, or drag himself to the nearest position of comparative safety, and there wait to be picked up by the stretcher-bearers.'[2] Many had spent the night in severe pain, and the appearance of a stretcher-bearer through the smoke and fire had a near miraculous effect. The bearers breathed hope into the soldiers' spirits while tending to their mutilated bodies:

> What [the bearer] can do for the physical hurt is little: a
> bandage, an improvised splint, and perhaps a tourniquet are
> his only aids. But what he can do for the mind is incalculable.
> Even if he does not speak a word, with a pair of strong arms
> he can raise a man from hell to heaven in half an hour.[3]

Not in all cases: Private Edward Lynch witnessed a stretcher party trying to carry away a young soldier who'd been buried alive in a collapsed dugout:

> They lay him on the stretcher and start off. He sits
> straight up and laughs hysterically; louder and louder
> he laughs as he is borne away . . . we see the bearers
> trying to force him down on the stretcher again. .[44]

Others seemed to endure the horror of being buried alive, such as the case of a buried soldier who, on being exhumed, smiled, dusted himself down and asked whether the men had saved his cherished Primus stove.

A unique kind of courage accompanied the stretcher-bearers' deliberate, slow and methodical work. They were not infantrymen charged with adrenalin. No starburst in the hypothalamus drove them to commit these acts of recurrent courage. They simply set off into no-man's-land again and again in search of the wounded, whom they bundled up and carried back, in and out of craters, along ridges, within sight of the enemy. Both sides often broke the unwritten rule not to fire on stretcher-bearers, whose work demonstrated 'a peculiar and . . . unnatural quality; not the instinctive response of the courageous animal to attack, but an acquired and "conditioned" inhibition of the instinct to flight'.[5]

An astonishing example of this selfless courage was Captain Noel Godfrey Chavasse, the English medical officer, doctor and former Olympic athlete who helped bring in the wounded during the opening battles of Third Ypres. His bravery earned him the accolade of being the only man in the Great War, and one of three of all time, to be awarded the Victoria Cross twice. He received the first in October 1916, for treating the wounded all day under heavy fire. The second, or Bar, he received 'for most conspicuous bravery and devotion to duty' when in action from 31 July to 2 August 1917,

> Though severely wounded . . . whilst carrying a wounded
> soldier to the Dressing Station, Capt. Chavasse refused to leave
> his post, and for two days not only continued to perform his
> duties, but in addition went out repeatedly under heavy fire
> to search for and attend to the wounded who were lying out.

During these searches, hungry, worn with fatigue, and faint from blood loss, Chavasse 'helped carry in a number of badly wounded men, over heavy and difficult ground'. Chavasse later died of his wounds.[6]

The famous photo, by John Warwick Brooke, of a stretcher party wading knee-deep through slime carrying a wounded man epitomised the experience of thousands of bearers. It was utterly exhausting work. After a day of this, the bearer would fall to the ground, dripping with sweat, roll over and sleep 'in his equipment in the adjacent mud'.[7]

Private R. L. MacKay, temporarily attached to a bearer section, recalled that his party 'could scarcely move one foot after the other'. He confessed that he would rather join the attack than carry out another body: 'I hope to goodness it is my last – [I] prefer going over the top.'[8]

The medical officers saw a dark dimension to the generals' much-touted victories. The 'great success' at Polygon Wood, for example, was 'not without disturbing features', a medical officer wrote to his division's deputy director. 'As the morning wore on our casualties were mounting up, and stretcher-bearer after stretcher-bearer was shot down,' said Private G. L. Davidson.[9] The casualties in his unit, about 70, raised the question of who would bear the bearers: 'If losses are severe during any further offensive it is likely that there will be a grave shortage of stretcher-bearers.'[10]

—

For the severely wounded, the journey home was gruelling in the extreme. Many died of their wounds on the way (or weeks or months later). The experience of Lieutenant Arthur Edmett, of the Queen's Own Royal West Kent Regiment, offers a shocking example: fresh back with his battalion after a long convalescence for a severe thigh wound, he joined the attack on the Menin Road on 21 September. Shot through the abdomen, he 'lay for twelve hours without shelter or protection in the midst of a terrific barrage with shells bursting all around him'.[11] He survived the journey home, by stretcher, lorry, train and ship, and endured three major operations in French and British hospitals. His heart failed on 16 March 1918, six months after his second wound. Or consider Private William Harkeness Evans, who, having survived wounds to the head and knee in 1916, found himself back at the front in time for Third Ypres. On 17 August 1917, he fell wounded in fourteen places, in his head, arms and legs. Hospitalised for months, he was discharged from the army on 20 December 1918. His body gave up in hospital, on 11 January 1919, a year and a half after his second wounding.[12]

Junior officers' average life expectancy was six weeks, and shorter during the great offensives of 1917. Consider Lieutenant Norman Collins, a nineteen-year-old subaltern in the 4th Seaforth Highlanders (51st Division), who survived an officer's six-week 'life' span – on three occasions. He was wounded on the Somme in December 1916, after six weeks' service; wounded a second time in May 1917, five weeks after returning to France; and wounded a third time in mid-July, at the start of Third Ypres, six weeks after returning to his unit. In all, Collins spent seventeen weeks at the front and fourteen months in hospital, giving him 'a lifetime of pain that no disability pension could compensate for'.[13] Yet he lived to the near miraculous age of 100, and died in 1998, truly the 'last man standing' of his unit, as he named his memoir.

To extract these and thousands of others, the bearers formed relay teams, each of which covered a distance of 500–800 yards. They were passed through a succession of aid posts and dressing stations, situated in concrete dugouts or under corrugated iron 'elephant' cupolas. Severe cases were treated in fifteen casualty clearing stations, which had expanded by 1917 to a size that 'staggered all precedent and expectation',[14] treating lachrymatory gas cases, head injuries, abdominal and severe chest wounds, compound fractures of the thigh and not-yet-diagnosed nervous cases (i.e. 'shell-shocked' – see below).

The wounded were accommodated in 1300 marquees (ten patients per tent) and sixty huts (twenty per hut), giving a total capacity of 14,200 casualties in 'normal' circumstances and 20,000 in an emergency. Total casualties at the end of the first two days of Third Ypres were 23,000, so the facilities were instantly pressed to the limit.[15] From the clearing stations, those with 'Blighty' wounds – which warranted rest and/or hospitalisation at home – were entrained to base hospitals in northern France, and then by hospital ship back to Britain. The German wounded who couldn't walk were similarly borne home, but theirs was a less jarring experience because the Germans were not attacking over a plain of mud and shell craters. Like their Allied counterparts, the German medical teams performed phenomenal feats on the Western Front, each month treating about 175,000 wounded at field hospitals, 66,600 at evacuation hospitals and 86,300 at base hospitals, most of whom suffered battle wounds caused by artillery and shrapnel. Of Germany's 25,000 doctors, about 70 per cent worked in war-related facilities.[16]

—

Doctors and nurses worked with ceaseless dedication in ghastly circumstances. During the worst periods, the British casualty stations and their German equivalents resembled charnel houses, the air heavy with the cries of the wounded and the smell of death, the floor a slick of blood and gore, the scenes heart-rending. 'I often wondered,' said Nurse Vera Brittain, a VAD, in August 1917, 'how we were able to drink tea and eat cake in the operating theatre, in the foetid stench, with the thermometer about 96 degrees in the shade and the saturated dressings, and yet more gruesome human remains heaped on the floor.'[17] The conditions were primitive. Remy Siding clearing station was erected in a field of shell holes, on grass, which became mud, recalled Sister J. Calder: 'Matron fell into a shell-hole one night . . . She'd been in it an hour and she'd just managed to prevent herself from being drowned . . .'[18]

The great battles of 1917 presented doctors with an array of medical conditions on an unprecedented scale: gaping flesh and head wounds, trench fever, trench foot, wound shock and shell shock. They offered an 'unrivalled opportunity', wrote one, to 'try-out' methods which 'experiment had shown worthy of further exploitation . . .'[19]

Nothing could prepare them for the kinds of wounds the new howitzers inflicted on human flesh. Norman Collins, blown up and then buried alive, regained consciousness in a field dressing station where all around him, under the corrugated iron, lay 'chaps with . . . their brains practically hanging out'.[20] Later, in a French hospital, he saw more of the 'real' wounded: soldiers who had been

By 1917, the British 'shell famine' was broken. Factories like this munitions plant in Nottinghamshire produced millions of heavy rounds for a war in which artillery would inflict about 70 per cent of casualties. Women did most of the work.

The British and Empire forces detonated nineteen enormous mines before the Battle of Messines in June 1917, creating huge craters – and instant mass graves for thousands of German soldiers, the prelude to the rout of the enemy.

Hundreds of thousands of Allied soldiers marched past the ruins of Ypres, on their way to the frontline. Here, men of the 1st Anzac Corps pass the wreckage of the city's thirteenth century Cloth Hall and cathedral, in the heart of the most bombed place on the Western Front.

British troops preparing to attack during the Flanders Offensive. Waves upon waves would be thrown at the German lines during Third Ypres, as part of Field Marshal Sir Douglas Haig's 'wearing down' war.

British troops advancing through a gas cloud during Third Ypres. The Germans were the first to use mustard gas, on 12 July 1917; the Allies soon followed. The new gas was more likely to cause excruciating pain than kill you.

A tank graveyard in the Flanders quagmire in August 1917. Unable to advance in the hellish conditions the early tanks were easily incapacitated, and spent the remainder of the war sinking into the mud.

Bringing forward the heavy guns to protect the infantry was critical. But as the weather worsened, it proved a nightmarish struggle. Here, Allied troops heave a 15-inch 'heavy' into place.

Australian troops wearing gas masks in an advanced trench at Garter Point, as they prepare for the Battle of Passchendaele, 27 September 1917.

'How it happened …' An infantryman tells his comrades of the day's exploits, safe in their dugout for the night. Their grinning faces reveal another side to the war, the extremely close friendships of men ordered daily to risk their lives.

Exhausted Australian troops walk along a duckboard through the remains of Chateau Wood after the Battle of Passchendaele, 29 October 1917, in which they were ordered into battle without artillery protection, with catastrophic results.

Canadian machine gunners near Passchendaele, sunk in the mud, await the final order to attack the village, which they overran in November 1917. The Canadians earned nine Victoria Crosses for the loss of 16,000 men during the final push.

Dead and wounded lie in a dugout railway bedding between Tyne Cot and Passchendaele, 12 October 1917. Photographers were often unable to distinguish the living from the dead in the groups that scattered the battlefields of Flanders.

Stretcher-bearers knee deep in mud carry a wounded soldier out of No Man's Land. Both sides tended not to fire on stretcher parties, but showed less restraint during the final battles.

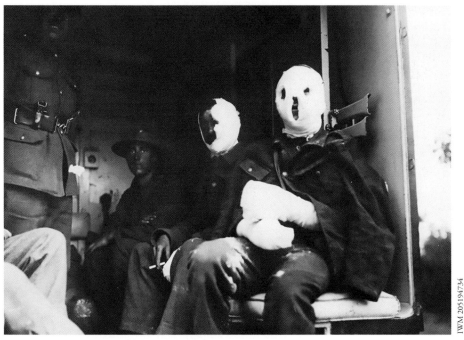

Two Canadian wounded, both heavily bandaged, one with face and hands almost completely obscured, in a motor ambulance during the Battle of Passchendaele. The terrible wounds to the face and brain forged the development of modern plastic surgery and neurosurgery.

Stretcher-bearers resting behind a concrete pillbox near Zonnebeke during the fighting at Passchendaele. Stretcher teams worked in relays over the worst of the terrain. Maori bearers often did away with the stretcher and carried men out on their shoulders.

In this famous photo of the battlefield the wounded are laid out at an aid post, awaiting evacuation. Rays of sunlight break through the clouds that shed torrential rain for most of August and October, turning the battlefield into a quagmire.

Tommy and Fritz share a smoke in No Man's Land: fraternisation was common among soldiers who grew to respect their opponents often more than their own commanders.

Prime Minister David Lloyd George would remember Passchendaele as the 'most futile and bloody fight ever waged in the history of war' – one that he did nothing to stop when he had the power to do so, despite his later claims.

Field Marshal Sir Douglas Haig, the British commander-in-chief on the Western Front. During several battles of Third Ypres, he ordered his armies to attack across fields of mud, in pouring rain, knowing they faced huge losses.

Haig meets Lloyd George, then Minister of Munitions, in France on 12 September 1916, during the Somme. Their relationship soon soured and they came to loathe each other, imperilling the Allied cause. In 1917, appalled by the losses, Lloyd George would try to transfer command of the British army to the French.

Accused of being a 'butcher' in recent decades, Haig returned to Britain after the armistice a war hero. Hugely popular, he would devote the rest of his life to serving veterans and their families. In later years, his reputation would never recover from Passchendaele.

General Herbert Plumer – 'Old Plum' – led the British and Anzacs to victory at the Battle of Messines. A champion of the 'bite and hold' tactics that almost broke the German lines, Plumer was reputed to be one of the better generals on the Western Front.

General Hubert Gough (above left) led the first attack of the Flanders Offensive, which ended in stalemate and his Fifth Army stalled in the mud. The Dominions would refuse to serve under him, such was his reputation for needless wastage of lives.

On the agony in Flanders in 1917 German commander Erich Ludendorff (above right), general of the infantry, would later write: 'the horror of Verdun was surpassed … It was mere unspeakable suffering'.

Field Marshal Paul von Hindenburg, Kaiser Wilhelm and Ludendorff (left to right) study their maps. The war would destroy the German empire, forcing the Kaiser into exile. His most senior commanders later fell under the sway of the lance corporal turned politician, Adolf Hitler.

Commander of the Anzacs, the British General William Birdwood (above left) proved popular with his men, donning the slouch hat and making an effort to understand their subversive spirit.

The Australian General John Monash (above right) challenged his superiors' decision to keep attacking in October 1917, when heavy rain made progress impossible. Overruled, he could do little more than reinforce his field ambulance before the attack.

Fiercely protective of his men, the rotund General Sir Arthur Currie (centre), commander of the Canadian Corps, also tried to resist orders to send thousands of Canadians to certain death at Passchendaele.

Theo, a friend, Keith and George Seabrook (left to right) rest before battle in Flanders, 1917. All three would die in a single action, 20–21 September. Their mother would never accept the official account of the 'disappearance' of George, whose body was never recovered.

Mrs Anne Alsop, of Winchelsea, Victoria, one of thousands of mothers who received an official letter after the war, notifying her that the remains of her son, Fred (inset), twenty, were unrecoverable and that his name would be inscribed on a monument.

'Known unto God': here lie the remains of three unidentifiable Australian soldiers, probably blown apart by a direct hit. By the war's end, tens of thousands of soldiers would be buried in anonymous graves.

11,956 soldiers are buried at Tyne Cot, Passchendaele, the world's largest Commonwealth cemetery (below), the walls of which bear the names of 34,857 men whose bodies were never found or identified, such as these members of the Black Watch (right).

München, 19. Juni 1917     Preis 35 Pfg.     22. Jahrgang Nr. 12

A. g. XIII

# SiMPLiCiSSiMUS

Begründet von Albert Langen und Th. Th. Heine

Abonnement vierteljährlich 4 Mark · Alle Rechte vorbehalten     Abonnement vierteljährlich 4 Mark · Copyright 1917 by Simplicissimus-Verlag G.m.b.H. & Co., München

Der Tod von Flandern    (Zeichnung von Thö)

„Ihr Menschen, hört auf — ich kann nicht mehr!"

The German nation felt the terrible weight of a war that killed two million of its men. Here the Grim Reaper, on the cover of the German magazine *Simplicissimus*, sits on a pile of corpses in Flanders and despairs: 'You people stop … I can't take anymore.'

disembowelled, scalped or castrated, and others with ghastly facial wounds.[21]

The hospitals were crowded with the chronic cases and the psychologically ruined. 'Kill me! Kill me!' was a familiar scream from a man who had just heard he'd never see, hear or make love again.[22] Day and night, Collins heard men, 'who were probably dying', cry out for their mothers. The dedication of the nurses, many the daughters of aristocratic families, made a deep impression on him: 'it must have been a great change to go and have to empty bedchambers as their first job in the morning'.[23]

The sheer scale of the medical challenge catalysed reforms and improvements, and great strides were made in hygiene and methodology. The Great War brought forth sterilised gauze, rubber gloves, mobile laboratories, intravenous saline solutions, blood transfusions, hypodermic syringes and lighter X-ray machines;[24] as well as huge advances in anaesthetics, wound disinfection, amputation, the setting of fractures, and plastic surgery.[25] Much of this came into use for the first time during Third Ypres. The hideous deformities to the face and body called on new skin-grafting techniques pioneered by the young exponents of plastic surgery. The clients of today's vanity industry might pause to thank the surgeons of the Great War the next time they buy a nip and tuck.

Men bore the loss of limbs with remarkable stoicism, as their letters attest. '[N]ow Mother,' wrote Private C. J. Joss, 'I have a piece of news for you that I'm afraid you won't like . . . about three days ago my leg hemoerraged [sic] and the result has been that I have had to lose some of it. Please don't be frightened . . .'[26]

New weapons, too, called on a new understanding of the horrors of war. The only treatment for mustard gas was to bathe the afflicted area in a soda solution and decontaminate the clothing. The gas clearing station received the first cases, about 1000 blinded and blistered men, on 22 July, of whom about twenty died, chiefly from bronchial troubles. 'Fortunately vision does not appear to be often lost,' observed an American medical officer, Dr Harvey Cushing.[27]

More deadly were chlorine and phosgene gas, the effects of which Edward Lynch witnessed after the battle of Polygon Wood:

I saw seven gassed men dying out behind a dressing station. They were in convulsions and black in the face and throat. Buckets of blood-specked foamy sort of jelly was [*sic*] coming from their mouths. The doctor and orderlies attending them wore gas masks. The poor gassed beggars kept grabbing at things and I saw one man grab at his own hand and smash his fingers out of joint. One man tore his mouth nearly back to his ear trying to pull the gas out of his throat. And as each man died, they threw buckets of mud over their head and shoulders. Been far kinder to have smothered them before they died not after.[28]

——

Not since the Somme had doctors encountered such extreme cases of 'wound shock' (often confused with the nervous complaint known as shell shock), in which a blast or projectile inflicted so powerful a shock to the body that it self-anaesthetised, shut down, and failed to exhibit any signs of recovery: 'The local analgesia produced might permit of the removal of shattered limbs and of much manipulation without obvious pain . . .' The pain, when it came, was often so intense as 'to make men beg for death'; yet with effective 'management', such as complete immobilisation, 'a smoke, hot tea, morphia', the worst pain might be 'surprisingly moderate'.[29] 'Wound shock' came to mean the collapse of vital organs and bodily functions: the heart rate fell dramatically, the blood pressure sank, the whole system yielded. Only immediate, intensive care might reverse the process.

As old as warfare, yet barely understood, and not taken seriously in 1917, was the mental disorder then known as shell shock. None of the British, Dominion or German armies recognised shell shock as a serious medical condition, 'though it undeniably existed', remarked the Australian surgeon general Major General Sir Neville Howse

VC. Commanders tended to dismiss shell-shocked men as 'malin-gerers', 'windy' and 'neurotic', whose condition, they believed, was a result of cowardice or a family predisposition to psychiatric illness, and not a nervous reaction to intense shellfire.[30]

Many sufferers were court-martialled for cowardice and pun-ished; a few were shot. Traumatised soldiers whose self-discipline collapsed under the strain – abandoning their posts, falling asleep on sentry duty, drunkenness, going absent without leave – were severely dealt with: fined, sentenced to hard labour, or subjected to Field Punishment No. 1, 'when the victim or culprit was spread-eagled on the wheel of an artillery wagon and strapped by the ankles and the wrists. He was in full sun and remained there for the requisite number of hours he had been sentenced to.'[31] About 200 men per division probably experienced the wheel.

Death sentences were few, and rarely enacted. Only 94 British sol-diers were shot, most for desertion, in the year to the end of September 1917 (and 95 in the next twelve months). Of the 3080 men sentenced to death by British courts martial between the start of the war and 31 March 1920, 346 cases went ahead. Haig was, however, an inveterate believer in capital punishment, in order to 'make an example to pre-vent cowardice in the face of the enemy . . .'[32]

Self-inflicted wounds manifested the broken spirit of a soldier who no longer cared what his fellow men thought of him. There were surprisingly few cases – about 30 convictions per month (5.5 per cent of total convictions) in July, August and September 1917. Only the most acute terror overrode the shame of deliberately shooting yourself in the foot. A crop of self-inflicted wounds usually occurred in the lull of battle or in the anticipation of its resumption, when blowing off a finger seemed preferable to enduring another moment. 'You could not help being sorry for these men, even though you despised them,' wrote A. P. Herbert.[33] When these 'haggard, miser-able wisps' recovered from their wounds, they were given a dressing down, paraded in disgrace and dispatched to the front, often in the worst section of the line, where few survived.

Nobody seriously asked whether the unnatural strain of putting a man in a trench under an explosive storm might have caused his trauma. Dr William Rivers, of the Craiglockhart War Hospital in Edinburgh, immortalised in Pat Barker's novels, under whose care fell Graves, Wilfred Owen and Siegfried Sassoon, believed that the soldier's trauma resulted from his repressing the memory of his battle experiences; Rivers spent his days coaxing the patient to recall what had happened, however ghastly.

A medical officer at one casualty station, said to have 'exceptional insight', described shell-shocked men as 'unfit simply through strain and war-weariness'.[34] If so, it was a strange kind of fatigue that engendered such bizarre symptoms. Homer had described them in *The Iliad*; Hotspur suffered them in Shakespeare's *Henry IV, Part 1*: in mild cases, nervous tension, flashbacks and terrible nightmares. The worst were reduced to laughing lunatics and shuddering wrecks who, at the sound of shells bursting, would go berserk or curl up into embryonic balls, the prelude to complete nervous breakdown. Two severely shell-shocked patients, recalled Rifleman J. E. Maxwell, in a ward within earshot of a bombardment, leapt up and ran amok 'with their hands over their heads screaming and screaming and screaming'. The lights were out, due to the air raid, and 'they were charging around banging into things'. The nurses managed to calm the men down and put them back to bed.[35]

Despite their dismissal of the condition, British and Dominion commanders at Third Ypres knew what to expect. The Somme had produced a 'vast increase in the incidence of psychological casualties'.[36] '[P]erhaps the most terrible thing of all,' recalled Reverend Julian Bickersteth, a senior chaplain, 'was the laughter and tears of the shell-shocked cases. I found that hard to stand. Every effort to quiet them failed.'[37]

Early in 1917, army doctors cited the 'psychic factor' as the chief cause of 'delayed recovery' in a large proportion of casualties of the Somme, according to the Australian official medical history.[38] In short, they had been warned: regimental aid posts during Third

Ypres were about to confront the same phenomenon, on a larger scale – due to the wretched conditions and more concentrated artillery.

During Third Ypres, the Royal Army Medical Corps reclassified cases of shell shock as 'Not Yet Diagnosed Nervous'. Such cases were to be set aside for special examination at a dedicated clearing station, as decreed by a General Routine Order dated June 1917. At first, they were sent to a station near the front, 'too noisy' for 'nervous' men. A quieter station at Haringhe apparently achieved a remarkable success rate: just sixteen per cent of 5000 cases of shell shock required evacuation to specialist base hospitals.[39] Most were sent back to the front. That did not mean they were 'cured'; simply, that they'd been rested and persuaded to fight on. Doctors knew little of the long-term consequences and were discouraged from sending shell-shocked cases to comfortable hospitals at home, from where, the military feared, they would be reluctant to return to active duty.

No-one then knew the long-term complications of 'nervousness'. Not until it was diagnosed as a genuine mental illness in 1980 would psychiatrists label a spectrum of war-related psychological conditions as post-traumatic stress disorders. In other words, the war, and chiefly heavy artillery, and not cowardice or a predisposition to mental illness had created these nervous wrecks. No military doctors were prepared to say that in 1917 (and even today, some military officials vehemently deny the existence of PTSD). Perhaps it was no coincidence that, until 1917, shell-shocked cases were ineligible for a war pension: the government was afraid that special recognition of the disorder would 'open up a floodgate of wastage'.[40]

—

Head wounds posed a terrific surgical challenge. The American neurosurgeon Dr Harvey Cushing, who served with the British Army in Flanders, recorded his experiences at the head wound clearing station at Proven in a diary of searing honesty. His work laid the basis for modern neurosurgery.

Consider a few days in the life of this extraordinary man.[41] Never had he performed so many major brain operations with so little time. During the heavy rains in early August, Cushing's station received 2000 'head cases' a day, a rate he expected to rise 'hugely'. Soon enough, his surgery was packed with 'untouched cases, so caked in wet mud that it's a task even to strip them to find out what they've got'.

Proven was one of the busiest of the fifteen clearing stations, treating about 30,000 casualties in the first weeks of the offensive, ten per cent of which were listed as 'GSW (gun shot wound) Skull'. Often, Cushing operated 'all day'. He ended one shift, he wrote, by extracting 'a large piece of shell from a man's badly infected ventricle with the magnet – then dinner, and now to bed'.

Next morning, 'a large batch of wounded were unexpectedly brought in – mostly heads – men who have been lying out for four days in craters in the rain, without food. It is amazing what the human animal can endure. Some of them had maggots in their wounds.' Again, he used a magnet to draw steel fragments out of damaged brains. On 5 August, he was engaged in 'Urgent operations on more rotting men'. One had 'a gross gas infection of the brain'. Another, brought in on the 15th, had the whole of his frontal lobe blown out, by a piece of shell almost an inch square. By this point, Cushing's team were operating on eight serious neurological cases a day; they included 'little East End Tommies', big 'Fritz' prisoners and terrified Belgian civilians.

In early September, Cushing proposed that a special hospital be set aside for head wounds. The sheer volume warranted the reform, he argued. His team were more than fit to run it, having reduced the mortality rate of penetrating head wounds from 56 to 25 per cent. The British Surgeon-General Bruce Skinner answered that he would 'look into it'. Nothing was done before Polygon Wood, during which Cushing experienced his busiest two days yet: twelve patients on 27–28 September, of which several had 'multiples', meaning that he operated on twenty major head wounds in 24 hours, 'our record so far'.[42] In peacetime, he would have been unlikely to do more than one such operation a day. Cushing was performing complex brain surgery; surgeons who performed so-called 'knife, fork and spoon' operations – amputations or flesh wounds – often exceeded 100 operations a day.[43]

Moments of black comedy punctuated Cushing's routine: in late August, Skinner appeared in Cushing's surgery, complaining of a bee sting. Was it a battle casualty? Cushing asked. Skinner 'didn't get it at all'.[44]

At night, Cushing operated by candlelight to avoid drawing the attention of German aircraft. Bombing hospitals was rare, but both sides did it. The density of the British barrage destroyed anything in its path, including German dressing stations. On at least one occasion, German aircraft deliberately targeted an Allied hospital: the 3rd Australian casualty clearance station near 'a town that begins with the second last letter in the alphabet' was shelled three times, Elsie Grant, a young nurse working there, wrote to a friend on 23 August (the cryptic clue to her whereabouts survived the censors): 'this last time was too dreadful those brutal Germans deliberately shell our hospitals with all our poor boys [sic]'.

She and the other sisters were immediately moved to deep dugouts. Not all the wounded could be evacuated in time, and four were killed during the bombardment. 'I can't tell you how cruel it was to leave those poor helpless patients,' she wrote. Two dozen officers decided they were needed in the dugout to comfort the nurses, and arrived bearing food and a gramophone. Soon the party was singing 'Pack Up Your Troubles in Your Old Kit Bag'. When they all emerged, the hospital 'was a total wreck'.[45]

—

A kind of heaven awaited the recovering soldier in the little town of Poperinghe, nine miles west of Ypres, the British troops' rest and rehabilitation centre. It was 'one of the seven wonders of the world' to men returning from the front, observed Edmund Blunden MC.[46] Throughout 1917, troops pounded its mediaeval square and filled the local billets, pubs, cafes and brothels, swelling its population from 10,000 in peacetime to tens of thousands during the war.

In the heart of 'Pop', as the men dubbed it, was a church-run haven for the soldiers' entertainment, called Talbot House, run by Chaplain Philip 'Tubby' Clayton, over whose rooms stood the sign, 'All Rank Abandon Ye Who Enter Here'. Tubby meant what he said: his parties often entertained a general, lieutenants and privates.

Talbot House staged comedies and singing nights, and its restaurant served British classics (roasts with Yorkshire pud, etc.). The library, a 'very large cupboard', was packed with books that the soldiers borrowed by 'pawning' their army caps. Services were held in the chapel in the attic, where 800 soldiers were confirmed and at least 50 baptised during the war.[47]

The happiest and saddest place in Talbot House was Friendship's Corner, the message board. Here, men who had been thought dead were brought back to life; and those who had been thought living were pronounced dead. The messages reunited thousands of troops over the years, with listings such as: 'Gunner H. STOOKE would like to see his brother BILL'; or 'Bdr [Bombardier] R. YEOMAN D/150 Howitzer Battery, RFA, would like to meet any old friends'; or 'Pte [Private] W. STAPLEHURST would like to meet Pte E. STAPLEHURST.'[48]

Talbot House distributed the soldiers' post and rations. When they arrived together, 'the post won every time', Tubby recalled. 'Letters were of more value than many biscuits. Tins of bully beef were not infrequently thrown away, but old letters never . . .'[49]

Most days on leave, the men took a hot bath in the bathhouse, a former brewery situated in the village of Reninghelst. They stripped and plunged into the brewing tub, or took a hot shower under a series of pipes pierced with holes. They attempted to 'delouse' their clothes in a variety of ways, chiefly by boiling them, but 'lice continued to live and thrive despite everything', observed Captain Philip Gosse, of the 69th Field Ambulance.[50]

The men played soccer and cricket, drank and relaxed here, and fraternised with the locals. The appearance of normality among the townspeople was a source of comfort and reassurance. Corporal Alfred Leahy, who served at Third Ypres with the Royal Australian Engineers, was reassured to see ordinary people going about their business. 'Harvesting is now in full swing over here and the fields are being mostly worked by women, girls and boys,' he told his mother, on 2 September 1917. 'Nearly every woman and girl are dressed in mourning for some dead relative or other who has fallen in the war. We all dread the approach of another winter but hope by the end of the year this great war will be terminated.'[51]

—

Even if the Channel was calm, the slightest rock of the troop ship jarred the seriously wounded, many of whom fell seasick. For them, the voyage home was 'a nightmare of nauseating pain'.[52] A buzz of voices, the honk of launches and the sound of automobiles on the wharves greeted their arrival at Southampton or Plymouth, where uniformed men with white armbands carried the stretcher cases off the ship and onto the hospital trains, bound for Charing Cross, London. These arm-banded men were conscientious objectors, whose religious beliefs had exempted them from combat. 'They are perhaps doing their bit on home service,' Ed Lynch recalled, 'but nevertheless we somehow despise them.'[53]

A dream-like experience attended the soldiers' return to Britain, in late 1917. A weary and divided nation awaited them. Anecdotally the home fires were still burning. The middle classes tended to carry a torch for the spirit of 1914. Children still dressed up in khaki; girl guides volunteered to make socks and mittens for the troops; boy scouts acted as lookouts or ran errands for the army; and babies were still being named after towns in France and Flanders.

Long coal and food queues were ubiquitous: sullen-faced women and miserable children would wait for hours to buy coal, in short supply since the government introduced strict coal rationing in April 1917. As winter approached, angry crowds besieged the coal trolleymen and tried to gather extra fuel from the railway sidings. Queues for scarcities such as meat, sugar, tea, bacon and butter, the price of which soared in 1917, often turned violent. In Birmingham, they were 'a pathetic and alarming spectacle' of bedraggled despair, according to one witness.[54] The queues lengthened alarmingly later that year, when thousands lined up in the hope of some butter or margarine. In response, from September 1917, the government introduced food rationing, along with a nationwide plan to boost tillage and cereal harvests.[55]

The British people, however, suffered none of the famine-like destitution of German civilians (see below). Potatoes were in plentiful supply, thanks to a good mid-year harvest, as were tinned fish and 'war bread', made out of wheat husks. People complained that the bread was inedible and fit only for pigs, but they ate it. Bread consumption was in fact higher than pre-war levels, because it was cheap, thanks to a government bread subsidy that kept the prices down, financed by taxes on the rich. Anyone caught wasting bread or giving crusts to pets was fined. One wealthy woman received a £20 fine for feeding her Pekingese a regular diet of rump steak.[56]

The rich and upper middle classes were rarely seen queuing; their income was able to absorb the black-market food prices. In fact, the well-off 'remained conspicuous consumers', notes Trevor Wilson.[57] London's butchers were fully stocked, according to one visitor, but only the wealthy could afford meat. Nor would the aristocracy let the war curb their demand for luxury goods, the trade of which the government exempted from higher taxes. 'New hats,' complained Auckland Geddes, in late 1917, 'alone absorb the work of millions of fingers, and whatever effect they may have, that effect certainly does not include helping to beat the enemy.'[58] The government defended the trade in luxury goods as economically beneficial, ignoring the fact that satiating the tastes of the members of the House of Lords and their ilk locked up labour that might have worked for the war effort. Yet surely there was nothing wrong in throwing a good party? One Lady Scott attended a lavish dinner at the Berkeley in May 1917, where, to her shock, champagne and strawberries were served, followed by the theatre.[59]

Nobody in Britain starved. Ration cards ensured a fairer distribution of scarce foodstuffs. And British food stocks were holding up very well. The Royal Navy's convoy system had protected merchant shipping. German Deputy Matthias Erzberger admitted as much in a speech to the Main Committee of the Reichstag on 6 July 1917. '[T]he submarine war,' he declared, 'was perfectly hopeless and it was quite impossible for us to win the war at all'. His words infuriated Ludendorff and the armed forces.[60] But Erzberger was right: German submarines had inflicted little damage on British food stocks, and had only seriously affected sugar, supplies of which were down by a third because they were wholly imported. True, the Germans were producing eight subs a month, the War Cabinet heard on 24 September,[61] but German success at sea 'had not been commensurate with their increased numbers'.[62] Indeed, on 21 September, the press announced the British victory over the German U-boats. '[T]he submarine is defeated,' reported *The Dundee Courier* and other papers. 'If the public knew what we know,' a 'high naval authority' had leaked to the Press Association, 'they would not have the slightest anxiety [about the U-boat] . . .'[63]

In sum, Haig's original strategic justification for Third Ypres – to destroy the U-boat bases on the Belgian coast – had ceased to exist. But nobody in the War Cabinet saw fit to ask: why persist with an offensive that is killing tens of thousands of men for an objective that no longer threatens us? Or for one that is no longer urgent enough, surely, to justify such heavy losses?

———

If the rich and middle classes were well fed and content – many women had jobs for the first time – the British workers were disenchanted. The inequity infuriated the poor. The perception that the wealthy were gorging themselves while the poor went hungry caused 'more discontent and dissatisfaction to the people of East London than anything we have known since the war started', noted the *East London Advertiser*.[64]

The unions were flexing their muscles, and thousands were going on strike: 1917 would prove the worst year for British industrial action since the war began, with 688 strikes and trade disputes, involving 860,000 workers.[65] An especially bad week ending on 26 September (the day of the battle of Polygon Wood) recorded 75 strikes, many against food shortages.[66]

Though disruptive, these were hardly the beginnings of an insurrection. British workers were not radicalised to the extent of the Russian proletariat, of course, who would soon dismember the ruling class in the coming October Revolution. Nor would the British worker find the enthusiasm to imitate the anti-war German Workers' and Soldiers' Councils, then being formed to seize power from the Prussian-controlled state.

The British workers' patriotism, love of country over class, and psychological affinity with subjection – of 'knowing one's place' – trumped their anger at food prices, poor factory conditions, wartime profiteering and even the extension of income tax to low-wage earners. They protested and went on strike, and then submitted, as so often, to their economic overlords.

In one respect, the salaried and working classes' feelings were indeed hardening – against the war. '[M]uch of the early enthusiasm' for military service had 'evaporated', claimed one report on the British recruitment situation, in July 1917: 'the voluntary system having exhausted most of those who were keen to fight, the later drafts under conscription consist mainly of men averse to doing so'. For this, the authors blamed the 'governing classes', who had 'forgotten . . . the ideals which were in men's hearts in the first months of the war'; and the 'military authorities' for not treating conscripts 'with human sympathy and consideration'.[67] The authors failed to see that the army's job was not to sympathise with soldiers but to train them to fight. The more likely cause of a lad's reluctance to enlist in 1917 was his very real fear of losing his life or part of his body.

By then, crippled and deformed veterans were commonplace in European cities.

—

One of the great myths about the Great War is that people hated it, and wished it would end. On the contrary, countless civilians, safe in their urban redoubts, revelled in the stories of great victories and huge armies on the march. Even in 1917, the anti-war movement made little impact on the war-approving majority. Fewer men may have wanted to fight it, but they did not openly oppose it. A small minority saw the tragedy as a catastrophe for civilisation, for which every European nation bore a measure of responsibility. The rest seemed to bear out some truth in Graham Greene's later observation: 'Perhaps to the soldier the civilian is the man who employs him to kill, who includes the guilt of murder in the pay-envelope and escapes responsibility.'[68]

Returning to this alien world, the soldier felt a jolt of estrangement, of dislocation, sharpened by the perception that so few at home seemed aware of, interested in or able to comprehend his experience in Flanders. Was anyone truly conscious of the scale of his sacrifice?

The newspaper version of the war struck the returning soldiers as the most glaring offender. The papers were wilfully blind. Government propaganda twisted the first casualty of war into an unrecognisable story of derring-do, a boisterous enfilade of jolly good news about a patriotic romp through Flanders in which our boys would skewer the Hun and return victorious. Lord Beaverbrook's Express Group was the loudest and most obscene offender, but Lord Northcliffe's *The Times* sometimes matched the *Daily Mirror*'s standards of wilful misinformation. 'Are we downhearted? – No' claimed the *Times* headline over a staged photo of troops waving their helmets on their way to the front on 8 August 1917, captioned, 'Cheering as they go forward'.[69] Away from the cameras, the soldiers were downcast and sullen, possibly at the thought of the huge losses of the battle of Pilckem Ridge their comrades had just fought.

The accredited journalists of the Press Section, the 'chateaux warriors' recumbent in their lavish French and Belgian billets, were made to understand that they should not report 'the truth', or the truth as they found it. Their dispatches were to provide a 'steadying' influence on the home population, in the view of Brigadier General John Charteris, whose Intelligence Section at GHQ controlled their activities. In Haig's view, the reporter had a slightly less demeaning purpose: to promote the justice of the British cause and impress upon the people the case for a long and costly campaign – in other words, to defend his strategy of attrition. Critical articles and facts that got in the way of the official line were censored.

Lloyd George would recall the residual press coverage with contempt, drawn from his conviction that Lord Northcliffe 'had, ever since 1916, been the mere kettledrum of Sir Douglas Haig, and the mouth organ of Sir William Robertson'. *The Times*'s reports were 'therefore ecstatic'.[70] After the September battles, the paper reported that 'we advanced about a thousand yards' and 'our losses were heavy'. Despite these meagre gains, the enemy's elaborate defensive system had been crushed, under the headline, 'GERMAN DEFENCE BROKEN'.[71] Later reports, after more terrible losses, referred to 'a smashing blow, the most smashing defeat we have inflicted on the enemy, a complete victory', concluding, 'We have him beat.'[72]

The media's misreporting was more a question of emphasis and omission than one of brazen lies. The censors filleted out any bad news. According to one study of the press coverage of Passchendaele, 'Military censorship, or the absence of news, had become the shock-troops of propaganda. As a result the media record was nothing like "reality", but rather an illusion of reality . . .'[73]

The most meretricious reports were the result of official, government-approved lies, such as the ridiculous stories of bayoneted babies, mutilated corpses and Berlin's alleged Corpse Conversion Factory, which boiled down soldiers' bodies to extract scarce soaps and lubricating oils. This nonsense was predicated on the idea that the British blockade had been so successful as to deny cleansing agents to the German people.

The succession of stories of British victories over the Huns bore out the guiding principle of Charteris, as he put it: 'to make armies go on killing one another it is necessary to invent lies about the enemy'.[74] Years later, it surprised nobody who knew him to learn that Charteris had made up the Corpse Factory story, to rally neutral nations behind the war effort.

So, during one of the most terrible conflicts on the Western Front, when Allied morale fathomed the lowest circles, the people at home learned that the British and Empire armies were 'in the best of spirits' (*The Times*, 28 September 1917); enjoying 'Complete Success' (*Daily Mirror*, 22 September 1917, in a report about 'the Battle of the Pill Boxes' – a verdict the paper reversed two days later); and delivering a series of 'smashing blows' or striking 'another blow' (*Daily Mirror*, 6 October 1917). The Germans were cast as savages who would bayonet your daughter, or as pathetic specimens, miserable, despondent, broken – a mirror of Haig's view. The Germans were neither; they were simply young men, like their British and Dominion counterparts, trying to survive the holocaust their governments had unleashed on the world.

There were jewels of journalistic excellence, splinters of clarity that broke through the official whitewash. Philip Gibbs, of *The Daily Telegraph* and *Daily Chronicle*, is often cited as the finest of the Great War correspondents, but Charles Bean, who later made his name as Australia's official historian, shared that accolade. Both sent vivid and arresting reports during Third Ypres, some of which survived the censors. Some correspondents tried to interpret the war, even if they erred in defence of Haig's strategy. Perry Robinson, in the *Daily News and Leader*, 20 September 1917, grasped the point of bite and hold: 'For a long time [the German wires] sought to represent each of our attacks as "an attempt to breakthrough". We have never attempted to break through. It is not that kind of war.'[75]

Of course, the German press were similarly manipulated to peddle myths about British barbarity (they had a point in the case of the naval blockade). All governments use the Fourth Estate as a launch pad for psychological warfare, and the press offensives of 1917 seem positively quaint by the totalitarian standards of the mid-twentieth century. Yet the propaganda campaigns were extremely effective, and won millions of people over to the war. In this light, it is absurd to suggest that the war went on simply 'because the peoples of Europe willed it so'.[76] Governments were not merely reacting to mass enthusiasm for war. The war 'the people' were supposedly willing had little to do with the reality of Third Ypres and the incessant 'wastage' of young men. In any case, the 'people', if represented by their ability to vote, ignored half the population: women. And from the summer of 1917, the people's enthusiasm began to collapse: workers were on the march against the war, families were distraught, and governments who counted on their support were experiencing a loss of nerve.

'We are losing the flower of our Army, and to what purpose,' Lloyd George confided in a colleague on 6 August.[77] Something had to be done to win back popular enthusiasm for the war, the Cabinet decided. Lloyd George set out to answer his own question: as Third Ypres began, he announced the formation of the National War Aims Committee, set up to sell the war to the people afresh. The committee subjected audiences around the country to fiery pro-war speakers such as Horatio Bottomley, instructed to put the bark back into the British bulldog: 889 meetings were held around Britain between 25 September and 10 October, promoting the 'good fight' during some of the worst battles of Passchendaele. The speakers made no reference, of course, to the war of mechanised slaughter then about to enter its most dreadful phase.

—

Towards the end of 1917, nothing could deflect public horror at the dreadful harvest of war: the ranks of the wounded inhabiting the cities and villages of Europe. Forty thousand British, hundreds of thousands of French and about half a million German soldiers would undergo amputations by the war's end, spurring the development of dozens of kinds of prosthetic arms and legs.[78]

The home front tried to normalise the horror. In British shires, for example, cricket matches were arranged between full-bodied local teams and 'Arms & Legs' sides, in which the local bowlers were told to bowl easily against one-legged or one-armed batsmen. Soldiers with severe facial wounds presented a terrible spectacle to the home front. Many men had lost their noses, ears, eyes or entire jaws, leaving ghastly scars and twisted flesh. 'Hideous is the only word for these smashed faces,' observed one hospital orderly. 'The socket with some twisted, moist slit, with a lash or two adhering feebly, which is all that is traceable of the forfeited eye.'[79] There were no mirrors and very few visitors in the wards set aside for the dreadfully deformed – the 'chambers of horrors', as they were known in the hospitals. If the patient returned to the community, he tended to shut himself away, rather than endure public revulsion at his appearance – as would the victims of Hiroshima and Nagasaki, 28 years later.[80] For such men, 'becoming a cinema projectionist was the ideal job'[81] – or a night worker.

Some cases were beyond surgery, and monstrous to the point of offending the public. For such men, in Britain, France and Germany, masks were moulded out of plaster, copper, wire and hair, to disguise what remained of the soldier's face. The masks gave a freakish, vaudeville appearance to the wearer, many of whom discarded them the instant they left hospital.

Hope for these men arose in the summer of 1917, when Professor Harold Gillies, a pioneering plastic surgeon, established a specialist hospital in a stately home in Kent where he conducted the world's first plastic surgical operations. Gillies had spent the war trying to find a surgical response to 'men without half their faces'.[82] In time, he would build the world's finest plastic surgical team, and make great advances in the reconstruction of human noses, jaw lines, cheeks and chins. A lot of good came out of his spirited reaction to the war.

—

Returning soldiers gazed in wonder at the strangeness of the cities and the people. 'In London the war is a very real thing,' the Australian medical officer Major George Alexander Birnie wrote to his parents in October 1917. Frequent air raids were a constant reminder:

> A huge bomb in Piccadilly the other night killed about
> 30 people and wounded some hundreds besides breaking
> every pane of glass within ¼ of a mile. The cost of living is
> enormous, practically no sugar is obtainable, very little tea
> . . . but rationing is not far off. The wounded are everywhere
> and the Hospitals are crowded. But still the shops are full of
> beautiful and costly things, the theatres are full and there
> is no lack of food in the restaurants. There is no mourning
> in England though, and though nearly everyone had lost
> someone, there is no parade of it, which is one thing in which
> we are superior to the French, I think, who are all in black.[83]

Some returning soldiers sensed a want of spine among the people. Colonel Wilkinson arrived in London in September, soon after an air raid. A few days earlier, he had witnessed the death or wounding of thousands of men in battle, and the media's disproportionate coverage of the air raids disgusted him. He wrote to his father:

> [T]o judge from the papers, the majority of people appear
> to be entirely demoralised. After there has been an air raid
> over London it is difficult to believe that there is still a war
> on out here. Columns and columns of what we consider to be
> entire nonsense are written on the subject . . . & there is an
> entire omission of any other war news. One reporter had the
> impertinence to say that 'under the circumstances cheerfulness
> would have been as offensive as panic'! He should see the British
> soldier undergoing a nice bombardment . . . Such drivel I have

seldom read . . . Seeing what the soldier, not so long ago himself a civilian, has to put up with, we think that the people at home might show a little more fortitude when they get a mild insight into the realities of war. For the women and children I am very sorry, but there are many women whom it will not harm to realise that this war is not quite the joke they thought it was.[84]

Neville Hind got closer to the truth about the soldiers' feelings on his return home. He wrote of civilians who 'cannot even approach comprehension' and whose 'glib commonplaces' and 'cheap sympathy' he found 'hideously exasperating':

Perhaps you are tempted to give them a picture of a leprous earth, scattered with the swollen and blackening corpses of hundreds of young men. The appalling stench of rotting carrion . . . of flies and bluebottles clustering on pits of offal. Wounded men lying in the shell holes among decaying corpses; helpless under the scorching sun and bitter nights, under repeated shelling. Men with bowels dropping out, lungs shot away, with blinded, smashed faces, or limbs blown into space. Men screaming and gibbering. Wounded men hanging in agony on the barbed wire, until a friendly spout of liquid fire shrivels them up like a fly in a candle. But these are only words and probably only convey a fraction of their meaning to the hearers. They shudder, and it is forgotten . . .[85]

On leave, Hind resolved never to talk about such things.

—

The British people were far better off than their German counterparts. The British blockade had inflicted a great deal more suffering on the Germans than unlimited submarine warfare had on the British.

Holger Herwig's exhaustive history of the German home front

reveals the full extent of German impoverishment as a result of the blockade. The domestic economy staggered under the demands of fighting a total war without access to a seaport. By late 1917, the nation was stripped to the bone. Berlin had exhausted the metal reserves in the occupied territories, and now appealed to the German people to surrender any metal possessions. Cartloads of old pots, kettles, candlesticks, lamps, cutlery and other metallic objects arrived at the collecting stations.[86] Churches yielded up their metals to the arsenal. By mid-year, few possessed a copper roof or church bell, virtually all of which would be melted down and used in weapons. The old Prussian Synod donated 10,312 church bells. Supplies of cotton, silk and fibrous materials vital for the manufacture of uniforms and blankets dwindled. 'Wooden' tyres were prescribed after supplies of rubber ran out (echoed in Japan in 1945 when kamikazes flew partly wooden planes). Oil and petroleum were in desperately short supply: after exhausting Romanian and Galician oil supplies, Berlin turned to ersatz measures such as 'gasohol', a blend of alcohol and petroleum.

The nation was slowly starving. German civilians were experiencing an epidemic of malnutrition. Most food necessarily went to the armed forces. A single corps of infantry, according to Herwig's study, devoured one million pounds of meat and 660,000 loaves of bread per month, while their horses needed seven million pounds of oats and four million pounds of hay.[87]

Yet it was never enough. To preserve the food supply, the German Government imposed 'meatless' and 'fatless' days; and an ingenious array of ingredients replaced the staple diet of bread, milk, sausage and sugar. Black bread, fatless sausage, one egg and a few potatoes and turnips constituted the average weekly diet, and the German people even consumed ground European beetles. These measures merely delayed the encroachment of hunger-related diseases (cases of tuberculosis, for example, soared). Since the start of the war, the weekly calorie intake had fallen by a third, to 1000, and the civilian mortality rate had increased by 37 per cent. The hardest hit were the weakest – young children, the sick and the elderly

– whose mortality rates rose by as much as 50 per cent.

In the spring of 1917, food shortages and soaring inflation led to the breakdown of civil life in Germany and the occupied territories. Annual domestic wheat production had almost halved, to about 2.5 million tons, and the meat ration was cut to half a pound per week, accompanied by the destruction of a million cows. With the terrible 'turnip winter' of 1916–17 high in their minds, the German people took to industrial action and mass protest against the soaring prices. In April, hunger strikes erupted in about 300 German factories, while about 150,000 Berlin workers in key war industries struck over the lack of food.[88] Thousands of workers in several German cities demanded an end to the war. To offset the wave of strikes, the Berlin Government subjected all industries and factories to military law. Anyone capable of working was forced to do so. Social misfits, homosexuals, prostitutes, the mentally ill were pressed into service in factories, hospitals and farms.

By mid-year, the blockade had reduced Germany to a beggar nation. Her foreign trade had collapsed, from US$5.9 billion in 1913 to US$800 million in 1917.[89] The treasury was technically bankrupt: tax receipts barely covered the interest on the soaring debt. In 1917, the worst year, the cost of the war topped 52 billion marks, while tax and other receipts were a mere 7.8 billion, creating a deficit of about 44 billion marks.[90]

The Germans could not rely on their main ally, Austria-Hungary: the Dual Empire had made no provision for a long, protracted war, and by 1917 was on its knees. Supplies of butter, fat, flour, potatoes and grains were exhausted or in short supply. The available potatoes were 'not fit for human consumption'.[91] As in Germany and Russia, inflation skyrocketed by late 1917, accompanied by food riots and destitution. On a typical day in Vienna, according to police, 250,000 hungry people formed some 800 queues outside the food markets and 54,000 people visited the soup kitchens.[92]

Sigmund Freud and other members of the bourgeoisie were

reduced to buying their cigars and liquor on the black market at huge prices. Many city residents flocked to the countryside on so-called 'hamster tours' to steal extra food, provoking a police crack-down. In the face of such shortages, Berlin and Vienna appropriated food and resources from the occupied territories: Romania supplied oil; Serbia cattle, sheep and hogs; Poland grain, potatoes, coal, eggs, horses and wood; and Albania some 50,000 turtles – most of which found their way to the black market and onto the tables of the rich.

By Third Ypres, most German civilians were living below the subsistence level and many were slowly dying of hunger or illnesses relating to malnutrition. Hoarding and ransacking of the rural food supplies were commonplace. German housewives engaged in fero-cious rows in queues and often 'brutally snatched' potatoes and fruits from farmers' stalls. Mothers lashed out at an obvious target, the owners of expensive, well-stocked Berlin department stores, most of whom were wealthy Jews. Such German women 'of little means' were indeed 'a potential time bomb' for the Prussian authorities, as Herwig concludes.[93]

With their sons and husbands dead, wounded or fighting, and their children malnourished and sick, millions of German people were ripe for exploitation by a demagogue who would soon articu-late their frustrations. Hitler had returned on leave in August 1917 and had witnessed with disgust the breakdown in civilian morale.[94] German civilian deaths attributed to the hunger blockade (and related diseases) were 762,796, according to British and German official figures, with a lower estimate of 424,000.[95] (Those figures exclude a further 150,000 German victims of the 1918 influenza pandemic, which 'caused disproportionate suffering among those already weakened by malnutrition and related disease'.) By the war's end, the loss of one million births were also directly attributable to medical conditions resulting from or exacerbated by the British hunger blockade, making it one of the first war atrocities of the twentieth century.[96]

—

Women drew the returning soldier's immediate attention: his wife, his girlfriend, his sister, his mother, women in the shops, women in the street, their apparent warmth, their security, the pleasure they gave . . . all this he longed for. George Winterbourne, the semi-auto-biographical hero of Aldington's novel, was amazed at their 'almost angelic beauty' on his return to London. He had not seen a woman for seven months.[97] These strange, smiling creatures, so alien, so adorable, with their soft skin and sweet voices, their delicious smells and colourful dresses, startled young men who had grown used to each other's stink and grunts, hard lines and dead colours.

Most were hard at work. War had become a woman's business as much as a man's. Behind every soldier were women, assembling his weapons, tailoring his uniforms, dressing his wounds, urging him to do his duty, tearfully willing his departure. The war offered middle-class women a job, in war factories, industries and hospitals, and financial independence for the first time. Most willingly embraced their duty. The war benefited them. The suffragettes had set aside their campaign for the duration. Many younger women, who had dispatched men (or dull boyfriends) to the front by planting a white feather on their chest (denoting a coward), enjoyed new freedoms they hadn't dreamed of in peacetime. By mid-1918, more than 7,310,000 women were employed in war-related jobs, of whom 947,000 worked in munitions production, 90 per cent of the arms industry's workforce.[98]

A mood of libidinous abandon rippled across Europe when the war began, and showed no signs of abating in 1917. Women found the danger, the risk of violence and so many men in uniform sexually arousing. And women rekindled the returning soldiers' desire, long dormant or limited to masturbation, fleeting acts of homosexuality (then illegal) and bleak moments with prostitutes, for whose rushed services the soldiers would form long, dismal queues outside the few legal brothels in France and Belgium. The tactile nature of trench friendships – the pre-battle embrace, the cradling of the wounded, the firm arm around a friend's shoulder[99] – were usually supportive, not homosexual, in nature (though homosexual feelings were common enough). They expressed the affection of brothers-in-arms acutely aware that they might die tomorrow.

The first woman a soldier saw after months of war was typically a nurse, for whom he often felt an 'extraordinary feeling of attraction', recalled Sister J. Calder. 'I've never known anything like it . . .', she said, describing it as mutual sympathy and understanding, rather than anything sexual, between young men and women far away from home in the vicinity of a war zone.[100]

On leave, men tried to rejuvenate their sexual relationships in the few short weeks allowed them. Their departure date hung over any passion or tenderness like the shadow of a cowl. Winterbourne's first encounter with the two women he loved left him feeling cold. He sat silently through a dinner party as his girlfriend and her fashionable set laughed and gossiped excitedly about nothing he understood: 'He felt uncomfortable, like a death's head at a feast.'[101] It was not the fault of his friends. After a terrible row with the girls dearest to him, Winterbourne perceived a truth about himself: while they remained human, he had become 'merely a unit, a murder-robot, a wisp of cannon fodder'. The girls sensed the change in him. One said, 'It's quite useless, he's done for. He'll never be able to recover. . . . What was rare and beautiful in him is as much dead now as if he were lying under the ground in France.'[102]

Winterbourne wandered the city, his thoughts mired in bitterness. He sat in a music hall and watched patriotic films about how all the girls loved 'Tommy': Tommy, who would defeat the Germans by dangling a sausage from his bayonet. And this estranged young man drew a brutal conclusion about leave in Blighty: 'one of the horrors of the War was not fighting the Germans, but living under the British'.

This severe personal judgement is an extreme case: Aldington's hero did not speak for the temperate and often loving reactions of other men on home leave. Yet many would feel the same sense of disillusionment, a feeling Aldington later described to his friend, the poet T. S. Eliot, whose poem *The Waste Land* is leavened with the imagery of a world destroyed.

—

As he sensed the ignorance of the people, heard the thunderous speeches in favour of war, and read the newspaper accounts of great victories he knew to be disastrous, a fissure opened in the soldier's mind. On one side, he experienced the fantasy war on the home front; on the other, the bloody reality of the Western Front. And as time passed, the fissure widened into two irreconcilable perceptions, sending the soldier to the margins of society, where, like Neville Hind, he stayed silent and dared not speak of his experiences. Winterbourne's girlfriend was not the only woman who yawned with boredom as she heard him describe the dreadful expression on the faces of gassed men.[103]

Some men raged at the whole political machinery that kept the country at war, the most sensational example of whom was Siegfried Sassoon, who had received the Military Cross for 'performing suicidal feats of bravery', according to Robert Graves. Sassoon's disillusionment drove him to toss the ribbon of the medal into the Mersey River, and to urge his fellow soldiers to 'throw their medals in the faces of their masters'. Though he hadn't served at Third Ypres, Sassoon's poem 'Memorial Tablet' immortalised the battle, with the line 'I died in Hell – (They called it Passchendaele)'. In June 1917, an MP read Sassoon's letter denouncing the war to a shocked Parliament. 'The War is being deliberately prolonged by those who have the power to end it,' he wrote (see Appendix 7 for full text).[104] For his pains, Sassoon was sent to an army doctor who diagnosed him as suffering from a nervous breakdown. He was confined to a mental hospital.

Many soldiers bitterly concluded that their correct place, the only place left to them, was back at the front with the men, where at least 'you were doing something real'.[105] The bleakest irony is that many sought solace in the war itself, and longed to return to the trenches.

And as the soldiers boarded the dark troop ship – their 'old friend' that would take them back to France – many shared a kind of love for the 'barbaric but not brutal' men on the voyage. 'I don't care a damn what your cause is,' thought Winterbourne. 'By God! I swear I'll die with you rather than live in a world without you.'[106]

# 12

# THE CRUELLEST MONTH

*You cannot fight machine guns plus wire, with human bodies.*
Sir Andrew Russell, commanding the New Zealand Division

---

*. . . no pen or brush has yet achieved the picture of that*
*Armageddon in which so many of our men perished*
Philip Gibbs, war correspondent, October 1917

---

'I am of opinion,' Haig wrote on 28 September 1917, 'that the enemy is tottering, and that a good vigorous blow might lead to decisive results.'[1] In such hopes, which he shared with Gough and Plumer at a conference that day, Haig brought forward the next attack from 6 October to 4 October, ordered up six infantry divisions and placed five cavalry divisions at Plumer's disposal behind the Yser Canal. High in his mind, as ever, was the prospect of a breakthrough, even if it involved the slow grind of 'bite and hold'. At a minimum, Passchendaele Ridge should be his by mid-October.

Spurring Haig's desire for swift action was Charteris, in whose wilful distortion of the truth the former retained a blinkered faith. Haig's intelligence chief now claimed that the Germans had 'used up' 48 divisions in the Flanders battles since 31 July, 'while we have only had 23 in the line so far'. Haig's generals tended not to share his faith in Charteris: 'it comes from Charteris I fear!!' Rawlinson lamented, a common reaction on discovering the source of the intelligence.[2] If the commander-in-chief 'allowed himself' to be deluded by Charteris,[3] Haig's decision to press on seemed, from one viewpoint, understandable: the soldiers' spirits were high after the September victories, and the weather had been fine for weeks. The bite and hold tactics had triumphed at Polygon Wood: why should they not continue 'working' – i.e. grinding the enemy back – if the weather held? 'In the air was the unmistakable feeling,' wrote Bean, '. . . that the British leaders now had the game in hand and, if conditions remained favourable, might in a few more moves secure a victory which would have its influence on the issue of the war.'[4]

Reinforce success, Haig insisted at the commanders' conference on 2 October. Don't make the same mistake as the Germans, who, on 31 October 1914, during First Ypres, failed to finish off the exhausted British forces.[5] The circumstances had been very different then, but Haig would not broach any dissent. He resolved to turn all his power on the Passchendaele offensive for as long as the weather held. He suspended parallel operations at Lens and on the Belgian coast, and postponed plans for an attack at Cambrai. At this point, his generals shared his determination to finish the job in Flanders: they believed they had found a way of cracking the enemy's lines and only a change in the weather could prevent their destruction of the German forces in Belgium. As Rawlinson noted in his dairy, 'If only the weather shall last . . . we shall do a very big thing.'[6]

Ah, the weather: the curse of High Command. The disobedient elements brawled in the commanders' faces, confounding their mortal plans. Three rainless weeks had been a critical factor in the string of victories between 20 September and 3 October. The field of mud was now a dust bowl; shells skidded on landing, throwing up clods of dry earth. Yet the dry spell was about to break, according to 'Meteor', the British weatherman, Lieutenant Colonel Ernest Gold.

'[A] miracle might save us from rain,' he told the Second Army's chief of staff in early October.[7]

Meanwhile, the German commanders, though alarmed by British advances, were far from demoralised or beaten. Ludendorff conceded the enemy had broken, for now, the system of flexible defence; the gruff old warrior now wrestled for an answer to Plumer's slowly grinding steps. 'Our defensive tactics had to be developed further, somehow or other,' Ludendorff later growled. '[But] it was so infinitely difficult to agree on the right remedy.'[8] He and his commanders settled on a radical reform: the Eingreif units would be brought up to the front lines, in the hope of shocking the British forces when or even before they attacked.

News of Russia's complete collapse gave a further boost to German spirits, with the prospect of reinforcements from the east: 82 German divisions were stationed on the Russian front; 36 could be moved west within sixteen weeks of the redeployment order.

—

The British and Dominion armies resolved to carry on, hopeful the good weather would continue. They would attack Passchendaele Ridge in three steps: the first, to be called the Battle of Broodseinde, would start at dawn on 4 October 1917. The New Zealand and three Australian divisions were chosen to lead the attack, across a 2000-yard front, the arrowhead of Plumer's Second Army spread between 'Bitter Wood' and the Ypres–Staden railway, a front of some 14,000 yards (see Map 5). Their objective was to seize Broodseinde Ridge, an arc of higher ground a few miles short of Passchendaele Ridge that the British had not held since 1915. The Germans lining it had a direct view onto the Salient, spread out beneath them like a life-size map. The Anzacs were to advance 1500 yards in the first bite, across an extremely concentrated battlefield.

And so, once more, the lorries, mule-drawn wagons and light tramlines dragged the giant British war machine forward. Once more, the heavy guns and great masses of men and matériel came up. Huge dumps of medical supplies, blankets and stretchers were established in the forward areas. Advanced dressing stations and gas treatment stations were set up where a suitable shelter could be found. Starting tapes were laid. All of this proceeded within range of German shellfire.

The four Antipodean divisions were fighting together for the first time, and they assembled in exuberant spirits. Tens of thousands of heavily laden Anzacs came up the dusty tracks from Ypres, along the Menin Road, past Hellfire Corner, through the Birr Cross Roads, past the rising, shell-torn ground of Bellewaerde Ridge towards the forward trenches and shell holes lining the jump-off point. 'The track from Bellewaerde to Westhoek Ridge,' remembered Ed Lynch, 'is . . . just a narrow strip of corduroy laid down across miles of unending muck, pock-marked by thousands of watery shell holes. The whole road is bordered by dead mules and mud-splattered horses, smashed wagons and limbers and freshly killed men who have been tossed off the track to leave the corduroy open for the never-ending stream of traffic.'[9]

A light rain fell on the night of 3 October, and turned the roads and tracks a bit muddy. Heavier rain would make them impassable to the gun carriages, warned an artillery unit.[10] The rain gathered strength and spat down around midnight, easing into a light drizzle in the early hours of the 4th. Just before dawn, low, dark clouds hid the full moon, portending something heavier. At 5.20 am, 40 minutes before zero, German flares illuminated the frontline Anzacs assembled in the mist below. The enemy shelled whatever they could see, killing or wounding about a seventh of I Anzac Corps before the battle began.[11]

The British and Anzac artillery produced a weaker, less dense barrage than previously: fewer Australian guns were in action that morning than the one for every five yards of front officially claimed.[12] The quality of the barrage varied, however, according to the location and timing: Monash described II Anzac's barrage as 'excellent'.[13]

At zero hour, 6 am, the first wave of infantry swallowed their tot of rum, lit their cigarettes and moved off, aglow with confidence, anticipating another victory. When the barrage reached the German trenches, the first line of Anzacs burst through the wall of smoke mingling with the morning mist. They met little resistance. As at Polygon Wood, the German defenders who were not dead or wounded surrendered or fled. Many sat immobilised with fear. A German blockhouse yielded to a single Australian officer, who captured 31 prisoners; another gave up as soon as the attack began, abandoning three machine guns. The pattern was repeated.[14]

Then, as if from nowhere, the Eingreif counter-strike units – normally further back – crowded forward with bayonets fixed, following Ludendorff's tactical reform. Ferocious hand-to-hand fighting ensued, in shell holes and around the pillboxes, several of which were set alight with phosphorus bombs. The leading Australian brigades swept on, silencing the enemy bunkers with Lewis guns and grenades. Monash's Third Division overran stubborn German holdouts in the ruins of Zonnebeke, and soon reached the 'valley' beneath Gravenstafel Ridge, a mere dip in the plain before it rose to Passchendaele. A Tasmanian battalion captured the concrete blockhouses that still stand at Tyne Cot Cemetery, suffering 50 dead and 204 wounded; one soldier sprinted 100 metres over open ground and subdued a pillbox single-handedly.[15] En route to their objectives, Australian patrols encountered an old trench the British had used in 1914–15, where the tattered remains of Tommy uniforms lay strewn.

The New Zealanders attacked the eastern slopes of Gravenstafel ('Abraham Heights') and the Gravenstafel spur itself, with similar, decisive results. With the help of a stronger barrage, they carried all before them up the wide, open slope. Dozens of enemy pillboxes were silenced and claimed.

At 8.10 am, having bitten hard, the Anzacs paused to hold their gains. Some were so confident they continued to give chase, pursuing the retreating Germans 'over the hilltop'.[16] Australian and New Zealand riflemen picked off the escaping enemy, who were 'fleeing in all directions'. 'It was always difficult to keep Australians from following an enemy who was on the run,' Bean observed.[17]

The British were abreast of the action, on the Antipodean flanks. The Fifth and Second armies, aided by tanks that could advance in the drier conditions, similarly captured all their objectives and thousands of prisoners. This great patchwork of actions culminated in another emphatic Allied success. In places, the Germans put up stiff resistance: officers defended their bunkers with revolvers and grenades, often to the last man. Fierce fighting surged around a huge crater on the ridge. At one point, the British and Anzacs had advanced so far that the German heavy guns were compelled to fire over open sights.

During and prior to the attack, some soldiers relished shooting down the Germans as they 'ran away from us', according to one Australian soldier.[18] So, too, did the British. 'It was great fun shooting at Germans,' Major Allhusen wrote to his mother. 'We saw any number running about & it cheered the men up enormously.'[19] By the end of it, he added, 'I was more alive than most people – some absolutely collapsed. Young Trotter . . . was carried away this morning. Nothing seriously wrong with him. Simply collapsed. He was too young for this sort of show.'[20]

Hand-to-hand combat, killing at a range of a few yards, mortified the more sensitive men. Nineteen-year-old Private Walter James Bradby shot dead three Germans as they fled a pillbox, two of whom, he later found to his distress, were younger than him. The memory would haunt Bradby for the rest of his life.[21]

By twelve minutes past nine, after three hours of battle, the Anzacs had secured most of Broodseinde Ridge and Abraham Heights, and routed the enemy in the area. German soldiers were continually seen bolting to the rear. Three hundred and fifty were found dead, many with bayonet wounds, within the first 500 yards of one brigade's front.[22]

For the first time in two years, the Allies enjoyed a view of the fields beyond the German lines. To the south-east, green pastures, copses and hedgerows spread out to the sky, and, when the shelling died and the smoke cleared, images of bucolic normality met their eyes: cows grazing, carts moving, smoke issuing from farmhouses. A few miles due east rose the ultimate objective of the battle: the ruins of the church in what remained of the village of Passchendaele, atop the highest ridge in the Salient. For now, they reversed the captured German trenches and awaited the final push, settling down to a breakfast of tea and black Bavarian bread.

—

Haig's headquarters revelled in the third decisive victory in fifteen days. Wild hyperbole permeated all ranks. Broodseinde was the greatest Allied triumph since the Battle of the Marne (in 1914), declared Plumer. '[D]ivision again brilliantly victorious in greatest battle of war,' Monash cabled Melbourne.[23] The Anzacs at Broodseinde had 'never fought better', Charles Bean concurred: 'An overwhelming blow had been struck and both sides knew it.'[24] Bean shared Haig's view that, 'for the first time in years', British and Dominion troops were poised to inflict a decisive victory on the Western Front.

'We have been very busy recently killing Germans,' Lieutenant Malcolm Kennedy wrote to this brother, the day after the battle. 'Our Australians have done very well.'[25] The personal messenger of General Sir Alexander John Godley, commander of II Anzac Corps, recorded the euphoria in the corps headquarters. The Anzacs had done 'far more' than expected of them: 'If only it keeps fine for a few more days Fritz will get the scare of his life but I'm afraid it will rain before long . . .'[26] Godley accepted without demur Haig's view of the 'demoralization not only of the [German] troops but of the enemy's commanders and staff . . . The whole of the battlefield of our successive advances is covered with dead Huns.'[27] Monash similarly believed that the Germans were now 'staggering' and that 'unless the weather balks me I shall capture P-village on 12th'.[28]

The newspapers were reliably ecstatic, trumpeting Broodseinde as the most complete success achieved by the 'British Army' (with whom the Anzacs were habitually bundled) thus far on the Western Front. The Battle of Broodseinde was 'The Turning Point of the War', 'Germany's Biggest Defeat' and New Zealand's 'Greatest and Most Glorious Day'.[29]

Nine Victoria Crosses were awarded that day, for 'most conspicuous bravery'. Sergeant Lewis McGee, for example, of the 3rd Australian Pioneer Battalion, had rushed a German machine gun armed only with his revolver;[30] Private Arthur Hutt, of the 1/7 Royal Warwickshire, having taken command of his platoon after all his officers were dead or wounded, led an attack on a pillbox, with the capture of 40–50 prisoners.[31] Captain Clement Robertson, of the Queen's attached Tank Corps, led his machines on foot across difficult terrain to their objectives.[32] And Private Thomas Henry Sage, of the 37th Division, threw himself on a grenade dropped by a fallen, neighbouring soldier, saving the lives of many.[33]

Only Lloyd George soured the mood, grumbling about illusory gains won at great cost. In part, he was right: Broodseinde was another mile-and-a-half bite, hardly the Marne (which had saved Paris). The accolades failed to recognise that the Germans still held part of the ridge and, ominously, were far from a spent force. Reinforcements were pouring into the second line, Flandern-II Stelling, which lay between Broodseinde and Passchendaele, and great numbers were assembling on the unseen eastern plain between Passchendaele and Roulers.

And Haig had sustained the usual, terrific casualties: some 20,000 officers and men had been killed or wounded that morning. Allied commanders were reluctant to describe these losses as 'excessive' in view of 'the magnitude of the results'.[34] Yet the British and Dominion forces had suffered a casualty rate of around twenty to 25 per cent, with some units (such as 1 Auckland Battalion) losing almost half their men – for a gain of, at most, 1900 yards closer to Passchendaele Ridge. A body or body part could be found every twenty paces along the main front, 'some frightfully mutilated, without legs, arms and heads and half covered in mud and slime', wrote

Australia's official photographer, Captain Frank Hurley, who had followed the men into battle. The battlefield, he observed, 'was littered with bits of men, our own and Boche, and literally drenched with blood'.[35] And this was a battle that had gone well, in which everything had proceeded according to the plan.

The Germans were more heavily battered. Many regiments had suffered their worst day of the year,[36] with some 35,000 casualties and, for some units, a very real sense of defeat; 5000 prisoners were taken (of whom the New Zealanders took 1159).[37] They presented a pitiful sight, many very young, in poor spirits, some crying, reinforcing Haig's view that the enemy were on the brink of collapse. The official German history called 4 October the blackest day of the war (in a spate of black days).[38] It was 'extraordinarily severe', Ludendorff later confirmed, 'and we came through it only with enormous loss'.[39] He conceded that his decision to move the Eingreif forward had failed.

Yet still the Germans were far from broken, if Ludendorff could be believed. Like Haig, he tended to cling to good news even as ghoulish evidence to the contrary congregated around him. Just two days later, on 6 October, he assured Rupprecht that the German Army would win the war by the end of the year so long as they held Flanders. Ludendorff even maintained that the U-boat offensive might save the day. This fantasy arose out of his refusal to accept that the Royal Navy–escorted convoys had already won the U-boat war.

Rupprecht drew a very different conclusion: after Broodseinde, he had nightmare visions of the rout of his entire army in Belgium. In early October, he even contemplated a general withdrawal from Flanders and the possible abandonment of the U-boat bases. He decided not to do so, for two reasons: the U-boats were still operational and many more were coming on-stream; and more importantly, it had started to rain again, a godsend to defenders on the higher ground. 'Most gratifying,' Rupprecht wrote, 'rain: our most effective ally.'[40]

—

The heavens denied Haig the miracle for which he prayed. The skies opened just after noon on 4 October, as Gold had forecast. On the 5th and 6th, the rain bucketed down; on the 7th, it fell in 'drenching squalls';[41] on the 8th, a drying wind yielded to more torrential rain. Gold surrendered to his instruments: great storm clouds 1000 miles west of Ireland were bearing down on Europe at 40 miles an hour and the rest of the month looked hopeless. (The rain would not ease for weeks: 107 millimetres would fall that month, compared with 31 millimetres in the same period in 1914, 32 millimetres in 1915 and 69 millimetres in 1916. That October, there would be only five rainless days in Flanders.)

By the 8th, the swamp-like conditions of August had returned. Yet the fighting would continue, Haig decided, into the valley of Gravenstafel, just below Passchendaele Ridge, a low-lying area prone to heavy flooding. Haig persisted with his belief that a few sharp blows would deliver Passchendaele; the recent victories even revived his hopes of clearing the coast before winter.

Wishful thinking clouded reality like a cataract. In such appalling conditions, the exacting preparations that Plumer had hitherto insisted on – a ready supply of fresh troops and the availability of enough guns to create a dense barrage – were not adhered to. In the rain-swept days that followed the battle, Haig decided to press on, in what many now regard as the most disastrous decision of his career (see Chapter 17). Most of his corps and divisional generals 'would have liked to stop the offensive', Bean observed.[42] Birdwood, commander of the Anzacs, advised Plumer 'against any further advance'. 'My men were weak and tired . . .'[43] Monash concurred, anticipating carnage. When Godley and even Plumer rejected Monash's protests, the Australian commander bowed to the inevitable and organised an ambulance system 'akin to a cab rank' and 200 additional stretcher-bearers.[44]

Few shared Haig's assessment of the Germans as a near-spent force. Junior officers and ordinary soldiers, watching the battlefield revert to an 'ocean of thick brown porridge' in which 'the wire entanglements had sunk into the mud', grabbing at their submerged legs,[45] were astounded at the decision to fight on: surely this would lead to wanton slaughter, with little chance of success? 'Now I fear that it must be a wash-out for the year – tough luck,' noted one private.[46]

Nor was there enough time to prepare – just two days – or to bring forward the available guns, as Haig's commanders knew. And yet, if they doubted their chief's wisdom, Plumer and Gough showed little inclination to challenge his orders. Their recent successes made Plumer uncharacteristically confident, and he and Harington 'allowed themselves . . . to be seduced into rushing preparations'.[47] Gough – chastened by the memory of August – made plain his reluctance to attack in the wet, but put up little resistance once he knew Haig's mind was decided. If both expressed reservations, even objections, at a meeting on 7 September (the occurrence of which is disputed[48]) neither took a strong stand against their commander's decision.

Exactly why Haig persisted has baffled military experts, historians and politicians for a century. Flush with confidence after the capture of Menin Road, Polygon Wood and Broodseinde, Haig could be forgiven, says Bean, for wondering, 'What will be the result of three more in the next fortnight?'[49] If fine weather returned, Bean concludes, 'was Haig's strategic design beyond the chance of attainment'?[50] Nor were the alternatives appealing. Staying put and wallowing in the mud beneath Passchendaele for the winter was militarily untenable, and withdrawing to Pilckem Ridge, after so many losses, politically unacceptable. The latter would have brought the wrath of the politicians and the press onto Haig's head. Balancing these arguments, Haig concluded that the only viable option was to attack and hold Passchendaele for the winter.

Countering his resolve was the great destroyer, the rain. An intelligence summary on 7 October described part of the valley the men would have to cross as 'saturated ground. Quite impassable. Should be avoided by all troops at all times.'[51] On the morning of the 9th, when the next battle, at Poelcappelle, was scheduled to begin, the field had been reduced to something worse than the porridge of August. Spread out before their eyes, for all to see, was a landscape pocked with depressions of unknown depth, each filled with a stinking brown liquid, set in a mash of mud, bodies and debris thrown up by thousands upon thousands of explosions that had busted the ancient drainage system and scalped the crust of the earth. Over this, the Anzacs and British were now ordered to attack.

—

What followed produced such scenes of human and animal misery as to render superlatives meaningless and the descriptive powers of historians inert. '[N]othing that has been written is more than the pale image of the abomination of those battle-fields,' wrote the war correspondent Philip Gibbs, 'no pen or brush has yet achieved the picture of that Armageddon in which so many of our men perished.'[52] Yet, to have any understanding of what these men went through, we must at least try to imagine the ineffable, and their eye-witness accounts together provide the best indication.

Tim Harington, Plumer's chief of staff, told war correspondents on the eve of the Battle of Poelcappelle – the second step in the assault on Passchendaele Ridge – that the high ground was dry as a bone. If true, which it wasn't, surely Harington spoke to German, not British, advantage? Bean, then in his role as Australia's official war correspondent, listened with dread to this recipe for a 'classical tragedy' in which the British commanders, in their eagerness to dismiss the Germans as a spent force, had overlooked the state of their own men.

'I believe,' Bean wrote, 'the official attitude is that Passchendaele Ridge is so important that tomorrow's attack is worth making whether it succeeds or fails. I suspect they are making a great bloody experiment . . .' This 'huge gamble', he added, would rely wholly for its success on 'German demoralisation'. Bean accused the generals of 'playing with the morale of their troops': 'They don't realise how . . .

desperately hard it will be to fight down such opposition in the mud, rifles choked, [Lewis guns] out of action, men tired and slow . . .' He plaintively concluded, 'I thought the principle was to . . . "hit, hit, hit, whenever the weather is suitable". If so, it is thrown over at the first temptation.' With his usual prescience, Bean believed the commanders failed to see 'how very strong our morale had to be to get through the last three fights'.[53] The coming battles would fail, he feared.

Such warnings had no truck with Haig, for whom the capture of Passchendaele was becoming something of an obsession, the fulfilment of which trampled over any obstacle: exhaustion, the lack of guns and even pouring rain . . .

Throughout the night of 8–9 October, one Anzac and two British divisions of Plumer's Second Army staggered up to the 13,500-yard front, the tip of another vast arrow-shaped formation flanked by the rest of the Second Army, the Guards Division, as well as French units and Gough's Fifth Army. Two cavalry divisions were within a day's march of the front – such was Haig's confidence of success. The question of how their horses would gallop across a swamp remained unanswered.

In the pouring rain, far fewer heavy guns could be assembled. The carriages sank in the quagmire. Mules were the only means of delivering ammunition: a one-hour journey now took between six and sixteen. 'If the animals slipped off the planks,' observed one historian, 'they often sank out of sight.'[54] On arrival, each slimy shell had to be cleaned before use. Gun platforms made of beech slabs nailed onto a foundation of fascines and metal required two days' work to construct. These, too, 'began to sink into mud after a few rounds had been fired'.[55]

And there was the question of Allied morale. Most British units were well below full strength. Many Australian brigades were severely depleted, their men exhausted from clearing tracks, hauling wagons and laying duckboards and telephone cables, 'tasks which appeared physically impossible to perform, and which no other army would have faced'.[56] Hundreds had been evacuated with trench foot or severe bronchial complaints, the result of sleeping on wet blankets or straw. Several Australian battalions contained just 150 men, out of the usual 750 or so, and a handful of officers. Some had 'temporarily deserted' and faded to the rear. Bean witnessed soldiers coming back down Menin Road, pale and drawn, placing one foot in front of the other, robotically, 'as I had not seen men do since the Somme winter'. They looked 'like a dead man looks, and scarcely able to walk'.[57]

The British, too, were battered and exhausted. An untested British division, the 66th, designated to spearhead the attack on one part of the front, lost hundreds of men en route to the starting line. The march, which should have taken 90 minutes, according to a diarist of the Lancashire Fusiliers, took eleven terrifying hours, as the heavily laden men were trying to cross a swamp under torrential rain and enemy shellfire. Duckboards over the water-filled holes collapsed or were shelled. Many drowned. The loathed staff officers were sent to goad the fitter troops forward to the starting tapes. One brigade arrived twenty minutes after zero hour (5.20 am), and were flung straight into battle.[58]

'It was an absolute nightmare,' recalls Lieutenant P. King, of the East Lancashire Regiment, '. . . all the time the duckboards were being blown up and men being blown off the track or merely slipping off . . . we were loaded up like Christmas trees, so of course an explosion near by or just the slightest thing would knock a man off balance and he would go . . . right down into the muck.'[59]

'[O]ur barrage had started,' recalled Private A. T. Shaw of the same regiment, 'but we had not then arrived at the jumping off point. Heavy German shells were already falling amongst us and shrapnel was flying all over the place. There were shouts and screams and men falling all around. The attack that should have started never got off the ground.'[60]

The opening barrage was thin and ineffectual, as many had feared. Shells burst in the mud, losing their power, fell short or veered off target; gun platforms sank with every shot. The barrage failed to break the German lines or destroy the belt of fresh wire in front of the enemy trenches. The German machine gunners fired on the enemy unhindered. 'No previous attack organized by the Second Army in the war had such an unfavourable start,' writes one historian.[61]

In spite of all this, the Anzac and British soldiers who had reached the starting tapes rose at the whistles and attacked. Some staggered or crawled or were even dragged into battle, exhausted, wet through and covered in mud.[62] They advanced into lines of pill-boxes crowded with machine guns that spat belts into the valley. Through all this, some British troops reached Passchendaele Ridge, and a patrol of British officers actually entered the ruins of the village, which they found deserted (as a result of Ludendorff moving the Eingreif to the rear again). The rain and German shellfire ended their audacity, and they withdrew. Thousands were left floundering below Passchendaele and Poelcappelle, easy targets for enemy machine gunners. Acts of searing bravery redeemed the failure; one action alone merited three Victoria Crosses.[63] Whole units disappeared: fourteen men out of an Australian raiding party of 85 returned unwounded; no traces of the rest were ever recovered.

The survivors fell back to the starting point, and scrambled for shelter. Some Australians dug in near the smashed Zonnebeke railroad, so exhausted and shell-shocked that Frank Hurley, lying near them, could not distinguish the living from the dead.[64] Bursting shells blew horse-drawn ambulance wagons off the track, hurling their damaged human cargo into the mire. Helplessly the bearers tried to gather up the wounded and right the wagons, under rain and shellfire. Acute demoralisation set in.

'My Dearest Mother,' wrote Alfred Leahy on 10 October (having been told he would be recommended for a Military Medal or high award), 'You have no doubt read in the papers of this great battle . . . Men were falling all around me, and the dying, dead and wounded lying about the field was indescribable. I do not wish to go thro' the same again or witness such shocking sights . . .'[65]

311

Through the crowded aid posts and field hospitals padres roamed, to deliver last rites. 'Even when a man was very badly wounded and unconscious,' recalled Padre S. Hinchcliffe, of the Northumberland Fusiliers, 'I always believed that you could penetrate right down through his consciousness.' He bent down and whispered in their ears, 'Put your trust in God.'[66]

—

In the shambles that now passed for the front, the men spent the night in shallow shell holes, many in the ruins of Zonnebeke, awaiting relief. But the relieving troops could not get through the German fire. Allhusen's company, part of a relief battalion, succeeded after an epic journey. His men approached the Menin Road on the night of 6 October, 'hopelessly depressed and exaggeratedly cheerful in turns', he wrote. They rested in the ruins of a village for three days, cold and wet. He likened the mood in the mess to that of 'a condemned cell'.[67] Past Dead Mule Corner, the road met the duckboards. Further up the slope, at Sanctuary Corner, the shellfire worsened. One of his men received a 'blighty': 'I have never seen anybody so pleased,' Allhusen observed.

Moving along Menin Road that night left him with a memory of:

> bursting shells, treading on dead men, frantic calls for stretcher-bearers long after the stretcher-bearers had gone, losing the way . . . everybody hurrying and swearing: then awful delays while the guide admitted that he was lost and made futile remarks such as 'there ought to be a broken tank 'ere' . . . all under heavy shelling with men being hit left and right.[68]

His men found the unit they were supposed to relieve, a company of Bedfords, many of whom were huddled in a captured pillbox, 'like ghosts, pale and wild-eyed, with long beards and coated in mud from head to foot'. Their present company commander (the first had been killed in the doorway to the pillbox) 'talked incessantly in a light-headed way'.[69]

Allhusen led his platoon to a trench filled with a foot and a half of water, 'where they were to live' amid men of strange regiments who were 'wandering about lost and swearing'. It rained all night. In the morning, the sun shone. Allhusen surveyed 'just the shapeless mess that remains when everything else has gone'. The mud rose 'in squashy heaps out of pools and lakes of slimy liquid that were sometimes black, sometimes yellow . . . sometimes bright green – but never the colour that water ought to be', he recalled. 'Mixed with everything were stores, arms and equipment . . . and dead men. Sometimes these were in groups, sometimes single, while often there were only bits of them.'[70]

This perceptive young lieutenant's 'strongest memory' was 'the hunted, haunted feeling which made men restless and sullen, wandering aimlessly about talking in disjointed monosyllables, and ultimately drove them mad'. The soldiers were always in a hurry, yet with nothing to do, as they waited to attack. They tried to improve the trenches – a hopeless task, 'as every shovel full of mud thrown out slithered slowly back again'.[71]

Shortly they prepared to leave the support trenches and enter the front line. Two men went down with severe shell shock: one shook 'like jelly' and 'couldn't speak'; the other 'became paralysed, and was not expected to live'. Allhusen, now second in charge of his company, reached the front to find his commander standing knee-deep in mud, his teeth chattering, and on the edge of going 'out of his mind'. In the distance, the German gunners were shelling their own troops, provoking laughter among Allhusen's men. Golden rain – the flare that was supposed to warn the gunners that their rounds were falling short – fell all day over the German lines as they blew themselves up.

An Australian unit managed to relieve the East Lancashires that night, to the astonishment of Lieutenant P. King: 'three tall figures', one of whom was 'actually smoking', jumped into his shell hole.

'Who the hell are you?' King asked. To which one soldier replied, 'Well, we're the Aussies, chum, and we've come to relieve you.' Delighted, King warned that he had no trenches, rations or ammunition, and could only offer a map. 'Never mind about that,' said the Australian. 'Just fuck off.'[72]

As the Australian reinforcements waited for dawn, they ate iron rations and drank cold tea. The cries of the wounded persisted all night. Every so often, a man fell into a crater and sank. 'We heard screaming from another crater,' recounts Sergeant T. Berry of The Rifle Brigade. Berry tried to create a chain of rifles to reach the man, now up to his neck:

> He went down gradually. He kept begging us to shoot him.
> But we couldn't shoot him. Who could shoot him? We stayed
> with him, watching him go down in the mud. And he died.
> He wasn't the only one. There must have been thousands . . .[73]

The Allies gained none of their goals that day. Their 'total repulse' by the Germans produced a further 13,000 British and Anzac casualties, of whom 4000 were killed: this by a supposedly broken enemy. Charteris was forced to face reality, as he revealed in his diary entry on 10 October:

> It was the saddest day of this year. We did fairly well
> but only fairly well . . . there is now no chance of
> complete success this year . . . there is no purpose
> in it now, so far as Flanders is concerned.[74]

—

The only man who could have ended the hell in the Salient remained mysteriously silent. The prime minister had insisted on retaining the power to halt the offensive should circumstances dictate, as they did now. Many years later, Lloyd George would defend his inaction by claiming that Haig and GHQ had kept him in the dark about the progress of the campaign – a piece of fiction as bogus as the casualties were real. In fact, the events on the Western Front were well known to the War Policy Committee, through which Lloyd George had by now acquired near dictatorial powers.

Instead, in early October, with his Italian campaign failing, Lloyd George busied himself with a scheme for a new front line, this time in Turkey. The prime minister's idea was to take Germany's southern ally out of the war via the stick of an attack through Palestine and the carrot of generous terms to Constantinople. He raised the Turkish card at War Committee meetings on 3 and 11 October, with all the zeal of his Italian adventure. Three of his colleagues were in favour; Bonar Law feared another Gallipoli.

The matter of Third Ypres rarely intruded on these deliberations. On the few occasions they discussed it, the War Policy Committee tended to dismiss it as a foregone failure, unworthy of their attention. Haig had failed even to reach Passchendaele, after two months of bashing, complained the prime minister on 3 October. Curzon argued in fairness that the weather had hampered the offensive. Regardless, Lloyd George barked, there was little chance of Haig seizing Roulers or Klerken Ridge (beyond Passchendaele) that year.

By the 11th, the prime minister had persuaded himself that a winter Palestine/Turkey campaign 'was the only operation to undertake', notwithstanding the firm objections of Major General Arthur Lynden-Bell, former chief of staff in Egypt, who knew better. The terrible battle at Poelcappelle that had ended two days earlier excited little comment. The prime minister merely regretted that he'd taken 'too sanguine a view of the Flanders offensive' and promised to raise the matter with the War Cabinet in three weeks if Haig's position had not improved: the nod, in other words, to continue the offensive until further notice.[75]

If any moment should have justified the prime minister's intervention, surely this was it. Every day, Lloyd George knew, thousands of men were being killed or wounded for little result. Yet neither he nor his committeemen saw fit to act. And again, the prime minister exhibited none of the thunderous moral energy with which he would later denounce the battle. The fact that the waging of the Flanders campaign was ultimately his to decide seemed not to impinge upon the committee's discussions at the time, as Prior and Wilson's devastating study concludes: 'It would continue not another day if they denied it authorization', yet the prime minister 'failed to raise a finger to stop it' when he had the chance.[76]

The prime minister was, of course, answerable to the Conservatives in his Cabinet. And there were other reasons for his inertia (as we shall discuss in Chapter 17). For now, Lloyd George put himself in the rare position of listening. He summoned a panel of military experts on 11 October to examine the whole panoply of war-related issues that were causing 'most anxiety in the War Cabinet': the Russian collapse; the delayed French recovery; the abandonment of the Italian offensive; the exhaustion of the supply of British manpower; the endless delays of the Americans; and the U-boat war (the only bright spot being that September's shipping losses had been 'exceptionally low').[77] Meanwhile, the rain poured down in Flanders and thousands of young men were on the move again, trudging to their doom.

—

Well aware that they would have weak, if any, artillery cover, Haig ordered his ragged armies up for another attack, which would be known as the First Battle of Passchendaele. They were given two days to prepare. The ensuing battles would thus rely on pure hope over hard experience. The commanders cast precedent aside, as if the lessons of Loos, the Somme, Gheluvelt and even the immediately preceding Poelcappelle, so profligate with soldiers' lives, were worth nothing. Haig continued to persuade himself, and told French President Poincaré, that enemy morale was at rock bottom and the German soldiers lacked the ability to fight.[78] Even Plumer believed one more push might carry the day. Old Plum, hitherto a model of caution, now tended to set goals that were beyond the capacity of his army. As the British official historian concludes, the task allotted the Anzacs on 12 October was 'beyond the power of any infantry with so little support'.[79]

A powerful dissenting voice intruded on the eve of the next bite. Lieutenant General George Macdonogh, director of military intelligence at the War Office, argued that the Germans were far from defeated, and that fresh formations were arriving from the Russian front. Macdonogh's sane intervention had no influence on Haig, who vented his feelings in his diary:

> I can't think why the War Office Intelligence Dept. gives such a wrong picture of the situation except that General Macdonogh (DMI) is a Roman Catholic and is (perhaps unconsciously) influenced by information which doubtless reaches him from tainted (i.e. catholic) sources.[80]

A charitable reading would set aside this squalid sentiment as Haig's personal prejudice, which had no place in a decision that would determine the outcome of a battle and the fate of thousands of men. Yet Haig's dislike of Irish Catholics was a palpable force in his thinking, and went hand-in-hand with his dim view of those under his command. One of Haig's apologists rather absurdly argues that the Pope's 'pro-German stance' somehow justified Haig's suspicions of Macdonogh's intelligence.[81] The Vatican's August peace proposal had condemned the war in general; the Pope had not taken sides.

In any case, as it happened, Macdonogh had not received tainted intelligence, and Haig had a responsibility to examine it: the Germans defending Passchendaele Ridge along the Flandern II-Stellungen were indeed gathering in strength. Macdonogh drew on the bigger picture, the situation in Russia and elsewhere in France, whereas Haig at this time tended to rely on his soldier's instincts and Charteris's wishful thinking. Obviously the Germans were heavily mauled – Haig was 'not totally wrong', writes Sheffield[82] – but they were far from defeated.

In the event, Haig ignored Macdonogh. He would continue bashing away with every man he could get hold of. If his geographical goal was Bellevue Spur, his actual goal was to kill or wound as many Germans as possible. Bellevue Spur juts out of Passchendaele Ridge above the Ravebeek Valley, through which flows the Ravebeek 'stream', now 50 yards wide and waist-deep. Surrounding it were hectares of thick brown stew. Few guns could be marshalled through this mess – not nearly enough to raise a barrage. 'Horses were useless in such mud so the guns had to be inched forward by manpower,' wrote one New Zealand gunner, 'pulled out of the muddy water in one shellhole to slide forward into another.'[83] Their carriages sank, their wheels buckled, their axles broke. The few guns that reached their intended positions had no firm ground on which to absorb the recoil shock, and sank deeper with every shot.[84] Topographers, too, with their heavy plane-tables and tripods on their backs, and trig observers with their theodolites, on whom the gunners relied to locate vital grid references such as Passchendaele church, faced a near-impossible task through the Flanders mud.[85] The pack mules took seventeen hours to deliver the ammunition: every time a mule got stuck, the eight rounds strapped to its back had to be removed and cleaned, and the animal dragged clear of the mud and reloaded, until it happened again.

A severe problem arose the day before the offensive: the 66th Division had failed to hold its section of front, in the Ravebeek Valley. An Australian officer went forward to find out why. He found scenes of despair. 'Never have I seen men so broken and demoralised,' he wrote. The Tommies were:

> huddled up close . . . in the last stages of exhaustion and fear.
> Fritz had been sniping them off all day, and had accounted
> for fifty seven . . . the dead and dying lay in piles. The
> wounded . . . groaned and moaned all over the place.[86]

The torrential rain prompted Gough, on the eve of the attack, to call Plumer and request a postponement. Plumer consulted his commanders and replied that the attack should proceed as planned. Both generals knew they would be sending men into battle with little or no artillery support – in other words, to certain death. Both knew that the few guns in place could not possibly destroy the German wire – a critical precondition for success, and a lesson so brutally learned on the Somme. None of this deflected Haig from his course. The Anzacs would again spearhead the offensive, this time 'virtually without protection', as Bean feared.[87] Their orders were to capture Passchendaele village that afternoon.

To reach the new starting line – a melange of mud, water, corpses and detritus – the fresh Anzac brigades had to move in single file along a few miles of duckboards, before plunging into the morass. The journey took the entire night. These men had heard stories of the previous battle, of thousands crawling through mud into the attack. And the stories had a lethal effect on morale. A gunner who had fought at Poelcappelle witnessed one relieving battalion pass him, on 11 October, on their way to the front:

> The reinforcements . . . shambled up past the guns
> with dragging steps and the expressions of men who
> knew they were going to certain death. No words of
> greeting . . . as they slouched along; in sullen silence
> they filed past one by one to the sacrifice.[88]

Many of these reinforcements got lost, fell into shell holes or were blown up on the way (such was the freedom with which the German gunners now operated). 'Before 5 am we had lost men like rotten sheep,' recalls Lieutenant G. M. Carson. 'I nearly got blown to pieces scores of times. We went through a sheet of iron all night and in the morning it got worse . . . at times we were bogged up to our arm pits and it took anything from an hour upwards to get out. Lots were drowned in the mud and water.'[89] Lieutenant Russell Harris found it 'impossible to shut one's ears' to the cries of men drowning: 'When silence came it was almost like a physical blow, engendering a feeling bordering on guilt.'[90]

The whistles blew at 5.25 am. If evidence for a miracle were needed, it lay here, in the sight of a fresh wave of Anzacs, rising once more under torrential rain. The barrage was a whisper of its usual strength and offered no protective screen. The batteries rustled up a few hundred shells, which burst harmlessly in the mud, or veered off target. The residue passed thinly over Passchendaele, too fast for soldiers moving along slippery duckboards; or it fell short, sending 'friendly' shells onto their heads.

Against all hope or expectation, some Australians and New Zealanders reached their first objective, the red line, 1200 yards ahead. Their second goal, the blue line, the starting point for the assault on Passchendaele, was a further half-mile on; and their final objective, the green line, 400 yards beyond the village. Bear in mind that these 'lines' were simply map references; the ground itself was all the same – a glutinous mass of mud and water on an upwardly curving plain.

Few got further than the red line. The belts of German wire were fully intact, as their commanders knew. Stuck in the open beneath the spur, without artillery protection, the men came under merciless German sniper and machine-gun fire, which spattered across the bog like a wave of hail. The entire Antipodean attack broke down in the swamps of the Ravebeek Valley. Thousands were shot standing knee-deep in mud, unable to move. Within hours, Australian casualties had reached 4500, dead and wounded. They included Captain Clarence Smith Jeffries, awarded the Victoria Cross posthumously, the last Australian to receive the decoration during Third Ypres, for leading the destruction of a machine gun that had blocked his unit's path.[91]

The battalion sent to seize Passchendaele got as far as 600 yards from the village church, where they encountered the remains of the 66th Division, whom they had been sent to relieve. The survivors included two forlorn Tommies sitting in a shell hole, one with a broken arm, the other with trench feet. At first glance, these dazed men took the Aussies for Germans, and panicked. When they realised their error, they exclaimed with relief, 'We knew the Australians would come. We prayed hard.'[92] Further on, a twenty-man Australian patrol managed to scramble into Passchendaele village and touch the ruins of the church steeple. Finding neither friend nor foe, they withdrew.

'Incredible, as it is not time yet,' noted Monash, in his headquarters beneath the Ypres ramparts. He had received the news at 10.28 am via the interrogation of a prisoner, and naturally assumed a large body of his men had taken Passchendaele. Reinforcing this belief was a message attached to a pigeon that flew in at noon, stating that an Australian battalion had reached the blue line. Firmer intelligence soon disabused the Australian commander, and by 4 pm the survivors had fallen back to their starting point, utterly exhausted.

Elsewhere, on the flanks to the north and south of Monash's men, a similar story unfolded, of countless futile blows, too numerous to recount, ending with the termination of the offensive – a near repeat of Poelcappelle. Yet, of all the casualties of those terrible October days, the New Zealanders suffered a uniquely tragic and ghastly end. Thousands who had set out to attack Bellevue Spur were never seen again.

—

New Zealand's sole division drew heavily on the youth of Auckland, Otago, Wellington and Canterbury, white and Maori, many of whom were fighting 'for home town first and New Zealand second', observed their historian Christopher Pugsley.[93] They numbered 20,000 young men, of great skill and proven courage. On the Somme, they had fought in the front lines for 23 consecutive days, longer than any other division, fulfilling every task assigned them, at a cost of 7408 casualties. At Polygon Wood and Broodseinde, along with the Australians, they had inflicted emphatic defeats on the enemy. Haig greatly admired this Antipodean fist in his arsenal, which was why he used them in the van of the October attacks.

Alas, in a year of 'black days', 12 October 1917 would go down as the blackest in New Zealand's military history. Their attack on Passchendaele Ridge broke one of the finest units on the Western Front. Even before the battle had begun, hopelessly bogged down, many New Zealanders found themselves caught between friendly fire from behind and German artillery in front. Their own guns fell short by about 200 yards, directly onto their heads. Dozens of Otago men and the commanding officer of the 1st Canterbury Battalion were cut to pieces, as they waited a hundred yards behind the starting tape.[94]

Private Leonard Hart of the Otago Battalion, among the few who survived the attack on Bellevue Spur, described what happened:

> What was our dismay on reaching almost to the top of the
> ridge to find a long line of practically undamaged German
> concrete machine gun emplacements with barbed wire
> entanglements in front of them fully fifty yards deep . . .
> Dozens got hung up on the wire and shot down before their
> surviving comrades [sic] eyes. It was now broad daylight
> and what was left of us realised that the day was lost.[95]

A 25- to 50-yard gap in the wire lured others into a 'lane of death', with German machine guns waiting on either side.[96] Others threw themselves onto the wire and wrestled to within a few yards of the German pillboxes. None got through – an impossible task. A regiment of the Black Watch, to the New Zealanders' left, experienced the same bloody shambles, cut down where they stood in the mud, or hanging from the German wire.

The survivors withdrew and tried to dig in beneath the spur, a 'ridiculous' notion to the New Zealand Machine Gun Company, who found themselves sitting in water. 'You can't dig water!' Private W. Smith observed.[97] Seeing their plight, the Germans emerged arrogantly from their pillboxes and started shooting the men floundering in the bog below. The New Zealanders were reduced to a leaderless rabble, staggering around in the mud, expecting at any moment to be picked off. Most of the officers and sergeants were wiped out. 'Everyone was scattered, wounded or dead,' recalled Smith. 'We had no idea what to do, for we had no NCOs, no officers, no orders.' In their pathos, he and a friend 'set off crawling towards Passchendaele', then thought the better of it and spent the night in a shell hole in pouring rain.[98]

'The stunt should never have been ordered under such conditions,' wrote Corporal Harold Green of the New Zealand Rifle Brigade. 'It was absolute murder.'[99]

'You cannot fight machine guns plus wire, with human bodies,' Sir Andrew Russell, commanding the New Zealand Division, later explained to the country's Minister of Defence. 'Without the wire to check them the men would've tackled machine guns despite their losses.' In a painful, almost insulting statement of the obvious, he added, 'As it was they tried heroically to tackle both. This was humanly impossible.'[100] The wire and weather were not the only culprits: a Scottish deserter had forewarned the Germans the night before that the New Zealanders were going to attack. The enemy were very well prepared.

Russell's acceptance of the blame deflected it from a more fitting source: Lieutenant General John Godley, the aloof English officer who commanded the New Zealand Expeditionary Force (as well as II Anzac Corps), of whom Birdwood charitably wrote, 'he does not seem able to command the affections of officers or men'.[101] Less politely, a New Zealand historian concluded that the soldiers 'hated' Godley.[102]

As reports of the disaster came in, Russell realised that Godley had no idea of the conditions at the front or where the front was. Nor, in fairness, had any commander at divisional level and above: all the telephone lines were cut; the runners, if they survived, took hours to deliver messages; the messenger dogs had taken heavy casualties; and the pigeons couldn't fly.

Godley would have none of these excuses. He had promised Haig that he would deliver Passchendaele, whatever the cost. Indeed, the seizure of the village and the ridge had become a near obsession, for both men. By the time the sun had risen on the attack, 117 New Zealand officers and 3179 men had been killed or wounded – a huge loss for so small a country – many hundreds of whom were found dead on the German wires. 'They had poured out their blood like water,' wrote Colonel Stewart. 'The bodies of 40 officers and 600 men lay in swathes about the wire and along Gravenstafel road.'[103]

Godley put a Haig-like gloss on the result: it had been 'a very good day's work', and a 'big success', he informed the New Zealand Minister of Defence on 16 October. He wrote in a similar vein to the assistant private secretary of King George V, claiming that his forces had cleared the way for the Canadians to take Passchendaele 'without undue difficulty'.[104] Godley added that the casualties were 'not unduly heavy' (in fact, they were a morale-cracking 60 per cent for the Anzacs in general, and 85 per cent in several New Zealand units). Buckingham Palace wrote back to say how delighted King George and Queen Mary – of the House of Windsor now, having changed their name from the German original, the House of Saxe-Coburg and Gotha – were to hear the news.[105]

Godley quoted with pride a German officer, taken prisoner, who 'exclaimed in astonishment that no troops in the world would have attempted an offensive' over such ground.[106] Indeed, no troops should have, and it was Godley's failure that they did, concluded the New Zealand historian. Thus ended the first defeat of the New Zealanders on the Western Front, in a battle in which, as Bean observed, 'No infantry in the world could have succeeded.'[107]

—

The medical teams fell upon a field more densely packed with bodies and body parts than any in their experience, heavier than the battles of August and September. The Third Australian Division had lost more than 35 men for every yard of front taken.[108] The 9th and 10th Brigades were virtually wiped out: the 9th went over with 79 officers and 1939 men, and returned with nineteen officers and 631 men; of the 10th's 64 officers and 1800 men, 23 and 767 respectively survived the battle unscathed.[109] The rest were killed, wounded, missing (presumed dead) or taken prisoner.

The mobile wounded had crawled into pillboxes or shell holes to escape German snipers. Many drowned, were blown up or expired slowly, by gas gangrene or blood loss, while awaiting stretcher-bearers, who sometimes took days to reach them. Some 500 New Zealand stretcher cases lay at a casualty clearance station near Waterloo Farm. Exposed to the hail and driving rain, they began sinking into the mud, 'just dying there where they'd been dumped off'.[110] His efforts to extract them left Brigadier General 'Bill' Braithwaite, a hard-driving brigade commander, who had witnessed the virtual destruction of his beloved regiment, a broken man. Having pleaded three times for assistance for the last 75 cases, he begged Russell, 'I am powerless to do more personally. As a last extremity I appeal to you personally.'[111] Alas, most of them drowned or succumbed to gas gangrene.

'A note of failure' was how the official medical record summed up the bearers' performance in early October, 'at times almost of despair' at their inability to reach the wounded.[112] Eschewing the use of stretchers, the powerful Maori relay teams were even seen carrying wounded men in their arms and over their shoulders, as if they were children.[113] The bearers' saving grace was the restraint shown by German snipers and machine gunners, most of whom refrained from firing on the six-man stretcher parties. Some Germans, amazed at what they had witnessed, even sympathised with the Anzacs and Tommies, pointing out where the wounded men lay, engendering, noted one British infantryman, 'a respect for the Hun I never had before'.[114]

Thousands of walking wounded hobbled back along the broken duckboards. A long line passed Private Edward Lynch:

walking, staggering, lurching, limping back. Men with
blood-stained bandages and men with none. Men carrying

smashed arms, others painfully limping on shattered legs.
Laughing men and shivering men. Men with calm, quiet faces
and fellows with jumping blood-shot eyes above strangely
lined pain-racked and tortured faces. Men walking back as
if there's nothing left to harm them and others who flinch
and jump and throw themselves into shell holes at every
shell burst and at each whistle of a passing bullet . . .[115]

Lynch was himself piggybacked from the field with a broken foot, and stretcher-borne into a long tent under 'dazzling lights', where 'the sight of a bed with snowy sheets seems to fly one into another world'. It seemed wrong, he thought, that such 'starched cleanliness' should 'hover so close to the mud and filth that is me'.[116] As he entered the operating theatre, he passed a bucket full of arms, hands and feet being carried out.[117] Emptying them was a daily chore.

The withdrawal was as perilous as the advance. Allhusen's men were relieved on the night of 16 October, and cheerfully began the long march back along the 'Menin Road handicap'. En route, enemy shells blew his platoon apart. What remained was 'something like the mediaeval idea of hell; pitch dark, except in the evil flashes of bursting shells; screams, groans and sobs; men writhing in the mud, men trying to walk and falling down again . . .'[118]

Discipline and self-respect ebbed away with every step towards safety, Allhusen recalled. The pace quickened 'into a stumbling run . . . a crowd of broken men, running for their lives'. Many were 'driven on mechanically by the terror which their minds were no longer able to resist'.[119] Half of Allhusen's platoon reached the lorries waiting at Shrapnel Corner, drawn by the promise of hot cocoa and rum, of which he drank half a bottle. 'We sat and wept copiously . . .'[120]

After a hot bath, Allhusen slipped into a pair of silk pyjamas and slept: 'Heaven can hardly be expected to come up to that standard.' He dreamed of 'a wonderful garden' that seemed more than a dream; rather, 'some sort of effort of the subconscious mind to sweep out the horrors of the war and get back to sanity'. Others woke up screaming, terrified of falling asleep again. His battalion had lost about 200 men, dead, sick or wounded, including all four company commanders. Allhusen had replaced the one who had 'gone mad'.[121]

—

One lucky survivor of the mid-October battles was Captain George 'Alex' Birnie, an Australian medical officer whom a German sniper decided not to spare. Birnie had received a blighty. On the 26th, he lay in a hospital bed in London, writing a letter about his extraordinary experiences to his parents. It evokes the reality of the First Battle of Passchendaele, through a medical officer's eyes:

> My Dear Mother and Father,
> Here I am once more in England in peace and comfort with a bullet hole through my neck. If it had been an inch closer in I would now be lying on the bloody Passchendale [sic] Ridge with many hundreds of our good fellows who went West on that day – but you see it didn't so let me try and give you an account of how 750 men went over the top and 50 came back.

His job had been to establish a medical aid post in the forward areas. After a five-mile march to the front, he located his commanding officer, Major Roderick Bell-Irving, in a hole under a piece of galvanised iron. They were 300 yards from the Germans, who were 'looking down on us'. Bell-Irving ordered Birnie to advance behind the infantry and set up an aid post in a pillbox out beyond no-man's-land.

At zero hour, 5.25 am, Birnie witnessed his battalion rise 'with a great cheer' and charge, 200 yards ahead of him. It was 'the most terrible thing I have ever seen for you could see them fall, see them blown high into the air and still pressing on, taking cover where possible, and then a bayonet rush again'.

Shortly he grabbed a Red Cross flag and, running through

geysers of mud and exploding shells, led four men towards the pillbox. One received a bullet through the heart. In that instant, Birnie told his parents, 'the most deadly fear got hold of me . . . the sort of thing that almost paralyses you'.

The thin barrage, he realised, had started *beyond* the German machine guns, freeing them to mow down the Australians, whose officers and NCOs had been killed within minutes. He found the dead 'lying in heaps; it was the worst slaughter I have ever seen'. There was nobody left to lead the men.

At the entrance to the pillbox, Birnie found himself face-to-face with 'seven Huns'. He waved his Red Cross flag. To his amazement, none of them fired. His three surviving stretcher-bearers met him there. Unable to carry anyone out, Birnie and his few men moved about the battlefield, dressing wounds, administering morphine, sitting with the dying. 'It was heartbreaking work,' he wrote, during which the Germans held their fire.

Then Birnie felt something hot shoot through his lower neck: 'a sniper bagged me'. He fell into a shell hole. One of his men shouted, 'Are you dead, Sir? Are you dead? God help those b----rs if they've killed you.'

Birnie crawled back to the shell hole that served as Bell-Irving's headquarters, dressed his wound, swallowed a dram of whisky and returned to work, moving around the battlefield, an act for which he was later awarded the Military Cross:

> To those in great pain and no chance of living, I gave enough
> morphia to put them out peacefully and it was pitiful to hear
> their thanks with white faces twisted into a smile, 'Thanks
> Doc – I'm not afraid but this damn pain gets you down', or a
> message to someone at home they would never see again.[122]

Just 48 of 750 men in his battalion had survived the battle, unwounded, he told his parents. His entire unit had ceased to exist.

—

The First Battle of Passchendaele had failed utterly: 13,000–15,000 British and Empire troops had been killed or wounded in a few hours, for no territorial gain and fewer German casualties.[123] German machine gunners had fired with impunity in scenes as depressing as the first day of the Somme. The demoralised enemy of Haig's imagination had proved themselves astonishingly resilient, and Macdonogh's intelligence had been borne out.

Touring the battlefield with Godley three days later, Sergeant Wilson wrote:

> I won't forget my experience today if I live for a thousand years
> . . . The Somme was pretty bad I'll admit but this is worse. I
> have never seen such destruction. It is hard to imagine that 4
> years ago peaceful people tilled this same soil and that it was
> one of the most prosperous districts in Europe. Now, as I saw it
> today, well its [sic] simply an awful nightmare, a hideous reeking
> swamp seething with living (and dead) beings. A place that
> stamps itself on one's mind and memory like a red hot iron.[124]

Platoon and company commanders wept with rage at the virtual obliteration of their units. Battalion and brigade commanders were shaken to the core at what they saw as futile bloodletting. Such carnage could not be allowed to persist. Plumer and Gough were now against continuing with the battle. In late October, Plumer's staff met at his headquarters in Cassel and decided that Third Ypres should be abandoned.

Yet no senior soldier, or politician, openly called on Haig to terminate the offensive: the field marshal's indomitable will seems to have overawed his commanders. Haig decided, on 13 October, that the battle would continue if and when the weather improved. Four fresh Canadian divisions under the command of Lieutenant General Sir Arthur Currie were ordered up to relieve the exhausted Anzacs, utterly broken after weeks of spearheading the offensives.

Haig's decision to persist amounted to 'one of the lowest points in the British exercise of command' during Third Ypres, concluded Prior and Wilson.[125] If so, Haig clearly did not share this assessment of his powers. Exceeding his own standards of unwitting understatement, he confided in his wife on 14 October that the 'rain has upset our arrangements a good deal'. The bad weather, he wrote, had also fouled an officers' afternoon garden party.[126] Haig was not being wilfully callous; his mind simply failed to rise to the occasion. His letters and diary suggest a spectator in the wings, at this stage of the battle, not a commander at the centre of events. He exhibited no sense of regret at the staggering losses. He writes as though they were inevitable, not his responsibility, simply the cost of attrition. No doubt, he wished to spare his wife the gruesome details (though he could be very candid with her when he chose). He ended this letter with the hope that 'before long' the weather would improve and the ground become 'as dry as it was in 1914 at the end of October'.[127]

The press echoed Haig's optimism, with the same curious detachment from reality. The *Birmingham Gazette* rejoiced in the Tommies' defiance of the weather, as if the want of an umbrella were their chief discomfort: 'The Germans could hardly have anticipated that we should strike again so soon in weather which would keep most troops under cover.'[128] Several papers, including the *Gazette* and the *Liverpool Echo*, quoted Haig's verdict on the battle: 'We have driven the Germans practically out of the whole depth of their defensive front . . . The early reports back from the fighting lines are very encouraging. At 7.40 a.m. it was reported that all was going splendidly . . .' Haig later corrected this: 'Since my last report the weather has closed in as thick as pease soup . . . and I understand operations have been brought to a temporary standstill.'[129]

Haig gave a pithy answer as to why he pressed on, in his 1917 report to the Cabinet: 'progress', he explained, 'had not yet become impossible'.[130] If these words meant anything, they meant that Haig would decide, not the rain or the mounting losses, when progress would become impossible. Until then, he would drive his men to the limits of endurance.

Haig justified this decision on the basis of the comparative wastage figures that he dispatched to the War Cabinet on 16 October 1917, which suggested he was 'winning' the battle of attrition. The figures stated that 32 of 66 British (including Anzac) divisions had been 'sent away exhausted' or soon would be, compared with 53 of Germany's 72 divisions (see Appendix 8).[131] This little chart of dubious accuracy neglected complicating factors such as the arrival of fresh German divisions and the severity of the collapse in morale in both armies. For Haig, however, the numbers were a restorative, and cemented his faith in his forces' resilience. They would simply go on and on until the Germans were destroyed or surrendered.

The next day, the War Cabinet examined Haig's wastage report alongside the total losses in Flanders up to 5 October. According to the latter, which excluded the terrible battles of Poelcappelle and First Passchendaele, British and Dominion casualties were 148,470 against German losses of 255,000.[132] The striking thing about these numbers is not merely that they were wrong – the reverse more accurately assessed the comparative body count, as later research has shown – but that they provoked so little discussion in the government. The War Cabinet concluded that it was 'not in the public interest' to publish the totals and wrapped up the meeting by deciding that Lloyd George would make an 'occasional statement' to Parliament to correct persistent 'false' rumours that 'Colonials' were doing most of the fighting (at that point, the Dominions were certainly leading most of the battles – see appendices 8 and 9).[133] So much for Lloyd George's later claim that the generals had hidden the truth about the extremity of the situation from the government. The Cabinet had all the information before them; they simply failed to act on it.

Instead, the government chose this moment (16 October) to send Haig a message of congratulations, in recognition of his 'dogged advance of 4½ miles in conditions of great difficulty':

Starting from the position in which every advantage rested
with the enemy, and hampered and delayed from time to

time by most unfavourable weather, you and your men have nevertheless continuously driven the enemy back with such skill, courage and pertinacity as to have commanded the grateful admiration of the people of the British Empire.[134]

What was Lloyd George's dark purpose, wondered Haig and Robertson, as they scanned this missive of silken praise, addressed to them at a time of reversal and crisis? Haig decided, with a mixture 'of conceit and cynicism', that public support for his leadership must have pressed the government to act.[135]

In truth, the prime minister had not a shred of faith in his commander-in-chief, and was busying himself with a fresh plan to subordinate Haig to French command. The prime minister believed that if Haig was not actually insane, then he was 'wholly indifferent to human suffering', according to one view of Lloyd George's thinking.[136] This time, however, the prime minister hoped to avoid the charge that he was undermining his field commander, thus enraging the conservative press. His letter of congratulations may thus be seen as a new tack in his 'wearing-down war' against Haig, to lull the target into a false sense of security: by congratulating his commander for doing everything he had asked him not to do, Lloyd George had prepared the ground to launch a fresh assault on Haig – under the cover of praise.

As he schemed, the prime minister drew renewed confidence from the continuing victory over German submarines: by the end of October, German U-boats had sunk just ten vessels out of 99 British convoys, or 0.66 per cent of the total.[137]

Meanwhile, the survivors of the October battles rested, wrote home and looked forward to mail. On the 18th, Allhusen thanked his mother for sending chocolate, toffee, Horlicks and apples. They were 'an absolute blessing. You've no idea what a difference these things can make . . . The chocolate kept the remains of my platoon going.'[138]

# 13

# THE FACE OF FEAR

*. . . the horror of Verdun was surpassed. It was no longer*
*life at all. It was mere unspeakable suffering.*
General Erich Ludendorff

---

Little is known of the German soldiers' experience of this relentless bashing. How the world looked and felt to a man sitting in a hole in the ground as the vast instrument of his destruction moved towards him tends not to be asked or answered in most histories of the Western Front. Many experienced a kind of negative epiphany, an annihilation of the self, a helpless resignation to a power that reduced him to the status of an insect; others discovered a strange, careless inner strength, coupled with a reckless indifference to his own suffering.

As with the British Army, indeed all armies, the German soldier's lot was a world away from that of his commanders: Rupprecht, Ludendorff, von Kuhl and von Armin. There he sat, in the path of a literal storm of steel, night after night, for weeks. How on earth had the German soldier resisted, for so long, the combined power of the British Empire, under the mightiest artillery bombardment ever unleashed? Why had his commanders insisted that he defend these wretched ridgelines to the death?

In early October, the German commanders surveyed the tactical war with rising alarm. Their heavy losses were admittedly disturbing. Morale had taken a serious blow. Yet they viewed the broader, strategic outlook with sanguinity. If the German Army could hold Flanders until the winter, Germany might win the war, Ludendorff believed.

Rupprecht, who commanded the German Fourth Army in Flanders, was less persuaded, but he shared Ludendorff's reasoning. It ran like this: the British were racing against time. By early October, the British commanders (as they themselves well knew) had no hope of capturing the U-boat bases on the Belgian coast. Yet if Haig had stopped the battle at that point all his efforts would appear in vain and his 'unimagined losses' a worthless sacrifice. So Haig had no choice other than to continue fighting, to salvage something from the wreckage of his doomed campaign. The only 'something' worth fighting for was the Salient's high point, Passchendaele Ridge, the possession of which would allow him to claim a partial victory and resume the struggle for Belgium in the spring of 1918.[1] By then, the full complement of the German Army would have arrived from the Eastern Front, a prospect Ludendorff relished, especially as they would arrive before the Americans. Until then, the German commanders resolved to commit all their resources to the defence of Passchendaele – and bleed the British and Dominion armies, as they had the French at Verdun. In short, the Germans, too, were fighting a wearing-down war – but from a position of defensive strength.

—

Certainly, the German frontline battalions had been badly mauled. The quick succession of British and Anzac bites had worn them down to the point of physical and nervous collapse. The incessant artillery battering had pinned the German forces to the front, so much so that it was extremely difficult to withdraw the infantry from the combat zone. 'Men had hardly departed when Command called them back again to the front,' notes the German history of Flanders, 'battalions often had to start a counter-attack in the middle of their relief time.'[2] Losses to sickness, such as gastric disorders and trench foot, were rising alarmingly.

Yet German morale would not reach the point of collapse until mid-1918, confounding the hopes of Haig and Charteris, and confirming the verdict of Macdonogh. Nonetheless, the German commanders were deeply concerned. On 18 October, von Kuhl proposed a general withdrawal from Flanders – an idea von Armin stoutly resisted, arguing that relinquishing any ground risked the destruction of the U-boat bases. For now, the German soldier would stay in the line.

So Fritz sat there, grimly hanging on to his position in the ridges above Ypres. How the ordinary German soldier found the 'inner combat strength' to withstand the British attacks is one of the mysteries of history. The sentiment 'Damn Fritz, he just won't die' spoke for the feelings of many Commonwealth troops in the face of an unbreakable wall of grey uniforms.

A few German soldiers took extreme measures to pre-empt the consequences of fear, such as chaining themselves to their guns. At Bullecourt, Norman Collins encountered a wounded German who had chained himself to his gun and thrown the key beyond reach: 'Some of the bravest men we've ever bumped into have been Fritz gunners . . .'[3] Or perhaps, at Flanders, these men had been reduced to an insensate state, whose 'deadening indifference' to suffering summoned 'an almost automatic and calm reaction to the terrible events on the battlefield', as one German history contends:

You are simply stuck in it, and you start to worry as little about the possibility of dying in the wet shell holes as you do about the even smaller possibility of leaving them alive. Death has lost its terror, since it has been standing next to you as a constant companion every hour of the day and night. The front instinct finds its best breeding ground in that state of 'couldn't care less': verve turns into patience, courage into calm, bravery into resilience against any events of an exterior or interior kind.[4]

In this light, the Battle of Flanders had created a 'new type of German soldier', one who, resigned to his fate, placed little or no value on his life, on medals or on words of praise. Such a man scorned military discipline, hobnobbed with his platoon and company commanders who lay in the mud beside him, and viewed every rear area commander with contempt. Such foot soldiers were affectionately known as *Frontschwein* (frontline hogs). In this light, they were not dissimilar to their British, Dominion and French counterparts, who held the red-tabbed staff officers in the rear in equal contempt.

The *Frontschwein*:

> upheld a kind of camaraderie amongst themselves which could not have been more self-sacrificing or loyal, but they considered it their right to 'pinch' the warm bread and rabbits from the field kitchens and the fresh vegetables and unripe potatoes from their garrisons. They knew whose shoulders the fate of the front was resting on at the decisive moment . . . and they accepted their duty as a matter of course and without pathos. That's how the indestructible, 100-times proven, never to be defeated, 'Frontschwein' was created.[5]

On the morning of the Battle of Broodseinde, the *Frontschwein* were actually preparing to *attack*, not to defend, contradicting everything Haig and his intelligence chief had assumed about the state of the enemy. The German commanders 'planned a large-scale counter-attack to retake the ground lost on 26 September to the south of Zonnebeke up to the Polygon Wood for this morning'.[6] All through the previous night, they had 'dithered' over whether the heavier British artillery was 'normal destructive fire' or the 'softening up' that usually preceded an infantry charge. Towards morning, they decided it was the former, and upheld the order to attack.

At 5.30 am, the German artillery opened up on the British and Dominion lines, killing or wounding, as we've seen, many Anzacs approaching the frontline.

At 6 am, when the British guns erupted, the German troops were still hoping to persuade themselves that the 'awful intensity' of the shelling was 'simply English defensive fire against the beginning of the German attack', according to the German history. The scale and density of the barrage soon corrected that assumption: '[T]he width across which this raging barrier of fire extended from the Houthulst Wood up to the canal to the south of Ypres soon taught them that the expected severe enemy raid had started.'[7]

—

The German experience of those October battles, the darkest month of the war in Flanders, bear witness to the capacity of the mind and body to endure unthinkable strain. Consider a few reactions of the men who survived the British barrage of 4 October, the worst day for Germany in 1917: 'The aim was to snuff out all life,' Unteroffizier Paul Stolz remembered thinking. 'Shell after shell smashed into our ranks . . . Many were buried alive . . . In amongst the dark clouds of the explosions, fountains of dirty yellow soup-like clay spouted out of the craters, along with huge clods of earth, tree trunks and chunks of concrete.'[8]

Major Freiherr von Sobbe, commander of Infantry Regiment 92, watched his men kneeling in their trenches and praying for salvation:

> The earth seemed to want to swallow up everything. The
> battalions clung on amidst a crazy maelstrom . . . Bodies
> trembled, pulses raced . . . Some of the men hunched there in
> silence, stripped of all their emotions . . . Many prayed, perhaps
> for the first time in a very long time: 'My God, do not forsake
> me' and, mixed in with their prayer was the glimmer of hope of
> men still trying desperately to hang on to life . . . One soldier
> after another was hit and rolled away into a shell crater . . .'[9]

Major Lincke, commander of a battalion in a Reserve Infantry Regiment, witnessed some of his companies lose 95 per cent of their strength before an Australian platoon captured him. Passed back through Anzac territory to an old German front line, Lincke beheld 'what, for me, was the most gruesome sight of the war. Hanging from one of the four metre long vertical steel reinforcing rods by his legs was the corpse of a German soldier, headless and with his chest torn open. He must have been thrown there by a shell.'[10] Something his interrogator, an Australian officer (and peacetime lawyer), told him he would never forget: the Germans could not possibly win the war because the 'cannon fodder of the entire world is at our disposal'.

—

The heavy rain before and during the Battle of Poelcappelle offered the German defenders a reprieve. Many assumed the enemy attacks would cease. On the contrary, they gazed down in stunned disbelief at the sight of thousands more British and Anzac soldiers slipping, stumbling and crawling towards them, unprotected by artillery. That the enemy had *chosen* to fight in such conditions seemed an act of wilful self-destruction. The Germans seized the advantage, as we've seen, and shot the Anzacs and British to a standstill in the bog below, or on the unbroken wires.

'[T]he battalions managed to push the enemy back to Broodseinde,' notes the German history. 'This meant the English [*sic*] were hardly two thousand metres away from Passchendaele now.'[11] And while 'precious ground' had fallen into Anzac and British hands, 9 October looked 'like a good German success': 'Human and material losses had decreased considerably compared to 4th October.'[12]

Despite the German victory at Poelcappelle, Rupprecht was alarmed at the enemy's progress. The Fourth Army had suffered 'very high wastage', he confided in his diary on 10 October. His artillery had used up 'twenty seven trainloads of ammunition' in defence of their lines that month:

It is really worrying that the fighting ability of our troops is
reducing all the time and that all the means we have employed
to attempt to counter the oppressive superiority of the enemy
artillery have failed to have any effect . . . there remains nothing
for it, but repeatedly to give ground in order to force our
opponents to waste time as they move their artillery forward.[13]

In this sense, the Germans were in the throes of a fighting withdrawal, holding each ridge until the last moment and then pulling back to the next. Their aim: to drag out and exhaust the British
advance. The heavy rain fell at just the right time, and became the
German saviour and Anzac destroyer.

—

On 12 October, the Germans delighted in the failure of the British
barrage: shells were misfired or fell short. One projectile strayed into
a German trench latrine and exploded harmlessly, flinging the con-
tents over a nearby platoon and its commander.

Yet the German infantrymen's nerves were near breaking point.
From behind, they had little hope of relief or rations getting through.
Many attempted to desert or 'trickle back' to the rear areas. These
men were summarily shot under an unsparing interpretation of the
military law issued by von Armin on 11 October. The German soldiers were thus sealed off for destruction: behind and ahead of them,
they gazed down the barrel of a gun.

Vizefeldwebel Zaske likened his grenadier regiment to a mob of
animals, in conditions he reckoned the worst he had seen in three
years of fighting:

Yes, we were in the Carpathians and took part in the
breakthrough in Galicia; we were there on the Somme, we
have got to know the worst of the Eastern and Western Fronts,
but here . . . words failed everyone. When we emerged from
our holes, we looked like animals whose natural camouflage

made them indistinguishable from the surrounding earth
. . . Our grey uniforms were coated with mud and earth and
it appeared as though every man was encased in terracotta
from his helmet to the nails of his boots. Here we endured the
uttermost limit of that which was humanly possible . . .[14]

———

By 20 October, German losses had far exceeded normal wastage.
Most counter-attack divisions had lost more than half their rifle
power (normally about 4000 men). Between 23 September and 9
October, for example, the 20th Infantry Division lost 257 dead,
878 wounded and 2588 missing (most presumed dead); in the
seven days from 6 to 13 October, the 195th Infantry Division lost
94 officers and 3231 men, killed and wounded. The overall losses of
the Ypres Group, the main German defensive shield in the Salient,
comprising six divisions (three trench, three counter-attack), were
about 30,000: 3851 dead, 15,202 wounded and 10,395 missing,
according to German figures.[15] Of particular concern were the
disproportionally high casualties among commanders at platoon,
company and battalion level: some regiments had lost virtually all
their officers.[16]

Food supplies and medical aid were failing to get through. By
late October, the meagre German rations were barely able to sustain normal human life, far less soldiers involved in a fight to the last
man. There was an epidemic of gastroenteritis. Ludendorff began to
despair, according to his memoir:

The world at large . . . did not see my anxiety, nor my deep
sympathy with the sufferings of our troops in the West. My
head was in the East and in Italy, my heart was on the Western
Front. My will had to bring head and heart together.[17]

On one point, he and his generals felt positive: the new British tanks
had not proved 'particularly dangerous'; nor did the men experience

the horror of the machines, dubbed 'tank fright'.[18]

In the last week of October, the Canadians began their frightful assault on Passchendaele Ridge. At that point, Ludendorff realised that this was not a battle that could be 'won', in any conventional sense. At Flanders, he later wrote, 'the horror of Verdun was surpassed. It was no longer life at all. It was mere unspeakable suffering.'[19]

—

As hope on both sides drained away, the soldiers' morale hit rock bottom. Scenes that earlier would have horrified or revolted them were now treated as commonplace. The sight of a soldier drowning in a shell hole was no longer shocking; it could not be helped. Nothing could be done, for example, for the British lad who got bogged to his knees, then the waist, when the combined effort of four men with rifles under his arms failed to release him. There were no footholds from which to dig or haul him out. Duty compelled the men to move up to the line; two days later, they returned along the same route and found 'the wretched fellow . . . still there but only his head was now visible and he was raving mad'.[20]

Their minds were numb, their senses sullen. The British and Anzac soldiers' letters home did not bear out their actual mood. If a buoyant tone imbued their September correspondence, with few complaints of 'war weariness', according to surveys of uncensored (Green Envelope) letters, that was no surprise: September had been a dry month of victories. In any case, soldiers rarely poured out their misery or fear to their families, not wishing to disturb their loved ones; nor did they think their families would understand. A mixture of both inhibited the expression of the truth. A cheerful letter did not denote a cheerful man.

The mood in the British, Anzac and German armies in late October more closely resembled John Buchan's description of morale, in his history of 1917 written a year later: 'For almost the first time in the campaign there was a sense of discouragement . . .

Men felt they were being sacrificed blindly [and] that such sledge-hammer tactics were too crude . . .'[21] (he was referring here to the mood post-August). The observations of 'Pompey' Elliott, the fiery Australian brigade commander, of the young troops he led in late 1917 echoed Buchan: 'They had not the same spirit at all . . . The difficulty once was to restrain their impatience for action. Now we find men clearing out to avoid going into the line at all.'[22] Philip Gibbs similarly reported that the British Army had 'lost its spirit of optimism and there was a deadly depression among many officers and men'.[23] In a letter to his mother in late 1917, Wilfred Owen observed an expression on the faces of the men in the rear training grounds that was 'not despair, or terror, for it was a blindfold look, and without expression, like a dead rabbit's'.[24]

The disciplinary figures added statistical fibre to these assessments: a record 2000 Commonwealth troops were reported absent in France in December 1917, ten per cent of whom were Australian.[25] Indeed, Australian morale fell sharpest if the rates of detention and courts martial were any guide. By the end of 1917, the number of Australian troops behind bars for disciplinary failure was six times that of the other Dominions combined, and eight times the British total.[26] Australians were being court-martialled at the rate of 400 cases per month in October and November 1917, double the Canadian rate. If fighting ability and discipline had thus far found no correlation, by the end of October the Anzacs were utterly finished as a fighting force, at least until early 1918.

The Germans had severe disciplinary issues of their own. 'Out of two train loads of Prussian replacement troops from the east,' Rupprecht noted in his diary, on 3 November, 'ten per cent went absent without leave during the journey.'[27] These men had not yet experienced Flanders. Perhaps they were reacting in anticipation of what awaited them, a last snatch of life while they had the chance. Their mood worsened on their arrival at Valenciennes, near the French border with Belgium, where many whistled and jeered at officers who were trying to control them. A sense of local mutiny was in the air, but no sign, yet, of a complete collapse in morale on the French or Russian scale.

By late October, the average 'frontline hog' was in a state of 'mental shock', and going through the motions of war. Many had abandoned hope, epitomised by a wounded German prisoner who sat beside Gibbs in late October. 'We are lost,' the German told Gibbs. 'My division is finished. My friends are all killed.' When Gibbs asked the prisoner what his officers thought, the latter made a gesture of derision with a finger under his nose: 'They think we are "kaput" too; they only look to the end of the war.'[28] He was half-right: at that very moment, the German commanders were arguing over whether the German forces should be withdrawn altogether or reinforced in readiness for one last push, a massive counter-attack.

Even in the worst of Passchendaele, the German commanders' fixation on good order never deserted them, as this directive sent to officers in Group Wijtschate on 20 November demonstrated:

> Recently, the standard of saluting by officers . . . has left
> a great deal to be desired. It is a rarity to come across
> junior officers who consider it necessary to salute senior
> officers first. In many cases the salute itself is extremely
> sloppy. Some gentlemen do not consider it necessary
> to take their left hands out of their pockets . . .[29]

Amid the harbingers of doom were blazing exceptions, on both sides, of men who simply would never give in, whose characters relished combat, conquest, action. Such men experienced war as the sublimation of the spirit, the highest and most noble sacrifice. On the German side, the highly decorated future novelist Ernst Jünger was one such soldier; Adolf Hitler another. Both were wounded (Jünger several times; Hitler twice), both returned twice to Flanders, and both received the Iron Cross twice (First and Second Class). Jünger would also receive Pour le Mérite, the highest award to men of his rank.

There the comparison ended: after the war, Jünger repeatedly refused to join or endorse the Nazi Party or put his name to any of their works, to Nazi fury. Near the end of Passchendaele, sitting in his billet in Lille on a leather armchair in front of an open fire, Jünger felt a different reality to his fellow soldier-author, Erich Maria Remarque, who would write of a sense of universal despair. Perhaps Jünger's vision was more selfish, or self-interested, yet it was filled with the hope of life, to be relished and enjoyed. 'We still couldn't quite grasp,' he wrote, 'that for the time being we'd given death the slip, and we wanted to feel the possession of this new lease of life, by enjoying it in every way possible.'[30]

That comfort was not possible for Remarque, for whom the war had smashed the filament of hope that sustained Jünger. For millions, Remarque's novel *All Quiet on the Western Front* would become the last word on the horror of the Great War, a catastrophe the world would not 'survive', etched in the human soul, never to be erased.

Perhaps Lloyd George should have the last word on the state of British morale. His memoir, for all its self-serving bombast, rises to the occasion on the question of why so many veterans of Passchendaele would break under the German onslaught of 1918:

> There can be no doubt that when [Third Ypres] came to an end, the fighting spirit of the troops that had passed through this prolonged horror was at its lowest. It was a calamity unforeseen by G.H.Q. that their frayed nerve was to be put to another test before they had been given time to recover. It was this Army [the Fifth] under the same General [Gough] that was doomed to bear the brunt of Ludendorff's great coup on the Oise in March, 1918. No soldiers in that condition could have sustained such an onslaught. It is no reflection on their valour to say that they broke. So much for the claim of the apologists of Passchendaele that German morale alone had been impaired. As if British troops were not also flesh, blood and nerves![31]

In late October 1917, the flesh, blood and nerves of Canada came forward, to take over the leading role in the attack from the Anzacs. After studying what this meant, and what his men were being asked to do, General Sir Arthur Currie, the Canadian commander, decided it was impossible and was determined to refuse his orders.

# 14

# PASSCHENDAELE RIDGE

*The positions already gained [at Passchendaele] fell short
of what I had wanted to secure before the winter.*
Haig to the War Cabinet, mid-November 1917

---

Now it was Canada's turn. Like a marathon relay runner snatching
the torch from his ailing teammate, the Canadian Corps – four divisions of rough-hewn Canucks – moved up to attempt to finish the
job the British and Anzacs had begun: to capture Passchendaele.

Their commander's 'concern for saving lives and avoiding senseless operations were among his most endearing leadership qualities,'
wrote one observer.[1] In this observation lay the essence of General
Sir Arthur Currie, whose cheerful pragmatism and careful planning
had not only saved lives but also won battles. He communicated
such qualities in his gruff, homespun way. For example, during the
Somme he wrote in his pamphlet 'Lessons Learned', 'The infantry
should be taught to follow the artillery barrage as a horse will follow
a nosebag filled with corn . . . It is far better to lose a few of our
men from our own artillery fire than to sacrifice hundreds by hostile
machine-gun fire.'[2]

Before the war, Currie had been a real estate agent and a

territorial officer in British Columbia. He managed to disgrace himself in both roles. Facing bankruptcy after a soured property speculation, he made up the losses by extracting C$11,000 (C$224,000 today) from the regimental fund that had been set aside for new uniforms. Sailing for Europe as a brigade commander, the now Colonel Currie – he had impressed powerful people – felt a mixture of guilt and fear, guilt over the theft and fear of discovery: 'It was the first thought that struck me when I woke in the morning, and the last thought in my mind when I turned in at night.'[3] The thought prevailed, and he repaid the debt in September 1917 with funds borrowed from wealthy subordinates. Currie's physique was even more prepossessing than his business dealings: aged just 41 in 1917, he presented a pear-shaped figure to the world, six feet four inches tall, weighing 250 pounds, prematurely jowled, saggy-bottomed and pot-bellied.[4]

His personality and brainpower overcame these physical defects. His startling common sense, quick mind, loyalty to his men, sincerity of intent (if not always of action) and sheer companionability marked him out as a leader. People warmed to and respected this 'good-natured, cheerful, imperturbable' soldier, observed a British officer attached to the Canadian headquarters.[5] As often happens, the school head prefect, prize-winner or 'good' man rarely rises to the occasion *in extremis*, to lead the charge. More often, it is the rogue, the outlier, the unexpected man, the thinker on his feet, who seizes the nettle. Currie was such a man.

The most exacting and least forgiving measure of the quality of a commander was his soldiers' opinion of him. By this, Currie was a great success. He received and repaid the intense loyalty of his men. He excelled at Vimy Ridge as a divisional commander, and at Hill 70 in August 1917 as a lieutenant general in command of the Canadian Corps, in which capacity he made very clear to his British masters how and where his men would be used. Currie *felt* every casualty.

Currie took charge of the Canadian Corps after their sensational victory at Vimy Ridge, where General Julian Byng had led them with great authority. He stamped his character on the unit at once, winning their admiration by angrily refusing to serve under the Fifth Army, whose commander, Gough, he regarded as profligate and incompetent.[6] Haig's chief of staff, Lieutenant General Kiggell, recommended that Currie's men serve instead with Plumer's Second Army, because 'the Canadians do not work kindly' with Gough.[7]

Perhaps that was a mixed blessing now, with Currie under instructions to relieve the Anzacs and take Passchendaele Ridge. On 13 October, the Canadian general was asked to submit plans for the capture of Passchendaele at once. Unlike many generals, Currie made it his duty to visit the front, to see the conditions into which he was being ordered to send his men. He took one look at the great expanse of watery bog, rising gently to the distant ridgeline, itself rimmed with German pillboxes, and told Plumer to cancel the operation. He strongly protested against using Canadian troops as another battering ram in a battle that, he felt, had run out of steam and amounted to the futile pursuit of a worthless point on a map. 'Our casualties will be high,' he told Plumer, 'at least 16,000 men . . . and we have to know if the success would justify the sacrifices.'[8]

Nor were his officers or men willing to die in what many saw as a suicide mission. 'Every Canadian hated to go to Passchendaele,' Currie wrote after the war. 'I carried my protest to the extreme limit . . . I pointed out what I believed the casualties were bound to be, and was ordered to go and make the attack.'[9]

In fact, Haig did not 'order' the Canadian to commit his men. Instead, the field marshal did something highly unusual. First, in a meeting with Currie, Haig calmly laid out the reasons for the offensive: to establish an effective 'winter line' in Flanders in readiness for the resumption of hostilities in spring 1918; to keep the enemy pinned down during preparations for the Battle of Cambrai, set for November; and to assist the forthcoming French attacks in Champagne (i.e. at Malmaison on 23 October 1917).[10] A fourth, unspoken reason was that Haig desperately needed Passchendaele as the trophy with which he hoped to validate the huge sacrifice of the preceding three months to a deeply dispirited prime minister.

Having persuaded the reluctant Currie, Haig made a personal visit to the Canadian headquarters, and delivered a speech to the officers that none would forget – a notable achievement given Haig's renowned inarticulacy. Haig had not come to order the Canadians to attack Passchendaele (which was entirely within his powers). He was asking, even pleading with them to do so.

'Gentlemen,' Haig said, 'it has become apparent that Passchendaele must be taken and I have come here to ask the Canadian Corps to do it. General Currie is strongly opposed to doing so, but I have succeeded in overcoming his scruples. Some day I hope to be able to tell you why this must be done, but in the meantime I ask you to take my word for it. I may say that General Currie has demanded an unprecedented amount of artillery to protect his Canadians and I have been forced to acquiesce.'[11]

By recognising Currie's reluctance to commit his men, Haig's speech had the effect of personalising the decision at troop level: this would be a battle for the officers and men to decide; together they would prove themselves, to their commander and their country, again, at a moment when the world looked to Canada to redeem the sacrifice on the Western Front. Haig had read the psychology of the young soldier precisely.

By now, Passchendaele village had become a sort of siren song to both sides. In Haig's eyes, it had to be taken, regardless of the cost. The Germans had accurately assessed his dilemma. Hadn't he told Lloyd George in June that his plan entailed the capture of Passchendaele within weeks? How could he end the year with his men floundering beneath the ridge on which the wretched village stood? It offered firmer, drier ground from which the Allies would have an unimpaired view of German positions to the north-east, far beyond the Salient. In turn, to deny Haig that advantage, the German commanders would defend Passchendaele to the last available man.

—

Currie imposed several conditions on the use of his men, chiefly that the attack would not proceed until his preparations were complete. Like Plumer and Monash, he was a great believer in meticulous planning. The guns had to be brought forward, intelligence gathered, and his men rigorously trained in specific tactics (such as destroying pillboxes). The guns must be able to produce the densest possible barrage. There would be no repeat of the Anzacs' disaster, of attacking without artillery cover. Dragging up enough guns was absolutely vital before he committed his men to the battle. Haig, in no position to argue, agreed at once to the Canadian's demands.

The struggle ahead would exceed anything in Currie's experience. He submitted his plans on 16 October; the first attack would go in on the 26th. After a quick inspection of his resources, he realised he had far fewer guns than he'd been led to expect. Of 250 Australian heavies that were supposedly in situ, he found only 227, 89 of which were out of action. Less than half the 306 18-pounders were in working order, and most were 'dotted about in the mud wherever they happened to get bogged'.[12] Somehow the full complement of guns and ammunition had to be got forward, but the roads were impassable and the tracks of the light railway submerged.

They got to work at once. Canadian sappers and pioneer battalions were deployed alongside Plumer's Royal Engineers to construct two miles of new 'plank' roads (using elm or beech planks, nine feet long and 21 inches thick), 4000 yards of new tramlines and hundreds of gun emplacements positioned wherever necessary to effect a dense barrage. Currie ordered any lumberjacks to the rear to fell trees, to build a new network of duckboards.

The work came at a high cost: German shellfire killed or wounded 1500 men at work on the new transport lines between mid-October and mid-November.[13] 'Dead men and horses all around. Thousands of men working,' Private P. H. Longstaffe, of a Canadian pioneer battalion, wrote in his diary on 21 October. At the time, he and his comrades were building a plank road: 'Rush job on road through swamp. Ammunition, mules and horses passing in continuous stream. Fritz shelling both sides.'[14] Their efforts would save more lives in the coming battle, by ensuring an effective barrage.

The pre-battle preparation conformed to Currie's chief priority: to preserve as many of his soldiers' lives as possible. 'Currie consistently sought to pay the price of victory in shells and not in the lives of men,' an officer with the Canadian Corps Heavy Artillery later observed.[15] And so, by the time the Canadian infantry reached their starting points, most of their guns were in place, pounding away at the German pillboxes and wire entanglements. A further 210 18-pounders, 190 howitzers and 26 heavy guns arrived from the Canadian divisional artilleries, delighting Brigadier General Edward Morrison, Currie's commander of artillery.[16] To complete this line-up, the Canadian machine-gun companies were rushed forward, and soon began sweeping the enemy's supply lines with nightly fire, to deny them food and relief.

The attack would proceed in three steps, of just 500 yards each: the first aimed to capture German positions up to the red line, on the high ground surrounding Passchendaele; the second would secure points along the blue line, from which to seize the village; and the third would capture the village itself and extend the gains to the ridge east of town (the green line). There would be pauses of three to five days between each step, to rotate the men and drag up the guns. A creeping barrage 700 yards deep, advancing at 40 yards every four minutes, would precede the attack.

Before battle, Currie addressed his men. 'With good judgement and guts,' he declared, Passchendaele could be taken.[17] He bluntly explained what they were up against: entrenched German forces lining the ridge, many of them encased in rows of concrete block-houses. What followed applied the lessons Currie had drawn from his first-hand experience, chiefly at the Somme and Vimy: 'if the Artillery preparation and support is good; if our Intelligence is properly appreciated; there is no position that cannot be wrested from the enemy by well-disciplined, well-trained and well-led troops attacking on a sound plan.'[18] As a pointed diagnosis of why a string of

Allied offensives on the Western Front had failed, this could hardly be bettered.

—

The Canadians moved up on 18 October, to relieve the Anzacs and Tommies along a line bound by the Ypres–Zonnebeke–Passchendaele road to the south-west and the parallel road running through Gravenstafel to the north. They came by light train through the usual miserable conditions. Passing the casualty clearing station at Godwaersveldt (Godewaersvelde), the lads hung out of the train and waved to the nurses, shouting, 'Keep a bed for us, Sister. We'll be back in a few days.'[19] The German gunners shortly shelled the hospital and the train, visible to enemy observation balloons, killing several nurses. The long march to the front wound past Ypres and up the Menin and Gravenstafel Roads, under shell-fire all the way.

Some of the Canadians had been here before, in April 1915, when the Germans used chlorine gas on them. The landscape was unrecognisable now: a brown stretch of treeless bog that extended east to Passchendaele Ridge. All the former landmarks – villages, woods, farmhouses – had disappeared, and only the 'roads', shelled lanes of mud-covered planks, offered familiar orientation points. From here, they gazed across the Ravebeek Valley, the Anzac graveyard, now covered in water, liquid mud and soldiers' remains, and utterly impassable. Some wondered how on earth their colonial predecessors had attempted to attack across such country. Instead the Canadians would attack Passchendaele from the flanks, along the slightly raised roads that bound the Ravebeek – the northern road heading along the Bellevue Spur and the Zonnebeke Road running from the south-west onto Passchendaele Ridge itself.

They arrived in situ amid a cacophony of falling shells. Corporal R. G. Pinneo of the 10th Canadian Infantry Brigade thought it a joke when he found his 'billet', a bombed cemetery: 'The graves and tombstones had all been knocked to hell by gunfire, and even the crypts and coffins had been blasted open. You could see the sheeted dead. We bivouacked as best we could.'[20]

No sooner had Private Reginald Le Brun, of the Canadian Machine Gun Corps, reached his billet, in the ruins of a church, than a shell blew up the cook pot and the cook, and he and his men were left to eat cold emergency rations.[21] The next morning, his commanding officer ordered him to take supplies up to the men in the frontline shell holes (there were no trenches this far up), as the mules could go no further. 'It was only a quarter of a mile or so from the front,' Le Brun recalled, 'and the whole way was nothing but shell holes with bodies floating in them . . . maybe just legs and boots sticking out from the sides. The shelling never let up.'

During the first trip back, he heard someone calling for help:

It was one of our infantryman and he was sitting on the ground, propped up on his elbow with his tunic open. I nearly vomited. His insides were spilling out of his stomach and he was holding himself and trying to push all this awful stuff back in. When he saw me he said, 'Finish it for me, mate. Put a bullet in me. Go on. I want you to. Finish it!' He had no gun himself. When I did nothing he started to swear. He cursed and swore at me and kept on shouting even after I turned and ran.[22]

British feinting attacks were launched on 22 October, at Poelcappelle and elsewhere, to deceive the enemy into thinking the battle would continue along the entire front. Then, at dawn on the 26th, the Canadian infantry attacked along the two roads leading to Passchendaele: the 3rd Division on the southern road, flanked by Monash's Anzacs and the 4th Division on the northern road, flanked by Gough's Fifth Army (see Map 7).

It started to rain, on cue, reprising the old joke that the heavy guns had punctured the clouds. The barrage was dense and slow enough to protect the Canadians' advance, thundering across the field at just 50 yards every four minutes.[23] Hugging the barrage, the

Canadians scrambled up the Bellevue Spur, curse of the unprotected New Zealanders.

The Germans thronged the ruins of Passchendaele village. Every corner hosted a sniper or machine gunner. It was a place of 'smashed walls' and 'wrecked and torn remains', recalled one German soldier, whose regiment arrived on 20 October. 'In all directions there was yawning emptiness, ruins, rubble and destruction . . . no trenches, just shellholes in which our men took cover. The crater field stretched forward for three kilometres.'[24]

When the first Canadians emerged from the barrage, a German gunner yelled, 'Look, here they come through the fog!'[25] Waves of them flooded over the crest of the Bellevue Spur, he recalled. Most were repelled, and forced back to their starting line. Lieutenant Robert Shankland DCM and his outsized platoon held on, shooting the dazed German resistance and seizing their shell holes. Then, under the cover of sharp diversionary fire, small raiding parties crept around the blind side of the bunkers and tossed grenades through the rear entrances and loopholes. Against all expectations, Shankland's men established a foothold on the spur and held it.

On the flanks, the Royal Naval Division, a famous British formation of pioneering 'marines', 'got stuck in the mud'.[26] By noon, the Naval Division was completely bogged down beneath a hail of fire from Paddebeek, site of a German command post. The future German author Leutnant Ernst Jünger happened to be reconnoitring the area with a detachment of fusiliers. He came upon 'traces of the dead everywhere; it was as if there was no living soul to be found in this wilderness'. The Naval Division made no further attempts to attack that day – or, in Jünger's words, to 'throw disorganised and cruelly depleted units' into the breach.[27] The marines' relief arrived under the cover of darkness.

All night, Canadian and British patrols probed the lines of the Germans, who sent up a multitude of flares to try to locate their attackers under an illuminated sky. All next day, small bands of infantry burst out of the barrage and fell upon the Germans in sudden, savage increments that slowly prised open the enemy's lines. Carrier pigeons bore the bad news back to German headquarters.

By the end of the 27th, the Canucks had seized the high ground on Bellevue Spur, breaching the main German defensive line (Flandern I-Stellung), repelling waves of counter-attacks and earning three Victoria Crosses: to Shankland; Acting Captain Christopher Patrick O'Kelly MC, who led the capture of six pillboxes; and Private Thomas Holmes, who 'singlehandedly knocked out two machine-guns, captured a pillbox and took nineteen prisoners'.

Several Germans responded in kind, notably platoon com-mander Leonhard Abt, who, though wounded in the arm, held his position in the ruins of a house for ten hours under terrific Canadian fire from three sides, before being relieved. He would receive a gold medal for bravery, one of Bavaria's highest military honours.[28]

The Canadians dug in along the two approaches to the village, and were rotated over the next three days while the guns were moved up. Their casualties were as high as Currie had feared, if fewer than the staggering losses of the Anzac battles. On the first day, the two divisions had lost 2481: 585 killed and 961 wounded, with the rest missing, presumed dead.[29] The 4th Division, represented by a single battalion (the 46th), lost almost 70 per cent of its men.[30] The bearers went forth to collect the living, drawing lots each day to see which squad would venture first into no-man's-land.

'Am I going to die, mate?' one terrified, badly wounded lad pleaded with his bearer, as they waited in a hole for a pause in the shelling. 'Don't be stupid, fella,' said the bearer. 'You're going to be all right . . . You're going to be back across the ocean before you know it.' The shelling eased, they set off, and the boy died on the way to the dressing station.

The Germans were no longer sparing stretcher-bearers, it seemed. His party passed the bombed remains of an earlier stretcher party: 'There were nothing but limbs all over the place. We lost ten of our stretcher-bearers that day . . .'[31]

—

At 5.50 am on 30 October, Currie ordered his fresh divisions to attack. The rain resumed. The Canadians were expected to capture the positions they had failed to reach on the 26th, to 'secure good jumping off points for the final attack on Passchendaele'.[32] By 8.30 am, some had reached the blue line, an astonishing achievement in the conditions – notwithstanding the tragedy that befell the Princess Patricia's Canadian Light Infantry, near 'Duck Lodge'. Relentless German fire tore apart this renowned unit, killing or wounding 363, including 80 per cent of the officers and 60 per cent of the men; just 200 survivors attended the Last Post at sunset that day.

The Patricias earned three Victoria Crosses during their decimation. Lieutenant Hugh McDonald McKenzie, married with two children, took command of a platoon who found themselves pinned down in shell holes near an undefeated German pillbox. From his hole, McKenzie hatched a plan to seize the box: he rounded up a few bedraggled men and led them off. Promptly shot through the head, McKenzie had inspired a comrade, Sergeant George Mullin, to creep around the side of the bunker and silence it with grenades and a revolver. Both men were awarded the Victoria Cross, McKenzie's posthumously.[33] His devoted men buried him beside the pillbox and put up a cross to mark the spot; his grave could not be found after the war. Today, he is listed as missing.

An astonishingly resolute company of about a hundred men led by Major George Pearkes stormed across the higher, less soggy ground towards 'Vapour' and 'Source' farms, and held these against frenzied German counter-attacks that steadily decimated Pearkes's party to about twenty. 'I have eight 2nd Canadian Mounted Rifles and twelve 5th Canadian Mounted Rifles,' he reported later that day. 'All very exhausted. Do not think we can hold out much longer without being relieved.' For outstanding courage, Pearkes would also receive the Victoria Cross.

Other Canadian units succumbed to the mud and rain and tremendous fire, and 'failed to reach the Blue Line', in the curt official summary. Some barely advanced a few yards before losing most of their men. The 49th Battalion was virtually shot to pieces as they went over the top: just four officers and 125 men (of the usual 750) remained alive and unwounded within a few steps of leaving their trenches. Among the casualties was Private Alexander Decoteau, a famous Canadian long-distance runner who had competed at the 1912 Olympic Games in Stockholm; the 29-year-old, of Indian extraction, was killed by a sniper.[34] Most of his battalion were destroyed during the course of the day: by 2 pm, the 5th Canadian Mounted Rifles had lost three-quarters of their men.

A bright spot was the capture of Crest Farm by a single brigade of the 4th Division, who exploited a perfectly executed artillery barrage and overran the German defence. Crest Farm was no longer a farm, of course, just another point in the bog that apparently offered a 'good springboard' for the final assault on Passchendaele. Thus far that day, the Canadians had advanced a few hundred yards, in places not at all, for the loss of 2321 men, of whom 884 were dead.[35]

One officer's explanation of the failure cited the usual culprits: impassable ground, troops unable to keep up with the barrage, poor communication, runners killed or wounded, pigeons too saturated to fly. One phrase in the draft seemed 'to him so damning' that he chose not to use it in the final version: if the infantry advanced upright, 'they were an easy target', he had written; 'if they advanced on all fours the men were exhausted in a few minutes'. He summed up: 'any prospects of success under these conditions was nil'.[36] To which the historians Prior and Wilson appended a comment that speaks for us all: 'Even today the vision of sections of Haig's army crawling into battle in an attempt to stay alive induces a sense of inexpressible melancholy.'[37]

—

And there it was. A few hundred metres in the distance, atop the ridge, the furthest Canadians beheld the remnant of a steeple rising out of the wreckage of a village, drawing them towards it like a totem to some lost civilisation. A few forward patrols even crept beyond the blue line and into Passchendaele itself, which the Germans appeared to be evacuating, they later said, under terrific bursts of British artillery.

The two Canadian divisions (the 3rd and 4th) were now utterly exhausted and their relief vital before the final push. Overall casualties were exactly in the order of what Currie had envisaged: of the 75 officers and 1706 men of the 3rd Division, a quarter remained alive and unwounded. The 49th Battalion had lost 80 per cent of its men; others were decimated in similar proportions.[38]

The survivors were relieved that night: the 1st and 2nd Divisions crept forward and exchanged places with their comrades in the frontline holes. Their orders were, first, to seize Passchendaele itself; then to capture the crest of the main ridge further east of the village. The Germans, too, were being relieved, with a new division coming up from Champagne, well aware that the British were fixed upon capturing Passchendaele and the heights 'at whatever cost'.[39]

The fresh Canadians resumed the attack at 6 am on 6 November behind another dense barrage that flattened whatever dared remain vertical. By now, the terrain resembled a scene from some sort of post-apocalyptic landscape, unrecognisable as part of our world. 'Dante,' wrote one British gunner, 'would never have condemned lost souls to wander in so terrible a purgatory. Here a shattered wagon, there a gun mired to the muzzle in mud which grips like glue, even the birds and rats have forsaken so unnatural a spot . . . You see it best under a leaden sky with a chill drizzle falling, each hour an eternity, each dragging step a nightmare. How weirdly it recalls some half formed horror of childish nightmare.'[40] Only a shattered tree trunk or the relic of a cottage occasionally pierced this unreality, reminding the dazed witness that this scene had once sustained life.

Across this terrain, the Canadians now pressed forward. From Crest Farm, the fresh troops hugged the inside edge of the barrage so closely that 'the Germans could not man their machine guns before the attackers were on top of them', prisoners later confirmed.[41] They were taken completely by surprise, utterly unaware that 2500

Canadians had gathered over the previous night just a few hundred yards in front of them.

On the wetter slopes out of the Ravebeek Valley, the Canadians literally advanced knee-deep, and in places waist-deep, through mud and water.[42] German aircraft launched low-flying strafing raids on their positions, the bullets whipping up the surface of the stew.

Passchendaele itself fell with a whimper under the final assault, which took a little under three hours. The Canadians raced into the village with bayonets fixed, taking few prisoners. German troops hiding in cellars and rubble were quickly dispatched. In the final stage, Corporal Colin Fraser Barron dashed forward under covering fire and overran three enemy machine guns, for which he, too, would receive the Victoria Cross.

The 27th Battalion eventually seized the centre of town, an expanse of rubble, thanks largely to Private James Peter Robertson, who burst into an unsilenced pillbox, bayoneted its occupants and swung their machine gun on a few fleeing Germans, in a display of lethal resourcefulness that earned him Canada's ninth Victoria Cross of the battle for Passchendaele.

By a little after 9 am, on 6 November 1917, all of Passchendaele, whose capture had obsessed Allied commanders and whose name would soon become a byword for senseless slaughter, was firmly in Canadian and British hands. 'Despite stiff German resistance the entire attack went like clockwork,' noted a recent Belgian history.[43] Total casualties that morning were 2238, of whom 734 were killed or died of wounds; 434 Germans were captured.[44] The remaining Germans had the worst of it: 'If they stood up to surrender they were mown down by their own machine gun fire aimed from their rear at us; if they leapfrogged back they were caught in our barrage.'[45] An act as farcical as it was ingenious marked the last day. Finding themselves bogged down and their weapons jammed under a horrendous German counter-attack, the 2nd Royal Munster Fusiliers saved themselves by hurling mud balls at the enemy, who, mistaking the projectiles for grenades, kept their heads down as the legendary Irish unit withdrew.[46]

A distinguishing footnote to the battle was that, for the first time, the Allies had transmitted messages using continuous wave wireless sets, which had proved more reliable than runners, dogs and pigeons with muddy wings.

The village that revealed itself to the Allied armies for the first time in three years was just a smear of rubble on a denuded plain. 'The buildings had been pounded and mixed with the earth, and the shell exploded bodies were so thickly strewn that a fellow couldn't stop without stepping on corruption,' wrote one Canadian soldier.[47] The dwellings and shops were a mash of bricks, tiles and rubbish. The tombs in the little cemetery had been tossed aside, and the open graves of the pre-war dead yawned to the sky. Fragments of the statues of Christ and the saints lay strewn about the wreckage of the church amid scattered splinters of stained glass. Surveying the whole area around the village, a British gunner discerned:

> fifty square miles of slime and filth from which every shell that burst threw up ghastly relics, and raised stenches too abominable too describe; and over all, and dominating all, the never-ending, ear-shattering artillery fire and the sickly reek of the deadly mustard gas.[48]

The village the Allies had hoped to seize within weeks had taken three and a half months of ceaseless 'wearing down' to claim, for more than half a million total casualties.

—

The village itself was, of course, merely a point on a map. The supposed military prize of the operation lay further: the lip of higher ground to the east of Passchendaele, the 'summit' of the last and highest ridge in the Salient. On 10 November, the Canadians turned their sights on this final objective of Third Ypres, the capture of which would hand the Allies, for the first time, a commanding view towards Roulers and the German positions to the north-east.

The German defenders did not go quietly. They abandoned the ridgeline with a bang. The last Canadian attack cost the leading brigade 45 per cent of its strength. Of the 99 officers and 2610 men who spearheaded the final push, 58 officers and 1838 men survived unwounded.[49] Days of usual horror awaited the medical teams: the bodies of the Canadian wounded mingled grotesquely with the putrid mud and water. Many could not be reached in time to save them, despite the furious efforts of the stretcher-bearers working beneath the muzzles of a few surviving German snipers.

Their victory in Flanders had cost the Canadian Corps 15,654 casualties, precisely 346 short of Currie's estimate. His artillery had fired 1,453,056 shells (40,908 tons) between 17 October and 16 November, 68 per cent of his total firepower. Mud had made it impossible to deliver the rest.[50] Currie's understanding of the conditions distinguished him from most of the other 'Higher Authorities', observed one Canadian officer, who thought it 'incredible that men equipped with even fewer than average brains could ever send troops into such terrain'.[51]

—

A section of Passchendaele Ridge was theirs at last. Was this the prize for which they'd slogged through mud and rain for months and watched so many of their friends die? For which hundreds of thousands had been shot, bombed, drowned, gassed and obliterated?

No, Haig decided. After initially expressing himself well satisfied with the result, this heap of rubble, this rain-swept spine, was not worth the trouble; it was not good enough at all. The village and the ridgeline had no tactical usefulness whatsoever. Haig confirmed this in a letter to Robertson on 15 November, in which he terminated the battle: 'Any further offensive on the Flanders front must at once be discontinued . . .' Aware of the shocking impact of this admission on the government and the people, he added: ' . . . it is important to keep this fact secret as long as possible.' As damning was the recognition of the strategic uselessness of what he had won: 'The positions already gained [i.e. Passchendaele] fell short of what I had wanted to secure before the winter.' He concluded that Passchendaele Ridge, between the village and the Ypres–Staden railway, 'may be difficult and costly to hold if seriously attacked . . . I think this latter contingency must be expected as soon as the enemy realizes that he has regained the initiative.'[52] Seizing the village thus fulfilled merely a symbolic goal in a battle that, since August, had lost any hope of achieving its ambition of conquering the Belgian coast.

At any rate, the main purpose of Third Ypres all along, Haig would later insist, was to pin the German soldiers in Flanders and destroy as many of them as possible before winter set in, buying time for the French to recover and the Americans to arrive. Haig did not openly say this until after the armistice. For now, Passchendaele was a tenuously held spoil of war, which played well in the press and spoke to civilian notions of the aims of battle – to seize and hold terrain. And so the village on the ridge began to insinuate itself into the public mind as sacrificial ground; a soldiers' Calvary, whose seizure had summoned a sacrifice that Winston Churchill, in similar circumstances after the Somme, had raised to the realm of martyrdom. Currie was unmoved: the wanton sacrifice of his men for so little infuriated the Canadian, and the memory would torment him for the rest of his life.[53]

The nature of the tragedy unfolding in Flanders had not fully penetrated the minds at home. The War Cabinet heard on 31 October – ten days before its official end – that the Flanders Offensive had been 'quite successful', and that the Canadians had gained more than they set out to take. The battle would end, under Haig's orders, at a line due east of the village, to which Major General Frederick Maurice, the director of military operations, alerted the meeting.[54]

The anticlimactic end of Third Ypres left no furrows on the face of the government. At a meeting on 2 November, the ministers reaffirmed the prime minister's power to decide the extent of British support for Italy and whether and when the Flanders Offensive should end[55] – the latter a seemingly perfunctory gesture given that

Haig had just informed the War Cabinet that it would end on 10 November. The Cabinet let the war drag on to Haig's deadline, nine days during which thousands of men's lives were lost. Even as these Canadians were hurling themselves at the village, Lloyd George and his ministers were fiddling with dates, having dismissed Flanders as a sideshow and a failure.

The government briefly acknowledged the capture of Passchendaele, on 7 November, as 'a good step forward' that had produced some casualties. This grotesque misrepresentation went unchallenged, with no debate. Their attentions were elsewhere, now: the eyes and ears of the press and the men in power were attuned to the fresh excitement in France, where the first massed tank offensive was about to start, in Cambrai.

On the 11th, Haig called off the Flanders operation: he needed men at Cambrai and, at Pétain's request, to take over part of the French lines on the Somme. At the same time, notwithstanding his protests, four of his divisions had left or were soon leaving for Italy, with the prime minister's blessing and Plumer in command. They were to restore the situation after the dismal failure of the opening battles of Caporetto on 26 October (a series of clashes that would kill or wound 700,000 Italians and lose 3000 Allied guns).

The thinning out of Haig's forces meant that a skeleton detail of British troops, under General Rawlinson, would be left to defend Passchendaele for the winter. Theirs would be the least enviable role on the Western Front: three fresh German divisions had arrived in Flanders from Russia over the previous fortnight, and on 14 November the Germans heavily bombed the British positions in the vicinity of the wretched ridge.[56]

—

'[N]othing could be worse for this country than that we should be driven back from the Passchendaele ridge,' Major General Maurice, the director of military operations, warned the War Cabinet on 15 November.[57] If true, the government had a curiously negligent approach to defending its most vital military asset. The British Army similarly talked up the tactical importance of Passchendaele. On 26 November, the commanders of the few miserable battalions sent to defend it received a cable:

SECRET [dated 26/11/1917, distributed to
offices of the 14th (Light) Division] . . .
Copies to be handed in before proceeding to the LINE
NOTES ON THE PASSCHENDAELE SECTOR:
. . . The possession of the PASSCHENDAELE Ridge by
the British is of the first importance, as it affords complete
observation in an Easterly and North Easterly direction
and may force the enemy to withdraw his artillery from
WESTROOSEBEKE and from in front of MOORSLEDE.[58]

In fact, Passchendaele was already terribly vulnerable, and in 'a really untenable position against a properly organized attack', Rawlinson wrote, in a blistering assessment of the situation. 'We must therefore be prepared to withdraw from it, if the Germans show signs of a serious and sustained offensive on this front . . .'[59] In short, within weeks of its capture, they were planning to abandon it. This made tactical sense, in a war of attrition, when only the body count mattered. But nobody was willing to use that argument on Lloyd George at that moment.

The Germans were already showing signs of serious and sustained counter-attacks to recapture the lost ground. Ludendorff himself visited the Western Front on 20 November, underscoring Passchendaele's importance in Germany's evolving offensive plans, which had already assumed a tactical dimension in Flanders: German gunners had withdrawn their long-range heavy cannon to safe positions from which to shell the British troops defending Passchendaele Ridge. The prospect of losing it so soon even prompted a question in Cabinet, on 28 November, to the effect that hadn't these long-range German guns rendered 'our position . . . very unfavourable?' To which Maurice replied that the British troops at Passchendaele were 'uncomfortable' but the Germans were worse off because 'we held the high ground'.[60] That not only failed to answer the question; it revealed his utter ignorance of the situation.

An Australian captain, Norman Nicolson, had a better grasp of reality than most staff officers and generals. Near the end of Third Ypres, suffering from gas poisoning and a bad cold, and having lost his voice, he sat down and wrote in his diary:

> The Canadians have taken Passchendaele but it is impossible
> to advance guns for the mud and shell holes. It is the
> Somme all over again. The fire eating old generals and
> the pretty boys on their staffs don't know what things
> are like up in front and keep ordering futile attacks that
> are doomed before they start because of the mud.[61]

A frequent refrain, which was no less true in November than it had been in August.

—

And here were Lieutenant Allhusen and his company, back in action after two months' rest, approaching Passchendaele Ridge in late November. The village resembled an island, he wrote, cut off from any support and under constant German shellfire; the British troops were sitting there, being slowly wiped out. The only road into the village to relieve them 'was naturally a death trap'.[62]

Allhusen's usual good cheer deserted him:

> The whole outlook had become unutterably black. All the
> battles of the Spring and Summer seemed to have been in
> vain . . . it had all ended in this, with fresh German troops
> streaming across from their long holiday on the Eastern front,
> to face our worn-out divisions and start it all over again.[63]

The individual soldier's mood, he observed:

> was one of complete and logical despair . . . The ideal was
> to lose a leg as soon as possible . . . the majority carried on
> mechanically, waiting for the next wound, while the weaker
> members went under, either to lunacy, desertion or self-inflicted
> wounds. The German army had reached the same state.[64]

On the way to the front, one of Allhusen's subalterns got a bullet in
the arm, 'and retired rejoicing'.

On reaching Passchendaele village, Allhusen set up his headquarters in an old cellar on what had been the high street, 150 yards
from the front. His platoons went forward, to relieve the men in the
shell holes. He kept back his officers, servant, cook and a runner
called Quicke, the last of six brothers, whose mother had appealed to
the army to give her surviving son a safe job. The army had declined
her request, so Allhusen kept Quicke 'in the safe end of the dugout'.[65]

By night, Allhusen went out to inspect the forward posts; by day,
he sat under constant shellfire in the cellar, reading. Each night, the
closest shots made the planks in the roof sag, the mud crumble and
the candles flicker. The cracks in the roof 'seemed to get bigger while
I watched. One had a distinct face, and eyes which followed me
about.' He speculated about what would happen if the cellar received
a direct hit.[66] Night liberated him to work in the line. By day, he
returned to the cellar, 'wondering how many men I was going to lose
that day'. His company were soon down to their last few; by early
December, his surviving corporals couldn't answer for the lives of
their men for another day.

On the night of 8 December, the last before his company's relief,
Allhusen counted a shell falling near the cellar every two minutes.
He and his staff sat in 'dead silence' like 'six criminals . . . uneasily
aware that the executioners must be coming soon'. The hours passed,
and he tried to imagine rum and food. Then he awoke, dazed, in
a shambles of dust and smoke. The direct hit had killed one of his

men, and wounded the rest except Quicke. A piece of shell had put a hole through Allhusen's foot, his boot a bloody mess.

With the roof gone, and exposed to enemy shelling, they waited for relief to arrive. Long hours passed. Allhusen couldn't walk. A big sergeant eventually appeared, picked him up and laid him on a stretcher. Thus began the 'worst five hours of my life', of being dragged back through Passchendaele, along Bellevue Spur, to an aid post, then a dressing station, always under falling shells. Six weeks later, he was on a hospital ship to England.

—

A few gunners and soldiers remained on the ridge through December, freezing in the chill blasts of a Flanders winter. One was young Ronald Skirth, the nineteen-year-old bombardier, who found himself in a captured pillbox – facing the 'wrong way' – on the crest of Passchendaele with his commanding officer, whom he contin-ued to detest, and another gunner, whom he claims was his friend Jock Shiels (although the Commonwealth War Graves register lists Shiels as having been killed on 18 July 1917). They were wet, dirty and lice-ridden, and lived on bully beef. Mules delivered ammuni-tion. Of their four heavy guns, one had sunk to its axles; another had received a direct hit, wiping out its crew; and a third had self-destructed when the crew loaded it with a faulty shell, killing them all. One gun remained operational, had there been the crew to load it. So the three men sat in the middle of 'a vast morass of flooded cra-ters', awaiting likely death.

'I was convinced by now,' Skirth would later recall, 'that our C.O. had taken leave of his senses and was no longer capable of responsible action.'[67] So intense was his hatred of his commander's 'blind pride and obstinacy' and 'complete indifference to the plight of his men', that had he possessed any suitable weapon, 'I would have had no hesitation in using it on him'.[68]

Lying awake in the pre-dawn hours, Skirth's despair drove him to commit 'the soldier's unforgivable sin' of leaving his post without his officer's permission. He donned his respirator and helmet, stepped softly through the gas curtains and out into a night ablaze in flares. The German guns were quiet. He dashed to the surviving No. 1 gun: the crew had gone, the gun abandoned. He crawled back to an old command post, where he found the crew and his second-in-command, who informed him that the gunners had all been ordered to withdraw. Skirth's commander, a Captain Ahab-like figure in this telling, had torn up the written orders to withdraw and refused to budge.

'I was right,' Skirth concluded. 'We had a raving lunatic in charge', who would only move 'when Haig told him to . . .' Skirth crawled along the duckboards back to his pillbox to deliver the news of the general withdrawal. On his arrival, his commander gave him a severe reprimand, which Skirth interrupted to report that the entire battery had withdrawn: 'There are no men at No 1 gun. Repeat, NO MEN.' To which his commander arrested him, muttered that he'd have him shot for desertion, and reached for his revolver. His friend intervened, and the two gunners backed slowly out of the pillbox.

At the gas curtain, Skirth shouted back at his officer to the effect: 'My pal and I have had enough of you and your bloody war. We're getting out of it, understand? We're getting out. Call it desertion if you like. Call it cowardice if you like . . .'[69] That was the last they saw of their commanding officer.

Outside, the German shelling had ceased. In the lull, the two men made a dash for it, scrambling back along the duckboards and through the Passchendaele graveyard. It was daylight, and the German guns resumed. Skirth prayed. Several shells fell on the graveyard and further obliterated the coffins and corpses. 'You're wasting your ammo, Fritz,' he thought, looking back. 'You can't make the dead any deader.' Further on, a shell killed his friend and wounded Skirth, who was eventually extracted and sent home, where he suffered a nervous breakdown.[70]

In the rear areas in the last days of 1917, the padres held

services for the survivors of Third Ypres. In November, the Reverend Tanner, who had just been recommended for a DSO for helping the wounded, felt moved to deliver a service that reiterated three things he felt had upheld the spirit of the men during Third Ypres. They were: 'courage, determination and dash when in action'; 'cheerful endurance'; and 'consideration and courtesy' to the local people. He ended his sermon with an appeal to the men to put their faith in their 'White Comrade', the Holy Spirit: 'When in action I know nothing better calculated to help a man control his fears . . . than the consciousness of the encircling presence of God . . .'[71]

—

The year of the Flanders Offensive began in a world thunderous with aggressive imperialism in which the divine right of kings held sway over millions and the monarchies that encrusted the face of Europe seemed unassailable. It ended in a harsh new light, in which kaisers and tsars and their senescent regimes were seen as eminently dispensable. Every monarchy in Europe trembled for its survival in the wake of the Russian Revolution, the removal of the Tsar and the plainly untenable reign of the Kaiser.

On 24 October 1917, hearing that Russia's Provisional Government was about to raise the bridges over the Neva River, Vladimir Ilyich Lenin fired off his famous Call to Power to the Soviet Central Committee: 'The government is tottering. It must be given the death-blow at all costs.'[72] The Bolshevik Revolution went into action in Petrograd that night, ousting Alexander Kerensky's Provisional Government. Kerensky fled the country and the Communists took power.

Lenin's 'Statement of Bolshevik Demands' sentenced to death the monarchies of Europe and the preservers of the capitalist system. 'The Bolsheviki,' he declared, 'refuse to leave to capitalist Governments the task of expressing the desire of the nations for peace. All monarchies must be abolished. The peasants must at once take all the land from the landholders. Order must be strictly maintained by the Councils of Peasants' Delegates.'[73] On 15 December, Germany and Lenin's newly minted dictatorship agreed an armistice, formalised as the Treaty of Brest-Litovsk on 3 March 1918, freeing the remaining two-thirds of Ludendorff's Ober Ost forces for service on the Western Front.

The planets had realigned against the Allies. In the closing weeks of 1917, the members of the War Cabinet responded with deep anxiety to the news of Britain's and France's dire situation, the very opposite of what Haig had intended six months ago. The prime minister raged at Haig's dispatches, which calmly informed him on 13 December that Passchendaele, though 'unsuitable to fight a decisive battle in', should be briefly held, in order 'to wear out and break up the enemy's advancing troops'.[74] Pouring out all his scorn, Lloyd George would later sum up the Passchendaele battles as forcing 'the British Army into a more dangerous position than it was in before the battle commenced'.[75]

The British forces now faced a critical shortage of men, Haig informed the War Cabinet, in a paper tabled on 6 December, and he urgently needed more recruits to continue the struggle. Haig was in earnest. From his perspective, the casualties were unavoidable and wholly necessary; the men had sacrificed themselves in the line of duty, a cost the nation must bear. That was the point of a war of attrition.

And now, by December 1917, Haig's forces were 100,000 below 'establishment' level. He would need 500,000 to make up the deficit in the next six months. If Lloyd George refused to provide them, 'the British infantry divisions in France would be 40 per cent below establishment by 31st March 1918'. In other words, the prospect of actual defeat loomed, Haig concluded. The War Cabinet concurred. In a debate on manpower on 6 December 1917, Lord Derby warned: 'So far from there being any question of our breaking through the Germans, it was a question of whether we could prevent the Germans breaking through us.'[76]

Winston Churchill, the Minister for Munitions, agreed that the situation was 'one of great danger'.[77] Where would they find the men? Could they squeeze the war industries and farms, and slow down production, to release workers for battle? No, the ploughs were already idle for want of men, and on 26 October the War Cabinet had called for 10,000 soldiers to be *released* to work the ploughs, even if they had to be withdrawn from the Western Front. Perhaps the government could raise the military age further? Or even appeal to Ireland? If all else failed, would France kindly rejoin the war, or the Americans arrive?[78]

On one point, the prime minister's mind was made up: he was determined not to meet Haig's demands. Dismissing the 'alarmist tone' of the army, he argued on 10 December that the French and British armies together outnumbered the Germans on the Western Front by 1.2 million and had 400,000 more rifles.[79] As usual, the prime minister glossed over inconvenient details. For one thing, the French continued to protest that they were unfit for action. Most importantly, the Allied defences were now extremely precarious. According to a long charge sheet that Robertson presented to the Cabinet on 19 December: the British troops were untested in defensive war; the trench lines were fragile; and fresh German regiments were continually flowing over from the Russian to the Anglo-French front. (Indeed, in the two months ending mid-December, Germany had moved fifteen divisions from east to west, and 100,000 further enemy troops were being 'combed out' of the German forces in the east,[80] delivering 154 German divisions and about 8000 extra guns to the Western Front by the year's end.)[81]

'Strategically we were in a bad position,' Robertson warned the War Cabinet, 'as there was very little depth behind our defences . . . Dunkirk was already within range of the enemy's guns, and a short advance by the enemy would bring him within range of Calais and Boulogne. A retirement for even a few miles westward might therefore be disastrous.'[82] The Admiralty even revisited the question of whether Britain was in danger of invasion. Nobody had

anticipated so dismal an end to a year that began with glad premonitions of victory, of clearing the Germans out of Belgium by
Christmas.

All this produced a mood of extreme tension in Parliament,
'almost amounting to panic' on 5 December when Brigadier
General Lowther, military secretary to the commander-in-chief,
Home Forces, told the House of Commons that the situation on
the Western Front was worse than it had been in 1914.[83] He only
slightly overstated the case: with Russia completely out of the war,
and France and America not yet ready, the British and Dominion
armies had been forced onto the defensive for the first time since the
outbreak of hostilities. They would stay that way for the foreseeable
future. Haig 'had no offensive plans in mind at present', Robertson
told the War Cabinet on 19 December, a complete volte-face from
the aggressive spirit of July.

And so, as the world entered its fifth year of war, the Allies were
forced to dig in again. In late December, France's new prime minister, Georges Clémenceau, recalled 270,000 Frenchmen to the colours 'for the purpose, not of fighting, but for digging trenches'.[84]
For their part, the British troops seemed to have lost their digging
skills. They were unable to 'dig their trenches properly', Britain's secretary of state for war, the Earl Derby complained to the Cabinet on
Christmas Eve. The German trenches were 'very much better than
ours', he said, reprising an old refrain of 1914–15. Robertson replied
that he had spoken to Haig about the matter, but unfortunately 'our
troops were not good at digging trenches'.[85]

An element of blackest farce might be said to hang over all this,
over the spectacle of men returning to the killing grounds whence
they had come, to re-dig trenches along the lines they had dug four
years previously, and resume the slaughter on the orders of their
Lilliputian commanders . . . were it not for the fact that millions of
lives were in play, rendering the farce grotesquely real.

If the world felt very much like 1914 all over again, facing the
same old battlefields, gridlocked along a trench line, the new

weapons, the smell of new gas and the evolution of the barrage reminded them that three and a half years had passed. In all other respects – the uncompromising politicians, the all-conquering generals, the acquiescent civilians – little had changed.

# 15

# THE BURIAL OF THE DEAD

*Here lies the noblest work of God.*
Epitaph to Private H. R. Sloggett, killed in action on 21 October,
aged twenty, buried at Tyne Cot Cemetery in Flanders

---

After swearing, a year earlier, that there would be no more Sommes, in December 1917 Lloyd George found himself staring at casualties on that scale. British and Dominion soldiers killed, wounded, missing (presumed dead) or taken prisoner in October totalled 4956 officers and 106,419 other ranks, according to the monthly return sent by the director of military operations to the War Cabinet on 2 November (the figures did not include the 'wastage' of the Canadian battles of early November).

Yet if 'normal average monthly casualties' – i.e. when there was no severe fighting – were 35,000, the return said, then the actual casualties in October 1917 'were about 76,000'.[1] If this macabre clarification was supposed to console the prime minister, it had the opposite effect. Lloyd George read the casualty figures in a state of stupefied rage.

Total losses during the whole of Passchendaele, between 31 July and 10 November, were 271,000 British and Dominion troops, compared with about 217,000 German. (For a full breakdown, see Appendix 1.) Factoring in their small populations, the Dominion forces suffered disproportionately. Passchendaele temporarily crippled the spirit of the Anzac divisions, killing or wounding 38,000 Australians, 15,654 Canadians and 5300 New Zealanders. '[F]or these smaller nations, Passchendaele was their most costly engagement of the war, indeed their entire military history,' writes Craig Tibbits, of the Australian War Memorial.[2]

Nobody can agree on the precise number of British and Dominion troops killed at Third Ypres, but it is likely to be between 80,000 and 100,000, or 10–13 per cent of the 750,000 British and Commonwealth soldiers, sailors and airmen who lost their lives on the Western Front. French losses at Third Ypres were 1625 killed or missing and 6902 wounded or taken prisoner. The six French divisions had fought in a quiet sector, under Pétain's policy of 'limited offensives', soundly defeating the Germans in the area and capturing 1500 prisoners.[3] Clearly they were not as unfit as Pétain had led Haig to believe.

German official medical records for the period between 21 May and 10 December 1917 tallied total casualties of 236,241, including 32,878 killed, 38,083 missing (killed or captured), and 165,280 wounded and evacuated.[4] Those figures refer to a period 40 days longer than the dates the British official historian set for Third Ypres. The comparable dates, of between 1 June and 10 November 1917, show German casualties of 217,194, of which the total killed and missing were 67,272 and total wounded 149,922. Thus Germany 'won' the body count, with 54,000 fewer casualties. Despite this, statistical fetishists continue to declare Third Ypres an Allied victory by body count; or a 'draw', with each side losing 'about 250,000'.

In their defence of Third Ypres, some historians cite the fact that British losses were fewer than the Somme (where 481,842 were killed or wounded, though the offensive lasted five weeks longer). Or they point to the daily average 'wastage' at Third Ypres as 'only' 2323, whereas the Somme killed 2943 on an average day; the

Hundred Days offensive in 1918 killed 3645; and the mother of all massacres, Arras, killed 4076 per day. Or they compare the number of men killed and wounded per square yard of front gained as a measure of progress. These macabre calculations are for the night owls of military history, ready to swoop on the remains of the most disturbing human tragedy to buttress a theoretical case for attritional massacre.

The long-running dispute over which side suffered the most casualties need not detain us beyond acknowledging that Britain's official historian, Brigadier General Sir James Edmonds, grossly overstated German losses at 400,000 in his book, almost twice the actual figure and 130,000 more than Commonwealth losses.[5] It is unthinkable that an official historian would wilfully miscalculate the body count on this scale, to support his case that Britain 'won' or to appease the British defenders of Third Ypres. Yet, unless one believes he made a genuine error, that is the only conclusion one can draw. Edmonds seems to have all-too-hastily overlooked a vital German source in reaching his figure.[6] Even without this source, it seems odd that the brigadier general failed to question a tally that contradicts basic military doctrine and the word of the great von Clausewitz, who stipulated that in a war of attrition the defending army almost always suffered fewer losses than the attacking one. Many historians have settled on a 'compromise' figure, of 250,000–260,000 casualties on either side, which they claim to be 'about right'. This also flies in the face of the basic military lessons they hold dear. Like Edmonds, they appear to have inflated German losses by adding every minor wound and sickness, as Sheldon charitably suggests, raising the question, 'when is a casualty not a casualty?'[7] The German answer seems reasonable: when the 'casualty' is able to carry a rifle.

Lloyd George's blood boiled as he pondered such catastrophic losses: a gain of five miles for so many dead? Had we really lost 17,000 officers, he railed, seven to every two of theirs?[8] Like most interested civilians, he saw the war's progress in terms of territory gained per man lost. The grim truth about attrition – that these casualty levels had been factored in as the cost of Haig's 'wearing down' war, in which it mattered little how much ground was gained – either eluded the prime minister or was too awful for him to face. In Lloyd George's eyes, Haig was a butcher and a madman and had to be stopped before he dismembered the nation's youth. Henceforth, if the British leader could not extract his commander's resignation by pressure and humiliation, he would try to manacle Haig to a defensive strategy by denying him the supply of men.

A dreadful scenario ran in tandem with these deliberations, and deeply troubled the British leader. Lloyd George well knew that someone would be held accountable for such catastrophic losses, and he henceforth resolved to ensure that it would not be him. He would be known to posterity as the prime minister who won the war, not the leader who had had the power to terminate the massacre and failed to do so. To which purpose he now set in motion the dark arts of political self-exculpation: Third Ypres may have ended, but the battle for the ear of history had just begun.

—

Tommies and Fritzes, Diggers and Canucks, Jocks and Kiwis, privates and generals, professional soldiers and nineteen-year-old conscripts, virgins and middle-aged fathers, Anglicans and Lutherans, Catholics and Jews, poets and postmen, farmers and clerks, Tyneside cottagers and heirs to grand estates, Bavarians and Saxons, Irish fusiliers and the Black Watch, Old Etonians and Australian stockmen, New Zealand rugby players and Canadian lumberjacks, Prussian officers and Coldstream Guards, the brave and the fearful, the dutiful and the dissipated, 'our beloved son', 'my dear husband', 'my love', 'our boy': Third Ypres killed them all, with the indiscriminate power of a natural catastrophe.

After battle, the dead were given a short field service, if that were possible, though many bodies lay in the field for days or weeks before burial. The padres tended to use II Timothy IV.7–8: 'I have fought a good fight, I have finished my course, I have kept the faith:

Henceforth there is laid up for me a crown of righteousness, which the Lord, the righteous Judge, shall give me at that day . . .' Or the words of John XI.25–26: 'I am the Resurrection and the Life, saith the Lord: he that believeth in Me, though he were dead yet shall he live: and whosever liveth and believeth in Me shall never die.'[9]

Field services were held in former battle zones and attended by small groups of the deceased's friends and his officer. The services catered for the major faiths, and were often moving. Nor were the exotic tribes of the Empire forgotten. The members of the New Zealand (Maori) Pioneer Battalion were buried according to the rites of the 'tangi' tribal service. A witness recorded the tangi of Lieutenant Colonel George King, the much-admired commander of 1 Canterbury Battalion, who had previously led the Maoris, perhaps the most feared soldiers on the Western Front. 'I do not think,' wrote the witness, 'I will ever forget that service, a cloudless sky and an aeroplane scrap overhead, the shallow grave, the body sewn in a blanket and covered with the New Zealand flag, the surpliced Padre, the short impressive burial service and finishing up with the beautiful Maori lament for a fallen chief, "Piko nei te matenga" ("When our heads are bowed with woe') sung by the Maoris present, and with its beautiful harmonies and perfect tune, it seemed to me the most feeling tribute they could offer.'[10]

Dr Harvey Cushing witnessed the burial of Paul Revere Frothingham, great-great-grandson of Paul Revere, the American revolutionary. Revere's body was laid to rest on a soggy Flanders field beside a little oak grove under an overcast autumnal evening. Chinese coolies in tin helmets served as the gravediggers, working in ditches half-full of water. As Revere had served with the British Army, in an ironic twist in the family story the lad's body was:

wrapped in an army blanket and covered by a weather-worn Union Jack carried on their soldiers by four slipping stretcher-bearers . . . Happily it was fairly dry at this end of the trench, and some green branches were thrown in for him to lie on.

The Padre recited the usual service – the bugler gave the 'Last Post' – and we went about our duties. Plot 4, Row F.[11]

—

Those were the lucky ones. At the end of Third Ypres, thousands of corpses lay in shallow graves or shell holes, on wires or in pieces. Crowds of the dead and wounded filled the pillboxes and trenches, and rows upon rows of stretcher-borne bodies – many alive, many dead or dying – accumulated at assembly points. The stench of decomposition hung on the chill wind that blew over the Salient, the harbinger of winter. December's snowflakes cast a natural sheet over the hideous scenes on the ground.

The burial details roamed Flanders fields for months after the end of Third Ypres, combing the Salient for soldiers' remains, often finding only a limb, a hand, a head. Whole bodies were sewn into blankets. Body parts that seemed to form part of the same individual were placed in sandbags and buried as the complete human being. It was a gruesome jigsaw puzzle, and often the identity of the soldier was impossible to confirm.

Lieutenant P. King of a regiment of East Lancashires led a burial party to inter the remains of hundreds of Scottish soldiers who were mown down during the attack on Frezenburg Ridge, on 20 September. 'It was an appalling job,' King later wrote. '[S]ome were so shattered that there was not much left. We did have occasions where you almost buried a man twice. In fact we must have done just that several times. There was one officer whose body we buried and then shortly after we found an arm with the same name on the back of a watch on the wrist. . . . If they had any identity discs, then we marked the grave – just put the remains in a sandbag, dug a small grave and buried him. Then I had to write it on a list and give the map reference location. Where the bodies were so broken up or decomposed that we couldn't find an identity we just buried the man and put "Unknown British Soldier" on the list.'[12]

The gravediggers were working in a wasteland:

There was no sign of civilization. No cottages, no buildings, no trees. It was utter desolation. There was nothing at all except huge craters, half the size of a room. They were full of water and the corpses were floating in them. Some with no heads. Some with no legs. They were very hard to identify. We managed about four in every ten. There were Germans among them . . .[13]

Each inhumation, whether the corpses were Allied or German, received a brief service. '[W]e didn't just dump them into a hole,' said King. 'We committed each one properly to his grave. Said a little prayer out of a book issued to us. "Ashes to ashes, dust to dust." The men all stood around and took off their hats for a moment, standing to attention. "God rest his soul." A dead soldier can't hurt you. He's a comrade. That's how we looked at it. He was some poor mother's son and that was the end of it.'[14]

—

When the war was over, the soldiers' remains, if they could be found, were exhumed from these temporary graves and relocated to dedicated Commonwealth war cemeteries.

Two organisations, founded by the indefatigable Major General Fabian Ware, undertook the immense task of identifying and burying them: the Directorate of Grave Registration and Enquiries, part of the War Office, was charged with identifying and reburying remains; and the Commonwealth War Graves Commission with marking graves and building and maintaining burial sites. Between 1919 and 1921, Ware's Exhumation Units fanned out across the Salient, to attempt to find, exhume and identify tens of thousands of soldiers' bodies buried in makeshift holes, collapsed dugouts or shallow graves, on or near the battlefield, marked with a wooden cross. Shellfire had obliterated many of these temporary resting places, along with the corpses, making the soldier difficult or impossible to identify from what remained (DNA testing had not been discovered). Every body and body part had to be unearthed and, if possible, identified or matched with other body parts.

For this immense task, Ware deployed 8559 men, divided into squads of 32, who worked in groups of four, each equipped with rubber gloves, two spades, a pair of pliers, stakes to mark the graves, tarpaulins to wrap the bodies, stretchers and disinfectant. Machine-gun-cleaning rods were commonly used to probe the earth, for signs of the dead.[15] Dog tags, papers, wallets, any unit numbers or identifying marks on belts, spoons, watches or ground sheets were the most useful means of identifying the dead man and his unit. Identified remains were then transferred to a designated Commonwealth cemetery.

By May 1920, the exhumation teams had recovered 130,000 bodies – many from earlier battles in the Salient, and many of them German.[16] The German dead were buried in mass graves, with little attempt to identify them. An unknown number of bodies were found embedded in trench walls, where they'd been flung 'to help build up the parapet', Ed Lynch recalled. 'It's not good burial but it's good warfare,' he wrote. 'We're not undertakers.'[17]

—

Telegrams were sent to the families, and then obituaries appeared, followed by local memorials and the inscription of an epitaph on the soldier's tombstone. There was no question of repatriating the remains to their various countries – an enormously costly and difficult exercise. In any case, the very concentration of burial grounds in Flanders and north-east France has given the area its special quality as a place of remembrance. The diffusion of the soldiers' bodies throughout the world would have 'caused remembrance to fade a lot faster or even to disappear altogether'.[18]

Once a soldier was confirmed dead or wounded, the telegrams were dispatched. The news arrived in the little official envelope every parent dreaded; for example:

REGRET REPORTED SON PRIVATE _____
WOUNDED WILL PROMPTLY ADVISE IF

## ANYTHING FURTHER RECEIVED[19]

Madam,
It is my painful duty to inform you that no further news having
been received relative to (No.) _____ (Rank) _____
(Name)_____ (Regiment)_____,
who has been missing since _____, the Army Council
has been regretfully constrained to conclude that he is dead
and that his death took place on _____ (or since).

An official letter followed, offering the families the 'deep sympathy of the King, Queen, and Government in the sad loss that you
and the Army have sustained'.[20] A death notice then appeared in
the local papers, often in the name of the late soldier's children.
Private Matthew Austin was one of 50 men in his unit killed on 12
October 1917; his two-year-old son Hugh's name appeared beside
the notice: 'In loving memory of my dear daddy . . . who was killed
at Passchendaele . . . The dearest spot on earth to me is where my
dear daddy lies.'[21]

The late soldier's officers or friends usually followed up with a
personal letter to the parents, enumerating their son's qualities and
the gallant manner of his death. Many performed the rite so often
that it became a reluctant chore, a benumbed duty. Norman Collins
often had to write 60 letters at a time, about men he barely knew.[22]
The officers tended to embellish their letters with lavish testaments
to the personal qualities, soldierly courage or popularity of the
deceased. Thus the phrases 'he died a soldier's death', 'he was loved
by all', 'he was a fine soldier', 'I cannot speak too highly of him' proliferated. These sentiments may have been true and heartfelt, but if
the dead man had been unpopular or a bad soldier or a coward, the
officers lied out of sympathy for the families. 'We always tried to
write a nice letter to the mother or father because we felt for them,'
Collins recalled.[23]

There is no doubting the sincerity of Lieutenant F. Taylor's letter to the family of Corporal John ('Jack') Ison, killed by shell-fire at the front line on 10 October 1917. 'When I lost him I lost a friend and one of my best corporals,' Ison's sergeant major, P. Kinchington, wrote to the dead soldier's father on 26 November 1917.[24] 'We went through Gallipoli, Egypt, France, Pozieres [sic], Belgium, the Somme, & again at Ypres together. I can honestly assure you that I miss Jack as much as my own brother . . . I know it is an awful thing to part with one's sons . . . You have no idea of the troop's sufferings . . . It really is a mercy from God to take us. I assure you at times I have asked God to take me from this life.'[25] The battalion's chaplain also wrote to Ison's parents, telling them of the 'splendid soldier' and 'fine man' their son had been: 'I can, I believe, give you the complete assurance that your son did not suffer any pain in his passing; he passed instantly to his rest & to the close keeping of God.'[26]

Four of Harold Leslie ('Les') Larsen's close friends wrote to console his mother after the stretcher-bearer's death, blown up while carrying out the wounded on 4 October, a week after he was awarded the Military Medal. '[W]hat a fine son,' began their deep-felt tribute to the 22-year-old baker's son from Queensland. 'He was ever ready to give assistance to those in danger or difficulty often at the risk of his own life . . . Never was a lad more popular amongst his comrades, his bright smiling face and splendid disposition inspired us all, in fact he was a general favourite in the unit.'[27] Many letters attested to the fact: before his death, Les Larsen had spent seven days in succession bearing the wounded to safety 'under heavy shell fire, through shell holes and knee deep mud'.[28]

Deeply moved, Mrs Larsen tried to express herself to one of her surviving sons:

> I want to write to you tonight and yet I don't know how . . .
> Our dear Les has gone; never shall I see him. We cannot realise
> it yet . . . this dreadfulness that has come upon us. Killed in
> action the cable said; so he got his wish. He once said, 'If I

have to go, Mother, I hope I am killed outright and not have to linger in agony.' . . . The thing I have dreaded has come to pass; but the awfulness of it, oh dear, when will the misery end?[29]

Quoting from the letters she had received from her son's fellow soldiers, Mrs Larsen wondered what 'Battlefield' his 'poor body is resting in . . .' In an earlier letter, Les had tried to console her in advance of his possible death: if it came, Mother, he wrote, it would be 'a happy relief' from the war. But she could not reconcile herself to his peace.[30] On 18 May 1918, she received a parcel containing Les's personal effects – identity disc, coins, letters, wallet, badge.[31]

—

Many soldiers sought to console the dead man's family by invoking the greater good of his sacrifice. After the death of her beloved brother Allan, Sister Elsie Grant, a young Australian nurse, received a letter from his sergeant:

> It is with regret I take up my pen to write these few lines
> telling you that your brother A.H. Grant was killed in action
> on 12.10.17; but Sister is it not a great consolation to know
> that he died a grand and noble death fighting for his God,
> King, Country and dear ones . . . he was so jolly; full of sport;
> & good-natured that he was soon known and loved by all
> of the boys, in fact his platoon used to just idolise him.

The sergeant included a few items in the parcel – the young man's wallet (containing £5), a letter and a mirror – that Grant had asked him, on the night before he died, to send to his sister should he not survive 'the Stunt' that killed him.[32] Elsie had last seen her brother in August, when he visited her after the shelling of the Australian casualty clearing station in the village where she worked. 'God must've sent him as a comfort,' she had told a friend at the time.[33]

Often the aggrieved widow, mother or father, sought further

information on their husband or son, usually by writing to the padre. Many also wrote if they had not heard from their loved one, to inquire whether their sons were alive. Their letters make some of the saddest reading of the war:

Dear Sir,
I have received . . . the sad news of the death of my dear son. It came as a great blow to us all. He was a good and devoted boy. . . . We are glad to know that his death was instantaneous . . .

Dear Sir
I am writing to thank you for letting me know about my dear husband's death. It came as a great blow to me but I am more than pleased to think you witnessed his death and berrial [sic] as I can rest quite comfortable that heisput [sic] comfortable away.

To the Padre . . .
. . . He was our only surviving son and it is, therefore a bitter grief. We would be so grateful for any little news of him . . .

Sir,
Would you kindly tell me what you know about my poor Boy . . . is he alive or dead, it is 8 weeks now since I heard a word . . .

Dear Sir,
I hope you wont [sic] mind me writing to you again . . . your kind letter of sympathy is of a great help to us poor mothers. I can't realise yet that I shall not see my dear boy again on earth but I do miss his bright cheery letters, they were such a help to me. It does seem so hard that we should lose them like that when you have brought them up so many years with no husband to help you but I musnt [sic] repine. God knows best and I pray that my dear boy and I shall meet again in a better land. Should you know of any boy who is lonely and gets no

letters from home if I could write him sometimes I should still
feel that I had someone out there I could help in that way . . .[34]

These are samples of thousands of letters sent to Reverend Victor
Tanner and the other padres. Tanner plainly did not relish the task
of replying to so much correspondence. The families' 'pathetic letters', he wrote, with exasperation, revealed their 'complete ignorance
of the conditions of modern warfare', questions such as: Was my husband's death instantaneous? Did my boy suffer? What were his last
words? Could you send me the ring he was wearing?[35] Tanner had a
standard card printed to respond to the deluge, to which he would
sometimes append a personal note.

—

One of the hardest post-mortem rites the family had yet to bear
was the arrival of their son's parcel or trunk containing his personal
effects – usually just his clothes, razor, pay book, a little money and
watch. Often, they amounted to a few cards and photos and his last
will and testament. Corporal John Ison's effects included a cigarette
case and a watch in the back of which he kept a lock of hair.[36]

Months passed before Australian, Canadian and New Zealand
families received the parcel, of which the army would pre-warn
them: 'transmission to your address, one package containing the
effects of the late [soldier's name and unit] received ex Transport
[ship's name], as per inventory attached . . .' The families were asked
to 'kindly let us know whether [the parcel] come [sic] safely to hand
by signing and returning the attached printed receipt'.[37]

Fearing a white feather in the post, Horace ('Horrie') Rex had
enlisted a month short of his twentieth birthday. He had a robust
military pedigree to live up to: his great-grandfather, John Mernagh,
fought the British in the 1798 Irish Rebellion and migrated to
New South Wales rather than face trial for murder if captured.
His uncle, Brigadier General Dr Patrick Farrell, had served with
the American Army in Mexico and in the Boxer War in China,

and had commanded the first company of US troops to land in the Philippines on 30 June 1898. During the Great War, General Farrell held a senior command in the US medical corps.[38]

In May 1917, Rex arrived in Flanders with an Australian machine-gun company. The average life expectancy of an officer of machine gunners was about three weeks. Horrie lasted a bit longer: fragments of a 'whizz bang' struck him on 7 October, at the entrance of his dugout. He was buried a few yards from where he was hit, but his temporary grave, marked by a little cross, did not survive the war. His remains were never found and he is now listed as missing on the Menin Gate.

From Flanders fields to London, by ship to Sydney, and then by train to Braidwood, New South Wales, a suitcase containing Horrie's personal effects finally arrived at the family home a few months after its dispatch. The 'Valise (Sealed)' contained:

> 2 Wallets, Letters, Postcards, Socks, Handkerchiefs, Ties, Collars, 2 Books (Fragments of France), 2 Towels, 1 Pr. Gloves, 1 Muffler, 2 Suits Pyjamas, 2 Singlets, 1 Shirt, 1 Pr. Underpants, 1 'Sam Browne' Belt, 1 Pr. Boots, 1 Pr. Leggings, 1 Safety Razor, 2 Shaving Brushes, 1 Brush, 1 Knife, Keys and Chain, 1 Whistle & Lanyard, 2 Razor Strops, 1 Pr. Spurs, 1 Belt, 1 Cap, 1 Fleece Lining, 2 S.D. Tunic, 1 Pr. Slacks, Rosary Beads, 1 Kit Bag.[39]

Further items arrived in a leather trunk, including his breeches, field glasses, golf balls, letters, postcards, a walking stick and prayer book. The family were informed that the Braidwood branch of the Bank of New South Wales held the original of their son's will.

Thousands of families received this one-paged document on which their son had typically bequeathed to 'my mother and father my personal estate', perfunctorily signed in the cheerful belief that the beneficiaries would never have to read it. On receiving it, the parents' desolation was complete: many broke, turned to drink, never recovered. Parents who outlived their sons did not 'move on' and 'get closure', in the callous usage of our times. Back then, people grieved.

———

Soldiers were listed as 'missing' if they failed to report at the Last Post of the day. Most were later recovered, wounded or dead. But a great number disappeared without a trace. During Poelcappelle, for example, an Australian raid on a line of pillboxes in Celtic Wood vanished into thin air: of the 85 men who went into the copse, fourteen walked out unwounded. The rest, it seemed, had ceased to exist: the War Graves Commission could find no trace of these men after the armistice.[40] Most of the missing had been obliterated in direct shell hits, making identification of the scattered body parts impossible. Families were duly updated, thus: 'the soldier who was previously reported missing is now reported Killed in Action'.[41]

The lists of the missing presumed dead soon entered the tens of thousands. The missing included those whose temporary graves were subsequently destroyed by artillery fire, tanks or battle. By 1918, 559,000 casualties were registered as having no known grave.[42]

Yet the soldier had existed: here was his kitbag, his military record, his razor and toothbrush. The missing presented governments and military authorities with the awkward question of how to inform the families of their son's disappearance; and how to commemorate a man whose body had vanished off the face of the earth.

It was eventually decided to carve their names in stone, in several monuments to the missing, the most famous of which are the great arch at Thiepval, on the Somme, and the Menin Gate, at the eastern entrance to Ypres, designed by Sir Reginald Blomfield and inaugurated on 24 July 1927. Addressing the ceremony, Belgium's King Albert said that Ypres had the same meaning for the British that Verdun had for the French.

Not everyone warmed to the imperialist overtones of the Menin Gate's triumphal design, and his dismay at the monument drove Siegfried Sassoon to compose his incendiary poem, 'On Passing the New Menin Gate' – 'this sepulchre of crime'.[43] And yet, great monuments tend to gather affection around them, perhaps in recognition of their awkwardness, or sober grandeur, and Menin Gate has powerfully served the purpose for which it was consecrated: to honour the missing. Inscribed in its panels of white Portland stone are the names of 54,896 soldiers of the British Empire with 'no known grave'.[44] The Last Post is performed here at 8 pm every evening (9 pm in summer), drawing crowds in their hundreds, sometimes thousands.

It would often take months, even years, before the missing were confirmed killed in action. The process was long and heart-rending for families, many of whom would never know what had actually become of their sons, husbands or brothers. One mother's search for her son's grave was a minor epic of unfolding despair. In late October 1917, Mrs Anne Alsop, of Winchelsea, Victoria, received a telegram informing her and her husband that their son Fred had been killed in action on 17 October 1917. His personal effects followed. His body had been interred in a temporary grave with two other Australians, a cross marking the spot, according to a letter from Fred's commanding officer:

> It is my painful duty to inform you of the death of your
> dear son, Frederick . . . your son, with two other boys,
> were killed instantaneously by a shell falling on the dugout
> which they occupied. I must express my deepest sympathy,
> as a more pleasant boy I could not have had in my section.
> He was liked by all who came in touch with him. I buried
> him just beside the cemetery, and a short burial service,
> which was read over him, was conducted by myself. I have
> made arrangements to have a cross put on his grave . . .[45]

After the war, Mrs Alsop presumed her son's remains had been transferred to a permanent grave with a headstone. Unable to afford to travel the great distance to see it, she wrote repeatedly to the

Australian Army barracks in Melbourne, Victoria, to ask for a photograph of her son's permanent resting place. On 2 October 1921, she requested:

> Please send me a photo of my son's grave as I wrote
> once before for it but got no answers. I do hope
> and trust you will do me this great favour.
> Sincerely,
> His Heart-broken
> Mother[46]

A week later, she received a reply from an unnamed major, the 'Officer in Charge, Base Records, Victoria Barracks, Melbourne':

> Dear Madam . . .
> I regret to state that no photographs of the grave of your
> son, the late No. 411 Private F.B. Alsop, 24th Machine Gun
> Company, have yet been received here, but arrangements
> have been made for three photographs of the graves of
> our fallen soldiers to be sent, free of charge, as soon as
> they can be made available. Owing to the magnitude
> of the task considerable delay is inevitable . . .[47]

Neither the promised photos nor an explanation was forthcoming. So Mrs Alsop wrote again. On 1 May 1923, she received this letter from another unnamed officer at 'Base Records':

> Dear Madam,
> With reference to your communication, I very much regret
> to inform you that no report of the burial of your son . . .
> has been received, and . . . it must be reluctantly concluded
> that the Graves Services have not succeeded in locating his
> resting place . . . Failing the recovery and identification
> of the actual remains, it is the intention of the authorities

to perpetuate the memory of these fallen by means of
collective memorials on which the soldier's full regimental
description and date of death will be inscribed . . .[48]

In other words, shellfire had destroyed her son's grave and his corpse.
She and her husband, like other parents of the missing, received a
British Commonwealth Memorial Plaque.

Among the thousands of missing was Lance Sergeant Donald
Gordon Douglas, a professional soldier born in Northern Ireland
in 1886. Douglas had served in the Boer War, in South-West Africa
in 1914, and in Egypt in 1915 and 1916, and had survived one of
the worst battles of the Somme, at Delville Wood. He was killed
in Flanders on 20 September 1917, and buried in the field. 'He was
struck in the stomach and died almost immediately,' wrote Douglas's
commanding officer to his parents: 'your son was a brave and great-
hearted man. I feel his loss very much indeed . . . Sixteen men and
myself were all that came out of that action, and all of these wish me
to express their sincere sympathy with you in your bereavement.'[49]
Douglas's battlefield grave was destroyed, and his name is commem-
orated on the Menin Gate.

Some families refused to accept that their missing sons were
dead. Often, they asked the Red Cross to investigate. This rarely
brought good news, such as in the case of Private Matthew H.
Austin, from a small mining town in New South Wales. 'We deeply
regret to inform you,' the Red Cross informed his parents, 'that we
have received an unofficial report which we fear leaves little hope
that he is alive . . . [A witness] stated that he saw your son lying dead
on Oct 12th, 1917 at the Regimental Aid Post . . . apparently killed
by a machine gun bullet in the head. Another man remarked . . .
"There is poor old Pies" (your son's nickname).'[50]

Many parents persisted in hoping their boys were alive against all
the evidence. 'I beg to ask leave for my son 2/Lieut R.H. Taylor who
left Canada two years ago,' a mother wrote to her boy's commanding
officer. 'He is my only son and I certainly if it is possible want him

back on leave as I am not well and I must see him.' Two days before she wrote this letter, her son, the only boy in a family of seven girls, had been killed in Flanders.

Born in the British colony of Newfoundland in 1892, Richard Taylor had been studying engineering at McGill University when he enlisted in the Princess Patricia's Canadian Light Infantry. He died of a shell burst on 20 September 1917. His mother refused to believe he had been killed because an earlier notice in the paper had reported him Wounded and Missing. She permitted one of her daughters to volunteer as a nurse on the Western Front, in the hope of finding him. A stretcher-bearer who saw the newspaper report revealed the truth: 'I found his body . . . and took his property, including his watch and wallet . . . No time for burial.'[51]

—

Many families lost all or several of their sons. South Australians Fred and Maggie Smith lost six of their seven sons to the war[52]; Lincolnshire mother Amy Beechey lost five of her eight sons, the biggest single loss to a British family.[53] The Gallaher family, from the Bay of Plenty, in New Zealand, had five sons: David and William served in New Zealand units; Charles, Henry and Douglas in Australian ones. All except Charles were killed. In 1905, David had captained the New Zealand All Blacks on their world tour, in which they predictably won every match except one. He married in 1906, and the couple had a daughter in 1908. A foreman in the Auckland Farmers' Freezing Company, he decided to enlist when he heard that his younger brother Douglas had been killed in France in 1916. David died on 4 October 1917 at the Battle of Broodseinde. His grave at Nine Elms British Cemetery in Flanders lists his age as 41; he was actually about 44 (he always claimed to be three years younger).[54]

The case of George, Theo and Keith Seabrook was unusual because all three men were killed in the same action, at Polygon Wood, on 20–21 September 1917. 'I knew two brothers called

Seabrook,' a witness later told the Red Cross. 'One of them was killed instantly beside me on 20th Sept in front of Ypres.' He could not say whether it was George's or Theo's death he'd witnessed, but felt sure the casualty was 'the taller of the two', adding, 'All brothers were I believe single . . . one was a good cricketer.'[55] Another witness said, 'Death was instantaneous. They were given Field Burial.'[56] It seems a Canadian unit coming up the line had buried George and Theo, 'as we had no chance of putting our own men under', said a fellow soldier.[57] A friend in the same unit said, 'I saw [George's] body put into a shell hole nearby. He was a friend of mine. Knew him well. Came from Sydney. I don't know if he got any other burial.'[58] The third brother, Keith, had been mortally wounded and lay in a casualty clearing station. Their parents were yet to receive the telegrams. Such was the confusion surrounding one set of brothers' deaths in Third Ypres.

Their mother, Fanny Seabrook, discovered the full story of what happened in increments, over several years. Rumours persisted they had been killed by the same shell, or at Gallipoli, or elsewhere; or that George was still alive and mentally ill. The family would not learn the full story until 1923; they never recovered from the trauma.

In the days following the battle that killed them, confusion reigned: yes, Keith had been confirmed dead, but George was initially reported 'Wounded', then 'Killed in Action'; and Theo was reported 'Wounded', then 'Wounded and Missing', and finally 'Killed in Action'. The family received a series of cables to this effect. Neither George's nor Theo's remains could be found. The family's mystification deepened when, on 7 November 1917, Private Tom Bowman, a close friend of the three boys – 'we were as four brothers and I cannot forget them', he later wrote[59] – sent the Red Cross his diary extracts relating to Keith's death:

> Sept 19. Troops left at midnight for the firing line. Keith
> (Lieut Seabrook) very pale and anxious, took my final
> handshake to be very spontaneous and affectionate.

20th Hop over this morning . . . Keith wounded.

21st Capt Barnett, our Adjutant tells me Keith is dead.

24th We arrive at Rest Camp near Poperinghe and boys tell me 'Keith was seriously wounded by a phosphorous shell (which also knocked out 8 of his men) . . .' Capt Allan our OC sent for me and told me Keith was dead and was buried on the 21st in the Military Cemetery at Poperinghe . . .

Of the two other brothers, Bowman heard that Theo had been killed and buried in a shell hole. But he had received no 'authentic news' of George: 'His Sergt Major and Quartermaster Sgt tell me they have heard many times unofficially that he is dead but others tell me he is not dead and until I get Official news I do not feel inclined to write their parents. Happy thought.'[60]

When the family saw Bowman's diary, Fanny Seabrook clung to the hope that there had been a mistake. George's tag had not been found, perpetuating the mother's hopes that her eldest son had survived, despite the fact that she had received an inventory of his personal effects on 12 November.[61]

'[I]t is all very confusing to our minds,' she wrote to Army Base Records in Melbourne on 27 November 1917, '& if you could explain it to me we would be much obliged and grateful. The blow of losing our three sons in one battle is terrible and we are heartbroken.'[62]

The army replied a week later. George and Theo Seabrook had been officially 'reported killed in action, 20/9/17', the officer wrote. 'I regret to state there is no room to suppose that a mistake has been made . . .'[63]

Still holding a candle for George, Mrs Seabrook asked the Red Cross to initiate an inquiry, with the help of Tom Bowman. In February 1918, they confirmed that Keith had died of multiple shell wounds and a fractured skull; and the two other brothers had been killed in action. George and Theo's bodies still had not been found. A witness told the Red Cross that he had seen George's body in a shell hole.

That did not satisfy the indomitable Fanny. In March 1918 she wrote to the army to request photographs of her sons' graves, on the understanding that these would be freely supplied. They were no longer free. A Belgian agency now handled the photos of war graves, as one scrupulously efficient captain informed her:

> it is not the intention of the Government to furnish next-of-
> kin with photographs of the completed graves of our soldiers,
> but copies of the permanent headstones may be obtained
> on application to [a Mr Kemp with a Belgian address], who
> will supply three (3) postal card sized prints . . . for the sum
> of seven shillings and sixpence (7/6), plus postage 3d.

In any case, she would receive no photos of George's and Theo's graves because the Commonwealth War Graves Commission had not succeeded in finding their remains. Now officially 'missing', their names would be inscribed on the Menin Gate.[64]

The messy aftermath continued to plague the family. In March 1918, Keith's personal effects arrived in Sydney (the parcel included two gold boomerangs, a whistle, a compass and a cigarette case).[65] Theo's were still at large, in pursuit of which, on 3 July, Fanny flourished her pen again: had her son's belongings been sent, she wondered, and could the army confirm a report she'd received from a soldier in George's unit who had seen his body 'half-buried' in a shell hole?[66] The army replied that Theo's kit had not yet arrived but that 'several heavy consignments' were en route, 'and there may be something included for you'.[67] George's identity disc had not yet been recovered, it added.

After the armistice, the Exhumation Units entered the battlefield. Fanny Seabrook hoped for news of her missing sons' bodies. They found nothing. They could only say that George's remains most likely lay north of Polygon Wood, where the battle occurred, and not – as the official records stated – 'in the vicinity of Westhoek and Anzac Ridge'.[68]

A letter from the Seabrooks' commanding officer on 10 December 1919 should have defused the mother's growing obsession with the fate of George: 'Your son George and his other brother [Theo] were killed during the attack . . . I can only think that George and his brother were so upset at Keith's death that they exposed themselves unduly in seeking their vengeance on the enemy . . .'[69]

If they were dead, where were their bodies, she continued to ask herself. The question tormented her. Like many parents, she had no conception of modern warfare or the effect of a direct hit by a howitzer shell on the human body. On 6 July 1921, she fired off another letter to the army: 'I am much concerned at no word having reached us to the whereabouts of the Bodies [*sic*] of our two eldest sons . . .'[70] Wearying of this unshakable woman, the army promptly replied that 'an intensive search is now being made over all old battlefields with a view to locating unregistered graves'.[71]

They found nothing. Fanny never stopped believing that her eldest son was alive. On 21 April 1923, almost six years after their deaths, the Australian Army confirmed that the remains of George and Theo were still missing and speculated as to the reason, in a letter of brutal honesty, to the three brothers' father: 'It is quite possible all traces of their graves were obliterated by shell fire . . .'[72]

Fanny Seabrook even refused to accept this; by now, the poor woman was delusional. On 14 March 1925, she wrote to the Defence Department to ask why no photograph of Keith's grave had arrived from Belgium and whether the Department had received any news of the bodies of her other sons: 'After all these years surely something should be known. This is very heart-breaking for us.'[73] She died on 28 August 1929, of stomach cancer, still clinging to the belief that her eldest son lived.

—

The Germans were similarly clearing the battlefield of their dead, of whom an enormous number had accumulated on the ridges of the Salient throughout the summer and autumn months. Of their

220,000 casualties sustained between 21 May and 10 December 1917, the heaviest concentration was in the first ten days of October, with 9034 men killed and missing and 14,217 wounded. The Germans were running out of manpower, unlike the Allies, who would soon be able to draw on the great pool of American manpower and the rehabilitated French Army. The British attacks were draining Germany's male lifeblood, as Haig intended. At this rate, the Allies would ultimately 'win', though at a cost in lives that Lloyd George and posterity would refuse to accept.

The German padres similarly went forth with their Lutheran bibles to console the wounded and deliver last rites to the dying. Feldgeistlicher K. Foertsch, padre with the 234 Infantry Brigade, witnessed the terrible scenes at Passchendaele on 26–27 October. 'All I could do was offer words of comfort,' he recalled.

He saw a Bavarian, 'deathly pale, with his arms folded across his chest. I whispered a short prayer of comfort to him . . . and over there was anther man from near Würzburg. Wracked with pain, he called repeatedly [for] Our Lady, "Mary, Help!" I sat a long time with him until he became quiet and resigned to his fate. Then there was another man, cold as ice. I laid my hands on his forehead and cheeks . . . Yet another cried out for thirst. I went and fetched him some water . . .'

The wounded found their voices. One young man pleaded, 'Don't leave me Padre.' So Foertsch dropped to the ground and took his hand. 'There was a short roar and another thunderclap . . . Quite involuntarily I ducked down toward the wounded man who lunged up and threw his arms around me. Finally he lay still, but he would not let go of my arm. As I crouched next to him he talked to me about his home, his parents, his relations with his God . . . We managed a really intimate discussion despite the fact that all hell had broken loose around us.'[74]

—

Scores of little monuments to the fallen rise out of the windswept fields of Flanders. The rows of white headstones flash white against the green land, like ancient tablets bearing a message for our times: 169 cemeteries were built here, in an area of 140 square kilometres, a density of at least one cemetery per square kilometre or three per square mile.[75]

Here is the New Zealand Division's memorial at Gravenstafel Junction, commemorating their breakthrough at Broodseinde. Here, the monument to the Scots, with the inscription, 'It is in truth not for glory nor riches, nor honours that we are fighting, but for freedom . . .' Every few hundred metres, another cemetery appears.

And here, on the plain beneath Passchendaele, lies the largest Commonwealth graveyard, the Tyne Cot Cemetery, named after the workers' cottages along the river Tyne, with which the British nicknamed the German pillboxes. The cemetery is the final resting place of 11,956 British and Dominion servicemen, more than 8300 of whom remain unidentified and whose stones bear the inscription, 'A Soldier of the Great War – Known Unto God'. Four German soldiers are also buried here. On the eastern boundary stands the Tyne Cot Memorial to the missing, listing the names of 34,857 men (33,690 British, 1166 New Zealanders and one Canadian). Their bodies could not be found or identified. Several famous and exotic regiments adorn the walls: the Black Watch, the Northumberland Fusiliers, the Auckland and Otago Infantry Regiments. Most of the men listed were killed during Third Ypres, but many also died in the 1918 Spring Offensive.[76]

Other nations lost many more over the course of the war than the Anglo-Saxon nations. The vast French ossuary at Verdun, for example, holds the remains of 130,000 soldiers; while the German mass grave at Langemarck contains about 44,000, including 3000 boys of school age killed in the '*Kindermort*' of 1914.

Such quantitative judgements end at the point where individual grief begins. Walking among the graves, past the lists of names, one feels helpless to explain losses on this scale. Here are the names of a father and son, inscribed in the panel to the King's Own Yorkshire Light Infantry; here a little cluster of head stones, set apart, signifying men killed by the same shell, their remains mixed up. Occasionally a Star of David or the absence of any religious symbol reminds the visitor that the dead were sometimes Jewish or atheist or held another belief.

The families were invited to choose the inscriptions. They often drew from the Bible, or hymns. The most popular Anglo-Saxon epitaph was taken from John 15:13: 'Greater Love Hath No Man than This, that he may lay down his life for his friends' – that their son had sacrificed himself, Christ-like, so that others may live in freedom. Or they accepted their loss as an act of God: 'The Lord gave and the Lord hath taken away' (Job 1:21). Or it was all a great mystery: 'God holds the key of all unknown'. Or they chose lines from poetry. To remember Captain Clarence Smith Jeffries VC, his family applied the mysterious line from Theodore O'Hara's poem 'Bivouac of the Dead': 'On fame's eternal camping ground their silent tents are spread'. Paper poppies pinned to little wooden crosses throng the base of Jeffries' headstone, as they tend to do at the graves of other recipients of the Victoria Cross.

Perhaps the most moving, however, are the parents' or wives' own personal messages:

'One of the best of sons'

'Though wounded in the morning he fought till evening when he fell'

'You have left behind some broken hearts that never can forget you'

'My husband and pal so dearly loved'

Further on is the epitaph, which one sincerely wants to believe, to a young Australian private called H. R. Sloggett, killed in action on 21 October 1917, aged twenty: 'Here lies the noblest work of God.'[77]

# 16

# FROM THE JAWS OF DEFEAT

*We are not going to lose this war, but its prolongation will spell
ruin for the civilized world and an infinite addition to the load
of human suffering which already weighs upon us . . . What will
be the value of the blessings of peace to a nation so exhausted that
they can scarcely stretch out a hand with which to grasp them?*
Lord Lansdowne, in a letter to *The Daily Telegraph*, 29 November 1917

---

*With our backs to the wall and believing in the justice of our
cause each one of us must fight on to the end. The safety of
our homes and the Freedom of mankind alike depend upon
the conduct of each one of us at this critical moment.*
Field Marshal Sir Douglas Haig, 11 April 1918

---

Stopping in Paris on 11–12 November 1917 on his way back from
Italy, Lloyd George expressed his displeasure with the course of the
war. 'We have won great victories,' he famously said. 'When I look at
the appalling casualty lists I sometimes wish it had not been necessary to win so many.'[1] The prime minister was in vintage, coruscat-
ing form: 'When we advance a kilometre into enemy lines, snatch

a small village out of his cruel grip, capture a few hundred of his soldiers we shout with unfeigned joy.'[2] How, he wondered, would the press celebrate a genuine military triumph?

Conservatives were appalled. In their eyes, Lloyd George had not only attacked Britain's field commanders, he had also gravely damaged the country's morale. The press brayed at this meddling 'amateur strategist'. *The Spectator* demanded Lloyd George's dismissal: 'a man capable of such levity, such irresponsibility, such recklessness, such injustice, is beyond endurance'.[3] An outraged House of Commons forced the prime minister into a humiliating retreat: days later, he told Parliament that he had complete faith in his top soldiers and denied that he had intended to damage the general staff. Soon, however, the prime minister would commit another volte-face: the terrible news issuing from Flanders had him raging once more for Haig's head.

If he could not sack Haig, Lloyd George would diminish him. The disaster of Third Ypres made another command reform inevitable. In October, he had set in motion a scheme to create another French-led command structure. That had been the main purpose of his trip to Rapallo in November: to forge a Supreme War Council, which he had warned Haig he intended to do in Paris in early October. The Council, approved by the War Cabinet on 2 November, would coordinate British, French, American, Dominion, Italian and Belgian forces in Europe. Leaders of the Allied governments would have a seat on the Council and joint command of the direction of war; a French commander would lead all Allied units on the Western Front. As Maurice Hankey wrote of the prime minister's motives, 'he would not go on unless he obtained control of the war'.[4]

The Council first met in Versailles at the end of 1917; not until March 1918 would it appoint the formidable Ferdinand Foch as supreme commander. Foch would be responsible for assembling the greatest army the world had seen, in a united will against Germany. His appointment was a body blow to Haig and Robertson, who once again found themselves sidelined. They railed against the new command structure as unnecessary and likely to fail; and kept the press fully abreast of their opinions. Wully Robertson's 'resignation' soon followed. Lloyd George offered him General Sir Henry Wilson's job on the Supreme Council in Versailles, a technical demotion, and all the more wounding in light of Wilson's eager acceptance of the CIGS job in return. Robertson's was the most powerful 'scalp' in Lloyd George's assault on his commanders – and it was to Haig's personal discredit that he failed to defend the man who had supported him so faithfully and for so long.

The new command structure, a great improvement upon the dismal Nivelle arrangements a year earlier, married a respect for the independence of national armies with a broad vision of how they should be cooperatively deployed. Its formation occupied a long and tedious debate in Parliament, on 19 February 1918, punctuated by the plaintive voice of James O'Grady, the little known Labour member for Leeds East, whose message hauled everyone back to reality: 'Men are dying at the front while all this is going on.'[5]

—

While Lloyd George was abroad, Haig made his own inquiries about casualties. On 15 November, he visited Lieutenant General Sir Sidney Clive, head of the British Mission at French Army headquarters, at Bavencourt, to examine the numbers. 'D.H. interested in the graphics of losses of resource,' Clive noted in his diary on 15 November 1917. 'Looking at our figures he said very quietly: "Have we lost 500,000 men!"'[6]

Haig had not lost that many, but he had lost enough to horrify the War Cabinet. And he wanted hundreds of thousands more to fill their places and to continue his offensives into 1918. The Flanders campaign would resume in the spring, he told Robertson on 10 November, at the end of Third Ypres: 'I pointed out the importance of the Belgian coast to Great Britain, and urged that nothing should be done to stop our offensive next Spring.'[7]

Into this distempered atmosphere, Haig sent his report for 1917.

It brought Lloyd George's simmering rage to boiling point. Haig had known since early August that the Flanders Offensive would fall well short of his goals, ending at best with the capture of Passchendaele. Here was the grim result: the ridge could not be held, and Haig had gained a few miserable miles at a staggering cost.

Hope in the outcome of Cambrai overshadowed the perception of failure in the Ypres Salient. For several months, Haig had been reluctantly planning this new offensive near the French village, using General Julian Byng's Third Army and the largest massed tank attack yet deployed. The question of how the new tanks would perform transfixed generals, politicians and war reporters.

Cambrai began well, on 20 November: 378 Mark IV combat tanks and two corps of infantry (against Germany's one), supported by 1000 guns (against Germany's 54) and fourteen squadrons of the Royal Flying Corps, broke though the German wires and rolled over their front lines, gaining 7000 yards.[8] The Germans had no answer to this shocking spectacle at first, no tanks of their own and limited anti-tank weapons. English church bells tolled a brilliant victory, prematurely: within days, a fierce German counter-attack drove the British off most of their gains, destroying scores of tanks and forcing the battle into another attritional stalemate. By the end, each side had lost about 45,000 men. British euphoria faded with another stalemate. It was an excruciating outcome so soon after Passchendaele, and demonstrated once again that the Germans were far from a spent force.

The Cabinet were in shock and Lloyd George apoplectic. After some 760,000 casualties in twelve months, Haig's huge drafts on manpower had plumbed the depths of the nation's reserves. The Cabinet had deep reservations about approving hundreds of thousands more, if Haig meant to stake their lives on biting off the next shell-shattered ridge. 'To political leaders,' Bean writes, 'fired to accept his plans, but shocked by the result, the obvious moral was: "Keep back the men!"'[9]

Enough, Lloyd George said: that month, the War Cabinet

devised a plan that aimed to halve the British casualty rate in the coming year. In January 1918, the government approved just 100,000 'A' class recruits, a sixth of what the War Office had demanded.[10] Volunteers would never make up the shortfall: the horrors of 1917 had impaired morale at home, and the enlistment rate had plunged. December set a new low in British recruitment, at 24,923 men. Haig thus entered 1918 facing a serious shortage of men, well below what he deemed necessary to meet the replacement rate. All this was the direct harvest of Third Ypres.

———

Military exigencies crowded Haig's mind: if the government demanded victory, only more men could deliver it. He failed to see that the government's determination to thwart his demands reflected the mood of a people experiencing a crisis of faith in the war.

On 29 November, Lord Lansdowne, spurred to action by the events in Flanders, reissued his plea for an armistice. This time, it appeared in a newspaper, *The Daily Telegraph* – after *The Times* refused to publish it – outraging the government and Conservatives, and garnering much public support. 'We are not going to lose this war,' Lansdowne wrote, 'but its prolongation will spell ruin for the civilized world and an infinite addition to the load of human suffering which already weighs upon us . . . What will be the value of the blessings of peace to a nation so exhausted that they can scarcely stretch out a hand with which to grasp them?'[11]

Auckland Geddes, the director of national service, made his feelings known in less apocalyptic, melancholy terms, in his review of the manpower situation after Passchendaele and Cambrai (tabled in June 1918). 'The heavy casualties which accrued . . .' he wrote, 'the effect of what was in common belief the unfruitful pouring out of life, upon the moral of the people and upon the willingness of the men to serve dogged for many years the war effort of the nation.'[12]

As for Cambrai, the Cabinet came close to accusing Haig of misleading the government over its prospects. According to one baleful minute, on 4 December, the enemy 'had gained a success which was inconsistent with the advice in regard to the strength and condition of the German army', which Haig had given the War Cabinet.[13] An inquiry would be held into why such overwhelming British superiority in guns, aircraft and men had been so swiftly repulsed.

Haig's star fell in December 1917. Lloyd George was determined to crush his authority and deny him men; senior military staff were privately calling for his removal; and even his press champions, the media barons Lords Northcliffe and Rothermere, sensing the popular mood, abandoned him. 'There is the memory of a dead man, or the knowledge of a missing or wounded man, in every house,' Northcliffe replied to a letter seeking support for Haig. 'I doubt whether the Higher Command has any supporters whatever.'[14] His papers *The Times* and *The Daily Mail* mauled the general staff as serial blunderers who had squandered British lives.

Haig held on to his job thanks to his conservative backers in government, a lack of suitable replacements and, most importantly, the prime minister willing that he should stay (exactly why is a murky matter, which we shall get to). And yet, whatever his enemies said about him, they all tended to agree that only Haig had the inner steel needed to lead, and endure the loss of, the numbers of men required to win the war.

———

The new French-led command structure was enacted just in time to confront Germany's revival. At the end of 1917, far from being demoralised, the German commanders were in high spirits. In their eyes, it had been a year of victories, albeit with terrible casualties: they had crushed Nivelle's offensive, signed a peace treaty with Russia, and held the line at Flanders. Mars had aligned in Berlin's favour: the bulk of the American Army would not start arriving until mid-1918; the French forces were still reckoned unfit; and the British and Dominion armies were battered and disheartened.

This confluence of events opened a window on victory,

encouraging Ludendorff to stake all on a massive counter-blow that might win the war. At a meeting on 11 November, the day after the end of Third Ypres, Ludendorff, Hindenburg and their generals began planning the first major German offensive since 1915. The Spring Offensive – Operation Michael – was scheduled to start in March 1918, by which time Germany would have amassed 192 divisions on the Western Front, opposing 156 Allied divisions. For the first time since October 1914, Haig was forced to fight a defensive battle, with fewer men and guns than Germany – a complete reversal of the situation at the start of 1917.

On 21 March 1918, this mighty German arsenal rolled across France and Belgium in a spectacular reprisal of August 1914. Passchendaele fell within three days; Messines and Hill 60 were quickly overrun. All the gains of the past two years, on the Somme, at Arras and the Aisne, yielded to Ludendorff's juggernaut.

Denied the manpower needed to resist this typhoon, the British and Dominion forces fell back, sustaining casualties that 'dwarfed the "butcher's bill" of Passchendaele'.[15] Not quite: some 254,740 British and French soldiers were killed or wounded or missing in the Spring Offensive, almost 20,000 fewer than the Allied casualties of Third Ypres.[16] Gough's Fifth Army nearly cracked: in the greatest mass capitulation in British history, 21,000 of his 90,882 casualties were taken prisoner. Gough was sacked, in the richest irony of his career: of all the sackable offences that fastened to his name, March 1918 should not have been one of them. The Fifth Army's surviving formations bravely held. Had they broken, 'the Germans would probably have won the First World War'.[17]

By April, the Allies had retreated as far as Amiens. Remarkably, the British held Ypres – at the Battle of *Fourth* Ypres. Yet Paris trembled under the threat of German occupation for the second time in four years. The British, Dominion and French armies, now fighting under Foch's supreme command, were staring at the prospect of defeat. On 11 April, in an emotional departure from his granite calm, Haig issued his famous 'backs to the wall' order, reminiscent of Joffre's plea to the French Army on the Marne in 1914:

SPECIAL ORDER OF THE DAY
By FIELD-MARSHAL SIR DOUGLAS HAIG
K.T., G.C.B., G.C.V.O., K.C.I.E.
Commander-in-Chief, British Armies in France
To ALL RANKS OF THE BRITISH ARMY
IN FRANCE AND FLANDERS
Three weeks ago to-day the enemy began his terrific attacks
against us on a fifty-mile front. His objects are to separate
us from the French, to take the Channel Ports and destroy
the British Army . . .
    There is no other course open to us but to fight it out.
Every position must be held to the last man: there must be no
retirement. With our backs to the wall and believing in the
justice of our cause each one of us must fight on to the end. The
safety of our homes and the Freedom of mankind alike depend
upon the conduct of each one of us at this critical moment.[18]

The British and Dominion armies held on. Then they rallied, and
struck back. The German offensive died hard, over a tortuous retreat
lasting months. Failed tactics, rushed training, demoralisation,
lack of food and ammunition, and overstretched supply lines were
blamed for their eventual collapse – aggravated by the astonishing
return to form of the British, Anzac and French forces and the arrival
of the first units of the 500,000-strong American Army. The tactical
sequence that had frustrated the Tommies, Anzacs and Canadians
for almost three years – attack, brief success, resistance, counter-
attack, and stalemate or defeat – now dragged down and destroyed
Ludendorff's great offensive.
    It culminated in the '100 Days' (8 August to 11 November 1918),
a rapid series of Allied victories that terminated the German war. By
now, the Americans were pouring into France: 39 divisions would
arrive by the end of September. The revived French had re-entered

the arena. Most importantly, a battle-hardened Commonwealth phoenix had risen out of the ashes of Flanders. The Australians were now fighting as part of a stand-alone national army, injecting fresh patriotic zeal into their ranks. The newly formed Australian Corps under General Sir John Monash were about to exceed what anyone imagined possible a year earlier, when they lay immobilised in the swamps beneath Passchendaele. A glimpse of their return to form was the capture of the village of Hamel on 4 July, an opening victory of great symbolic value. Indeed, Monash would emerge as one of the outstanding commanders of the war, largely due to his generalship during the 100 Days and his mastery of the synchronisation of the new 'weapons system' of infantry, machine guns, artillery, tanks and aircraft – a role he likened to that of the conductor of an orchestra.

On 8 August 1918, the British, Anzacs and Canadians burst out of Amiens, broke the German lines, captured 12,000 prisoners and 450 guns, inflicted 15,000 further casualties and advanced eight miles, the furthest achieved on the Western Front in a single day (the Flanders Offensive had taken three and a half months to capture the same distance). Over the next five days, the Canadian Corps defeated or put to flight ten full German divisions, capturing 9131 prisoners and 190 artillery pieces, advancing fourteen miles and liberating more than 67 square miles.

Blow by blow, the Germans were heaved out of France and Belgium. Over the next three months, with terrific losses to both sides, the Allies regained all the ground they had lost in France and in Belgium. In late September, the British retook Messines and Passchendaele, in the *Fifth* Battle of Ypres. By the beginning of October 1918, the Germans were back to where Operation Michael had begun. Later that month, British forces occupied the Belgian coast and seized the U-boat bases, fulfilling the original goal of the Flanders Offensive the previous year.

Ludendorff would never recover from the nightmare of Amiens, another 'black day' for Germany, and the ensuing 100 Days, during which some of his finest units were destroyed or utterly broken. The

German forces surrendered en masse or were annihilated. They were comprehensively defeated on the battlefield, not 'stabbed in the back' by Jews and communists as Lance Corporal Adolf Hitler would later claim.

Haig's men – the British and Dominion armies – had spear-headed the Allied victory, capturing 188,700 prisoners and 2840 guns by the 100th day, just shy of the combined total of the much larger American and French armies. By this measure, the great Allied counter-offensive of 1918 'was, by far, the greatest military victory in British history', Sheffield concludes[19] – not without a little Anzac and Canadian help.

# 17

# WHAT THE LIVING SAID

*Whilst hundreds of thousands were being destroyed in the insane
egotism of Passchendaele, every message or memorandum from Haig
was full of these insistences on the importance of sending him more
men to replace those he had sent to die in the mud. If Britain said,
'Where are my lost legions?' then anyone who asked such a question
on her behalf was betraying the Army and attacking our soldiers.*

David Lloyd George, *War Memoir*

---

*Still swept the rain, roared guns,
Still swooped into the swamps of flesh and blood,
All to the drabness of uncreation sunk,
And all thought dwindled to a moan, Relieve!*

Edmund Blunden, 'Third Ypres'

---

No other battle in British history has inspired so much righteous indignation, passionate debate and biting satire as Passchendaele. On the 100th anniversary of the campaign, it is time to attempt a fresh understanding. Was Passchendaele 'worth it'? How did it contribute to the final victory, if at all? Should it have been fought in the first place? Perhaps we should start by asking that oddly juvenile question, 'Who won?'

It seems perverse to speak of winners and losers in a struggle that ended so piteously. Commanders on both sides claimed Third Ypres as a great victory, of course. The cold verdict, however, is that the British and Empire forces 'lost' Third Ypres: they lost the body count; they lost the original strategic case for Third Ypres, in failing to capture the submarine bases on the Belgian coast; and they lost the tactical battles in August and October. Those they won were largely thanks to September's dry weather.

And yet, in every battle, the men far exceeded what any commander could expect of a soldier. They were ordered to attack again and again, in battles that Haig and his generals knew had little or no chance of success and would inflict huge casualties. They were used as thousands of little battering rams, hurled against the enemy lines without realising that their commanders had lost hope of achieving the original goals of Third Ypres. Most were unaware that they were fighting a war of pure attrition, the point of which was to drain German lifeblood, at higher cost than to their own ranks. And that is why the Allies ultimately 'won' the Great War, as we've seen: they had a deeper pool of manpower to draw upon. They could have kept going until every last German man was dead or wounded.

—

How then would Haig reconcile his serial losses between 1915 and 1917 with the extraordinary triumph of 1918? He did so with a splendid flourish of his pen, assisted by the thriller writer John Buchan. In 1919, they sat down to write his final dispatch to the government, in which Haig recast Passchendaele and every other offensive under his command as 'victories', according to a set of criteria that overrode his previous, specific objectives (e.g. to clear the Belgian coast).

A striking example of Haig recasting the goal of an offensive to suit the result followed the Somme. In the aftermath, he described the Somme as the 'Opening of the Wearing Out Battle', suggesting that his chief aim had always been to wear down the enemy. In fact, the planning of the Somme prescribed a major breakthrough and the resumption of mobile warfare; its attritional 'benefits' were a distant second. Lloyd George would not let Haig forget it, and the Somme's staggering casualties cursed their relationship. Indeed, even Haig's staunchest admirers have baulked at this *ex post facto* justification of the slaughter.[1]

Haig then extrapolated the justification for the Somme forward and backward in time, armed with the great validator of final victory. By this reading, he had always intended Passchendaele as another stage in his master plan to crush the enemy's power to wage war; the U-boats were a secondary consideration. It bore out his general war plan, to 'wear down the enemy but at the same time have an objective'.[2] This meant also winning the *Materialschlacht*, the battle of material attrition over the supply of munitions and war resources (which the British blockade was already winning, at great cost to German civilians).

Passchendaele was thus transformed into one battle within a great, four-year struggle that Haig had planned from the start. The war should thus be seen as 'a single continuous campaign', he wrote in 1919, broken into three 'stages': first, 'the creation of continuous trench lines from the Swiss frontier to the sea' (1914); second, 'close and costly combat' to wear down his opponent (1915–16) and 'to pin him to his position' (1917); third, the decisive blow, 'when signs of the enemy becoming morally and physically weakened are observed' (1918). At every stage, casualties 'will necessarily be heavy on both sides for in it the price of victory is paid'.[3]

Here, then, under the astonished gaze of Lloyd George, was Haig's strategic assessment of the Great War: a four-year process of chronic slaughter, which he had planned from the start. Every other rationale for the offensive, all the strategic and territorial imperatives that Haig had pinpointed on his great maps, were secondary aims of a war whose primary purpose was human annihilation.

While the commanders all understood what this meant, they did not spell it out to their political leaders. It would not play well in the press or with politicians, of course. Yet army commanders made no bones about the meaning of attrition among themselves. Well before Third Ypres, Haig's chief of staff Sir Launcelot Kiggell was saying, 'Boche killing is the only way to win war', not territorial gain.[4] Ludendorff said as much in April 1917: 'Basically, this war comes down simply to killing one another.'[5] Robertson had been saying the same since 1915. The generals were thus inured to 'normal wastage' at 7000 dead and wounded per week, as the price of attrition. That was planned for. During the Somme and Third Ypres, normal wastage ran at 20,000–50,000 casualties per week. That, too, was planned. A certain level of wastage was, in fact, desirable, because it implied the enemy had sustained similar losses. Allied generals would often bemoan their own low casualties as evidence of a want of offensive spirit. Haig himself had complained in his diary, on 4 September 1916, at the height of the Somme: 'The unit did not really attack, and some men did not follow their officers. The total losses of this division are under a thousand! [i.e. too low].'[6]

Haig's 1919 despatch, his last, makes no mention of the original goals with which he justified Third Ypres to the government and his generals in May and June 1917. The British, Anzac and Canadian soldiers thought they were fighting to capture a ridge or a submarine base or some other 'objective'; in fact, they were fighting chiefly to kill or wound more Germans than the Germans could kill or wound of them.

Haig thus recast Passchendaele as a victory, part of the second and third stages of his four-year offensive: it had worn down the enemy and pinned the German forces to Flanders, denying them the freedom to attack the weakened French. Had he not attacked in Flanders, Haig argued, the German Army might have broken through the weak French defences and won the war.

Haig's argument has since formed the bedrock of the case for Passchendaele as a 'decisive', war-winning offensive, as he wrote:

The rapid collapse of Germany's military powers in the latter half of 1918 was the logical outcome of the fighting of the previous two years. It would not have taken place but for the period of ceaseless attrition which used up the reserves of the German Armies . . . It is in the great battles of 1916 and 1917 that we have to seek for the secret of our victory in 1918.[7]

At the same time, however, Haig's war drained the manpower of the British and Dominion armies. Addressing this point, he remarked, 'our total losses in the war have been no larger than were to be expected. Neither do they compare unfavourably with those of any other of the belligerent nations . . .'[8]

The slaughter of millions seems to have had no greater purchase on Haig's moral sensibility than a cavalry charge across a Sudanese desert. His losses, he wrote, were examples of 'splendid gallantry'. His moral compass was of a different age: Haig was a Victorian gentlemen and a Christian fatalist. He believed himself predestined to do what had to be done, in the name of God, King and Empire. He brought the morality of John Calvin and Queen Victoria to the monstrosity of the howitzer.

—

There are deep flaws in Haig's case. The most damning is that it failed on its own terms: at Loos, the Somme, Arras and Third Ypres far more of his own forces were killed or 'worn down' than Germany's. Passchendaele ravaged the morale of the British and Dominion soldiers, whose spirit fell into the darkest slough of despond since the war began.

Nor did Haig's French counterparts support his Flanders operation, despite his claim that it saved them from a massed German attack. The French High Command had little faith in Third Ypres and did not encourage Haig to pursue it.[9] Foch famously scorned the Flanders Offensive as a 'duck's march through the inundations to Ostend and Zeebrugge' and Haig's plan as 'futile, fantastic and dangerous'.[10] Nivelle thought Flanders a low priority. And General Wilson claimed that Pétain had told him, in May 1917, 'Haig's attack towards Ostend was certain to fail, and that his effort to disengage Ostend and Zeebrugge was a hopeless, hopeless one!'[11]

Pétain habitually exaggerated French weakness to secure Anglo-Saxon help, as we've seen.[12] And Haig went along with Pétain because it served his cause in Flanders. In truth, the French forces were in much better shape than Pétain pretended. Some units were in rude good health, shown by their emphatic victory at Malmaison on 23 October 1917 – a 'brilliant success', as Robertson told the War Cabinet, against 'good' German troops, who had been well-prepared.[13] Haig later suggested that Pétain had begged him to continue fighting in Flanders, to avoid a French collapse: there is no evidence of Pétain or any French commander pleading for Haig to continue. Nor is there any evidence of Pétain visiting Haig to urge the British commander to press on with the Flanders offensive (as Haig later claimed).[14] In short, the French commanders reckoned their Army had recovered and were ready to defend France. Pétain said as much to Charteris in 1917: 'the British as well as French Armies should confine their fighting to small operations with limited objectives'.[15]

—

The Germans were confused about the outcome: had they won it or lost it? In the immediate aftermath, Crown Prince Rupprecht claimed Germany had triumphed:

> The sons of all German tribes . . . have made the English
> and French attempt to breakthrough a failure . . . In spite
> of the unheard of mass deployment of men and material
> the enemy has gained nothing. So the Battle of Flanders
> is a heavy defeat for the foe, for us it is a great victory.[16]

Distance yielded a different conclusion. The verdict of General der Infanterie Hermann von Kuhl, Rupprecht's chief of staff, played into

Haig's hand. Von Kuhl did not say that British forces had won the battle; he wrote that they had had no choice other than to fight it in 1917, given the collapse of Russia, the French exhaustion and the American delay:

> The one and only army capable of offensive action was
> the British . . . If they had broken off their offensive, the
> German army would have seized the initiative and attacked
> the Allies where they were weak . . . For these reasons the
> British had to go on attacking until the onset of winter ruled
> out a German counter-attack. Today, now that we are fully
> aware about the critical [state of] the French army . . . in the
> summer of 1917, there can be absolutely no doubt that through
> its tenacity the British Army bridged the crisis in France.
> The French army gained time to recover its strength; the
> German reserves were drawn towards Flanders. The sacrifices
> that the British made for the Entente were fully justified.[17]

Third Ypres, Kuhl added, was Germany's 'worst ordeal of the World war'; his men had suffered their 'greatest martyrdom' in Flanders fields, which had inflicted irreparable damage on German morale. 'The former sharp German sword became blunt.'[18]

Further distance produced fresh German interpretations, in histories and memoirs. Ludendorff's and Hindenburg's memoirs acknowledge that Passchendaele had depressed German morale, though no more so than British morale. Yet Third Ypres had failed to break the German spirit. 'The enemy,' wrote Ludendorff, years later, 'charged like a wild bull against the iron wall which kept him from our submarine bases . . . He dented it in many places, and it seemed as if he must knock it down. But it held, although a faint tremor ran through its foundations.'[19]

The German history of Flanders cast Third Ypres as both a German and a British victory. Haig lost the tactical war to Germany's 'flexible defence' (and the weather!) and lost the strategic war because the ridges he gained had no strategic value and were easy targets for German counter-attacks.[20] At the same time, however, the British forces had won at Passchendaele, 'by tying up the Germans with the most severe of exertions' and wearing them out. 'In the year 1918, it turned out that this victory played a decisive part in terminating the war in favour of the Allied Forces . . .'[21]

It is a rich irony that the German commanders became Haig's biggest cheerleaders. Yet their case cannot go unchallenged. For one thing, it is impossible to calculate the extent to which Passchendaele helped or hindered the Allied victory. To call Passchendaele 'decisive' retrospectively endows a strategically useless slaughter (as the Germans described it) with the status of a turning point in the war. This ignores a multitude of more forceful long-run 'causes' of the eventual Allied victory: the British blockade, Germany's economic and logistical collapse, the American reinforcements, the French recovery, and the extraordinary revival of the British and Dominion forces.

One could persuasively argue that Passchendaele prolonged and almost lost the war for the Allies, given the staggering casualties and collapse in morale it produced, which directly led to the near-vanquishing of the British and Dominion armies in early 1918. Certainly, Lloyd George thought so. 'The Passchendaele fiasco imperilled the chances of final victory,' he concluded.[22] And Paul Harris, a senior lecturer in War Studies at the Royal Military Academy, Sandhurst, and a trenchant critic of Haig's war, writes of Third Ypres:

> some phases had a quality more nightmarish than anything
> previously experienced. Whereas the British Army came out
> of the Somme campaign with remarkably good morale, Third
> Ypres seems to have left much of it distinctly despondent
> . . . It seems clear, therefore, that, in terms of morale, Haig
> had done proportionally very much more damage to his
> own army than to the Germans. The British Army (and

their Dominion ranks) had been the only army of the Allies
in a fair state of both morale and efficiency when Third
Ypres began. Haig's conduct at Third Ypres, especially
in the latter stages of the campaign, can be regarded as
amounting to reckless endangerment of the Allied cause.[23]

—

It is often asked why Britain did not join France's defensive war. For
one thing, 'defending' ran counter to all of Haig's instincts. He was a
basher, always 'on the offensive', physically and temperamentally. Yet
Lloyd George and the French commanders, for different reasons, saw
a defensive war as an appealing alternative to profitless attrition.

Their pressure spurred Haig to devote a whole section of his
1919 report to justifying his offensive. Under the heading 'Why We
Attacked Whenever Possible', Haig wrote, 'The idea that a war can
be won by standing on the defensive and waiting for the enemy to
attack is a dangerous fallacy, which owes its inception to the desire
to evade the price of victory . . .' – that is, a higher casualty rate.
'A defensive strategy,' he continued, implied a 'distinct lowering of
the moral [sic] of the troops, who imagine that the enemy must be
the better man, or at least more numerous . . . Once the mass of the
defending infantry become possessed of such ideas, the battle is as
good as lost . . .'[24]

His argument pivots on the flawed assumption that braver soldiers, or 'better men', fight offensive actions, while cowards or lesser
men fight defensive wars. This ignores the extraordinary courage of
the German Army, which had successfully fought a three-year defensive war. Morale had held up throughout. Indeed, the Germans
would lose the war as a result of their over-ambitious offensive in
1918.

Should Britain and the Dominions have fought a defensive war
in 1917? There were compelling points in favour. First, the Germans
could not afford to lose men at the rate of Britain and were thus
reluctant to mount major offensives. Second, the attacking force

usually lost more men than the defending one (which is one reason why the German Army had been defending for so long). Third, the Allies together would have imposed a formidable defensive barrier, as the British showed at First Ypres in 1914. Fourth, the French were committed to a defensive battle until the Americans arrived, under Clémenceau's leadership, and wanted the British to join them. Fifth, British forces fielded far more heavy guns and machine guns than the Germans in 1917 and were producing them at a faster rate. And sixth, the Germans had *fewer men than the Allies* on the Western Front in 1917, and were unable to mobilise the bulk of their eastern forces until the end of the year and into 1918. And as every general knew, a vast numerical advantage, in the order of three to one, was needed to win a major offensive in an entrenched war of attrition. Haig never had that advantage.

That is not to suggest they should have sat and waited for victory to come. Rather, in 1917, Britain would have been defending, from a position of strength, until the Americans arrived and French returned. That was not the case in early 1918, when they had fewer men, fewer guns and dreadful morale, *as a result* of Passchendaele. It is something of a miracle that they held on, and won. Indeed, the Allies won by waging a defensive war (a 'fighting withdrawal') deep into French territory, drawing out the German supply lines then hitting back with the full complement of the American and French armies and the revived Commonwealth forces.

Against this, a defensive war did not sit well with the press and public, who, like Haig and his generals – though from a position of ignorance – were overwhelmingly in favour of great offensive actions. They wanted bold thrusts and gallant victories. And that is why Flanders went ahead despite the prime minister's strong opposition to it before it began.

—

Since the end of the Great War, a chorus of voices have variously praised or condemned it. Thousands of books have examined the legacy of the war and whether it was just or unjust, inevitable or avoidable. Since the 1960s, the Great War has been variously and near-unanimously condemned as a tragic bungle, state-sponsored mass murder and/or a crime against humanity, which destroyed the best part of a generation and plunged the world into economic chaos and tyranny. The rise of Nazism and the Soviet Union would not have been possible without the conditions created by the Great War: on that, most experts are agreed.

In recent years, however, a new breed of self-described 'revisionist' historians have emerged to champion the Great War as just, 'worth it', and absolutely necessary. They hail the Somme and Passchendaele as vital battles in a necessary war against German aggression. They defend the war of attrition, more or less, as the only option open to Haig, and praise him for making the best of a botched hand. They have no truck with what they derisively call the war poet's view of the Western Front – dispatching, at a stroke, some of the finest writers on the *experience* of the Great War (who also happened to fight it with great courage). On an operational level, some revisionists defend the huge attritional struggles as valuable lessons in the use of new weapons, such as howitzers, gas, flame-throwers and grenades; and new applications, such as the creeping barrage. They tend to aim their hostility at harmless targets – poets, artists, musicians and comedians (chiefly the late twentieth-century serial, *Blackadder*) – betraying an oddly fragile sensitivity.

The revisionists' high priest is John Terraine, who bludgeoned the popular horror of the war in the 1960s with a stringently argued case that Haig had done all he could to win, within the limitations imposed on him. Terraine's heirs are numerous, but their most recent ranks include Gary Sheffield, Sir Max Hastings and Gordon Corrigan. Sheffield's central theme is that the Great War was a 'forgotten victory' over German aggression, which also provided the Allied commanders with a good education in strategy and weaponry. Hastings' position is confused: he is absolutely convinced that Britain had no choice other than to go to war against Prussian aggression; on the other hand, as he stated in a debate recently, he admits that 'if the Germans had not gone into Belgium, I would find it very difficult to say I would assuredly have said that we could and should have fought in 1914'.[25] This does not cohere. If Germany really was the terrible threat to world peace and liberty that he claims, then surely Britain should have gone to war to defend France – and Europe – from Berlin's aggression regardless of whether the German Army respected Belgium's neutrality. Would the threat have disappeared had Germany bypassed Belgium?

The revisionists have no doubt that the war was worth fighting, despite the catastrophic cost. Passchendaele was 'worth it', some argue, as part of a victorious four-year struggle – here, they tend to march in lockstep with Haig's last dispatch – that ended with the greatest feat of arms in British history. That may be true, in a pure military sense. But they fail to explain exactly what advantages accrued to Britain from fighting the war in the first place, or just how the war achieved anything worthwhile for Europe.

Victors tend to justify the act of winning, no matter how atrocious, wasteful or wrong-headed the conflict, on the spurious grounds that the end justifies the means: for them, victory is self-validating. Few British historians critically examine, for example, the illegal Naval Blockade, which they pass over as a valid instrument of war. Though effective in crushing the German economy, by any other definition it was a war crime that killed almost 800,000 German civilians. Many strategists argue that winning is all that matters, regardless of the means, or the human or material cost. They discuss the strategic usefulness of poison gas as though it were a variant on the cavalry charge. In a world of banned weapons and laws against war crimes that is nonsense, of course: if might were right, the use of gas, firebombs and nuclear weapons would all be justifiable, as would torture and civilian slaughter.

It would be unfair, however, to cast the pro-First World War brigade as warmongers, as some critics have done. A curious emotional dissonance leavens their prose. Their conclusions seem ruptured, torn between the heart and the head, as if doubt lurks in the margins of their minds. On the one hand, they plunder the stock of popular phrases to describe the Great War – thus they agree that it was 'catastrophic',[26] and 'tragic', in which the 'butcher's bill'[27] was 'appalling'[28]; on the other hand, they claim the war was absolutely necessary and worth the cost. This jarring of word and thought begs the question: at what point would the catastrophe not have been worth it? How many millions would have had to die, how many nations destroyed, how many fascist and communist seedlings sown, how many families struck down with grief, before politicians, the press and military revisionists would concede that the First World War was *not worth it*?

Perhaps those who argue that the First World War was 'necessary', and that the Somme and Passchendaele were 'worth it', should submit their views to my Scroll Back Test. Knowing what we know now, of the cost in blood, grief and economic loss, imagine you're able to travel back in time to 1914 to serve as a mediator between the governments of Europe. How would you advise them to act on the brink of hostilities? Would you urge the Entente to go to war because you genuinely believe, in accordance with the views you hold today, that Germany was a tyranny intent on world conquest and had to be crushed (ignoring the fact that Germany's political system at the time was just as democratic and progressive as Britain's, and the Berlin government negotiable, well into 1914)? Or would you advise the governments of Europe to pull back from the brink and negotiate a peaceful settlement (as they succeeded in doing in the crises of 1905, 1911 and 1912–13)? In the first instance, you would have unleashed the Four Horsemen, but your advice would cohere with your views today. In the second, you would have saved the world from a holocaust, and yet contradicted everything you've said or written since in support of the case for a 'necessary war' against Germany.

The Great War was an avoidable tragedy that condemned Europe, the fount of Western civilisation, to political degeneracy,

WHAT THE LIVING SAID

economic collapse and totalitarian rule. Even many of today's 'revisionist' historians, who argue that the war was necessary, recognise this. 'The British,' writes Sheffield, 'could have perhaps have been [sic] more generous in [their] response to the emergence of German power.'[29] Nor was war inevitable, he concedes: as late as July–August, Germany and Austria 'might have got their way without fighting'.[30] By then, it was too late: Russia had mobilised and the Prussian commanders were effectively in charge in Berlin.

—

In this light, the recent process of 'normalising' Passchendaele as 'worth it' appals sensitive-minded civilians who, in the intervening years, have longed to find some redemptive meaning in all this.

Many ordinary people despair of the 'expert' view of the Somme and Passchendaele as 'necessary' battles in a 'just' war. They find deeper meaning in the war poets' portrait of the Western Front as pointless butchery, the rupture of the human soul, conveyed in the most powerful lines ever to emerge from a battlefield: those of Wilfred Owen, David Jones, Edmund Blunden, Siegfried Sassoon, Robert Graves and Richard Aldington. Graves's *Goodbye To All That* and Aldington's *Death of a Hero* are surely the most bitter expressions of this sensibility; Owen's poetry and Jones's epic, *In Parenthesis*, the noblest. The greatest literary voices on the German side were the veterans Erich Maria Remarque, whose novel and memoir *All Quiet on the Western Front* gave the German nation a heartfelt morality play; and Ernst Jünger, the highly decorated German officer, whose novel *Storm of Steel* delivered the unadorned truth about the professional soldier.

A subtler literary response was that of the British soldier-poet Edmund Blunden. He was one of the few who fought at Passchendaele, the memory of which became a ceaseless torment, so much so that his friends worried for his sanity. His poem 'Third Ypres' summoned a nightmarish vision of devolved humanity in 'uncreation sunk':

The more monstrous fate
Shadows our own, the mind swoons doubly burdened,
Taught how for miles our anguish groans and bleeds,
A whole sweet countryside amuck with murder;
Each moment puffed into a year with death.
Still swept the rain, roared guns,
Still swooped into the swamps of flesh and blood,
All to the drabness of uncreation sunk,
And all thought dwindled to a moan, Relieve!
But who with what command can now relieve
The dead men from that chaos, or my soul?

Blunden's was a calm patriotic soul. The bitter volleys of Graves and Aldington he eschewed as 'a betrayal of the experience of the war, and of those . . . who died in it'.[31] In one poem, 'Illusions', he asks the reader's forgiveness for finding beauty, loveliness, in the trenches, before the 'Terror' shatters his reverie, and he sees 'death's malkins dangling in the wire'.[32] The 'steely glitter' of Blunden's eye, to whom the horror is ironic, aberrational, redeems him from the charge of enclosing a charnel house in lyricism, of composing 'quatrains in an abattoir'.[33] Long after the war, he continued to believe in the possibility of love, rendering him unacceptable to the 'Modernist' literary set, for whom love was a perversion and compassion a sickness – a style of 'cultural criticism' to which the German philosopher Theodor Adorno appended the grim epitaph: 'To write poetry after Auschwitz is barbaric.'[34]

—

It is time to offer some of my own conclusions about Passchendaele, based on my work in the preceding pages. Primarily, I believe that the poisonous relationship between Lloyd George and Douglas Haig offers a fresh, human perspective through which to understand the battle. Their mutual hatred and furious disagreement on how to fight the war led to a near-complete breakdown in communication between the prime minister and his commander-in-chief. The collapse of a partnership so vital to British security needlessly prolonged and thus, to a real extent, exacerbated the tragedy of Passchendaele.

Let us ask ourselves, for example, the question that has vexed historians, soldiers and academics since 1917: why did Haig prolong the battle after 9 October, when heavy rainfall, terrible losses, the advice of senior officers (though not Gough or Plumer) and the evidence of his eyes pointed to futile slaughter and counselled against continuing? We already know the official military explanation: Haig pressed on because he felt he was on a winning streak; perhaps the weather would hold; the Germans were on the brink of collapse, etc. He could hardly halt below the village, on a mud plain within German sights, where nobody would have lasted 'any more minutes than necessary', as Harington observed.[35] Nor could Haig withdraw to Pilckem Ridge and regroup – a sensible option in military terms, as Sheffield states, but 'to give up territory so recently captured at such heavy cost, was psychologically and politically impossible'.[36] And militarily unsound, he writes, in a remark of devastating consequence that he curiously underplays in his recent book: 'To accept the logic of a battle of pure attrition, that ground [Passchendaele] was unimportant . . .'.[37] The 'logic' was to destroy as many of the enemy as possible; it didn't really matter where.

There is a darker explanation for Haig's decision to keep slogging away, rooted in the psychology of power and pride. Haig was a proud man who had been brutally used by a politician he loathed. According to Haig's original plan, the capture of Passchendaele had always been his 'fall-back' position if the battle failed to advance as he hoped.

In this light, had Haig failed to reach the village, the prime minister would have been the first out of the blocks to damn him as a total failure. Not only Haig's job but his entire reputation and legacy were at stake. Had he called off the battle on 9 October, at such immense cost in soldiers' lives, having fallen so short of the goals he had laid before the War Cabinet, Haig would have handed Lloyd

George the perfect chance not only to sack him but also to destroy his name under a barrage of schadenfreude.

Lloyd George admits this in a revealing paragraph in his memoir:

> There were two courses open to Sir Douglas Haig [around
> 9 October]. One was to go to the Cabinet and admit that
> the campaign was a complete failure based on an absurd
> miscalculation of essential facts. He would have to own up
> that the criticism directed against the scheme by the Prime
> Minister had been justified by the event. The other course
> was to persevere stubbornly with his attacks, knowing that
> at the worst he would gain some ground, with a chance that
> one day the enemy morale might break . . . He gambled
> on the latter chance rather than face the dread alternative
> of a confession of failure to the politicians . . .[38]

There is a further, metaphysical dimension to Haig's persistence: the lavish religious tones of the word 'Passchendaele' resonated with politicians, civilians and journalists as a symbol of redemption, of Christ's sacrifice, of Easter. Passchendaele was 'popular'. By this reading, the Allies were fighting a righteous war towards a shell-strewn Calvary. Possessing Passchendaele exerted a near-mystical hold on certain soldiers' minds. None paused to ask *why* or *when* Passchendaele had become a vital military target. (By November, it had no strategic value as an end in itself; its value as a jumping-off point as part of an attack on the coast had ceased to exist). The men simply assumed it must be, and not only the ordinary soldiers. When General Godley ordered thousands of New Zealanders to their deaths in a battle he knew they couldn't win, he was acting in the thrall of Haig's orders to seize the village.

Haig, too, a man of keen religious faith, fell under the siren-like allure of the little cross on the hill. Capturing Passchendaele became something of an obsession for the field marshal who, on several occasions in his life, imagined himself a tool of the Almighty. At the end of 1914, he started to experience a 'Higher Power' commanding his destiny.[39] We have already seen him on the eve of the Somme, confiding in his wife that he felt a higher power working through him. On the eve of the battles of Passchendaele, Haig felt similarly guided: he prayed and frequently visited his favourite chaplain, and his faith acquired a deeply personal dimension, as Charteris observed:

> He came to regard himself with almost Calvinistic faith as the predestined instrument of Providence for the achievement of victory for the British armies. His abundant self-reliance was reinforced by this conception of himself as the child of destiny.[40]

With this spiritual armour, Haig went in person to implore the Canadians to finish the job that the British and Anzacs had started.

In this light, is it fanciful to suggest that Passchendaele had acquired in Haig's mind the aura of the last station on a terrible and unremitting Via Dolorosa, along whose bloody path his armies had staggered Christ-like, past the 'stations' of Pilckem, Gheluvelt, Broodseinde and Gravenstafel, before their final sacrifice on Passchendaele Ridge?

—

Lloyd George presents the other face of this Janus-like duo. The prime minister had approved the Flanders Offensive in the last week of June 1917 on the understanding that he would end it should it fail to progress. It failed and he didn't – contrary to his later claim that he had done his best to terminate the battle:

> I resisted to the very last the whole project before it was ever commenced, and confidently predicted its failure, giving reasons for my prediction. After its failure was beyond reasonable doubt, I did my best to persuade the Generals to break it off.[41]

True, Lloyd George opposed the offensive before it began; but there is no record of him telling Haig to end it *after* it began. Nor did the prime minister have much to say about the progress of the battle; the subject surfaced fleetingly in Cabinet, as we've seen. Had the prime minister more important things on his mind than one of the bloodiest military encounters in British history? Or did he withhold his disgust behind the steeliest exertions of self-restraint? The answer to both questions is no: Lloyd George lived and breathed the war effort; he was a stranger to self-restraint.

He had his own reasons for deciding not to call off the offensive. Those reasons were not the ones he later gave, such as ignorance: 'I was a layman and in matters of military strategy I did not possess the knowledge and training that would justify me in overriding soldiers of such standing and experience. Accordingly, the soldiers had their way.'[42] That rings hollow in light of his brash intervention to put Haig under French command, and his solo crusade for the Italian campaign.

A less risible case for Lloyd George's decision not to intervene was that he bowed to conservative pressure. 'Passchendaele could not have been stopped without dismissing Sir Douglas Haig,' he later wrote. 'But I could not have done it without the assent of the Cabinet. I sounded the Members of the Cabinet individually on the subject and I also spoke to some of the Dominion representatives. They – or most of them – were under the spell of the synthetic victories distilled at G.H.Q.'[43] Again, this fails to convince. Are we led to believe that this rowdiest of political animals, leader of a nation at war, yielded to a few colonials and conservative politicians, who were in no position to replace him?

There is a Machiavellian explanation for Lloyd George's inertia: he was giving Haig enough rope to hang himself. This scenario courts power politics at its most brutal, but it has substance in the context of their bitter personal struggle and eye on their place in history. The prime minister certainly recognised the cost to Haig personally of failing to take Passchendaele, as we've seen. In which case, if Lloyd George overruled his commander, and called off the offensive on 9 October, he would have rescued Haig from any responsibility for its failure. The press would have leaped to defend their favourite commander against a meddling politician. And Haig would have been able to blame Lloyd George for preventing his men from capturing Passchendaele and perhaps breaking through. Lloyd George might even have gone down as the prime minister who lost the war.

Lloyd George later conceded as much. Had he tried to stop Passchendaele, he remarked, 'they would have said I had spoilt the chance of a decisive success, and of saving us from the danger of submarines'.[44] At the time to which he refers, he knew Britain had won the U-boat war. In other words, here speaks the consummate politician, pursuing his personal legacy ahead of thousands of lives. And so, throughout October, the prime minister stood quietly watching, letting Haig pursue an offensive that Lloyd George already thought a spectacular, bloody failure – but one that must be seen to be Haig's failure.

—

Lloyd George would not reveal the true state of his mind for decades. When it showed itself, with the publication of his memoirs in the 1930s, his wrath was terrible to behold. Guilt tormented him: he had long brooded on the tragedy of Flanders, and by molten increments the demon of conscience had worn him down. In the post-war years, in a terrific outpouring of rage, blame, grief and regret, he sat down to write his memoir. With his hair hanging long and white, and his mind as agile as ever, the retired politician then in his late 60s took up his pen and with every weapon in his formidable intellectual armoury sallied forth to clear his name and excoriate the man he held solely responsible for 'the most gigantic, tenacious, grim, futile and bloody fight ever waged in the history of war'.[45]

First published in 1933, the memoir devoted an entire chapter to Passchendaele, under the title 'The Campaign of the Mud'. A few extracts convey Lloyd George's mood and intent. Passchendaele was a 'ghastly fiasco'[46], fought according to the 'unimaginative' and 'commonplace' strategy of attrition, 'an afterthought of beaten Generals to explain away their defeat . . .'[47]

It got worse: 'But as soon as the troops went over the top, they found that they had to pass through exactly the same experiences as those to which they had been subjected in the discredited offensives of the past few years – machine guns playing upon their crumbling ranks from positions which had not been touched by their artillery . . . the enemy still entrenched behind a line of impregnable earthworks.'[48]

'The troops felt that they had been fooled and sold and their comrades butchered.'[49]

'When it was finally concluded, the attack had completely failed in all the purposes for which it was originally designed . . .'[50]

'Whilst hundreds of thousands were being destroyed in the insane egotism of Passchendaele, every message or memorandum from Haig was full of these insistences on the importance of sending him more men to replace those he had sent to die in the mud. If Britain said, "Where are my lost legions?" then anyone who asked such a question on her behalf was betraying the Army and attacking our soldiers.'[51]

—

The question of 'blame' is always fraught. On the one hand, there are many who follow Lloyd George's lead and hold Haig chiefly responsible. Among them are millions of tender souls who defend the war but condemn the way it was fought, as if humane methods were at the commanders' disposal. Theirs is a decent hypocrisy. Yet to criticise Haig or Ludendorff for not fighting a 'nicer' or more restrained war is akin to criticising a lion for not showing mercy to a zebra; or decrying the lack of morals in a virus. That is not to suggest the commanders were 'willing executioners' – most were deeply affected by their soldiers' sacrifice. It is simply to state the unpalatable fact that the commanders on the Western Front had little choice other than to fight the war as they did; the casualties were not only planned for, they were inevitable, in the absence of the political will to stop the carnage.

In this sense, Haig's or Ludendorff's *characters* were irrelevant, because force of will ultimately had little bearing on the *kind* of war being fought in France and Belgium. Every commander – to the dismayed incomprehension of their civilian leaders – was condemned to fight or defend within the straitjacket of attrition. Over and again, the British, French, Dominion and German armies explored ways to end the struggle of the trenches, to return to open, mobile battle: Nivelle's 'two-day miracle', Gough's 'breakthrough', Plumer's 'bite and hold', clouds of gas, huge mines, the creeping barrage, shock troops, lightning counter-attacks, massed tanks . . . None changed the fundamental conditions of the bashing war of the trenches. No army or weapons system was able to break the deadlock until the last do-or-die onslaughts of 1918, when the Allies' numeric supremacy and the Germans' exhaustion determined the outcome. In sum, if the Great War was *not inevitable* – there 'are always choices', as the historian (and Lloyd George's great-granddaughter) Margaret MacMillan reminds us[52] – the methods of fighting it were.

This powerlessness manifested itself at government level, too. Having declared war, the European powers had little control over the monster they had unleashed, or how it should be fought. Once they had said 'yes' to war, they had said 'yes' to the creeping barrage, frontal assaults and enormous casualties – an equation the civilian rulers misunderstood or refused to accept. It meant unleashing every available weapon on the enemy's lines, no matter how horrible or 'illegal'. International law had banned but failed to prevent the use of mustard gas, of course (just as it would fail to prevent firebombs in the Second World War and napalm in Vietnam).[53]

On the other hand, to exonerate the commanders and politicians as helpless pawns who were 'unable to impose their will on events' is to remove the human agency from the machinery of war.[54] What men had begun, they were able to end, had there been the political and moral will to do so. Yet nobody took responsibility. The politicians stood aside. As with the Vietnam and Iraq wars, those in charge escaped any punitive action for their colossal misjudgements. A soldier who lost control of himself and deserted faced severe punishment, possibly execution. A commander or politician who lost control of the war, or whose errors caused thousands of needless casualties, could expect to be forgiven, lauded and ennobled.

Though he was later rewarded with an earldom, greatness would always be denied Field Marshal Haig. 'Why has not Haig been recognised as one of England's greatest generals?' asked a newspaper eighteen years after the armistice. 'The answer may be given in one word – "Passchendaele".'[55]

—

Humanely, then, we are driven to conclude with a question. A war armed with the technology to kill a generation of men, doomed to use it because the generals could find no other way: did this not place an unprecedented responsibility on the political leaders to intervene and agree a compromise peace? That is the question Passchendaele forces upon us. Haig himself believed a negotiated truce the only option, when his spirits were lowest, in early 1918. Knowing, by 1917, that the trenches were unbreakable without appalling losses, the governments of Europe had a historic duty to find a way to end it, to save the flower of European youth. They chose not to, and utterly failed the societies they ruled or represented.

The people were ignorant of these issues, of course, so it is no good defending the continuation of the war on the grounds that 'the people' wanted it (as some historians have suggested). Few knew what had actually happened in Flanders until well after the war. Lloyd George knew, and this is how he carried the burden of truth:

If people really knew, the war would be stopped tomorrow,
but of course they don't – and can't know. The correspondents
don't write and the censorship won't pass the truth . . .
The thing is horrible and beyond human nature to bear
and I feel I can't go on with this bloody business. . .[56]

# EPILOGUE

# REQUIEM FOR DOOMED YOUTH

*What would our fathers do if one day we rose up and confronted them, and called them to account? . . . Our knowledge of life is limited to death. What will happen afterward? And what can possibly become of us?*
Erich Maria Remarque, author of *All Quiet on the Western Front*

————————————————

*[I felt] the heart-breaking realisation that I'll never get the warm, friendly grip of welcome from my own proud father. The dear father, whom I loved as few men ever loved a father . . . May God rest his dear soul . . .*
Private Edward Lynch, author of *Somme Mud*, on his return to Australia

————————————————

On the 100th anniversary of Passchendaele, poppies and medals will be worn, wreathes laid, tears shed. Armchair generals, academics and journalists will mourn the 'catastrophe': 'Ah, yes, Passchendaele, appalling business. Shocking.' Then comes the 'but': 'But it had to be done. All part of a just war, you know. Absolutely necessary. Saved the world from tyranny.'

And so the true meaning – *the warning* – of the sacrifice slides away from our understanding, and this avoidable slaughter is cast as another battle in a 'necessary' war in which millions had to die, over whose bodies millions mourn and learn nothing.

No doubt, many soldiers and civilians were sad to see it all end. On Armistice Day, 11 November 1918, Colonel Wilkinson was standing by his old friend, Sergeant Oscar Warner, watching the fireworks. After a while, Wilkinson said to Warner, 'Well, what do you think of all this?' Warner 'looked at me for a moment and then he said, "I'm sorry it's all over, Sir, we'll never have times like this again!"' He repeated those words to troops in training for many years after the war.[1]

Many more would never forget the horror, their post-war trauma brutally articulated in Richard Aldington's autobiographical novel, *Death of a Hero*. Aldington came home nursing 'a vendetta of the dead against the living', born of survivor's guilt. 'What right have I to live?' he asks. No answer came, and he felt 'icily alone'.[2]

Implicit in his fury at being alive in a world he despised was a longing for a 'hero's death', like the one he awards his main character, Winterbourne. On hearing a badly wounded runner cry out, 'Oh, for God's sake, kill me, *kill* me', Winterbourne bursts over the top into a hail of fire. 'Something seemed to break in Winterbourne's head,' Aldington writes. 'He felt he was going mad, and sprang to his feet. The line of bullets smashed across his chest like a savage steel whip. The universe exploded darkly into oblivion.'[3]

How can the living atone, Aldington wondered:

for the lost millions and millions of years of life, how atone
for those lakes and seas of blood? . . . Somehow or other we
have to make those dead acceptable, we have to atone for
them, we have to appease them. How, I don't quite know.
I know there's the Two Minutes' Silence. But after all, a
Two Minutes' Silence once a year isn't doing much . . .
What can we do? Headstones and wreaths and memorials
and speeches and the Cenotaph – no, no; it has got to be

something in us. Somehow we must atone to the dead . . .

It is poisoning us, this inability to atone, he writes: 'It is the poison that makes us heartless and hopeless and lifeless – us, the War Generation, and the new generation too. The whole world is blood-guilty . . .'[4]

———

Old men tend to write the history of war. Old men often forget they're writing about very young men. They unwittingly project their cynicism and experience onto lads just out of school, idealistic young men with little knowledge of life, love or loss, and whose adult lives were just beginning.

In a similar misperception, the young tend to think of 'war veterans' as old men. They forget that the defining moments of a veteran's life, relived for many years later, draw on the most extreme experiences of his youth.

And in his idealism, the young soldier believed in and cherished those qualities of friendship, loyalty and self-sacrifice. He cheerfully offered up his body to the grizzled politicians and hoary generals, who hungrily dispatched it to the front, with the proud complicity of his girlfriend, parents and society.

Once he started fighting, the British, Dominion and German soldier did not stop – until he was killed, wounded or ordered. And it is often asked why, after so much bloodshed, knowing what he risked, did he persist? The soldier's answer is always the same: he kept fighting for the sake of his friends . . . in the name of the dead buried beneath him and the esteem of the living marching beside him.[5]

If we are to understand what went through their minds, and grasp a deeper truth about war, we need to listen to them: to Neville Hind's frustration, Ronald Skirth's defiance, Richard Aldington's bitterness, Patrick Campbell's fear, the Seabrook brothers' innocence . . . and the courage in them all, in Allfree, Allhusen, Lynch, Birnie, Wilkinson, Yoxall, the War Poets, Remarque, Jünger and hundreds of thousands of other voices – British, Anzac, Canadian, German, French – whose feelings imbue these pages. For theirs are the true voices of the history of war. But who is listening to them anymore?

—

The Tommies returned to a mean-spirited and ungrateful nation, a far cry from the 'land fit for heroes' the British Government had promised them. In fairness, the British people could be forgiven for wanting to forget the war. But the soldier could not. So traumatic was the memory of Passchendaele that, 27 years later, in his third attempt to take the Italian town of Cassino during the Second World War, the New Zealand lieutenant general Sir Bernard Freyberg VC, GCMG, KCB, KBE, DSO (with three bars) merely had to utter the word 'Passchendaele' to bring the entire operation to a halt.[6]

The Battle of Passchendaele touched hundreds of thousands of young men, who could never forget it. Private Neville Hind wrote his war memoir between October 1917 and April 1918, while in hospital in Sheffield, recovering from a gunshot wound to the shoulder. There, he loved the big breakfasts, Woodbines, books and theatre, and for a time he lived in heaven: 'my dream has been fulfilled,' he wrote of his luck at getting a 'Blighty' wound that sent him home to these comforts.[7]

Hind was demobbed in January 1919, and he prepared to start studies at Cambridge University in October that year. 'This was a miserable time,' his daughter Dorothy recounts, 'as his mother had remarried while he was away and "home" was no longer Newcastle, so he seems to have buried himself in reading the daily press.'[8] Hind graduated in 1922 with a BA in History and the next year married his Newcastle girlfriend. He got a job as a teacher at a school in York, and was later appointed headmaster at Keighley Boys' Grammar School, a job he held until 1958. He rarely spoke about his war experience. After years of silence and awkwardness, he let his fiancée read his memoir. 'She felt that they were able to talk together as easily as they did before he joined up,' his daughter

Dorothy recounts. 'Before that, he was like a brick wall.'

Hind never mentioned the war to Dorothy, 'or the Military Medal which I think he felt he did not deserve', until she was well into adulthood: 'On reflection, I guess it was the years at Cambridge which turned him round from becoming a bitter, introverted person to being a successful teacher and a caring, thoughtfully optimistic husband and father.'[9] Hind made a success of his life, a chance so cruelly denied millions of similar young men.

So, too, did Lieutenant Patrick Campbell, the young officer who had feared his men would never accept him. Immobilised with terror at the start of Passchendaele, he went on to earn a Military Cross. He returned home, then went up to Oxford, and soon married. He lived to the age of 88. He loved his chosen career, a teacher – many veterans turned their minds to the young – and became master of Westminster Under School. In retirement, he wrote several memoirs of his years as a soldier and teacher, and lived to see the publication of his autobiography, *Blade of Grass*.[10]

Corporal Skirth suffered shell shock and amnesia after Passchendaele. On his recovery, he was transferred to the Italian front, where his disillusionment with the war was complete. He made a pact with God in the church in the village of San Martino never again to take human life. He confided in Ella that he had become a pacifist. During the ensuing battles, he was as good as his word: he targeted the guns away from the enemy, building in minor errors to his trajectories so that the shells 'never once hit an inhabited target' on the first attempt, giving the enemy a chance to evacuate.[11] His superiors never discovered the sabotage.

Skirth declined a Military Medal, offered for his part in trying to prevent a fatal accident, and returned home in 1919 to his childhood sweetheart. He and Ella married in 1923. He, too, became a teacher, at a school in West London, and in 1929 Ella gave birth to a girl. During the Second World War, Skirth's school was evacuated to South Wales, where he was branded a communist and a crank for his pacifism.[12]

Skirth's memoir was published in 2010, entitled *The Reluctant Tommy: Ronald Skirth's Extraordinary Memoir of the First World War*, to critical acclaim, notwithstanding some question marks over its accuracy. Ella and he lived happily together. They holidayed in Italy, and he rediscovered his love of poetry. Years after the war, he wrote that the Western Front had deprived him of the one thing that was as precious to him as life itself: 'my love of beauty'.[13]

Millions of men would not live to see beauty. A few thousand had their lives cut short by firing squad, as emblematised by the fate of Lieutenant Harry Penrose, the pseudonymous young officer in A. P. Herbert's novel *The Secret War* (based on a true story). Soon after Penrose's voluntary return to France in 1917, a violent terror came over him, a fear so powerful that he turned and walked away from the enemy. He walked *back from the front line*. His trial was brisk, his sentence a foregone conclusion and his execution swift. He was shot for cowardice seven days later in a little orchard in northern France. According to the padre, Penrose faced the firing squad 'bravely and quietly'. '[M]y friend Harry,' Herbert wrote, 'was shot for cowardice – and he was one of the bravest men I ever knew.'[14]

—

Field Marshal Sir Douglas Haig returned from the war a conquering hero. For his pains, he accepted a grant of £100,000 and an earldom. He devoted the remainder of his life to ex-servicemen with the energy of a man possessed – 'working himself to death', in one doctor's opinion. He would stay up late writing letters to soldiers. 'I think that they rather prefer to get a letter in one's own handwriting,' Haig said. 'The personal touch, I think, counts for something, and I can do so little for them.'[15]

Perhaps Haig's finest hour was the roasting he gave the Medical Boards and Trade Unions for their indifference and hostility to war veterans. He condemned the government for failing to provide proper care and financial support for returned soldiers, especially the disabled.

The British commander-in-chief enjoyed great popularity in his waning years (Lloyd George would not try to vilify him as a butcher until well after his death). Vast crowds attended his funeral, on 3 March 1928, reportedly bigger than those at the funeral of Princess Diana, in 1997.[16] Like hers, Haig's body was borne along on a gun carriage, to Westminster Abbey. Among the pall-bearers were Marshals Foch and Pétain.

———

For the little Dominions, the emotional toll would be disproportionately hard. Passchendaele tore the heart out of New Zealand and left many veterans psychologically devastated. The tough Brigadier 'Bill' Braithwaite suffered a nervous breakdown after the battle, and was removed from his post.

One rumour – credible in the circumstances – circulated that Braithwaite had been sacked for refusing to send his men to their certain deaths, on 12 October 1917, the bloodiest afternoon in New Zealand's history. Braithwaite 'refused to order his men to be murdered and of course that was the end of his military career', one soldier recalled. 'He was returned to England and we never saw him again.'[17]

Homes were plunged into grief; families could not outlive the memory of their loss. Years later, one New Zealand mother, who lost two sons in the war – one at Passchendaele – and a third soon after, would suddenly break down in tears at the dinner table, 'weeping and railing against the injustice of war'.[18]

Many men would not survive the peace, as at least one young bride found on her wedding day (recounts the New Zealand poet Robin Hyde):

> You could get engaged, triumphantly, to a good-looking
> fine-faced returned man . . . Then, perhaps on the eve of the
> wedding, there would be an incoherent note, a policeman
> around in the morning, and an inquest on a man who had

put a bullet through his head. Somebody would explain
that he had been badly shell-shocked at Ypres, badly gassed.
Poor old Jack, everybody said. Yes, but nobody thought,
in the same degree, poor young Laura or Mavis.[19]

—

In Australia, confirmation of the death of their three eldest sons
blackened the Seabrook family's home. The younger siblings grew
up in the shadow of death. None spoke of their three lost brothers.
In March 1919 their father, William, suffered a nervous breakdown,
forcing his wife, Fanny, to apply for a government living allowance.

The government refused her application at first, on the grounds
that she was not a war widow and had provided insufficient evidence
of her husband's condition. On 26 March, she wrote in despair to
a family friend, enclosing the government's 'curt answer to having
given our three boys as a sacrifice to the country. Their loss I will
never recover, and now my husband is a complete wreck, he collapsed on Sat. last, almost mad . . . I am afraid he will have to be put
away.'[20]

On 1 May 1919, the government revised its decision. The
deputy comptroller wrote to the comptroller of the Department of
Repatriation, in Melbourne, thus:

[A]lthough Mrs Seabrook has been hit very hard by the
late war, three sons having paid the supreme sacrifice, her
husband is alive, and at ordinary times quite able to provide
necessary support. For some weeks, however, the husband has
been prostrated with Neurasthenia, and unable to work.[21]

Her allowance was granted.

The Seabrooks could never afford to visit Ypres, where the Menin
Gate lists George's and Theo's names, nor to see Keith's grave at
the Lijssenthoek Military Cemetery, near Poperinghe, in Flanders.
Fanny took an active role, however, in prolonging their memory

in Australia, and was invited to lay a wreath at the Australian War Memorial in the 1920s.[22]

———

Bitterly cold, standing in line on a snow-covered parade in northern France, awaiting the arrival of the King, was the Australian Private Ed Lynch and his battalion. It was 24 November 1918, and the war was over. The men stamped their feet and blew their benumbed fingers. The King was an hour late. Then a long car arrived and passed slowly by, bearing King George, who stared out at the Australian survivors, at attention in the winter cold. The King didn't leave his car.

'How's it for a loan of your overcoat, King?' yelled one soldier, to roars of recrimination from the sergeant major.

'Hip, hip, hooray,' shouted Lynch's company, as the King's car passed on.

Lynch counted himself lucky to be there: of the 250 men and two officers with whom he had joined his battalion, as reinforcements, just nineteen were left, and every one of the nineteen had been wounded at least once.

Lynch left Le Havre on 15 April 1919 and sailed for England, sad and glad to be leaving France. On the morning of 25 April, he found men cleaning their boots, shaving, removing stains from their uniforms. 'Today's Anzac Day, don't you know,' said one.

'We didn't know, or much care either.'[23]

At that night's gala dinner, Lynch was told to 'uphold the honour of Australia' in front of 'British officers and gentlemen of the town'. Any display of larrikinism would be sternly dealt with. Lynch's 'old general' arrived at the event, apparently drunk, to loud applause. 'We're proud of him, for the first time in the war,' Lynch recalled. The general then delivered a rambling speech about Gallipoli, with apparently no mention of Passchendaele, and quickly lost his audience.

The general took the loud applause for an encore and began

'to clear his nearly drowned vocal cords for a fresh affliction upon us', when the chairman rose and sat him down. The men were then asked to be upstanding, to sing, 'Back Home in Tennessee', at the end of which a 'fat parson' said 'very good' three times.[24]

Lynch sailed for Australia from Devonport on 30 May 1919, aboard the *Beltana*, and arrived in Melbourne on 19 July, to cheering crowds. Then he travelled by train to Sydney: 'Station after station flits by, each with its little cheering crowd . . .'

In Sydney, he passed through more cheering crowds, who were searching the soldiers' faces. Some turned away in tears, their worst fears confirmed. 'Hey, where's ya rifle and machine gun, mister?' asked a disappointed boy.[25]

Lynch caught his mother's eyes, 'waiting to give me her lonely welcome'. Grandparents, brothers, sisters, friends soon crowded in, 'mercifully allowing no time for brooding'. His father was not among them, having passed away a few weeks earlier. He then experienced the 'heart-breaking realisation that I'll never get the warm, friendly grip of welcome from my own proud father. The dear father, whom I loved as few men ever loved a father . . . May God rest his dear soul . . .'[26]

—

The German soldiers' lot was worse, far worse, than that of their British, Anzac and Canadian counterparts, and beyond our scope to recount. They came home with a sense of shame and despair, to a nation in revolt, an economy in ruins, and a country experiencing the first rumblings of a brutal political movement intent on tyrannising the world. It is therefore fitting that the finest literary evocation of Germany's Great War – Remarque's *All Quiet on the Western Front* – should also conjure a universal statement of the homecoming soldier's experience:

Now we wander around like strangers in the landscapes of our youth. We have been consumed in the fires of reality

. . . We are free of care no longer – we are terrifyingly indifferent. We might be present in that world, but would we be alive in it? We are like children who have been abandoned and we are as experienced as old men . . .

I am young, I am twenty years of age; but I know nothing of life except despair, death, fear, and the combination of completely mindless superficiality with an abyss of suffering. I see people being driven against one another, and silently, uncomprehendingly, foolishly, obediently and innocently killing one another. I see the best brains in the world inventing weapons and words to make the whole process that much more sophisticated and long lasting . . . What would our fathers do if one day we rose up and confronted them, and called them to account? . . . Our knowledge of life is limited to death. What will happen afterward? And what can possibly become of us?

—

On 11 May 1922, the man in whose name the British and Dominion forces had ostensibly fought the war visited Tyne Cot Cemetery. As King George V roamed the aisles of the largest Commonwealth war cemetery, he saw a point to the soldiers' sacrifice that eluded the generals, politicians and journalists and had little to do with laying down their lives for him.

'We can truly say,' he said, 'that the whole circuit of the earth is girdled with the graves of our dead. In the course of my pilgrimage, I have many times asked myself whether there can be more potent advocates of peace upon earth through the years to come, than this massed multitude of silent witnesses to the desolation of war.'[27]

# APPENDIX 1

## CASUALTY FIGURES

British Empire, German and French Casualties of the Great War, 1914–18 – Killed, Wounded and Missing

| Nation | Population (millions) | Combat deaths and missing in action (included in total military deaths) | Total military deaths (from all causes) | Civilian deaths (military action and crimes against humanity) | Increase in civilian deaths (malnutrition and disease excluding Influenza pandemic) | Total deaths | Deaths as % of population | Military wounded |
|---|---|---|---|---|---|---|---|---|
| Australia | 5.0 | 61,527 | 59,330 to 62,149 | | | 59,330 to 62,149 | 1.19% to 1.24% | 152,171 |
| Canada | 7.2 | 56,638 | 56,639 to 64,996 | 2,000 | | 58,639 to 66,996 | 0.81% to 0.93% | 149,732 |
| India | 315.1 | 64,449 | 64,449 to 73,905 | | | 64,449 to 73,905 | 0.02% to 0.02% | 69,214 |
| New Zealand | 1.1 | 18,166 | 16,711 to 18,060 | | | 16,711 to 18,060 | 1.52% to 1.64% | 41,317 |
| Newfoundland | 0.2 | 1,204 | 1,204 to 1,570 (included with UK) | | | 1,204 to 1,570 | 0.6% to 0.79% | 2,314 |
| South Africa | 6.0 | 7,121 | 7,121 to 9,726 | | | 7,121 to 9,726 | 0.12% to 0.16% | 12,029 |
| United Kingdom (and Colonies) | 45.4 | 744,000 | 744,000 to 887,858 | 16,829 | 107,000 | 867,829 to 1,011,687 | 1.91% to 2.23% | 1,675,000 |
| Sub-total for British Empire | 380.0 | 953,104 | 949,454 to 1,118,264 | 18,829 | 107,000 | 1,077,283 to 1,244,093 | 0.28% to 0.33% | 2,101,077 |
| France | 39.6 | 1,150,000 | 1,357,000 to 1,397,800 | 40,000 | 300,000 | 1,697,000 to 1,737,800 | 4.29% to 4.39% | 4,266,000 |
| German Empire | 64.9 | 1,800,000 | 2,037,000 | 720 | 424,000 to 763,000 | 2,198,420 to 2,800,720 | 3.39% to 4.32% | 4,215,662 |

SOURCE: 'World War I Casualties', Wikipedia, https://en.wikipedia.org/wiki/World_War_I_casualties

## British Empire and German Casualties of Third Ypres ('Passchendaele') – Killed, Wounded and Missing (31 July–10 November, 1917)

### British and Dominion Casualties:

TOTAL: 271,600

of which (approx.):

British: 212,100

*SOURCES: Various, including the Imperial War Museums, Australian War Memorial, Edmonds, Sheffield, Sheldon, Terraine and War Cabinet Papers (see Bibliography for source details)*

Australian: 38,000

*SOURCES: 'Third Battle of Ypres', Australian War Memorial, www.awm.gov.au/military-event/ E104*

Canadian: 15,600

*SOURCE: R. H. Roy and Richard Foot, 'Battle of Passchendaele', 31 May 2006 (last edited on 4 March 2015), Historica Canada, www.thecanadianencyclopedia.ca/en/article/ battle-of-passchendaele*

New Zealand: 5300

*SOURCE: 'Passchendaele: Fighting for Belgium', updated 29 May 2015, NZ History, Ministry for Culture and Heritage, www.nzhistory.net.nz/war/passchendaele-the-battle-for-belgium; and 'Third Battle of Ypres', Australian War Memorial, www.awm.gov.au/military-event/E104*

### German Casualties:

TOTAL: 217,000

| Date | Casualties | (Missing) |
|---|---|---|
| 21–31 July | 30,000 | 9,000 |
| 1–10 Aug | 16,000 | 2,000 |
| 11–21 Aug | 24,000 | 5,000 |
| 21–31 Aug | 12,500 | 1,000 |
| 1–10 Sept | 4,000 | – |

APPENDIX 1

| | | |
|---|---|---|
| 11–20 Sept | 25,000 | 6,500 |
| 21–30 Sept | 13,500 | 3,500 |
| 1–10 Oct | 35,000 | 13,000 |
| 11–20 Oct | 12,000 | 2,000 |
| 21–31 Oct | 20,500 | 3,000 |
| 1–10 Nov | 9,500 | 3,000 |
| 11–20 Nov | 4,000 | * |
| 21–30 Nov | 4,500 | 500 |
| 1–10 Dec | 4,000 | * |
| 11–31 Dec | 2,500 | 500 |
| **Total** | **217,000** | **49,000** |

*Missing totals for 11–30 November and 1–31 December are combined*

*SOURCE: Reichsarchiv, 1942, p. 96; German casualties were counted in ten-day periods. A discrepancy of 27,000 fewer casualties recorded in the Sanitätsbericht could not be explained by the Reichsarchiv historians*

# APPENDIX 2

# A COMPARISON OF MANPOWER BETWEEN THE BRITISH AND DOMINION ARMIES, 1917

## TABLE 1

A General Comparison Of The Man-Power Of The United Kingdom And Of Each Of The Four Self-Governing Dominions

| Country | Total Enlistments from all sources, United Kingdom, up to 2.12.16. Dominions up to 30.10.16. | Estimated population, United Kingdom, July, 1914, Dominions, 1911 Census. | Percentage of total population represented by enlistments. | Estimated white male population, United Kingdom, July, 1914. Dominions, 1911 Census. | Percentage of male population represented by enlistments. |
|---|---|---|---|---|---|
| England | 2,911,474 | 35,013,346 | 8.31 | 16,890,181 | 17.24 |
| Wales | 183,500 | 2,094,202 | 8.76 | 1,059,284 | 17.32 |
| Scotland | 410,350 | 4,849,500 | 8.46 | 2,351,843 | 17.45 |
| Ireland | 108,388 | 4,374,500 | 2.47 | 2,184,193 | 4.96 |
| Total | **3,613,712** | **46,331,548** | **7.80** | **22,485,501** | **16.08** |
| Canada | 328,020 | 6,500,000 | 5.1 | 3,400,000 | 9.6 |
| Australia | 265,417 | 4,750,000 | 5.6 | 2,470,000 | 10.7 |
| New Zealand | 68,819 | 1,080,000 | 6.4 | 580,000 | 11.9 |
| South Africa | 11,552 | 1,280,000 | 0.9 | 685,000 | 1.7 |

Note: The population figures of the Dominions, being mainly taken from the 1911 Census, probably err on the side of under-estimation.
In population of England, Isle of Man (50,000) is included, but Channel Island figures (100,000) are not included.

*SOURCE: British War Cabinet Papers, 23 January 1917*

# APPENDIX 3

# LORD KITCHENER'S SPECIAL INSTRUCTIONS TO (THEN) GENERAL SIR DOUGLAS HAIG, 28 DECEMBER 1915

Instructions of the Secretary of State for War (Lord Kitchener) to the General Commanding-in-Chief, British Armies in France (General Sir Douglas Haig), 28 December 1915

1. His Majesty's Government consider that the mission of the British Expeditionary Force in France, to the chief command of which you have recently been appointed, is to support and co-operate with the French and Belgian Armies against our common enemies. The special task laid upon you is to assist the French and Belgian Governments in driving the German Armies from French and Belgian territory, and eventually to restore the neutrality of Belgium, on behalf of which, as guaranteed by Treaty, Belgium appealed to the French and to ourselves at the commencement of hostilities.

2.  You will be informed from time to time of the numbers of troops which will be placed at your disposal in order to carry out your mission, and in this connection you will understand that, owing to the number of different theatres in which we are employed, it may not always be possible to give the information definitely a long time in advance.

3.  The defeat of the enemy by the combined Allied Armies must always be regarded as the primary objective for which the British troops were originally sent to France, and to achieve that end, the closest co-operation of French and British as a united Army must be the governing policy; but I wish you distinctly to understand that your command is an independent one, and that you will in no case come under the orders of any Allied General further than the necessary co-operation with our Allies above referred to.

4.  If unforeseen circumstances should arise such as to compel our Expeditionary Force to retire, such a retirement should never be contemplated as an independent move to secure the defence of the ports facing the Straits of Dover, although their security is a matter of great importance demanding that every effort should be made to prevent the lines which the Allied Forces now hold in Flanders being broken by the enemy. The safety of the Channel will be decided by the overthrow of the German Armies rather than by the occupation by our troops of some defensive position with their backs to the sea. In the event, therefore, of a retirement, the direction of the retreat should be decided, in conjunction with our Ally, with reference solely to the eventual defeat of the enemy and not to the security of the Channel.

Notwithstanding the above, our Expeditionary Force may be compelled to fall back upon the Channel ports, or the circumstances may be such that it will be strategically advantageous that, while acting in co-operation with the French Army, it should carry out such a retirement. The requisite steps required to meet this contingency should therefore receive due attention.

5.  In minor operations you should be careful that your subordinates understand that risk of serious losses should only be taken where such risk is authoritatively considered to be commensurate with the object in view.

6.  You will kindly keep up constant communication with the War Office, and you will be good enough to inform me regarding all movements of the enemy reported to you as well as those of the French Army.

7.  I am sure that you fully realise that you can rely with the utmost confidence on the whole-hearted and unswerving support of the Government, of myself, and of your compatriots.

SOURCE: *Haig*, War Diaries and Letters 1914–1918, *p. 514*

# APPENDIX 4

# HIERARCHY OF COMBAT RANKS: BRITAIN (AND DOMINIONS), GERMANY AND FRANCE

The table below provides a (simplified) hierarchy of combat ranks within the British, French and German armies, and gives an idea of the job men at each rank might perform. The reality was considerably more complex. The Dominion armies followed the British structure. The numbers of combat soldiers in the British units tended to be considerably greater than their German counterparts.

| Rank | Command | Approximate number of men under command | German equivalent | French equivalent |
|---|---|---|---|---|
| Field marshal | Army group | 2,000,000 | Generalfeldmarschall | Maréchal de France |
| General | Army | 300,000 | Generaloberst | Général d'armée |
| Lieutenant general | Corps | 60,000 | General der Infanterie/Kavallerie/Artillerie | Général de corps d'armée |
| Major general | Division | 12,000 | Generalleutnant | Général de division |
| Brigadier general | Brigade | 3,500 | Generalmajor | Général de brigade |
| Lieutenant colonel | Battalion commanding officer | 1,000 | Oberstleutnant | Lieutenant colonel |
| Major | Battalion second in command | | Major | Commandant |
| Captain | Company | 200 | Hauptmann | Capitaine |
| Lieutenant or second lieutenant | Platoon | 50 | Oberleutnant or Leutnant | Lieutenant or sous-lieutenant |
| Sergeant | Platoon second in command | | Feldwebel or Sergeant | Sergent |
| Corporal or lance corporal | Section | 12 | Unteroffizier or Gefreiter | Caporal |
| Private | None | 0 | Soldat | Soldat |

SOURCE: Jonathan Boff, 'Military Structures and Ranks', British Library, www.bl.uk/world-war-one/articles/military-structures-and-ranks

# APPENDIX 5

# SKELETON ORDER OF BATTLE, THIRD YPRES

**SECOND ARMY**

| | |
|---|---|
| G.O.C. | General Sir Herbert Plumer |
| Major-General G.S. | Major-General C. H. Harington |
| D.A. & Q.M.G. | Major-General A. A. Chichester |
| M.G.R.A. | Major-General G. McK. Franks to 7th July, then |
| | Major-General C. R. Buckle |
| C.E. | Major-General F. M. Glubb |

**FIFTH ARMY**

| | |
|---|---|
| G.O.C. | General Sir Hubert Gough |
| Major-General G.S. | Major-General N. Malcolm |
| D.A. & Q.M.G. | Major-General H. N. Sargent |
| Major-General R.A. | Major-General H. C. C. Uniacke |
| C.E. | Major-General P. G. Grant |

**1 CORPS**

| | |
|---|---|
| G.O.C. | Lieut.-General Sir Arthur Holland |
| Br.-General G.S. | Br.-General G. V. Hordern |
| D.A. & Q.M.G. | Br.-General N. G. Anderson |
| Br.-General R.A. | Br.-General M. Peake (k. 27.8.17) |
| Br.-General H.A. | Br.-General A. Ellershaw |
| C.E. | Br.-General E. H. de V. Atkinson |

**II CORPS**

| | |
|---|---|
| G.O.C. | Lieut.-General Sir Claud Jacob |
| Br.-General G.S. | Br.-General S. H. Wilson |

| D.A. & Q.M.G. | Br.-General R. S. May |
| Br.-General R.A. | Br.-General A. D. Kirby |
| Br.-General H.A. | Br.-General D. F. H. Logan |
| C.E. | Br.-General C. Godby |

## V CORPS

| G.O.C. | Lieut.-General Sir Edward Fanshawe |
| Br.-General G.S. | Br.-General G. F. Boyd |
| D.A. & Q.M.G. | Br.-General H. M. de F. Montgomery |
| Br.-General R.A. | Br.-General R. P. Benson |
| Br.-General H.A. | Br.-General A. M. Tyler |
| C.E. | Br.-General A. J. Craven |

## IX CORPS

| G.O.C. | Lieut.-General Sir Alexander Gordon |
| Br.-General G.S. | Br.-General J. S. J. Percy |
| D.A. & Q.M.G. | Br.-General B. H. H. Cooke |
| Br.-General R.A. | Br.-General G. Humphreys |
| Br.-General H.A. | Br.-General G. B. Mackenzie |
| C.E. | Br.-General P. Scholfield |

## X CORPS

| G.O.C. | Lieut.-General Sir Thomas Morland |
| Br.-General G.S. | Br.-General A. R. Cameron |
| D.A. & Q.M.G. | Br.-General W. K. Legge |
| Br.-General R.A. | Br.-General H. L. Reed, V.C. to 11th October, then Br.-General G. Gillson |
| Br.-General H.A. | Br.-General H. O. Vincent |
| C.E. | Br.-General J. A. S. Tulloch |

## XIII CORPS

| G.O.C. | Lieut.-General Sir William McCracken |
| Br.-General G.S. | Br.-General I. Stewart |
| D.A. & Q.M.G. | Br.-General S. W. Robinson |
| Br.-General R.A. | Br.-General R. A. C. Wellesley |
| Br.-General H.A. | Br.-General L. W. P. East (k. 6.9.17) |
| C.E. | Br.-General E. P. Brooker |

## XIV CORPS

| G.O.C. | Lieut.-General Earl of Cavan |

| Br.-General G.S. | Br.-General Hon. J. F. Gathorne-Hardy |
| D.A. & Q.M.G. | Br.-General H. L. Alexander |
| Br.-General R.A. | Br.-General A. E. Wardrop |
| Br.-General H.A. | Br.-General F. G. Maunsell |
| C.E. | Br.-General C. S. Wilson |

## XV CORPS

| G.O.C. | Lieut.-General Sir John Du Cane |
| Br.-General G.S. | Br.-General H. H. S. Knox |
| D.A. & Q.M.G. | Br.-General G. R. Frith |
| Br.-General R.A. | Br.-General B. R. Kirwan |
| Br.-General H.A. | Br.-General C. W. Collingwood |
| C.E. | Br.-General C. W. Singer |

## XVIII CORP

| G.O.C. | Lieut.-General Sir Ivor Maxse |
| Br.-General G.S. | Br.-General S. E. Hollond |
| D.A. & Q.M.G. | Br.-General P. M. Davies to 14th Aug., then |
| | Br.-General B. Atkinson (acting) to 8th Nov. |
| Br.-General R.A. | Br.-General D. J. M. Fasson |
| Br.-General H.A. | Br.-General H. E. J. Brake |
| C.E. | Br.-General H. G. Joly de Lotbinière |

## XIX CORPS

| G.O.C. | Lieut.-General H. E. Watts |
| Br.-General G.S. | Br.-General F. Lyon to 25th Sept., then |
| | Br.-General C. N. Macmullen |
| D.A. & Q.M.G. | Br.-General A. J. G. Moir |
| Br.-General R.A. | Br.-General W. B. R. Sandys |
| Br.-General H.A. | Br.-General C. G. Pritchard |
| C.E. | Br.-General A. G. Bremner |

## CANADIAN CORPS

| G.O.C. | Lieut.-General Sir Arthur Currie |
| Br.-General G.S. | Br.-General P. P. de B. Radcliffe |
| D.A. & Q.M.G. | Br.-General G. J. Farmar |
| Br.-General R.A. | Br.-General E. W. B. Morrison |
| Br.-General H.A. | Br.-General R. H. Massie |
| C.E. | Br.-General W. B. Lindsay |

## I ANZAC CORPS

| | |
|---|---|
| G.O.C. | Lieut.-General Sir William Birdwood |
| Br.-General G.S. | Br.-General C. B. B. White |
| D.A. & Q.M.G. | Br.-General R. A. Carruthers |
| Br.-General R.A. | Br.-General W. J. Napier to 14th Oct., then |
| | Br.-General W. A. Coxen |
| Br.-General H.A. | Br.-General L. D. Fraser |
| C.E. | Br.-General A. C. Joly de Lotbinière |

## II ANZAC CORPS

| | |
|---|---|
| G.O.C. | Lieut.-General Sir Alexander Godley |
| Br.-General G.S. | Br.-General C. W. Gwynn |
| D.A. & Q.M.G. | Br.-General A. E. Delavoye |
| Br.-General R.A. | Br.-General E. W. M. Powell |
| Br.-General H.A. | Br.-General A. S. Jenour |
| C.E. | Br.-General A. E. Panet |

Guards Division (Major-General G. P. T. Feilding):
1 Gds., 2Gds., 3Gds. Brigades

1st Division (Major-General E. P. Strickland):
1, 2, 3 Brigades

3rd Division (Major-General C. J. Deverell):
8, 9, 76 Brigades

4th Division (Major-General T. G. Matheson):
10, 11, 12 Brigades

5th Division (Major-General R. B. Stephens):
13, 15, 95 Brigades

7th Division (Major-General T. H. Shoubridge):
20, 22, 91 Brigades

8th Division (Major-General W. C. G. Heneker):
23, 24, 25 Brigades

9th (Scottish) Division (Major-General H. T. Lukin):

26, 27, South African Brigades

11th (Northern) Division (Major-General H. R. Davies):
32, 33, 34 Brigades

14th (Light) Division (Major-General V. A. Couper):
41, 42, 43 Brigades

15th (Scottish) Division (Major-General H. F. Thuillier):
44, 45, 46 Brigades

16th (Irish) Division (Major-General W. B. Hickie):
47, 48, 49 Brigades

17th (Northern) Division (Major-General P. R. Robertson):
50, 51, 52 Brigades

18th (Eastern) Division (Major-General R. P. Lee):
53, 54, 55 Brigades

19th (Western) Division (Major-General C. D. Shute acting to 19th June,
then Major-General G. T. M. Bridges, wounded 20th September; Br.-General
W. P. Monkhouse acting to 22nd September, then Major-General G. D.
Jeffreys):
56, 57, 58 Brigades

20th (Light) Division (Major-General W. Douglas Smith):
59, 60, 61 Brigades

21st Division (Major-General D. G. M. Campbell):
62, 64, 110 Brigades

23rd Division (Major-General J. M. Babington):
68, 69, 70 Brigades

24th Division (Major-General L. J. Bols):
17, 72, 73 Brigades

25th Division (Major-General E. G. T. Bainbridge):
7, 74, 75 Brigades

29th Division (Major-General Sir B. de Lisle):
86, 87, 88 Brigades

30th Division (Major-General W. de L. Williams):
21, 89, 90 Brigades

33rd Division (Major-General P. R. Wood):
19, 98, 100 Brigades

36th (Ulster) Division (Major-General O. S. W. Nugent):
107, 108, 109 Brigades

37th Division (Major-General H. Bruce Williams):
63, 111, 112 Brigades

38th (Welsh) Division (Major-General C. G. Blackader):
113, 114, 115 Brigades

39th Division (Major-General G. J. Cuthbert to 20th August, then
Major-General E. Feetham):
116, 117, 118 Brigades

41st Division (Major-General S. T. B. Lawford):
122, 123, 124 Brigades

47th (2nd London) Division (Major-General Sir George Gorringe):
140, 141, 142 Brigades

48th (1st South Midland) Division (Major-General R. Fanshawe):
143, 144, 145 Brigades

49th (1st West Riding) Division (Major-General E. M. Perceval):
146, 147, 148 Brigades

50th (Northumbrian) Division (Major-General P. S. Wilkinson):
149, 150, 151 Brigades

51st (Highland) Division (Major-General G. M. Harper):
152, 153, 154 Brigades

55th (1st West Lancashire) Division (Major-General H. S. Jeudwine):
164, 165, 166 Brigades

56th (1st London) Division (Major-General F. A. Dudgeon):
167, 168, 169 Brigades

57th (2nd West Lancashire) Division (Major-General R. W. R. Barnes):
170, 171, 172 Brigades

58th (2/1st London) Division (Major-General H. D. Fanshawe to 6th
October, then Major-General A. B. E. Cator):
173, 174, 175 Brigades

59th (2nd North Midland) Division (Major-General C. F. Romer):
176, 177, 178 Brigades

61st (2nd South Midland) Division (Major-General C. J. Mackenzie):
182, 183, 184 Brigades

63rd (Royal Naval) Division (Major-General C. E. Lawrie):
188, 189, 190 Brigades

66th (2nd East Lancashire) Division (Major-General Hon. H. A. Lawrence):
197, 198, 199 Brigades

1st Canadian Division (Major-General A. C. Macdonell):
1 Cdn., 2 Cdn., 3 Cdn. Brigades

2nd Canadian Division (Major-General H. E. Burstall):
4 Cdn., 5 Cdn., 6 Cdn. Brigades

3rd Canadian Division (Major-General L. J. Lipsett):
7 Cdn., 8 Cdn., 9 Cdn. Brigades

4th Canadian Division (Major-General D. Watson):
10 Cdn., 11 Cdn., 12 Cdn. Brigades

1st Australian Division (Major-General H. B. Walker):
1 Aust., 2 Aust., 3 Aust. Brigades

2nd Australian Division (Major-General N. M. Smyth):
5 Aust., 6 Aust., 7 Aust. Brigades

3rd Australian Division (Major-General Sir John Monash):
9 Aust., 10 Aust., 11 Aust. Brigades

4th Australian Division (Major-General W. Holmes, killed 2nd July;
Br.-General C. Rosenthal acting to 16th July, then Major-General E. G.
Sinclair-Maclagan):
4 Aust., 12 Aust., 13 Aust. Brigades

5th Australian Division (Major-General J. Talbot Hobbs):
8 Aust., 14 Aust., 15 Aust. Brigades

New Zealand Division (Major-General Sir Arthur Russell):
1 N.Z., 2 N.Z., 3 N.Z. (Rifle), 4 N.Z. Brigades

## NOTES

### 8TH DIVISION:

25th Brigade. Br.-General C. Coffin was awarded the V.C. on the 31st July,
1917.

### 9TH DIVISION:

27th Brigade. Br.-General F. A. Maxwell, V.C., was killed in action on the
21st September, 1917. Lieut.-Colonel H. D. N. Maclean acting till Br.-
General W. D. Croft took over on the 23rd.

### 21ST DIVISION:

62nd Brigade. Br.-General C. G. Rawlings was killed in action on the
28th October, 1917; Colonel G. M. Sharpe acting till 1st November, when
Br.-General G. H. Gater assumed command.

### 29TH DIVISION:

86th Brigade. Br.-General R. G. Jelf was invalided on the 16th August, 1917.
Lieut.-Colonel H. Nelson acting till the 24th August, when Br.-General G. R.
H. Cheape assumed command.

## 41ST DIVISION:
123rd Brigade. Br.-General C. W. E. Gordon was killed in action on the 23rd July, 1917. Br.-General W. F. Clemson (124th Brigade) acting until the arrival of Br.-General E. Pearce Serocold on 3rd August.

## 49TH DIVISION:
146th Brigade. Br.-General M. D. Goring-Jones left on the 18th October. Br.-General G. A. P. Rennie assumed command.
148th Brigade. Br.-General R. L. Adlercron left on the 24th October; Br.-General L. F. Green-Wilkinson assumed command.

## 58TH DIVISION:
173rd Brigade. Br.-General B. C. Freyberg, V.C., was wounded on the 19th September, 1917. Lieut.-Colonel W. R. H. Dann acting till 3rd October, when Br.-General R. B. Worgan assumed command.

## NEW ZEALAND DIVISION:
1st Brigade. Br.-General E. H. J. Brown was killed in action on the 8th June, 1917, Br.-General C. W. Melvill taking over on the same day.

SOURCE: *Brigadier General James E. Edmonds,* Official History of The Great War: Military Operations France & Belgium 1917, *Vol. 2, pp. 388–95*

# APPENDIX 6

# HAIG'S CASE FOR THE FLANDERS OFFENSIVE, SUBMITTED TO THE WAR CABINET 17 JUNE 1917

O.A.D. 502

To assist the War Cabinet in considering the various possible courses of action open this summer, I submit, in continuation of my O.A.D. No. 478, of the 12th instant, the following, fuller, statement of my views as to the strategical advantages which would be gained by successful operations to secure the Belgian coast.

Even a partial success in the operations for which I am preparing will give very useful results, apart from the effect on the German army and nation of another defeat.

A very limited advance will enable our guns to make OSTEND useless to the German navy, and will, at the same time, render DUNKIRK – one of our most important ports – immune from long-range hostile gunfire.

The enemy's communications with the coast are not numerous, and run through such a narrow space between our lines and the Dutch frontier that an advance sufficient to bring the ROULERS–THOUROUT railway within effective range of our guns would restrict his railway communications with the coast to those passing through GHENT and BRUGES.

A short further advance, bringing us within effective heavy-gun range of BRUGES, would most probably induce the evacuation of ZEEBRUGGE and the whole coastline.

The consequences of extending our front to the Dutch frontier would be so considerable that they might prove decisive. Following on the successes we have already gained such a failure to stop our advance would leave little room for German hope of success-fully opposing our further advance, even if temporary exhaustion imposed a halt on us for a time.

Realizing this, the enemy would find himself faced by a most serious situation. His main lines of retreat run through bottle-necks north and south of the ARDENNES, and any reasonable possibility of our being able to continue the advance on GHENT and BRUSSELS would probably suffice to determine the enemy to undertake a retreat, if not to accept our terms at once, in view of the dangers and difficulties of retreat under such conditions.

In addition, as neutrals would recognize the imminence of a German collapse, it is conceivable that the attitude of Holland towards us might be such as to add seriously to the German anxieties.

At present it is not in our power to give Holland any direct help if Germany committed a breach of neutrality against her. With the Germans driven from the Belgian coast, and our flank resting on the Dutch frontier, however, the situation would be very different; and if Holland then decided to join the allies a way would be opened to turn ANTWERP and the German lines through Belgium com-pletely, and to sever the German Lines of Communication through LIEGE.

Germany would then have to choose between accepting terms, or undertaking a retreat likely to prove disastrous, or attempting to forestall the danger by violating Dutch territory. If she had failed to stop our advance, it is reasonable to assume that she would not have sufficient forces left at her disposal to justify the last mentioned course.

In short, it is clear that very great possibilities will be opened up by the operations now in preparation. These operations have long been recognised as offering the possibilities stated whenever we had sufficient strength to carry them out. If it be questioned whether that time has yet come my considered opinion, as stated in my paper of the 12th instant, is that by concentration of our resources now the operation has sufficient prospects of success this year not only to justify our undertaking it, but – in view of the general situation – to make it most advisable to do so. Even if the full measure of success is not gained I see no reason to doubt that the results attained will at least be sufficient to have a great effect on Germany and her allies, who will realize that, although a respite has been gained, it is likely to be a short one.

Comparing this operation with anything that we might do in other theatres its advantages are overwhelming.

It directly and seriously threatens our main enemy, on whom the whole Coalition against us depends.

It is within the easiest possible reach of our base by sea and rail and can be developed infinitely more rapidly, and maintained infinitely more easily, than any other operation open to us.

It admits of the closest possible combination of our naval and military strength. It covers all the points which we dare not uncover, and therefore admits of the utmost concentration of force; whereas, for the same reason, any force employed in any other theatre of war can never be more than a detachment, with all the disadvantages of detachments.

Even a short advance along the Belgian coast, in addition to considerable moral results, would assist our navy appreciably in securing our lines of communication; while the value of that coast to the enemy as a base for air raids against England would be reduced in proportion to the extent of our advance.

In no part of any theatre of war would so limited an advance promise such far-reaching results on Germany, and through Germany, on her allies and on neutrals.

In short, after the fullest consideration, it is my earnest conviction that the arguments in favour of the course I propose in comparison with the possibilities open in any other theatre of war are incontrovertible. In other theatres we can only employ detachments, seeking to attain results by indirect methods, and under most difficult conditions of maintenance. Time and space considerations would be so unfavourable to us that if any indirect threat appeared dangerous to Germany it would be well within her power to take timely steps to counteract it either by direct attack on us at a more vital point or by moving troops to meet our indirect threat.

Lastly, while an increase in our forces in the Western theatre would have an encouraging effect on France, where encouragement is of very high importance now, any reduction of our forces here at this juncture might have most serious consequences.

I cannot urge too strongly the importance of a whole-hearted concentration of our forces for the purpose in view.

Amid the uncertainties of war one thing is certain, viz, that it is only by whole-hearted concentration at the right time and place that victory ever has been or ever will be won.

In my opinion the time and place to choose are now beyond dispute. We have gone a long way already towards success. Victory may be nearer than is generally realized if we act correctly now. But we may fall seriously short of it if at this juncture we fail to follow correct principles.

SOURCE: *Haig Papers, National Library of Scotland, Edinburgh (contained in letter, Haig to Robertson, 17 June 1917)*

# APPENDIX 7

# SIEGFRIED SASSOON'S LETTER OF PROTEST AGAINST THE WAR AND EXTRACT FROM COMMONS DEBATE

Lt. Siegfried Sassoon.
3rd Batt: Royal Welsh Fusiliers.
July, 1917.

I am making this statement as an act of wilful defiance of military authority because I believe that the war is being deliberately prolonged by those who have the power to end it. I am a soldier, convinced that I am acting on behalf of soldiers. I believe that the war upon which I entered as a war of defence and liberation has now become a war of agression [*sic*] and conquest. I believe that the purposes for which I and my fellow soldiers entered upon this war should have been so clearly stated as to have made it impossible to change them and that had this been done the objects which actuated us would now be attainable by negotiation.

I have seen and endured the sufferings of the troops and I can no longer be a party to prolonging these sufferings for ends which I believe to be evil and unjust. I am not protesting against the conduct of the war, but against the political errors and insincerities for which the fighting men are being sacrificed.

On behalf of those who are suffering now, I make this protest against the deception which is being practised upon them; also I believe it may help to destroy the callous complacency with which the majority of those at home regard the continuance of agonies which they do not share and which they have not enough imagination to realise.

SOURCE: 'Finished with the War: A Soldier's Declaration', Letters of Note, www.lettersofnote.com/2011/04/finished-with-war-soldiers-declaration.html

## Commons Debate, 30 July 1917

In the following Commons debate, Mr Hastings Lees-Smith spoke on the subject of Sassoon's protest:

Mr. LEES-SMITH: I wish to raise the case of an individual officer which has some connection with the subject which the hon. Member for Haggerston raised. It is the case of Second-Lieutenant Sassoon, of the 3rd Battalion Royal Welsh Fusiliers. This young officer, I think, appears to have one of the finest and most gallant records of service in the Army. He enlisted as a private – without waiting for the War to break out – on 3rd August, 1914, and I imagine would be one of the first 1,000 men to enlist. He has been wounded, and has been awarded the Military Cross for conspicuous gallantry. He has received formal recognition from the General Commanding for distinguished service in the field. About three weeks ago this young officer came to see me, and told me he had written this letter to his commanding officer. The Under-Secretary will see that this letter raises the question of policy which has to be considered in the light of the treatment which is meted out to those soldiers who break up meetings. It raises a question of policy, and why there should be differentiation of treatment between soldiers who hold one set of opinions and those who hold another. The writer says: [QUOTES SASSOON'S LETTER TO THE HOUSE]

This young officer asked me if I would follow up his case and, if necessary, bring it to the notice of the House. What he anticipated has occurred. After some delay he was forced to appear before a medical board, and the board, having heard the opinions he had expressed in the letter, informed him that he must be suffering from the effects of a passing nervous shock due to his terrible experiences at the front. He was sent to a hospital for officers suffering from shell shock and other minor ailments. I read that letter, because I think, however profoundly hon. Members may disagree from it, that it contains no indication whatever of having been written by a man suffering from any kind of nervous shock. This young officer is known to Members of this House. I myself had a long interview with him only a few weeks ago, and he certainly impressed me as a man of most unusual mental power and most extraordinary determination of character. The fact is, that the decision of the medical board is not based upon health, but based upon very easily understood reasons of policy.

SOURCE: *The text of the debate over the Sassoon letter appears to be missing from the official record in Hansard. See: http://1914-1918.invisionzone.com/forums/index.php?/topic/202759-sassoons-statement-hansard/. Yet, it assuredly occurred, as numerous sources attest. See David Gray, 'Protest',* Siegfried Sassoon: His Life and Illustrated Bibliography, *http://siegfried-sassoon.firstworld-warrelics.co.uk/html/protest.html*

# APPENDIX 8

# STATEMENT OF BRITISH AND GERMAN WASTAGE IN FLANDERS

SECRET

No. O.A. 216.
General Head Quarters,
British Armies in France.
16th October, 1917.

Chief of the Imperial General Staff.

As requested by your cipher telegram No. 43274, dated 15th instant, a statement is attached showing the comparative British and German wastage by divisions in the Flanders battle.

(Sd.) D. Haig.
Field-Marshal.
Commanding-in-Chief,
British Armies in France.

SECRET

## Comparative Statement of British and German Wastage by Divisions in the Flanders Battle.

|   |   | British | German |
|---|---|---|---|
| **A.** | Divisions engaged for the first time | 43 | 57 |
| **B.** | Divisions engaged for second or third time and included in A | 23 | 15 |
| **C.** | Divisions included in A and B which have been sent away exhausted | 23 | 40 |
| **D.** | Divisions included in A and B which are likely to be sent away exhausted very shortly | 9 | 5 |

*NOTE. The above figures do not include German divisions engaged in front of First French Army.*

(Intd.)  D.H.

16th October, 1917

*SOURCE: British War Cabinet Papers, CAB24/29/19*

# APPENDIX 9

# DEBATE ON ALLIED CASUALTIES AND DECISION NOT TO PUBLISH TOTALS

## War Cabinet Meeting, 17 October 1917

Casualties.

The Director of Military Operations, in reply to an enquiry, referred to the estimate of the comparative British and German losses since the commencement of the recent offensive, up to the 5th October, which had been circulated to the War Cabinet. The figures were:-
British, 148,470; German, 255,000
The Secretary of State for War stated that the British losses since the 1st October were about 41,000. Attention was called to a telegram, No. 2993, from Stockholm, dated the 13th October, 1917, containing a newspaper announcement, on German authority, to the effect that during August the average officer casualties as published in the British casualty lists were 511 a day, the highest total recorded during the War.

Publication of
Casualties.

Attention was called to the exaggerated reports circulated from time to time in this country in regard to our casualties. It was suggested that these rumours, which were often made in the most definite manner, would never be checked till publicity was given to the true facts.

Attention was also drawn to the false rumours that had been circulated to the effect that the bulk of the fighting was being done by the Colonials – rumours which also would be effectively disposed of by the publication of Casualty Lists. Mention was made of the statement recently communicated to a French newspaper by the Director of Military Operations, in denial of certain false rumours in this respect.

The War Cabinet decided that –

It was not in the public interest to publish the whole of the casualties, but that opportunity should be taken from time to time to dispose of the various rumours in circulation by an occasional statement by the Prime Minister.

Note: the British Cabinet were misinformed. British casualties were about 230,000 at this stage of the battle, and the German casualties about 180,000.

SOURCE: *War Cabinet Papers, 17 October 1917*

# ACKNOWLEDGEMENTS

I'd like to thank a few people without whose commitment to this book I could not have written it. They are: my agent, Jane Burridge; my publishers, Alison Urquhart (Australia) and Bill Scott-Kerr (Britain); and my editor, Kevin O'Brien. Three researchers were helpful in gathering the reins of an epic that spans several continents, and I'm grateful for their work: Glenda Lynch in Australia, Simon Fowler in Britain and Elena Vogt in Germany. Veterans' families similarly gave their time and interest at short notice, and I'm particularly thankful to Kristie Harrison and Dorothy Hind. War memorials and museums were patient and attentive to my requests, especially the staff at the Imperial War Museum in London, the Australian War Memorial in Canberra, and the Memorial Museum Passchendaele 1917 in Zonnebeke, Flanders. Finally, I'd like to thank Shane Munro and Adam Courtenay for their interest and suggested source material; and Nathalie Hoornaert and Claus Arschoot, who run B&B Noja, the best in Ypres, for their wonderful hospitality.

And, of course, my dear family, who are always there in spirit. Thank you.

# NOTES AND REFERENCES*

## Introduction

1. 'In Flanders Fields' was written by John McCrae in 1915 but has come to represent all casualties of that terrible battlefield.
2. See Fussell, *The Great War and Modern Memory*; Winter, *Sites of Memory, Sites of Mourning: The Great War in European Cultural History*; Eksteins, *Rites of Spring: The Great War and the Birth of the Modern Age*.

## Chapter 1: Servants of Attrition

1. Wolff, p. 38.
2. Collins, ebook, loc. 1137.
3. Quoted in Holmes, p. 37.
4. Harris, pp. 153–77.
5. Simkins, 'Voluntary Recruiting in Britain, 1914–1915', British Library, http://www.bl.uk/world-war-one/articles/voluntary-recruiting.
6. Herwig, p. 256.
7. Ibid.
8. Prost, p. 65.
9. For the range of casualty estimates at Verdun, see Terraine, *The Smoke and the Fire*, p. 65; Dupuy and Dupuy, p.1052, Clayton, p. 110; Doughty, p. 309; Philpott, p. 226; Churchill, p. 1004; Foley, p. 259.
10. Bartholomees, 'The Issue of Attrition', www.strategicstudiesinstitute.army.mil. p. 10.
11. For the range of estimates of casualties at the Somme see: https://en.wikipedia.org/wiki/Battle_of_the_Somme.

* Ebook sources refer to the location number ('loc.') on a standard Kindle or Kindle for Mac.

12. Bartholomees, 'The Issue of Attrition', www.strategicstudiesinstitute.army.mil. p. 15.

13. See Clausewitz, Book Six – Defense, *On War*, pp. 357–90.

14. See https://en.wikipedia.org/wiki/Battle_of_the_Somme.

15. Collins, ebook, loc. 384.

16. Herbert, *His Life and Times*, p. 36.

17. Herbert, *The Secret Battle*, p. 2.

18. Aldington, p. 204.

19. Hind, memoir, p. 29.

20. Ibid., p. 29.

21. Ibid., p. 30.

22. Ibid., p. 30.

23. Ibid., p. 30.

24. Wolff, p. 28.

25. Herbert, *The Secret Battle*, p. 43.

26. Wolff, p. 29.

27. Interview with Kristie Harrison, family relative, 24 April 2015.

28. William Keith Seabrook, private papers.

29. Ibid.

30. Kristie Harrison, email, April 2008.

31. Seabrook family, private papers, postcard, 13 January 1917.

32. Ibid., 9 January 1917.

33. Ibid.

34. Allhusen, private papers, diary.

35. Ibid.

36. Ibid.

37. Ibid.

38. Ibid.

39. Skirth, private papers, memoir.

40. Ibid.

41. Ibid.

42. Ibid.

43. Ibid.

44. Ibid.

45. Ibid.

46. Allfree, private papers, p. 9.

47. Ibid., p. 10.

48. Ibid.

49. Ibid., p. 53.

50. Campbell, private papers, diary.

51. Ibid.
52. Ibid.
53. Ibid.
54. Ibid.
55. Aldington, p. 182.

## Chapter 2: The Human Factor

1. Lloyd George, p. 49.
2. Piketty, Technical Appendix, http://piketty.pse.ens.fr/en/capital21c2.
3. Herwig, p. 299.
4. McKernan, p. 181.
5. Vincent, pp. 21–2.
6. 'Public Opinion of Lord Lansdowne's Letter', cited in JSTOR paper, 'British Strategy and War Aims', p. 246.
7. Ibid., p. 246.
8. War Cabinet Papers, 12 December 1916.
9. See Grigg, *Lloyd George: War Leader, 1916–18*; Hattersley, *David Lloyd George: The Great Outsider*; Rowland, *David Lloyd George: A Biography*.
10. Hattersley, p. 53.
11. Quoted in Hattersley, p. 13.
12. JSTOR paper, 'Lloyd George's Premiership: A Study in Prime Ministerial Government', p. 130.
13. Ibid.
14. Quoted in Hattersley, p. 221.
15. Quoted in Rowland, p. 286.
16. Quoted in Hattersley, p. 357.
17. Rowland, p. 340.
18. Hattersley, p. 377.
19. Dugdale, p. 125.
20. Asquith, p. 158.
21. JSTOR paper, 'Lloyd George's Premiership: A Study in Prime Ministerial Government', p. 132.
22. Cassar, p. 26–7.
23. Wolff, p. 65.
24. JSTOR paper, 'Lloyd George's Premiership: A Study in Prime Ministerial Government', p. 133.
25. War Cabinet Papers, 9 December 1916.
26. Ibid., 19 January 1917.
27. Ibid., 21 December 1916.
28. Ibid., 22 January 1917.

29. Ibid., 23 January 1917.
30. Ibid.
31. Jablonsky, p. 77.
32. Haig, p. 22.
33. Sheffield, *The Chief*, pp. 19 and 37.
34. Quoted in ibid., p. 25.
35. Corrigan, p. 8.
36. Sheffield, *The Chief*, p. 23.
37. Ibid., p. 32.
38. Haig, p. 149.
39. Secrett, p. 114.
40. Haig, p. 14.
41. Ibid., p. 27.
42. Haig, pp. 161–2.
43. See Harris, *Douglas Haig and the First World War*.
44. Quoted in Haig, p. 516 (see Appendix 3).
45. Corrigan, p. 45.
46. Haig, p. 106.
47. Quoted in Sheffield, *The Chief*, p. 132.
48. Haig, p. 187.
49. Sheffield, *The Chief*, p. 155.
50. Quoted in ibid., p. 132.
51. Haig, p. 195.
52. Ibid., p. 197.
53. Ibid.
54. Ibid., p. 13.
55. Ibid., p. 231.
56. Quoted in Holmes, *The Western Front*, p. 238.

## Chapter 3: Death by Water

1. Paxman, p. 201.
2. JSTOR paper, 'Wellington House and British Propaganda During the First World War'.
3. War Cabinet Papers, 26 October 1916.
4. Edmonds, pp. 2–5.
5. Lloyd George, p. 45.
6. Vincent, p. 38.
7. Ibid., pp. 21–2.
8. Ibid.
9. Quoted in Vincent, p. 45.

10. Wilson, ebook, loc. 10802.
11. Lloyd George, p. 44.
12. Herwig, p. 309.
13. 'Official German Documents Relating to the World War', II, pp. 1154–63.
14. Ibid.
15. Ibid.
16. Ludendorff, p. 3.
17. Herwig, p. 311.
18. 'Official German Documents Relating to the World War', II, pp. 1320–1.
19. Ibid.
20. War Cabinet Papers, 30 December 1916.
21. War Cabinet Papers, 8 March 1917.
22. Herwig, p. 301.
23. 'Official German Documents Relating to the World War', II, pp. 1320–1.
24. Herwig, p. 312.
25. German Chancellor Theobald von Bethmann-Hollweg on the prospect of war with the U.S., April 1917, 'Source Records of the Great War', Vol. V.
26. War Cabinet Papers, 21 December 1916
27. Ibid.
28. War Cabinet Papers, 23 December 1916.
29. War Cabinet Papers, 21 December 1916.
30. Lloyd George, p. 76.
31. War Cabinet Papers, 15 March 1917.
32. War Cabinet Papers, 20 December 1916.
33. Ibid.
34. War Cabinet Papers, 13 February 1917.
35. War Cabinet Papers, 15 March 1917.
36. Herwig, p. 313.
37. Gray, p. 180.
38. Wilson, ebook, loc. 10829.
39. War Cabinet Papers, 11 April 1917.
40. War Cabinet Papers, 13 April 1917.
41. War Cabinet Papers, 30 May 1917.
42. Quoted in Wiest, pp. 104, 107.
43. War Cabinet Papers, 25 May 1917.
44. Herwig, p. 313. Wilson gives slightly different figures.
45. War Cabinet Papers, 8 February 1917.
46. 'How Was Information Shared?', BBC Schools, World War One, www.bbc.co.uk/schools/0/ww1/25332968.
47. 'Germany's Policy of Unrestricted Submarine Warfare, 31 January 1917', First

World War.com, www.firstworldwar.com/source/uboat_bernstorff.htm.

48. 'The Zimmerman Note', WWI: The World War One Document Archive, wwi. lib.byu.edu/index.php/1917_Documents.

49. War Cabinet Papers, 2 March 1917.

50. Ibid.

51. Ibid.

52. War Cabinet Papers, 30 May 1917.

53. War Cabinet Papers, 11 May 1917.

54. War Cabinet Papers, 31 May 1917.

55. JSTOR paper, 'British Strategy and War Aims', p. 246.

56. Grigg, pp. 49, 51, 53.

57. War Cabinet Papers, 8 March 1917.

58. 'Wilson's War Message to Congress', 2 April 1917, WWI: The World War One Document Archive, wwi.lib.byu.edu/index.php/Official_Papers.

59. War Cabinet Papers, 10 April 1917.

60. War Cabinet Papers, 11 April 1917.

## Chapter 4: Knights and Pawns

1. Quoted in Mead, p. 277.

2. Terraine, *The Road to Passchendaele*, p. 17.

3. Edmonds, p. 8.

4. Terraine, *The Road to Passchendaele*, p. 23.

5. Ibid., pp. 28–9.

6. Spears, p. 37.

7. War Cabinet Papers, 10 January 1917.

8. Terraine, *The Road to Passchendaele*, p. 23.

9. Ibid., p. 24.

10. Haig, p. 261.

11. Quoted in Terraine, *The Road to Passchendaele*, p. 25.

12. Terraine, *The Road to Passchendaele*, pp. 25–6.

13. Spears, p. 40.

14. Ibid., p. 130.

15. Ibid., pp. 134–52.

16. War Cabinet Papers, 24 February 1917.

17. Terraine, *The Educated Soldier*, p. 267.

18. Haig, p. 272 (footnote).

19. Quoted in Spears, p. 139.

20. Haig, p. 270.

21. Ibid., p. 271.

22. Quoted in Spears, pp. 141–2.

23. War Cabinet Papers, 22 May 1917.

24. Spears, p. 143.

25. Ibid., p. 141.

26. Ibid., p. 143.

27. Haig, p. 271.

28. Mead, p. 280.

29. Haig, p. 272.

30. Quoted in Spears, p. 150.

31. Quoted in Spears, p. 155.

32. Haig, p. 273.

33. Spears, p. 158.

34. War Cabinet Papers, 9 March 1917.

35. Quoted in Wolff, p. 75.

36. Haig, p. 269.

37. Quoted in Wolff, p. 75.

38. Ibid.

39. War Cabinet Papers, 28 February 1917.

40. War Cabinet Papers, 14 March 1917.

41. Quoted in Wolff, p. 76.

42. War Cabinet Papers, 12 March 1917.

43. War Cabinet Papers, 9 March 1917.

44. Ibid.

45. War Cabinet Papers, 19 March 1917.

46. Ibid.

47. Ibid.

48. Wolff, p. 82.

49. Quoted in Terraine, *The Road to Passchendaele*, p. 24.

50. Quoted in Wolff, p. 83.

51. War Cabinet Papers, 10 April 1917.

52. Spears, p. 247.

53. Gibbs, pp. 26–7.

54. JSTOR paper, 'Environments of War', p. 158.

55. Ibid.

56. Ludendorff, ebook, locs. 151, 163.

57. Ibid., loc. 151.

58. Quoted in Wolff, p. 86.

59. Prior and Wilson, ebook, loc. 758.

60. War Cabinet Papers, 10 April 1917.

61. Simkins, ebook, loc. 393.

62. Sheffield, ebook, loc. 3599.

63. Ibid., loc. 3595.
64. Spears, p. 605.
65. Bean, Chapter IX, p. 351.
66. Wolff, p. 90.
67. Herwig, p. 322.
68. Spears, p. 507.
69. Doughty, pp. 354–5. Some historians claim that Nivelle's offensive was a 'limited success', but elsewhere argue that the capture of a few miles of terrain was of little military value in a war of attrition.
70. War Cabinet Papers, 25 April 1917.
71. Herwig, p. 320.
72. Ibid.
73. War Cabinet Papers, 23 April 1917.
74. Stevenson, p. 157.
75. Quoted in Hattersley, p. 444.

## Chapter 5: The Bloody Salient

1. Edmonds, p. 23; see also Woodward, p. 73.
2. See Ham, *1914*, Part 4, chapter 41.
3. Ibid.
4. Chapman, p. 187.
5. See Ham, *1914*, Part 4, chapter 41.
6. Haig, p. 73.
7. Conan Doyle, https://archive.org/details/ahistorygreatwa00doylgoog.
8. Monash, ebook, Ch. 10.
9. Ibid.
10. *Simplicissimus*, 19 June 1917.
11. McNab, p. 197.
12. *Wipers Times*, p. 215.
13. *Wipers Times*, p. 223.
14. Gordon, p. 42.
15. http://www.bl.uk/world-war-one/articles/military-structures-and-ranks.
16. Simkins, p. 14.
17. Officers' Training Manual, p. 124.
18. Campbell's bloodthirsty lessons seem to appeal to some military specialists. See, for example, Paddy Griffith, *Battle Tactics of the Western Front: The British Army's Art of Attack, 1916–18*, pp. 71–2, and Rob Engen, 'Steel Against Fire: The Bayonet in the First World War', *Journal of Military and Strategic Studies*, Spring 2006, Vol. 8, Issue 3.
19. Engen, 'Steel Against Fire: The Bayonet in the First World War', *Journal of*

*Military and Strategic Studies*, Spring 2006, Vol. 8, Issue 3, p. 19.

20. Livermore, pp. 46–7.
21. Graves, p. 195.
22. Collins, ebook, loc. 1137.
23. Engen, 'Steel Against Fire: The Bayonet in the First World War', *Journal of Military and Strategic Studies*, Spring 2006, Vol. 8, Issue 3, p. 15.
24. King, p. 101; Liddell Hart, p. 219.
25. Officers' Training Manual, p. 126.
26. Allfree, private papers, diary; see also Aldington's account, p. 209.
27. Butler, p. 333.
28. Ibid.
29. Graves, p. 159.
30. Allfree, private papers, diary.
31. Ibid.
32. Hind, private papers, memoir.
33. Lewis-Stempel, p. 75.
34. Skirth, private papers, memoir.
35. Bourne, J., 'The British Working Man in Arms', in Cecil and Liddle (eds), p. 336.
36. Holmes, ebook, loc. 244.
37. Ferguson, Norman, p. 100.
38. Holmes, ebook, loc. 339.
39. JSTOR paper, 'The Armed Forces and the Working Classes', p. 595.
40. Quoted in Holmes, ebook, loc. 244.
41. Roy, R. H. and Foot, Richard, 'Battle of the Somme', *Historica Canada*, 21 December 2006 (last edited 4 March 2015), www.thecanadianencyclopedia.ca/en/article/battle-of-the-somme.
42. JSTOR paper, 'Not Glamorous but Effective: The Canadian Corps and the Set-Piece Attack, 1917–1918', p. 429.
43. Haig, p. 186.
44. Seabrook private papers, postcard, 25 May 1917.
45. Mackenzie, pp. 179–80.
46. Ibid., p. 180.
47. Ibid., p. 186.
48. McNab, p. 51.
49. Thomas, p. 20.
50. Ibid., p. 18.
51. Holmes, ebook, loc. 5489.
52. Graves, p. 239.
53. Nicholson, p. 291.
54. McNab, ebook, loc. 639.

55. Ibid., loc. 608.

56. Ibid., loc. 691.

57. Richard, M., 'The Weapons and Equipment of the British Soldier at Passchendaele', in Liddle (ed), p. 339.

58. McNab, ebook, loc. 695.

59. Ibid., loc. 697.

60. Simkins, p. 13.

61. Griffith, P., 'The Tactical Problem: Infantry, Artillery and the Salient', in Liddle (ed), p. 69.

62. Leinberger, p. 30.

63. Bostyn (ed), p. 183.

64. Sheffield, *Forgotten Victory*, p. 99.

65. Campbell, private papers, memoir, p. 10

66. Ibid., p. 20.

67. Ibid., p. 25.

## Chapter 6: The Mines of Messines

1. Wynne, p. 262.

2. Bostyn (ed), p. 13.

3. Stanhope Papers, quoted in Holmes, ebook, loc. 4092.

4. Passingham, pp. 30–33.

5. Prior and Wilson, p. 57.

6. Ibid., p. 59.

7. Bean, p. 588.

8. Ibid., p. 600.

9. Davies, ebook, loc. 1188.

10. Beumelburg, p. 6.

11. Ibid.

12. Ibid.

13. Edmonds, p. 42.

14. Allfree, private papers, memoir, p. 71.

15. Ibid., pp. 72–3.

16. Ibid., pp. 76–7.

17. Prior and Wilson, p. 56.

18. Allfree, private papers, memoir, p. 103.

19. Ibid., p. 105.

20. Ibid.

21. Yoxall, private papers, letter to mother, 1 June 1917.

22. Ibid.

23. Ibid., 5 June 1917.

24. Edmonds, p. 47. See pp. 46–9 for full details of the barrage used at Messines.
25. Yoxall, private papers, diary, 3 June 1917.
26. Yoxall, private papers, letter to mother, 5 June 1917.
27. Yoxall, private papers, diary, 3 June 1917.
28. Ibid., 4 June 1917.
29. Ibid., 3 June 1917.
30. Bean, p. 589.
31. Quoted in Prior and Wilson, p. 61.
32. Bean, p. 591.
33. Davies, ebook, loc. 394.
34. Ibid., loc. 407.
35. Grieve and Newman, p. 35.
36. Holmes, ebook, loc. 2722.
37. Grieve and Newman, p. 35.
38. Davies, ebook, loc. 915.
39. Edmonds, p. 37.
40. Ibid.
41. Ibid., note, p. 39.
42. Ibid., p. 60.
43. Ibid., note, p. 60.
44. Sir Douglas Haig, '4th Despatch (1917 Campaigns), 25 December 1917', www.firstworldwar.com/source/haigcampaign1917despatch.htm.
45. Davies, ebook, loc. 1584.
46. Quoted in Sheldon, p. 4.
47. Ibid.
48. Edmonds, p. 55.
49. Herwig, p. 321.
50. Quoted in Sheldon, p. 26.
51. Bean, p. 593.
52. Quoted in Sheldon, p. 14.
53. Edmonds, p. 62.
54. Ibid.
55. Bean, p. 594.
56. Ibid.
57. Bean, p. 594.
58. Bean, p. 595.
59. For the official British history of these and other battles during Third Ypres, see Edmonds, pp. 61–8. For the best account of the German experience at Messines, see Sheldon.

60. Quoted in Johnstone, pp. 290–1.
61. Quoted in Sheldon, p. 23.
62. Ibid., p. 7.
63. Ibid., p. 12.
64. Ibid., p. 5.
65. Ibid., p. 9.
66. Edmonds, p. 71.
67. Yoxall private papers, letter to mother, 8 June 1917.
68. Ibid., 9 June 1917.
69. Edmonds, p. 73.
70. Bean, p. 618.
71. Edmonds, pp. 79–80.
72. Bean, p. 621.
73. https://www.thegazette.co.uk/London/issue/30215/supplement/7905.
74. Bean, p. 625.
75. Bean, p. 624.
76. Skirth, private papers, pp. 116–28.
77. Ibid.
78. Edmonds, p. 87.
79. Sir Douglas Haig, '4th Despatch (1917 Campaigns), 25 December 1917', www.firstworldwar.com/source/haigcampaign1917despatch.htm.
80. War Cabinet Papers, 11 June 1917.
81. Edmonds, p. 87; Sheldon, p. 315; Vandiver, F., 'Field Marshal Sir Douglas Haig and Passchendaele', in Liddle (ed), p. 35.
82. JSTOR paper, 'The Psychology of Killing', pp. 239–40.
83. Ludendorff, ebook, loc. 493.
84. Rupprecht, *My War Diary*.

## Chapter 7: A Fatal Delay

1. Gollin, p. 448.
2. War Cabinet Papers, CAB 27/6, 7th Meeting of Committee on War Policy, 19 June 1917.
3. War Cabinet Papers, CAB 27/6, 2nd Meeting of Committee on War Policy, 12 June 1917.
4. Ibid.
5. Ibid.
6. Ibid.
7. Haig, 14 June 1917.
8. Ibid.
9. Ibid.

10. Haig to Robertson, 17 June 1917, quoted in Terraine, *The Road to Passchendaele*, pp. 138–9.
11. Ibid.
12. Ibid., pp. 139–40.
13. Haig, p. 239.
14. The following discussion is based on the Minutes taken by Cabinet secretary Maurice Hankey, Haig's diary, Lloyd George's memoir and various secondary sources; see Terraine, Lloyd George, Wolff, Haig's Diary.
15. Wolff, p. 142.
16. Lloyd George, p. 363.
17. War Cabinet Papers, CAB 27/6, 7th Meeting of Committee on War Policy, 19 June 1917.
18. Ibid.
19. Ibid.
20. Lloyd George, p. 366.
21. War Cabinet Papers, CAB 27/6, 7th Meeting of Committee on War Policy, 19 June 1917.
22. Lloyd George, p. 367.
23. War Cabinet Papers, 16 March 1917.
24. War Cabinet Papers, CAB 27/6, 7th Meeting of Committee on War Policy, 19 June 1917.
25. War Cabinet Papers, 15 June 1917.
26. War Cabinet Papers, CAB 27/6, 7th Meeting of Committee on War Policy, 19 June 1917.
27. Lloyd George, p. 367.
28. Ibid.
29. War Cabinet Papers, CAB 27/6, 9th Meeting of Committee on War Policy, 20 June 1917.
30. Lloyd George, p. 375.
31. War Cabinet Papers, CAB 27/6, 9th Meeting of Committee on War Policy, 20 June 1917.
32. Ibid.
33. Lloyd George, p. 378.
34. War Cabinet Papers, CAB 27/6, 9th Meeting of Committee on War Policy, 20 June 1917.
35. Edmonds, p. 101.
36. Wolff, p. 149.
37. War Cabinet Papers, CAB 27/6, 10th Meeting of Committee on War Policy, 21 June 1917.
38. Lloyd George, p. 367.

39. JSTOR paper, 'Lloyd George's Premiership: A Study in "Prime Ministerial Government"', p. 9.
40. War Cabinet Papers, 27–28 June 1917.
41. Wolff, p. 145.
42. Haig, Diary (Blake edition), pp. 240–1.
43. War Cabinet Papers, 13 and 20 July 1917.
44. Lloyd George, pp. 391–4.
45. Ibid., p. 385.
46. Ibid., p. 391.
47. Farrar-Hockley, pp. 71–2.
48. Ibid., p. 165.
49. Robbins, p. 33.
50. Ibid., p. 16.
51. Ibid., p. 33.
52. Ibid., p. 33; see also Beckett, Chapter 4 and p. 85.
53. Beckett, p. 85.
54. Prior and Wilson, p. 70.
55. Edmonds, p. 17.
56. Beckett, p. 39.
57. Edmonds, p. 131.
58. Quoted in ibid.
59. In Sheffield (ed), *Leadership and Command*, p. 90.
60. Sheffield, *Haig*, p. 228.
61. *Frankfurter Zeitung*, 1 July 1917.
62. Quoted in Macdonald, p. 87.
63. Rupprecht, II, pp. 195, 199.
64. Ibid.
65. Jones, p. 233. Though here he refers to the Somme, the description is apt.
66. Prior and Wilson, p. 72.
67. Hagenlück, H., 'The German High Command', in Liddle (ed), p. 51.
68. Ibid.
69. War Cabinet Papers, 30 July 1917.
70. Rupprecht, II, p. 232.
71. Werth, G., 'Flanders 1917 and the German Soldier', in Liddle (ed), Chapter 20.
72. Dearden, private papers, diary, p. 50.

## Chapter 8: August 1917

1. Ibid.
2. Hind private papers, memoir, p. 56.
3. Macdonald, p. 95.

4. Dearden, private papers, diary, p. 75.
5. Wilkinson, private papers, letter.
6. Dearden, private papers, diary, p. 71.
7. Bewsher, p. 198.
8. Hind, private papers, memoir, p. 216.
9. Van Bergen, p. 184.
10. Allhusen, private papers, memoir.
11. Ibid.
12. Ibid.
13. Ibid.
14. Ibid.
15. Beumelburg, p. 7.
16. Allfree, private papers, memoir, p. 124.
17. Ibid., p. 130.
18. Allfree, private papers, diary, p. 137.
19. Ibid., p. 138.
20. Ibid., p. 146.
21. Ibid., p. 143.
22. Ibid., pp. 140–1.
23. Ibid., p. 146.
24. Ibid.
25. Ibid., p. 149.
26. Hagenlück, H., 'The German High Command', in Liddle (ed), p. 51.
27. Quoted in McNab, p. 74. See also Von Kuhl's chapter on Flanders.
28. See Sheldon for a good explanation of the German concept of 'flexible defence'.
29. Dearden, private papers, diary, p. 72.
30. Quoted in Sheldon, p. 43.
31. Quoted in ibid., p. 59.
32. Beumelburg, p. 10.
33. Bostyn (ed), p. 15.
34. Dearden, private papers, diary, p. 75.
35. War Cabinet Papers, 20–21 July 1917; see also in Edmonds, p. 105–6.
36. Edmonds, p. 106.
37. Quoted in Terraine, *Douglas Haig: The Educated Soldier*, p. 336.
38. Beumelburg, p. 10.
39. Bostyn (ed), p. 21.
40. Beumelburg, p. 10.
41. Kuhl, pp. 121–2.
42. Hagenlück, H., 'The German High Command', in Liddle (ed), p. 52.
43. Beumelburg, p. 10.

44. Ibid.
45. Prior and Wilson, p. 88.
46. Fifth Army intelligence reports, quoted in Prior and Wilson, p. 88.
47. Edmonds, p. 136; see also Haig's diary, 25 July 1917.
48. Beumelburg, p. 10.
49. Campbell, private papers, memoir, p. 80.
50. Quoted in Sheldon, p. 54.
51. Macdonald, ebook, loc. 2149.
52. Edmonds, p. 151.
53. Macdonald, ebook, loc. 2149.
54. Ibid., loc. 1954.
55. Ibid.
56. Bostyn (ed), p. 23.
57. Ibid.; see also Edmonds, p. 156 (note).
58. Macdonald, ebook, loc. 2149.
59. Quoted in Sheldon, p. 56.
60. Quoted in Edmonds, p. 24.
61. Edmonds, p. 152.
62. Ibid., p. 157, plus note.
63. Quoted in Wolff, pp. 198–9. See alternative translations: http://www.casinapioiv.va/content/accademia/en/magisterium/benedictxv/1august1917.pdf; and https://repository.library.nd.edu/view/370/838948.pdf.
64. *The Times*, quoted in Wolff, pp. 198–9.
65. Ludendorff, ebook, loc. 1802.
66. Campbell, private papers, memoir, p. 91.
67. Quoted in Edmonds, p. 170.
68. Edmonds, p. 171.
69. Macdonald, ebook, loc. 2377.
70. McCarthy, p. 11.
71. Yoxall, private papers, diary, 2 August 1917.
72. *Daily Mail*, 2 August 1917.
73. Allfree, private papers, diary, p. 130.
74. Ibid., p. 165.
75. Ibid., p. 166.
76. Ibid., pp. 170–1.
77. Wolff, p. 169.
78. Macdonald, ebook, loc. 2211.
79. Prior and Wilson, p. 97.
80. Wolff, p. 170.
81. Robertson, II, pp. 250–1.

82. Ibid.

83. Lee, J., 'The British Divisions at Third Ypres', in Liddle (ed), p. 217.

84. Haig, 10 August 1917.

85. Campbell, private papers, memoir, p. 111.

86. Ibid., p. 101.

87. Ibid., p. 104.

88. Ibid., p. 105.

89. Ibid., p. 112.

90. Ibid., pp. 117–18.

91. Quoted in Terraine, *The Road to Passchendaele*, p. 228.

92. Prior and Wilson, p. 102; Falls, *History of the 36th (Ulster) Division*, p. 116.

93. Prior and Wilson, p. 102.

94. Bostyn (ed), p. 39.

95. Ibid., p. 42.

96. Ibid., p. 43.

97. Haig, 17 August 1917.

98. Bostyn (ed), p. 44.

99. Falls, *History of the 36th (Ulster) Division*, p. 116.

100. Lee, J., 'The British Divisions at Third Ypres', in Liddle (ed), p. 218.

101. McNab, p. 96.

102. Haig, 16 August 1917.

103. Ibid.

104. Ibid.

105. Prior and Wilson, p. 105.

106. Gough, ebook, loc. 142.

107. Bostyn (ed), p. 33 (note).

108. Quoted in Macdonald, ebook, loc. 2413.

109. Wohlenberg, p. 302–3.

110. Ibid.

111. Quoted in Macdonald, ebook, loc. 2605.

112. Gold, letter to *The Spectator*, 17 January 1958.

113. Fletcher, C. R. L. and Atkinson, C. T., 'The Flanders Battleground', *Army Quarterly*, Vol. I, October 1920, p. 155.

114. Sir Douglas Haig's Despatches, Full Text, December 1915 to April 1919, https://archive.org/details/sirdouglashaigsd00haiguoft.

115. Hussey, J., 'The Flanders Battleground and the Weather in 1917', in Liddle (ed), p. 147. Hussey's excellent essay draws on admirable graduate research by Philip Griffiths, a geography student at Birmingham University.

116. Ibid., p. 143.

117. Ibid., p. 148.

118. Ibid. See also Sir Douglas Haig's Despatches, 1917, Full Text, December 1915 to April 1919, https://archive.org/details/sirdouglashaigsd00haiguoft.
119. McNab, p. 99.
120. Edmonds, p. 209.
121. Ibid.; see also Wolff, p. 197.
122. Bostyn (ed), p. 31 (note 31).
123. McCarthy, p. 27.
124. Quoted in Edmonds, p. 177.
125. Edmonds, p. 177.
126. Edmonds, p. 210; Sheffield, *Forgotten Victory*.
127. Rupprecht, Diary.
128. Edmonds, p. 209; Wolff, p. 197.
129. Kuhl, II, p. 114.
130. Ludendorff, p. 92.
131. Quoted in Sheldon, p. 120.
132. Rupprecht, Diary, 16 August 1917.
133. Carrington, p. 190.
134. Yoxall, private papers, diary, 7 August 1917.
135. Bean, *Anzac to Amiens*, p. 349.
136. War Diary Administrative Staff, HQ 3rd Australian Division, August 1917, regimental medical officers' reports, 7th and 8th Field Artillery Brigades.
137. Edmonds, p. 209.

## Chapter 9: Those Who Walked Beside You

1. Harris, p. 364.
2. Haig, 7 November 1914.
3. Charteris, p. 243.
4. http://www.bbc.co.uk/guides/zq2y87h.
5. Quoted in Langer and Pois, p. 144; see also: http://www.firstworldwar.com/bio/kiggell.htm.
6. Quoted in ibid., p. 143.
7. Quoted in Wolff, p. 169; and Lloyd George, p. 405.
8. War Cabinet Papers, 2 August 1917.
9. Ibid.
10. Ibid.
11. Prior and Wilson, p. 96.
12. War Cabinet Papers, 27 August 1917.
13. Quoted in Wolff, p. 213.
14. Ibid., pp. 197–8.
15. See Piketty's conclusions.

16. Quoted in Macdonald, ebook, loc. 2532.
17. Hind, private papers, memoir, p. 96.
18. Wilkinson, private papers, letter to father, 28 June 1917.
19. Ibid., letter to father, 30 July 1917.
20. Ibid., letter to father, 5 August 1917.
21. Ibid., letter to father, 4 August 1917.
22. Ibid., letter to father, 25 August 1917.
23. Yoxall, private papers, letter to mother and family, 1 June 1916 and 2 June 1916.
24. Ibid., letter to mother and family, 1 June 1916.
25. Ibid., letters to family; see especially between December and February (1916–1917).
26. Ibid., letter to mother, 1 June 1916.
27. Ibid., letter to mother, 2 January 1917.
28. Ibid., letter to mother, 5 February 1917.
29. Ibid., letter to mother, 5 April 1917.
30. Tanner, private papers.
31. Ibid.
32. Allfree, private papers, memoir, p. 133.
33. Tanner, private papers.
34. Hind, private papers, memoir, p. 116.
35. Tanner, private papers, sermon preached in Weymouth College Chapel, Sunday 1 January 1915.
36. Tanner, private papers, diary, 12 January 1917.
37. Ibid., 20 January 1917.
38. Tanner, private papers.
39. Allhusen, private papers, diary.
40. Skirth, private papers, memoir, p. 105.
41. Ibid., p. 136.
42. Ibid., pp. 137–8.
43. Ibid., p. 111.
44. Ibid., pp. 138–9.
45. Herwig, ebook, loc. 6727.
46. Lynch, ebook, loc. 1348.
47. Holmes, ebook, loc. 2992.
48. Ibid.

## Chapter 10: September 1917

1. Lynch, p. 58.
2. Ibid., p. 103.
3. Williams, ebook, loc. 110.

4. Herbert, pp. 238–9.
5. Hawkings, p. 20.
6. Roe, p. 87.
7. Dolden, p. 110.
8. Blacker, p. 237.
9. Haig, 19 August 1917.
10. Prior & Wilson, p. 108.
11. War Cabinet Papers, 7 September 1917.
12. Edmonds, p. 232.
13. Skirth, private papers, memoir, p. 73.
14. Liddell Hart, pp. 323–4.
15. Beckett and Corvi, ebook, loc. 3815.
16. See Eden, *Another World*.
17. Beumelburg, pp. 7–8.
18. War Cabinet Papers, Cabinet Committee on War Policy, 25 June 1917.
19. War Cabinet Papers, 4 September 1917, CAB23/13/17.pdf.
20. Edmonds, p. 233.
21. Ibid., pp. 233–4.
22. Wolff, p. 207.
23. Edmonds, p. 234 (see footnote).
24. Beckett and Corvi, p. 36.
25. Ibid., p. 37.
26. Ibid., p. 41.
27. Bean, p. 738.
28. Ibid., p. 739.
29. Ibid.
30. Ludendorff, ebook, loc. 1431.
31. Edmonds, p. 238.
32. Bean, note, p. 744.
33. McNab, p. 106.
34. Bean, pp. 757–8.
35. Edmonds, p. 245.
36. Davids, pp. 183–5.
37. Wolff, p. 211.
38. Bean, p. 757.
39. Edmonds, p. 252.
40. Schwenke, pp. 259–60.
41. Pirscher, p. 73.
42. Wohlenberg, p. 333.
43. Pirscher, p. 71.

44. Bean, p. 760.

45. Mackenzie, pp. 188–91.

46. Edmonds, p. 258.

47. Van der Fraenen, 'Passchendaele September 1917: A Terrible Loss in an Australian Family. The Story of the Three Seabrook Brothers', Archives, Memorial Museum Passchendaele 1917, Zonnebeke.

48. 'William Keith Seabrook', AWM, Red Cross file, 2440806, 7 November 1917.

49. Mackenzie, p. 191.

50. 'William Keith Seabrook', AWM, Red Cross file, 2440806, 7 November 1917.

51. Ibid., 4 November 1917.

52. Ibid., 11 November 1917.

53. Van der Fraenen, 'Passchendaele September 1917: A Terrible Loss in an Australian Family. The Story of the Three Seabrook Brothers', Archives, Memorial Museum Passchendaele 1917, Zonnebeke.

54. 'Theo Leslie Seabrook', AWM, Red Cross file, 2440805, 11 February 1918.

55. Lee, J., 'The British Divisions at Third Ypres', in Liddle (ed), p. 220.

56. Edmonds, note, p. 272.

57. Prior and Wilson, p. 121.

58. Pirscher, pp. 78–9.

59. Quoted in Bean, p. 761.

60. Bean, p. 761.

61. Prior and Wilson, p. 119.

62. Nasson, W., 'South Africans in Flanders: Le Zulu Blanc', in Liddle (ed), p. 301.

63. Bean, p. 788.

64. Quoted in Bean, p. 790.

65. War Cabinet Papers, 21 September 1917.

66. Wohlenberg, p. 332–4.

67. Ibid., pp. 340–1.

68. Bean, p. 769.

69. Grant, pp. 141–7.

70. Prior and Wilson, p. 128.

71. Bean, p. 792.

72. Ibid., p. 793.

73. Bostyn (ed), p. 75.

74. Edmonds, p. 279; other sources place the total at 20,441 – see McNab, p. 107.

75. Bostyn (ed), p. 76.

76. Bean, p. 813.

77. Edmonds, p. 284.

78. Bean, p. 813.

79. Bostyn (ed), p. 76.

80. Bean, p. 826.
81. Ibid., p. 820.
82. Edmonds, p. 290.
83. Quoted in Sheldon, p. 176.
84. Quoted in Sheldon, p. 177.
85. Terraine, *Road to Passchendaele*, p. 279.
86. Ludendorff, ebook, loc. 1319.
87. German Official History, xiii, p. 77.
88. Prior and Wilson, p. 131.
89. Bean, p. 827.
90. German Official History, xiii, p. 77.
91. See: https://www.awm.gov.au/people/P10676380/; and Edmonds, p. 285.
92. See: http://www.iwm.org.uk/collections/item/object/30006584; and Edmonds, p. 262.
93. See: http://www.victoriacrossonline.co.uk/hugh-colvin-vc/4586221939; and Edmonds, p. 263.
94. Bean, p. 772.
95. Lloyd George, p. 419.
96. Ibid., pp. 416–17.
97. Suttie, p. 240, note 122.

## Chapter 11: Odyssey of the Wounded

1. Butler, pp. 209–10.
2. Butler, pp. 275–6, note 14.
3. Ibid.
4. Lynch, p. 167.
5. Butler, p. 282, note 31.
6. *The London Gazette*, 14 September 1917; see: https://www.thegazette.co.uk/London/issue/30284/supplement/9531.
7. Butler, p. 282; see also Gristwood, p. 87.
8. Whitehead, I., 'Third Ypres – Casualties and British Medical Services: an Evaluation', in Liddle (ed), p. 180.
9. Butler, pp. 275–6, note 14.
10. Butler, p. 211.
11. Bostyn (ed), p. 180.
12. Ibid., p. 181.
13. Collins, ebook, loc. 62.
14. Butler, p. 359.
15. Ibid.
16. Herwig, p. 296.

17. Vera Brittain, quoted in Talbot House Museum, Poperinghe.
18. Macdonald, ebook, loc. 2469.
19. Butler, pp. 331–2.
20. Collins, ebook, loc. 2189.
21. Ibid., loc. 2201.
22. Paxman, ebook, loc. 3691.
23. Collins, ebook, loc. 2215.
24. Herwig, p. 296.
25. Butler, pp. 331–2.
26. Whitehead, I., 'Third Ypres – Casualties and British Medical Services: an Evaluation', in Liddle (ed), p. 180, in Liddle (ed), p. 184.
27. Cushing, p. 166.
28. Lynch, ebook, loc. 4542.
29. Butler, pp. 331–2.
30. Miller, p. 171.
31. Collins, ebook, loc. 2104.
32. Oram, p. 55.
33. Herbert, ebook, loc. 1427.
34. Butler, p. 463.
35. Macdonald, ebook, loc. 2922.
36. Whitehead, I., 'Third Ypres – Casualties and British Medical Services: an Evaluation', in Liddle (ed), pp. 175–200.
37. Reverend Julian Bickersteth, quoted in Talbot House Museum, Poperinghe.
38. Butler, p. 462.
39. Whitehead, I., 'Third Ypres – Casualties and British Medical Services: an Evaluation', in Liddle (ed), pp. 175–200.
40. Ibid., p. 193.
41. From Cushing, *From a Surgeon's Journal*.
42. Cushing, p. 213.
43. Witnessed by Sapper Harold Clarke, Royal Engineers, Autumn 1917, quoted in Talbot House Museum, Poperinghe.
44. Cushing, p. 192.
45. Elsie Grant, Australian nurse, letter, AWM PR00596.
46. Edmund Blunden, quoted in Talbot House Museum, Poperinghe.
47. Talbot House Museum, Poperinghe.
48. Talbot House Museum, Poperinghe.
49. Tubby Clayton, quoted in Talbot House Museum, Poperinghe.
50. Captain Philip Gosse, quoted in Talbot House Museum, Poperinghe.
51. Leahy, pp. 42–3.
52. Lynch, p. 254.

53. Ibid.

54. Brazier and Sandford, p. 210.

55. War Cabinet Papers, 7 May 1917.

56. Quoted in Chambers, p. 559.

57. Wilson, ebook, loc. 13331.

58. *New Statesman*, 15 December 1917, p. 248–9.

59. Wilson, ebook, loc. 13331.

60. Ludendorff, ebook, loc. 844.

61. War Cabinet Papers, 24 September 1917.

62. Ibid., 18 September 1917.

63. *The Dundee Courier*, 21 September 1917.

64. *East London Advertiser*, 11 January 1918.

65. Simkins, p. 183.

66. Wilson, ebook, loc. 13236.

67. Quoted in ibid., loc. 13288.

68. Greene, p. 45.

69. *The Daily Mail*, 8 August 1917.

70. Lloyd George, p. 420.

71. Ibid.

72. Ibid., p. 423.

73. Badsey, S., and Taylor, P., 'Images of Battle: the Press, Propaganda and Passchendaele', in Liddle (ed), p. 372.

74. Quoted in Best, pp. 50–1.

75. Ibid., p. 123.

76. Sheffield, *Forgotten Victory*, p. 50.

77. Riddle, p. 267.

78. See Herwig, Chapter 7: Death, disease and doctors.

79. Muir, pp. 143–4.

80. See Ham, *Hiroshima Nagasaki*, Chapter 20: Hibakusha.

81. Paxman, ebook, loc. 3695.

82. Quoted in Biernoff, p. 30.

83. Birnie, private papers, letter to parents, 26 October 1917.

84. Wilkinson, private papers, letters.

85. Hind, private papers, memoir, pp. 74–5.

86. Herwig, p 253.

87. Ibid., p. 280.

88. Ibid., p. 291.

89. Ibid., p. 284.

90. Ibid., p. 254.

91. May, p. 332 .

92. Herwig, p. 273; Herwig's description is drawn from Healy.
93. Ibid., p. 292.
94. See Ham, *Young Hitler*.
95. 'Spotlights on History: The Blockade of Germany', The National Archives, United Kingdom, www.nationalarchives.gov.uk/pathways/firstworldwar/spotlights/blockade.htm; see also Grebler, p. 78.
96. Ibid.
97. Aldington, p. 276.
98. Simkins, p. 81.
99. Santanu Das, 'The Dying Kiss: Gender and Intimacy in the Trenches of World War I', World War I Centenary, JISC, http://ww1centenary.oucs.ox.ac.uk/body-and-mind/the-dying-kiss-gender-and-intimacy-in-the-trenches-of-world-war-i.
100. Macdonald, ebook, loc. 2469.
101. Aldington, p. 278.
102. Ibid., p. 182.
103. Ibid., p. 287.
104. See: http://www.lettersofnote.com/2011/04/finished-with-war-soldiers-declaration.html; see Commons Debate: http://siegfried-sassoon.firstworldwarrelics.co.uk/html/protest.html.
105. Aldington, p. 201.
106. Ibid., p. 202.

## Chapter 12: The Cruellest Month

1. Haig, 28 September 1917.
2. Quoted in Wilson, ebook, loc. 12086.
3. Wilson, ebook, loc. 12086.
4. Bean, p. 833.
5. Edmonds, p. 297.
6. Quoted in Wilson, ebook, loc. 12066.
7. Hussey, J., 'The Flanders Battleground and the Weather in 1917', in Liddle (ed), p. 145.
8. Quoted in Bean, p. 857.
9. Lynch, p. 232.
10. Bean, p. 838, 2nd Division Artillery Diary.
11. Edmonds, p. 304.
12. See Bean, p. 839.
13. Bean, note, p. 849.
14. Edmonds, p. 305.
15. Tyne Cot Cemetery, exhibit.

16. Bean, p. 852.
17. Ibid., p. 855.
18. Otto, private papers, postcard, 10 October 1917.
19. Allhusen, private papers, letter to his mother, 18 October 1917.
20. Ibid.
21. Bradby, W. J., 'Polygon Wood and Broodseinde', *Stand-To*, vol. 8, no. 5, September–October 1963, pp. 19–22, 27–28.
22. Edmonds, p. 308.
23. Quoted in Leahy, p. 32.
24. Bean, p. 875.
25. Kennedy, private papers, letter, 5 October 1917.
26. Quoted in Harper, p. 45.
27. Ibid.
28. Ibid.
29. Ibid., p. 48.
30. Edmonds, p. 308.
31. See: http://www.warwickfusiliers.co.uk/pages/pg-60-private_arthur_hutt_vc/; Edmonds, p. 310.
32. See: http://www.queensroyalsurreys.org.uk/vc/vc11.html; Edmonds, p. 313.
33. See: http://www.devonheritage.org/Places/Tiverton/ThomasSage.htm; Edmonds, p. 315.
34. Bostyn (ed), p. 97.
35. Hurley, pp. 52–4.
36. Bean, p. 876, see note about German regimental history.
37. Harper, p. 42.
38. Edmonds, p. 316.
39. Bean, p. 876; and Ludendorff, ebook, loc. 1470.
40. Rupprecht, vol. II, p. 271.
41. Bean, p. 883.
42. Ibid., p. 884.
43. Birdwood, p. 316.
44. Perry, ebook, loc. 5674.
45. Sherriff, ebook.
46. Quoted in Bean, p. 883.
47. Haig, 26 and 28 September 1917; see also Beckett, ebook, loc. 3894.
48. Edmonds claims the meeting occurred; Prior and Wilson could find 'no contemporary record' of the conference.
49. Bean, p. 881.
50. Ibid.
51. Ibid., p. 885.

52. Quoted in Harper, p. 9.
53. Bean, pp. 884–88. See also undated diary entry, item 89, 3DRL, 606 AWM.
54. Anstey, p. 189.
55. Edmonds, p. 328.
56. Ibid., p. 329.
57. Quoted in Bean, p. 891.
58. For details, see Bean, p. 886.
59. Macdonald, ebook, loc. 3742.
60. Ibid., loc. 3754.
61. Lee, J., 'The British Divisions at Third Ypres', in Liddle (ed), p. 221.
62. See account by Sherriff, R. C., in, McNab, ebook, loc. 1500.
63. Edmonds, p. 336.
64. Hurley, p. 64.
65. Leahy, letter to mother, 10 October 1917.
66. Macdonald, ebook, loc. 3793.
67. Allhusen, private papers, diary, 5–8 October 1917.
68. Ibid.
69. Ibid.
70. Ibid.
71. Ibid.
72. Macdonald, ebook, loc. 3835.
73. Ibid., loc. 3807.
74. Charteris, p. 259.
75. Quoted in Prior and Wilson, p. 154.
76. Ibid., p. 155.
77. War Cabinet Papers, 11 October 1917, Conclusion, General Military, concern at situation, CAB23/13/21.
78. Haig, 10 and 11 October 1917.
79. Edmonds, p. 342.
80. Haig, 10 and 11 October 1917.
81. Sheffield, *Haig*, p. 243.
82. Ibid.
83. Quoted in Harper, p. 63.
84. Bean, pp. 903–4.
85. See Chasseaud, P., 'Development of the Survey Organisation', in Liddle, (ed).
86. Quoted in Bean, pp. 906–7.
87. Quoted in Wilson, ebook, loc. 12150.
88. Wade, pp. 57-8.
89. Quoted in Ekins, A., 'The Australians at Passchendaele', in Liddle (ed), p. 243.
90. Ibid.

.

91. See: https://www.awm.gov.au/people/P10676249/ .
92. Bean, p. 917.
93. Pugsley, C., 'The New Zealand Division at Passchendaele', in Liddle (ed), p. 275.
94. Phillips, Boyack and Malone, p. 145
95. Quoted in Phillips, Boyack and Malone, p. 145.
96. Quoted in Harper, p. 70.
97. Macdonald, ebook, loc. 3910.
98. Ibid., loc. 3964.
99. Quoted in Harper, p. 74.
100. Pugsley, C., 'The New Zealand Division at Passchendaele', in Liddle (ed), p. 275-280.
101. Quoted in Harper, p. 28.
102. Ibid.
103. Pugsley, C., 'The New Zealand Division at Passchendaele', in Liddle (ed), p. 285.
104. Quoted in Harper, p. 87.
105. Ibid., pp. 87–8.
106. Pugsley, C., 'The New Zealand Division at Passchendaele', in Liddle (ed), pp. 287-88.
107. Quoted in Harper, p. 90.
108. Ekins, A., 'The Australians at Passchendaele', in Liddle (ed), p. 243.
109. Bostyn (ed), p. 125.
110. Harper, p. 83.
111. Quoted in Pugsley, C., 'The New Zealand Division at Passchendaele', in Liddle (ed), p. 286.
112. Butler, p. 219.
113. Macdonald, ebook, loc. 3997.
114. Quoted in Ekins, A., 'The Australians at Passchendaele', in Liddle (ed), p. 244.
115. Lynch, ebook, loc. 3506.
116. Ibid., loc. 3688.
117. Ibid., loc. 3709.
118. Allhusen, private papers, diary, 16 October 1917.
119. Ibid.
120. Ibid.
121. Ibid.
122. Birnie, private papers, letter to parents, 26 October 1917.
123. McNab, ebook, loc. 1572.
124. Harper, p. 91.
125. Prior and Wilson, p. 169.
126. Haig, 14 October 1917.
127. Ibid.

128. *Birmingham Gazette*, 13 October 1917.

129. Ibid., and *Liverpool Echo*, 12 October 1917.

130. Sir Douglas Haig, '4th Despatch (1917 Campaigns), 25 December 1917', www.firstworldwar.com/source/haigcampaign1917despatch.htm.'

131. War Cabinet, 16 October 1917, Statement of British and German Wastage in Flanders, CAB24/29/19.

132. War Cabinet, 17 October 1917, Casualties, not in public interest to know, CAB23/4/25.

133. Ibid.

134. War Cabinet Papers, 16 October 1917.

135. Hattersley, ebook, loc. 8758.

136. Neillands, ebook, loc. 9364.

137. Lloyd George, p. 126.

138. Allhusen, private papers, letter to his mother, 18 October 1917.

## Chapter 13: The Face of Fear

1.  Beaumelberg, p. 25.

2.  Ibid., p. 27.

3.  Collins, ebook, loc. 2545.

4.  Beaumelberg, p. 27.

5.  Ibid.

6.  Ibid., pp. 31–2.

7.  Ibid.

8.  Blankenstein, pp. 314–15.

9.  Sobbe, pp. 411–13.

10. Quoted in Sheldon, p. 196.

11. Beaumelberg, pp. 31–2.

12. Ibid.

13. Rupprecht, Diary, 11 October 1917.

14. Quoted in Sheldon, p. 232.

15. Beaumelberg, p. 36.

16. Ibid.

17. Ludendorff, ebook, loc. 1445.

18. Ibid., loc. 1462.

19. Ibid., loc. 1486.

20. Wilson, ebook, loc. 11976.

21. Buchan, p. 592.

22. Quoted in Pedersen, 'The AIF on the Western Front: The Role of Training and Command', in McKernan and Browne (eds), p. 183.

23. Gibbs, *Realities of War*, p. 396.

24. Owen, p. 521.
25. Ekins, A., 'The Australians at Passchendaele', in Liddle (ed.), p. 245.
26. Ibid.
27. Rupprecht, Diary, 3 November 1917.
28. Quoted in Gibbs, *From Bapaume to Passchendaele*, p. 139.
29. Quoted in Sheldon, p. 243.
30. Jünger, p. 203.
31. Lloyd George, p. 435.

## Chapter 14: Passchendaele Ridge

1. Oliver, D., 'The Canadians at Passchendaele', in Liddle (ed), p. 259.
2. Ibid.
3. Neillands, ebook, loc. 3625.
4. Ibid., loc. 3646.
5. Ibid., loc. 3652.
6. Nicholson, p. 312.
7. Ibid.
8. Neillands, ebook, loc. 9793.
9. Quoted in Hyatt, General Sir Arthur Currie, p. 79.
10. Nicholson, p. 312.
11. Neillands, ebook, loc. 9796.
12. Quoted in Nicholson, p. 313.
13. Nicholson, p. 314.
14. Macdonald, ebook, loc. 4163.
15. Quoted in Nicholson, p. 315.
16. Nicholson, p. 318.
17. Neillands, ebook, loc. 9438.
18. Quoted in Oliver, D., 'The Canadians at Passchendaele, in Liddle (ed), p. 263.
19. Macdonald, ebook, loc. 4135.
20. Ibid., loc. 4106.
21. Ibid., loc. 4188.
22. Ibid., loc. 4208.
23. JSTOR paper, Brown, I. M., 'Not Glamorous, but effective: The Canadian Corps and the Set-Piece Attack, 1917-1918', p. 430.
24. Quoted in Sheldon, p. 258.
25. Ibid., p. 254.
26. Bostyn (ed), p. 130.
27. Ibid., pp. 135–6.
28. Sheldon, p. 257.
29. Nicholson, p. 323.

30. Bostyn (ed), p. 130.
31. Macdonald, ebook, loc. 4250.
32. Bostyn (ed), p. 133.
33. Ibid., p. 151.
34. Ibid., p. 149.
35. Neillands, ebook, loc. 9496.
36. Prior and Wilson, p. 177.
37. Ibid.
38. Bostyn (ed), p. 156.
39. Ibid., p. 161.
40. Quoted in Prior and Wilson, p. 178.
41. Nicholson, p. 324.
42. Ibid.
43. Bostyn (ed), p. 161.
44. Nicholson, p. 325.
45. Prior and Wilson, p. 179.
46. Lee, J., 'The British Divisions at Third Ypres', in Liddle (ed), p. 223.
47. Ibid.
48. Wyrall. p. 239.
49. Bostyn (ed), p. 179. check figs
50. JSTOR paper, Brown, I. M., 'Not Glamorous, but effective: The Canadian Corps and the Set-Piece Attack, 1917–1918', p. 428.
51. Quoted in Oliver, D., 'The Canadians at Passchendaele, in Liddle (ed), ebook. loc. 7122.
52. Blake, pp. 267–8, see also Terraine, *The Road to Passchendaele*, pp. 331–332.
53. Churchill, p. 750.
54. War Cabinet Papers, 31 October 1917, Flanders 'successful', CAB23/4/35, pdf.
55. War Cabinet Papers, 2 November 1917, On Italy, DLG has full discretion to decide, CAB24/4/38, pdf.
56. War Cabinet Papers, 14 November 1917.
57. War Cabinet Papers, 15 November 1917.
58. Quoted in Allhusen, private papers, Intelligence: General Staff, 14th (Light) Division.
59. Prior and Wilson, p 181.
60. War Cabinet Papers, 28 November 1917.
61. Nicolson, private papers, AWM 3DRL/2715, P1040087, https://www.awm.gov.au/collection/3DRL/2715.
62. Allhusen, private papers, diary.
63. Ibid.
64. Ibid.

65. Ibid.
66. Ibid.
67. Skirth, private papers, memoir, p. 149.
68. Ibid., p. 153.
69. Ibid., pp. 166–7.
70. Ibid., pp. 174–5.
71. Tanner, private papers, pp. 93–4.
72. 'Lenin's Call to Power, 24 October 1917', www.firstworldwar.com/source/callto-power.htm.
73. 'Lenin's Statement of Bolshevik Demands, 24 October 1917', www.firstworldwar.com/source/lenin_24oct1917.htm.
74. Lloyd George, p. 431.
75. Ibid.
76. War Cabinet Papers, 6 December 1917.
77. Ibid.
78. Ibid. See full Minutes of the debate.
79. War Cabinet Papers, 10 December 1917.
80. War Cabinet Papers, 12 December 1917.
81. War Cabinet Papers, 2 November 1917 and 26 December 1917.
82. War Cabinet Papers, 19 December 1917.
83. War Cabinet Papers, 5 December 1917.
84. War Cabinet Papers, 26 December 1917.
85. War Cabinet Papers, 24 December 1917.

## Chapter 15: The Burial of the Dead

1. War Cabinet Papers, 24 December 1917.
2. https://www.awm.gov.au/blog/2007/10/06/passchendaele-an-almost-universal-experience/
3. Bernède, A., 'Third Ypres and the restoration of confidence in the ranks of the French Army', in Liddle (ed), p. 99.
4. Quoted in Sheldon, p. 315 (see also Note 58).
5. Edmonds, p. 363; for details of this dispute, see Sheldon, pp. 313-315
6. Sheldon, p. 314.
7. Ibid.
8. Lloyd George, p. 429.
9. Tanner, private papers.
10. Quoted in Harper, p. 81.
11. Cushing, pp. 197–8.
12. Quoted in Macdonald, ebook, loc. 4032.
13. Ibid.

14. Ibid.
15. Bostyn (ed), p. 227.
16. Ibid., p. 229.
17. Lynch, ebook, loc. 1590.
18. Bostyn (ed), p. 234.
19. Ison, private papers.
20. Larsen, private papers.
21. Austin, private papers.
22. Collins, ebook, loc. 1505.
23. Ibid.
24. Ison, private papers.
25. Ibid.
26. Ibid.
27. Larsen, private papers.
28. Ibid.
29. Ibid.
30. Ibid.
31. Ibid.
32. Grant, private papers.
33. Ibid.
34. Tanner, private papers.
35. Ibid.
36. Ison, private papers.
37. Rex, private papers.
38. Ibid.
39. Ibid.
40. Bean, p. 900.
41. Austin, private papers.
42. Commonwealth War Graves Commission.
43. Sassoon, poem.
44. Inscription on Menin Gate.
45. Alsop, private papers
46. Ibid.
47. Ibid.
48. Ibid.
49. Bostyn (ed), p. 65.
50. Tyne Cot Memorial, exhibit.
51. Bostyn (ed), p. 70.
52. http://www.heraldsun.com.au/anzac-centenary/six-of-seven-sons-of-frederick-and-maggie-smith-died-in-ww1/story-fnmeodwa-1226895364091

53. http://www.dailymail.co.uk/news/article-2060179/Armistice-Day-2011-The-mother-lost-sons-WW1.html
54. Bostyn (ed), p. 95.
55. 'George Ross Seabrook', Red Cross file, 2440806, AWM, 4 December 1917.
56. Ibid., 10 December 1917.
57. Ibid., 7 February 1918.
58. Ibid., 9 March 1918.
59. Seabrook Family, private papers.
60. Ibid.
61. Ibid.
62. Ibid.
63. Ibid.
64. Ibid.
65. Ibid.
66. Ibid.
67. Ibid.
68. 'Private George Ross Seabrook', 11586728 (service record), NAA, B2455.
69. Seabrook Family, private papers.
70. Ibid.
71. Ibid.
72. Ibid.
73. Ibid.
74. Quoted in Sheldon, p. 263.
75. Derez, M., 'A Belgian Salient for Reconstruction: People and Patrie, Landscape and Memory', in Liddle (ed), p. 451.
76. Tyne Cot Memorial, exhibit.
77. Tyne Cot cemetery, from Pope, A., 'Essay on Man', see also: http://www.epitaph-softhegreatwar.com/155.

## Chapter 16: From the Jaws of Defeat

1. Grieves, *The Politics of Manpower*, p. 161.
2. Ibid.
3. JSTOR paper, 'Britain in a Continental War.pdf', p. 57.
4. Ibid.
5. Hattersley, ebook, loc. 8937.
6. Grieves, K. 'The Recruiting Margin in Britain: Debates on Manpower during the Third Battle of Ypres', in Liddle (ed), p. 396.
7. Haig, 10 November 1917.
8. Travers, pp. 19-30.
9. Bean, p. 946.

10. Grieves, K. 'The Recruiting Margin in Britain: Debates on Manpower during the Third Battle of Ypres', in Liddle (ed), p. 396.

11. *The Daily Telegraph*, 29 November 1917.

12. Quoted in Grieves, K. 'The Recruiting Margin in Britain: Debates on Manpower during the Third Battle of Ypres', in Liddle (ed), p. 401.

13. War Cabinet Papers, 4 December 1917.

14. Wilson, ebook, loc. 1374.

15. Sheffield, *Forgotten Victory*, ebook, loc. 1970.

16. Edmonds, Military Operations: France and Belgium, 1918, p. 490.

17. Sheffield, *Forgotten Victory*, ebook, loc. 4175.

18. 'Sir Douglas Haig's "Backs to the Wall" Order, 11 April 1918', firstworldwar. com, www.firstworldwar.com/source/backstothewall.htm.

19. Sheffield, *Forgotten Victory*, ebook, loc. 4695.

## Chapter 17: What the Living Said

1. See the Introduction to Haig's Diaries, p. 31.

2. Bean, p. 945.

3. 'Sir Douglas Haig's Final Despatch, 21 March 1919', firstworldwar.com, www.firstworldwar.com/source/haiglastdespatch.htm.

4. Quoted in Grieves, K. 'The Recruiting Margin in Britain: Debates on Manpower during the Third Battle of Ypres', in Liddle (ed), p. 391.

5. Quoted in Herwig, p. 341.

6. Haig, 4 September 1916.

7. 'Sir Douglas Haig's Final Despatch, 21 March 1919', firstworldwar.com, www.firstworldwar.com/source/haiglastdespatch.htm.

8. 'Sir Douglas Haig's Final Despatch, 21 March 1919', firstworldwar.com, www.firstworldwar.com/source/haiglastdespatch.htm.

9. See Liddell-Hart. B. H., 'The Basic Truths of Passchendaele', *RUSI Journal*, November 1959, pp. 433-439.

10. Callwell, Vol 1, p. 359.

11. Lloyd George, p. 350.

12. See Liddell-Hart. B. H., 'The Basic Truths of Passchendaele', *RUSI Journal*, November 1959, pp. 433-439.

13. War Cabinet Papers, 24 October 1917.

14. See Prior and Wilson, p. 33; Nicholson, p. 309; Callwell, p. 359.

15. Quoted in Lloyd George, p. 346.

16. Quoted in Beumelburg, p. 168.

17. Kuhl, p. 126.

18. Ibid., p. 131.

19. Quoted in Harper, p. 117.

20. Beumelburg, p. 8.
21. Ibid., pp. 41–2.
22. Lloyd George, p. 431.
23. Harris, p. 382.
24. 'Sir Douglas Haig's Final Despatch, 21 March 1919', firstworldwar.com, www.firstworldwar.com/source/haiglastdespatch.htm.
25. Intelligence Squared Debate: Britain Should Not Have Fought in The First World War, 15 April 2014, http://www.intelligencesquared.com/events/britain-first-world-war/
26. Hastings, *Catastrophe: Europe Goes to War 1914*.
27. Sheffield, *Forgotten Victory,* ebook, loc. 2022.
28. Corrigan, p. 50.
29. Sheffield, *Forgotten Victory*, ebook, loc. 848.
30. Ibid., loc. 946.
31. JSTOR paper: Fussell, P., 'Modernism, Adversary Culture, and Edmund Blunden', p. 593.
32. Ibid., p. 597.
33. Matthews, p. 54.
34. Adorno, T., 'An Essay on Cultural Criticism and Society', *Prisms*, p. 34.
35. Harington, C., *Tim Harington Looks Back*, pp. 63–4.
36. Sheffield, *The Chief*, p. 93.
37. Ibid.
38. Lloyd George, p. 410.
39. Quoted in Harris, p. 188.
40. Ibid.
41. Lloyd George, p. 329.
42. Ibid., p. 401.
43. Ibid., pp. 415–16.
44. JSTOR paper: Woodward, D. R., 'Britain in a Continental War', p. 56.
45. Lloyd George, p. 320.
46. Ibid., p. 571.
47. Ibid., p. 322.
48. Ibid., p. 337.
49. Ibid., p. 338.
50. Ibid., p. 419.
51. Ibid., p. 429.
52. MacMillan, p. 645.
53. The Hague Conventions of 1899 and 1907 banned poison gas, aerial bombardment and the killing of civilians. See: https://archive.org/stream/hagueconventions00inteuoft/hagueconventions00inteuoft_djvu.txt

54. Steel and Hart, p. 302.

55. *News Chronicle*, quoted in Edmonds, p. iv.

56. As Lloyd George confided to the editor of the *Manchester Guardian* in December 1917. See Greenslade, R., 'First World War: How State and Press Kept Truth Off the Front Page', *The Guardian*, 28 July 2014, www.theguardian.com/media/2014/jul/27/first-world-war-state-press-reporting.

## Epilogue: Requiem for Doomed Youth

1. Wilkinson, private papers, letter home.

2. Aldington, p. 201.

3. Ibid., p. 372.

4. Ibid.

5. See Lynch, Holmes, Williams and the private papers cited, for many examples. In literature, the soldier's willingness to sacrifice himself for his friends is a central theme. See: Herbert, Aldington, Remarque, Jünger and Jones, for examples.

6. Harper, p. 100.

7. Hind, private papers, memoir.

8. Dorothy Hind, email to author, 12 July 2016.

9. Ibid.

10. *The Times*, 26 July 1986.

11. Barrett, p. 182.

12. Barrett, p. 344.

13. Skirth, private papers, memoir.

14. Herbert, p. 216.

15. Barr, p. 37

16. Todman, p. 73

17. Harper, p. 102.

18. Ibid., p. 109.

19. Quoted in ibid.

20. Seabrook family private papers, letter, Fanny Seabrook to Mr Varley, 26 March 1919.

21. Seabrook family private papers, letter, deputy comptroller to comptroller, Department of Repatriation, Australian Government, 1 May 1919. See also 'Mrs F. I. Seabrook (Application for living allowance)', 153197, NAA A2487, 18 July 1919.

22. Wilkinson, private papers, letters.

23. Ibid., p. 409.

24. Ibid., p. 411.

25. Ibid., p. 421.

26. Ibid., p. 424.

27. King George V's visit, Tyne Cot Memorial at Tyne Cot cemetery, 11 May 1922.

# BIBLIOGRAPHY

## Private Papers

(Personal memoirs, letters, diaries)

Imperial War Museum, London
Allfree, E. C.
Allhusen, Desmond
Bradbury, Stanley
Campbell, Patrick
Cushing, Harvey
Dearden, Harold
Dennis, Gerald
Ferrie, William Stavert
Hind, Neville
Lyne, C. E. L.
Magill, V. R.
Nettleton, John
Ponting, George
Skirth, John Ronald
Tanner, Reverend Victor
Wilkinson, W. A. C.
Whitfield, Gerald Herbert Penn
Yoxall, Harry

Cadbury Research Library, Special Collections, Birmingham University
Eden, Sir Anthony, Earl of Avon

National Library of Scotland, Edinburgh
The Haig Papers

Australian War Memorial
Alsop, Fred
Austin, Matthew
Baldwin, Rupert
Birnie, Alexander
Blake, George
Bryant, Leonard
Cumming, William John
Cunningham, Alexander Jackson
Edmonds, Adrian Henry
Gatliff, Charles Edwin
Grant, Elsie
Hickman, Keith
Ison, John
Kennedy, Malcolm
Ketterer, Victor
Larsen, Harold Leslie
Leahy, Alfred
Morris, Hart
Moseley, Arthur Henry
Murray, Ernest
Nicolson, Norman
Pearson, Leslie
Regan, Hughie
Rex, Horace
Richey, George Henry Mills
Seabrook, George Ross
Seabrook, William Keith
Seabrook, Theo Leslie
Sheldrick, Robert
Vincent, William Percival


Mitchell Library, Sydney
Otto, Robert


German Soldiers
Gelshorn, von (first name n/a), Offiziersstellvertreter, 6th Battery Field
    Artillery Regiment 62

Kotthoff, Reserve Leutnant (first name n/a), Reserve Infantry Regiment 77
Lincke, Major (first name n/a), Commander, 2nd Battalion, Reserve Infantry
    Regiment 212
Wohlenberg, Alfred, Reserve Leutnant, Reserve Infantry Regiment 77
(See also German soldiers in the text, sourced to their battalion histories and
    *The German Army at Passchendaele*, by Jack Sheldon)

Note: Canadian and New Zealand case studies are sourced to their official
and other histories.


## Official Documents and Publications

Australian War Memorial: Australian Imperial Force, Unit War Diaries,
    1914–18.
British War Cabinet Papers and other documents, 1914–1918, The National
    Archives, Kew (UK): CAB 23, CAB 24, CAB 27, CAB 63: http://www.
    nationalarchives.gov.uk/cabinetpapers/
First World War, General Archives: http://www.firstworldwar.com/
Horne, Charles and Austin, Walter, *Source Records of the Great War*, Internet
    Archive, American Library Association, San Francisco, California, 1923:
    https://archive.org/details/sourcerecordsofg03horn
Liddle Collection, The University of Leeds: https://library.leeds.ac.uk/
    special-collections-liddle-collection
Officers' Training Manual, The British Army
Official Histories of the Great War – British, Australian and Canadian. See
    works by Bean, Charles; Butler, Arthur; Edmonds, James; and Nicholson,
    Gerald – in Books section)
Official German Documents Relating to the World War, translated under the
    supervision of the Carnegie Endowment for International Peace, Oxford
    University Press, New York, 1923
World War One Document Archive: https://wwi.lib.byu.edu/index.php/
    Official_Papers and https://wwi.lib.byu.edu/index.php/1917_Documents


## General Online Sources

Australian War Memorial: https://www.awm.gov.au
Australian War Memorial, Blog: https://www.awm.gov.au/blog/
Blockade of Germany, Spotlights on History, The National Archives, United
    Kingdom: http://www.nationalarchives.gov.uk/pathways/firstworldwar/
    spotlights/blockade.htm

Blackadder comedy series, controversy: http://www.bbc.com/news/
    uk-politics-25612369; https://rusi.org/search/site/Blackadder;
    http://www.historyextra.com/feature/blackadder-bad-first-world-war-
    history

Brigadier General Edward Spears on the Calais Conference, January 1917:
    http://discovery.nationalarchives.gov.uk/details/r/C373605

British Journal of Military History: http://www.bjmh.org.uk/index.php/
    bjmh/pages/view/about

Commonwealth War Graves Commission: http://www.cwgc.org/

Fischer Controversy, 50 years on: http://www.open.ac.uk/Arts/
    fischer-controversy/

Germany's Policy of Unrestricted Submarine Warfare, 31 January 1917: first-
    worldwar.com, www.firstworldwar.com/source/uboat_bernstorff.htm

Haig, Field Marshal Sir Douglas, 'Backs to the Wall' Order, 11 April 1918:
    www.firstworldwar.com/source/backstothewall.htm

Haig, Field Marshal Sir Douglas, complete transcripts of Despatches: http://
    www.firstworldwar.com/source/haig_despatches.htm

Intelligence Squared, Debate, 'Britain Should Not Have Fought in the First
    World War', 15 April 2014: http://www.intelligencesquared.com/events/
    britain-first-world-war/

Lansdowne Letter for a negotiated peace:
http://onlinelibrary.wiley.com/doi/10.1111/1467-8497.00249/abstract

Lenin's Call to Power, 24 October 1917: www.firstworldwar.com/source/
    calltopower.htm

Lenin's Statement of Bolshevik Demands: www.firstworldwar.com/source/
    lenin_24oct1917.htm

Pope Benedict XV's Peace Proposal, 1 August 1917, World War I
    Document Archive, 7 July 2009: https://wwi.lib.byu.edu/index.php/
    Pope_Benedict_XV%27s_Peace_Proposal

Prime Minister Lloyd George on the British War Aims, 5 January 1918, The
    World War One Document Archive:
http://wwi.lib.byu.edu/index.php/
    Prime_Minister_Lloyd_George_on_the_British_War_Aims

Reichstag Peace Resolution, 19 July 1917, The World War One
    Document Archive: https://wwi.lib.byu.edu/index.php/
    The_Reichstag_Peace_Resolution

Scheck, Raffael, 'Military Operations and Plans for German Domination of
    Europe', http://web.colby.edu/rmscheck/contents/germanyc2/

Wilson's War Message to Congress, 2 April 1917, The World War One
    Document Archive: wwi.lib.byu.edu/index.php/Official_Papers

World War One Battlefields: http://www.ww1battlefields.co.uk/flanders/
    passchendaele.html
World War One Diaries, Memoirs, The World War One
    Document Archive: http://wwi.lib.byu.edu/index.php/
    Diaries,_Memorials,_Personal_Reminiscences
World War One Timelines, 1917: http://www.firstworldwar.com/
    timeline/1917.htm
Zimmerman Note, The World War One Document Archive: wwi.lib.byu.
    edu/index.php/1917_Documents

## JSTOR Essays and Articles

Baussan, Charles, 'General Foch', *Studies: An Irish Quarterly Review*, Vol. 7,
    No. 25 (March 1918), pp. 65–79.
Beckett, Ian., (Review), 'A Month at the Front: The Diary of an Unknown
    Soldier', *The Journal of Military History*, Vol. 71, No. 2 (April 2007),
    pp. 546–547.
Bond, Brian, 'Soldiers and Statesmen: British Civil-Military Relations in
    1917', *Military Affairs* 32, no. 2 (1968): 62–75.
Bowman, Kent, 'Echoes of Shot and Shell: Songs of the Great War', *Studies in
    Popular Culture* 10, no. 1 (1987): 27–41.
Brown, Ian M., 'Not Glamorous, But Effective: The Canadian Corps and the
    Set-Piece Attack, 1917–1918', *The Journal of Military History*, Vol. 58, No.
    3. (July 1994), pp. 421–444.
Burke, Tom, 'The Royal Dublin Fusiliers in the Great War', *History Ireland*
    13, no. 5 (2005): 29–33.
Cowdrey, Albert E., 'Environments of War', *Environmental Review: ER* 7, no.
    2 (1983): 155–64.
Cowley, Robert, 'Ghosts on the Plain', *New England Review (1990)* 13, no. 3/4
    (1991): 45–66.
Curry, Andrew, 'Under the Western Front', *Archaeology* 62, no. 4 (2009):
    49–54.
De Schaepdrijver, Sophie, 'Death Is Elsewhere: The Shifting Locus of Tragedy
    in Belgian Great War Literature', *Yale French Studies*, no. 102 (2002):
    94–114.
Egerton, George W., (Review), 'The Lloyd George "War Memoirs": A Study
    in the Politics of Memory', *The Journal of Modern History* 60, no. 1 (1988):
    55–94
Englander, David, and Osborne, James, 'Jack, Tommy, and Henry Dubb: The

Armed Forces and the Working Class', *The Historical Journal* 21, no. 3 (1978): 593–621.

Falls, Cyril, (Review), 'Canadian Expeditionary Force 1914–1919 by G. W. L. Nicholson' *International Journal* 18, no. 2 (1963): 229–30.

French, David, 'Sir Douglas Haig's Reputation, 1918–1928: A Note', *The Historical Journal* 28, no. 4 (1985): 953–60.

Fussell, Paul, 'Modernism, Adversary Culture, and Edmund Blunden', *The Sewanee Review* 94, no. 4 (1986): 583–601.

Hoffenberg, Peter H., 'Landscape, Memory and the Australian War Experience, 1915–18', *Journal of Contemporary History* 36, no. 1 (2001): 111–31.

Hucker, Jacqueline, '"Battle and Burial": Recapturing the Cultural Meaning of Canada's National Memorial on Vimy Ridge', *The Public Historian* 31, no. 1 (2009): 89–109.

Isham, R. H., (Review), 'From A Surgeon's Journal, 1915–1918, by Harvey Cushing', *The North American Review* 242, no. 1 (1936): 215–18.

Jones, Edgar, 'The Psychology of Killing: The Combat Experience of British Soldiers during the First World War', *Journal of Contemporary History* 41, no. 2 (2006): 229–46.

MacLeod, James Lachlan, '"Greater Love Hath No Man than This": Scotland's Conflicting Religious Responses to Death in the Great War', *The Scottish Historical Review* 81, no. 211 (2002): 70–96.

Maier, Charles S., 'Wargames: 1914–1919', *The Journal of Interdisciplinary History* 18, no. 4 (1988): 819–49.

McGerr, Rosemarie, '"It's Not All That Easy to Find Your Way Back to the Middle Ages": Reading the Past in "A Month in the Country"', *Criticism* 47, no. 3 (2005): 353–86.

Millman, Brock, 'A Counsel of Despair: British Strategy and War Aims, 1917–18', *Journal of Contemporary History* 36, no. 2 (2001): 241–70.

Morgan, Kenneth O., 'Lloyd George's Premiership: A Study in "Prime Ministerial Government"', *The Historical Journal* 13, no. 1 (1970): 130–57.

Nevinson, Henry W, 'Lloyd George: The Leader of British Liberals', *Foreign Affairs* 9, no. 3 (1931): 457–68.

O'Leary, Daniel, 'Censored and Embedded Shaw: Print Culture and Shavian Analysis Of Wartime Media', *Shaw* 28 (2008): 168–87.

Sanders, M. L., 'Wellington House and British Propaganda during the First World War', *The Historical Journal* 18, no. 1 (1975): 119–46.

Sidebotham, H, 'Civilian or Military Strategy', *Journal of the British Institute of International Affairs* 3, no. 5 (1924): 247–63.

Strachan, Hew, 'The British Way in Warfare Revisited', *The Historical Journal* 26, no. 2 (1983): 447–61.

Strachan, Hew, (Review), 'The First World War: *The Arming of Europe and the Making of the First World War* by David G. Herrmann; *Armaments and the Coming of War: Europe 1904–1914* by David Stevenson; *Authority, Identity and the Social History of the Great War* by Frans Coetzee, Marilyn Shevin-Coetzee; *Dismembering the Male: Men's Bodies, Britain and the Great War* by Joanna Bourke; *Passchendaele: The Untold Story* by Robin Prior, Trevor Wilson; *Battle Tactics of the Western Front: The British Army's Art of Attack, 1916–1918* by Paddy Griffith; *Government and the Armed Forces in Britain, 1856–1990* by Paul Smith', *The Historical Journal* 43, no. 3 (2000): 889–903.

Ware, Thomas C., '"Shepherd in a Soldier's Coat": The Presence of Arcadia on the Western Front', *South Atlantic Review* 68, no. 1 (2003): 64–84.

Woodward, David R., 'Britain in a Continental War: The Civil-Military Debate over the Strategical Direction of the Great War of 1914–1918', *Albion: A Quarterly Journal Concerned with British Studies* 12, no. 1 (1980): 37–65.

Woodward, David R., 'Did Lloyd George Starve the British Army of Men Prior to the German Offensive of 21 March 1918?', *The Historical Journal* 27, no. 1 (1984): 241–52.

## Further Essays & Reports

Anstey, Brigadier E. C., 'History of the Royal Artillery', Anstey Papers, Royal Artillery Institution, Woolwich

Bartholomees, Jr., J. Boone, 'The Issue of Attrition', *Strategic Studies Institute*, US Army, Spring 2010, www.strategicstudiesinstitute.army.mil

Biernoff, Suzannah, 'Flesh Poems: Henry Tonks and the Art of Surgery', *Visual Culture in Britain*, 11(1), 2010, 25–47

Bradby, W. J., 'Polygon Wood and Broodseinde', *Stand-To*, vol. 8, no. 5, September–October 1963, pp. 19–22, 27–28

Das, Santanu, 'The Dying Kiss: Gender and Intimacy in the Trenches of World War I', World War I Centenary, JISC, http://ww1centenary.oucs.ox.ac.uk/body-and-mind/the-dying-kiss-gender-and-intimacy-in-the-trenches-of-world-war-i

Edmonds, A. H., 'In Flanders Fields', IWM, 1960

Engen, Rob, 'Steel Against Fire: The Bayonet in the First World War', *Journal of Military and Strategic Studies*, Spring 2006, Vol. 8, Issue 3, Centre for Military and Strategic Studies, Canadian Defence & Foreign Affairs Institute, 2006

Greenhalgh, Elizabeth, 'Myth and Memory: Sir Douglas Haig and the Imposition of Allied Unified Command in March 1918', *The Journal of Military History*, Vol. 68, No. 3 (July 2004), pp. 771–820

Greenslade, Roy, 'First World War: How State and Press Kept Truth Off the Front Page', *The Guardian*, 28 July 2014, www.theguardian.com/media/2014/jul/27/first-world-war-state-press-reporting

'How Was Information Shared?', BBC Schools, World War One, www.bbc.co.uk/schools/0/ww1/25332968

Jewell, John, '"Our Casualties Not Heavy": How British Press Covered the Battle of the Somme', History News Network, 30 June 2016, http://historynewsnetwork.org/article/163259

Liddell Hart, Basil, 'The Basic Truths of Passchendaele', *RUSI Journal*, November 1959

Roy, R. H. and Foot, Richard, 'Battle of the Somme', *Historica Canada*, 21 December 2006 (last edited 4 March 2015), www.thecanadianencyclopedia.ca/en/article/battle-of-the-somme

Simkins, Peter, 'Voluntary Recruiting in Britain, 1914–1915', British Library, www.bl.uk

Singleton, John, 'Britain's Military Use of Horses 1914–1918', *Past & Present*, No. 139 (May 1993), pp. 178–203

Todman, Daniel, 'Sans Peur et Sans Reproche: The Retirement, Death, and Mourning of Sir Douglas Haig, 1918–1928', *The Journal of Military History*, Vol. 67, No. 4 (October 2003), pp. 1083–1106

Van der Fraenen, 'Passchendaele September 1917: A Terrible Loss in an Australian Family. The Story of the Three Seabrook Brothers', *Passchendaele Archives*, Zonnebeke

Toye, Richard, 'Lloyd George's War Rhetoric, 1914–1918', *Academia.edu, http://www.academia.edu/2533280/Lloyd_Georges_War_Rhetoric_1914-18*

Wynne, Graeme, 'The Development of the German Defensive Battle in 1917 and its Influence on British Defensive Tactics', *Army Quarterly*, vol. 34, April 1937, pp. 15–34

## Email discussions

Harrison, Kristie, April 2015
Hind, Dorothy, 12 July 2016
Diana Richey (various)
Ketterer, Walter, 13 April 2015
Munro, Shane (various)

Vandenbussche, Steven, Director, Memorial Museum Passchendaele,
    Zonnebeke (various)


## Museums & Exhibits
Australian War Memorial, Canberra
Imperial War Museums, London
National Army Museum, London
Memorial Museum Passchendaele, Zonnebeke, Flanders
Tyne Cot Cemetery, Exhibit, Passchendaele, Flanders
Talbot House Museum, Poperinge, Flanders


## Newspapers (from 1917 unless otherwise stated)
*Birmingham Gazette*
*Daily Record and Mail*
*Daily Mirror*
*Dominion* (NZ)
*Dundee Courier*
*Dundee People's Journal*
*Edinburgh Evening News*
*Evening Despatch*
*Fife Free Press*
*Grantham Journal*
*Guardian* (2014–16)
*Herald Sun* (2015–16)
*London Gazette* (various)
*Lincolnshire Echo*
*Liverpool Daily Post and Mercury*
*Liverpool Echo*
*Manchester Guardian*
*Middlesbrough Daily Gazette*
*Newcastle Journal*
*Observer*
*Rochdale Observer*
*Sunday Pictorial*
*Sydney Morning Herald* (2014–16)
*The Times* (various)
*Yorkshire Post*

# Books

Adorno, Theodor, W., *Prisms*, MIT Press, Cambridge, Massachusetts, 1983

Aldington, Richard, *Death of a Hero*, Penguin Classics, London, 2013

Arthur, Max, in association with the Imperial War Museum, *Forgotten Voices of the Great War*, Ebury, London, 2006

Asquith, Herbert Henry, *Memories and Reflections: 1852–1927*, Cassell, London, 1928

Barton, Peter, Doyle, Peter and Vandewalle, Johan, *Beneath Flanders Fields: The Tunnellers' War 1914–1918*, Spellmount, Staplehurst, Kent, 2004

Baker-Carr, Brigadier General Christopher, *From Chauffeur to Brigadier: Founder of the Machine Gun Corps and Pioneer of the Development of the Tank,* Leonaur, Driffield, East Yorkshire, 2015

Barr, Niall, *The Lion and the Poppy: British Veterans, Politics, and Society, 1921–1939*, Praeger, Santa Barbara, 2005

Barwick, Archie, *In Great Spirits: The WWI Diary of Archie Barwick*, HarperCollins Publishers, Sydney, 2013

Beach, Jim, *Haig's Intelligence: GHQ and the German Army, 1916–1918*, Cambridge University Press, Cambridge, 2013

Bean, Charles, *The Australian Imperial Force in France, 1917*, Official History series, Volume IV (11th edition, 1941), Australian War Memorial, Canberra, https://www.awm.gov.au/collection/RCDIG1069753/

—*Anzac to Amiens*, Penguin Books, Melbourne, 2014

—*Making the Legend: The War Writings of C. E. W. Bean* (selected by Denis Winter), University of Queensland Press, St Lucia, Queensland, 1992

Beaumont, Joan, *Broken Nation: Australians in the Great War*, Allen & Unwin, Sydney, 2013

Beckett, Ian, *The Making of the First World War*, Yale University Press, New Haven, Connecticut, 2012

Beckett, Ian and Corvi, Stephen (eds), *Haig's Generals*, Leo Cooper Ltd, Barnsley, South Yorkshire, 2006

Bergen, Leo van, *Before My Helpless Sight: Suffering, Dying and Military Medicine on the Western Front, 1914–1918*, (translated by Liz Waters), Burlington, VT Ashgate Pub., Farnham, Surrey, 2009

Best, Brian, *Reporting from the Front: War Reporters during the Great War*, Pen & Sword, Barnsley, South Yorkshire, 2015

Beumelburg, Werner von, *Flandern 1917*, Gerhard Stalling, Berlin, 1928

Bewsher, Major F. W., *The History of the 51st (Highland) Division: 1914–1918*, William Blackwood and Sons, Edinburgh, 1921

Birdwood, Field-Marshal Lord, *Khaki and Gown: An Autobiography*, Ward, Lock & Co., London, 1941

Blacker, Charles Paton, (John Blacker – ed), *Have You Forgotten Yet? The First World War Memoirs of C. P. Blacker, M.C., G.M., M.A., M.D., F.R.C.P., M.R.C.S*, Leo Cooper, London, 2000

Blankenstein, Dr, *History of the Reserve Infantry Regiment no. 92 in the World War, 1914–1918*, Kampfgenossenverein R.I.R. 92, Osnabrück, Germany, 1934

Blunden, Edmund, *Undertones of War*, Richard Cobden-Sanderson, London, 1928

—(Greening, John – ed), *Edmund Blunden's 'Undertones of War'*, Oxford University Press, Oxford, 2015

Bonham-Carter, Victor, *Soldier True: The Life and Times of Field-Marshal Sir William Robertson, Bart. GCB, GCMG, KCVO, DSO, 1860–1933*, Frederick Muller, London, 1963

Bostyn, Franky (ed), *Passchendaele 1917: The Story of the Fallen and Tyne Cot Cemetery*, Pen & Sword Military, Barnsley, South Yorkshire, 2007

Brazier, Reginald H. and Sandford, Ernest, *Birmingham and the Great War, 1914–1919*, Cornish Bros., Birmingham, 1921

Buchan, John, *A History of the Great War*, Biblio, London, 2009

Bull, Stephen, *Trench: A History of Trench Warfare on the Western Front*, Osprey Publishing, Oxford, 2014

Busch, Briton C. (ed), *Canada and the Great War: Western Front Association Papers*, McGill-Queen's University Press, Montreal, 2003

Butler, Arthur Graham, *Official History of the Australian Army Medical Services, 1914–1918: The Western Front*, Vol II, Australian War Memorial, Canberra, 1940. https://www.awm.gov.au/collection/RCDIG1069846/

Callwell, Charles Edward, *Field-Marshal Sir Henry Wilson, Bart, G.C.B., D.S.O.: His Life and Diaries*, Cassell, London, 1927

Campbell, Patrick J., *In the Cannon's Mouth*, Hamilton, London, 1979

Carrington, Charles, *Soldier from the Wars Returning*, Hutchinson, London, 1965

Cassar, George H., *Lloyd George at War, 1916–1918*, Anthem Press, London, 2011

Cave, Nigel, *Hill 60 – Ypres*, Leo Cooper, Barnsley, South Yorkshire, 1998

—*Passchendaele: The Fight for the Village – Ypres*, Leo Cooper, London 1997

Cecil, Hugh and Liddle, Peter (eds), *Facing Armageddon: The First World War Experienced*, Leo Cooper, London, 1996

Chambers, Frank, *The War Behind the War, 1914–1918: A History of the Political and Civilian Fronts*, Arno Press, New York, 1972

Chapman, Guy, *A Passionate Prodigality: Fragments of Autobiography*, Buchan & Enright, London, 1985

Charteris, John, *At G.H.Q.*, Cassell, London, 1931

Christie, N. M., *Slaughter in the Mud: The Canadians at Passchendaele, 1917*, CEF Books, Nepean, Ontario, 1998

Churchill, Winston, *The World Crisis, 1911–1918*, Odhams Press, London 1938

Clark, Christopher, *The Sleepwalkers: How Europe Went to War in 1914*, Harper, New York, 2013

Clausewitz, Carl von, *On War*, Princeton University Press, Princeton, New Jersey, 2008

Clayton, Anthony, *Paths of Glory: The French Army 1914–18*, Cassell Military, London, 2003

Clements, Captain Robert N., (Tennyson, Brian Douglas – ed), *Merry Hell: The Story of the 25th Battalion (Nova Scotia Regiment), Canadian Expeditionary Force 1914–1919*, University of Toronto Press, Toronto, 2013

Collins, Norman, (Van Emden, Richard – ed), *Last Man Standing: The Memoirs of a Seaforth Highlander During the Great War*, Leo Cooper, Barnsley, South Yorkshire, 2002

Conan Doyle, Arthur, *A History of the Great War*, George H. Doran, New York, 1916

Corrigan, Gordon, *Douglas Haig: Defeat Into Victory*, Amazon Kindle Single, Endeavour Press, London, 2015

Courtenay, Adam, *The Thirty-One: The Bankstown Anzacs who never came home*, Bankstown Youth Development Service, Sydney, 2015

Crerar, Duff, *Padres in No Man's Land: Canadian Chaplains in the Great War*, McGill-Queen's Press, Montreal, 1995

Creveld, Martin van, *The Changing Face of War: Combat from the Marne to Iraq*, Presidio, Novato, California, 2008

Cushing, Harvey, *From a Surgeon's Journal 1915–1918*, Little, Brown & Co, Boston, 1936

Dancocks, Daniel, *Sir Arthur Currie: A Biography*, Methuen, Toronto, 1985

Davies, Will, *Beneath Hill 60: The Extraordinary True Story of the Secret War Being Waged Beneath the Trenches of the Western Front*, Bantam, Sydney, 2011

Dickson, Paul Douglas, *A Thoroughly Canadian General: A Biography of General H. D. G. Crerar*, University of Toronto Press, Toronto, 2007

Dolden, Stuart A., *Cannon Fodder: An Infantryman's Life on the Western Front, 1914–18*, Blandford Press, New York, 1980

Doughty, Robert, *Pyrrhic Victory: French Strategy and Operations in the Great War*, Belknap Press of Harvard University Press, Cambridge, Massachusetts, 2005

Doyle, Peter and Walker, Julian, *Trench Talk: Words of the First World War*, The History Press, Stroud, Gloucestershire, 2012

Dugdale, Blanche Elizabeth Campbell, *Arthur James Balfour, First Earl of Balfour*, G. P. Putnam's Sons, New York, 1937

Dupuy, Ernest and Dupuy, Trevor, *The Harper's Encyclopaedia of Military History: From 3,500 BC to the Present*, (4th ed.)., Harper Reference, New York, 1993

Eden, Anthony, Earl of Avon, *Another World, 1897–1917*, Doubleday, Garden City, New York 1977

Edmonds, Brigadier General James E., *Official History of the Great War: Military Operations France & Belgium 1917*, Vol 2, Naval & Military Press, Uckfield, East Sussex, 2013

Eksteins, Modris, *Rites of Spring: The Great War and the Birth of the Modern Age*, Papermac, London, 2000

Ellis, A. D., *The Story of the Fifth Australian Division*, Hodder and Stoughton, London, 1920

English, Allan D. (ed), *The Changing Face of War: Learning from History*, published for The Royal Military College of Canada by McGill-Queen's University Press, Toronto, 1998

Evans, Martin Marix, *Passchendaele: The Hollow Victory*, Pen & Sword Military, Barnsley, South Yorkshire, 2005

Falls, Cyril, *The Great War*, G. P. Putnam's Sons, New York, 1959

—*The History of the 36th (Ulster) Division*, M'Caw, Stevenson & Orr, Belfast, 1922

Farndale, General Sir Martin, *History of the Royal Regiment of Artillery: Western Front 1914–1918*, Brassey's, London, 2001

Farrar-Hockley, General Sir Anthony, *Goughie: the Life of General Sir Hubert Gough CBG, GCMG, KCVO*, Hart-Davis, MacGibbon, London, 1975

Ferguson, Norman, *The First World War: A Miscellany*, Summersdale Publishers, Chichester, West Sussex, 2014

Ferguson, Niall, *The Pity of War*, Allen Lane, London, 1998

Fischer, Fritz, *Germany's War Aims in the First World War*, Chatto & Windus, London, 1967

Fletcher, Anthony, *Life, Death and Growing Up on the Western Front*, Yale University Press, New Haven, Connecticut, 2013

Foley, R. T., *German Strategy and the Path to Verdun: Erich von Falkenhayn and the Development of Attrition*, 1870–1916, Cambridge University Press, Cambridge 2007

Fosten, Donald and Marrion, Robert (authors), Embleton, Gerry, (illus.), *The German Army 1914–18*, Osprey Publishing, London, 1978

France, John, *Perilous Glory: The Rise of Western Military Power*, Yale University Press, New Haven, Connecticut, 2013

Fraser, Donald, (Roy, Reginald – ed), *The Journal of Private Fraser, 1914–1918*, Canadian Expeditionary Force, CEF Books, Nepean, Ontario, 1998

Fraser, William, (Fraser, David – ed), *In Good Company: The First World War Letters and Diaries of the Hon. William Fraser, Gordon Highlanders*, Michael Russell, Salisbury, Wiltshire, 1990

Fremantle, Michael, *Gas! Gas! Quick, Boys! How Chemistry Changed the First World War*, Spellmount, Stroud, Gloucestershire, 2013

Fussell, Paul, *The Great War and Modern Memory*, Oxford University Press, London, 1975

Gammage, Bill, *The Broken Years: Australian Soldiers in the Great War*, Melbourne University Publishing, Melbourne, 2010

Gibbs, Arthur Hamilton, *Gun Fodder: The Diary of Four Years of War*, Little, Brown, Boston, 1919

Gibbs, Philip, *From Bapaume to Passchendaele, 1917*, William Heinemann, London, 1918

—*Realities of War*, William Heinemann, London, 1918

Gilbert, Martin, *The First World War: A Complete History*, Weidenfeld and Nicolson, London, 1994

Gollin, Alfred, *Proconsul in Politics: A Study of Lord Milner in Opposition and in Power*, Macmillan, London, 1964

Gordon, Huntly, *The Unreturning Army: A Field-Gunner in Flanders, 1917–18*, Doubleday, London, 2013

Gough, General Sir Hubert, *Soldiering On: Being the Memoirs of General Sir Hubert Gough*, Arthur Barker, London, 1954

Grant, Ian, *Jacka VC, Australia's Finest Fighting Soldier*, Sun Books, Melbourne, 1990

Graves, Robert, *Goodbye to All That*, Penguin, London, 2009

Gray, Edwyn A., *The Killing Time: The U-boat War 1914–1918*, Pan, London, 1972

Grebler, Leo, and Winkler, Wilhelm, *The Cost of the World War to Germany and Austria-Hungary*, Yale University Press, New Haven, Connecticut,1940

Green, Revd Samuel Frederick Leighton, (McLaren, Stuart – ed), *Somewhere in Flanders: Letters of a Norfolk Padre in the Great War: The War Letters of the Revd Samuel Frederick Leighton Green MC, Army Chaplain, 1916–1919*, Larks Press, Norfolk, 2005

Greene, Graham, *The Quiet American*, Penguin, New York, 2002

Grieve, W. Grant and Newman, Bernard, *Tunnellers: The Story of the Tunnelling Companies, Royal Engineers, during the World War*, Herbert Jenkins, London, 1936

Grieves, Keith, *The Politics of Manpower, 1914–18*, Manchester University Press, Manchester, 1988

Griffith, Paddy, *Battle Tactics of the Western Front: The British Army's Art of Attack, 1916–18*, Yale University Press, New Haven, Connecticut, 1994

Grigg, John, *Lloyd George: War Leader, 1916–18*, Faber Finds, London, 2011

Gristwood, A. D., *The Somme, including also, The Coward*, Jonathan Cape, London, 1927

Haig, Field Marshal Sir Douglas, (Sheffield, Gary and Bourne, John – eds), *Douglas Haig: War Diaries and Letters, 1914–1918*, Weidenfeld & Nicolson, London, 2005

—(Blake, Robert – ed), *The Private Papers of Douglas Haig, 1914–1919: being Selections from the Private Diary and Correspondence of Field-Marshal the Earl Haig of Bemersyde*, Eyre & Spottiswoode, London, 1952

Ham, Paul, *1914: The Year the World Ended*, William Heinemann, Sydney, 2013

—*Young Hitler*, Amazon Kindle Single, Endeavour Press, London, 2014

Harington, Sir Charles, *Tim Harington Looks Back*, John Murray, London 1940

—*Plumer of Messines*, John Murray, London, 1935

Harper, Glyn, *Massacre at Passchendaele: The New Zealand Story*, FireStep Books, Eastbourne, 2011

Harris, Paul, *Douglas Haig and the First World War*, Cambridge University Press, Cambridge, 2008

Hastings, Sir Max, *Catastrophe: Europe Goes to War 1914*, William Collins, London 2014

Hattersley, Roy, *David Lloyd George: The Great Outsider*, Little, Brown, London, 2010

Hawkings, Frank (Taylor, Arthur – ed), *From Ypres to Cambrai: The Diary of an Infantryman, 1914–1919*, Elmfield Press, Morley, UK, 1974

Headlam, Cuthbert, *History of the Guards Division in the Great War, 1915–1918*, J. Murray, London, 1924

Healy, Maureen, *Vienna and the Fall of the Habsburg Empire: Total War and Everyday Life in World War I*, Cambridge University Press, New York, 2004

Herbert, Sir Alan Patrick, *The Secret Battle*, A. A. Knopf, New York, 1920

—*A. P. H.: His Life and Times*, Heinemann, London, 1970

Herwig, Holger H., *The First World War: Germany and Austria-Hungary, 1914–1918*, Bloomsbury, London, 2014

Hodges, Clive, *Cobbold & Kin: Life Stories from an East Anglian Family*, The Boydell Press, Woodbridge, Suffolk, 2014

Høiback, Harald, *Command and Control in Military Crisis: Devious Decisions*, F. Cass, London, 2003

Holmes, Richard, *Tommy: The British Soldier on the Western Front, 1914–1918,* Harper Perennial, London, 2005

—*The Western Front*, BBC, London, 2008

Howard, Michael (ed), *The Theory and Practice of War*, Indiana University Press, Bloomington, 1975

Hurley, Frank, *Hurley at War: The Photography and Diaries of Frank Hurley in Two World Wars*, Fairfax Library in association with Daniel O'Keefe, Sydney, 1986

Hussey, A. H. and Inman, D. S., *The Fifth Division in the Great War*, Nisbet & Co, London, 1921

Hyatt, A. M. J., *General Sir Arthur Currie: A Military Biography*, University of Toronto Press in collaboration with Canadian War Museum, Canadian Museum of Civilization, National Museums of Canada, Toronto, 1987

Jablonsky, David, *Churchill and Hitler: Essays on the Political-Military Direction of Total War*, F. Cass, Portland, Oregon, 1994

Jack, General James Lochhead, (Terraine, John – ed), *General Jack's Diary*, Eyre & Spottiswoode, London, 1964

Jackson, Julian, *France: The Dark Years, 1940–1944*, Oxford University Press, London, 2001

Jeffreys, Richard Griffith Bassett, (Dodd, Conor & Liam – eds), *Lieutenant Colonel R. G. B. Jeffreys, 2nd Battalion Royal Dublin Fusiliers: Collected Letters 1916–1918*, Old Tough Publications, Blackrock, Co. Dublin, 2007

Jerrold, Douglas, *The Royal Naval Division*, Hutchinson, London, 1923

Johnstone, Tom, *Orange, Green and Khaki: The Story of the Irish Regiments in the Great War, 1914–18*, Gill and MacMillan, Dublin, 1992

Jones, David, *In Parenthesis: Seinnyessit e gledyf ym penn mameu*, Faber & Faber, London, 1963

Jünger, Ernst, *Storm of Steel*, Penguin, London, 2004

Keegan, John, *The First World War*, Hutchinson, London, 1998

Kennedy, Paul, *The Rise of the Anglo-German Antagonism 1860–1914*, Allen & Unwin, London, 1980

King, Anthony, *The Combat Soldier: Infantry Tactics and Cohesion in the Twentieth and Twenty-First Centuries*, Oxford University Press, Oxford, 2013

Kuhl, Hermann von, *Der Weltkrieg 1914–1918: Dem Deutschen Volke dargestellt* [The World War, 1914–1918, for the German people], Wilhelm Kolk, Berlin, 1929

Larsson, Marina, *Shattered ANZACs: Living with the Scars of War*, UNSW Press, Sydney, 2009

Lawrence, Brian, (Fletcher, Ian – ed), *Letters from the Front: The Great War Correspondence of Lieutenant Brian Lawrence, 1916–17*, Parapress, Tunbridge Wells, UK, 1993

Leese, Peter, *Shell Shock: Traumatic Neurosis and the British soldiers of the First World War*, Palgrave, New York, 2002

Leinburger, Ralf, *Fighter: Technology, Facts, History*, Parragon Books, Bath, 2008

Lewis, John E., (ed), *On the Front Line: True World War I Stories*, Constable, London, 2013

Lewis, Wyndham, *Blasting & Bombardiering*, Calder & Boyars, London, 1970

Lewis-Stempel, John, *Six Weeks: The Short and Gallant Life of the British Officer in the First World War*, Orion, London, 2011

Liddell Hart, Sir Basil Henry, *History of the First World War*, Papermac, London, 1992

—*Strategy*, Meridian, New York, 1991

Liddle, Peter H., *Passchendaele in Perspective: The Third Battle of Ypres*, Leo Cooper, London, 1997

Livermore, Bernard, *Long 'Un: A Damn Bad Soldier*, Harry Hayes, Batley, UK, 1974

Lloyd George, David, *War Memoirs of David Lloyd George,* Odhams Press, London, 1942

Longmore, C., *The Old Sixteenth Being a Record of the 16th Battalion, A.I.F., During the Great War, 1914–1918*, The History Committee of the 16th Battalion Association, Perth, Western Australia, 1929

Ludendorff, General Erich, *My War Memories: 1914–1918*, Hutchinson & Co, London, 1919

Lynch, Edward, (Davies, Will – ed), *Somme Mud,* Kindle Edition, RHA eBooks Adult, 2010

Macdonald, Lyn, *They Called it Passchendaele: The Story of the Third Battle of Ypres and of the Men who Fought in it*, Atheneum, New York, 1989

Mackenzie, K. W., *The Story of the Seventeenth Battalion A.I.F. in the Great War, 1914–1918*, Naval & Military Press, East Sussex, 2010

MacMillan, Margaret, *The War That Ended Peace: How Europe Abandoned Peace for the First World War*, Profile Books, London, 2013

May, Arthur, J., *The Passing of the Hapsburg Monarchy, 1914–1918*, University of Pennsylvania Press, Philadelphia, 1966

McCarthy, Chris, *Passchendaele: The Day-by-Day Account*, Arms and Armour, London, 1995

McKernan, Michael, *Victoria at War: 1914–1918*, NewSouth Publishing,

University of New South Wales Press Ltd, in association with the State
Library of Victoria, Melbourne, 2014

McKernan, Michael and Browne, Margaret (eds), *Australia: Two Centuries
of War and Peace*, Australian War Memorial in association with Allen &
Unwin Australia, Canberra, 1988

McMullin, Ross, *Pompey Elliott*, Scribe, Melbourne, 2008

McNab, Chris, *Passchendaele 1917*, Stroud Spellmount, Stroud,
Gloucestershire, 2014

McNicoll, Ronald, *The Royal Australian Engineers 1902–1919: Making and
Breaking*, The Corps Committee of The Royal Australian Engineers,
Canberra, 1979

Mead, Gary, *The Good Soldier: The Biography of Douglas Haig*, Atlantic Books,
London, 2007

Messenger, Charles, *Trench Fighting 1914–18*, Pan Books, London, 1973

Miller, Emanuel (ed), *The Neuroses in War*, Macmillan and Co, London,
1940

Monash, General Sir John, *War Letters of General Monash*, Black Inc. Books,
Melbourne, 2015

Muir, Ward, *The Happy Hospital*, Simpkin, Marshall, Hamilton, Kent,
London, 1918

Naylor, John F., *A Man and an Institution: Sir Maurice Hankey, the Cabinet
Secretariat and the Custody of Cabinet Secrecy*, Cambridge University Press,
Cambridge, 1984

Neate, Margaret, *Not Bad Coves: Alfred Leahy with the Tenth Field Company,
Australian Engineers, 1st A.I.F.,* Peacock Publications, Norwood, South
Australia, 1999

Neillands, Robin, *The Great War Generals on the Western Front 1914–1918*,
Magpie Books, London, 2004

Newman, Bernard and Evans, I. O., *Anthology of Armageddon*, Greenhill,
London, 1989

Nicholson, Gerald W. L. and Canadian Army, Historical Section, *Canadian
Expeditionary Force, 1914–1919*, R. Duhamel, Queen's Printer and
Controller of Stationery, Ottawa, 1962

—*The Fighting Newfoundlander: A History of the Royal Newfoundland
Regiment*, McGill-Queen's University Press, Montreal, 2006

Nicholson, Walter, *Behind the Lines*, Jonathan Cape, London, 1939

Oram, Gerard, *Military Executions during World War I*, Palgrave Macmillan,
New York, 2003

Owen, Wilfred (Blunden, Edmond – ed), *The Poems of Wilfred Owen*, Chatto
& Windus, London, 1946

—(Bell, John – ed), *Wilfred Owen: Selected Letters*, Oxford University Press, Oxford, 1998

Passingham, Ian, *All the Kaiser's Men: The Life and Death of the German Army on the Western Front*, The History Press, Stroud, Gloucestershire, 2013

—*Pillars of Fire: The Battle of Messines Ridge, June 1917*, Spellmount, Stroud, Gloucestershire, 2012

Parsons, W. David, *Pilgrimage: A Guide to the Royal Newfoundland Regiment in World War One*, DRC Pub., St. John's, NL, 2009

Paton, Alexander Watson, *Occasional Gunfire: Private War Diary of a Siege Gunner*, Bishop-Laggett, London, 1998

Paxman, Jeremy, *Great Britain's Great War*, Penguin, London, 2014

Pedersen, Peter, *Monash as Military Commander*, Melbourne University Press, Melbourne, 1992

Perry, Roland, *Monash: The Outsider Who Won a War: A Biography of Australia's Greatest Military Commander*, Random House Australia, Sydney, 2004

Phillips, Jock, Boyack, Nicholas, and Malone, Edmond Penn (eds), *The Great Adventure: New Zealand Soldiers Describe the First World War*, Allen & Unwin/Port Nicholson Press, Wellington, New Zealand, 1988

Philpott, William, *Attrition: Fighting the First World War*, Little, Brown, London, 2014

Piketty, Thomas, *Capital in the Twenty-First Century*, Harvard University Press, Cambridge, MA, 2014

Pirscher, Friedrich von, *Das (rheinisch-westfaelische) Infanterie-Regiment Nr. 459 [(Rhineland-Westphalian) Infantry Regiment no. 459]*, Verlag Gerhard Stalling, Berlin, 1926

Pois, Robert and Langer, Philip, *Command Failure in War: Psychology and Leadership,* Indiana University Press, Bloomington, 2004

Pope, Alexander, *An Essay on Man in Four Epistles to H. St. John, Lord Bolingbroke*, Mirick West Brookfield C.A., 1843 (electronic book)

Powell, Geoffrey, *Plumer: The Soldier's General: A Biography of Field-Marshal Viscount Plumer of Messines*, Pen & Sword Military Classics, Barnsley, South Yorkshire, 2004

Prior, Robin and Wilson, Trevor, *Passchendaele: The Untold Story*, New Haven, Connecticut, Yale Nota Bene, London, 2002

Prost, Antoine, *Republican Identities in War and Peace: Representations of France in the Nineteenth and Twentieth Centuries*, Berg, New York, 2002

Quigley, Hugh, *Passchendaele and the Somme: A Diary of 1917*, Methuen & Co., London, 1928

Reid, Richard, *Ypres 1917: Australians on the Western Front*, Dept. of Veterans' Affairs, Canberra, 2008

Remarque, Erich Maria, *All Quiet on the Western Front,* Ballantine Books, New York, 1982

Repington, Lieutenant Colonel Charles à Court, *The First World War, 1914–1918*, Houghton Mifflin Company, New York, 1920

Riddell, George Allardice Riddell, 1st Baron, *Lord Riddell's War Diary, 1914–1918*, Nicholson & Watson, London, 1933

Robbins, Simon, *British Generalship on the Western Front 1914–18: Defeat into Victory*, F. Cass, London, 2005

Robertson, Field Marshal Sir William Bart, *Soldiers and Statesmen, 1914–1918*, Cassell, London, 1926

Roe, F. P., *Accidental Soldiers*, F. P. Roe, London, 1981

Rowland, Peter, *David Lloyd George: A Biography*, Macmillan, New York, 1976

Rupprecht, Crown Prince of Bavaria, (Frauenholz, Eugen von – ed), *Mein Kriegstagebuch* [My War Diary], Deutscher National Verlag, Munich, 1929

Russell, Henry, *Slaves of the War Lords*, Hutchinson, London, 1928

Sassoon, Siegfried, *The Complete Memoirs of George Sherston*, Faber, London, 1972

—*Collected Poems, 1908–1956*, Faber and Faber, London, 1961

Schwenke, Alexander, *Geschichte des Reserve-Infanterie-Regiments Nr 19 im Weltkriege 1914–1918*, *[History of Reserve Infantry Regiment No. 19 in the World War 1914–1918]*, Oldenburg, Oldenburg, Germany, 1926

Secrett, T., *Twenty-Five Years with Earl Haig*, Jarrolds, London, 1929

Sharpe, Robert J., *The Last Day, The Last Hour: The Currie Libel Trial*, published for the Osgoode Society for Canadian Legal History by University of Toronto Press, Toronto, 2009

Sheffield, Gary, *The Chief: Douglas Haig and the British Army*, Aurum, London, 2012

—*Command and Morale: The British Army on the Western Front 1914–1918*, Pen & Sword Praetorian Press, Barnsley, South Yorkshire, 2014

—*Forgotten Victory: The First World War – Myths and Realities*, Review, London, 2002

Sheldon, Jack, *The German Army at Passchendaele*, Pen & Sword Military, Barnsley, South Yorkshire, 2007

Sherriff, Robert Cedric, *No Leading Lady: An Autobiography*, Gollancz, London, 1968

Simkins, Peter, *The First World War (3): The Western Front, 1917–1918*, Osprey, Oxford, 2002

Skirth, Ronald, (Barrett, Duncan – ed), *The Reluctant Tommy: Ronald Skirth's Extraordinary Memoir of the First World War*, Charnwood Publishing, Coalville, Leicestershire, 2011

Smith, Melvin Charles, *Awarded for Valour: A History of the Victoria Cross and the Evolution of British Heroism*, Palgrave Macmillan, New York, 2008

Snelling, Stephen, *VCs of the First World War: Passchendaele 1917*, The History Press, Stroud, 2012

Sobbe, Freiherr von, *History of the Brunswick Infantry Regiment No. 92 in the World War, 1914–1918*, Verlag Tradition, Wilhelm Kolk, Berlin, 1929

Spears, Major General Sir Edward, *Prelude to Victory*, Jonathan Cape, London, 1939

Staniforth, John Hamilton Maxwell, (Grayson, Richard S. – ed), *At War With the 16th Irish Division 1914–1918: The Staniforth Letters*, Pen & Sword Military, Barnsley, South Yorkshire, 2012

Steel, Nigel and Hart, Peter, *Passchendaele: The Sacrificial Ground*, Cassell, London, 2001

Stevenson, Frances, (Taylor, A. J. P. – ed), *Lloyd George: A Diary*, Hutchinson and Co., London, 1971

Stewart, Colonel Hugh, *The New Zealand Division, 1916–1919: A Popular History Based on Official Records*, Whitcombe and Tombs, Auckland, 1921

Strachan, Hew, *The First World War*, Oxford University Press, Oxford, 2001

Stevenson, David, *Cataclysm: The First World War as Political Tragedy*, Basic Books, New York, 2004

Sulzbach, Herbert, *With the German Guns: Four Years on the Western Front*, (translated from the German, *Zwei lebende Mauern*, by Thonger, Richard), Pen & Sword Military, Barnsley, South Yorkshire, 2012

Suttie, Andrew, *Rewriting the First World War: Lloyd George, Politics and Strategy, 1914–1918*, Palgrave Macmillan, New York, 2005

Terraine, John, *Douglas Haig: The Educated Soldier*, Cassell Military Paperbacks, London, 2005

—*The Road to Passchendaele: The Flanders Offensive of 1917 – a Study in Inevitability*, Leo Cooper, London, 1977

—*The Smoke and the Fire: Myths and Anti-Myths of War, 1861–1945*, Leo Cooper, London, 1992

Thomas, Nigel and Bujeiro, Ramiro (illustrator), *The German Army of World War I*, Osprey, Oxford, 2003–2004

Todman, Daniel, *The Great War: Myth and Memory*, Bloomsbury, London, 2013

Travers, Tim, *How the War Was Won: Command and Technology in the British Army on the Western Front, 1917–1918*, Routledge, London, 1992

—*The Killing Ground: The British Army, the Western Front and the Emergence of Modern War 1900–1918*, Pen & Sword Military, Barnsley, South Yorkshire, 2009

Tregoning-Lawrence, Heather, and Siers, Robyn, *Forever Yours: Stories of Wartime Love and Friendship*, Dept. of Veterans' Affairs in association with the Australian War Memorial, Canberra, 2011

Tsouras, Peter G. and Jones, Spencer, *Over the Top: Alternate Histories of the First World War*, Frontline Books, London, 2014

Vaughan, Edwin Campion, *Some Desperate Glory: The Diary of a Young Officer, 1917*, Macmillan, London, 1985

Vincent, Paul, *The Politics of Hunger: Allied Blockade of Germany, 1915–1919*, Ohio University Press, Athens, Ohio, 1985

Wadsworth, Jacqueline, *Letters from the Trenches: The First World War by Those Who Were There*, Pen & Sword Military, Barnsley, South Yorkshire, 2014

Warner, Philip, *Passchendaele: The Story Behind the Tragic Victory of 1917*, Pen & Sword Military Classics, Barnsley, South Yorkshire, 2005

Wade, Aubrey, *The War of the Guns: Western Front, 1917 & 1918*, B. T. Batsford, London, 1936

Whitehead, Ian R., *Doctors in the Great War*, Pen & Sword Military, Barnsley, South Yorkshire, 2013

Wiest, Andrew, *Passchendaele and the Royal Navy*, Greenwood Press, Westport, Connecticut, 1995

Williams, Harold, *An Anzac on the Western Front*, Pen & Sword, Barnsley, South Yorkshire, 2012

Wilson, Trevor, *The Myriad Faces of War: Britain and the Great War, 1914–1918*, Faber & Faber, London, 2010

Winter, Jay, *Sites of Memory, Sites of Mourning: The Great War in European Cultural History*, Cambridge University Press, Cambridge, New York, 1998

*Wipers Times: a Facsimile Reprint of the Trench Magazines, The Wipers Times, The New Church Times, The Kemmel Times, The Somme Times, The B.E.F. Times*, H. Jenkins, London, 1918

Wolff, Leon, *In Flanders Fields: The 1917 Campaign*, Penguin, London, 2001

Woodward, David R., *Trial by Friendship: Anglo-American Relations, 1917–1918*, University Press of Kentucky, Lexington, Kentucky, 1993

Wright, Matthew, *Shattered Glory: The New Zealand Experience at Gallipoli and the Western Front*, Penguin, Auckland, NZ, 2010

Wynne, Graeme, *If Germany Attacks: The Battle in Depth in the West*, Greenwood Press, Westport, Connecticut, 1976

Wyrall, Everard, *The History of the Fiftieth Division: 1914–1919*, Percy Lund, Humphries & Co., London, 1939

# INDEX